The Divisible Republic

THE DIVISIBLE
REPUBLIC

Matthew Holden, Jr.
University of Wisconsin, Madison

ABELARD-SCHUMAN
An Intext Publisher
NEW YORK • LONDON

Library of Congress Catalog Card No. 72–9407
International Standard Book No. 0–200–71975.0

NEW YORK
Abelard-Schuman
Limited
257 Park Avenue So.
10010

LONDON
Abelard-Schuman
Limited
450 Edgware Road W2 1EG
and
24 Market Square Aylesbury

Printed in the United States of America

For the families of Holden, Welch, and Clark
  whose histories embody the peril,
  the hope, and the staying power
  of the black "nation" in America

Contents

PART I

The Politics of the Black "Nation"

PART II

The White Man's Burden

Preface

In the year 1968, the Kerner Report warned the President, and the United States as a whole, of what it deemed the potentiality for the United States to become permanently two societies, separate and unequal. It was fashionable at that point to describe the race schism as "the most serious domestic crisis since the Civil War." But the symbols of public discontent have since moved on. The year 1968 was also the year of that now-remote event, McCarthy's victory in the New Hampshire primary, and the clear transformation of the Vietnam conflict into an issue that bitterly divided American society, and most bitterly divided the Democratic party. It was the year in which that division focused on the Chicago Convention and, around the violence of that convention, focused as well on a "generation gap" and a "youth culture" as serious political phenomena. The country has moved beyond that division, too. For many observers, the milieu now is one of social conservatism rather than social change, one in which the severest domestic economic fear is not of unemployment but of inflation, in which talk of rapid advancement and compensation for past deprivation refers to the status of women and not of blacks, in which perhaps the most fundamental issue being discussed is the purported conflict between environmental protection and economic growth.

If nothing else, political moods change rapidly. It is as if citizens and political observers were but theater-goers, and political issues but a form of amusement, so that one act follows another—each producing new sensations. And there is, indeed, a certain amount of theater in the political world. People become satiated with the sensations of any given moment, growing first weary and then bored with the clamors of any particular group. And so their attention passes on to something new. When a political issue is viewed as theater, boredom follows weariness in the face of unwanted repetition of any particular "act." But the passage of attention, or even the apparent quiescence of a dissident group, does not necessarily mean that the structural relations producing conflict have altered.

This interpretation, I maintain, applies to any important political question. But its relevance to race schism in contemporary American politics is deep. Race schism, though muted (and even reduced in some ways), remains a fact in American politics. And that fact also remains the one fundamental domestic threat to the viability of the political system. The latent tensions between groups of younger people—in situations as various as universities, military facilities, high schools, and prisons—are a straw in the wind. The psychological and structural materials of future conflict are all about us. The question is how we should think about current problems, anticipating a future when the present superficial quiescence shall have worn off and racial dispute once more have become volatile.

This volume undertakes two tasks in this light. One is to examine the dynamics of the internal politics of the black "nation," without which the nature of black pressure upon the polity cannot be understood. The other task is to examine the nature of racial hierarchy in the United States and the capacity of the white population—particularly that segment adhering to *conservative* values and interests—to adjust to that pressure.

If this book is about American politics cast as a study of race relations, it is also about an issue that encompasses most of the world: the problem of social peace in political systems that have very different populations next to each other. The underlying theme, regarded in this way, is that the problem of social peace may be conceived as a problem of *republican* government. That is to say that, since the key idea of democracy is the right of "the people" (translated as the majority) to rule, then racial issues are pertinent chiefly as they raise questions of what "rights" a minority ought legitimately to have. But the idea of the republic—the commonwealth, the political system as the common or shared enterprise of its participant—gives racial issues a different cast. The problem of republican government in many contemporary societies (notably Ulster, Belgium, most of Africa and Asia) is that of creating the terms of internal social peace, of reconciling different socio-cultural "nations" within the same polity.

The Politics of the Black "Nation"

I

Centrifugal
Influences in Black Politics

INTRODUCTION

Benjamin Disraeli, later famous as a Tory Prime Minister, early in his career wrote political novels. One of these, *Sybil,* characterized rich and poor in Chartist England as "two nations." Disraeli's use of the term may have been a literary convenience, but it is also a reasonable and realistic way of describing the black-white relationship in the United States today. The term used here has nothing to do with the idea that separate "nations" are, as a matter of right, entitled to separate governments or juridical institutions. It is a way of describing the social and economic relationship of one group to another. It is not necessary here to delineate the vast range of statistically measurable indicators on which blacks, *en bloc,* differ significantly for whites *en bloc* (Flax, 1971; Bureau of Labor Statistics, 1971).[1] All that is sufficiently well known for present purposes.

If any two groups differ significantly as to physical places of residence, cultural styles and outlooks, levels of capital and income, political habits, legal rights, and habits of communication and exchange, then it may be quite reasonable to describe them as separate "nations." The case for doing so is virtually conclusive if we have evidence that they regard each other as constituting different and exclusive *moral communities.*[2] In this light, it is sensible to speak of blacks as constituting a separate socioeconomic "nation," though domiciled in North America and constrained

1

within the legal system of the United States.[3] If one looks at blacks in this way, then one must also accept that the internal politics of the black "nation" is independently interesting and important.[4] Indeed, one must argue that it is particularly important from the normative aspiration for a more republican politics in the United States,[5] because it will not be possible to achieve that more republican politics without a significant black contribution. Yet the available literature on black politics tends to convey hardly more enlightenment than the literature which the ordinary citizen reads on the internal politics of Vietnam.

The best evidence that we need much greater sophistication on the subject is the wide acceptance of the hypothesis that there is no leadership in black politics; that blacks constitute an essentially disorganized, dispirited, demoralized group. If one needs evidence that blacks hold this view, one may but note the frequency with which they say to each other "Why can't we get ourselves together?" "We have got to get ourselves together," "We need some real leadership," and so on. If one needs evidence that whites hold this view, one needs but note that, virtually every year, several major magazines and newspapers will run a feature musing over the presumably curious fact that blacks "no longer" have any "commanding" leaders (like Martin Luther King, Jr., Walter White, Booker T. Washington, or whomever). The presentation of this mode of thought has been going on for a long time, and has its obverse in another series of features celebrating the emergence of the newest "commanding" leader. King, Stokely Carmichael, Imamu Amiri Baraka (LeRoi Jones), Adam Clayton Powell, Roy Wilkins, and a number of others have also been received in this fashion.

For many blacks, however, the constant inquiry into "why you [blacks] haven't got authoritative leaders" is an irritant. Their response is virtually inevitable. "Why," it will be asked, "should *we* be expected to have one source of leadership and authority, when white people have not? How could anyone expect one source of leadership and authority for a group so numerous as blacks in the United States?" The response is fair, so far as it goes, but hardly satisfying. Even those who offer it are likely to be found, at other times, arguing or working for caucuses, common fronts, and concerted positions. The incessant calls for "unity" make sense only on the presumption that "real unity" is possible.[6] One suspects that blacks who offer the responses I have just mentioned secretly agree with the white critics, that they also think of the black population as demoralized, disorganized, and dispirited.

THE BLACK "QUASI GOVERNMENT"

I propose a different interpretation. Black politics actually takes place through a fairly well-defined and stable set of relationships which one may call the black "quasi government." One can observe the stability of this quasi government by observing patterns of interdependence between institutions in black communities both local and nationwide; by observing the consistency of symbolism in black politics; and by observing the remarkable stability in the groups of people who provide leadership. Under extreme conditions, when very specific issues are presented and those issues have a strong emotional aspect (as in the Chicago Panther deaths), blacks are very likely to perceive themselves as attacked by the outside world, and to move toward some form of common front. But the decisive fact is that combination of specific issues plus emotional intensity is likely to be transitory. Life soon returns to its normal condition, and black leaders recurrently face powerful centrifugal (or factional) tensions which limit their success. Organizations make promises to other organizations which they do not keep, suspicions run high, and the collective effort declines.

This is the essential conception, and the problem to be explained. But we should approach this by exploring a little more definitely that set of relationships that we call a "quasi government." The politics of the black "nation" may be explained, at least partially, by reference to the local black communities out of which it is aggregated.[7] Within each such community there is a political system, by which we mean a system of influence and control, based upon the wide variety of institutions that serve people's ordinary needs. These institutions are manifold as to their size, permanence, resources, degrees of social respectability, appeal to different social classes, and legal status. But most of them can probably be related, without too much injury to reality, to three sorts of central focuses.[8] Some are *service* ("uplift") and *mutual-aid* institutions (such as the Urban League or the Prince Hall Masons) out to do good works in behalf of the black population or some part of it. Some are *self-interested* (the Great Lakes Mutual Life Insurance Company or the Dawson political machine) in the sense that, whatever side benefits may accrue to "the community," their central driving force is the remuneration and prestige of their leaders and their active members. Such are the political-party groups, trade-union locals, and—obviously—the business institutions. Some are essentially *recreational* (Alpha Phi Alpha) in the sense that they are not so much dedicated to the uplift of their members (or others) or to the profit of their members (or others), but rather more to the provision of leisure-time activities for compatible people.

Any local community, and the "nation" as a whole, is these institutions operating as a system, wherein one depends upon the other—regardless of approval or disapproval. The system becomes a system of *influence* (or *power*) which may operate almost *as if* it were invested with at least some degree of legal governmental authority: not that it sits in collective legislative judgment or holds formal court, *but that the constant interplay between the elites of these various institutions produces a central tendency which becomes the judgment of "the black community."* Such a judgment has substantial moral and political influence over some options available to anybody living within the territorial ghetto. Moreover, it frequently has influence over some of the options open to people living quite beyond the physical bounds of that ghetto. Why has it this influence? Because, since the social world of black America is centered in the ghetto, he who would play any role in that social world needs acquaintanceship within it—and that acquaintanceship must be sufficiently intensive and extensive that other people may indentify him as trustworthy, efficient, wise, militant, or whatever qualities may be in demand. How might one illustrate this? Imagine a black physician who desires to launch a new health center, but whose entire professional life has been conducted beyond the scope of the black "quasi government." Such a physician is not destined to failure, but it is obvious that his chances of being successful, by a specific time, are less than those of a man well known to all the persons whose cooperation he needs —and well known because they have already seen him in everything from church to fraternity-ball planning committees to medical society.

In short, the "quasi government" is held together by the interdependent elites of the major black socioeconomic institutions. It would thus be quite realistic to regard anyone holding a key role in such an institution as a "black leader." As a term of art, however, the term refers to men and women who have at various times been regarded, or have sought to have themselves regarded, as conscious architects of some definite strategy for "race uplift," "redemption," "race advancement," "equality," "civil rights," or (the most recently fashionable word) "liberation." Black leadership thus *generally means those who seek (or claim to seek) the interest of the "whole" black population* (Daniel Thompson, 1963; Ladd, 1969; Wilson, 1960) and who purport to do so by defining for blacks how they should relate to whites. In order to function as well as they can, they have to do what other political leaders must do—within the limits of their circumstances. They must try to assemble and utilize various combinations of the fundamental political resources: money, office, prestige, technical knowledge, the capacity for eliciting a mass response, or the capacity for utilizing physical force.

At various historical stages, depending upon the development of the black population and the condition of the United States as a whole, black leaders (as defined) have tended to operate from one among three resource bases. Prior to the Civil War, the predominant (but by no means the only) mode of operation was that of *prophetical publicity.* Money, office, and prestige were virtually nonexistent; some limited use could be made of technical knowledge (chiefly in such ventures as the Underground Railroad) and of physical force (which usually proved abortive and counterproductive). But the prophetic publicizers could and did seek to energize both blacks and receptive whites by appeal to powerful symbols of good and evil, as in Frederick Douglass's and Sojourner Truth's speaking crusades against slavery. Seeking to elicit some mass response is a style of operating that has never left black politics, and may now in some respects be more potent than it was before.

After the Civil War, the most prominent leadership resources were based upon *electoral politics,* and the most prominent black leaders were those who had prominent roles in the Republican party. Once the Republican party made the decision to unload the black electorate (*The White Man's Burden,* Essay IV, "The Republicans: Historical Note on the Southern Strategy"), the resources of leadership passed to those who could otherwise command some attention among highly placed whites. In this way, much leadership passed to social workers and educators—the two sorts of black people who could perform roles valued by whites and, at the same time, perform roles which they and other blacks would also regard as valuable. The importance of securing access to the holders and managers of white capital and/or the holders of national power is a persistent theme in the history of the Urban League (Strickland, 1966; Dancy, 1966), and it also accounts for the peculiar importance which a few college presidents had in black life for so many years.[9] These men and women had a special access—which other blacks often sought to utilize— into the foundations, the world of high finance, and the world of high politics that most blacks never saw and hardly comprehended.[10] Booker Washington, his successor Robert R. Moton, and Mary McLeod Bethune (*The White Man's Burden,* Essay V, "The Democrats: Racism, Black Votes, and White Liberals")—three college presidents in a row—had a near monopoly as the only black personages able to get to see the President of the United States, or even get into the White House.

For most of the time since World War I, however, the principal sources of black leadership have come via certain rather well-known *formal organi-*

zations. The National Urban League occupies a rather ambiguous position, for it is profoundly influenced by a latent control mechanism that runs outside the black "nation." That control is based upon the need of the League for relatively large amounts of money, which can come only from foundations and private industry, and which is symbolized by the presence on the League's national board of a large number of representatives of these white sources. Control is "latent," however, in the sense that when the League has active professional leadership—of the sort provided by the late Whitney Young—the organization tends to follow the disposition of its staff to associate itself very closely with black interests, ambitions, and moods. The dualism, the internal strain, which the League experiences affects other organizations, as well. But it is far less apparent. The National Association for the Advancement of Colored People (NAACP)[11] may be both "integrated" and "integrationist," but it is essentially an organization rooted in the black population. So are (or were) the Southern Christian Leadership Conference (SCLC), the Student Nonviolent (National) Coordinating Committee (SNCC), and the Congress of Racial Equality (CORE).[12]

At the national level, and in local communities, these organizations and their managers have tried to provide structures within which deliberation about purposes and strategies might take place, doctrinal disputes might be mediated, means for action arrived at, resources aggregated, and techniques devised for adjustment in the light of feedback. As a plain reality, such leaders do not, within their own organizations, command a sufficient share of the resources of the black community to be effective on their own. Interdependency implies that someone else is able to veto one's own course of action, or the course of action that still another party might take consistently with one's own course of action.

As one illustration, some deacons of a working-class Baptist church in Chicago were also active in their trade-union local. Through the union, they were enlisted in a campaign to raise funds to support one of Martin Luther King, Jr.'s campaigns. In the deacon role, they sought to get a contribution from their church—which is one of the largest and best-financed in the country. Their proposal brought on much strain, however, for the pastor—a theologically fundamentalist gentleman who had founded the church fifty years before and who ran it dictatorially—said "No." This King campaign was not his conception of the work of God, and he made an issue of the deacons' being loyal to his conception or leaving the church.[13]

Interdependency can take other forms as well. In recent years, for instance, one prominent Baptist preacher (let us call him Pastor Z) has attained some renown as a "conservative" critic of Martin Luther King, Jr., of "direct action," and of those who are heirs to the King view. It is possible that his stance rests entirely on ideological grounds. But one cannot ignore the possible importance of clique politics. For the Kings (father and son) were, in their preacher roles, central members of a faction opposed to Pastor Z within denominational politics. Further, much of Pastor Z's continuing support seemed to come from the more conservative Southern Baptist preachers—men more sensitive to the needs of peace with their white environment than to demands for change—and one could interpret Pastor Z's position as reassurance of his central supporters. His position would do much to convey an image of safeness which would help them at home, and thus assure their continuation as part of his faction.

Both examples make the same point. Those who profess to be black leaders, in the sense that I here give that term, cannot get very far unless they can mobilize and coordinate the resources of the various "nonpolitical" organizations, at least some of the time. The precise importance of the King movement, in an organizational sense, was that it often managed to escape the perils of the two cases just mentioned. Other organizations seek the same device—to call upon the resources of people who are linked to still other people, in the widest networks across the black "nation." That they are able to do so at all is what gives continuity to campaigns and provides muscle and leverage.

Within the black "quasi government" there is not only interdependence but also a high degree of stability of symbolism. At any moment, the things to be believed, admired, rejected, denied, debated are well known to most people. Over the years, at any moment, people would react favorably, unfavorably, or neutrally to "Jim Crow," or "Walter White," as they now do to "Roy Wilkins," "Black Panthers," or "oreo cookie." These symbols have their meaning in that people organize them rationally, that is, in a pattern about which they have taken thought. Through such symbols, there is *a decided stability to the ideological cleavages over the question how to meet the white world.*

Finally, there is a certain *stability in the continuation of persons in leadership roles over very long times while—over the same times—new leadership personnel are constantly added as competitors,* but *seldom merely replace* or displace their predecessors. In public politics, for instance, Congressman Ralph Metcalfe may be associated with the political style and organization of Mayor Daley for more than a quarter century and grow in strength. At the same time, one may observe the entrance of an August Savage[14] or an A. A. (Sammy) Rayner, men of different style and appeal, neither of whom can have been much beyond teen age when Metcalfe began to operate. Or one can think of a Jesse Jackson, who can barely have been ready for nursery school. An examination of the networks of trade-union leaders, churchmen, lawyers, and physicians (and—to be candid—underworld participants) in the black population would show a similar process, as would the networks of PTA board members, neighborhood leaders, and bowling-league presidents whose names virtually never reach the papers.

This very same kind of stability would apply to those who make a specific effort at organizing politics to change the structure of race relations. If one reads *The Autobiography of W. E. B. DuBois* or that of his adversary Walter White, one sees the entry of (then) young men who are now becoming elder statesmen—William Hastie, Robert C. Weaver, Thurgood Marshall, Roy Wilkins. To read the black press in the 1940's and 1950's is to see Hastie, Weaver, Marshall, and Wilkins at their apogee, but it is also to see other newcomers—James Farmer, James Forman, with King overshadowing all. To come into the 1960's is to see Farmer, Forman, and King operative, and also to see *still other newcomers* —Julian Bond, Charles Evers, Stokely Carmichael. To note that Roy Wilkins was an NAACP official, risking *his* life in Mississippi ten years before Carmichael was born, is—if one notes that Wilkins was moving in the company of presidents when Carmichael in turn was risking *his*—to note the stability of a leadership-recruitment process which incorporates both personalities in the political world of black folk.

If institutions are interdependent within the black population, if symbolism is relatively consistent, and if leadership recruitment is stabilized, then it is not possible to argue that the black population is simply demoralized or leaderless. It is not possible to deny a good deal of stability to the internal politics of the black "nation." On the other hand, it is not possible to ignore all the signs of internal confusion and apparent disorientation. There is, I would argue, a pattern of stability to even that apparent confusion. We should regard it as the expression of factional or centrifugal tendencies that arise from an inevitable competition over scarce organizational resources; from cultural limitations on the moral authority of those who would be leaders; and from limitations on moral authority due to class tensions.

COMPETITION OVER SCARCE ORGANIZATIONAL RESOURCES

Collective action frequently does require substantial popular participation and support, but such support does not arise spontaneously. It requires somebody to mobilize it. The mobilizers are either people found in the leadership and subleadership strata of existing organizations or they are people capable of manipulating such leadership. In order to be effective within the "quasi government," it is necessary to have a certain measure of power as well as moral authority. Power—the ability to coerce those potential supporters who are resistant or to protect those who are exposed—depends on some combination of technical-bureaucratic skills, money, favorable internal attention, and external recognition.

TECHNICAL BUREAUCRATIC SKILLS

The importance of technical bureaucratic skills is well indicated in the one arena where commentators seldom mention its pertinence: the more successful aspects of nonviolent direct action (moral opposition) in the South. King's capacity to manage that movement depended on more than charisma. He was most successful when he found and could cooperate with something one might call at least a protobureaucracy—a network of people possessing the management competences necessary to anticipate, counteract, and outmaneuver the white forces. He himself demonstrated this capacity and necessity by referring to the problem of insuring the voluntary car pool which made the Montgomery bus boycott successful. At one point, the car pool lost its liability insurance, without which the drivers could have been run off the streets. Through some channel, King (or someone else in the community—he did not say) was informed that a contract could be negotiated with Lloyd's of London (King, 1958, pp. 128–129). And this—not charisma—made continuity possible. It is inconceivable that a small-town Alabama Baptist preacher in (say) 1923 could have worked out such a deal in time to keep his car pool operating.

To know how to make contact with an insurance company and conclude a deal with it is but one of many skills required. Some others are apparent. If a community can succeed in a particular venture only by getting a federal agency to overrule its field representative, someone must know how to get access to that agency, at the right moment, and how to put the argument in terms which the agency will find persuasive. If the problem is defeating an entrenched political party, someone must know whether it is better to rely on public media or on face-to-face canvassing, how to prevent voting-machine frauds, and how to raise political funds. If the problem is conducting an Alinskian campaign against the town's largest bank, someone must know what makes a good community organizer, how one gets such an organizer, and how to protect adherents from the retributive action of the party being attacked. In short, the varieties and combinations of skills are numerous and complicated.

In the available-skills pool of a black community, the range of pertinent skills has usually been relatively narrow, owing to the narrow range of occupations in which a significant number of persons would be found. The community leader was likely to be the clergyman or the schoolteacher, the lawyer or the physician, the dentist or the social worker, the civil servant or the small businessman—simply because those were the commonest occupations for educated blacks. But such a community leader was not likely to have a pool of other competences to which he could turn for backup. Moreover, as one would expect, the proportion of any existent pool which would be disposed, free, and competent to undertake collective organization would be small. Consequently, the black community leader (or potential leader) would likely be even more overburdened than would the white community leader. The overburden meant, in turn, that many tasks were not performed well and might not be performed at all. One need not omit recognition of skills born of common sense and experience[15] (as against training) to observe that this limited skills pool is a direct consequence of limited occupational scope plus limited educational scope. It is the behavioral consequence of the institution of segregation.

MONEY

Skills limitations may be overcome, in part, *by using money to hire people.* But if a community is going to follow this strategy, *there must be a sufficient number of people or organizations that have money,* that believe they can afford to spare part of their money economically, and whose money if spared will aggregate to an amount sufficient for the purpose. On the whole, this requirement would mean large gifts rather than an aggregation of small gifts, and the economic facts of life have precluded large gifts on a significant scale.

It is widely remarked that the communal institutions of black America are grossly underfinanced relative to the tasks which they are pressured to undertake. Underfinancing is usually explained by passing reference to the absence of a "tradition of giving," but what seems more relevant is the sheer capital starvation of the black community. The absence of a tradition of giving can hardly be an adequate explanation, for it has been shown beyond doubt that the development of welfare institutions has frequently been generated (although ill-sustained) on the basis of the small contributions which people could afford in black communities. (Moreover, one would have to deny the evidence of one's eyes and not take cognizance of the large number of church buildings which, like other buildings, have mortgages that must get paid.) In all probability, comment on the absence of a tradition of giving misses what seems a rather compelling point. Except in very unusual situations, the ability to raise large sums from small gifts depends on skillful fund raisers (around which a whole occupation has now developed) *and* a special occasion (such as the Stevenson, Goldwater, McCarthy, or Wallace campaigns). In addition, it is powerfully assisted by the catalytic presence of a few sources able to contribute large sums, which not merely help the total but lead the small contributors to believe that they are part of a significant enterprise.

The economic environment of black institutions does not provide that catalytic condition at all (or, until recently has not done so). Black-owned business enterprise, which is the basic source of funds (either directly from firms or from shareholders and executives who are personally wealthy by virtue of the well being of the firms) cannot alone provide it. No one expects banks or insurance companies to be charitable institutions. The point rather is (a) that in most black communities there has been very little opportunity for the development of a class of individuals who out of their business connections could have been sufficiently wealthy to support much collective activity personally, and (b) that the institutions through which people in black communities might have gotten an understanding of other available financial resources were relatively few.

The problems of capital and personnel translate into each other. There is almost no black community (if there is any) effectively capable of providing useful activity by which a man might support himself without lowered standard of living, if in consequence of his politics, he were to lose his job. Nor is there any community in which an institution can be effectively supported if, in consequence of its activities, some of its major financial sources begin to withdraw. The institutions will not die, but they will be forced to operate at a reduced level, probably for a substantial time.

Given both personnel and capital scarcities, any organization has always to look at what will happen if it becomes deeply engaged with other organizations in collective enterprises. In what sense will it change the balance between the friendly and the unfriendly members of its constituencies? (By constituencies one means any group, body, or interest which can either increase or diminish the resources off which an organization operates.) If the organization can maintain the supporters it wants, and keep down (or away from) the enemies it does not want, while cooperating in some common venture with other organizations, then it will cooperate. If not, not. The principle is simple, but the practicalities of daily life are not. The situation is usually ambiguous, so that even those with the least need to look beyond the black community may be reluctant to commit themselves too far.

The church is the best example, because it is usually regarded as the strongest black institution. It has been a vehicle of emotional satisfactions, of social control (indeed, once having a sort of "quasi-judicial" role in settling personal disputes), and appears to have been a prime organizer of black economic and social welfare ventures. Its resources are the enthusiasm and loyalty of its members, its personnel reservoir in the clergy, and its funds which (however limited) come most regularly from within the black community. It is part of no larger authority system, and has no significant white competition. Nonetheless, it is not the church as an institution but rather a certain number and type of individual clergymen that have been deeply engaged in efforts to push back the limitations of the racial frontier.

This distinction is partly attributable to self-maintenance problems. At one level, it could be evidence of self-seeking and nothing more. But there was (historically) a quite different level. Maintenance of the church as an institution was important from a doctrinal point of view. If the mission of the church were to save souls, then it might be questioned how far the church should risk injury to its organizational position in quest of secular change. When this position was important and ministerial involvement in secular problems deemed somehow inappropriate, then to move the church organization into race advancement questions was to create an important internal strain. Even if the church's ordinary expenses may be met by the contributions of its members, those contributions may frequently be insufficient for capital ventures. If the clergyman has had need to accept financial help from a black party politician who is associated with the white party organization, the clergyman may be hesitant to repudiate the implicit obligation by taking a forceful role in some move which injures that party organization, and thus contravenes the interests of his former benefactor. This was precisely the position of the minister who (according to James Q. Wilson) said that he would not offend Congressman Dawson, because Dawson could be helpful while the political figure most respected by the militants of the day could hardly help him at all. This is similarly the position of the minister in Philadelphia who could be observed getting a black intermediary to help his church with some zoning problems. The extreme cases, of course, are those of the Southern clergy from whose pattern King and his associates represented so decisive a break. The role of these clergy was often to tranquilize the black community and placate the white. It was never very difficult to resolve this problem when the institutional interests of the church coincided with racial interests, as when the black church wished to defend its "territory" against white churches. It was not so easy when the question was whether a Christian minister should touch the pitch of the secular world, and risk the consequent spiritual defilement, to serve the secular interests of his flock.

Even if ministers found nothing doctrinally inappropriate in external activity, the ultimate "economics" of any politics—the allocation of the scarce resources of time and energy—often led them to pay attention strictly to internal matters as a function of clique politics. Because black church politics offered so many opportunities for esteem and regard, not otherwise equally available, men put a good deal of themselves into pursuing the posts of honor. To become a bishop of the African Methodist Episcopal Church, the successful episcopal candidate was likely to have to invest the same sort of time that a successful candidate for governor or senator might have to invest. He would also have to follow their rule of minding his own business if he were to keep in control of his business and not generate too many enemies.

INTERNAL ATTENTION AND EXTERNAL RECOGNITION

Rather obviously, favorable internal attention is a source of power, provided that it can be enhanced to such a degree that criticism from others has to be muted or can be ignored. It can be decisive in the short run, but on the whole is not a stable source of power precisely because public opinion is subject to dramatic fluctuations. Moreover, for any particular set of organizational leaders or leadership claimants, internal attention may be undermined by the necessity to seek *external* recognition. External recognition is important for the same reasons that diplomatic recognition is important to a new regime in a small country. Such recognition sometimes provides the prestige which comes from having overawed the outsiders. But more important, it usually provides the access to technical bureaucratic skills which come from outside.

Historically, the greatest practitioner of this form of power seeking was Booker T. Washington. Washington's advocacy of *self*-improvement, and his de-emphasis of the overt challenge to white supremacy, made him congenial to Eastern industrial leaders, presidents of the United States, the academic establishment, and moderate white leadership in the South to a degree never repeated in the case of any claimant for black leadership. They provided resources that made it possible for him to overawe most black opponents. He became the client of these white elites and, by subtle use of their support, made himself the *de facto* ruler of the black "nation." Washington was able to establish himself as the center of a black network which ran into the politics of Mississippi and Louisiana, educational administration in Texas, newspaper management in New York City, and hospital services in Chicago. It was this pervasive network which W. E. B. DuBois would call "the Tuskegee machine."

The Washington style may be called clientage in the sense that the practitioner becomes dependent, to some substantial degree, on resources which outsiders have the capacity to confer or to withhold. Clientage as a style is not praised, and would be vigorously disavowed by most practitioners of black politics. Yet the fact is that there are almost no institutions within the black population which have the objective capacity to operate free of some form of clientage, whatever their moral preferences.

If the logic of politics usually advanced in black communities were followed to its conclusion, black politicians—raised to some position of influence on the black vote—would be foremost in the advocacy of racial concerns. In fact, however, the experience indicates a considerable reluctance on the part of politicians to agitate racial issues or even to become involved in them, unless and until the community is virtually uniformly supporting one side of those issues. The Martin Luther King experience in Chicago—where black Democrats led the opposition—is not at all mysterious. (They opposed him, not overtly on the merits of the issues, but by the deflective tactics of creating alternative strategies on the ground that his way of proceeding was wrong, and that he—as a stranger—did not understand the city.) These politicians no more enjoyed subordination than anyone else, but had vital interests to protect and which could not be protected if there were a decisive challenge to the party organization as a whole. They thus chose to adopt a different style of tactics, and to pursue their hope of raising themselves within the party by other means.

The similar problem arises within the trade-union movement.

The trade-union experience is somewhat different, but it is impossible to miss the strain which the new black politics has put on those people who are active in the black community, but who are also active in the labor movement. The problems are particularly important because the trade-union movement has been in more direct contact with large numbers of black people, on a regular basis, than any other organization outside the black community, not excluding the political parties. Black unionists are an important slice of the membership, particularly in the mass-production industries organized by the old Congress of Industrial Organizations. On the whole, the union movement has served their interests fairly well—possibly more so as employees than black men, although the requirements of unionization forced some unions to deal more directly with the problem of in-plant discrimination. As the industrial unions sought, in the 1930's, access to the black work force, some of them found it useful and desirable to adopt at least a symbolic support of racial equality, and to permit local-union officers, staff members, and others, to take active roles in the civil rights organizations. There are still other complications. In the case of some unions, notably the United Automobile Workers, the early experience showed how much management had tried to use the black clergy as liaison in the black community. Many years ago, Ford Motor Company hired a substantially greater proportion of its employees from the black community than did the other companies. One sort of unofficial employment service was the black clergy, particularly—it seems—the Baptists. The predictable happened. The ministers' ability to help people get jobs enhanced their internal influence, and the enhancement of their internal influence gave them an incentive to oppose unionization in the 1930's. As it happened, the black professionals and small businessmen—who earned their incomes directly from the Ford laborers or got other benefits from Ford, also were opposed to unionization. (This opposition was presumably furthered by the fact that the union movement then generally was accurately understood to be antiblack.) As a matter of self-defense, the UAW leadership set out to penetrate the clergy-professional sector, and did so with success. By the late 1950's, the leadership based in that sector was quite closely associated with the UAW and with the Mennen Williams-Neil Staebler faction of the Democratic party. If now the black unionists entirely go over to the militant position, they destroy (or believe they destroy) their leverage in the union. If they do not, they undermine themselves inside parts of the community.

The external recognition and clientage process comes most sharply to the fore now in the action of those who choose the most vigorously "black" rhetoric. Many varieties of overtly militant politics—from black caucuses in white churches to the Panthers—find that their effectiveness depends upon being able to secure and retain white allies, in the course of which they must establish themselves as the "authentic" black spokesmen by destroying the idea that any others than themselves are or could be authentic. This is actually very little different from Washington's use of his foundation connections to exclude the Talented Tenth advocates from serious effectiveness in his own time.

In this light, we are driven to a reconsideration of "militant" and "moderate." These are not, in fact, program positions for the same programs are differently defined as "militant" and "moderate" from one time to another. Nor are they genuinely ideological positions, for there is no coherent statement of an ideological position which at one place (in the same time) might not be called "militant" and in an other place (in the same time) be called "moderate." Nor is there any position which, over time, may not be appropriated by one or another side. "Militant" and "moderate" are, rather, identifying marks for specific factions (networks of people) aligned against each other in the internal politics of the black "nation" at a given moment. They are *party* positions taken in the competition over which side should have external recognition and all that is entailed thereby.

The centrifugal tendency is, thus, partly dictated by the needs of organizational development and organizational maintenance. In general, organizations within the "quasi government" operate on something approaching a hunger budget of skills, money, internal attention, and external recognition. Only if a leader is prepared to see his own organization go down can he fully abstain from the competition. But the fact of the competition at any moment means that those trying to impose collective decisions and strategies have a capacity smaller than their task would seem to imply.

CULTURE AND CENTRIFUGALISM

Scarcity naturally tends to breed conflict, but not all groups facing scarcity situations experience the same amount of internal conflict. How much centrifugalism occurs is also related to the cultural orientation of the population in question. In our interpretation, a second element of black centrifugalism depends on the partially distinctive attributes of Afro-American culture. People interested in racial equality have often been reluctant to accept the idea that Afro-Americans were, in any significant way, culturally different. Their political reasons were sound.[16] Anglo-conformity was so powerful that whites could hardly accept even modest meliorism until fairly recently, and it seemed likely that accepting the black-white cultural difference would merely increase the difficulties. This is one sense in which the much abused word "racism" has a certain practical meaning. For example, we would suggest that the reason Daniel P. Moynihan's report received such wide publicity was not that matriarchal family systems are known to produce bad results. (We may waive the question how far the black family system *is* matriarchal or what "bad" results are.) Instead, it is that (a) the patriarchal pattern is strongly valued by white Americans, (b) the patriarchal pattern is itself under attack, which makes whites extremely uncomfortable, and (c) the fear really was that the black family was the archetype of what the white family would become.

The difficulty is, however, twofold. One is that intellectual responsibility simply dictates the best appreciation of reality that the mind of man can conceive. The second is that unsound analysis, however lofty its political motivation, has a way of coming out wrong, so that the prescriptions for behavior which are based on such analysis are themselves shown to be unsound. Since culture is behavior learned in cohorts, it follows that when two groups are separated by legal or behavioral frontiers over any significant time, some tendency toward cultural difference must develop.[17] (The obverse is also true, at the same time. If they coexist within the same linguistic, economic, or political system, they must develop significant commonalities.)

But how may we know something about the Afro-American culture and its political significance? The answer is not easy, for the problem has largely been ignored, except by psychiatrists who offer a series of unconvincing and apparently unverifiable assertions about the "castration" of the black male. It would be methodologically wrong to argue that the psychiatric explanations could not possibly be correct. The difficulty is that psychiatrists are in the habit of not explaining what their ground rules are, but of leaving us as priests left medieval peasants to take their conclusions on faith.[18] We prefer our own speculations to theirs, speculations which are based on our understanding of the common-sense language that Afro-Americans use as they go about their daily business—somewhat as that language might be interpreted by a latter-day Ruth Benedict (Benedict, 1946).

The ordinary language of Afro-Americans expresses *five themes,* as we see it, which reflect a culture somewhat averse to the sustained coordination required by scarce resources. These themes reflect five characteristics: the hope for deliverance; the wish for defiance; Dionysian independence; moralism; and cynicism-and-fear.

THE HOPE FOR DELIVERANCE

Perhaps the single most common theme in all Afro-American culture is the hope for deliverance some day. For years and years (and perhaps even now), older people looked at their captivity and said "God will deliver us some day." At times, the hope took a more concrete form, a little separated from the doctrinal content but not the spirit of evangelical Protestantism. The Second Coming took on a secular tone, and the Young-as-Deliverers came into focus. There has probably never been a generation in which people did not look at their parlous state and say, "We've had to put up with this, but these young folks ain't gonna take it forever." One could hear this theme during World War II, about the expected return of black soldiers from Europe and the Pacific, as one now hears it about the expected return from Vietnam and (one suspects) as one could have heard it about the Spanish-American War and World War I. The expectation of the Young-as-Deliverers animated much of the passionate concern with schooling—whence the strain to sustain a hundred small colleges—and can even be found in the language of present-day Panthers, who speak of the expectation that the whole emerging generation will be Panther-minded.

THE WISH FOR DEFIANCE

Virtually all black people who speak about their condition look forward to some undefined future when the suffering will be over. But there is another cultural theme which is nearly as deep and profound—defiance. The spirit of defiance serves a need that prudence has usually forbidden people to gratify: to compensate for the pervasive insults and humiliations of past and present by telling "the white man" where to go and what to do, and making him go and do it! Defiant heroism is represented by the plantation folklore of the "bad nigger" or the "crazy nigger" who, pushed beyond his tolerance limits, retaliated with the simple self-help of personal violence, even if doing this guaranteed his own death. The stories are too widespread in black folklore to be underestimated.[19] Sometimes they refer to actual events, and sometimes they refer to mere wishes and dreams. But the hero-figure is not some mere psychotic. Instead, he is a man asserting an elemental right, in a situation where the legal order would almost surely deny that right. Earl Long, not ordinarily noted as a social commentator, understood this syndrome well enough. Telling Louisiana legislators that they had brought the racial strife upon themselves, he chose to illustrate with the story of the black man who killed Earl Long's uncle, when the Long uncle had forced him out of his own bed and raped his wife. The story is recounted in A. J. Liebling's *The Earl of Louisiana* (Liebling, 1961).

The wish for defiance runs all through Afro-American history, in large events and small. The rhetoric of David Walker advocating slave rebellion (1829) is akin to the *Baltimore Afro-American*'s editorial comment (August 8, 1919) that there would be a riot after every Southern lynching "if Southern colored folk knew how to meet violence with violence." The spirit is also manifest in action beyond rhetoric: situations as various as the slave revolts or the thirteen-year-old Walter White's being given instructions during the Atlanta riot (1906): "Son, don't shoot until the first man puts his foot on the lawn and then—don't you miss!"

The wish for defiance is buttressed by a belief in the black capacity to endure. The civil rights movement, in the days of massive nonviolent protest, was a testimonial to the belief that blacks could endure and outlast the worst pain and violence that the Bull Connor types might inflict. But this belief in the capacity to endure is not limited to the advocates of nonviolence. William Brink and Louis Harris report (1964; table, p. 4) survey evidence that blacks themselves believe that, in a contest of violence, black performance would be superior to white.[20] This belief is an important clue to the willingness of people to risk death and danger in the violent urban confrontations of the last eight years.

The greatest responsiveness to the wish for defiance, in all likelihood, was and is to be found among the black peasantry. But it would be a decisive error to believe that it is found only there. It is particularly important to the belletristic writers—the intellectuals with most influence inside the black communities. In contrast to the rather mundane care of social scientists, aiming at a systematic exploration of institutions and processes, the writers of novels, plays, and poems have worked in the mold of protest, prophecy, and the evocation of anger and disgust. The spirit of defiant heroism is given electric expression in a poem by Claude McKay, written under the psychic pressure of much brooding and fear about lynching at the time of World War I:[21]

> If we must die, let it not be like hogs
> Hunted and penned in an inglorious spot,
> While round us bark the mad and hungry dogs,
> Mocking their mock at our accursed lot.
> If we must die—oh, let us nobly die,
> So that our precious blood may not be shed
> In vain; then even the monsters we defy
> Shall be constrained to honor us though dead!

Probably no other verse is known to so many blacks, except James Weldon Johnson's hymn, "Lift Ev'ry Voice and Sing."[22] And McKay himself expressed amazement at "the general sentiment for the poem," saying that "I am so intensely subjective as a poet, that I was not aware, at the moment of writing, that I was transformed into a medium to express a mass sentiment." Imamu Amiri Baraka (LeRoi Jones) and James Baldwin, dissimilar as they are otherwise, are spiritual heirs to McKay. For what they have said was seldom devoted to hard-headed examination of alternatives for action with a calculation of costs of the alternatives.[23] Counting costs is not part of the game, but assuaging the sense of insult is.

The latent spirit of defiant heroism runs even through the sedate politics of the NAACP. Three episodes illustrate the case. One was the punishment of the chapter in Monroe County, North Carolina, then led by Robert F. Williams, for arming that violated not only the national leadership's strategic best judgment but also the sense of propriety in politics. One need not fault the national leadership on either count to observe that many blacks would be more sympathetic to the local chapter, the more so because few blacks would have confidence in the fairness and good discretion of the local authorities. Another episode involves the appearance of then Vice President Nixon at an NAACP Convention. These superbly respectable (and largely middle-class) people, angry at the go-slow posture of the Eisenhower administration, hissed and booed the Vice President until Roy Wilkins rebuked the audience and brought the convention under control. Wilkins's action brought some criticism from such a journalist as James L. Hicks *(The Amsterdam News)*, who thought he ought to have "let them loose" on Nixon, and it surely indicates that the delegates —who may be supposed more "restrained" than an audience randomly selected would be—wanted something more dramatically defiant.[24]

Only by the same hypothesis could we make sense of the dispute within a Midwestern NAACP branch about how to handle the surrender of the city's largest bank, at the end of a long fight over employment policy. The bank, one of the thirty largest in the country, had had the most rigorously discriminatory policies since its foundation just after 1900. As late as 1963, its sole black employee was a uniformed doorman. Following public picketing and other pressures, the bank negotiated an agreement with the local NAACP chapter, by which it would begin to add black staff. As a face-saving device, the bank officers refused to hold a press conference themselves, but said that they would not contradict a public statement by the NAACP president, whose negotiations with them had been public knowledge. Only with great difficulty did the NAACP president suppress a revolt in his own group, since other members of the negotiating team *wanted the bank officers to go through an act which both they and the bank officers regarded as publicly humiliating to the latter.* There are many examples of similar transformation of specific issues into symbolic issues. It is in the same spirit that one comprehends the proclamation of a "curfew" against whites' entering the black areas of Chicago after the Panther killings of 1969—under circumstances when this action might have been deemed provocative beyond the actual capacity of the black population to sustain it. It is in the same spirit that the Panthers' resort to guns draws approval now from people who will never themselves touch a gun. If the ritual of heroism takes different forms for different social classes within the black "nation," one should not fail to understand its importance as a response to enforced subordination.

DIONYSIAN INDIVIDUALISM

Daniel Moynihan once exemplified his conception of the of the weak black male by saying that young black males don't swagger. Ralph Ellison retorted: "I wonder if he has ever *looked* at a bunch of young black men on the street!" Ellison's comment embodies deep insight, for to see groups of young men is to watch a twentieth-century personification of *The Autobiography of Benvenuto Cellini.* Far from the controlled (Apollonian) style which is the Anglo-Protestant norm (and the norm learned by young black men of a certain class), the *standard* is a "culture of the swagger." One of the powerful themes of the culture is, in short, a kind of Dionysian individualism. Psychiatrists may think that boys' juvenile gang wars somehow derive from boys' low self-esteem. But this explanation seems no more valid for gang wars than for the *code duello* among Elizabethan aristocrats or among American politicians a hundred years ago,[25] for the showdowns at High Noon which are celebrated in movies and television, or for the underworld battles on the streets of Chicago in the years of Capone.[26] *Honor*—understood not as fidelity to social obligation but as the maintenance of pride—is a far more persuasive explanation (Miller, 1967, 127–141).

The passion for honor requires a more penetrating discussion than we can give here. But it has at least three elements which seem to have something to do with the centrifugal tendency of black politics.

1. *Self-Expressive Assertion.* The black culture is a culture in which, relatively speaking, oratorical-debating competence is far more praiseworthy than technical bureaucratic skill or the investment of oneself in the tedium of organizational detail. Black audiences, unless very well educated, will not sit still for the sort of dullness which passes in white Episcopal, white Methodist, white Baptist, sermons. A black preacher—even one of the great church political manipulators—had also better be a good talker! The same thing is more often than not true for the black politicians. Such an organizational genius as William L. Dawson was, in his heyday, a brilliant orator. He almost never talked for white audiences, but in the confines of his own ward club could be as cultivated as Adlai Stevenson, as phosphorescent as Adam Clayton Powell, or could relapse into the plain rough-and-tumble of black-alley slanging.

The importance of oratorical debating skill shows up in affairs which purport to be serious, but which are often a political version of the young men's game "playing the dozens." (Playing the dozens is rather like the situation in Vailland's *The Law.* The object is to insult someone else brutally, skillfully, wittily—by aspersion upon his legitimacy—but the loser is not supposed to lose his cool.)[27] In the last five years, when the black middle class has been at a public discount, even meetings under the auspices of so professional a group as the National Urban League are a study in one-upmanship. Conferences become rap sessions, in which people who freely describe themselves as "field niggers" make other people uncomfortable about being "Negroes," preferring to berate them for being "house niggers" who won't face "The Man" and "tell it like it is." That behavior is merely playing the dozens, with one side programed in advance to lose. It is even more striking to see the game played in black-white sessions—such as Urban Coalition meetings—because there the more restrained blacks dare not appear to side with whites (and may even enjoy seeing white corporation presidents cussed out by young black high school dropouts).

The point about all this is that, while it often reflects serious political concerns, it is also a game in which blacks get back their own and vindicate their sense of honor and cleverness.[28] It is not, however, the orientation to the world of the cool-headed calculator, with a clear conception of a major strategic end and a careful appraisal of the tactics which will and will not work. It is not political pragmatism, but self-expression.

2. *Authoritarian Leadership.* The Dionysian preoccupation with honor also affects the behavior of leaders. It enhances the tendency—found in all sorts of organizations, black and white, in any case—for leaders to run their organizations with a minimal sense of due process and a maximal sense that their followers ought to do as they are told. The manifestation of this tendency can still be seen in many sorts of organizations. The clerical dictatorship in an ordinary Baptist church (not to mention the National Baptist Convention) could teach lessons to many a ward boss; but this may also be observed in those organizations explicitly dedicated to racial liberation.[29] Disagreement may be vigorous, but calls for "black unity" are more often means to suppress the minority than to remind all of their common purpose and common necessities. Why this behavior occurs is not clear, but we may hypothesize that black people have tended to be limited to precisely those situations most adverse to due process, and to learn in these situations their political rules-of-the-game. This quality is patent in the kind of big-city party organization where blacks have had some scope, and the operational lessons of which they have had to learn, as it is patent in the cumulative experience of Southern politics and the organizational life of the trade union—the other settings in which blacks have most experience. The Southern experience is one of living with, and observing, situations in which due process was entirely withheld in black-white relations, and also, as could be observed, was frequently missing in

the relationships between white competitors in politics. The experience which most black men have in the North, outside the black community but translated back into that community, is the trade union. It is common knowledge that the trade union is one of the least "constitutional" private organizations in American life, and that it is one in which coercion and intimidation of an overt sort are likely to play the most significant roles. Since men learn from the environments in which they exist, unless there are constraints which impede their learning, it seems likely that these exposures would contribute to the difficulties that even the civil rights organizations have in maintaining due process criteria for their internal decisions.

3. *Segmentation and Secession.* Dionysian individualism is expressed, finally, in the adoption of segmentation and secession as a means for the defense of honor, in those cases where honor cannot be reconciled with continuing in an existing organization. This defense would explain the fissiparous tendency in black organizations. Black men, like others, do not like to operate in organizational situations where they have no options but to go along or shut up. In all likelihood, they have frequently dealt with the situation by operating from a model in the church world with which most are familiar: the model of segmentation and secession. In the Baptist experience—where ever so many blacks have learned their organizational behavior—there is a strong tendency toward *de facto* autocracy, even though the Baptist polity emphasizes the equality of the conscience of each man. Church leaders, whether pastors in individual congregations or denominational leaders, have tended to develop quasi-machines, such that once in control a leader could hardly be challenged except by those who might mean entirely to destroy him. The defense against autocracy— legitimated by the doctrines of the church—is withdrawal to form a new and purer unit.

MORALISM

Life is interpreted through still another Protestant residue: a moralistic language which expresses the view that men ought to do "right." The ordinary conversational language of black people seems to express the self-image that black men, in contrast to white men, possess a greater "sensitivity," a greater "humaneness," or (in one version) "more soul." This is not to say that such concerns are not present in other languages,[30] but that they are acutely present in the current language of the black Americans. One got this message in a conversation with a justice of the peace in a small Michigan city. He could, he said, understand Stokely

Carmichael, even though Carmichael was a little radical: "Somebody, sometime, must have hurt him." This man knew that white people had "hurt" him (and went off into a long discussion of his experiences in the Navy and with his white fellow-unionists in the General Motors plant). The same spirit is barely veiled in the language of the Brooklyn housewife who said she favored community (black) control of the schools because "white people don't really care about us" (New York Times, September 16, 1968). If one were but dealing with a woman of little experience, this could be dismissed easily. But it has the same tone from two women of international repute and great sophistication: "The white man is dirty!" and "White people have used such *despicable* tactics!" If one knows the ways of realist politics, is even capable of using them—and still protests —something deeper remains about one's own values. That something comes through in even the most melodramatic and threatening language of most "Black Power" advocates; the theme that "the white man is *dirty"* and "does not *care* about you," is so often advanced that it is quite striking. "What *morality?* This *country ain't got no morality!"* was the theme which, in the speeches of Mr. Stokely Carmichael, could get overwhelming responses from black audiences.[31] The moralistic demand is not merely turned outward, but inward as well. It demands of leaders that they should approach perfection *in their heroism,* and the more nearly they do so the more their other failings can be excused.[32] But the absence of heroism activates the bitter cynicism and the *almost* paranoid fear of being sold out.

CYNICISM-AND-FEAR

The same experience which teaches people to wish for defiance and hope for deliverance also teaches them to be cynical about the prospects and fearful of trying. In part, this cynicism-and-fear is utterly realistic. One may admire other people's defiance and yet recognize the likelihood that such defiance will be destructive to oneself, when one is not ready to be destroyed. In part, it may be delusory—the idea that in all things white people know some tricks and devices unknown to blacks. The political repercussions are important. For it is usually the case that most black leaders neither do, nor could, go the uttermost distance commanded by the wish for deviance and deliverance.

Not seeing heroism, it is natural for those themselves fearful to interpret black leaders who are not *demonstrating heroism* as equally fearful. Cynicism is also related to the historic experience with the fact that clientage has been a crucial instrument by which some black men ("leaders") have secured influence over other black men.[33] That is, it has been quite useful for some leadership figures (Booker T. Washington is surely the archetype) to make themselves important by playing the role of Herod to the white man's Caesar. Self-evidently, within the values we have been describing, Herodianism can never have been the most fully approved mode of operation. Yet the matter is still more complex.

(1) Herodianism may be denounced in black political mythology, but its practice has never ceased and one may even argue that the institutions most immediately responsive to the *economic* problems of blacks have been and have had to be cast in the Herodian format. For instance, until just after World War II, the vast bulk of higher schooling for blacks—an essential prerequisite though not a sufficient condition for any sort of economic progress—has come through the black colleges and universities of the South. It is not only in fiction but also in sober fact that the institution builders who made the continuance of those colleges and universities possible, beyond the meager support level which blacks themselves could afford, had to adopt the strategy of "keeping powerful friends." Such a practice has been visible not only in the strategies of those administrators who seemed perfectly comfortable doing the bidding of whites, but to some degree also in the strategies of those who were quite uncomfortable yet nonetheless did what they deemed necessary. (2) Nor is this strategy merely an artifact of Southern life. In the urban North from World War I on, the main institution which devoted itself to the economic welfare problems of *blacks as such* has been the Urban League, which is reputed for its "conservatism." But the memoirs of Urban League staff, no less than academic studies of League operations, amply document the painful strategy of "keeping powerful friends" and the constant search for some other viable strategy. (3) In this sense, Herodianism has been in black politics like other practices in broader politics—uncomfortable, denounced in the symbol system, yet a source of desired goods which people have been unable or unwilling to forego. The analogy is, perhaps, to a practice like corruption in urban politics—uncomfortable, denounced in the symbol system, yet a source of the influence which parties have needed in order to achieve office, with the achievement of office as a necessary (but not sufficient) condition for achieving policies which people have wanted. Yet this concession to necessity by no means reduces the disposition of people to treat Herodianism cynically, and to be deeply suspicious of those who practice it.

These five themes (the hope of deliverance; the wish for defiance; Dionysian individualism; moralism; cynicism-and-fear) seem to us regularly perceptible in the common speech of Afro-Americans.[34] They are major ingredients in a culture which is still in the process of formation.

The question which is pertinent is how these elements impede coordination of the already severely limited resources which, by their very limitation, produce a high degree of centrifugalism in the "quasi government." Our hypothesis is that the hope for deliverance, the wish for defiance, and moralism jointly produce a disposition to treat the problem of racial liberation as a morality play rather than as a pragmatic problem in political tactics. The people as a whole are deemed an audience rather than responsible participants. Collective advancement is deemed the business of leaders. Leaders are expected always to "do right," never to shirk danger, and soon to produce the most dramatic results.

At the same time, Dionysian individualism and cynicism-and-fear undermine the capacity of individuals to participate on a large scale and responsibly. The passion for honor diminishes the willingness of leaders to extend due process to followers. The end result is that many followers withdraw in a segmentation process in defense of their own honor, and —being suspicious—treat any assumption of elite roles as a form of supererogation. Dionysian individualism means that if individuals do enter the process on a large scale, they will do so expressively, so that the political morality play is also a form of collective psychiatry, which makes the participants feel better about themselves in a hostile world. In encourages members of the group to believe that all failures are a function of "bad" leaders or malevolent adversaries. The net effect is to diminish the capacity to make prudent use of those limited resources which are available in a hostile world, for that task is very difficult to carry out under a combination of very high demands and very low support.

CLASS AND CENTRIFUGALISM

Our main argument has been, we may recall, that resource competition has limited the power of leaders to exercise effective direction over the "quasi government." In addition, we argue, even those resources available have been used less effectively than in principle they might be, because the cultural strains tend to limit the moral authority of leaders. Moral authority is limited, however, by still another factor: tension among the social classes within the black "nation." By a "social class" I mean a collectivity the members of which have somewhat similar economic status, somewhat similar prestige aspirations, and somewhat similar life styles and cultural values.

It used to be appropriate to identify social classes among blacks in the United States by their positions relative to each other, recognizing that the characteristics which gave them their relative positions would have put them farther down any scale of classes in white America. For instance, we are all familiar with the image of a black upper elite which—at the turn of the century—was unlikely to contain men of wealth, but did contain some professionals and, at the same time, independent tradesmen, and was likely to contain the personal servants of wealthy whites. Later on, the uppermost portion of the black middle class was likely to contain public school teachers and social caseworkers, in a variegated mix with literati, postal employees, and Pullman porters (Garraty, 1966). It is now broadly possible to identify social class within black America by placing the same class labels on individuals in both black America and white America, although there is the significant distinction that black America still does not possess the full range of classes to be found in white America. Within our definition of class, it is convenient to divide the black population into two major classes, each of which is further divisible into subclasses. Following more or less conventional practice, we may describe these two classes as *the bourgeoisie* and *"the folks."*

THE BOURGEOISIE

No part of the Afro-American class structure is very well understood, but the least understood element is what one may call the *"Gentry,"* a class broadly possessing the tastes and style of an aristocracy, but lacking the capital and power to function as an aristocracy.[35] The origins of the gentry seem to come from three historical streams: the covey of black families—Northern, but to some limited extent Southern—free from before the Civil War (Chesnutt, 1953); some of those irregular white man-black woman unions that were occasionally maintained about as stably and publicly as if they were legal marriages (see Torrence, 1948); and finally, from families that got a leg up during the Civil War or in the Reconstruction politics that followed (Uya, 1970; Fox, 1970).

The distinctive quality of the gentry is that they would now be embarrassed by Nathan Hare's derisive term, "the black Anglo-Saxons." But their grandparents would not have been. It seems reasonably clear that color snobbery (most of them were phenotypically Caucasoid) was an important regulator of their private social lives, and that they were not quite comfortable with the ordinary black peasant families. The life styles which they prized were clearly and explicitly those of the Anglo-Protestant tradition of New England: a respect for learning and *belles lettres,* a sense of duty, and a passion for respectability and citizenship.

The gentry remain as a class, though very small and much changed, but they have never managed to establish themselves as an upper class with moral authority. One of the impediments was probably scalar. The number of persons who might fit these traits is too small to make them a self-sustaining group. Moreover, few acquired the *capital* to perform the supporting functions of a stable upper class with respect to the rest of the population. Most gentry from preceding generations have tended to fall back into some lower stratum.

The second element of the bourgeoisie, and that most commonly mentioned, is what we may now call the *"Solid Middle-Class"*—probably about 25 percent of the black population. This is no longer the assemblage of postal clerks and Pullman porters so often remarked in literature as late as World War II. Instead, they are people whose middle-class status is defined in the same terms as the middle-class status of their white counterparts. Their opportunities are not equal to those of their white counterparts, for they may earn less money than those counterparts and even, on the average, less than white working-class persons (Ross and Hill, 1967, notably Chapters 1–3).

But their qualities are similar. Their cocktail parties are more and more likely to be attended by a lot of couples where at least one member is sure to have been to college, and where it is not remarkable if both have college degrees at least to the baccalaureate. They are the junior-management personnel in large national firms,[36] the various sorts of bureaucratic personnel who have direct contact with "the public," department store salespeople, accountants with some college training, or struggling lawyers in one- and two-man offices. The participation of the solid middle class in the large economy is perceptible in a number of ways, obviously by means of visual inspection ("eyeball methods"). It used to be said that middle-class blacks were those who could pay the rent regularly. Now, these are the people—in any Eastern or Midwestern metropolis—who can buy $20,000 *used* houses,[37] whenever credit is not too tight to make FHA mortgages inoperable. They may also buy truckloads of new furniture to put into those houses, have wardrobes of new clothing, and—under the most favorable circumstances—spend $100 per couple for an NAACP dinner or take vacations in the West Indies and Europe. Above all, the offspring of these persons are likely to be able to go to school longer, with less risk of having to drop out for financial reasons, than were the middle-class offspring before World War II. This last is probably the most important single factor, for the ability of a large number of such people to keep their children in school through the college years predicts a certain future status security which this class, on the whole, has not before had.

THE FOLKS

One might, in keeping with current fashion, refer to "ghetto people" and convey a certain fairly definite image. Or one might speak of "lower-class blacks" or "the black poor." But all these terms have so many other implications that we dare not think them useful. It may more adequately convey our present meaning to speak simply of "the folks"—a grouping in whose no-nonsense social world "pretending to be white" is a devastating charge likely to be thrown at those who suddenly seem to be adopting the life styles of the gentry. This world is not all of one piece, though until recently, most observers did not bother to distinguish its components, presumably because the usual overt ("objective") indicators seemed so much the same. "The folks" all occupied the same poor portions of the territorial ghettoes, had the same sorts of schooling, and—when employed —had the same sorts of jobs. Moreover, since the various components of the world of "the folks" are members of the same extended family networks, they do have genuine relationships to each other. Nonetheless, they fall into three main patterns: the Working-Class Respectables, the Striving Poor, and the Immobile Poor.

The size of the whole category of "the folks" can be guessed only roughly, but if we suppose that the solid middle class are about a quarter of the black population (roughly 5.5 million people) and the poor (by government definitions) are about 10 millions, then the Working-Class Respectables must be about 30 percent of the black population (or about 6.5 millions).

Historically, the *Working-Class Respectables* may have been very insecure economically. They are still so, but their economic insecurity is similar to that of the working-class whites, with whom they are comparable. Economic slumps hurt them badly, for they constitute part of the work force most likely to be laid off. An economic cool-out freezes them. But when the economy is booming, they benefit—particularly since they are under the protection of mass unionization as well. As a result, they are an important segment of the consumer economy, living with the expectation that life will continue to get better.

The expectation is fully consistent with their historic perceptions, for they used to describe themselves as "poor," which was a respectable term —in contrast to "lower class," which *meant* in their language "low class" (low life, morally inappropriate, and similar derogations). To be poor had no moral connotations, or implications of apathy and anomie. These people did (and do) *believe* in work, hate laziness, and feel superior to "these welfare people," just as does the white working class. They are the deacons of the Baptist church or, if no longer religious, regular attenders at something like the bowling league, and they despise the income tax. Anyone who doubts their rational calculation of their own interests should watch carefully, for they dislike Rap Brown, distrust the police (they know all about shakedowns and brutality), would be Wallace voters if they were white,[38] know that "the white man can't be trusted," but generally do not participate in racial organizations. (They do participate in other organizations, e.g., the Democratic party, social clubs, the church.)

They may not know how to evaluate an educational program, but they believe in school and their kids had better not be found playing hooky. (Not knowing how to evaluate school programs, they are strongly in favor of the one item they can easily appreciate—effective discipline.) Similarly not knowing how to explain failure, they are disappointed and chagrined when their kids drop out.

The significant difference between the Working-Class Respectables and the *Striving Poor* is mainly one of objective likelihood that they can satisfy themselves, at least partly by their own efforts. The Striving Poor may not be so intent on lifting themselves upward, or may lack the educational skills to do so, and are certainly still more handicapped by racial discrimination. From one case to another, within this group—and from time to time with respect to the same person in this group—one may encounter the faith that somehow things will work out if one keeps trying, along with a contradictory, despairing "What's the use? It won't work for me."

Finally, there are those who may be called the *Immobile Poor*. Change in the economy since 1946 has benefited them least, except to the extent that it is represented by an increase in public assistance payments. The Immobile Poor are those most likely to be in more or less permanent trouble with the police, the occupants of public housing projects, and the least defended victims of the public school system. They are those who constitute the 2,000,000 black persons on Aid to Families with Dependent Children, and the most likely among the AFDC recipients to have children who become recipients. It is also they who are the least likely to be involved in any of the forms of organizational life within the black community, and the most likely to live virtually all their lives—day and night—in the territorial ghetto as well as in the black social system.

CLASS TENSIONS AND CENTRIFUGALISM

Contrary to the dominant image, widely believed among "the folks" (and spread to the world at large by a misinterpretation of Franklin Frazier), *the initiative for a politics of liberation has persistently come from within the black bourgeoisie.* Historically, the role of the gentry was particularly important in this regard. For all their color snobbery, the gentry were also strongly committed to old-fashioned ideas of "manhood" and "citizenship" which made it the more essential for them to press their claims to equality of treatment before the law.[39] Moreover, as a practical matter, their very careers depended immediately upon widened opportunities, which explains the fact that they fought Booker Washington whenever they could. (See Essay II, following.) And some—notably DuBois and John Hope—were committed to a kind of cultural freedom for which claims are only recently resuscitated (DuBois, 1969; Torrence, 1948). As the gentry's power in the black community declined, leadership passed to "the solid middle class," which again provided those people who were "out front" on racial issues. Nonetheless, the moral authority of the bourgeoisie—gentry *or* "solid middle class"—has been rather limited, so that this group never developed an effective capacity to make its leadership effective. Indeed, nothing has been more significant a barrier to collective action than the distrust of the black bourgeoisie by the black "folks." This distrust has not, at least until recently, taken the form of any class struggle, but merely of class tension. There have been no sustained efforts to transform the distrust into actual political action, meant to displace bourgeois leadership by "folk" leadership.[40] The tension exists because of the powerful spirit of moralism, which led "the folks" to believe that the bourgeoisie did not "care" about them; a belief which the bourgeoisie were unable to reduce since they could not produce defiant or liberating results. But even if moralism were not pertinent, other structural constraints would tend toward the same results.

There has been, and remains, a natural and overt conflict of interest between that part of the bourgeoisie based in independent business-professional activity and the large popular audience required for moral authority. Businessmen, for instance, are hardly generous and are little part of the mechanism for lending ritual approval to collective projects. This is a function both of their style and of their economic necessities.

Since the center of gravity of black entrepreneurship must be in relatively small retail trade and service enterprises, one may regard black business as a sort of urban peasant economy. Its participants are competitive, but not in the economic sense that implies substantial volume and turnover, relatively low mark-up, and innovation, all of which depend on a certain solidity of capital backing. Rather, they are, perforce, individualistic in the sense of being little disposed to cooperate in ventures which do not clearly serve their immediate interest and of being conservative in the sense of preferring the absolute minimum of risk.

Undoubtedly, many black businessmen have engaged in pricing and other policies which made their black customers pay more than white customers would have paid. But there was a harsh logic even here. For the black businessmen, the white customers did not exist. The black customers would not have yielded enough to make the enterprise worthwhile, if they had been charged at the same rate that might have been applied to white customers. In some sense, such exploitative policies were a necessary condition for any capital aggregation by black men at all. In a sense, here is another version of the developmental process for any poor "nation," whether that nation have a formal government or not. It is not a pretty process, and in *moral* terms becomes justifiable only if it *later* produces rewards which the people would otherwise not have had. It is functionally useful only if it leads to deferred gratification. If the process produces no later gratification, then it is exploitative. The question "How much later?" is hard to answer, both in economics and in moral philosophy. In the same sense, block-busting tactics by black real estate men could simultaneously be condemned and understood. At the minimum, block busting—so long as the duality of housing markets would remain rigid in any case—also served to increase the volume of housing available to black occupants.[41]

Apart from this problem, most of the black bourgeoisie will be found earning their daily incomes in other situations which either distract them from collective action or provide disincentives for solid cooperation (as against ritualistic discussions of cooperation). For example, many of the members of this group now earn their incomes in private industry, and are likely to feel (as their white colleagues at the same level often feel) that they should not become engaged in "controversial" matters if they wish to fare well on the job. It is not essential that the employers should actually discourage them, but only that they should suspect that the employers want to discourage them.[42]

A third factor is that many of the same sorts of professionals who would engage in the generation of collective action, who talk about doing so, and who actually do so work in exposed situations where their activity produces backlash. If, for instance, the executive director of an Urban League seriously pursues a policy of antidiscrimination in housing or employment, he may find that his agency becomes the object of criticism and inquiry on the next round of United Fund budget decisions. But if he withholds his hand, then he is subject to criticism. This decision is particularly important since his role, under the latter condition, hardly becomes distinguishable from clientage, that is, leadership dependent on external sponsorship. He is, therefore, in a peculiarly exposed position for he could hardly fail to live better than the average man, unless he systematically gave away his salary and refused to own property. It was natural for such people to be seen as exploitative, as they sometimes were calculatedly and more often must have been unwittingly. At the minimum, they sometimes declined to raise relevant racial issues lest they anger white supporters. Caution was used not only to save their salaries but also to keep their institutions operating (Dancy, 1966; Strickland, 1966). Adverse criticism rests on a presumption which deserves more examination: that a social functionary—operating an intermediary role between two audiences—can always consistently advance the maximum demands of one, always reject the other, and still be effective.

Economic reasons apart, the bourgeoisie experienced difficulties due to uncertainties and conflicts within itself. Competition within any sort of leadership class usually tends to become somewhat personalized. Hyper-"rational" theories of decision making to the contrary, leaders do not usually remain wholly detached from the issues and alignments in which they are entangled. (Witness the Johnson-Fulbright strain.) But the larger the organizational system, and the more the competitors can rationalize disagreement as due to some external demand ("my district demands this"), then the more the competitors can rationalize their divisions without losing friendship or the ability to cooperate in other situations. Members of the black bourgeoisie do not normally have this kind of constituency relationship, which is both clear and accepted as morally legitimate by their fellows. Disputes, when they arise as they must, consequently tend to leave residues of conflict which, over time, become the nuclei of personal factionalism, such that A is automatically suspicious of *anything* B proposes.

The black bourgeoisie has experienced what one may call the "small-town syndrome," even in the urban North. The number of people disposed to engage in collective action, capable of doing so, and free to do so has been sufficiently small that they would have tended to become acquainted with each other as persons. Even in so large a city as Detroit, this interpersonal awareness among the top echelon is rather high.

Finally, a leadership class, to be effective, must have a certain clarity about the appropriate values and the confidence to hold these values forth as those which other people ought to accept. But to reflect upon the small size of the gentry is to see a group too small to communicate its values very widely, and to reflect upon the growth of the solid middle class is to see a group inherently unstable due to its rapid rise from a different social status. As a class in transition, looking both to the cultures of the white and to the cultures of the black, the bourgeoisie thus lacked the occasion to develop a firmly set system of values by which action could be guided.

If one started with the black gentry, one began with a rather clear adherence to the political values of democratic constitutionalism and in addition a general acceptance of the body of Anglo-Protestant cultural values. Recruitment from the world of "the folks" into the bourgeoisie brought in a whole cultural approach in which the values of constitutionalism were far less explicit. But no substitute intellectualized values were offered until the rise of the nonviolent direct-action movement. There was, instead, a distinct ambivalence, reflected in recurrent debates over "segregation" versus "integration," "political" versus "economic" approaches, and the conditions for "mass organization." Moreover, within the black bourgeoisie there was a profound discomfort with the observable behavior of the black poor, which led to a kind of common belief (asserted too stridently to have been really *believed*) that if black men acted "properly" they would be accepted "as Americans, not Negroes."

SUMMARY AND CONCLUSION

The internal politics of the black "nation" is—as one might expect—a politics which white social scientists and journalists have found particularly difficult to understand, even when they have thought the contrary. This difficulty is no surprise. It is always terribly difficult to understand the politics of *any* other people whose experience is quite unlike one's own, and difficult to overcome this disability. Protestants clearly do not understand the politics of the Roman Catholic Church, else they should never have thought it a monolithic ecclesiastical dictatorship. Europeans have great difficulty understanding United States politics, which is reflected in their constant puzzlement at the absence of "left" and "right" class-based parties. Americans similarly do not understand the dynamics of the Sino-Soviet relationship, the rigidities of Protestant-Catholic politics in Ulster, or the intricacies of Vietnam. So it is also that social scientists—and journalists even more—persistently fail to understand the structure of influence within the "black population."[43] They have written a great deal about black voting behavior, officeholding, and party participation; the claims and strategies of race-advancement organization, as those strategies and claims are manifest in the public arena; and somewhat about black attitudes toward the governmental system and urban rebellion as a form of "unconventional" political participation. But in all this the tone is that the territorial ghettoes of the cities (and most of the rural South) are simply demoralized, disorganized, dispirited reservations, lacking structure and leadership.

The uncertainty and confusion of scholars and commentators is easily represented in two questions. "What do you people want anyway?" and "Why don't you have accepted leaders with whom we can deal?" Generally speaking, black people find both these questions immeasurably irritating. Some judge these very questions themselves to be indicia of a perverse "racism" to which the answer is obvious: "Get your foot off my neck!" But whatever the irritation may express about blacks' state of mind, the conversation has three deficiencies. First, the answer is not "operational." It does not indicate the sorts of white behaviors which would be satisfactory if—like Paul on the Damascus Road—whites suddenly experienced a flash of light. Second, the questions imply what is not correct: that blacks fully agree on what is important or how one ought to go about what is important. Indeed, there are those blacks who find the questions irritating not because any answer is obvious, but because they deem it perverse (if not stupid) to talk as if a group more numerous than the national populations of most members of the United Nations could possibly have the sort of unanimity which the questions imply. The third deficiency is the most important. *Not only is it hard to understand somebody else's politics, but it is very hard to understand one's own.* Very careful reflection and very careful attention to fact and logic may reveal much that is crude and lacking in nobility. Black people, *like others,* avoid as much as possible the examination which threatens both their preferred self-images and the images of the "others" which they find most agreeable and comforting.[44]

Neither approach clarifies very much. The idea that the black "nation" is simply leaderless, demoralized, or disorganized cannot be supported. Instead, there is an extensive pattern—relating a wide variety of specific institutional centers and operated within a well-understood set of symbols. These centers possess no legal authority over any black person, but they do possess some degree of real influence which few black people can effectively escape. In addition, there is a considerable stability in leadership personnel. It is not actually the case that one group is displaced rapidly by another, so much as that successive additions bring in new sorts of personnel who compete with their predecessors. The important problem is not the absence of organization. It is, instead, the incapacity of existing leadership to develop a relatively stable process for identifying goals and methods, and a relatively effective method for inducing the members of the group to lend their efforts in a stable manner.

That problem exists, we argue, as a function of three factors: the intensive competition between organizations, due to limited organizational resources; an imbalance in a culture yet being formed, so that there is a pattern of high demands and low support; and a natural tension between the social classes of the black "nation." This tension has, as the very record of black politics of the last sixty years shows, not prevented a substantial measure of collective action. It has prevented collective action at a level high enough to produce results which people find adequate.

All three factors reduce the capacity of the "quasi government" to be effective *vis-à-vis* the white world. The process then becomes circular. Every failure at cooperation tends to exacerbate issues which are adverse to cooperation, even if people want to cooperate. Factionalism has not, however, prevented the black bourgeoisie from maintaining themselves as the prime source of black leadership, perhaps only because there were (until recently) no other sources. If this group has maintained itself, it has not been able to redeem the promises which—as a leadership group—it has overtly and implicitly made to produce racial change on a scale, and in a form, suitable to most of the black population. This is the process which we call centrifugalism (or factionalism): a tendency toward severe internal conflict.

The next question is what the implications of centrifugalism are for the external politics of the black "nation." The more stable a group is, the more it can make the adjustments without claiming that past strategies were, *in their contexts,* wrong or that the advocates of different stagies at any moment are either fools or traitors. Of course, there is no perfection in any case. The world of political strategy making is always rather like an ocean which, to the casual observer, may seem like one indivisible entity, but which the political oceanographer knows to be a medley of clashing and underflowing currents and cross currents. In the next two essays we consider some of these currents and cross currents as they are manifested in the external politics of the black "nation" and in the evolution of the main strategies which have been advanced as calculated means of changing the racial structure of power. We consider also the relative success and failures of those strategies and the problems involved in adapting those strategies to present conditions.

NOTES

1. Also, for further discussion of the white-black differences and their political implications, see Holden, *The White Man's Burden,* published simultaneously with this present volume. Occasions for referring to *The White Man's Burden* will be numerous, and the form for reference will hereafter be simply the title.

2. My thought on the problems on this essay has been much influenced by the

works of Pieter Geyl and Karl W. Deutsch, which I here acknowledge with respect.

3. A very interesting book which raises some of these issues in the context of Ulster politics is Rose, *Governing without Consensus* (1971). Unfortunately, Rose's book appeared too late for me to make good use of its insights in the present analysis.

4. By "politics" I mean much more than electoral competition or even "public policy." I mean, instead, the whole complicated process by which, within any group X, some people seek to organize control and give direction and other people either accede or resist. This then leads to thought about patterns of enmity, friendship, and alliance; of domination, subordination, and rebellion; of coercion, pragmatic bargaining, and moral suasion. See Hamilton (1957) and Masao Maruyama as quoted in Paige (1966, 57, n. 16).

5. Above, Preface, and *The White Man's Burden*, Essay I.

6. In my view, the advocacy of "unity" makes sense at some levels, but can easily be overdone. I return to this briefly, in the first two pages of Essay V, below.

7. By "black communities" we mean mainly the *territorial* ghettoes within Northern cities, although we would argue that the analysis can be extended to Southern localities.

8. One sort of institutional center which I do not discuss, for lack of personal knowledge or a research base, is that of illegal activity ("the numbers" operations and so forth). It would be naive to ignore the presence of such activity as represented in street-level conversation, but information suitable to publication is harder to achieve. No book, to my knowledge, has even attempted this since the publication of Drake and Cayton's *Black Metropolis* more than twenty-five years ago.

9. Indeed, a study of the social role of the college president would be greatly merited, for there is little on the record except a few biographies (most not very good) and the portraits drawin by such novelists as Saunders Redding and Ralph Ellison.

10. Something of that role-defined access may remain even now. I would note, for instance, that the political circumstances permitted (and possibly required) President Nixon to postpone meeting the Congressional Black Caucus for a very long time in 1971. On the other hand, when the Cambodian crisis led to the appointment of President Alexander Heard (Vanderbilt) to report on student discontent in relation to public policy, President James Cheek (Howard) was assigned to work in tandem with Heard, and had a half-time office in the Executive Office Building while continuing his direction of Howard University.

11. The most quickly read piece I know is the poet Langston Hughes' book *Fight for Freedom* (1962). Among the books by persons involved in the foundation of the organization, I have found profit in W.E.B. DuBois, *Autobiography* (1969); and Ovington (1947). The NAACP's national reputation was, for many years, as closely associated with the name of Walter White as it is now with the name of his successor, Roy Wilkins. The development of the organization and its role in

national politics, from White's perspective, is represented in White (1948). For a detailed academic account, in what is apparently meant to be the authoritative book for many years to come, see Kellogg (1967).

12. On the background leading up to SCLC, Martin Luther King, Jr., *Stride Toward Freedom* (1958); and, on CORE and SNCC, Muse (1968).

13. For this information, I am obliged to Mr. Odie Parker (Chicago), who has close personal connections with both the union leadership and with the deacon board mentioned. Naturally, judgment precludes identifying the specific congregation.

14. For those not familiar with the details of Chicago politics, August A. Savage is a youngish neighborhood newspaper publisher who has been active in black insurgent politics in the Democratic party. A. A. (Sammy) Rayner is an undertaker who beat the Daley organization in his campaign for election to the City Council.

15. All the denunciations of the Office of Economic Opportunity should not obscure the great importance of the enlargement of the black communities' skills pool which came simply because "maximum feasible participation" got a lot of people used to doing things.

16. This is still not irrelevant. One indicator is contained in the remark of a Miami secretary that black people ought to have rights comparable to those of white people to the extent that they should become "more like us." See the Harris Survey as reported in *Detroit Free Press*, September 16, 1968.

17. Our formulation here has been influenced substantially by Pieter Geyl, *History of the Low Countries*, (1964, 15–16 and *passim*).

18. This is the central problem with the use of the case histories in William H. Grier and Price M. Cobbs, *Black Rage* (1968). The authors do not tell us what the rules of interpretation are. We have to take their word that the case histories mean what they say they mean, unless we are all to become psychiatrists ourselves. As thoughtful people in a highly educated society, we are entitled to a better exposition than that. Even if we *assumed* the case histories to be correctly reported and analyzed, we should still be entitled to ask the psychiatrists: Upon what theory and rules do you interpret these cases to explain the behavior of twenty-two million people?

Precisely because psychiatry has such enormous authority in American society, it is important to notice that the problem of evidence and intepretation seems to elude the profession, and gives us some reason to pause and wonder if this emperor is really clothed. See, Erik H. Erikson, "The Nature of Clinical Evidence," in Lerner (1958), 73–95.

19. Social scientists should not too hastily decide, however, that the anecdotes themselves are either fictitious or unrepresentative. In this connection, it is worth noting that recent refinement in oral history techniques have shown, at least in the African context, far more literal accuracy in folklore than those who conceive of "history" as embodied in *paper* evidence would normally concede. If folklore is accurate in one social context, it merits examination in another; for there is no *a priori* basis to assume that it is limited to the African context. However, accuracy

in these stories *is* an empirical question which can probably best be examined by a serious study of the folklore.

20. This may, of course, surprise those whites who have precisely the reverse image fixed in their minds.

21. McKay's own thoughts on his fumblings and trials toward a poem on this theme are mentioned in his book, *A Long Way from Home* (1937), 20–22, 31–34, 98–99, and 227–228.

22. Indeed, the Johnson hymn—which used to be called "the Negro national anthem" when I was a child—and the McKay poem together brilliantly represent the hopeful and the defiant themes in the culture of black America.

23. However, this statement does not apply so much to Imamu Amiri Baraka, the self-conscious political strategist of current Newark, as it does to LeRoi Jones, the poet of the years before 1967.

24. But dramatic defiance was not within the cultural frame of the Association's leadership, given the leadership's strong commitment to constitutionalist values and their noticeable respect for political pragmatism as ordinarily defined; but one would be surprised if Wilkins has not sometimes regretted his prudence.

25. John Carl Parish, *George Wallace Jones* (1912), shows this in discussing the personal style of the first United States Senator from sober, moderate Iowa. For a brief discussion of the pattern in Congress, see Polsby (1968), 167–168.

26. There is a very insightful discussion of the similarity between Elizabethan aristocrats and Chicago gangsters in Stone (1965), 234.

27. He usually does lose it. See also Hannerz (1970). 129–133.

28. The critique of E. Franklin Frazier, *Black Bourgeoisie* (1962 ed.), says that this vindication of cleverness is a conspicuous feature of black-college faculty life. We, however, have insufficient experience to deal with that confidently.

29. We were given illustrations of this by the heads of two major national organizations within the past two years. Mr. A said that he, and his headquarters staff, were appalled at the procedural irregularities which they sometimes found in local branches. The problem was not so much ballot-box stuffing as outright arbitrariness, for example, rulings from the Chair that those who seemed to be in opposition could not exercise elementary membership rights, such as voting in local branch elections.

Mr. B described the national convention of a third organization—which he attended as a guest. At a heated moment, one delegate arose to say that he had a point of order, to which the Chair replied: "You've got *what?* You'd better sit down."

30. If we are to believe the social historians, something of this sort must have been very important in the evangelical culture of the nineteenth-century English working class. See, for instance, Postage (1951).

31. For a much more restrained statement of the same theme, see the vignette, "Whites Can Be So Nasty," in Brink and Harris, (1967), 117–118.

32. This, we would argue, is the most important single reason for the long-standing popularity of Adam Clayton Powell. Powell was respected not so much for those occasions when he adroitly and shrewdly used the power of his commit-

tee chairmanship in the House, as for all those other occasions when he spat symbolically in the white man's eye by violating the more obvious conventions of political decorum.

33. This is the nucleus of the "Uncle Tom" syndrome, the black equivalent of the term "quisling." Later in the next essay, we shall point out some other aspects of clientage.

34. As we have noted above (Preface), we have not done the research which the argument implies, so the argument is purely hypothetical. We *believe* (hypothesize) that this is what one would find if one adopted the methods of something like Ruth Benedict, *The Chrystanthemum and the Sword* (1946).

35. See, for instance, McCain *et al.* (1967).

36. The few people who have reached senior-level positions in the major firms are more likely to have come from the gentry.

37. The pattern of discrimination in the housing market usually means that new housing is not open to them—except in central-city urban renewal projects (such as Southwest Washington or Lake Meadows in Chicago)—because that new housing is in suburbia. The private government of real estate mostly keeps that closed, and is reinforced in this exclusion by the reluctance of such purchasers to expose themselves to the privation of living in isolated environments. What they buy, therefore, is the best available housing being vacated by whites at any moment.

38. They are not, and they know the active prejudices of their fellow union members.

39. See Fox (1970) for some insight into this aspect.

40. James Q. Wilson (1960), discusses a fight between a certain group of professionals and a trade-union group for control of the Chicago NAACP. But this was a fight within the bourgeoisie. The trade unionists were merely bourgeois types (within our definition), who operated from a different institutional base.

41. See, for instance, the discussion of the Harlem realty pioneer Philip A. Payton, in Osofsky (1966) and in Cruse (1967), 21–22.

42. Within the past five or six years, such a problem made the headlines in Pittsburgh. A new technician, imported into the city to work for Gulf Oil, became engaged in a suit to force a dealer in Mount Lebanon (an upper-income suburb) to make a house available. The usual problems of discrimination and allegations of discrimination were involved. In the course of the case, it developed that many people in Pittsburgh thought that Gulf had tried to persuade the man not to pursue that case. Whether Gulf did or did not is immaterial. It is simply that *if* people think this is happening, and are discouraged in such simple cases as individual suits to enforce existent legal rights, then *a fortiori* they will be more reluctant when it involves action calculated to produce larger changes in the structure of the situation.

43. Our guess is that the most important white politicians have been more

insightful, but have been temporarily disoriented by the fluidity of the last half-dozen years. In general, they have shown remarkable ability to know how to move within that population to serve their ends.

44. I would argue, for instance, that this is an important obstacle to clear thought about black factionalism, *just as a similar reaction by white people is an obstacle to clear thought about white racism.*

II

Clientage, Opposition, and Withdrawal: Three Forms of External Politics

INTRODUCTION

White supremacy is the single most important fact in the *environment* of black politics. How to cope with white supremacy is the single most important issue overtly debated within black politics. The answers proposed and/or practiced fall into three major forms of external politics. One set of claimants for black leadership have generally assumed that no direct challenge to white supremacy is likely to be fruitful, and have consequently sought to acquire the resources of change from external (white) support. The practitioner of this strategy accepts, in other words, the role of *client* to some external source. *Opposition* as an external procedure is similar to clientage in one way and dissimilar in another. It is similar in believing that the connection between black and white is inescapable, but dissimilar in the proposed adjustment. Opposition is a political technique which seeks to activate rules and norms that those preferring change can, as they see it, validly claim to share with those whose behavior they have to change. In the specific case of black-white relations, opposition is an effort to activate white people's real or presumptive commitments to "the Constitution," "democracy," and related values, in order to overcome the violation of those values believed to be inherent in "discrimination," "prejudice," "segregation," and so on. The third main approach—*withdrawal*—is different from both clientage and opposition in the sense that it does not accept the inescapability of the black-white connection. It differs further from clientage in the refusal to accept the

42

proposition that white supremacy cannot be challenged directly; it differs further from opposition in rejecting the idea that black-white associations are inherently useful. Indeed, it is more likely to activate the symbols of "independence" and very open and explicit defiance of almost all "white values."

Advocacy or practice of these strategies is sometimes explicit—in fact and in words—sometimes covert in the sense that the advocate or the practitioner understands what he is doing, but prefers not to make it very clear; and sometimes implicit in that the advocate or the practitioner does not fully recognize what he is doing. Advocacy and practice have also been influenced by some other variables, notably the culture and class structure (above, Essay I) of the black "nation"; the degree to which black leadership is constrained by the approval and disapproval of a recognized "mass" constituency; the scale and subtlety (or simplicity) of the problems being addressed; and, perhaps above all, the North-South differential. Not all the three strategies are equally reputable at any given moment. Rather, over the past seventy-five years there has been a tendency for clientage to be replaced by opposition, and opposition by withdrawal as the strategy which can be most openly advocated or practiced with greatest emotional appeal and least injury to the reputation or good name of the advocates or practitioners. Yet it is not true, even now, that any one has been wholly displaced. Within the black population one may find pockets of popular support for any, and within leadership groups one may find even more the practice of any.

CLIENTAGE

Clientage is one of those relationships in black-white politics which merits scholarly attention, not only because it tells something about blacks and whites *per se*, but because it is so fundamental a relationship in nearly all politics.[1] The rule of thumb which the practitioners of clientage seemed to follow, as far as one may be able to extract a rule from what they said and did, might be stated as follows: *Find a basis for coexistence by choosing objectives which the more influential outsiders* (in this case whites) *will support, and by their support offer protection against those outsiders who are your irreconcilable enemies.* Isaiah T. Montgomery,[2] a onetime (slave) personal clerk to Jefferson Davis, put the rule most pithily: "If you haven't got power yourself, keep powerful friends." If the strategy of dominant outsiders may be called "divide and rule," this strategy for weaker parties may be called "divide and survive." It was the daily common-sense strategy of the man in the cotton fields, and was played on a larger scale by professed leaders and organizers. So far as I know, there is no systematic examination of black client-leaders as a type. But the most reasonable hypothesis would seem to be that they were most likely to be drawn from men whose property or institutional interests left them exposed to white retaliation.[3] This expectation is consistent, at any rate, with one of the few items which approximates being a datum on the subject. "When the Atlanta *Constitution* in 1890," says Meier, "interviewed a number of the most prosperous Negroes in Atlanta about their views on the Lodge Bill,[4] it was able to report that—for white ears at least—these men, several of whom were well-to-do merchants with white customers, were either indifferent or opposed to the legislation" (Meier, 1966, 77).

One could regard such men as hostages, in a way that a completely poor man[5] (or an equally prosperous man) in the North would not necessarily be. It would be entirely reasonable to believe that much of this was specifically associated with *self*-interest. If a man somehow acquired property and felt that his property rights *really* were not fully protected by the law, one would predict a very conservative (trouble-avoiding) strategy on his part.

Montgomery's career may represent an extreme case. He, his father, and his brother first took over the old Davis plantations in the Vicksburg area after the Civil War. But when white neighbors brought pressure on the father, for having accepted appointment as justice of the peace—from the military government then in control of Mississippi—the Montgomerys gave way. When Jefferson Davis's widow laid claim to the properties they occupied, the Montgomerys again gave way. By some unknown method, they got a township grant from the Illinois Central Railroad in the then swampy, but rich and underpopulated, plain ("the Delta") about a hundred miles south of Memphis. With a company of blacks from the old Davis area, they settled the town of Mound Bayou in 1887.

For the remainder of his life (until 1924), Montgomery was preoccupied with making and maintaining a truce with the surrounding whites. On that truce depended his town, his estates, and his own position in the Republican party—each of which was closely linked to the others. In that search for security, he was constantly giving some ground in the hope of buying a little more. As the lone black delegate to the Mississippi Constitutional Convention (1890), he publicly acquiesced in the constitutional disfranchisement of blacks. No one has ever revealed what pressures he was under then, nor what deal he thought he made. But he clearly was not a "nonpolitical" type, and—in private correspondence with Booker Washington—later reversed his position on the blacks' need for the franchise (Meier, 1966, 148, n. 23). When the "lily-white" movement was challenging black participation in Southern Republican politics (*The White Man's Burden;* see footnote 4 above), he again yielded some ground—favoring the seating of a white delegate instead of a black in the 1920 national convention (Nowlin, 1931)—but this was also an equivocal situation. For his family and heirs remained active in Republican politics for many years later.[6] The politics of Montgomery is a virtual study in the politics of the hostage.

The problems of the political hostage are even more sharply defined when he is the leader responsible for some exposed, but presumably essential, insitution. W. C. Handy, the great musician, gives us remarkable insight into one of these men—William Hooper Councill, president of Alabama A. and M. College—with whom Handy himself had a bad experience. At one stage in his career, Handy taught music at the college. He and Councill had some unpleasant moments, partly because Handy was turning the college toward the emergent music based on folk experience, while Councill's image of genuine music was more classical. In the manner of small colleges, this came to a head when Handy was downgraded by being assigned what he thought unrelated and unprofessional chores (essentially accounting). In open faculty meeting, with students also present, Councill denounced minstrelsy (which Handy deemed "at that time one of the greatest outlets for talented [black] musicians and artists")—a denunciation which virtually all the faculty members repeated one by one. After Handy's own "impassioned defense" of the genre,

> The students gave me a big hand. Many of the teachers congratulated me at the close of the service. Councill stood apart, silent and grim. He appeared to be convinced that he had guessed right, that I had actually received new minstrel offers and that I was on the verge of accepting them. He looked disappointed and sad. Suddenly I lost my bitterness. I had no further wish to show up those who had derided the minstrels. I found no pleasure in adding to the burdens of the lonely man who was trying so hard to keep his school going against great odds. Perhaps it was not his fault that we didn't see eye to eye. Perhaps he was too worried about the threatened withdrawal of the state's small appropriations. (Handy, 1957, 63)

All this was many years ago, but it provides an insight into the pattern so often reported for the black state college: the president who seems to students and much of the black world outside a mere egocentric dictator (and both egocentrism and dictatorship are present), obsequiously crawling before whites (which was also true), undercutting opposition to himself (also true). This much of the image is continued by a current historian who described Councill as "a notorious accommodator . . . widely known for his unctuous sycophancy" (Meier, 1966, 77). There must have been something in that portrait. Booker T. Washington, even, with his usual care for his reputation, hesitated "to appear on the same platform with W. H. Councill, who 'has the reputation of simply toadying to the Southern white people' " (quoted in Meier, 1966, 100). Washington's hesitation clearly said something about Councill's reputation, but we know that good and bad reputations may be misleading—especially when the men whose reputations are in question have problems difficult to explain in public. One political scientist who spent two years as a participant-observer with black activists in Bolivar County, Mississippi, and who was himself sympathetic to militant action, said that he would feel morally inhibited about calling anybody an "Uncle Tom" for making accommodations to that difficult environment. But this principle surely applies far more to retrospective judgment about Alabama in the late 1890's than to Mississippi in 1963 or 1964.

Councill had the task of securing white toleration and support for a school that was entirely on the public treasury, whereas even Washington had the advantage of very substantial private money from industrialists in the North. Against this background, even Handy's account becomes sympathetic. The strategy, he observes, was to persuade whites that industrial education for blacks, "to make them better cooks, nurse maids, mechanics, and share farmers" was good for whites. "With this sort of logic to chew on, the authorities were *sometimes* willing *to suffer the existence* of a school for blacks, but not always. Night riders set fire to Councill's school at one time and burned the buildings to the ground." (Handy, 1957, 58–59; emphasis additional—M.H.)

According to Handy, Councill was at one point faced with a 50-percent cut in the state's appropriation, from the magnificent sum of four thousand dollars ($4,000!) to two thousand ($2,000).

I admired the way [he took the state legislators] to task. . . . He showed them how much money the institution spent in the town of Huntsville, how it employed twenty-six teachers and generally proved itself an asset to the community. Then he chided the politicians who could vote a ten-thousand-a-year salary to one white college president while showing themselves so small[7] as to renege on the paltry four thousand they had appropriated to a whole Negro institution. *I gave him credit for handling this sort of problem in such a way as not to antago-*

nize those who really had the destiny of the school in their hands. (Handy, 1957, 59; emphasis additional—M.H.)

The style is that of the supreme realist, who does whatever he judges necessary to a given situation. That realism was very clear in Councill's effort to make Democratic friends as early as 1875—the year before the Hayes-Tilden election, remember!—though he himself had originally been a Republican. With remarkable foresight, he estimated that the white Southerners would return to full political power within twenty-five years. "[I]f they have found that you go en masse against them right or wrong, on all political occasions, . . . [they] will take from you the ballot which you continue to cast against them." In the colorful language so common to Southern politics, Councill continued:

The Republicans will grow tired of you, and seek to unload the Negro element, and like the bat which is disowned by the beast and not recognized by the birds, you will find favor with neither Democrats nor Republicans. (Handy, 1957, 59)

The political record of the South suggests that whites would have tolerated black suffrage under virtually no conditions, so that element of Councill's *explanation* is doubtful. But the forecast of the Republican party's attitude was nearly as sound as his forecast of the time within which the ex-Confederates would regain control in the South. *It was defective only in being too optimistic.* The Republicans did not wait until 1900, the date called for in Councill's forecast, to begin "unloading" the black man. They clearly started down that path in 1890 with their willingness to give up the Federal Elections Bill (the Lodge Bill[8]); and no like effort to protect the black franchise was again attempted for sixty-seven years until the Civil Rights Act of 1957.

Montgomery was one of Washington's close allies. Councill was apparently not, since Washington scrupled even to appear on the same platform because of Councill's reputation for "toadying." But both operated on a political logic that *blacks must be willing to withdraw from open political competition with whites,* because white antagonism was so great that it could not be reduced so long as the possibility of direct electoral confrontation or influence existed. That logic is also an essential key to the strategy of clientage politics as practiced by Washington himself.

Contemporaries could not, of course, be sure at the time how it would all work out.[9] Washington's interpretation of unremitting white resistance to the black franchise was coupled with a basically different three-point strategic conception. It assumed (1) that political development would never be secure without *prior* economic development, (2) that economic development would have to be based on widespread improvement for the rural black peasantry, and (3) that economic improvement for the rural peasantry depended on improved efficiency which could only come with "industrial (vocational) education" rather than "classical" (liberal arts) education. (The debates between Washington and the many others who shared his view, on one hand, and his "classical" critics, on the other, should not obscure two central points. In fact, neither side ever really opposed the form of education proposed by the other, but there was a real disagreement about the relative emphasis. This disagreement was, however, particularly important in a competition for resources at a time when a large section of Southern white opinion accepted the proposition that "to educate a Negro is to make a fool.")[10]

The essential element of the Washington program was, in fact, to create a property-owning peasantry. For this purpose, Washington was prepared to go to great lengths to secure support among "powerful [white] friends" —and to secure his monopoly over that support by undermining, browbeating, or buying off actual or potential critics.[11] All this really shows how complicated any form of politics is, and how subtle the connections between symbols, methods, and objectives. For the central point is that everything about the Washington record indicates a *purposiveness* in his method. The purposiveness was that of a Herod the Great, prepared to be disliked (but not happy about it) and to work with the dominant outsider, in the interest of the *ultimate* increase in the power and stability of the constituency which he identified for himself (see A.H.M. Jones, 1967).

Until A. Philip Randolph emerged as a *national* figure in the March on Washington Movement (Garfinkel, 1969), there was never again a black organizer who devoted so much of his time to a primary concern with the economic problems of the black poor. (Indeed, one of the problems with the later civil rights movement was its difficulty in developing an economic focus; (see pages 57–59, later in this essay). In this respect, Washington was actually at the time the antithesis of (and by some values "ahead of") the more militant critics (DuBois and others) whose reputations we now value more highly.

Even more, the Washington program was that of a propagandist—a master propagandist whose talents would now command a high price in Madison Avenue—addressing his propaganda to a white audience when most white audiences were decidedly uninterested. The avenue to the attention of those few audiences which might become interested, and which might have the capacity to be helpful (Washington spent no time on the coterie of contemporary "radicals") was through presentation of his program in nonthreatening terms. But the Washingtonian practice was by no means as simple as the rhetoric. Even the rhetoric was not simple. If political abstemiousness were deemed appropriate, there was never a suggestion that blacks ought not to have the right to the vote. (In fact, it is doubtful that so practical a man would have uttered such a suggestion, considering that it could only anger black audiences and dim their reception of the rest of his message.) Instead, he argued the perfectly intelligible proposition (which—being a good Victorian like the New Englanders who trained him—he probably believed) that the vote had to be exercised "intelligently," and that it was appropriate to disfranchise the "unintelligent" until they were "ready." The unintelligent included for Washington not only the rural black poor but the white poor as well. Beyond that proposition, his admonition to black voters was not so much nonvoting as carefully "consulting" their own interests by looking as well to the interests of their white neighbors.

Washington's personal *modus operandi,* like that of his black allies across the South, was anything but lacking in political activism. If Herod pretended to submit, he never willingly forsook Caesar's ear. It was critical to Washington's power and purposes that he should become, and remain, the prime consultant on black social problems across the country. It was similarly critical that, so long as possible, he should maintain an important role in presidential patronage in the South, for whites and for blacks. But the role was even more complex. He went about in secret stirring up blacks to resist disfranchisement in the several states—sometimes expressing annoyance that they were not sufficiently vigorous about that; in secret, he supported constitutional challenges to the peonage legislation which virtually tied the sharecropper to his landlord; and openly, he agitated for action against lynching (which was probably the most elemental problem facing blacks at the time).[12] Clientage, particularly in the manner practiced by Washington, should be regarded not as "nonpolitical" but rather as the most fundamentally political conception one could imagine. That is, *if it worked,* it could not but have penetrating effects on the structure of social competence and power. But there are two important questions. Under what circumstances could its open advocacy and practice be adopted? Could clientage have worked under those (or any) circumstances?

Clientage in black politics, though practiced in the North, has been—and is—preeminently occasioned by the power imbalance between blacks and whites in the South. That imbalance has never been greater, except during slavery, than during the last quarter (and particularly the last ten years) of the nineteenth century. At that juncture, Southern white tolerance for black participation in politics was about as great as Soviet tolerance for a nonsocialist Czechoslovakia in the 1960's. At the same time, it was the South which contained more than nine-tenths of the entire black population, most of that being in the rural South on plantations. In this context, Washington (and others) chose this unmistakably Southern strategy, and sought to implement by focusing upon the most elemental problems of the largest number of black people. If one takes this view, two problems appear. What was the viability of the strategy, regardless of the reputational consequence? What was the reputational consequence?

It is impossible to measure the *effects* of clientage as practiced by Washington (and by others who adopted the same style). Their apologists would necessarily say that they laid the foundations for such secondary and higher education as blacks did receive before the 1930's depression—without which the black "nation" would have been even worse off. That proposition is probably true (though not demonstrable), although one cannot show that no other system of education would have arisen had that one not been created. If they did lay the foundation, it is no mean achievement, unless one wants to say that all black education before the 1930's depression was valueless. On the other hand, the detractors could say equally pertinent things, particularly that the constant admonitions that blacks should improve (not that they, or anyone, should not) only encouraged black self-distrust and provided whites with psychological encouragement to ignore the main focus of the problem.

That the strategy did not work was apparent before Washington's death. Not only did unsympathetic critics see this, but so did faithful allies. Isaiah T. Montgomery wrote in 1904 of changing his mind on the importance of the franchise. And Washington himself might well have observed a good deal of discouraging evidence. The cities of the United States came dangerously close to official apartheid. President Theodore Roosevelt made a decision on the Brownsville case remarkable for its harsh thoroughness, cashiering whole companies of black infantry for an escapade which could not be proved against any member of any company. Presidents Theodore Roosevelt and Taft hemmed and hawed on black federal appointments, but the reverse march on that road became clearer and clearer. Congressional measures to defend the black franchise, which once had been the subject for serious debate, became the quixotic interest of individual members who could not any longer get serious attention from their colleagues when they brought up that subject. The black convention delegations from the South, deprived of an opportunity to compete in serious politics, became mere pawns in convention brokerage, and were already being reduced to a trivial vestige of their former role. By the time of Washington's death (1915), the Republican party had virtually finished its "unloading" job, and the country was more than half-way through Wilson's first administration—with no sign of improvement.

Not only is it apparent the strategy did not work as its authors predicted, but the logic of politics might suggest that neither its political nor its economic proposals could then have worked in the South in the manner prescribed. As has already been mentioned, Washington was like the good white Victorians who had trained him in believing that the "ignorant"—both white and black—should be excluded from the franchise. If this meant most blacks, it also meant many whites. But in the late nineteenth century there was literally no possibility that the remaining white franchise would be curtailed. As a general matter of policy, the "qualified" franchise (rather than some approximation to the universal male franchise) was already an anachronism. If, moreover, the administration of franchise restrictions were going to be exercised by whites—a problem only now being overcome—it followed that paper "qualifications" would be activated mainly to diminish black voting. At the very moment that Washington was urging upon blacks the skilled trades as the route to economic solvency, those very trades were beginning to be closed by deliberate acts of managerial policy, North no less than South. If Andrew Carnegie, Theodore Roosevelt, and Henry Grady found attractive the idea of a vast new class of black artisans, economically productive but largely excluded from the polity, we may be sure that the white common man and his political representatives did not. The Tom Watsons and James Vardamans —those populist precursors of George Wallace and Orville Faubus—were not so naive as to exclude the blacks from electoral politics only to meet them on the next corner as an even greater economic menace. Finally, no one could question—even without economic determinism—that one of the critical limitations upon the black population is that, in the aggregate, it is without significant working capital. But what is questionable is that the entry into the sorts of skilled trades to which Washington so often referred would have produced the capital which he clearly envisaged. From this perspective, we may reasonably suppose that Washington was simply overoptimistic about the possibility of covering the distance between the baseline where he found the blacks when he began and the point where he wanted to see them go.[13]

Washington's second strategic problem was the reputational. His obvious dependence on white support brought doubtful rewards for the black population as a whole—though good ones (in material terms) for himself —and simultaneously violated the symbols of bravery and heroism which many people might have preferred seeing. Accordingly, his client-leadership violated both the material interests and the symbolic necessities of the emergent black gentry (as has been mentioned in Essay I). Their images of rectitude and their self-respect were closely associated with "manhood" (meaning a fervent belief in protest against invasion of their rights), with the symbols of citizenship, and with the ideals of a "higher" culture. Their interests were consonant with these values. Politics was a particularly important instrument. Not only did it provide an avenue for the defense of their rights, but it also provided a leverage and an upward mobility they could not otherwise have.

Many of these people were among the Southerners then being displaced from politics, and it could not have been comfortable for them to hear Washington counsel that this ejection was relatively unimportant. Nor could it have been comfortable for their Northern counterparts, whose weight in Republican politics declined precisely as the black Southern franchise declined. Even if one treats Washington as oriented to the necessities of the rural black peasantry, it would have been reasonable for the gentry to regard Washington as a "self-seeker." To wipe out the last remains of Reconstruction was to wipe out themselves. In the end, they would win. For it was they who would evoke the symbols of resistance to white supremacy, they who would teach the emergent younger generation what "race advancement" *really* meant (that is, what they said it meant), they who would write the editorials and books in which Washington's reputation was downgraded. Their preference was for *opposition* (or, as some would put it, "protest"). Opposition as a political method is similar to clientage in assuming an inescapable connection between white and black. It is different in that it explicitly seeks to change the very *structure* (pattern) of race relations, where clientage purports to accept the pattern. The specific quality of opposition, finally, is that it purports to move within rules and norms which the opponent holds, which constitute commitments for the opponent that one will seek to activate, and which one can claim legitimately to share with the opponent. If the Washington critics were never able wholly to *eradicate* Washingtonian ideas within the black "nation," they nonetheless made opposition ("protest") the predominant symbol of respectability within the decade. So strong was their influence that only within the last five years has the idea of "self-help" (usually meaning economic self-development) been respectable.

OPPOSITION

CONSTITUTIONAL OPPOSITION

For most of the time between World War I and the rise of Martin Luther King, the principal (though not exclusive) version of opposition was *constitutional* opposition. Where clientage overtly accepted the white man as master, and sought to subvert him, constitutional opposition interpreted him as opponent and sought to activate him to accept that interpretation under his own rules of law and conventional politics. Constitutional opposition arose from the convergence of Washington's black-gentry critics with a curiously mixed group of white allies. The mix was curious because it included people who had not much to agree on except the "unconstitutionality" of gross racial discrimination; these were members of the Jewish community, upper-class Anglo-Protestant conservatives, a few white reformers of the muckraker tradition, and even a few socialists. Their experience was virtually identical with the organizational history of the NAACP, and their techniques those most widely regarded as "normal" and "legitimate": voting, open propaganda, lobbying, and, particularly, litigation.

Constitutional oppositionists have had more success in federal than in state-local politics and, indeed, have invested more attention there. There are several reasons. For many years the outcomes they wanted to influence were Southern, but access to state and local politics there was virtually nonexistent. Even in the North, success in state and local politics was often limited, partly because such success required either great amounts of money or substantial access through the party machinery. Moreover, the leadership of constitutional opposition often came from white collar and professional personnel who had to earn their livings through methods susceptible to the pressure of state and local politicians, examples being the lawyers who were presidents of NAACP branches. Such people could campaign against Southern practices with impunity, but not necessarily against other practices at home. Finally, state and local decisions often had little strategic impact. There was no way to translate a favorable outcome in one state into a favorable outcome in another part of the country where the problems might be similar. From this perspective, it made more sense to focus upon federal politics.

Since the passage of the Civil Rights Act of 1957, the first such act since 1875, the constitutional oppositionists have come to have a large reputation for success in national lobbying. Much about the record, including the rejection of Messrs. Haynsworth and Carswell, as well as the adoption of the voting rights extension of 1970, suggests that there is a lot of merit in the reputation. But the practical limitations of constitutional opposition (as expressed in lobbying) are also revealed by a closer look at the historical record. The first major success, which set this group (again best represented by the NAACP) on the lobbying road, was the campaign against John J. Parker, President Hoover's nominee to the Supreme Court in 1930.[14] Parker, a Republican lawyer in North Carolina, had a "lily-white" record in North Carolina Republican politics. He was also on record with what the American Federation of Labor interpreted as antilabor views. (In these respects, Parker's nomination was remarkably similar to the Haynsworth nomination in 1969). In the end, the Senate narrowly rejected the Parker nomination. How much the NAACP counted in this is naturally hard to tell after the fact. What is not disputable is the Parker rejection, the fact that the NAACP tried to stir both Northern black and trade-union opposition, and that several Northern senators who voted for Parker were defeated in the immediately following election.[15] At the minimum, this was sufficient to establish the belief that the Association had been a decisive factor.

Obviously, it was in the interest of the Association to claim credit for itself (as any organization needs credit for organizational maintenance), the more so because this was probably the first time in the twentieth century that the black side had won on a major national issue. Defeats in the next few years reinforced the idea that the Association *needed* a serious lobbying effort. Such a defeat was that suffered on antilynching legislation in the 1930's, when even President Franklin D. Roosevelt refused to intervene on the ground that he could not risk the punitive retaliation of Southern congressmen. This image of a need for improved lobbying practices was still more strongly influenced by the rejection of bills to ban the poll tax, the failures to secure federal fair-employment legislation during the 1940's, the defeat of the proposals for such legislation in most of the states, and the similar defeat of proposals for fair-education legislation to regulate the admissions policies of private universities. Only with the Civil Rights Act of 1957, acceptable to the NAACP mainly on the ground that it set a precedent, did the legislative tide begin to turn. In federal politics, constitutional oppositionists were least successful in administrative action, with certain rare exceptions. For example, they seldom proved able to get the Justice Department to interpret federal statutes in their favor, even in such matters as applying the Lindbergh Law to lynchers when lynchers had taken the victims across state lines.[16] Nor were they able to have much effect on the discriminatory employment policies of federal agencies, although it was long clear that such policies clearly existed.

The big success in administrative politics was the initial fair-employment-practices order (Executive Order 8802) issued by Franklin D. Roosevelt in 1941. Under pressure of racial exclusion at a time when defense-production manpower shortages existed, and in the face of a threatened March on Washington, Roosevelt created the first Fair Employment Practices Committee, an agency which subsequently died at the end of the War when Congress terminated appropriations for a number of unpopular executive agencies. The reliance on litigation has not been due to any peculiar belief in the magic of court pronouncements, but rather to the problems of access to governmental institutions and the problems of having the resources necessary for access. Constitutional oppositionists have never believed that the courts alone were sufficient, nor have they ever relied on the courts alone. But it is there that they have, on the whole, been most successful.

If the over-all experience in administrative and legislative politics was discouraging for most of the years before the 1960's, the experience in judicial politics was rather different and constitutional oppositionists learned to rely on litigation. The fact that it was rather different was due, in part, to the greater ease of getting one's issues into the court system of the United States. The adversary process permits individuals to present their own grievances, if they can get a lawyer and raise the court fees. This combination was, given other constraints, made to order for the politics of black constitutional oppositionists. Judicial review, as practiced in the United States, permits the courts to determine what is or is not constitutional, and a determination of unconstitutionality is an almost ineluctable handicap for the proscribed policy unless it has a strong and active popular support. If blacks could secure determinations, therefore, that the practices of which they complained were unconstitutional, they would—it was reasoned—have a substantial advantage over their previous position. This was a workable procedure for making strategic impact. Lawyers are in sufficient supply among blacks, and have sufficient personal and professional incentive to intervene, to make the possibilities of raising such questions relatively great. From the first, the Association had been available to assist in such matters. It was in this context that the NAACP placed a great deal of its early effort in the provision of legal services in courthouse after courthouse throughout the rural South. At this distance in time, such an activity seems routine, but there are two vital points to remember: that at the time the appearance of a black lawyer, usually from the North, in a rural courthouse was the same order of symbolic defiance as the more recent appearance of a SNCC organizer for voter registration; and, that some (though by no means all) of the crucial issues in criminal procedure were thus moved from the local scene to the federal judiciary.

It was at least as crucial that partial access to the franchise was opened, well before the Civil Rights Acts, by a continuous assault upon the mechanisms of racial discrimination in voting. This access made it possible for black men in the South to begin minimal political organization within standard channels, and thus to create incentives for at least a few Southern politicians to take a different posture on racial issues.

At the time of the depression, a peculiarly skillful combination of lawyers (managed by Charles Houston of the Howard Law School, and later by Thurgood Marshall), undertook a systematic campaign to develop the constitutional grounds for a challenge to racial hierarchy. For a series of reasons, the legal advice was that this might best be done in education, and it is thus that the Association conducted the detailed series of cases which eventuated in *Brown v. Board of Education*. This decision undermined the legal supports for segregation, not only in education but through many other sectors of life. By the early 1950's, most of the critical legal rights which had been denied in principle three or four decades before were now affirmed in principle.[17] But the affirmation of rights only in principle is, self-evidently, not satisfying. And what the constitutional oppositionists proved to lack was a capacity for strategies to turn this affirmation into wide practice. Our hypothesis is that constitutional opposition, though as much oriented (in the minds of its practitioners) to the well being of the whole black population, was actually a form of *leadership with minimal popular participation*. Conceded, there was no intent to exclude wide participation. Indeed, one of the laments of NAACP leadership was its incapacity to induce that participation. But the fact is that the wide participation—as opposed to romantic approval—did not exist.

Leadership with minimal popular participation is possible, and effective, if the objectives are objectives which leaders can by themselves secure. If the courts are disposed to rule in one's favor (or even are open to one's arguments), the main requirement is good lawyers. But if the objectives require more intensive pressure, require more contributions from more people, then it is necessary either to have a following which will move at request (as the Teamsters moved for Mr. Hoffa or the Mine Workers for Mr. Lewis) or a following which is itself highly energized and somewhat self-starting. In the South, the requirement was for a wide popular movement to implement the legal rights thus secured. In the rest of the country, the problems were even more complex, and one may say that the central failure of the constitutional oppositionists was the failure to develop a strategy of participation simultaneously applicable to the South and to the Northernization and urbanization of the black population. This grew out of failure to understand the dynamics of collective action, a failure which had been latent for many years. While the rest of American politics was becoming increasingly collectivistic, the constitutional oppositionists were still focused upon the classical liberal doctrine that the problem was to abate unreasonable restrictions upon individuals. Aspects of this narrow focus are associated with several problems, among which four may be specified and discussed: economic issues, alliance patterns, cultural bias, and organizational practice.

Economics: One important problem was the incapacity to come to terms with economic issues, although economic issues obviously were central to the notion of collective benefits from a series of useful indicators. This is not a new observation, for the challenge to the Association on economic grounds was sharply stated in the 1930's by diverse black intellectuals (including DuBois and Ralph Bunche). Nor would it be accurate to say that the Association was uninterested in economic questions. Quite the contrary. The examples of local boycotts in the interest of black employment are legion. From the earliest, the NAACP found it necessary and useful to support black workers (such as railroad firemen) seeking equal pay with white workers (and in this sense the campaigns for equal teacher pay in the South are also economic strategies). In the New Deal era, it played an important role in the creation of a black consortium, the Joint Committee on National Recovery, for the purpose of trying to assure that the welfare and recovery programs of the New Deal reached blacks no less than whites, at a time when it would have been mere administrative routine to distribute those benefits differentially. And one need but mention its critical role in the evocation of the fair-employment-practices idea, leading to the presidential proclamation on the subject in 1941.

The problem has, however, been that the Association has never given the economic problems of blacks sustained attention comparable to its attention to the question of segregation *per se.* The NAACP, and groups of similar bent, have been most confident and most energetic in economic matters only if they could choose antidiscrimination grounds on which to stand. This helps to explain why, despite the overconcentration of black people among the poor, the literary attack on poverty came from outside the black community (Harrington's *The Other America*), while the policy responses were developed within the government and the foundations (abetted intellectually by the social workers). In similar manner, one need not adopt the Nixonian version of "black capitalism," although one need not reject that version without careful thought, to recognize that the black oppositionists never faced seriously the question of capital accumulation.

Alliance Patterns: A second factor limiting the constitutionalists' ability to think of *collective* action in a form appropriate to the urban North lay in some necessary alliance patterns. The constraints existent in American society meant that to be able to make a case against racial discrimination required the supportive prestige of whites, the financial support of whites, and the availability of skills which were not so easily available in black communities. Conservative constitutionalists of the Moorfield Storey variety, for instance, could reason their way to advocating the same constitutional rights for the individual black as for everyone else. In the same way, some part of the "assimilationist" leadership of the American Jewish community could adopt the same stance. The Jewish community placed great store on reducing adverse restrictions—official and unofficial—and it was only natural that an organization in which both Jewish and upper-middle class black participants worked should emphasize such goals. It was not even necessary then to contemplate that the actual adoption of such legislation as might reduce such restriction (fair-employment legislation, for instance) might be of more significance to Jews than to blacks, although of considerable significance to both.

One of the most important developments was the emergence of the alliance with the trade-union movement. Before the depression, the broad policy of the trade-union movement was exclusionary where possible and discriminatory in any case. Comprehensibly, this policy meant that there was little, if any, basis for pragmatic cooperation between black leaders and trade-union leaders, either on matters of the economy or on broader political issues. It seems probable (although not yet demonstrated) that the Parker nomination fight was the first occasion where the interests of the two clearly dovetailed and were understood to dovetail.

In the 1930's, the unionization of the mass-production industries opened some additional bases of cooperation. In the case of the automobile industry, for instance, Walter White, then the NAACP national leader, reports having made special trips to Detroit for the purpose of persuading black-community leaders that they ought to cooperate with unionization rather than to oppose it. It would be reasonable to believe that such an effort would constitute part of the nexus between NAACP leadership and UAW leadership which has continued over the ensuing thirty years. Some particularly visible connections ran to other unions of the CIO group, notably the electrical workers under James B. Carey. A study of the boards of directors in NAACP urban branches would reveal many connections to black members of the international-union staffs, union-local presidencies, and so on.

If one tries to put oneself in the position of the NAACP leaders as they then operated, the development of the white alliances must have seemed a tremendous gain. For it had not been long since very few respectable whites took any position except to say "let the South handle its own problems." The retention of these alliances must also have seemed of crucial importance, lest the fight against white supremacy slip backward once more. It was important to have the help of major trade-union leaders —with their entree to the white workers, the Democratic politicians, and the Catholic Church.

But difficulties also arose from the alliance pattern. If the NAACP, or similar groups, made much effort to eliminate discrimination within the plants, they would necessarily have alienated union supporters. The price of getting a secure foothold within the plant at all was to accept a certain amount of subordination. I do not mean that accepting it was a conscious strategy, but that people behaved as if it were, and that the situation left them with little option. Only since World War II, when the presumption of a wider public consensus made union support seem less urgent, has the NAACP leadership undertaken a direct attack upon problems of union discrimination. Theoretically, one might find this progression hard to understand. But it is not hard to understand if one recognizes that most people, white and black, who have raised the question of economic growth have raised it as a substitute for, not a complement to, governmental action at a moment when governmental action seemed the only productive mechanism.

It seems equally likely that the negative attitudes of big-business leadership were just as important a consideration. If one moves back of World War II, one will find that most companies now in the *Fortune* "500" explicitly practiced racial exclusion and that after World War II they continued to practice racial exclusion without admitting it. It is *still* possible to see the evidence, not only statistically but with the naked eye: stand outside a headquarters at 5 P.M. and watch the color distribution of the emerging staff. Moreover, insofar as it was possible to secure the interest of firms at all, the separation of "rights" issues from "welfare" issues put the latter within the purview of the Urban League. To have invaded that domain would have precipitated bitter organizational rivalries which neither group could easily afford.

Cultural Bias: If one may define "ideology" as a part of "culture," it seems reasonable to believe that the constitutional oppositionists were led away from the nonlabor (or capital-accumulation) side of the economic problem for ideological reasons. No one has (even now) discovered how to deal with capital accumulation except in the framework of the idea of a separate black economy. As economics, this is a very deficient idea. Andrew Brimmer has recently pointed out that the better-financed and better-staffed large national firms are surely not going to overlook any portion of the black market if there are profits to be earned there. They have precisely that superior competitive capability which one sees in the fact that Metropolitan Life apparently has more black policyholders than all the black companies combined.

But there is also a cultural aspect which is not directly tied to ideologies for or against economic development. Collective action can also be thought of in racial terms, without a primarily economic emphasis. The economic analysis is not what deterred the constitutional oppositionists. They were deterred by images of Washingtonian separatism which simply violated their *basic doctrines* that race should be given no official cognizance as a basis for action. The battle against segregation had not been launched because the advocates of constitutional opposition wanted black and white association *per se. It was launched because the purpose of official recognition of race* (except in the Freedmen's Bureau and, possibly, the Bureau of Negro Economics during World War I), *was to provide white men with advantages over black men.* If the constitutional oppositionists perceived this purpose —and there was good reason why they should—their intellectual recourse was simple: to argue that every man, black or white, should be given a "fair chance" and left to sink or swim. If the implicit supposition that all would work out well in the absence of active discrimination seems optimistic, it is also important to realize that the emergent black bourgeoisie were ready to take advantage of the social options coming their way in the absence of active discrimination. Their optimism about the possibilities in the absence of active discrimination was justified by the recognition that they were subject to the most intense discrimination, and by the observable fact that whenever that discrimination has diminished they have moved ahead rapidly. Since this new bourgeoisie was also the central source of support for the civil rights movement, it is reasonable that their optimism should have guided that movement and, by the same token, obscured its capacity to think in broader collective terms.

There is a closely related point which has to do with the cultural disparity between the leadership of such organizations as the NAACP and the black population taken as a whole. The organizations have always sought the strategic conception of constitutional government. But *constitutional* government, most of the time, has taken a form and reflected a value which has little visceral meaning to most people. Nothing is more apparent in, for instance, the public declarations of Roy Wilkins than a dedication to that concept. But constitutional opposition alone has been far too tame to tap the psychic themes of deepest meaning to most blacks. Reports of striking legal *victories* could command enthusiasm—not so much because the audience shared the values of constitutionalism as because such victories were reported as victories over the white man! But the legalistic *method,* however essential, could not usually command such enthusiasm, for no matter how decisive a shrewd move might be in the eyes of lawyers, such moves are almost always incomprehensible to other people until translated into concrete results. As the grosser constraints began to diminish, the latent spirit of defiance came closer and closer to the surface, and it was the tragedy of the constitutionalists that they had no language and style in which to capture this spirit.

Organizational Problems: A fourth consideration is that the Association's leadership had an emotional vested interest in continuing their former pattern. It seemed necessary to maintain the dominance of the National Office as the expositor of policy, with local branches as instruments of action and—particularly—as "tax-collection" units. Apart from any bureaucratic pathology inherent in large organizations, this outlook be interpreted as a function of an early policy decision about structure and a function also of the particular class characteristics which the Association's local branches later took on.

When the Association was formed, its oligarchic structure had been devised to prevent local branches falling into the hands of "conservatives." Presumably, "conservatives" in the atmosphere of 1909 meant local blacks under influence by hostile whites and, particularly, local blacks under the influence of "the Tuskegge machine". The Communist party's effort to penetrate the Association in the 1930's and 1940's was profoundly repugnant to the national leadership, and the fact that there was some Communist success in taking over a few branches made the Association the more determined to prevent a takeover of the whole organization. The grounds of objection were various. Two relevant considerations were that Communism itself was ideologically repugnant to the leadership and that the Communists toyed with various notions of territorial separatism which the Association thought smacked of "Jim Crow." Political realism indicated that the last way to black success was the adoption of a revolutionary program. Finally, it is probable that the importance of the Jewish alliance and the trade-union alliance played some role in bringing the Communist fight into NAACP. For both the Jewish community and the trade-union movement were bitterly torn by fights between the Communists on one side and the nexus of social democrats and pragmatic liberals on the other. It was quite natural that the fight should spill over into NAACP politics as well.[18] The successful effort to repel Communist penetration led, however, to a considerable reinforcement of the tight National Office control over what local branches were free to do. This control constituted an unintended source of organizational imcompetence to elicit mass participation, since it was impossible to get mass participation if National Office disapproval were likely to bring a suspension of the branch-office charter at any moment.

Organizational competence was also impeded by the class basis of recruitment into local leadership. If the organization began essentially with the black gentry, we have to recognize that this was possible because as a national group the black gentry constituted a sufficient critical mass to provide some leadership. In all except the largest cities, however, the black gentry were too small a *local* group to constitute a similar *local* critical mass. Leadership thus fell to the emergent solid middle class (people now approaching sixty or so). They were the main source of local leadership and active participation in the years down to 1954, and somewhat after. Such leadership did not possess the unaided capacity to generate broadly conceived programs which could serve both the economic and the cultural needs of a large proportion of the black population.

If one takes these two considerations jointly, one finds a situation wherein the National Office possessed the capacity to control local units and possessed some capacity to inspire. But it did not possess the capacity to offer effective, large-scale coordination for a systematic program in matters with which it was unfamiliar. Under these circumstances, one might suggest that the constitutional oppositionists did what other sensible men do. They tended to revert, in the new situation after *Brown v. Board of Education,* to the skills and strategies at which they knew themselves to be competent, and to avoid contesting the grounds on which they might prove incompetent. Apart from ideological reasons, this is one extremely important explanation of the focus on school desegregation in the urban North, which became *the* dominant issue for a few years. The constitutional oppositionist knew how to manage the litigation process, but they knew little about the economic development process. As committed people, and as organizational participants, they felt the necessity to "move." The principle of desegregation was established beyond question, and it was a relatively simple step to extend this principle from the *de jure* segregation which had been killed in *Brown* to the *de facto* segregation which existed in every major metropolitan center and many minor ones. The difficulty was, in fact, that they also knew nothing of the requirements of large-scale application of a principle, in a complicated circumstance where the management both of highly emotional people and of technical issues come together. It was in this context that the constitutional oppositions proved unable to show people how to implement the "rights" which had been "secured," and it was in this context that the initiative passed from the entrepreneurs of constitutional opposition to those of moral opposition.

MORAL OPPOSITION

Moral opposition is a term describing what people normally called "nonviolent direct action." Like constitutional opposition, it accepted the notion of some common framework of legitimacy between white and black. But it stated that common framework in terms of *human rights or moral rights,* rather than in conventional political terms. Moral opposition was part of no master plan, yet had it not been produced, some other technique would have been necessary in its place. Moral opposition contained the capacity, which constitutional opposition lacked, to popularize large-scale participation in the civil rights movement. Moral opposition did not attract support from black men because of its "morality," but because it offered a form of defiance more extensive than any before practiced by black men on a large scale. Black leaders have been deemed heroes whenever their actions pushed against the boundaries of what black men before could not do—regardless of what language they chose. It is in this context that one must appreciate the antisegregation boycotts in Southern cities *sixty years before King emerged in Montgomery,* the popular appeal of the Garvey Movement, and the response to the March on Washington Movement which utterly astounded its very sponsors. So moral opposition made a new kind of militancy fashionable, a new extremity of defiance beyond the act of filing a lawsuit against the county clerk in Mississippi which had once been an act of extreme defiance. Moral opposition made all-or-nothing-demands upon whites. It asserted that the condition of black men was a result of what whites had done or failed to do, that alteration of the racial structure of power was a moral obligation of white men and one that ought to be fulfilled in fidelity to conscience and in justice to black men.

The years of litigation had focused attention upon the most intimate details of Southern racial exclusion, by creating a milieu in which such details were increasingly unable to stand against the pressure of national public opinion. Not only the Southern Christian Leadership Conference (formally organized in 1957), but also the Congress of Racial Equality, the Student Nonviolent Coordinating Committee, and a variety of local groups (including NAACP branches) began to find "direct action" the most appropriate weapon. They sought to force the confrontations which would, as they imagined, lead to a translation of technical legal rights into substantial reality. And they had a decisive effect.

The real success of the moral-opposition movement, beginning with Montgomery but going beyond, was to activate black people in the South, where—in the absence of such direct organization—technical legal rights would have been ignored for years to come. In part this success came because the moral oppositionists proved more readily responsive to the concept of collective benefits, partly because their religious base made the notion of "justice" a more inclusive one and partly because the atmosphere in which they were born encouraged a collectivist approach to politics. Moreover, moral opposition in the 1950's had the capacity to provide a cultural framework which would energize those who wanted to behave with a sense of "propriety" yet also wanted to go beyond the technicalities of law to a more overt demonstration of their deep feelings. Its critical element was the capacity to provide a bridge across the emotive gap between the gentry and upper bourgeoisie, on one hand, and the lower-class respectables and the newer bourgeoisie who were the sons and daughters of the lower-class respectables). The educational process had now raised up a bourgeoisie which was technically competent but emotionally and culturally closer to the black working-class respectables. This process would, by infusing the historical memories and cultural norms of the black poor into the black middle class, change the attitudes of the middle class toward politics by diminishing its cultural kinship to the white middle class. Much of this upwelling was simply the reassertion of the traditional spirit of evangelical Protestantism. The young clergymen who rallied to King, and the students who acted on their own, probably were strongly responsive to a basic utopianism which suggests that if one can convert (or overcome) the sinful *men* exercising power, and get them to do the right thing, then a whole glorious future will open. The students and the clergy, to the extent that they were rooted in the popular culture, were thus intellectually and emotionally made free to violate defined conventions of ordinary politics.

But the novelty also lay in some other, and more mundane, dimensions which made it possible for Dr. King to lead his movement. Its practitioners came into the organizational life of black America at a time when, despite remaining difficulties and limitations, the prior experience had left a residue of skills and sophistication far greater than anything seen before. The relationship between the direct-action movement and the previous forms of action (notably the NAACP's reliance on litigation) was not entirely comfortable. (One might even suspect a certain competitiveness between organizations for the resources of popular approval and—per-

haps more important—the financial contributions from outside the South.)
Nonetheless, the usefulness of the NAACP's role in arranging bail, in
carrying on the legal argument which was necessary for the ultimate
vindication of the direct-action strategy, and in other technical matters,
must be fully acknowledged.

There was surely a new sophistication in making use of public-relations
appeals to white audiences far beyond the South. This, too, depended on
a certain historical experience. It may, perhaps, be impossible to measure
the strategic value of the favorable reception which King got in white
Protestant denominations and churches across the country (even when
these denominations and churches have their own internal racial difficulties), through the medium of the National Council of Churches.

Moral opposition was to prove attractive not only because it expressed
defiance, but because it was peculiarly adapted to be effective in the South
of the middle and later 1950's. It could be directed to such very concrete
objectives as the desegregation of a school or a lunch counter, where the
person whose compliance was needed could be well identified. Except,
possibly, for psychic insult, no third party had to be injured by compliance,
and the consciously self-restrained tractics of moral oppositionists put any
white violent response in a bad light. In the most successful cases (Montgomery and Birmingham), moral coercion was very successful within its
defined limits.

If the moral oppositionists possessed the capacity to turn the civil rights
movement into a popular-participation movement, they nonetheless experienced strategic limitations which made their entry into the urban
North less productive than they might have hoped or anticipated. The
prime limitation is that moral coercion is a weapon best directed toward
specific objectives, where the specific target may be separated from the
watching audience for whose sympathies the protester and the target
contend. This limitation has proved a stumbling block to moral coercion
in the urban North because, for the most part, the issues which can be thus
divided and made specific do not command the measure of black support
which is needed. The issues which have commanded the support have
been extraordinarily diffuse, with the result that much of the audience
sympathizes with the target rather than with the protester, or is simply too
ambivalent to be of much use to the protester.

Moral coercion could, for instance, be used to attack school segregation
only so long as the attack did not adversely affect the watching audience.
If the watching audience imagines that it, too, stands to lose, then all bets
are off. Yet this is precisely what has been at stake in the school desegregation issues (on which so much effort was expended until the last year or

two). It has been clearly shown that Americans are very likely to believe that students of a lower status (compared to their own children) will adversely affect the school situation for their own children. If white Americans believe this about differences in social class, for instance, it is all the more likely that white Americans would believe their children disadvantaged by close association with black children. Accordingly, moral coercion would be met not by discomfort and guilt, but by moral *resistance*. "Justice for the black man" would be met by "justice for our children," *even if the evidence actually indicated no loss to the children*. Once such a situation is reached, and if no "swing" party exists, the contending moralities become incompatible with the bargaining which plays so central a role in American politics under normal circumstances. Moral coercion may thus obstruct the pragmatic liaisons with those ambivalent white groups which could be brought into cooperation only through a long series of *tentative* engagements.

Not only did moral opposition obstruct tentative engagements, but it also obstructed the black demonstration of willingness to accept at least some "white" values, *in ways meaningful to whites*. The moral oppositionists failed to deal with this problem, partly because they were resistant to it, and partly because they thought they had dealt with it. Because they emphasized "nonviolent" change, they felt, they *had* shown their desire to abide by the moral community of "the Judaeo-Christian ethic." What they missed was a realization that protest strategies become self-defeating when "protest" reinforces the supposition that blacks desire freedom as a "gift" or repudiate the hard-core value of "self-help." Even the most responsive, morally oriented white advocates of civil rights share in the broad American consensus that *self*-support is better than charity, but charity is what they are called upon to offer in the event of a commitment to civil rights. If they are willing to offer charity, they do so out of a reinforced sense of pity and guilt; but pity and guilt are extremely weak grounds for serious policies. They amount to a form of sentimentality which is dispelled as soon as the object of pity or the beneficiary of guilt does (or is perceived as doing) something which makes him no longer "worthy" of this special consideration.

On this basis, moral opposition could be productive only so long as its active participants maintained their preternatural self-discipline *and* so long as no significant number of other black people obscured this self-discipline by more obstreperous behavior. Here is the precise point at which anomic urban violence becomes pertinent. Some small measures of such violence could awaken whites, not sensitive to moral opposition, to the extremity of black experience. But once it tended to become part of a regular pattern, and could be associated with political "agitation," it broke the bonds of pity and guilt, permitting many white people now to identify all blacks with the violent actors. The moral oppositionists were unprepared for this pattern because they had not understood their own experience. The pattern was rooted, as other patterns had been rooted, in the cultural-historical experience of black Americans. If a folk culture disciplines its members to believe, as the black folk culture does, that other men (in this case, white men) will eventually resort to brute force, and that only counterforce is a response, then one may also predict that at some point their capacity to act without utilizing that folk teaching will be exhausted. The self-discipline for which the moral oppositionists called could, it should be emphasized, be sustained only if there were a serious prospect of an early victory, and only if the participants were those who had been carefully selected and tutored.

In the urban North, however, the generalized attitude that it was "time to get the white man off our necks" activated the interest of all sorts of people in a hundred different ways and on a hundred different issues. When the moral oppositionists, like the constitutional oppositionists, found that they could not produce symbolic victories meaningful to the new audience, their effective capacity to give direction to events in the North was at an end. (Dr. King's failure in Chicago is testimonial to this problem.)

The Northern significance of moral opposition was not its success in attaining major goals, but in providing a rhetoric and a technique which has been transformed into Militant politics. Moral opposition applied to the urban North was more capable of activating the latent theme of defiance because it was and is more "militant" than constitutional opposition, in the sense that it makes more "extreme" demands and is less respectful of systemic constraints. But moral opposition was not, in fact, insensitive to constraints. The best test of the sensitivity to constraint is the formulation of issues in moral terms which the opponents could accept, and the professed willingness to accept the penalty for denying "unjust laws." In the more secular atmosphere of the urban North, however, the rhetoric of "righteous" and "love" and less meaning than in the South. People were more ready to think of "direct action," and sometimes to resort to it, as a form of sheer power play. Within the past five years, both constitutional opposition and moral opposition have lost much of their symbolic esteem, the Militant camp itself has been split, and the respected new language has become "self-determination" (or "black liberation"). Out of this, we now have the politics of withdrawal.

WITHDRAWAL

Within the past five years (since 1966), and particularly within the past four years (since the great urban crisis of 1967), there has been a change in the external forms of black politics which everyone recognizes in some way. The advocates and practitioners of opposition (and even of clientage) have not disappeared, changed their minds, or even became silent. But they have—relative to the advocates of "self-determination," "separatism," or "black power"—lost influence in the setting of agendas and in the presentation of symbols which will be widely believed and widely honored. There has been a shift which once more brings to the fore ideas and symbols that have always been present in the black culture.[19] There are essentially two elements of this change. First, *the wish for defiance*[20] *has become the basis for a virtually institutionalized form of expression.* It is open and widely disseminated. More and more blacks are open and explicit about telling white people, in all sorts of settings, "we neither like you, nor respect you, nor will we tolerate you, nor do we want you." Second, *within the black world, those who want the approval of their audiences and constituencies are more likely to get that approval,* and more likely to retain it, *if they maintain that black-white associations in common activity are neither very practical nor (often) desirable instruments to satisfy the hope for deliverance.*

Various symbols have been used to represent the central meaning of this shift, among them "black power," "self-determination," "separatism," and "nationalism." If there is a really common element, I argue, it is that of withdrawing from various values and institutions which black strategists have commonly thought essential to their purposes. The positive strategic or tactical conceptions do not agree, but this negative conception is identical to all.

VARIETY I: SEPARATISM

The least important but by no means *un*important variety of withdrawal is *genuine separatism*—cultural, political, or both. Political separatism is taken seriously only by small groups, but it nonetheless is the subject of considerable debate. The basic position is very simple. Institutional separatism, as conceived by some, calls for a full separation from United States political institutions, on the presumption that they are inescapably corrupt and/or doomed. Others merely argue that black and white cannot inhabit the same physical territory in peace, in consequence of which physical separation is the logical inevitability. Historically, political separatists have variously sought a separate place on the North American continent (say a black state in the Oklahoma territory) and abroad (as by the annexation of Santo Domingo or Haiti to the United States as a place in which to settle black men, or Marcus Garvey's dream of an African nation state.) Since it is not possible to imagine an African nation today which would give over any substantial portion of its land to black "foreigners,"[21] the idea of a large-scale "return to Africa" now would be a kind of colonialism which the political separatists could hardly champion in ideological good conscience. Present proposals focus, therefore, on North America. Perhaps the most widely advertised such proposal is that of a group known as "The Republic of New Africa"—which elected Robert F. Williams as its president. The RNA, drawing upon work by Brother Imari (formerly Richard B. Henry), a nationalist intellectual of Detroit, calls for the creation of a separate nation state out of five states on the Gulf of Mexico (Imari, 1968). Imari's interesting proposal is that these states should become receiving areas for the present Northern urban black populations, or so many as should desire to move, and that the state should be given its economic sendoff by United States aid as reparations for the historic damage of slavery and postslavery subordination. Imari also concedes, candidly, that few black people would presently be interested in his proposal, but argues that as the situation naturally matures—as black-white relations become worse—the level of interest and support will rise. The proposal does not contemplate merely waiting in the interim. Imari thus proposes a sort of advance guard—comparable to the Jews who settled in Palestine before World War II.[22] The return of 3,000,000 blacks from the North, to settle, to purchase land county by county and, under the present suffrage laws, take over control of the local government would throw the key areas into black hands, and open the way to the rest of his process (Imari, 1968, 40–41).

Political separatism on this scale has other advocates,[23] but this conception has suffered a number of limitations on its general acceptability. In part, it is that it has also been advocated—at various times in American history—by major white figures whose commitment to black purposes seemed dubious: the American Colonization Society before the Civil War (out of whose efforts Liberia is a byproduct), the late Senator Theodore G. Bilbo (Mississippi), and the Communist Party of the United States.[24] More practically, no doubt, it has called for an unimaginably great effort and sacrifice, with a relatively small foreseeable payoff. Pertinently, who wants to live in the poorest part of the country—from which he has made such great effort to escape?

If political separatism seems to make sense to very few people, cultural separatism is unquestionably more widespread, possibly growing, and related to the emergence of the black intellectuals into a new position of prominence. By the term "black intellectuals" we do not mean merely those persons of African ancestry who functioned as part of the larger intellectual community. We mean, more exactly, those persons who provided, or tried to provide, intellectual leadership on what they conceived to be the peculiar problems of the black "nation."[25] "Cultural separatism" or "cultural nationalism" may not be a specific political proposal, but calls for the emotional and intellectual separation of black from white and the cultivation of a mystique of blackness. Cultural separatism is likely to be associated, in practice, with withdrawal from active participation in the normal institutions of United States politics—as none of the other forms is—simply because cultural separatists do not conceive that this is where the essential priorities lie. Cultural nationalism has long been Harlem-centered,[26] based in groups which have tended to hold in common an extraordinary *racial self-consciousness* translated into intellectual terms. Because Harlem is in New York, and because New York is the center of the American communications system, the ideas of the Harlem-centered nationalists have been recurrently transmitted through the black press, *belletristic* literature, and (more recently) television into the consciousness of black intellectuals across the country. This circumstance has been the more important because the Harlem-centered intellectuals have been persistently critical—indeed, condemnatory—of what they perceive to be either the "superficiality" or the "sellout disposition" of whatever has happened to be existing black leadership at any given time. Thus, in the Harlem intellectual culture, there lay for many years a psychological and intellectual readiness to repudiate what had been the normal conceptions and ways of acting, a readiness to withdraw from relationships with white America.

VARIETY II: TACTICAL WITHDRAWAL

There is much discussion of "separatism" which is not really referent to separatism at all but rather to what one may call *tactical withdrawal*. A great many people seek withdrawal from those areas in which they think themselves unlikely to win (or in which they see nothing of importance) to an area in which they think they are likely to win (or in which they do see something of importance). In general, this withdrawal takes two forms: "caucus separatism" and "street-level populism." By "caucus separatism" I refer to a means of action which does not really propose much genuine institutional separation between black and white, but which does propose to reallocate decision-making authority in such a way that some specific members of the black bourgeoisie gain a larger role. One version is the "black-caucus" format (hence, "caucus separatism") which shows up in the world of the university, in social work, in professional societies, and notably in the predominantly white churches. The attack in these circles does not really mean rejection of American society at all. Instead, it responds to such an obvious fact as that the prime interpreters of race—from the point of view of white decision makers in education, industry, and government—are usually white, and that almost no black can (to judge from the behavior of white decision makers) ever be deemed "equally" competent with a white[27] Caucus separatism poses the questions: "Shall perquisites be given white interpreters who, as careerists, have a natural interest (psychological and economic) in establishing *their* credentials above and beyond the credentials of blacks?" Or shall "blackness" be defined as a prime credential so that perquisites go to blacks? This is naturally a vital issue. For it is a political fight over who shall be defined as the presumptively valid and authentic expert on black people, in a society where expertise is itself a form of power. The problem is the more important for those who participate in "caucus separatism" because their normal experience is that if they do not accentuate blackness—if they depend exclusively on their professional competence as otherwise defined —they will regularly be relegated to uninfluential roles, regardless of what the actual level of competence may be.

Street-level populsim[28] is a term which I apply to the growing participation of lower-middle class and lower-class persons in black-community ventures, and to their growing resistance against the participation of "professionals," "middle-class people," and "Ph.D.'s." The essential claims are that *"only* the brothers and sisters on the street know where it's at," and that they should control programs which "affect their destinies." Street-level populism has many roots and manifestations. In part, it is a function of genuine differences of interest, specifically associated with class position. Insofar as street-level populism is successful, it does create numerous advancement opportunities which people of the lower-middle and lower classes would ordinarily not have. In part, it is a kind of doctrinal and organizational effect, not of "the black revolution," but of the Office of Economic Opportunity. That is, for several years during the Johnson administration, the doctrine of "participation" was assiduously cultivated by the OEO staff and spread through the population at large by the mass media. The availability of OEO resources (money), and the availability of the doctrine, provided opportunities for much wider development and cultivation of organizational skills, by formally uneducated people, than had ever been possible before.

The merger of this effect with the "black revolution" gave strong organizational and cultural support, in a way which proved electrifying for a good portion of the ordinary black population ("the folks"—see above, Essay I) across the country who had long been in a state of ambivalence. If they were frequently prepared to show some enthusiasm for the black oppositionist leadership—particularly when that leadership was seen to be challenging white supremacy vigorously—it was also true that there was a certain emergent cultural distance between them and that leadership. The civil rights movement—particularly in its constitutional oppositionist form—spoke of "opportunity" for the black lower-middle and lower classes, but it never managed to coopt members of these classes or to give signs of its own respect[29] to the symbols with which the lower-middle- and lower-class black people were most comfortable. Indeed, until recently, only the churches and the political "machines"[30] managed to do this on a large scale and for a large number of people. The symbols which are here pertinent—less overtly "political" than "social," as dress, manner, speech, personal associations, and the like—and which the previous black leadership fell into most easily were (and are) "white" symbols, with which it was simply too much to expect that the lower-middle- and lower-class persons would be comfortable. We see the importance of this only if we remember that people are acutely sensitive to signs of status, and to implications that other people do not hold them in high esteem. They will leap at opportunities to achieve esteem. Thus, once it started to become fashionable to be "black," being black meant something more than admission of one's genotype.[31] *It meant the elevation of the cultural styles of the lower-middle- and lower-class black people to places of premier esteem, and the increasing payment of deference to those styles by black people whose ordinary cultural styles would be somewhat different.*[32] In politics, this change means an increasing activity by people who would normally be less overt and in a manner which has been less frequently used. It means the appearance of people uninvited and shouting, issuing demands for instant action and *never mind the context!* One of the advantages which street-level populism does offer is that it presents certain immediate needs in an abruptly direct manner: the need for improvement in a given school *now;* the need for police action to clean out heroin peddlers on the block *now;* the need for satisfaction about local-area housing *now.* While there are many advantages associated with street-level populism, and while decision makers in some existing institutions (notably *local* government institutions) find this new mood inconvenient or even nerve-wracking, my hypothesis is that street-level populism neither has, nor could have, nor is intended to have any decisive effect on American social structure.[33] In that sense, it is part of a withdrawal process.

VARIETY III: VALUE WITHDRAWAL

The most important form of withdrawal is also the most confused, for it is a complex and undisciplined tendency to withdraw not from specified institutions, as is the case with tactical withdrawal, but from major values, in terms of which oppositionists have normally formulated their political preferences. Such withdrawal is still primarily a Northern phenomenon, although it had its breeding in the South. Moreover, it was planned or foreseen by virtually no one; its natural Northern home was discovered after the fact, and the people involved had virtually no beforehand appreciation of what they were doing. This unexpectedness is particularly applicable to the catalytic element in value withdrawal, the resonating cry of "Black Power!" which emerged in the King-Carmichael debate on the Meredith March near Greenwood, Mississippi, in the hot summer of 1966.

Each of these remarkable men "failed" a test which Erikson (1958, 242) argues—I think rightly—that most leaders must ultimately meet: "The crisis of an ideological leader naturally emerges when he must recognize what his rebellion—which began with the application of a more or less disciplined phantasy to the political world in the widest sense—has done to the imagination, the sense of reality, and the conscience of the masses." In a certain sense, King had brought the generation of young men with whom Carmichael was associated to "the Movement," and in a certain sense they took "the Movement" away from him.

As the leader of the Student Nonviolent Coordinating Committee, Carmichael was the exponent of those who had once followed the King doctrine, and come increasingly to doubt it. The roles were even more complex, for the Southern Christian Leadership Conference, though not literally a parent of the student group, had some role similar to that of officiating midwife in its birth. Intellectually and psychologically, King and SCLC had—with the aid of the mass media—done more than anyone else to make their direct-action methods both popular and socially legitimate. In the atmosphere of 1960 and 1961, one black college after another produced a cascade of sit-ins. The students in these Southern schools were quickly joined by many of their Northern counterparts, black and white. At that time also, the spirit and accepted rhetoric were of "nonviolence," and dozens of "committees," "action groups," "protest groups," and their like arose—in the same spontaneous way that much antiwar agitation later spread.

SNCC came into being as a sort of coordinating entity for all this activity, vaguely related at the organizational level to SCLC in the sense that SCLC could not but encourage the students and even paid the bill for the session which put the formal organization together. If the broad objectives of the student movement coincided with those of the leadership presented by King and others, there was also a fundamental difference in tactics. This difference was something none of them could help, but it would in the end produce an unmistakable and major breach. King and his allies functioned as major national figures, and their tactics were those of artillery bombardment: break up the enemy's strong points, leaving until later the detailed occupation. These tactics meant, for instance, choosing carefully the places into which the forces of SCLC—with their ability to draw the television cameras—would be thrown. But these same tactics meant that many places just as bad by any objective standard had to be left alone—at least for the time being. They also meant that when a particular local fight was going too badly, or lost its broader strategic utility, the SCLC forces might withdraw. Conceptually, this approach was very sound, but it meant also that the local black people—who might have been involved—sometimes were left "holding the bag," left to face an even more embittered and hostile white population, against whom no protection was easily forthcoming.[34]

The student movement, on the other hand, was more attuned to some combination of the spirit of George Patton's use of armor (hit *fast,* hit *often*) and of the infantry spirit (dig out every last foxhole). In terms of field tactics, this approach gave SNCC a reason to emphasize working intensively to develop the confidence, skills, and self-defensive capacity of people in the hardest and toughest counties where the white supremacists had hardly yielded so much as a millimeter. But these were the places where many a white man would as soon kill you as look at you, and where the chances were that he could do it and get away with it. To live and work in such places was to live and work in the valley of the shadow of death. It would have been too much to expect people who lived that way for a purpose—*particularly young people* with all the predictable excitability of young people—also to hold on to the restraint which moral opposition demanded. The disillusionment had been growing for some time, and the debates at Greenwood were but the occasion on which it came breaking through to the surface, in a way that none could miss. From the Debates at Greenwood onward, the shouts of "Black Power" nearly drowned out all other voices. But if "Black Power" was a new emotional spirit, there was very little new content. If one reads Carmichael's book (1967, with Charles Hamilton), one meaning is clearly political, but hardly unconventional except that it was being applied in the Deep South, where anything new and black was by definition "revolutionary." The idea of "grass-roots" organization is one with which the church has been comfortable since the travels of St. Paul or, if one needs more immediate examples, one fully evinced in the American trade union and the political party in the large city. Applying that idea, consistently with their notion that the best way to work was "with the people" in ordinary circumstances, SNCC had already set about creating a base in a tough Alabama county. They rejected—as Great Plains farmers have at some times, and New York Jewish trade unionists at other times—the idea that "third parties" are always quixotic absurdities in American politics.[35] In Lowndes County—near Montgomery, but utterly unaffected by the civil rights movement, except that whites were probably angrier than they had been for years—they set out to use certain quirks of the Alabama electoral law to create a third party in the form of the Lowndes County Freedom Organization (LCFO)[36]—the "Black Panther party."[37] They were guided by the good strategic logic of "break the hard case and the easier cases will fall naturally." Perhaps they had learned the lessons of their five years' existence, that one could not be everywhere at once and do everything. For, as Carmichael and Hamilton (1967, 101) say:

Lowndes County was a truly totalitarian society—the epitome of the tight, insulated police state. SNCC people felt that if they could help crack Lowndes, other areas—with less brutal reputations—would be easier to organize. This might be considered a kind of SNCC Domino Theory.

At the time, there were some tactical reasons to expect that the white vote might split. But there were also reasons to fear that blacks would not benefit from the split since plantation owners might control their tenants' votes, thus also splitting the black vote. In that context, black electoral solidarity made good sense as a tactical objective, and one almost wonders how much the projection of "Black Power!" upon the television screen was meant to encourage the folks back in Lowndes County, and others in similar circumstances. One wonders, for no other serious political meaning can be attached to the slogan at the time—but one finds it difficult to believe that an intelligent man would show forth sound and fury of no import or intent.[38]

The thrust of the argument, thus far, is that "Black Power," though emotionally important, was actually a reiteration of some conventional notions about political organization and social action. This view seems applicable when one considers the problem of violence. SNCC was soon charged with, or praised for, advocating aggressive violence. But this charge or praise seems to have been, at first, overreaction by both white and black. Clearly, in the Debates near Greenwood, Carmichael was suggesting that "turn the other cheek" was no longer a valid policy (if it ever had been). And later in the course of the Meredith March, says Muse:

> The [white] bullies, who are essentially cowards, had made the disconcerting discovery that the Negro was no longer safe and submissive game. Carmichael lieutenants shouting—"If anybody touches one of our workers we're going to tear this place up!" or even "white blood will flow!" —was something new in Mississippi. (Muse, 1968, 240)

Hyperbole aside, this was a stance which the NAACP might just as easily have taken, consistently with its own principles and tradition.[39] For it was nothing more than a claim to self-defense,[40] "radical" only by Mississippi criteria under which a black man still had no rights a white man was bound to respect. Nonetheless, a wave of near-panic ran through the body politic, even though no one has ever shown that SNCC engaged even in retributive violence under any circumstances. But the wave of near-panic is related less to what SNCC did than to the imagery of incipient black revolt.

White people were aware that there had been major urban riots in 1964 and 1965, and this awareness was intensified by the latent cultural fear of black violence. (See *The White Man's Burden,* Essay II, pp. 32–39.) Those who were fearful believed themselves proven right when another wave of urban uprising occurred in the summer of 1966, and were made to feel absolutely right when the great crises occurred in Newark and Detroit in 1967. Indeed, the belief in some deliberate conspiracy was reportedly held even in the White House, and the Kerner Commission computerized Stokely Carmichael's movements to determine if such a conspiracy actually existed. In fact, they found nothing, except oratorical incitement (Wicker, 1968). My hypothesis is that they found nothing because there was nothing to find. Instead, it seems much more likely that SNCC fell accidentally into the posture of *appearing to advocate aggressive* violence. (One says "appearing" because a statement about the actual advocacy of violence has legal meanings, requiring standards of proof we are unable to offer.) Having done so, it found political benefits in never discouraging the idea that this was its policy.

My belief that this apparent advocacy was accidental is dependent on the fact that, *before the 1966 riots,* SNCC showed virtually no interest in the cities and no sign of recognizing the volatility of the cities. Once the 1966 riots occurred, at the time when SNCC was abandoning "nonviolence" as doctrine, a leadership vacuum developed which the SNCC activists could fill, but only if they did appear to advocate violence. The vacuum existed because the major civil rights leaders had to repudiate violence unless they were going to adopt an entirely new strategic posture, which they then were unable to do. The riots had begun in 1964 and continued in 1965, but the civil rights leaders so greatly feared "white backlash," a phenomenon which was appearing as early as 1964, that they could not afford to let even themselves see that this violence might be a new pattern. Political realism alone forbade them to predict it, lest they seem to encourage it. Moreover, as men dedicated to law, they were themselves opposed to such activity, and at first urged vigorous action to suppress it.[41] The best they could do was to say, "It's bad, it doesn't really represent the black people, but it cannot be stopped *permanently* unless there is real reform." Any other course would have rendered them even less influential politically, for what white leaders would want to deal with them if they could not, in fact, promise physical order *in return for* social reform? And how could they maintain credentials of "responsibility" if they did not deprecate physical disorder?

By the summer of 1966, the civil rights leadership was, if not paralyzed, beginning to be palsied. Many whites—particularly the newly alerted business leadership and the emergent advocates of a "new politics"—doubted (or even denied outright!) that these men and women represented anybody or even understood what was happening.[42] This aspersion was not wholly correct; they still represented the people who had been their followers in the past, even though many of their followers now wished they were more aggressive. But it was not wholly incorrect; there was a leadership vacuum. The civil rights leaders could not then provide the right symbols of action. What they did not understand was that, in addition to people accustomed to violating the law or being in trouble with the police—whose participation in riots could easily be predicted—there was a substantial reservoir of more respectable black people who were at least *sentimentally* friendly to violence. They did not perceive how many black people—hard-working, taxpaying, and responsible—would permit themselves to "get caught up in the situation," let alone how many more would say "I wouldn't do it myself, but I can 'understand' those who do." Even less did they seem to appreciate how much their authority would be undermined by a new coalition of young people to whom "civil rights" was irrelevant, "nonviolence" naive, and "integration" a middle-class sellout. The factor of being young was, and is, acutely important in motivating the members of this coalition. They were at that stage when self-discovery is still under way, and at that peculiar stage when "self-respect" requires some action. The character of that action may be even more accentuated by the peculiar importance of honor—in the Mediterranean sense of the term—in black culture, even though the *word* "honor" is seldom used. Honor requires a response to the provocation which lies in the very facts of history and ordinary social experience, in the very fact that someone they know was roughed up by some policeman within the past day or so, the very fact that being subjected to white violence or the threat of white violence is part of the natural history of the black American.

The new coalition had two main elements. The leadership element proved to be the most strongly disaffected part of the black university-student population in the urban North. I mean those who were insulted by higher education as it stood. As they saw it, it could at best trap them into being pawns in a white man's world if they were successful.[43] More likely, it would lead them into the graveyard of personal ambitions which they knew all too well the United States Post Office might be. Others transformed their purely personal needs into political problems, and interpreted every thing which made them uncomfortable as a racial problem (as *frequently,* but not always is correct). Still others were "refugees" from black colleges in the South—often expelled or suspended for forms of racial protest which the college administrations found incompatible with their assessments of institutional necessity (i.e., the necessity to get along with the local white environment).

If being young was an important consideration, so I suspect was social class. For, in all likelihood, the students who proved to have the greatest effect were those who, though formally enrolled, really never made much of a transition to "academic" status. If they went to college, they nonetheless, wanted to retain all their emotive ties and credibility on the block.[44] This reference was most likely to be expressed in the behavior of those lower-class and lower-middle-class youngsters who found it difficult to adapt to the cultural idiom of higher education. At the same time, they would have been somewhat changed themselves by their exposure to higher education, for it would have— by sharpening their sense of ideological concepts—have sharpened their sense of being at an unfair disadvantage relative to white people.

The disaffected students' strong racial passion simply could not be fulfilled within the civil rights organization. When these latter had "youth" components—which they did not always have—these were mainly cannon fodder; youth leaders got no closer to organizational power than student Democrats or student Republicans get to internal party power. Moreover, the civil-rights organizations were "too slow," too much given to refined calculations of conventional political tactics, had too many connections to white organizations sufficiently to express this racial passion. Were the disaffected to assert themselves they would have to find a vehicle of their own, and it would need to be one with which many people sharing their emotions could identify. Consequently, it had to be known. This much was certainly thought out by some, as by the young man in Detroit who said "we have got to bring the Panther North."[45] The next strategic problem, of course, was that potential leaders would have to have a following. Whether anyone thought this out specifically, in advance, is impossible now to say. But the result is clear. Those who brought the Panther North elevated themselves into a leadership position by coopting a following from a different sort of young urban black person.[46]

The followers coopted were people of high-school age, but likely to be dropping out; or of college age, but likely not to have gone on. Educated poorly in the schools, which they often found more like prisons, they were knowledgeable in the ways of the fighting factions which are ordinarily called "street gangs" and which I should here prefer to call "street commandoes."[47] The normal street commando would be a boy (or young man) of lower-class background, sometimes working-class and sometimes of the "immobile poor" (above, Essay I). (If the former, command participation would be extremely worrisome and incomprehensible—even infuriating—to parents anxious to see their children "make something of themselves.")

Long before anybody provided them with ideological posture, these groups of young men (and associated young women) clubbed together for conviviality, and at times for other less harmless activity. Inevitably, they became "juvenile delinquents" in the social definition, if not in their actual behavior.[48] They were almost sure to have encountered the juvenile court if not the police court, or to have had some unpleasant contact which engrossed their names upon some policeman's notebook. They also learned that, whatever others might say, "the rule of law" in the urban ghetto was likely to be the rule of the billyclub or the police revolver. They also knew something of the methods of those people (professional criminals) who created their own systems of private "law," if only because it was impossible to hang about the block and not learn this. In principle, and in practice, they learned to display their own assertive pride, and their own organizational talents, in the acquisition and consolidation of turf (territory in which their own writ might run), in the negotiation of treaties with their opposite numbers in other neighborhoods, and in the application of simple coercion against anybody who might obstruct their own rule of their own turf. Perhaps such young people actually engage in far more threat than violence,[49] but there is clearly enough violence to frighten most other people. The commandoes and the most disaffected students did not then, and do not now, necessarily understand each other well. They did have certain qualities in common which made them important to each other, and which made it possible for them to obscure from each other their common misperception. For one thing, the "street" young people were not comfortable in any other language, because they spoke no other. The disaffected college young people were not comfortable in standard college English (not the grammatical forms, but the whole complex of ideas), because it was culturally alien and politically repulsive. Neither the language nor the experience nor the rules of social behavior it called for were in fact "real." Thus, in their search for a genuine language, "street" language was the only place to turn. They showed no obvious sign of holding "street" people in contempt, but rather signs of valuing them.

Second, each group was tough, full of the assertive pride which I have called Dionysian individualism, ever ready for a fight. This is one reason, I suspect, that the most important role soon came to be played by those disaffected students who had never, emotionally or physically, long removed themselves from the block. The account of Huey Newton emphasizes how much combat-readiness, both in disposition and in competence, was one of his outstanding qualities. He could, and would at the slightest provocation, beat anybody on the block. (See Seale, 1969.) In contrast to such people, most black students—however threatening their words may sound—remain rather close to the campus. However strong their feelings may be, they know what life on the roughest block can be like, and have no real desire to be there mixing it up.[50]

The combat leaders' credibility was further enhanced, it would seem, by their very careers as students. For if they learned to be tough on the block, they learned in school the *words* with which to impress and intimidate not only their street counterparts but frequently the public authorities as well. Nothing would impress their followers more than making fools of the police and having the police unable to retaliate. It would be like playing the dozens![51] Consequently, these disaffected students were not only ready, but able, to constitute role models for emerging young black people—of the high-school (and even junior-high) age ranges—who would and do show *their* rebellion in readiness and willingness to take on their white counterparts, their teachers and administrators, or others, with their fists, with sticks, and bricks, and sometimes with guns or lighter fluid. The nature of this collaboration is revealed—if inadvertently—in the very language of the Panthers' 10-Point Program as adopted in 1966.[52] That program emphasizes, with the exception of Point 10 (which calls for a United Nations plebiscite in black America), what would be the basic demands of a lower-class constituency: material security,[53] relief from military service (which particularly burdens the urban black poor)[54] and protection from police violence and judicial maladministration.[55]

The elements of the formal Panther program are, at one level, entirely conventional. They may best be regarded as the rituals with which an ideologically motivated leadership catalyzes the value-withdrawal of its constituency. The constituents (young black poor) withdraw not so much from the broader complex of American values, about which they have had less reason to be concerned, as from rules (such as nonviolence) which have never made sense in their experience. But if their withdrawal is to be more than inane confrontation with policemen—virtually for its own sake—it needs a more rational frame which they can easily master. Hence, the strong emphasis on bread-and-butter issues and the issues of military service and judicial administration.

If one looks more closely, one also sees the tribute which the leadership pays to itself, its own withdrawal being at a deeper level. Thus, the more general emphasis on "freedom" and "power to determine the destiny of our people" (Point 1): "education for our people that expresses the true nature of this decadent American society" and "education that teaches us our true history and our role in the present-day society" (Point 5); and, most far-reaching (but by no means really revolutionary), the somewhat exaggeratedly expressed call for "a United Nations-supervised plebiscite to be held throughout the black colony in which only black colonial subjects will be allowed to participate, for the purpose of determining the will of black people as to their national destiny" (Point 10). All this is assuredly beyond the natural thought pattern, let alone language, of any lower-class population—black or white. Whether it is persuasive to the lower-class constituents is by no means clear. If they believe in these more complicated matters, it is because they have found their leaders to make sense on the gut issues. But the program is offered as part of the disaffected students' self-defined teaching mission—to make "revolutionaries" out of their "street" brothers, who may provide what no other element of the black population can provide: cadres of tough men, available for any rough-and-ready action.

Where all this will lead one cannot say. Too many elements are un-known. What, for instance, is the Panther response to police coercion?

One could imagine a great internal debate between those preferring to expand the retaliation and those preferring a discreet withdrawal. And what if the movement grows, possibly replenishing itself from the same youngsters involved in so many school disputes around the country? We should then expect the educated leadership to be swamped, and thus to have the movement adopt more of a "street" style—with less ideology still. If this development occurs, we might expect a peculiar combination: more physical confrontations between black street groups (*called* Panthers or not), but also more practical calculation of when to withdraw. Whatever may be predictable about all that, the form of politics discussed in this section shares one crucial common thread with both genuine separatism and tactical separation. That thread is some kind of inclination to detach black politics from white society. Withdrawal is different from its predecessors in several ways. It has been particularly important that withdrawal gives places of esteem to the symbolism and styles of the lower-middle classes and lower classes. Even more, it actually enhances lower-middle- and lower-class leadership options. But it is also critical that the emergence of a language of "black pride" has fed back to modify the posture of parts of the middle class. I mean those middle-class persons whose *effective* higher education has been essentially vocational, that is, calculated to convey skills for the economy. These students found the conquest of a degree program contingent on—for example—an interpretation of American literature which valued Mark Twain, but ignored Paul Lawrence Dunbar; which treated Mary Cassatt in the history of painting, but took no cognizance of Henry O. Tanner; which for so long treated jazz and spirituals as a species of exotica beyond the scope of real music. For many, many persons, this curriculum meant that the nonvocational education did not interest them or (with its Anglo bias) made them feel uncomfortable or "inferior." Those who carried with them a great residue of the lower-middle- and lower-class culture from which they had come, were (as they felt) obliged to disguise their continued emotional attachment to that culture, or even to destroy that attachment. A substantial proportion of the black middle class (though by no means all of it) has had this experience in formal education.

Many people thus felt the necessity to pretend to something which they neither were, nor wanted to become. When it was said (derogatorily) that they were "trying to be white," the statement was correct. Consequently, they were in desperate need of some way to assuage the guilt they felt for having made the effort to pretend.[56] When symbols drawn from the residual culture were pushed onto the public consciousness by the young people's rebellion, and quickly circulated through the mass media, it was natural that these particular middle-class blacks should find it exciting. The respectabilization of "blackness" provided a genuinely liberating effect for them, and made their acceptance of nonblack symbols seem much less respectable. "Integration" thus ceased to be so attractive a symbol as it had been; members of the black middle class (and even black gentry) could confess their discomfort at moving into situations and roles which exiled them among whites, and thus could adopt a rhetoric of staying with "the folks." Indeed, it even became psychologically—or politically obligatory —for many who did not really participate in that residual culture to seek to "return"[57] to it, or to pretend such a return. The new orthodoxy has tended to become a belief that even those who are genuinely comfortable with Euro-American culture must have something "wrong" with them, or must be pretending and refusing to admit that they are not comfortable in the white man's culture.[58]

SUMMARY AND CONCLUSION

The three major conceptions of external strategy—clientage, opposition, and withdrawal—have been laid one atop the other. It is through an appreciation of this unfolding pattern—so similar to the unfolding sequence of strategies in the politics of "the new nations"—that one may seek to impart some clarity to the question "Why haven't you got accepted leaders?" It is the white man's version of the black man's question "Why can't we get ourselves together?" In the post-Reconstruction years the American republic came so close to total exclusion of blacks that we have found it profitable to describe the pattern as "unofficial apartheid." Against this background of intense coercion and suppression, there was always a latent will to defiance which could be found in the black culture. When it was utterly impossible to express this will systematically and on a large scale, the preponderant form of black politics was Herodian clientage of which the arch apostle and practitioner was Booker T. Washington. It is not possible to be sure that the Washingtonian version of Herodianism did more good than harm (or the converse), but it seems possible to maintain (retrospectively) that it could never have the large-scale results anticipated. Its possible base of support in the white population was too narrow, at the same time that it ran counter to the desires and needs of the black gentry, who became the seeding-ground of constitutional opposition.

Constitutional opposition was generated from this black gentry—a small but highly significant group—who were simultaneously comfortable in the cultural world of the Anglo-Protestants but much afflicted with an awareness of the burdens of blackness. Both their values and their sense of the necessary white alliances led them to focus upon the strategic problem of achieving "rights" for individuals within the framework of the Constitution, as they chose to interpret the Constitution. Constitutional opposition provided the decisive intellectual break with submission. Constitutional opposition was successful in establishing the *principle* that the United States is a single republic with a common citizenship. The *formal rights* which the constitutional oppositionists sought, and which had been substantially denied as late as the end of World War II, were well on toward achievement by the early 1950's, and nearly unchallenged by the early 1960's. But they were *formal* rights, not effectively implemented on a scale wide enough to make a decisive difference to Everyman. Moreover, they were *individual* rights, which could not easily be transformed into collective benefits on a scale appropriate to overcome the residues of unofficial apartheid. Accordingly, the rights so achieved seemed somewhat empty, not only in the South but in the urban North as well. But the constitutional oppositionists were, by the 1950's, reaching a point where within the black community they had to do what they had not had to do at any time in the prior forty years: justify their existence and their methods.

In this atmosphere, the initiative passed to the entrepreneurs of moral opposition, whose strategy of "nonviolent direct action" provided a scope for just any black man to participate directly in "the cause." Moral opposition articulated black claims to equality in the language of religious and humanistic values, abjuring force, declaring a willingness to suffer as the price for defying "unjust laws." As constitutional opposition had received the active attention of a small part of the black population and the romantic approval of the rest, so moral opposition now was capable of activating large parts of those best educated and most prosperous and also of linking that activity to the incentives and values of good parts of the black lower-class "respectables" and lower-middle class. Moral opposition encountered its limits, however, in the urban North, where the issues could be seen as contending moralities by whites and where, at the same time, the more secular atmosphere reduced the effects of the powerful discipline of "nonviolence." In the urban North, thus, one came to see a somewhat exaggerated form of moral opposition that soon came to be called "Militant" politics. Militant politics converted itself from "defiance of unjust laws" to the use of hostility toward whites as an organizing principle. Militant politics in this sense was frequently tactical, and carefully contained itself within the boundaries of the system it purported to denounce.

But the movement of the issues from South to North, on a large scale, brought to light a new situation: a set of issues which provoked more and more controversy between "Moderates" and "Militants." At the time (and since), the Moderate-Militant controversy was represented as one between those who "really" wanted to be free (Militant) and those who did not (Moderate). This representation seems erroneous. The controversy was one in which, given limited resources of money and public support, different groups had to compete for attention and in the competitive process grossly exaggerated their differences. It is true that the Moderates advocated mainly constitutional tactics within the ground rules already accepted as legitimate. It is true that the Militants advocated "direct action"—both with and without the Gandhian patina—more with in the South, more without in the North. (It is also true that both sometimes still practiced Herodian politics—although with no mention that they were doing so). But the rapid shifts of the 1960's brought to the fore the *avant-garde* elements of the Militants: those who—by professing to write their own rules *de novo*—were able to exploit the more fundamental cultural bias toward rejecting the symbols and practices associated with "whiteness." That these should come forward is easily comprehensible. There was an impatient audience waiting, for—while the line could not easily be represented in class terms—the newer forces did tap both class and generational stresses in a new way.

Concretely, the politics of withdrawal has taken three forms: (a) the minor—but not trivial—element of separatism; (b) tactical withdrawal which contains both "separatism" as a bourgeois self-promotion device and street-level populism as a mode of carrying on the lower-class and lower-middle-class assertion of its own cultural style and its own rebellion against black middle-class leadership; and (c) above all, the critical withdrawal from the conception of a rule of law which is represented in the propensity toward justification of a politics of violence. Each form makes clear that withdrawal is not a politics of passivity, but one of withdrawing from certain institutions and values which the oppositionists had long—and still do—regard as essential. This politics of withdrawal does not have the field all to itself. But it has acquired a special psychological power by making it respectable—and frequently necessary—for black people to make a concerted effort to be free by "thinking black," "feeling black," and discovering a cultural milieu in *which the standard to be respected is "blackness."* This isolated people is far more receptive, than five years ago, to the interpretation that it must simply withdraw from the white environment which surrounds it and "go it alone."[59] The attractiveness of withdrawal, and the possibility of its continued growth under some imaginable circumstances, can—except for the highly pragmatic forms of tactical with-drawal—best be explained if we emphasize the function of politics as collective psychiatry.

Politics in its most general sense is a calculated means of ordering social relations, of setting ground rules.[60] These rules set a framework for get-ting on about our "nonpolitical" business. Most such rule making is done by instrumental politics which demands that participants pay careful atten-tion to their power relative to that of other people, weigh their objectives carefully, sacrifice objectives which cannot be achieved in the interest of other and "more important objectives," count the costs, and look to the future. All of this "cold-bloodedly" emphasizes what is possible much more than what is desirable. Most people recognize that this kind of politics exists, and possibly even that it is necessary. But they do not like it. What they prefer is a form of politics which makes them feel better about themselves, which permits them to express their own genuine feel-ings about right and wrong, to assert their own personalities, to cultivate their own images of heroism and virtue.[61] In short, they prefer politics as a form of collective psychiatry.[62] Politics as collective psychiatry may take many forms,[63] one of which is politics-as-theater, an entertainment which reaffirms or inspires the audience in feelings which it may have but not see recognized and respected by others, or which it even may have dis-guised from itself. Politics-as-theater allows leaders to build their relation-ship upon ritual practices[64] which may have little or no effect upon achiev-ing declared objectives (Boudling, 1960, 94). But the harder it is to achieve declared objectives, the more likely it is that a theatrical and ritualistic politics, serving the function of collective psychiatry, will in face predominate!

The questions in black politics are, however: What does withdrawal produce? How should we evaluate a politics of collective psychiatry?

NOTES

1. As an analytical problem one could comfortably place clientage in a number of other fields. Economics, sociology, and industrial relations might find it perti-nent insofar as some trade unions are, from time to time, clearly under the wing of other unions which provide funds and organizing support. Economics, law, and political science might find it pertinent in dealings with the domination of one industrial firm by another, the domination of a firm by the banking house with which it deals, or the domination of distributors by manufactures (see Palamoun-tain, 1955; Macaulay, 1966). Sociology, political science, history, and the special-

ists in education might find some interests in the relationships between foundations and the universities which have constant relationships with them. Thus far, the discussion of clientage is not very clear in the social sciences, not even in international relations where its pertinence would seem obvious since *client* states (having little more than formal independence) probably outnumber genuinely independent states in the world today. James N. Rosenau (1966, 65–71) represents a rare and useful contribution toward the study of this topic.

2. Montgomery's personal history illustrates the remarkable intricacies of the black-white relationship in the United States. His entire family (which, unlike many slave families, seems to have lived as a functioning unit even before the Civil War) was part of the Davis brothers' (Jefferson and Joseph) estate, and seems to have been used for managerial and clerical functions about the estate. Isaiah was educated in the Davis household (with the Davis children) by the Davis tutor. As a young boy (probably in his teens although that is not certain), he was put to work keeping the estate accounts and handling the Davis business and political correspondence. One could hardly imagine a better (if unintended) education in the subtleties of politics than to have an intelligent boy learning in this manner from regularly reading his master's most intimate correspondence and records. For a portrait of Montgomery, see Redding (1958, 100).

3. August Meier (1966, 77–82) discusses this problem a little, but is inconclusive.

4. See *The White Man's Burden,* Essay IV, "The Republicans: Historical Note on the Southern Strategy."

5. A poor man in the South at that time would have been even more a hostage in a different sense, namely his complete absence of legal protection for his physical person and his probable dependence on the landlord even for food (through the commissary system).

6. In 1929, Democrats tried to create a sensation with the charge that President Hoover had danced with a black woman at a White House ball—the black woman being Montgomery's daughter (who was many years the Republican National Committeewoman for Mississippi).

7. The tactic of emphasizing "bigness" as a personal virtue and "smallness" as a defect runs through all the things written by Booker T. Washington in the same way. It is the device of shaming the man who has the whip hand.

8. The Lodge Bill and its contexts are discussed in *The White Man's Burden,* Essay IV, "The Republicans: Historical Note on the Southern Strategy."

9. On the difficulty of discerning the importance of bewildering and contradictory signals at the time they are forthcoming, see Wohlstetter (1962).

10. On the discouragement experienced even by respectable white conservatives prepared to argue for any sort of education for blacks, see *The White Man's Burden,* Essay III, in particular the section on "The Unconscious Retreat from Apartheid."

11. Everyone who studies Washington sooner or later notes how much time and effort he invested in this process. For one among many examples, see the

accounts of his success in detaching William H. Lewis, a Boston lawyer, from the group of anti-Washington gentry who clustered in that city (Fox, 1970, 445 and 159–160). Through Washington's support, Lewis was appointed to the United States' Attorney's office in Boston and later became Assistant Attorney General under President Taft, the last black appointee of comparable rank until J. Ernest Wilkinson became Assistant Secretary of Labor under President Eisenhower.

12. In a decade when, once more, there is broad public recognition of how important violence can be in politics—and how perilous life is when men cannot feel safe in their common affairs—Washington's public role as the opponent of lynching merits notice. Lynching was not, as common opinion came to believe, merely an informal way of handling cases which the courts had not taken care of. It was a fundamental tactic in a strategy of terror, inflicted for such simple matters as failing to show "sufficient" deference to whites, and inflicted not by a "mere hanging, but by castration, mutilation, and burning alive." The brute fact of life was that no black man was safe anywhere in the United States and that control in Southern politics depended upon a structure of violence.

13. But why should Washington not have been excessively optimistic? Men commonly measure what is possible by their personal experiences, and he himself had traveled a fantastic distance from the slave cabins of West Virginia to the company of presidents of the United States and of Harvard. This experience must surely have been consistent with the Victorian ethic he had learned and to which he always gave every sign of adhering. If white men believed in Horatio Alger, should he not also? But one does not have to believe that it was all *naive* optimism. One may quite consistently believe that, in the characteristic manner of the institution builder, he professed optimism even when he did not feel it. Agitators and charismatic leaders may be able to afford gloom and doom, but institution builders usually feel that they have to operate on the principle that one "catches more flies with honey than with vinegar." *Even if he realized how long a shot he was playing, one might ask what options he actually had* in the races being run in the 1890's and the early 1900's? Would strikes, civil disobedience, or even violent organized revolt (a black Southern *jacquerie?*) have been more productive? The answers are not self-evident.

14. See also *The White Man's Burden,* Essay IV, "The Republicans: Historical Note on the Southern Strategy."

15. A study of these 1930 elections would be rewarding, particularly if one takes account of the fact that the depression must have worked against the Republicans and the fact that the administration party tends to lose in midterm elections.

16. The Department of Justice characteristically took the position that lynching was murder, hence a state crime. After the Lindbergh Law was passed, it still declined to intervene even in cases where the person killed had been taken across state lines for that purpose.

17. It would be grossly inaccurate to say that nothing else counted in the shift of the American structure of race relations. One would have to take account of other forms of black politics, of other pressures in white politics, and of broad

changes in values and economy which also contributed to alteration of the pattern. But it is unmistakable that it was the constitutional oppositionists who made it their business to press the issues of race in the public arena. This pressure, mixed with whatever other factors were present, produced a large transformation in public opinion. Race began to be discussed in a different way, and the presumptions of public policy—though hardly the full conduct of public policy—were stated in terms which increasingly minimized the legitimacy of explicit racial hierarchy. See *The White Man's Burden,* Essay V, "The Democrats: Racism, Black Votes, and White Liberals."

18. The excesses of McCarthyism so disturbed liberal writers (among whom most social scientists might have been counted until recently) that they have found it emotionally impossible to examine the actualities of Communist penetration in the 1930's and 1940's. Communist penetration into voluntary and private organizations dedicated to social reform was no mere chimera of the Martin Dies, Parnell Thomas, and Joseph McCarthy investigations. It is another matter that the investigators' attack, ostensibly on the Communists, was in great measure really aimed at the social-reform organizations as "Communistic."

19. For historical documents expressing this spirit, see Bracey, Meier, and Rudwick (1970).

20. See the discussion of cultural themes in Essay I, above.

21. Interestingly enough, the specific points of departure for various black leaders may be quite similar, even when the ideological justifications are far apart. Thus, the Rev. J. H. Jackson (President of the National Baptist Convention of the U.S.A., Inc., and not to be confused with the Rev. Jesse Jackson)—a very conservative man, much admired by white conservative writers—announced in early 1970 that he had secured a grant of 100,000 acres in Liberia, to be filled by any black Americans who might desire to go there.

22. The Jewish settlement in Palestine is noted at p. 26 in Imari's 1968 book.

23. One group based in New York offers a proposal for a twelve-state area, the former Confederacy plus Maryland.

24. After the riots of 1967, the same idea arose (with none of the ideological trappings) in Jerome P. Cavanagh's idea that United States policy should be calculated to discourage further internal migration, and Orville Freeman's idea that United States policy should be calculated to encourage city-to-rural migration.

25. One should be most careful about such matters. "Black intellectuals" in the two senses used here were (and are) neither separate nor coterminous and coextensive but rather intersecting categories.

26. There is some evidence that Atlanta is now competitive in this regard.

27. The merits of Daniel P. Moynihan need not be in question when we note that in less than five years he became *far more influential* with two presidents than Kenneth Clark, St. Clair Drake, James Dumpson, or Hylan Lewis—all of whom are his seniors in years and had professional experience on various aspects of race-in-society.

28. The best study of street-level populism is Ellis (1969).

29. There are some interesting signs of change on this dimension, although these signs must be at once superficial and probably a little painful for all parties. One indicator of the type I mean is contained in the *Washington Afro-American*, August 19, 1969, showing a photograph of an upper-middle-class black women's function at which an award was being presented to Mrs. Fannie Lou Hamer.

30. By much personal observation, I can testify that this was so for the Dawson organization of Chicago's South Side.

31. This is what people mean when they say that "Black is a state of mind."

32. In this respect, Martin Kilson is right, although I *fundamentally* disagree with his interpretation of what the lower-middle- and lower-class black cultural style is. See his 1970 paper and my Essay I above.

33. Ellis (1969) takes a different view.

34. The best available analysis of this problem is Lewis (1970).

35. I refer, of course, to the Farmer-Labor parties which once were influential in the Great Plains and to the Liberal Party which still is influential in New York State.

36. The Lowndes County project is described in Carmichael and Hamilton (1967), 98–120.

37. The term "Black Panther" got wide currency, but my *impression* is that Carmichael was initially rather annoyed by it. In a television interview with Martin Agronsky and others (which I saw, but have not taken the trouble to look up as to exact date), he said that he saw no reason to call the Lowndes County Freedom Organization "the Black Panther party" any more than anyone called the regular Democratic party "the White Rooster party." The Panther symbolism, he said, had to do with white people's hang-ups about blacks and about sex.

38. There is still another aspect of "Black Power" which may have been pertinent. The newspapers published what they alleged were internal memoranda, the authenticity of which I have been unable to verify, claiming an intention by some black members of SNCC to reduce the influence of their white counterparts. If there were such memoranda (and it would have been reasonable under the circumstances to imagine that there were), then an emphasis on *black*ness would also have been rational.

39. As a practical matter, however, the organization has generally restrained itself to the defense of individuals when said individuals were clearly within their legal rights, and has punished officials (Robert F. Williams for one) who have attempted to organize a more aggressive collective force. This almost surely has resulted from calculations as to the over-all political effect of aggressive collective force, in contrast to the over-all gains. That the more "conservative" black leaders were capable of recognizing the same *logic* of deterrence was indicated to me in a speech by Roy Wilkins in Detroit in 1969. At a large public dinner, Wilkins adverted to the self-defense theme in connection with disputes over the job rights of black firemen on Southern railroads in earlier years. Quoting him more or less literally: "Every time one of the black firemen would go up the tower to put water in the engine, a rifle would crack, and he would go down. After a while, when

a white fireman would go up, a rifle would crack, and down he would go. Well, pretty soon, the rifles stopped on both sides, and the black men went on with their jobs" (from which an effort was being made to exclude them).

40. On the NAACP's consistent maintenance of the theory of a legal right of self-defense, see White (1948, 75–79, and Kellogg (1967, I, 57–64).

41. Muse (1968) provides some details.

42. This is actually a continuation of an old process in American racial politics. The authenticity of black leadership has almost always been challenged by whites. The irony was now that the same civil rights leaders who—within the past five to ten years—had been deemed unrepresentative because they were "too radical" now were deemed unrepresentative because they were "too conservative."

43. It is not clear how far the deep value withdrawal here suggested characterizes a great proportion of black college students. Studies of the people actively embarked on college life are themselves quite preliminary, and are still oriented toward developing instrumentalities for research. (See, for instance, Friedman, White, and Epps, 1970.) Consequently, it is natural that they should still be asking question which—though instructive for other purposes—would not suffice to distinguish between active members of the Black Panthers and young men headed for the Chrysler Corporation's personnel department. At best, one must rely on very general impressions. At the University of Wisconsin—of which I have some knowledge—the most *avant-garde* students are those who participate in the "All-African Peoples' Union," but at the outside, this seems to account for about one in six (75 to 100 in 500) black students on the Madison campus. Moreover, the active participants include a wide range of views, from Third World devotees to people seeking careers in industrial relations. The proportion seemed even smaller in Wayne State University, where there were more than 2,000 black students, but fewer than a hundred active in the Association of Black Students. Again, among the active students the same wide range of orientations seemed to prevail. Moreover, these impressions extend only to those who are actively attending college, not those who—though out of high school—have never been college students, those who have dropped out, and those still in high school.

44. The desire to remain at home was emphasized to me by a black counselor, associated with a social service agency in an eastern city where a very prestigious small university with very tight admissions criteria is located. This counselor found young people asking him to get them into this university. "I said to them, 'Look man, you don't want to go there and flunk out. Why don't you go to ——?' You know what? They don't wanta leave home. They wanta be able to get back to the block every day."

45. My memory is clear about the conversation, except that I cannot place it more precisely than some time late in 1966.

46. However, one should note another sort of black student who has also risen to leadership roles. These are the active leaders of student protest on campus, whose activities have made them visible to the national media and to the national and local community black leaders—who have felt obliged to support them even

when they had doubts (as in San Francisco) to the national-foundation leadership, and to the academic community leadership. Despite much talk about "putting our skills at the service of the community," most such people have been gradually absorbed into the more conventional elite system (as could be seen in Detroit when the leader of the Wayne State black students' organization was a featured speaker at the biggest McCarthy meeting in 1968, later a member of various local elite committees, and similar organizations).

47. I am merely searching for a term which is as nearly descriptive as possible, without overpraising or over condemning. "Gang" is clearly a pejorative term. The most precise term probably is "faction" (particularly if one uses that term in its old Roman sense), but this is not common usage. The term "commando" seems to me best adapted to indicate a group which has some structure, which nonetheless allows a good deal of leeway for the derring-do of its individual members, and which operates in a hit-and-run method.

48. As far as I am concerned, the most insightful man on the "juvenile delinquency" question in recent years was James B. Conant. Regardless of the merits of his *particular* ideas about big-city school reform, Conant was entirely right in describing the "juvenile-delinquency" phenomenon as "social dynamite." Few, if any, other people seemed to understand this, although Conant's language was widely used. For example, I remember a discussion nine years ago at Wayne State University between several faculty members, some local social-agency officials (including a black woman on the staff of the Mayor's Commission on Children and Youth), and a representative of the President's Committee on Juvenile Delinquency and Youth Crime. In the course of the discussion, I asked the federal representative why juvenile delinquency was important *as a matter of public policy,* by which I mean *what reasons pertinent to the political order made it important.* The official—himself a black social worker with long experience in two large cities, and later to occupy a senior post in a federal line agency—had no answer, which proves merely that he did not understand the situation facing the committee to which he was then assigned. But neither did anyone else in the room, including myself.

49. This is the claim offered in Miller (1967, 127–141).

50. For this reason, I argue further, their enthusiasm for such figures as Newton and Seale is actually compensatory for their own knowledge of their own limitations.

51. On the importance of verbal facility and the ability to make a putdown, see above, Essay I, "Internal Politics of the Black 'Nation'." On the extraordinary detail which Huey Newton commanded on matters which interested him, such as the right to carry weapons, and on his use of that knowledge in confrontation with the police, see Seale (1969).

52. Obviously, the views of the Panthers have developed a good deal in four years. However, the 10-Point Program is still being published. See *The Black Panther,* 5:17 (October 24, 1970), 22. Presumably, this would not be so if the program no longer embodied the organizational policy. Moreover, if Bobby

Seale's book, published in 1969, is at all representative, there is very little development which goes beyond the 1966 program.

53. *Point 2:* We want full employment for our people. *Point 3:* We want an end to the robbery of the CAPITALIST of our Black Community. *Point 4:* We want decent housing; fit shelter of human beings.

54. *Point 6:* We want all black men to be exempt from military service.

55. *Point 7:* We want an immediate end to POLICE BRUTALITY and MURDER of black people. *Point 8:* We want freedom for all black men held in federal, state, county and city prisons and jails. *Point 9:* We want all black people when brought to trial to be tried in court by a jury of their peer group or people from their own black communities, as defined by the Constitution of the United States.

56. This, I maintain, is the psychological basis for the political support which middle-class blacks so quickly extended to the black-studies movement. If this basis had not existed, there would not have been such an instant and electric *political* response in behalf of "black studies." In the same way, I should predict that there will be an even wider political response in the next several years to the emergent (white) "ethnic studies" idea, in support of which Congressional legislation has already been introduced. I believe it also true that a substantial proportion of the South European-descended and East European-descended white middle class had something like the same psychological experience, because the cultural bias of higher education is not merely Euro-American but Anglo-American (see *The White Man's Burden,* particularly Essay VIII), with certain deference to France and Germany (and to Italy for specified periods, mainly the Renaissance) in studies of art and literature.

57. This process was strikingly akin to the search for Jewish "uniqueness," the French-Canadians' linguistic *rassemblement,* the current move in Belgium to separate French-speaking and Flemish-speaking students and faculties into separate universities, the futile Irish effort to revive Gaelic, or the Israeli pattern of renouncing European names. (Note, for instance, that Moshe Shertok became Moshe Sharett and that Golda Meir was once Golda Meyerson.)

58. In reality, some of this is fake. *Third-generation* Harvard blacks have, in general, no more *cultural*—as against political—kinship to "the folks" than the Kennedys had to the last remnants of the old-style Irish.

59. In this respect, blacks are analytically similar to the Quebecois (with whom they would not necessarily find comparison repulsive), Israeli (with whom some would find the comparison repulsive and some not), and Afrikanders or *Protestant* Northern Irelanders (with whom the comparison probably would be repulsive). Each group is relatively small compared to a large, mainly hostile *surrounding* mass —that mass also being more or less culturally homogeneous. When compared to the isolated people. This is in contrast to South European ethnic politics, for instance, where groups may be surrounded by enemies, but the enemies are themselves enemies to each other.

60. There are so many ground rules that it would be exhausting to try to

enumerate them, but we may try two: rules of *property* and rules of *speech*. I would suppose the number of musicians who have given much thought to "property" as a social institution must be very few, yet some system of property rules is essential to the musician. He may cultivate his talent on the piano or violin only if he has a piano or violin. He gets such an instrument, normally, only by receiving it as a gift, borrowing it, renting it, buying it, or if he is a complete genius, making it. He can never have a chance to practice unless his right to hold and use that instrument (given, borrowed, bought, or made) is protected against some other person who might desire to take it away physically. The instrument is property, which he "owns" (or otherwise has the "right" to use), only because there is a system of rules which prescribes that right, and those rules have to be made by people in a political process. (The problem of property is one of the most complicated and troublesome in human society, whether in the simple forms of which child in the household "owns" the particular toy or pencil or the larger ones of who has the "right" to control General Motors' assets.)

The same point holds for speech. If a man is mentally ill, most people will agree, we have no right to invade his clinic and scream at him "you are crazy." Whether a black man ought to be free to go on television and call white people "honkies" (or a white man to go and call blacks "niggers") will be debated. Most people will not doubt that it is appropriate to say "Franklin D. Roosevelt was a man who often spoke ambiguously." Most people will doubt, probably, that a militant atheist has the right to enter the pulpit of the Baptist church without "proper" invitation. In short, prior to the "law" on free speech, there is some political settlement which must be arrived at about the scope and limits of free speech.

61. Perhaps this is why men deemed cynical (which may merely mean that they let too much be known about their political methods) are so often unsuccessful, whereas those deemed "sincere" may elicit great enthusiasm, as they draw forth the fantasies, hopes, and discontents of the audiences they cultivate. The importance of the psychiatric patina may also explain why many people so often ignore the politics which is objectively important (in the sense that it will have great effect on their lives) if it is "dull" in preference to the politics which is "dramatic' " (but which may or may not have similar influence). The fact that most people pay very little attention to bureaucratic politics is a case in point.

62. The pioneer in the effort to understand politics as a process having psychiatric utility for the *individual politician* is Harold D. Lasswell. See for instance, his *Power and Personality* (1948). Here I am suggesting its utility for the politician's audience. One could, possibly, assimilate the conception of collective psychiatry to the collective portrait of the political ideas of fifteen "common men" in Robert E. Lane (1962).

63. War itself is one of them. War is not *simply* an "instrument of policy," for governments frequently attempt to maintain wars even if it is transparent that those particular wars cannot rationally be justified because they are not serving the purposes desired. And citizens or subjects will frequently evince great sorrow at "defeat," and great joy at "victory," far beyond what one might expect from any

threat or sense of relief from real physical threat. The "jingoism" which so captured many parts of the British population in the Boer War was collective catharsis, and so is the "war fever" in most times.

64. People who know nothing of how to produce artificial rainfall engage in rain dances or other forms of prayer for supernatural intervention. People who know how to produce artificial rainfall ignore the dances and prayers, although—if they lack the capacity for using their knowledge—they may engage in other rituals, such as curtailing the watering of lawns.

III

Politics as Collective Psychiatry: A Critique of Withdrawal

INTRODUCTION

Without collective psychiatry, a healthy politics is not possible. But a politics which relies almost entirely on collective psychiatry though it may permit people to express themselves, ultimately serves them ill. For in the end, it becomes a self-defeating morality play in which none of the more mundane but terribly "real" problems are managed. This shortcoming is now a real problem in black politics. The broad spirit of withdrawal has helped black people to show their chagrin and rage at a world ruled by whites. Naturally, it has more emotional appeal than the spirit of opposition, and surely far more than the spirit of Herodian clientage which now has emotional appeal for very few. Withdrawal strikes a responsive chord when it appeals to black people to "get themselves together," the more so because it claims to offer a practical method for doing so. But under close examination, it seems increasingly irrelevant to the purposes which its advocates espouse. It does not, in fact, offer a new kind of leverage for reducing the strength or impact of white rule—and indeed may enhance it.

The politics of rationality, seen from this viewpoint, demands an answer to the overriding question of whether there is a black interest in the improvement and future viability of the United States, or whether there is not. The answer here is clear from the central theme: that from a demographic and ecological point of view, the United States contains "two nations," whose fate is inevitably common. The two do not have the option of separable outcomes. Nor do they have the option of continuing in the imperial relation, except by paying so high a price that no sane man could—did he understand the issues—genuinely prefer it. Accordingly, each "nation" has a natural interest—whether it so perceives or not—in what has yet to come to the fore of public discussion: *a politics of peacemaking (The White Man's Burden,* Preface and Essay I). The problems which must be overcome, if there is to be a white contribution to peacemaking, run through the companion volume. But in this essay, I wish to discuss some rituals and illusions which must be surmounted if there is to be an effective black contribution.

THE RITUAL OF THE THIRD WORLD

The term "Third World" is used in two separable ways. One use actually refers to the fact that black politics may, on occasion, intelligently interlock with the politics of other ethnic minorities in the United States: various Spanish-speaking peoples, Nisei, Chinese-Americans, Indians. But that is not the essence of the Third World conception as the term is often used. The term is often used to refer to the nations that have (mostly) economies based on primary production (raw materials) as distinguished from the industrial nations. The Third World in this concept consists of nations subject mainly to the world economy in which the decisions that count are largely those of the Group of Ten plus the Soviet Union. Since this Third World is a collection of relatively poor countries,[1] there is sometimes a certain common interest in opposition to the richer countries. Moreover, these countries are—individually and collectively—not merely poorer but militarily inconsequential and politically weak compared to the United States, the Soviet Union, or the major states of Europe. Finally, the key factor—to which some are once again sensitive—is that most such countries are nonwhite. If we define the world majority as nonwhite, then it is possible to say that "we are a minority within this country, but we are a majority in the whole world." If that proposition is taken seriously, and if it is reasoned that white power on the global scale is declining relative to nonwhite power, the whole approach changes. It is psychologically comforting to entertain such an idea.

As practical politics, this idea is nonsense.

One consideration is that being *non*white does not establish either common images or common interests among peoples so various as Andean Indians, Guyanese Hindus, and North American blacks.

Nor is the economic consideration truly convincing. No one need deny the profound concentration of world economic power which rests in the American business firm, nor suppose that that has nothing to do with the policies of the United States government. Contrariwise, it is reasonable to predict that the United States government will seek to protect such nationals' large investments abroad. The incentive to do so will be even greater when the foreign countries involved produce *strategically* valuable commodities. This kind of consideration is what makes South Africa—critical for its role in the international monetary system, its location on the sea routes, and its massive quantity of private American investment—so worrisome a prospect. If South Africa were to face a serious black revolution, United States decision makers would have a predictably strong inclination to support the South African government actively. But blacks in the United States could only have a contrary disposition.

I do not overlook the likelihood of increasing pressure from various Third World countries upon American capital and the United States government, in the interests of enhancing their own options.[2] (The experience of the mining firms in both Peru and Zambia is obvious contrary evidence.) There are thus some extremely threatening issues which will be directly relevant to black Americans. Nonetheless, economic reality means that no Third World country can afford to pay any serious or sustained attention to the internal racial politics of the United States. If they did, it would only be on the supposition that internal racial division in the United States would weaken the power of the United States relative to themselves. African governments, Zambia for instance, have negotiated (or withheld negotiating) arrangements, with American companies, for the satisfaction of their internal economic and political needs. They have not made, and intelligently would not make, the racial policies of those companies inside the United States a matter of concern to themselves. They could not afford to do so, could not ordinarily have the leverage to do so, and would be forsaking the necessities of their own citizens if they tried to do so. To imagine otherwise is to be naive in the extreme.

To mingle domestic racial issues in the broader issues of global revolution implies that blacks in the United States would (or should) be willing to invite the risks of a concentration-camp society for themselves. Even if one were less apocalyptic, it would clearly require that blacks be willing to accept an actual aggravation of material poverty—an actual decrease in material well being—*compared to their present state*. Why so? Because if we granted the fantasy of Third World revolution, and if we granted that it could come about without nuclear war, we could imagine its coming only by two other circumstances. (1) If the American political-economic elites were so threatened into terror as to meet Third World demands, those demands would unquestionably involve an international redistribution of wealth from the United States to other countries. But, since the black American standard of living is so much higher than the Third World standard, it is hardly to be believed that any material improvements in the black United States standard would be part of the Third World demand. Indeed, meeting their demand would depress the domestic black standard, for the same reason that any depression of the American economy depresses the black standard. (2) But suppose, instead, that the American political-economic elites did not submit to threat, but were actually beaten by some newer version of nonnuclear war. Such a process would take several years (probably a decade, at least) and would utterly immobilize the American economy. In the end, the international redistribution problem would still have to be faced. But then the problem of reviving the economy and of meeting the international demands would similarly mean that little would be left for material improvement in black Americans living—and that that little would have to be developed over a revival period of many years. (Remember that under the fantasy conditions here specified, there would be no rich victor outside to revive the American economy in Marshall Plan fashion.)

The essence of political rationality—for blacks in North America no less than others—is that they must play the hands which they have been dealt by history. The Third World is not a social system, but has its own internal divisions born of its own internal necessities. In this perspective the "Third World" conception as ordinarily formulated is closely akin to suicide prescriptions if taken seriously, or if taken less seriously is but another form of ritualism not really meant to affect the social structure of the United States.

THE LIMITATIONS OF TERRITORIAL SEPARATISM

The modern proposals for some form of black *nation-state* in North America are nothing short of romanticism. Since people, white and black, are where they are, we have to recognize what the requirements would be to create separate national units. They would be created only by large-scale population exchanges: movements of whites out of the Deep South region on which territorial separatists set their minds; movements of blacks out of the urban-industrial centers where perhaps 40 percent of them now live and where more go each year. The population exchange requires an incentive on the part of people to leave where they are and go somewhere else, a mechanism for organizing their movement, and a process for resettling them into a healthy life in their new locations.

What is clear enough is that most people, at any given movement, do not want to go somewhere else. Despite the Partition of 1947, about a third of Indian Muslims remained in the Republic of India; most Jews remained in Europe until forced out under the most extreme and brutal circumstances known to modern history. It is indeed possible to imagine that self-selected colonies of particularly motivated blacks might move from Harlem or the South Side to Mississippi or Georgia. But it is not possible to imagine that many would do so. The attractions of urban civilization—even with crowding and noise pollution—exert the same attractions upon black people as upon those who are forcing themselves into urban centers around the world. Simple realism makes this clear. The life of a working-class black man in New York City is rough, but if he has aspirations for his children there is more access in the City University system than he ever could expect in the Mississippi university system— even if all whites were expelled from Mississippi. Nor need we make this all. The emotional requirements of people are terribly important in where they decide to live—as witness the country boys of all races who think New York "a good place to visit," and the confirmed Brooklynites who think the Alleghenies are washed by the Pacific Ocean. Man needs a way to relieve his boredom, but he who is accustomed to do so from 125th Street and Amsterdam Avenue will have little interest in contemplating the nightly frog calls of the Mississippi Delta.[3] Even the depression in the 1930's did not reverse the net inflow from country to city. There have been only two motivations in all migration history that caused large numbers of people to move: the pressure of fear and the lure of opportunity. People could be subjected to such intense physical pressure that they would flee in anger or despair or fear. Some effect of this sort would emerge under conditions of internal war,[4] but only madmen would regard that as an improvement over the *status quo* or over the future which might "naturally" flow from the *status quo*. The alternative depends mainly on the charges for perceptible economic improvement, but this requires conditions not encompassed by separatist thought.

If we were, however, to assume some incentive for black movement out of the cities, we should have to face the logistical economic problems of the movement. If by some miracle, large numbers of blacks wanted to leave Chicago and return to Mississippi, a white exodus from Mississippi would have to be its natural counterpart. Otherwise, one would have a biracial state, with all the political problems which the authors of separatist proposals seek to avoid. One would think a biracial state no more accepta- ble to them (or to whites) than a binational state was (or would have been) to Arabs and Jews in Palestine. If a biracial state were to be avoided, simple technical problems become pertinent. Do whites and blacks move simultaneously? If so, they will be passing each other on U.S. 51 and U.S. 61? Would they really be in the ordinary happy humor of travel, or would they be more likely to pay their hateful goodbyes? The answer is obvious, and so is the carnage implied. One need but recall the slaughter of half a million people in the Indo-Pakistani exchange or the similar brutalities of the Greek-Turkish exchange in the early 1920's.

Or would one expect whites to move out, and then have blacks move in? But which Mississippi whites, asked to risk their comfort, familiar surroundings, and economic well-being would do this without a fight? Would the life of blacks in Chicago, waiting for their turn to move, be made more comfortable if the City of Chicago and the State of Illinois knew that they soon would be gone (hence, would have no need to worry about their future political role) at the same time that the City and the State knew that the Mississippians would soon be there forever (and, hence, would have need to worry about their political role)? Or, possibly, one might expect blacks to move in—and then have whites move out. How would one cope in the interim with the pressure on food supply, living space, transportation, school facilities, hospitals, and so on? The last point makes itself felt very forcibly. There are but four circumstances in which people can move into a new place—on a large scale—comfortably. The first is when they are welcome. That self-evidently does not apply here. The second is when they are strong enough to take what they like, as was true in the New World settlement after the first hundred years or so. The third is when there is a vast space largely unfilled with present human occupants, which was also a factor in the New World settlement. The fourth is when they move in to fill lowly positions and are prepared by necessity to submit to those already present (the European immigrant experience in the United States between 1880 and 1920). Clearly, none of these four applies to the idea of some massive black migration from North to South.

Again, if we assumed away the difficulties and imagined the black people somehow to have made their way into a "New Africa," we should have to ask how they would get the arrangement going in such a way that they would be perceptivly better off. We might imagine that a certain amount of "pioneer spirit"—of building for future generations—would lead people to invest more of themselves than they had ever thought possible. Here is the model of the kibbutz. But it requires more than pioneer spirit. It requires the sustaining effect of skill and capital. One might even ignore the fact that the educated black population—no less than its less well-educated brethren—actually has no interest in resettling anywhere, and suppose that every black scientist, administrator, physician, engineer, teacher had put himself or herself in the vanguard. By careful management, the skill problem might be reduced—if not overcome. But, whence the capital? In the Malcolm X Society's proposal, the new unit would be financed through subsidies from the United States government, as reparation for the past damages suffered by black men. In principle, an excellent case can be made for some reparational scheme. The principle is the same as that which says that a man is entitled to be paid for years which he spent in prison on a completely false charge. It is like the principle that John Doe is entitled to be paid for Richard Roe's use of his property—contrary to Doe's knowledge, will or consent—over, say, the past seventy-five years. In theory, it would be valid to claim that blacks might be repaid for the contribution that their labor made to the growth of the American economy, as one might also claim that American Indians might be repaid for land inappropriately seized and used. It would be intellectually interesting—and of some possible policy value—to attempt to devise a mode for calculating such claims. However, to evaluate the Malcolm X Society's proposals, we may leave aside the judgment that such a reparational measure would have no success at all, since any proper calculation would probably constitute a lien against the whole United States budget. Which senator, willing to pay for the privilege of living in a wholly white country, would sponsor the bill for a ten-year domestic austerity program in order to put "New Africa" on its feet?

The political realities are patently averse to the idea of development by subsidy from the truncated United States. In addition to all the other reasons, two merit some attention. The first is that, under present conditions (not imaginary conditions about some unreal future), more than 90 percent of Americans are opposed to any form of job preference for blacks. Now job preference is such a simple thing, practiced within the existing political economy and could—in a growing economy—be implemented without too much pain to other people. If this is objectionable, why would a large subsidy program be less so? The second is the impact of refugee politics. Illinois, Missouri, Ohio, Pennsylvania, New Jersey, and New York would be natural receptacles for the white refugees from the South. But one should not expect them to be inert. Instead, one should expect them to be as active as the German refugees opposed to the Oder-Neisse boundary or the members of al-Fatah whose constant threat keeps King Hussein from settling with Israel and makes Lebanon submit to operations from its soil, even with Israeli bombers in action. And would not these white refugees *from* this new state—themselves desiring subsidies in order to be resettled without loss—be bitterly opposed to subsidies for those who had taken their homes and properties?

Moreover, there is another economic point. Black Americans usually reject comparisons between their economic well being and the economic well being of persons in other countries, on the ground that what they are entitled to (particularly in light of past exploitation) is an appropriate share of the national wealth of the United States. This objection seems indisputable. But consider. To create such a new black nation-state, in which enormous disruptions of the present economy would occur, would be to create a new regime with an economic level closer to that of the countries of the Third World than is the present economic level of black Americans. Could this be a net gain in the short run, or provide the foundation for substantial growth in the long run (considering how difficult it is to narrow the gap between poor and rich nations)?

The military side is equally curious. Under the Malcolm X Society's proposal, it is implicitly recognized that such a new nation-state would face the unremitting hostility of the revised United States. How, then, would it be protected? By the threat of action against the United States from nuclear-armed Chinese submarines cruising the Gulf of Mexico! Yet there is surely a fundamental law of international politics. The nation-state which is wholly dependent on a single foreign state for its physical protection is also wholly subject to the dictates of that state. Accordingly, such a proposal urges that black Americans resolve their present problems of subordination by accepting a dependency, which they would not have the power to alter, upon another foreign power. But to define voluntary acceptance of colonial status as "liberation" is a very strange definition, indeed!

The idea of a black territorial unit, one of wealth and power, located on the North American continent has a certain attractiveness. Were we able to deal in imaginative might-have-beens, we could suppose it a historical misfortune that the realities of the nineteenth century forbade some black equivalent of the Mormon settlement in Utah, such as the now-dead dream of a black state in Oklahoma. But the dreams of history can have no merit unless they are reconcilable with the logistical-economic-technological-administrative realities of the present.

THE POLITICS OF "VIOLENCE" AND "ARMED REBELLION"

If territorial separatism is romantic, its limitations are less troublesome than those of "violence" and "armed rebellion." Those who believe in territorial separatism may force us to waste our time, by forcing us to debate points which have no value, although the debate is perhaps not entirely waste if it has an educative effect. But, in any event, territorial separatism cannot be practiced simply because people believe in it. Blacks who imagine such a result in the future might go away by themselves, individually or in colonies. One could never imagine this operation actually eventuating in territorial separation, though one could imagine positive results at other levels. (As it happens, only the Nation of Islam has done this, and in a minuscule fashion, but that is not to be criticized.) The doctrines of "armed rebellion" are much more seriously open to criticism because they can be initiated by anybody who wants to act on them and who can collect a few people, and because they can have two decisively adverse consequences: eroding that very black unity which its advocates profess to want, and eliciting measures and forms of white coercion upon the whole black population, against which the advocates of armed rebellion themselves are inherently unable to offer serious defense.

RETALIATORY COERCION

Until only a few years ago, there were but few black people who believed and were prepared to act on the belief that violence could ever have any political utility. People may well have believed that violence was the only instrumentality to which whites would really be responsive, but most did not believe that it could be utilized without bringing more severe retribution than anyone could withstand. Caution was perfectly natural, for the historical circumstances ensured that an isolated people would be excessively conscious of their own limitations and thus timidly seeking "good behavior" on their part as a way of persuading a hostile world to be less hostile. This is the "Uncle Tom" syndrome in its classic sense. But, once activated to reject that syndrome, the isolated group is likely to fall into the opposite error of insisting that it itself has "no choice" except to insist that *only* its adversaries have either responsibility or latitude for producing satisfactory joint outcomes. It is likely—partly in reaction to its former self-abnegation—to need dramatic "proof" that it is really capable of going it alone under all circumstances, no matter what the other side may do. This is a particularly debilitating ritual because it means that the group will almost certainly define all conditions which an adversary could meet as "insignificant" or "insufficient" and insist upon conditions which the adversary could not but reject.

Black people are seriously burdened by the growth of an ideology which not merely states the obvious point that deliberate violence may at

times be necessary, but states further that violence is appropriate whenever one feels "frustrated." Beliefs have now been modified to the point
at which there is a virtually ritualistic advocacy of, if not the practice of,
violence. Nothing in our critique of such politics argues that *under all
conditions and circumstances* men avoid or ought to avoid the calculated use
of physical force. No one except a committed pacifist could doubt that
there are occasions when violence is at once a rational strategy, a morally
appropriate strategy, and the only available strategy. It is patent that
individuals have and ought prudently exercise their legal rights of self-
defense. Moreover, it is conceivable that there would be circumstances in
which a prudent and rational organization of collective self-defense would
be legally defensible and otherwise be appropriate. But prudent and
rational men ordinarily desire not to introduce violence into society if they
can possibly avoid it. And they are particularly aware that it is unwise and
irrational to impose pain (whether immediate physical pain or the threat
of physical pain) upon third (or nth) parties who have some justifiable
claim that the disputed matter does not concern them. The verbal violence
which is spread upon the airwaves does not make it possible for a white
man who has done nothing hostile himself (or who may have been actively
aiding blacks in physical danger) to feel comfortable. And such limited
physical violence as occurs has little rational relationship to the activity of
the party against whom it is directed. What significance, then, has the
verbal violence? Its significance is that it permits blacks, knowing as they
do that they stand in some physical peril (although they may overrate it),
to assuage their feelings by "talking big." But it is irrational for it has little
effect in introducing greater safety, and it alarms people who ought not
to be alarmed. It is merely stupid to go about aimlessly and randomly
scaring white people, *in general,* by a rhetoric of violence which will always
exceed the *activity,* but which will encourage other people to foolish
activity.

If we go beyond this rhetoric to real rebellion, we find that none of the
advocates of armed rebellion has yet given serious attention—of which I
am aware—to either the political or the technical requirements for the
successful use of private force. Any government would *attempt* to suppress
a spreading pattern of violence if that pattern threatened to immobilize the
normal activities of daily life. This much is inherent in the nature of
government, which may not have a monopoly of force but which certainly
tends to seek a monopoly of force and tends also to oppose any pattern
which obstructs that monopoly. The enhancement of the coercive capabili-
ties of government is predictable. No government is likely to avoid such
a response for long, whatever the source of disruption. This is acutely

important in understanding the *limitations* of force as a means for blacks in North America.

Governments will try to anticipate the behavior of groups which they understand to be likely sources of trouble. In the racial context, this means that intelligence units—national, state, and local—would seek to penetrate organizations whose public reputations are questionable or stigmatic. But the logic of intelligencing requires the maximum pursuit of all sorts of information which might conceivably be relevant. Thus, the natural consequence is that the intelligencing operation would be extended, by degrees, from keeping watch over such organizations as SNCC or the Black Panthers to keeping watch over almost any organization operating in a black community.

In addition to gathering intelligence about its adversaries—whether armed rebels against the system or nonviolent opponents within the system—a ruling group or a government quite naturally tries to hamper their movements. And governments today have the instrument in hand, namely the curfew, which has been so often used in cities in recent years that we may think it "institutionalized."[5] It provides control over the movements of persons, at the discretion of administrative officers, who do not have to explain to individuals why their individual movements are being interdicted.

If surveillance and curfews do not sufficiently assuage the fears of a government, and the white public has been led to share those fears, the next level of repression is preventive detention.

Intensive surveillance, movement control, and preventive detention would be more likely still if black politics inside the United States were to be associated, in the minds of decision makers, with the interests of foreign governments opposed to the United States. Defense against an ever more elaborate structure of coercion might be either technical or political, but the advocates of armed rebellion have shown no signs of having given serious thought to either. By "technical" we refer to such considerations as what physical terrain would be covered, how many people would provide support, how these people would be protected against unacceptable retribution by the other side, how much anger the other side would be expected to have because of being challenged with force, or what psychological capacity each side has to outlast the other in the agonizing struggle.

It would, self-evidently, be easy for any small body of determined men to wreak havoc upon an industrial society highly dependent on technology. This much is a recognized matter of public record. Imagine the effect of disrupting the New York subway system or the communications lines which link national corporations to their plants around the country. But such a disrupting group could not fully understand itself and adjust to its changing situation for, say, one year without a good deal of concerted planning. This planning would require a political high command and a communication system linking one part of the black population in, say, New York with another part in, say, Memphis. How would such a group protect itself against wiretapping if it lacked a body knowing all the tricks already known to professional wiretappers? How would it protect itself against the penetration of existing intelligence agencies when those agencies should be fully motivated to penetrate such a body? These are technical matters.

There is a still more fundamental technical question. *How would such a body protect the minimum requirements of the black population in whose interests it purportedly would act?* Revolutionaries would have the advantage in guerrilla war within the ghettoes, but the ghettoes themselves could be sealed off—left with no more than a couple of weeks' food and medicine. Where would even the minimum milk supply come from to meet the needs of thousands of black babies? Where would the minimum amounts of coal and oil come from to prevent thousands of persons freezing in Detroit and Chicago winters? And how would people in densest ghettoes be protected against bombing? Or, how would any significant mobility be possible if gasoline could be purchased only at stations in white neighborhoods and in business centers, and if a policeman or sheriff's deputy were stationed at each to make sure that only people who appeared to be white could buy gasoline? One could regard Harlem, North Philadelphia, Detroit's 12th Street, the South Side, *et al.*, as a kind of archipelago inhabited by the weaker side. No matter how much *soi-disant* revolutionaries may study *The Battle of Algiers,* there is a basic military fact. Algiers was surrounded by a friendly hinterland, but the urban ghettoes are enclaves surrounded by a hostile countryside. The *land,* unlike the sea, cannot be traversed in any direction, but mainly in directions established by modern highways and rail lines along routes dictated by nature, and used for thousands of years by the Indians of this continent. The parts of the land which provide even the minimum requirements for a large number of people (and 22 million is a large number!) are already occupied by some of the most hostile parts of the white population. From a strictly technical point of view, neither Mao nor Giap nor Che Guevara provides any clues for warfare in behalf of a large *minority* population in an industrial society.

These technical considerations are so basic that one would almost not discuss them except for one simple reality. There are those who speak of armed rebellion and encourage others to think of this as a realistic possibility. But it is no more a realistic possibility, insofar as producing an eventually desirable result is concerned, than military resistance by Costa Rica against the United States, Cambodia against China, or Czechoslovakia against the Soviet Union.

If technical defense against large-scale coercion is not possible—*in such a way as to produce a future better than the present*—then a politics of violence could make sense only were one to imagine the existence of favorable political conditions. Favorable political conditions would have to mean the existence of significant, and strategically located, white groups with a compelling self-interest in alignment with blacks. Unless these exist, we cannot treat the advocacy of political violence seriously.

The second major problem with ritualized acceptance of force is that it is fundamentally adverse to the short-run *and* the long-run interests of the black collectivity. A vague ideology which legitimates violence—in and of itself—leads inevitably to a terrorist politics, in which any man (rational or not) is free to "do his own thing" with a gun. A prime danger of such doctrines is that they are particularly appealing to the few genuine revolutionaries and to the relatively large number of young people who (in the manner of young people) take to sporadic violence as a way of acting out their rebellion against authority. The passionate dissemination of doctrines of violence "teaches" children and adolescents the "lesson" that self-motivated uncontrolled force is the sovereign "remedy." Consider, for instance, the turmoil in the big-city public school systems. The most striking fact about urban educational politics is the extent to which high-school students (and even younger students) are absolutely immobilizing such systems. Students in the big cities, most of whom are black, go through an agony-producing set of experiences. They have learned that even modest increments of violence—beating teachers, for instance—can virtually bring a system to a halt. But they have never learned to calculate *real* consequences. It is folly to use language which encourages high school boys to beat up teachers inside a ghetto high school building, an activity which does nothing to diminish violence against blacks in society at large, and which when reported in the papers scares still more people who are quite far removed from the situation and leads them also to do foolish things.

TERRORISM IN THE BLACK COMMUNITY

A major danger associated with terrorist doctrines is that all of the instruments of political action which have been used (or discussed widely enough that they are ideologically acceptable, even if not yet used) against other people will at some time be used *within black* politics even more than against whites. The excitements of disruptive power are learnings which the same cohorts of students carry on into their university lives (if they make it to there), and into the nonschool community—the black community. What they do there is act in the same fashion (which is the only strategic fashion they have learned to utilize). To that extent, terrorist doctrines pile up the future source of "forceful," self-motivated, uncontrolled disruptions within black politics.

If doctrines of violence are widely held, there will always be some ready to resort to terror. A politics of terror, however, is more likely to represent the highly sectarian (and sometimes irrational) perceptions of individuals and small groups who appoint themselves outside any responsible structure and beyond any authenticating process. It will, almost inevitably, be beyond the control of leaders who represent broad support, and cannot be used strategically, for ends which they choose. In their situation we find the first of many potentials for fratricide. Moreover, a politics of terror (such as bombing public centers) would have to be carried on beyond the control of most organizational leaders and would frequently interfere with the strategic conceptions of such organizational leaders. Just as the Jewish Agency found it necessary to criticize the Irgun, so would the NAACP (or even more radical, but legal, groups such as CORE) find it necessary at some point to denounce terrorism. If they did not, they would have no basis for any form of cooperation or alliance with any groups beyond the black community.

Such a relationship of repudiation and antagonism would exist not only between groups committed to legality and those committed to action beyond the law. It would also exist between groups committed to different forms of radical or revolutionary politics. Imagine, for instance, one group which should have adopted some conception of Marxian socialism as its guide, and imagine (as would be likely) splits and purges within such a group. Given the intense feeling which occurs under those circumstances, it would be virtually impossible for such groups (if they also adopted gun politics) not to spend a good deal of time killing each other. Or imagine a dispute between some groups committed to "cultural nationalism" in conflict with some other groups committed to "socialism." Similar results would ensue.

Those who disagree will be stigmatized as "Toms," and from social isolation—one natural consequence of stigma—there will be a natural tendency to develop a rationale for "dealing with" such people, and to make "dealing with" them mean their physical deaths. This is the normal experience of all groups which resort to terrorist politics, and has already been foreshadowed in public evidence on the hostile relationship between such a group as US, led by Ron Karenga in Los Angeles, and such a group as the Panthers.

A second source of fratricide would arise because some people would just desire to stay outside the whole enterprise. Since they would be able to see that the enterprise might have high costs for themselves (such as too much official intervention), they would try to remain disengaged. But if terrorists are to remain in action, they must be able to melt into some larger population, which would mean that detached people would have to be compelled to give aid and comfort.

The third potential source of fratricide lies in the fact that radical rhetoric may be mimicked by people who have no particularly radical purpose. The lessons of the Mafia are not to be ignored. Some groups within the urban ghettoes would be essentially unconcerned with "restructuring," but would be concerned with the material gains which they might achieve if they should be able to assert effective control over the ghettoes. Because no matter how rapid the growth of black leaders' economic and political power, they will never be in a position instantaneously to erase the heritage of discrimination. But if they do not provide immediate satisfactions, then their political credibility will be challenged within. This much cannot be helped. When this happens, there will be—as there now is for "middle-class" black leadership—a certain tendency to be apologetic, precisely because they know how little they have achieved. But if they are serious, they will also have to be confident in their method and resolute in their purpose. It is not to be thought that controversy (and even bitterness) will be absent. The task of leaders and followers is to handle such controversy and bitterness well and without bloodshed. For no leadership can be valid if it signals that it will yield to terror. To do so will render it powerless without and contemptible within. In the disputes which would logically ensue, doctrines of violent action would only increase the propensity for people in black politics to be fearful of each other, suspicious of each other, and prone to adopt an internal politics of coercion and assassination.

THE WASTE OF INTELLECTUAL RESOURCES

There is another aspect little noticed, but of great importance. While students are practicing some version of overt barricade-style politics, they are not learning the other sorts of skills which constitute a part of their armory at the next level of living. No matter what else may happen, the last third of the twentieth century will be dominated by sophisticated natural science (astrophysics, molecular biology, and others), by sophisticated social science (econometrics and the like), *and by policy and technology based upon their combination.* Those who encourage students to play the currently exciting games of disruptive politics are costing the black population of the United States at least half a generation of people effective and competent in these ways—at the first time when the institutional resources for providing them with training are beginning to be available. This is the more serious because it threatens to bring about a failure to fill the reservoirs of future competence. Perhaps the white upper-middle class can afford this price, but blacks surely cannot.

ILLUSORY OPTIMISM AND ILLUSORY DESPAIR

The understanding of the bad effects of violence-as-doctrine, expressed here, is not original. Its external and its internal effects have been understood before in many social movements, as they are now understood by many serious blacks of even very radical persuasions. Why, then, do people adopt a language which sounds *as if* they meant political violence to be taken seriously? Our suggestion is this. *The language of menace is sometimes an expression of an unreasonable optimism, and at other times becomes a pronouncement of utter despair.* The element of optimism was brief, but perceptible. After the dramatic summer of 1967, all sorts of whites who before had seemed inattentive or quiescent began to talk about the need to "solve the urban problem," and the great national symbolic gesture was the Kerner Report. Blacks who believed in taking force were able to say to those who did not, "You see, we have produced results where you could not." The advocates of force could not, technically, claim "credit," for the events of 1967 which were unplanned eruptions. Yet they were not wholly wrong, at least in the sense that a substantial proportion of the *Fortune* "500" elite began to pay a sort of attention which it had never before paid. Yet there was a gross illusion in the optimistic belief that this process of explosion could continue on an escalating scale without spillovers unfavorable to blacks themselves.

But the element of despair is still more important, since few people any longer entertain the optimistic assumptions. It is especially from an understanding of despair that we believe the politics of armed rebellion is not a serious effort to change social structure in an improved direction. Despair is the tone of a young black woman whose job was to work in films about racial issues. After viewing one of her firm's own productions she said, "I feel so helpless after seeing this kind of film. My only answer is to go out and buy a gun. Black children are dying while we wait for white

Americans to understand a couple of points." This tone is precisely the same as that represented by the folk belief in heroic defiance, and *damn* the consequences. This comprehensible reaction is akin to Japanese pilots' crashing their planes onto United States warships, or (even more) to the rage in which Samson killed himself while pulling down the pillars of his enemies' temple. It is the bravery of those who expect imminent death and care not what comes later.

We should not leave this point, however, without noticing that still another important element of fantasy and sentimentalist politics is the growing image of "the Second American Revolution" as some grand coalition of blacks, students, and whom else not yet specified. It is critical not to be misled by any of the activity associated with student disaffection in recent years. That disaffection is healthy to the extent that it alerts people to the need for reconsidering the web of relations which hold a society together. But the disaffection represents quite disparate elements. One element is an extremely small, though influential, body of doctrinal student revolutionaries whose scope is partly the result of the fact they have not been very forcibly restrained; partly due to an emergent youth "culture" in which "violence" has its own value; partly due to sheer self-interest in the desire to be free of the burdens of the war; and partly due to the shock of young adults' discovering that the sentimental pieties of fifth-grade civics do not represent reality—as they never did and never could. But to think of that element as a serious revolutionary nucleus is absurd. This is particularly important to the now-widespread language of "revolution." It is possible, and may even by likely, that physical resistance to governmental authority will grow for a time. But the essential fact is that there is no likelihood of a successful revolution in any major industrial society. No matter how great the capacity of disruptive groups, the ultimate balance of force in industrial society lies on the side of authority.

The fundamental fact is that all the elements of society averse to the student left are surely not going to roll over and play dead. Support in the population for conservative politics runs deep whenever the sacred symbols of the nation are touched. Private property is part of the civil religion in the United States, and popular antagonism against left politics, as soon as that politics goes beyond the "reform" parameter, is even more intense than popular antagonism against blacks. It is not the rich only who resist "communism" (as one left symbol), but the poor as well. It is precisely for such a reason that now, as in the 1930's, the left has sought to assimilate a large degree of black participation in order to establish a sounder foothold for itself. Black participation is, in some respects, more important now because a good share of the urban white population derives from

European immigrants who have sentimental ties and sometimes real ties to the home countries. These Americans of East European background often have some of the same reasons to be antagonistic to Communists who killed their relatives after World War that blacks have to be antagonistic to those who defend Deep South lynch mobs.

Even if a left revolution were to occur, those who would come to power would prove incapable of doing much about the racial structure of society which is not already being done or which cannot be done through a new politics of legitimate reform. If a Second American Revolution were to occur soon, its beneficiaries could not be the student elite, for they lack command over three things which are required for consolidation. They lack command, first, over the coercive and organized force (police and military) required for systematic organization of the population. A revolution could be consolidated only if (a) the military were brought over, or (b) a new military were created to destroy the old, both of which are beyond the capacity of the students as they are or as they will be in ten years. They lack command, second, over the appropriate order of administrative and technical skills to replace the existing administrative regime. How would they manage atomic research or the currency system or price-wage guidelines? These two requirements (force and administration) could be supplied only if those who took over were, in fact, those of the 35 + generation, but it is not to be supposed that these new rulers would be less sensitive to the problems of what one must really do to achieve consolidation than are people who now hold key positions. It would soon be revealed how fatuous is the slogan "power to the people!"

The third consideration in postrevolution consolidation has to do with building political support. In order to build political support, two things are required. The resistance must be eliminated (which would mean murdering at least a third of the white population),[6] and new support would have to be achieved by providing some on-the-fence people with benefits they did not have before. The lesson is unmistakable. The language of revolution may be widespread, but people use it mainly because they do not have other language with which to describe the departures from ordinary norms. It is not to be taken, however, as a serious politics capable of improving the position of blacks within the next ten or twenty years.

"STREET-LEVEL POPULISM" AS BANTUSTAN POLITICS

In the previous essay, I have noted the rise of street-level populism which, unquestionably, has some important virtues. However, it is also worth noting that, as a general rule and not merely in black politics, the fusion of rituals of "unity" and of "street-level populism" takes some curious forms which are, in fact, disadvantageous. There is a demand for a higher level of internal unity than any group, except possibly a totalitarian state, could possibly produce—thus making it impossible for group members to cooperate if they disagree on anything important, and by so doing to reduce the actual level of unity which might be achieved. The second is to overemphasize the actual unity of the adversaries ("monolithic communism" is such an instance) and by so doing to reinforce the effort to achieve purposes which simply cannot be achieved. Finally, in contemporary politics, one very important ritual is a romanticization of what "good" leadership could achieve (above, Essay I, "Internal Politics of the Black 'Nation' ") and, by this behavior, *so to undermine any leadership which could exist that it has to fail beyond the acceptable limits of failure.* This latter problem merits notice at present. For it takes the form of a ritualistic populism which frequently results in the systematic destruction of whatever may be the existing leadership at any moment.

THE DESTRUCTION OF LEADERSHIP

In black politics, the discount of "middle-class" leadership through an emergent popular mythology that it is "alienated from the black community," "uninterested," "self-interested," or "exploitive" is quite observable. Some part of such allegations must probably be accounted true. Some part of the matter is associated with class conflict and with a cultural gap between the older gentry-bourgeoisie cluster and the black lower classes. Blindness toward needs was not unknown. Some part of the middle-class leadership is fully satisfied with its won performance, and is thereby ready to cut itself off by retreating to earlier slogans which it will in no sense reconsider. Such is the pathology with which some (but by no means all) elements of the NAACP leadership is afflicted, particularly in those cities where the leadership is still drawn almost exclusively from the older gentry-bourgeoisie nucleus. Such a leadership is almost unable to come to terms with the moods out of which "black power" and "self-determination" emerge.

Conceding these criticisms, it is entirely fair to regard the achievements of that leadership as mammoth. At the same time, it is true that the black "nation" has not been able to consolidate its past gains in any very clear way, and it is also true that some matters remain very much as difficult as they were before. But the image, greatly encouraged by the demands of the black culture, is that leaders ought to have been heroic in style and efficient in accomplishment. Accepting this image, the middle-class leadership feels "guilty" and uncomfortable with an authority role. Moreover, some of the guilt is associated with two natural consequences of leadership. One is that any important leader has to go well out of his way in order not to be "better off" in some sense than he was before he became a leader. The other is that, because leadership is an ambiguous role, a leader may well be forced to worry about whether he did all that he could have done (obviously he did not, or he would have destroyed himself).

In order to cope with impossible expectations, there have been two main responses. One is that middle-class leadership elements attempt to adopt overt "folks" styles—nitty-gritty styles. But they do this not in order to provide substantial leadership, not really in order to be able to "communicate" with some larger black audience, but instead to court popularity, *hoping* that somehow if they hold popularity they will discover what else is necessary. This behavior is the black equivalent of Gene Talmadge and Theodore Bilbo, both well-educated men, playing the role of uncouth know-nothing. Even more, however, there is another response, which accedes to a populistic mythology that "true" leadership springs from "the brothers and sisters on the street." There is no doubt that a need exists for greater communication with, and responsiveness to, all strata of the black population. Nor is there any doubt that the sheer human capacity for leadership is found among the poor and the ill-educated as well as among the not-so-poor and the better educated. Indeed, one useful byproduct of recent experience has been the greatly enhanced number of people who—with wide ranges of formal schooling and other "normal" leadership accoutrements—have emerged into vital roles.

But in the "complex modern society" of which we all speak so often, it is sheer folly to maintain that the well being of a collectivity is served if the not-so-poor and the better educated merely stand aside. This is what they have been criticized in past for doing, not entirely unfairly, but what an emergent populist ideology now demands that they do. Politically, this demand is irrational for it means that technical-bureaucratic skills—the one organizational resource which now exists in fair measure within the black "nation"—are appraised at a discount and cannot be used effectively. The point is not at all mysterious. Any man in Detroit's 12th Street ghetto knows when he and a lot of his friends are jobless, and any such man will have a better sense of how much it hurts *him* than anyone else will. But only an economist, capable of holding his own with the Council of Economic Advisers' staff, can develop economic policy alternatives more appropriate to the 12th Street situation than those of which the CEA will think of in any case. Any family on public assistance will be able to offer profound insight, not otherwise available from the statistician's reports, on what it means to live "on welfare." But only someone competent to meet Health, Education, and Welfare people in their own ground can offer really useful guidance on the ways in which that desperate experience can be absorbed into some more humane policy. Any student from a poor family can express his or her disenchantment with the normal modes of education beyond high school. But only a skillful educator, with experience of the university system, is likely to make good judgments about how to transform that disenchantment into the stuff of a Malcolm X Community College (Poinsett, 1970). When these people stand aside —pretending to have nothing to offer—"the brothers and sisters on the street" are forced to do one of two things: either to act without the benefit of skills and guidance from the rest of the black population or else to receive those skills and guidance from such whites as put themselves forward (young college radicals, social workers, or corporate urban-affairs types) in the spirit of missionaries looking for primitives to practice upon. The net effect is not to enhance the contribution of "the brothers and sisters on the street," but to destroy the black authorities to whom they would give respect and to replace them with outside authorities instead.

COMMUNITY CONTROL

Probably, the idea that the largest number of blacks have recently found appealing is known as "black control of black communities." It proposes to dismantle the existing public school bureaucracies and replace them with neighborhood school authorities having authority over plant, personnel, and curriculum. "Community control" can be extended to many other public activities: police, garbage collection, tenement inspection, health centers. Black control would have certain values, if only because it would function as a training ground for a certain order of administrative skill which is presently hard to come by. No one should underrate the value of increasing the total pool of people who have had to learn through experience in decision making. But it does not follow that their decisions would automatically produce superior results (although they might not produce inferior results). Black-made decisions ought to be free from the taint of racism. Certainly, "police brutality" might not decrease, but it could not so easily become a racially charged matter if offender and victim were both black. (It *could*, of course, become a class issue or something else.)

Certain fundamental problems would not be eased, and could be exaggerated, by this kind of institutional change, unless other social changes went with them. One is the problem of living space. If the United States develops institutional mechanisms for black control of black communities (territorial units), it must by the same principle grant a recognition to white control of white communities beyond that which now exists. The critical decision must be: Where shall people live? If we grant that Blacktown (Ferry's term) is somehow to be organized separately, we must ask what is to happen when its population expands (by natural increase or migration) so that the original area is no longer adequate. A solution to this problem is one of the practical objectives—apart from philosophical considerations—implied in "open occupancy." Insofar as open occupancy may be made effective, it prescribes that the purchaser (or renter) may occupy any space which his income will permit him to command. But what is he to do when his side of the line is filled, and the market offers possibilities on the other side of the line? If sheer pressure for living space drives him well across the line, what is he to do if the local school there is so thoroughly adjusted to "white" criteria that his children have as hard a time as the original enrollees in Little Rock?

Education presents other problems of the same order. It would be possible more easily to get rid of patently unacceptable teachers. But the question is: How would the employer unit generate a sufficiently large supply to keep recruiting acceptable ones? What would it do when the situation showed that students emerged with self-concepts fully agreeable to the ideas of Malcolm X, but no competence at all in mathematics?

Health is of the same order. What would happen when one got community control of the health center's board of directors, only to fit find that the economics of the situation left the center without adequate staff?

Law enforcement presents still another problem of the same order. If a market for illegal narcotics exists within a community area, how will one prevent supplier's bribing black policemen (as they have done before), just as they once bribed white policemen? Those who operate with the suburban and small-town image in mind might more carefully study this part of the record, particularly since most big-city black communities would be considerably larger and more complex than many small towns.

The problems of new institutions and the commitments which the managers of new institutions develop as they get those institutions firmly established has also to be faced. Such local projects will, from their very birth, usually have to spend most of their time fighting (or maneuvering) for their very existence. The experience of the Ocean Hill-Brownsville school plan points up this fact, as does the experience of numerous Community Action Agencies launched under the authority of the Office of

Economic Opportunity. And, as any intelligent bureaucrat knows, the agency which has to spend most of its time fighting for its own life is, in the language of Norton Long, "an object of contempt to its enemies and despair to friends" (1960, 50). It cannot do much for its constituents.

As the institutions which community-control strategies call for are created, those who have advocated them will inevitably acquire a vested interest in them—regardless of their effectiveness. It is impossible to develop institutions without developing a commitment to the maintenance of those institutions. This inevitability raises all of the ordinary problems of government, except that both rulers and ruled would be black. It is the same problem as new nations trying to safeguard foreign investment. In practical terms, the Ferry proposal seeks local control over governmental and economic decision making. Community-controlled corporations might direct new investment, aimed at improving the economic base of the ghettoes. But they would first have to induce external investors to put money in, which would develop the same real problems associated with foreign investment in the new nations, or even in such relatively prosperous countries as Canada[7] If one has begun to work out subtle relationships with the Jewish financial community, relationships in which veiled anti-Semitic threats have become a bargaining weapon, one cannot so far encourage popular anti-Semitism that the weapon itself is unveiled, for at that point it is useless as a weapon. No one, as we noted before, will deal with you if everything "bad" you promise or threaten is going to happen anyway! Apart from securing new investment, such corporations could control existing investment—which mostly would mean taking over the current retail and service establishments. As soon as one owns the supermarket in the ghetto, it is no longer practical to say, "If the people are fed up with ghetto colonialism, I can't try to stop them from burning." And it is certainly impossible to say, "I can't try to stop them from burning until they come to my supermarket."

What has happened is that from a simplistic view of power, many blacks have permitted themselves to believe that "the power structure" (an unreal entity) in the local community is of major importance. One student revealed this interpretation when he said; "All we really want is to have the same control over our communities that the white people have over theirs." Albert Cleage made the same point, in almost the same language, using the Detroit suburbs as his model. For a young man of twenty, this is excusable. But for a major leader (as Albert Cleage once showed signs of becoming), it is less so. The local community is simply not the critical decision unit but a mere subordinate facilitator and no amount of decentralization will ever cure that.

There is very little that a *local* community controls which can make a difference to black liberation. In economics, the most important issues concern macroeconomic policy and special policies to deal with lagging sectors and regions of the United States economy. These are matters open to Federal decision—White House, Treasury Department, Office of Management and Budget, Council of Economic Advisers, Commerce Department, Labor Department, Congress, and the regulatory agencies. Matters affected by public finance depend on whether Congress maintains the categorical-federal-grant programs or moves to some block-grant revenue scheme. Law enforcement policies increasingly depend on what is done in the Justice Department, housing on the Department of Housing and Urban Development, and welfare on the Department of Health, Education, and Welfare.

In the Integral State, so tied into the complex world economy that the price of gold becomes a matter of daily attention for the politically concerned, the idea that "black control of black communities" depends upon controlling the neighborhood grocery store is similar to placing a .38 revolver against a 155 howitzer, if not against an ICBM. The decisions of most pertinence to blacks in the United States have to do with major decisions in the government and the economy, not the minor decisions which can be made at the local level. Now, developments of any sort which improve the conditions of black life, notably life in the poorer ghettoes, are to be encouraged. But the proposals for community control are but an *urban* edition of the rural resettlements proposed by George F. Kennan. Kennan maintains that he himself accepts the legitimacy of "integration" (in the conventional sense, apparently, rather than that which we have adopted here; see above, Preface and Essay I). But he goes on to say:

> . . . I suspect that there is a considerable part of [the black] community that does not [want integration]; and I think that provision should be made . . . for them, as well as for the others [who do]. That this would mean helping great portions of the Negro population *to remove from the big-city ghettos* (sic) and *freeing for them areas where they can live their own life, under their own administration,* with better propects for employment and health, I can well conceive. (Kennan, 1968, 234)

No public policy yet exists to implement the precise Kennan idea, nor has any black spokesman taken it up, although it is closely related in substance to the first phases of the Republic of New Africa proposal (Imari, 1968). Indeed, that may be impossible. But it is not even necessary if blacks convince themselves to accept in the urban territorial ghetto something like the spurious "local control" which the South Africans call the "Bantustan" policy (Leonard M. Thompson, 1966, 79–85). Bantustans are simply administrative units in which the visible administrators are of one genotype with those in the service area. They have, however, nothing to do with the major policy processes which set the contexts for administration. In the urban case, we have steadily been pressured to demand as "self-determination" or "community control" what is in reality very little different.

THE POLITICS OF EXTERNAL RECOGNITION

The final issue is the problem of relations to white groups and influence within the black population. Rhetoric to the contrary, most white influence centers need to find some black group with which they can come to terms, overt or implicit, whether they like it or not. And most black groups need to find some white group with which they can come to terms, whether those terms are overtly declared or merely implicit in the method of operation. The internal black "party" which can secure external recognition has an advantage. Inherently, all of this means that complete "self-determination" is an illusion and that when one fosters this image for other people one is creating a delusion. Why is this so?

The fundamental point is that "self-determination" may be reasonably interpreted as a symbol of intent, but that it is utterly delusive to try to make it mean complete independence of all external sources. No political unit—not even the most powerful nation—is able "to determine its own destiny" fully, completely, without let or hindrance by others. The revolutionary regime in Cuba has been able to make itself secure because the Soviet Union offers military equipment and buys the Cuban sugar crops. No one could have been more sensitive to sovereignty than President DeGaulle, yet the French Government proved unable to stop General Electric's taking over the assets of Machines Bull, now Bull GE, a stratagem by which GE got into the European computer market. If nothing else limits national sovereignty, the global market surely does.

Nor is there any such thing as a polity in which external influence has no effect on the choice of leadership or goals (Rosenau, 1966). Achieving a leadership role is some combination of doing something to indicate that one wants to be a leader and of receiving the approval of those who can lay on hands. Elections, for instance, are ways for those within the group to lay on hands. But some of the laying-on of hands comes from external recognition. In diplomacy, external recognition is often said to be *merely* declaratory of the state of fact that a regime, for example the Communist regime (and not the Kuomintang), is in control.[8] In reality, diplomatic recognition usually provides advantages which the nation-state could not have gotten without recognition. This inter-action becomes more subtle still in the relationships between the richer or more powerful nation-state and the poorer or weaker nation-state. The richer or more powerful nation-state needs to find some group, within the smaller or weaker nation-state, with which it can work. And groups within these smaller of weaker nation-states overcome at least some of their *internal* competitors by finding richer or more powerful nation-states with which they can work.[9] For example, in this age when "development" is a major Third World goal, the internal party which can secure diplomatic recognition and foreign aid has an advantage over its competitors which cannot.

The relationship is simply basic to politics in any case. It is compelling in American racial politics. This fact is more or less explicitly recognized in the ways of all groups except the rejectionists. But *it is also a vital part of their practice, contrary to their doctrine,* which is why comment here is appropriate. All the ramifications cannot be traced here. But one important version is the essentially defensive white posture which seeks the restoration of order. Apart from the directly coercive posture (which has appropriated the honorable concept of "law and order" to uses which are a parody), there is another sense best symbolized by the Urban Coalition and the National Alliance of Businessmen. It is time to recognize explicitly that, within the past three or four years, the Militant party in black politics has been raised to a position of eminence as much by the *de facto intervention of this part of the white population as by any opinion changes within the black population.*

When it became clear that the civil disturbances of 1967 could not be halted by any leadership already "recognized" by existing white leadership, the message that "we have been talking to the wrong people" quickly permeated the corporate elites. The search for new points of contact began. The Militants were able to make a persuasive case that the disturbances were grass-roots disturbances and that they "represented" the grass roots and that they *had to be consulted.* The implication was that if they were consulted and satisfied, urban order could be re-created. Even though one may presume that the Militants genuinely believed their preferences would be for the good of the community, their *organizational* positions did not (before the summer of 1967) permit them to override their Moderate antagonists and enforce their own preferences upon the community. They could acquire the power to suppress (or at least limit) their Moderate antagonists when they were *publicly recognized* by whites, not blacks, *as Militants* and when whites concluded that influence over the black community could be exercised more effectively through supporting Militants than through supporting Moderates. The very fact that the Militant leadership, formerly avoided or proscribed, began to be consulted by the powerful white leaders, increased the power of such Militant leadership within the ghetto relative to the power of their Moderate counterparts. This could hardly have been otherwise. If a major national corporation has been known to resist employing blacks, it is inevitable that the man who is able to penetrate not the personnel department but the office of the chairman of the board will acquire new power. (If capital for black entrepreneurs has been extremely limited, it is obvious that the man who is able to locate funds for cooperative stores or new light industry will acquire new power.)

Intervention is also demonstrated in the behavior of white groups in adopting a more radical language than that of conventional liberalism, while they nonetheless have some kind of commitment to the American polity. This phenomenon is perceptible in the history of something like James Forman's "reparations" movement. No one remotely familiar with the history of SNCC will, presumably, doubt that James Forman has a visible record of concern for black liberation which most people cannot match. Yet Forman's recent campaign for $500 million reparation arose from no apparent widespread base among blacks. The press (black and white) seemed ready to treat it with ridicule, if not hostility. The proposal was suddenly made respectable, at least as something to discuss, when prestigious white denominations began to offer it a hearing. Moreover, one may be sure, considering the limited dollars available to black organizations, that putting even 1 percent ($5 million) of these "reparations" under Forman's personal control would make him into a major power figure (not a mere agitator) in the black world.[10]

The natural evolution of this process could be seen in 1969 when a certain element of the "church left" and "cafe-society left," which used to support the NAACP and Martin Luther King, withdrew at least some of their patronage from the oppositionists to redistribute it to rejectionists. This intervention is exemplified in the Episcopal grant to Malcolm X University—a school for avowed separationists—or in the Massachusetts Council of Churches' grant to Forman's movement. The fact that this was an intervention, which did hurt another black "party," is manifest in Roy Wilkins's protest that the churchmen did not even give the black integrationists a hearing.

The process of intervention has most recently been seen in the extension of patronage, by the cafe-society left, to the Panthers, an event catalyzed by the killing of Fred Hampton. Figures such as Leonard Bernstein —who used to lend their aid to the NAACP and then to Dr. King—could now sell their glamour to raise money for Panther legal fees. But it goes further. Suburbanites, who used to think a face-to-face discussion with Wilkins a thrill, could now meet real live Panthers in living-room dialogue. Whites of the respectable left could believe that the police were not really pure (particularly after the summer of 1968 and other events). And, after the rise of "black power" rhetoric, they could reasonably find a Panther "rap" more authentic than anything from the black middle class. But this is but the latest link in the chain of events, It began earlier with the Panthers' cooptation by and of the white left radicals who believe that United States society is not salvageable in its present form, and that *revolutionary* reconstruction is required. Patently, those who believe this have no incentive to work with blacks who believe that American society is reformable. They do have an incentive to work with blacks who share their conception—even if for different reasons—that only the utter destruction of the present polity can be useful. This program means not only that they must do what they can to make such blacks visible and acceptable in the white part of society, but they must also do what they can to destroy the influence—within the black "nation"—of those whom they cannot accept as partners. *To do so enhances their own potential influence over the future of American society.*

This process can be well seen in the emergence of Eldridge Cleaver as a public figure and the Black Panthers as a political movement. (To say this, by itself, no more challenges the moral purposes of Cleaver or the Panthers than to describe Booker T. Washington's dependence on white elites challenges his moral purposes. It is merely to describe an ineluctable fact.) On the sheer face of his works, Cleaver would have to be regarded as a man of wit and energy, a potential leadership claimant in any case. But the question is how this potential leadership claimant came to be an actual and major leadership claimant for a certain part of the black population. In a mass-media society, he did not and could not rise above local importance until he was first "recognized" by external sources as an authentic voice of the ghetto. Once his message was accepted by such a vehicle as *Ramparts,* it was a natural candidate for such a publication as *The New York Times.* Once it was received by the *Times,* it was a natural candidate for national television, which in turn transmitted the message to the whole country, black and white. Precisely because the message created emotional and intellectual turmoil in the white community, it began to receive favorable opinion in the black community. Such a process made its author a "controversial" figure, one to be at least avoided and more likely to be denounced—by various elements of white leadership, from the liberal "center" to the conservative "right." Such avoidance and opposition made the message carrier a potential candidate to those blacks awaiting a new leadership. His recognition was strongly influenced by *preexisting white radical conceptions of what an "authentic" voice ought to be saying.* Had the message been contrary to the preexisting conception, it would probably have been edited out in favor of a message which fitted the conception more accurately.

If black and white factions, having something more in common with each other than with other black or other white factions, do cooperate, they will tend to adopt common symbols to sustain that cooperation. In the radical-Panther case, it becomes simply necessary for whites to adopt the language of "a racist society," but they cannot do that—without condemning themselves—unless they reinterpret racism. Hence, racism becomes a byproduct (in their language) of a more complex structure of "capitalist imperialism." In the same case, it becomes necessary for Panthers to adopt the language of "capitalism and imperialism" as the enemy out of which racism grows, otherwise they cannot sustain their collaboration with white radicals. When the Panthers adopted a Marxist language and white radicals convinced themselves that Pantherism was an element of "the revolutionary vanguard," the *relationship* was no longer different from the relationship between black integrationists and UAW liberals. Only the doctrine was different. Nor is it really possible for this kind of case to be escaped. Each time a mayor (governor, president, corporation executive, bishop) is faced with claims from some black group, he has to decide whether he will recognize those claims or not. Under some conditions, refusal to recognize the group may generate a reaction in the black population which gives that group new strength. In turn, such a group may be able to enforce a recognition it would otherwise not have received. But, in the end, it is simply inevitable that, whatever rationale is used, the white counterparts will choose to deal with blacks whose interests and purposes they believe are reconcilable to their own. Every decision of white leaders to treat someone as the authentic spokesman for a black community is an exercise in patronage, and every decision by a spokesman to be so treated is potentially an exercise in clientage. Those recognized derive strength, relative to their competitors, from the fact of being recognized.

By this process Militants in many cities, and their more vociferous successors, began to acquire added influence *within black communities* by a form of clientage quite as realistic as that practiced by Booker T. Washington, a process which they would denounce as "Tomism" *were it openly practiced by others not of their own persuasion.* This is merely the way of politics. But it points to the final question that rejectionists do not answer. If it is presently legitimate for black "revolutionaries" to *violate black "unity"* by seeking allies among white "revolutionaries," *why is it not equally legitimate for black "liberals"* (or even "conservatives," should they exist) *to do the same?*

CONCLUSION

It can hardly be denied that blacks face what is, on the whole, a hostile environment. The language of "self-determination" expresses a will to overcome that environment in terms consistent with self-respect. That will cannot be denied; neither could one do other than praise it. But the political process has its own logic which will, in the end, not be denied; and those who would survive that logic must also learn to manage realities effectively. The central issue—stated by Frazier a quarter century ago— still remains: "The change in the relation of Negroes to American life requires a new philosophy and new techniques of adjustment. Survival in the modern world demands scientific knowledge and a rational, as op- posed to a sentimental, attitude toward the world."[11] The strategic-tactical conception most likely to be productive will be one scrupulously rational, ruthlessly unsentimental. The politics of withdrawal simply fails to meet this test. It fails to consider what political rationality demands, that is, not only dreams and possibilities but also inherent limits.

To shut one's eyes and ears to realities is precisely what Frazier meant by "sentimentality." The task before blacks, therefore, is to find those ways of coping with their own development in a hostile environ- ment which will be effective rather than self-defeating, rational rather than sentimental. The approaches to "self-determination" which we have sketched may be psychologically appealing, but they all evade some twentieth-century realities which will become more compelling in the next century. In this sense, they are snares and delusions. It is natural that, from most black perspectives, black adaptation to (or self- restraint in the light of) white limitations as a condition of social peace seems malevolent, unfair, ineffectual and (when asserted *by* blacks) cowardly. There is *no just reason*—from such a viewpoint—to accept this idea. But rationality consists precisely in avoiding the temptations of self-confirming kamikaze politics which everyday existence thrusts in one's path. In one sense, this says that a weaker population within a nation-state, must achieve an imagination and skill superior to that of the Great Powers.

Advocates of withdrawal do not, in reality, deal with such problems.[12] They do not accept the fact that the basic logic of instrumental politics—anybody's instrumental politics—and the rhetoric of withdrawal must be in conflict. Their "community-control" version merely calls for measures of no greater probable benefit than the South African Bantustan policies, while the genuinely separatist version utterly fails to comprehend either the mechanics of population exchange or the requirements for the economic and physical survival of new states. The most troublesome version, however, is the doctrine of armed rebellion. One cannot deny that *some* readiness to use force has always been an essential ingredient of social change, nor that the severe application of force has been, *and to a considerable degree remains*, part of the mechanism which accounts for the subordinate place of blacks in American society. In this sense, withdrawal is more realistic, or possibly just more candid than the relative optimism of the oppositionists. What is missing, however, is a sober and mature appreciation of three points. (1) Anybody who really advocates armed rebellion on a large scale is either hopelessly naive in believing that retribution will not be severe in the extreme or is sunk in despair and advocating a kind of kamikaze politics. (2) The requirements for armed rebellion would so utterly divide the black "nation" that its internal life would be suffused with a politics of assassination—some believing genuinely that their victims were traitors deserving to be executed and others being mere opportunists seeking to apply Mafia tactics to their own enrichment. (3) The technical requirements for armed rebellion and the political requirements for armed rebellion are both absent, and likely to remain absent, in the United States—so that such an enterprise would be an invitation to the genocide which some advocates of armed rebellion foresee, and exercise in self-confirming prophecy.

Finally, the rhetoric and doctrine of withdrawal—of all schools—calls for resolute defense of "self-determination", yet withdrawal politics like all other is affected by the ecological interdependence of white and black in North America. In reality, that interdependence is so thorough that withdrawalism, as much as (and perhaps more than) any other variety of black political outlook, is substantially enhanced in black life when it receives white support and somewhat depressed when it does not. We conclude, therefore, that apart from legitimate normative and philosophical objects this strategic approach—like all its predecessors—has weaknesses no less than strengths, and that its weaknesses, as to desired effects in the republic, are greater than its strengths. Altering the pattern of

American politics so that *white rule* ceases to be the prime political fact is the serious objective. That objective is obscured by various psychiatric displays of protest against white rule, which, in fact assume its undiminished permanence. In this respect, the problems of black politics call for the same kind of ultimate realism which would be called for if the black "nation" were not merely a sociocultural unit but an actual and legally separate polity.[13] The achievement of such realism, and its translation into action, depends on a substantial trust between constituencies and those who purport to represent and lead them. If, in other words, most people who concern themselves with the issues of racial liberation think in slogans, unrelated to serious options, then no leadership will be able to make a useful contribution at the same level that it would had it a firmer base of understanding support. But it is not helpful to formulate political problems as problems to be appreciated by "the people" (in the classic language) or "the brothers and sisters" (in the current black parlance). Political issues have to be formulated by leaders (or aspiring leaders) who have some sense of purpose, much as questions for debate in large assemblies have to be formulated by somebody. The assembly does not by itself arrive at a formulation. Purposive political leadership must always keep in mind the limits which popular acceptance will permit, but it must also be willing and able to take the risks of defeat, repudiation, and even denunciation if the hardest issues are to be put up for serious consideration.

It may well be that the problem of racism in society is fundamentally insoluble, in the sense that no one could imagine a full and complete solution, as neat as a problem in algebra. This possibility people are understandably reluctant to confront, for its very enunciation may be thought to diminish the incentive to attack the problem without a sense of foredoom. But it remains real, whether or not discussed. As noted before, one part of the problem simply is that *ethnic* conflict is one of the most persistent forms of social division in human society, even in societies which are "racially" homogeneous, and in societies which are very different from the United States as measured by size, political form, or economic structure. Moreover, the very nature of politics involves many problems which cannot be solved in any final sense, but which people can find the wit and purpose to manage well in the interest of a more civilized existence. Thus, no one has solved ("eliminated") economic inequality in any society, but it is patent that many societies have a great deal less economic inequality than has been characteristic through most of history. Nor has any society solved ("eliminated") violence, but it is also the case that many contemporary societies have far less internal violence than most human societies have had in the past. When a problem has been reduced to "trivial" proportions, it still remains a potential threat, yet if the problem is already on a grand scale, the rational objective is to reduce it to those "trivial" proportions so that it is no more than a threat, rather than a daily and inescapable and pervasive fact.

In the approach to such problems, as in the approach to war, the task is thus to maintain at once *a grand strategic conception* of what the major outcomes ought to be, and to *achieve* those *interim tactical adjustments which* will serve the grand strategic outcomes. It is, of course, particularly important to define the grand strategic outcomes properly, for otherwise the interim tactical adjustments will be either incidental or even counterproductive. This view of the task accords with what we mean here by political rationality. Political rationality depends upon the emotional self-discipline which allows one to master both unreasonable optimism and unreasonable despair. There is no likelihood of unreasonable optimism in the black population at the moment. But there is a certain tendency toward despair which—though psychologically comprehensible—is politically unhelpful. Despair leads to two self-destructive behaviors. One is the continuous counting of all the signs of evil and danger in the world, without a similar counting of the signs which offer serious basis for hope. Despair leads, for instance, to sharp appreciation of the potentiality that the United States might yet rival South Africa, but a failure to explain why it has not yet done so. As a corollary, it leads to a preference for politics as collective psychiatry, ending in a kind of Samsonian or kamikaze politics which provides the evil results feared.

Secondly, rationality demands that, in order to cope with a hostile world, there be a recognition of the *extremely limited political rationality* thus far displayed by American public leadership. Over the long past, the dominant leadership in American society has shown such a limited capacity to deal rationally with racial dispute than one might almost be astonished. Indeed, were one given to biogenetic explanations, one would almost have to turn A. R. Jensen upon his head and argue that the capacity for rational political adjustment is something not contained in the white "gene pool."

Lord Acton and Senator Fulbright offer much better clues. The limited political rationality of white Americans comes from the extraordinary power which white people have been able to muster over blacks. The "arrogance of power" is precisely that rationality (flexibility, sophistication, insight, foresight) is not seen as necessary when one has truly overwhelming power. On the whole, the culture of white Americans contains no clues about what to do in situations when power (and the rules of life associated with it) is perceptibly diminishing. It provides no clues about the transition to some new relationship, and by that fact the most important sources of leadership and influence are immobilized. To a considerable degree, an increase in rationality depends on black action which liberates white leaders (and their followers) from their own developed incapacity. If one were able to apply moral judgment to an historical result, it would be possible to say that this dependence is "unfair," but moral judgment is (at his level) less pertinent than prudential clues for future human action. The question is: What considerations might—if taken seriously—enhance political rationality within the black nation?

NOTES

1. China and India, the two biggest of these countries, would—if their GNP could be divided evenly amongst all their residents—come out at a little over $100 per head, in contrast to something over $4,000 per head in the United States, around $3,500 per head in Canada, around $2,000 per head in Britain, France, and Germany, around $1,300 per head in Italy, and around $1,000 per head in Japan (the only rich Asian nation).

2. It *is* also patent that, if the United States is to do well in the last third of the twentieth century and in the twenty-first, it will have to arrive at a relationship to the rest of the world different from that which presently exists. It is not surprising that United States policymakers—suffering the disabilities of policymakers everywhere—have given little evidence of thought about this consideration. But it is more disturbing that there seems to be so little evidence that scholars or other serious commentators on foreign policy or world politics have thought about it either.

3. The ennui which city boys faced in Job Corps camps located in rural areas, or in military service at a post where the nearest town is a metropolis of 10,000, witnesses to this point.

4. See *The White Man's Burden,* Essay VII, "A Look at Medusa's Face."

5. This proposition could be tested by a study of the metropolitan daily newspapers (or the legal newspapers) during each of the years 1964 through 1968. We are predicting that such a study would show a phenomenal increase in the number of such curfew orders and in the number of cities in which they were ordered.

6. We have to assume that the genuinely racist third would not be good revolutionary material.

7. Many Canadian politicians wish to restrict United States investment in Canadian firms to a minority position. But the Canadian government seems reluctant to adopt such a policy because it wants the capital and American investors apparently will not come in on minority terms. *Toronto Globe and Mail,* July 30, 1970, B2.

8. The same might have been said when, in the late 1930's, General Motors *accepted* (but surely did not like) the fact that the United Automobile Workers was in control of the work force.

9. For some insight into this process, see Eldridge (1969), Feis (1964, Chapters 4–5 and 10–12), and Perloff (1969).

10. This could be interpreted in the light of the political consequences of scarce money as discussed in Essay I above, "Money."

11. Alumni Dinner Award Speech, Howard University, March 2, 1945, as quoted in Caliver (1948), 41.

12. These deficiencies mean that withdrawal politics simply cannot be taken seriously as a form of "revolutionary politics," even though many who adopt this pattern of thought use the rhetoric of revolution. There is not time nor space here to develop the additional critique that, on the available record, *the beneficent results of "revolutionary politics" are themselves greatly exaggerated.*

13. This is not to say that black people would get such realism under that hypothetical condition any more than anyone else seems to get it, but it is to specify more clearly what is called for.

IV

Toward Black Regrouping

THE PROBLEM OF RATIONAL STRATEGY

Among many black intellectuals today, "sincerely yours" (and similar phrases) is often replaced with "in the struggle," a symbol of commitment to black liberation. *The problem* before those who share that commitment, regardless what symbolic language they adopt, *is to discover what is rational strategy in the struggle.* Rational strategy would be aimed, I argue, at saving the opportunity for a decisive break with *institutionalized* racism. Such an opportunity is beginning to present itself, and will become increasingly realistic over the next twenty years, *provided that degenerative* incrementalism and catastrophic errors are avoided in the short run. The year 1991 should be as much a jump over 1971 as 1971 was over 1951. The reason is that the underlying thought patterns of the elite which should be emergent by 1991 will be far less permeated by conscious and semiconscious racial prejudice. This is one of the few things one probably can predict confidently—and favorably—about the outcome of the so-called youth culture of the early 1970's. To make clear the basis for such reasoning, we should discuss intergenerational change. Social change is partly a function of generational change, not so much because any generation directly changes the preferences of its elders nor because the elders step aside, but because of the complex way in which a new generation slowly displaces an older. In somewhat simplified fashion, we may interpret this as the interplay of three generational "layers." At any given moment, stable society tends to be gerontocratic, in the sense that strategic positions are

131

most likely to be held by relatively elderly people. One may speak thus of the *ruling elders*. Congressional seniority is the most advertised manifestation of this phenomenon in American politics. But gerontocracy appears also in the age level of the editors of the most influential newspapers, of the presidents of major corporations, trade unions, and nonprofit institutions, the general officers of the military, the bishops, and so on.

Behind this age grade are those who have every reason to believe that they will, if nothing goes wrong, inherit the strategic positions at some time in the future. These *heirs apparent* (typically Congressmen just becoming subcommittee chairmen, newspapermen just becoming syndicated columnists, professors just beginning to be part of some potential presidential entourage) obviously have a great deal at stake, The "system" into which they are entering makes a good deal of sense to them, even if or even though they are alert to its imperfections or critical of the ruling elders' slowness and rigidity.

The third layer are the *novices*, which is to say students (or people of that age) and young professionals (or college or graduate school dropouts looking for something "meaningful"). The novices have an image of social reality and strongly moralistic judgments about the way in which society is governed. But these novices have little constructive influence directly. They are still in a transitional world, and must wait at least ten years before they begin to enter the realms whence the *heirs apparent* ultimately will be recruited.[1]

No generation is intellectually, psychologically, or sociologically homogeneous. But there are common tendencies in the dominant themes acceptable and plausible to each. This is surely clear in music, sex habits, or childrearing styles and enters politics in the same way. Each generation tends somehow to crystallize its view of the world in late adolescence or early adulthood. Each changes its mind about fundamental interpretations and values relatively little thereafter, although it may grudgingly adopt new policies under pressure. But each new generation, having learned somewhat different things from those which its predecessors learned, brings somewhat different grounds of choice into decision making.

The process is well illustrated in industrial relations, where newer waves of managers (in the wartime 1940's and after) proved more amenable to dealing with trade unions than did their predecessors. In the same way, there are newer waves of managers in current industry who are much more amenable to the doctrines of "social responsibility." This process has been visibly operative in United States racial politics over a very long time. In a sense, the Republican retrenchment on black rights in the nineteenth century represented the emergence of a new wave, who reasserted white supremacy. By the early twentieth century, Henry Cabot Lodge was an old-fashioned man whom time had passed by. But the process is never in a straight line. From the late nineteenth century until the early 1920's, the white-supremacist consensus included ruling elders, heirs apparent, and novices. By the 1920's, the current turned.

The college-age population of the late 1920's and in the 1930's was the first to learn that black inferiority was *not* self-evidently true, and might be false. The change which crystallized in the 1920's would have hardly any effect until a few of that generation of novices actually began to occupy critical posts as heirs apparent. The relative smallness of the "white 'liberal'" coterie during the New Deal, however, tells us that not many heirs apparent had such a concern. It was only after World War II that the next wave of novices *began* to learn that race relations should be seen as a *major social issue,* not merely as one to be felt by those few people with "humanitarian" concerns. The college-age population of the 1940's and 1950's was the first to learn that public action to achieve equality of opportunity was, in fact, legitimate and desirable. Consequently, we may also understand why no important proportion of the heirs apparent experienced any severe moral conflict about the status of blacks until some time near the Kennedy generation in government.

The college-age population of the 1960's (the Peace Corps-VISTA-OEO generation) was the first to learn (or perceive) in any significant numbers that *substantial* racial equality ought to be a major objective. This progression is even more clearly accentuated in the 1970's. Such a view is not universal. Nor will those who hold it go out eagerly missionizing.[2] But we do mean that members of this age grade will begin to approach major positions of responsibility in about twenty years.[3] As the present novices enter responsible positions, they will be somewhat restricted by obligations of those positions. But they will also modify significantly the assumptions on which their functions are carried out. Accordingly, the assumptions within which black politics will be conducted must widen a good deal. On the other side, however, there is a significant and persistent conservatism in American politics.[4] Not only will aspects of this conservatism persist into the indefinite future, but some aspects will be particularly powerful in the immediate future.

The values and perceptions of white people—of a "middling" disposition—constitute a decisive set of outer limits on social policy. Those values and perceptions have a definite, though moderate, conservative bias. This conservatism does not mean that they are anything like completely satisfied. Certainly a large number of people—white, no less than black—consider that they have been treated "unfairly" by society. The idea that the rich and the well born get most of what is to be gotten is not only accurate, but widely held. However, no one should interpret this outlook as a repudiation of the legitimacy of the system. Such an idea has been present throughout the history of the United States polity but has never really shaken the solidity of the system.[5] For it is counteracted by the belief that, on balance, the system is superior to any which the protestants could imagine and certainly superior to any of which they have heard. "Love it or leave it!" could, under some circumstances, become a cry throughout all social classes, but it is, and always has been, most viscerally accepted by the people of the lower middle and lower classes. Moreover, complaints about the "big shots" are counterweighted by a wide belief in the importance of "self-help" under legitimate rules. The problem, therefore, is to formulate the projects of black action in terms which can be pertinent to these ordinary white people. It is utterly fatuous, and a mark of great fear, to avoid the task of defining the problems in terms which can be reached by that portion of the white population which is neither morally committed to "integration" nor morally committed to some modern version of a Ku Klux Klan state. If the United States is to move irreversibly in the desired direction, and at the desired rate, participation by this audience is essential. The problem of current black strategy, therefore, is to save the future. Saving the future implies giving consideration to two other important problems: (a) the relationship of blacks to whites, and the ways in which that should affect black action; and (b) the development of a stronger objective capacity for action by the black "nation."

THE INESCAPABLE INTERDEPENDENCE

In order to develop a more rational strategy, blacks will have to take account of three problems: an objective capacity for action, morale, and sheer barefooted realism. We return to the first two later, but the point here is to present a certain minimal realism without which effective action is simply not possible. One element of this realism is the interdependence of black and white. Recently, black leaders have shrunk from admitting this obvious interdependence. Indeed, many have virtually denied it, even when their very own practices contradicted their words. (See my further analysis in Essays II and III above.) This political escapism has something of the same intellectual stature as the idea that the United States can function well without coming to terms with China or with the facts of global poverty. Obviously, the escapism can be explained. The black experience has been so brutal, and the historical memory of that experience remains so acute, that to admit interdependence almost surely will earn a black leader some temporary obloquy.[6] Black political leaders, like others, prefer to avoid harsh criticism from their followers.[7]

All the same, the pervasiveness of black-white conflict does not negate the fact of interdependence or unmake the common interest which such interdependence dictates. This idea of common interest should be understood precisely as it is understood in international politics. It does not mean identity of views about what is morally right. Naturally, it is stronger if there is such an identity, but that identity is not essential. Common interest means some necessity common to both parties. It means that they can take care of the necessity only by some joint action—whether open or tacit—and that the failure of either will probably result in severe loss for both. If George Wallace and Huey Newton were aboard a two-man raft in shark-infested waters, each would have a vital interest in keeping the other aboard! Or, if Newark were imminently threatened with a great explosion at the airport—or with a cholera epidemic—the forces of Imamu Amiri Baraka (LeRoi Jones) and those of Anthony Imperiale would have a common interest in doing their utmost to arrest the catastrophe.[8]

The common black-white political interest grows out of *irreversible demographic and ecological* interdependence. Neither 30 million blacks nor 180 million whites are going to emigrate. They may each be foolish enough to contribute to internal war, but the costs of internal war are far beyond anything a reasonable man could regard as sanely tolerable.

Political rationality, in the most self-interested sense, thus dictates that each element seek its own role in avoiding ill consequences and in achieving favorable results. There is, of course, no guarantee that blacks, *not to mention whites,* will see the issues in this light. It is always satisfying, in conflict situations, to persuade oneself that meeting the needs of the situation is solely the obligation of the antagonist. But to act effectively upon this kind of perception requires an extraordinary concentration of power on one's side. More important, to try to make the opponent crawl, to make him meet one's unlimited demands, is irrational, from the viewpoint of one's own self-interest. The relevant point may be stated somewhat abstractly: If some party (X) conceives that he has gone a long way to meet the demands of the second party (Y), he will at some point revert to his prior resistance unless (a) he conceives that he is utterly beaten, or (b) he conceives that Y is also being "reasonable." This alternative casts a little clarity upon the strategic problems of blacks *vis-à-vis* whites. For a very long time, whites projected bitter-end resistance to virtually all demands from blacks, with the consequence that—in due season—blacks tended to revert to the most rigid position. This reality governs black-white politics in our time.

People do not naturally modify their preferences or positions to suit others. Change will be initiated primarily when the demands of those who stand to benefit become irresistible, but that is not all. Those who stand to lose (however much or little the prospective loss may be) must to some degree modify their initial objections. Obviously, this is a power problem. If the adversaries do not at all modify their position, the battle will go on until one side forces the other to crawl. Whoever makes it clear that he means to make the antagonist crawl acts irrationally. For he merely stiffens the antagonist's back. Even if he does possess the strength to force the antagonist to crawl, he should try to avoid doing so. Otherwise, he will leave a reservoir of poisonous hostility and the time will come when the antagonist will regain strength and seek to redress the balance.

This is the meaning of "sowing the wind and reaping the whirlwind".[9] White America sowed the wind in a long history of sheer domination. It now reaps a whirlwind of black rebellion. The question is whether black America will also now sow the wind.

"INTEGRATION" AS OBJECTIVE

The saving of the future implies a clarification about the nature of what is to be attained. No significant forward movement is likely without a fuller appreciation of *what "integration" really is* and why any of the objectives ordinarily discussed in black politics is actually inferior to "integration." To achieve such an understanding is not easy. The very word has been so far brought into disrepute that it excites alarm, anger, despair, and disgust in the minds of many who contribute to symbol-making in black politics, being often deemed in opposition of "self"-development. The idea that "integration" and "self"-development exclude one another is utterly false, when the concept is treated seriously. Integration has been confused with one procedure or technique which sometimes serves integration: namely desegregation. Desegregation is necessary in any case where the intent is to achieve racial diversity within some specific institution (such as a school) or some specific place (such as a neighborhood). If anyone has ever thought the integration objective meant primary emphasis on racial diversity (varied phenotypes) within specific settings, *for its own sake,* he has been in error. Why has diversity been sought? Desegregation has been sought for two reasons. First, segregation has been imposed as a means of white supremacy, and resistance to segregation has been, symbolically and practically, necessary to the struggle for liberation. Second, desegregation has been sought as a means of widening the opportunity structure, since the *white* institutions have been (and are) the loci of greatest opportunity. But desegregation is a mere technique, not equivalent to "integration." Nor is integration precluded by, or incompatible with, the mere fact of autonomous ethnic institutions. "Integration" in the broad political sense is not a matter of "integrating" some group A into the society and life of some group B. Rather, it is a matter of the spirit, process, and frame of mind in which the diverse parties approach each other. Integration is the result which exists when two (or more) diverse parties are brought together in what is a common political enterprise and a common structure of respect, even though each of the parties may also have certain additional enterprises and structures (self-development) peculiar to itself.[10] Perhaps it would even clarify matters to borrow the language of German industrial relations and speak of "codetermination."[11] Obviously, I do not mean that the specific German institutions provide a model to emulate. But the language expresses well the change in the major industrial nations in the twentieth century. At the beginning of the century, the industrial owner or manager possessed nearly autocratic power. To hire, fire or retain; to promote or not to promote; to pay higher or lower wages; to provide pensions or not—all these decisions the owner or manager could and did make without worker participation. The growth of worker power, through the union, means that some form of negotiated contract now sets the ground rules for such decisions. Thus the essentially "royal" managerial prerogative is enormously curtailed and the managing and working classes occupy a different relationship to each other, not only in the politics of the nation but in the internal "politics" of the factory and the industry as well. Even areas which are still theoretically subject to managerial prerogative, such as pricing decisions and plant-location decisions, are significantly if indirectly influenced by the union. Thus, the government of industry is decidedly subject now to *co*determination by managers and the representatives of organized workers.

The term "codetermination" can be misleading, for it can all too easily be taken to refer only to the operations of specific public institutions. My meaning, in speaking of "integration," includes this aspect. But it goes much further to refer not only to ordinary "politics" but also to changes in the racial hierarchy of the whole society and culture. How would we actually know an "integrated" polity if we saw one! We should know it by substantial evidence that race would not predict the distribution of either material benefits or psychic esteem in any significant degree. We should be unable to predict that a disproportionate number of the individuals treated with contempt and disesteem, a disproportionate number of the children dying at birth, a disproportionate number of the prisoners in jail, or a disproportionate number of educated men would be of one race rather than another. It would be this spread of life chances, individual and "institutional,"[12] across a wide range within each group that would indicate integration. The objective of "integration," as it has been presented, is superior to many objectives stated in more "radical" terms, because most of what is represented as "radical" would, if pursued to its essentials, settle for much more limited results than any here discussed.

SETTING A TIME HORIZON

The argument has been, let us recall, that the possibilities over the next twenty years are relatively encouraging, provided that short-term errors may be minimized. This calls for an estimate (or even a reasoned guess) about the time horizon which seems to make sense. The assumption is that the next five years (1971–1976) constitute the critical zone in which certain strategic measures ought to be initiated or accomplished. This does assume, of course, a certain stability in the world and that not everything comes loose at the same time. One could certainly imagine alternate developments[13] which would frustrate such an estimate. But in the absence of those developments, the five-year zone seems terribly important.

The number of years chosen is not arbitrary, but is deemed a reasonable span—as the way in which one would speak *if one could start with a clean slate.* The birth of the new infant is the closest to starting with a "clean slate." A black child born this year will be ready for kindergarten or first grade within five years. By the end of those five years (1976), measures should be *operational* which—for the first time in history—would be calculated to guarantee that this child should begin his school life (which is the route to the rest of his life) with more than a fighting chance of approximating the results available to his white counterpart. By the end of his first eight school years (1984), those measures should have so operated as to create a climate which loads the dice in favor of his going into high school with a real chance to succeed. By the end of his twelfth year (1988), those measures should have produced a climate which loads the dice still more in favor of the chance that the new graduate will either (a) go on successfully into higher education, of (b) go on successfully into a fruitful form of employment or other economic activity.

The five-year time horizon is not selected with reference solely to the new infant. We could also say that a child now in first grade should be, by 1976, more reasonably assured of what is not now the case: that from about sixth grade on he is *not* more and more dropout material. It may be even more important that the junior high school boy should, within the five years, begin to have much more realistic chances for successful performance in a competitive economy than he has now. We could say that the twenty-year-old black man, getting married this year, should at the end of five years have what no twenty-year-old black married in 1966 could count on: reasonable assurance that measures are afoot which will prevent his going onto an economic junk heap just at the time his children are beginning to get beyond the toddler stage. Seventeen years is a long time, but it is not nearly so long if there is a serious purpose—active year by year —to produce a viable world into which the black new parent of 1971 may release his or her graduating senior in 1988. This total time is thus short enough to lie within the horizons of quite ordinary people, but long enough to permit decisive social change if there is a political will.[14] I am aware that many black critics—and white ones—will say it is "too long." But it is realistic to know that *such result as I deem essential could not come instantaneously.* In the world of human affairs no major result of any sort comes instantaneously. It is correct, however disturbing, to recognize that large-scale political change does take time and cannot be produced magically.[15] Hence I shall remain unmoved until the critics present viable alternatives, which do not disguise—as most proposals do—the time it will take to show definite results.[16] (Considering that it has taken seventeen years since *Brown v. Board of Education* to make some change erratically and without design, we may ask whether it would not have been more fruitful to have been more systematic at that time about what was to be achieved when.)

There is also a "narrow" and "realistic" political reason for the five-year span. If a more reasonable course cannot be discovered by that time, the chances are that the Republican party will have chosen to consolidate a national majority on an antiblack basis. We do not have to suppose that the GOP would become a party of "prejudice" in the narrow sense. Indeed, that may be unlikely if—as seems to be the case—about two-thirds of the white population regards "racism" and prejudice as rather vulgar.[17] We may believe that the party would become—indeed, has become—the center of resistance born of a *generalized* unease about "things going sour," that this generalized unease is antireform and would, under some circumstances,[18] be functionally equivalent to "antiblack." To capitalize upon such unease would simply become the most economical way for the party to take care of its own organizational interests. In such an eventuality, the Democratic party could have little recourse but to follow—both for managing its own internal antiblack problems and in order to maintain its competitive position.

By the same process, the agencies of coercion would acquire a vested interest in more restrictive policies. This change need not be seen as malevolence, but as a normal human process. Events of the past several years have challenged publicly the moral probity, the insightfulness, and the technical competence of the military, the Federal Bureau of Investigation, and the police. It is but natural that they should seek to recoup their own self-esteem, regain the signs of public esteem, and renew the capacity to provide satisfying careers for their members. If degenerative incrementalism[19] cannot be arrested, then these agencies should be predicted to re-establish themselves partly on the presumption that blacks are especially dangerous people whom "society 'has to' control by whatever means are 'necessary'."

Doubtless, there are still other considerations. Doubtless, also, others might reasonably choose another time span. But the reasons offered seem sufficient to make the point that, prospectively, the year 1976 occupies a place of greatly important symbolism. It will be the 200-year anniversary of the Declaration of Independence, and the 100-year anniversary of the retreat from Reconstruction. Much of how people feel about the country, and their place in it, will depend upon whether the next five years show more degenerative incrementalism or whether they show reason to believe once more in a politics of hope.

Finally, there are the external influences. The fact is that the continuous external inquisition—from press and television, OEO reformers, social workers, and many others—into what is the "real" leadership of black communities constitutes an assertion that existing leadership is probably unreal.

Limited effectiveness and crisis of conscience, problems of perquisites, popular suspicion and external criticism will erode leadership self-confidence. These threats to self-confidence are understandable. But those who surrender to them help no one. For the real task of men, *by virtue of their very capacity to reason,* is to understand the social world well enough to overcome threats and to guide action rationally. If blacks share the view expressed here, what should they do?

NOTES

1. In a certain sense, the "youth revolt" is an attack by the novices upon the heirs apparent who do share some of their orientation to the world, because the

rulers who share very little of it are nearly invulnerable to the novices. The rulers typically would not compromise with change but would suppress it if they had full and free choice. One could therefore regard the youthful upheaval as an effort to force the apprentices to force the rulers to move over or to change. But the heirs apparent cannot entirely do that without destroying too much that is valuable to themselves.

2. Moreover, one should not neglect the possibility that the most radical might ultimately reverse themselves and adopt a racist politics. This reversal would be the most likely if, as I do not believe, the truly radical should win (be it five years or fifty) political power. This presupposes successful revolution. In that event, they would—in their necessity to consolidate themselves—jettison weaker allies such as the blacks (or at best relegate them to "second-class citizenship" as the Soviets have tended to do with Jews).

3. The assumption is that members of this age grade will not, in fact, commit political suicide by opting out of social responsibility (which is to say, out of elite roles).

4. Discussed in *The White Man's Burden*, Essay VIII, "Public Opinion and Everyday Behavior: I—Notes on Confusion and Ambivalence."

5. In my opinion, the system could be shaken seriously only if such an idea became widespread among those who actually command in their own hands the instrumentalities of force, or if the potential technocrats became so much alienated that the normal upper middle-class educated roles in society could not be filled.

6. The decline of Bayard Rustin's reputation since 1963 is precisely a demonstration of this point.

7. The fear of harsh criticism and disdain, by those whose respect one would rather have, has also deterred many black writers as well. The one thing which an analyst, in contrast to an active leader, owes an audience is—to adapt Burke —not his agreement but his judgment. If there has been a "failure" of black intellectuals, it has been less a disinterest in the black "revolution" and more a failure to offer *critical* judgment on matters where such intellectuals presumably have insights not equally available to all their brothers. There is no magic which gives an intellectual better judgment about anything than anybody else has. Insight comes, instead, from hard work and close application to some subject matter. That is, obviously, not the only way to learn important things. However, it is one way to learn things, and that way can validly be rejected if, but only if, one concedes that street-level populism is actually a superior way. (On street-level populism, see Essay III, above.) If one accepts the superiority of street-level populism, then one cannot criticize black intellectuals for their failure. One merely judges them guilty of presumption in saying anything.

8. Obviously, the parties in question might not cooperate and there is a good deal of human experience with parties' ignoring their common interest and letting each other go down.

9. The cases in international politics are too numberous to warrant detailed discussion. The cases of ethnic conflict in situations where there is a common

government, but not even the pretense of a political community, are equally demonstrative: India in 1947, the BaHutu-BaTutsi strife since 1960, Cyprus since World War II, Arab-Jewish contests in Palestine between World War I and the proclamation of Israel.

The problem of poisoned relationships in cases where there is a presumption —contrary to fact?—of political community is also very sharp. The point is driven home by the morning paper which, on the day this draft is being written, reports the death of Quebec Labor Minister Pierre LaPorte. This grim event cannot be considered apart from the history of Anglo-Canadian dominance.

10. For instances, see Ake (1967), Deutsch *et al.* (1957), and Jacob and Toscano (1964).

11. I have not consistently used the term throughout this analysis. To do so would require a reformulation of the entire argument, in ways which would now take too long to accomplish. There is a second—and perhaps more important— reason. The term "codetermination" has already been used by another author who thus has rights of priority. But I saw the term in his (or her) anonymous manuscript which I read for a scholarly journal. Not knowing his (or her) name, *I am unable to give proper credit* and thus do not feel free to use the term. For some notes on codetermination, see Fleming and Edelman (1965).

12. When I speak of "institutional" life chances, I stretch a point. But I mean to refer to the fact that one can predict with great accuracy the likelihood that an institution will be regarded respectfully by knowing with whom it is identified. If an institution is identified with blacks in the United States, there is a profound tendency to define that institution as immediately less worthwhile than a compara- ble institution not so identified. The problem of the black colleges is indicative.

13. The development which could supersede anything here discussed, of course, would be global nuclear war. Other imaginable (and not entirely fanciful) developments might include the following.

(a) The further racialization of international politics, so that "white" and "non- white" states should be more obviously aligned against each other, would tend to isolate American blacks either from (i) other Americans, by emphasizing the color tie, or (ii) nonwhites outside the United States by making it essential for them to "prove" their loyalty to the United States.

(b) The development of a world system in which the military would govern each major nation-state would have its effect, since military regimes would presum- ably be "security-minded" in a stricter sense. Accordingly, internal political debate would be less open and constraints and supervision tighter.

(c) The descent of Canada into ethnic-linguistic strife (of the sort which the murder of the late Pierre LaPorte made many people fearful in 1971), capable of being displaced into the United States. (This would, paradoxically, reverse the situation about which Prime Minister Pierre-Elliott Trudeau has been apprehen- sive, namely the displacement of American ethnic antagonisms into Canada and Mexico, creating class and ethnic revolutions in those countries.)

14. This lies within the compass of what *is* practical in American politics.

15. American public policy ordinarily takes something between 15 and 20 years to execute a major change in domestic direction. Even "revolutionary" change produces little *quickly,* except change in the major symbols. For example, it is possible to kill off all the landowners and redistribute titles to property. But it inevitably requires the passage of much time before a stable redistribution of actual wealth takes place. That is, it will be a long time before the new peasant-owners (or the new collective farms, or whatever) *actually* experience the benefits of more money widely spread among more people.

16. How long, for instance, will it take for the Panther program to be adopted and show definite results? How long for "community control"? Etc.?

17. This is touched on in *The White Man's Burden,* Essay IX, "Public Opinion and Everyday Behavior: II. Is There Latitude for Peacemaking?"

18. As, for instance, the circumstances discussed in *The White Man's Burden,* Essay VII, "A Look at Medusa's Face."

19. *The White Man's Burden,* Essay VII.

V

The Next Five Years: I.
Morale and Objective Capacity

THE PROBLEM OF MORALE (SELF-CONFIDENCE)

Black and white are inevitably interdependent. They can fight against that fact, but they cannot change it. A repeated theme in these essays is that they are unwise to fight against it. Instead, it is argued, strategies must be predicated upon it. Insofar as black leaders are concerned, such strategies will be acted upon only ineffectively, unless there is a revival of self-confidence on the part of such leaders and the constituencies they represent. Self-confidence and rational strategy are not very important when one is doing what is obviously easy, or what obviously will work. A man walks on solid ground in open daylight, virtually without thinking about it. His problems arise when he has to walk in a fog through a booby-trapped field. Self-confidence is not required for holding a conversation with an old and trusted friend. It is essential when being interrogated by an adversary whose purpose is to trap you into a serious error. Self-confidence is a major determinant of the effort which people make to overcome their difficulties, and is an essential attribute for those who would be leaders. It is essential because, while part of leaders' obligation is to advance whatever may be the case for their constituencies—even at the risk of some pain, another part of their obligation is to call to their followers' attention certain basic realities and certain alternative approaches—even at the risk of being cut down within the group. Those who cultivate leadership only by saying what the audience already wants to hear deserve the most severe censure, for their effect is to encourage the

144

audiences to engage in self-delusion which is at best wasteful and at worst self-destructive.[1]

This need for self-confidence would not be a problem for black leaders if they were able to achieve dramatic victories. Since they are not presently able to achieve such dramatic victories, it may be possible only to show why they feel insecure and, by raising the roots of insecurity to consciousness, provide some prelude to overcoming it and achieving a black regrouping. The erosion of black leadership, which must be overcome, arises from three sources.

1. *Black leaders suffer chronic crises of conscience.* Why crises of conscience? Part of the reason is cultural, the sense of shame at not getting the job done. Those leaders who do have very strong feelings about their missions —particularly young people of limited experience—themselves have acute strokes of conscience for "not having done more," although it is usually the case that they did all they knew how to do. Shame is increased when one directs at oneself powerful values of defiant heroism and moralism.[2] Crises of conscience are exaggerated, of course, for those leaders who share the cultural attachment to the Young as Deliverers. For that attachment means that one must value the opinions of the young, and the young (if taken seriously) in almost any culture can be counted to tell their elders that the elders did it wrong. In addition, nothing is more likely to accentuate the crisis of conscience than to know (or believe) that one's good fortune comes out of the misery of "the brothers and sisters."

2. *Black leaders also are likely to encounter certain perquisites of leadership which come whether they get the job done or not.* The mere fact of being a recognized leader—particularly a controversial one—procures invitations to share cocktails with cafe society liberals, rewards of the lecture circuit (which not merely assuage self-esteem but also increase income) or even a corporation position as "director of urban affairs" or a university appointment as "vice president for community relations." Perquisites are normal accompaniments of leadership in almost any politics. Only the most profoundly ascetic—indeed, often priggish—elites can refuse all perquisites[3]—and only the lovers of hairshirts can renounce perquisites once they have been received.

3. *Every leader is suspect as a possible "tool," witting or unwitting, and can never fully vindicate his authenticity.* He can never *prove conclusively* that he is beholden exclusively to "black people" and not to some whites by whom he has been recognized. Consequently, the more perquisites are advertised and the more they change a man's life style, and the more certainly will they threaten his reputation among the original following. The popular audience sees the leader's personal status change rapidly, and

it hears his rhetoric. But it does not see its own benefits increase nearly so rapidly. Thence arises the cynical view that "He had become a 'Tom'," regardless whether the statement is at all valid or not.

FACING THE "POWER" PROBLEM

One of the reasons self-confidence is important is the necessity to think clearly, and to act realistically, about the "power" problem. No idea permeates black social discourse more than the need for "power." Yet most discussion of "black power" focuses more on the problems which people experience—particularly the problems of self-image—than on the nature of power or the requirements which people must meet in order to be powerful. The very meaning of "power" is, in fact, obscure. Persons and groups reputed to be very powerful find themselves treading cautiously, on the defensive, unable to enforce orders which they are "entitled" to issue. No one doubts that Mayor Daley is powerful, yet the mayor reportedly takes the initiative on as few issues as possible, in order to save himself trouble. No one doubts that the general (and flag) officers of the United States armed services are powerful, yet draft evasion is rife and they have been unable to get full support for their preferred course in Southeast Asia. No one doubts that presidents of the United States are powerful, yet they have great difficulty making their wills effective throughout the bureaucracy. *There is no magic about power.* Yet people who are accustomed to being dictated to by almost everyone else naturally have a sharp sense of power. What they really seek is some means to attain at least some of their most important ends.

There is a better approach than merely verbalizing about "power" and that is to focus more intently upon the development of an objective capacity for action. In objective capacity I include such things as money and relevant operational skills. The growth of college-educated black persons as a proportion of all college-educated persons in the same age-groups is an improvement in the basic materials of an objective capacity for action. This growth will have its effects in due course, simply because it improves the personnel supply for collective action even if these people have low morale.

Black politics in recent years has been oriented mainly to morale (or "collective psychiatry"). A drive toward "black pride" is a search for higher morale, through the discovery of something which is "ours" in a social world where nearly everything valued is "theirs." I have expressed doubts about this kind of politics, which serves mainly as a public theatrical catharsis. I do not maintain that politics can, or should, be entirely divorced from this function. On the contrary, it is good that people should be helped to feel good about themselves. But when politics as collective psychiatry is dominant, then it is likely to offer no contribution to the fundamental problems of the group in which it is practiced. That kind of morale politics leads to choices that are sometimes counterproductive and very frequently of limited value.

The most important substantive problem is to devise a social program which can produce a net improvement in black capacity. Such a social program cannot be geared simply to what people might, want important though that may be. Nor can it be mainly "cosmetic," though cosmetic programs have utility.[4]

EDUCATION

One critical problem which requires new attention within the next five years is education. No one has any illusion, one presumes, that any merit attaches to the old-fashioned argument that equal opportunities and treatment will come simply as a consequence of education. The point is, rather, that educational achievement confers upon the achiever a skill which the achiever can use, even against the bitterest resistance of his adversaries. Over the past seventeen years (since the *Brown* decision), we have tended to experience a diversion from this basic conception of education because we lost sight of the need for a strategic conception.

For the first four or five years after *Brown,* black leadership paid relatively little attention to the problems of education in the urban North. As in most other cases of inattention by such leadership, this was explainable, and thus is not subject to mere "denunciation" even though it also had adverse effects. The explanation simply was that thinly stretched *local* leadership had far too few resources, and far too many problems, to pay any serious attention to education without giving up other emphases also deemed important. National leadership had the problem of focusing most of its attention on the South, where the resistance to Brown was even more formidable than it is now, and where desegregation had real strategic significance.

When education began to rise as a major issue in the North, local leadership—with national collaboration—copied the specific Southern thrust by emphasizing desegregation. Though commanded by symbolic necessity and demanded for morale, this was a tactical mistake for very simple reasons. Demography alone—the distribution of populations by race—simply worked against a really effective program of desegregation, and would have done so even if white parents had not adopted the "neighborhood-school" mythology in the form that they did. Within the past three years, "community control" has come to be the predominant substitute.

Unfortunately, community control, for all its values, is still formulated mainly as a morale proposition. There is a definite realization that something is wrong (as it has long been) and that realization usually can be broken into three parts. (1) There is clearly widespread racism, both of the subtle version represented by cultural ethnocentrism and of the more specific kind represented by prejudice and hostility. Consequently, the curricula placed before black students often contain little with which the students can identify. Worse, they are handled by teachers who understand nothing of the meaning of being black, or even by those who are more distinctly hostile. (2) Even more, there is such a widespread difference between the recorded learning of black students, in contrast to white students, that we can be very sure of one thing: Drop all discriminatory practices in extraschool activity (for example, in employment) tomorrow, and these students still will not be able to compete effectively. Parents know this very well, and react in decided anger when they see schools doing nothing about it. (3) There is widespread discrimination[5] in the assignment and management of educational personnel. Consequently, not only is there a certain educational limitation for black students, but there is also a decided and unacceptable limitation on the career options of black teachers themselves.

Consequently, it is quite reasonable for people to insist upon "community control." However, this objective itself indicates no better sense of the strategic objective—pertinent to the future emerging out of the situation in which we now live—than any previous formulation of the objective. Realism dictates a recognition of two points. (1) A group is not, by virtue of being a "community" group, either more representative or more competent. Much depends on specific cases. In addition, as some cities come under black control it is—from a political standpoint—worse to dismantle central structures than to maintain them. (2) As soon as one gets beyond the *big* cities (more than 500,000) one starts to encounter situations where community control makes no sense because the units will simply be too small! "Community control" is not everywhere a meaningful conception on any terms; in demanding it, sometimes the central task is forgotten. But in all situations there is a central task to which attention should be directed. The central task is to provide education for black students, as individuals, sufficient and sufficiently good that in the aggregate they will occupy new social roles with adequate capacity to make a difference in the life chances of the black collectivity.

How do we define the central task? We do so by noting that "education" has many purposes, but the central purpose must be to equip people to perform vital roles, roles such that their capacities will be in demand and their places in the economy be assured by the normal working of the economy. This purpose requires that black education be governed by a sense of the future of the economy. How should we expect that future to shape up?

It is estimated that total employment in the economy will increase (over that of 1968) by something approximating 20 percent (from 81 million people in 1968 to 101 million people in 1980). Total employment in the manufacturing portion of the economy will increase by about 10 percent (20 million to 22 million). Total employment in the service sector will increase about thirty percent (from something like 35 million to something like 46 million) (see Burck, 1970). Thus the biggest increase in numbers of jobs will not be in the manufacturing sector but in the service sector—and service does not mean "domestic work" but finance, business, the professions, and commerce. If blacks are to get their share of these new jobs (however "their share" is computed), they will have to compete for them.

From this forecast, it follows that policy must be based upon a conception of what educational content should be—apart from material meant to improve self-images—and how one should think about scale. As to content, Black education must be oriented to the essentially technological nature of the society. The competences which will be most valued are those based in knowledge of economics, administration, science, and technology. As to scale, we have to recognize the problem inherent in having a large number of people fall by the wayside. Under present circumstances, all too small a percentage of black students who enter the public high schools actually graduate. Similarly, all too few of the public-high-school graduates actually go on to some form of education beyond high school. Let us say "college" for the moment, although this may mean various kinds of technical and vocational schools as well. It would be ideal if each of these percentages were to be raised to 100 percent at once. But no one, however far-reaching his ideas, has even conceived that possible, and it is not possible.

There is *in no city of my knowledge*—and certainly in no organization viewing the country as a whole—any conception of specifying such objectives in the next five years. Yet it is obvious that this is essential. It is essential to consider measures which will achieve step-by-step increases, year by year. What is the grand objective? To enhance the likelihood that at any given level of the economy, and particularly in those levels which lead to the most desirable prizes in industrial and financial enterprises, the proportion of blacks should steadily increase.[6] What competences are required? A layman's answer to this question probably is "advanced skills based upon mathematical and scientific-technological knowledge." If one wants to increase the rate at which blacks may penetrate managerial ranks, and the rate at which they may ascend the managerial ladder, then one must constantly scan the probable industrial requirements and develop educational programs which will ensure that blacks are found in increasingly large numbers in the reservoir from which such industrial personnel requirements are filled.

ECONOMIC EQUALIZATION

My approach to the economic problem is akin to the approach to education suggested above. In the numerous papers and reports on the economic position of blacks, there seems to have been remarkably little attention to the objective to be achieved. In view of the conception of "integration" repeatedly emphasized in these essays, the realistic objective is simplicity itself. It is not to create Utopia, nor to remedy all the deficiences in the United States economic system—some of which would be profound even if race were not a consideration. The objective is merely to create an effect such that the general accessibility of blacks to money and what money will buy will not be in 1988—as it is now—notoriously different from the general accessibility of whites to money and what money will buy. If however, the economy—and public decisions about the economy—were to operate over that period as it characteristically does, then such a result could not possibly emerge for many, many years into the twenty-first century.

In dealing with the economic problem, it is just as well to recognize that there are natural differences, based upon class and income, within the black "nation." No single set of measures will meet all the interests involved, nor will any combination overcome all the splits which those different interests dictate.

INCOME SUPPORT

The fundamental division is between the economic measures which are required for some minimum level of acceptable living, and those which are required for substantial economic growth. The former are absolutely indispensable if one is to be serious about the immobile poor, and they probably involve adaptations of ideas receiving much current discussion —some of which have been in general currency for a fairly long time. It is essential to achieve a much higher floor than any thus far discussed. The most far-reaching proposal is that of the Welfare Rights Organization (and Senator George McGovern) calling for income support at about $5,500 per year. The McGovern-WRO proposal looks dramatic compared to the Family Assistance Plan proposed by the Nixon administration (under which a maximum family allowance would rise to $3,920). But something beyond either is necessary. Some years ago, the Bureau of Labor Statistics calculated that an "adequate minimum budget" for a four-person family would cost $5,950 per year. If this were adjusted to 1971 costs, taking account of inflation, it would exceed the McGovern-WRO proposal by more than 40 percent and come out at about $8,000 per year.

Such a figure seems completely visionary, but it makes a fundamental point. It simply is not possible to agree that present income support programs, or even the most far-reaching alternative proposals, are at all adequate. Thus, at whatever levels adequacy may be defined—in order to match in some degree the economy's capacity to support people—certainly the policy must go well beyond the present level. However, there are certain obvious political problems as well. One is the problem of invidious comparisons. Obviously, the working poor—*black no less than white*—will compare their incomes earned by working to the incomes of other people, earned by right of citizenship alone, and will not tolerate the idea that the latter right should produce as much as (or more than) the former.

Hence, it is politically realistic to accept, if one is to have a sufficiently high income-support level, what the social workers' doctrine has taught us to resist: some form of "means test" and some set of incentives to move people into the active economy. The means test should not, in fact, be troublesome in principle; it is not inherently evil, and we accept it in other regards. Indeed, an income tax exemption is but a means test in reverse! Moreover, there is evidence that a means test—administered in a civilized manner and not for the purpose of exploiting the persons involved—elicits no more resistance and imposes no more stigma than any other form of administrative regulation (Handler and Hollingsworth, 1969). Nor are incentives to work bad in themselves. Moreover, "work" is desirable not merely because it builds moral character (if it does), or because it is part of the price one may pay for political support of a subsidy for the poor. Work is also important because it is essential to social welfare in general ("the division of labor" and all that) and because it is an essential form of social participation. Beyond income maintenance there is a threefold problem.

ECONOMIC GROWTH

The problem of income support is one that requires earliest attention in a program of economic equalization for blacks, but a threefold additional problem must be discussed and attacked. This problem is here presented under the headings of economic growth, job discrimination, and capital formation.

Growth is even more important in economic policy than support of income at some floor level. It is simply fatuous to believe that a *primarily* redistributive politics will make any sense. But a growing economy which contains within itself a *tight* labor market serves the needs of both the working-class and middle-class black populations. Growth is of major importance in order to change the persistent black:white unemployment ratio of 2:1. The policy objective, specifically is to reduce the ratio to parity within ten years. Economists are fond of seeking "nonadministrative" (economic) incentives to solve (or reduce) noneconomic problems. In so far as the Working-Class Respectables and the black middle-class interests are considered, however, it may be more emphasis should be placed on "noneconomic" (administrative) incentives to solve economic problems.

JOB DISCRIMINATION

Cognizance of the importance of economic growth leads to the extremely hard problem of discrimination in promotion, advancement, and pay—even in firms and industries which seem to comply with the existing civil rights legislation. This issue, virtually as omnipresent as the atmosphere, has largely dropped from the center of black politics, despite the construction-industry disputes which have arisen in Buffalo, Chicago, and a number of other cities. Why is not clear. I suggest, but only suggest, three factors.

First, black politics in the last several years has so much emphasized the rhetoric about "the poor brothers on the street" that it conveyed the image of a vast *Lumpenproletariat*—a group utterly unable to perform any useful roles in the economy.

Second, this image converged *conveniently* with the conveniences of bureaucrats, unionists, and company officials. All could seem to be doing something useful by focusing on "the disadvantaged," defining the disadvantaged as those who would—if properly trained—be employable *some day!* But each (bureaucrat, unionist, and company official) could thus at the same time escape responsibility for dealing with the problem of people whose main difficulty is not lack of skill, but limited opportunity for use of the skill.

Third, it is virtually impossible to talk about "equality of economic opportunity" within a framework of anti-integration and "separatism." This difficulty led to a peculiar situation. Just at the point that the United States government *began* to develop tools for enforcing antidiscrimination policies, the ebb of black pressure in this well-defined and fully legitimate area (as black withdrew into exercises of collective psychiatry), left the government with all too little political incentive to proceed. The test of the government's failure to follow through (in this absence of incentive) is clear. James E. Jones, formerly assistant solicitor of the Labor Department, reports that in the three years 1966–1968, the three main federal agencies responsible for antidiscrimination action had a total budget of $37,361,000 (James E. Jones, 1970). If budgets are ever a test of will to act, particularly when the problem is protean, then it could only be concluded that the federal will was weak. Consequently, new attention to this problem is deserved. Essentially, three main approaches seem feasible.

1. *Third-party intervention in behalf of black potential employees needs to be institutionalized in all the major metropolitan areas.* This is required in order to make possible the refinement of "boycott power"—developed so effectively by the clergy[7]—in relation to those enterprises where the boycott is an effective instrument. It is not possible to have the boycott mechanism work, moreover, unless one can get standardized agreements by black-community leadership about what private mechanisms they will employ and support. But if such institutions can develop, then it is reasonable to expect that business and leadership will find it necessary to meet them on agreeable terms.

2. *Government should be pressured to develop a rational industry-by-industry scheme for black employment.* Such a scheme should be oriented toward those industries naturally capable of absorbing new black employment seekers who will be coming into the work force at any early stage, thus reinforcing the economy-oriented educational bias suggested in the previous section. The objective is, in part, to provide realistic options so that people will know that they are not wasting their time in school. However, each industry (and firm) must be required not only to hire, but to take definite measures for achieving a randomized (rational and racially diversified) distribution in its various occupational lines and at various levels of pay and promotion.

3. *In addition to judicial measures, and possible cancellation of government contracts, it is also necessary to think of monetary penalties and rapid measures for review and enforcement.* In other words, it is not realistic to expect that many government contracts will actually be canceled, simply because the political feedback will be more than government can usually tolerate. However, it is eminently realistic to design money penalties. Thus, if Company C were to promise (in an adaptation of the Philadelphia-Plan principle) to achieve X percent black in Y job categories by Z date, then the failure to achieve the ratio might be treated as nonperformance and subject to (a) a fine to be paid, or (b) a deduction to be made from the payment which the firm would normally receive. Precisely because monetary penalties would not provide any disadvantage for any existing white employee, the problem of massive political feedback would be reduced. But because it would provide an extra cost to the company, the responsible managers in question would wish to avoid shouldering that responsibility, and would thus have a reason to be positive about meeting the objective.

CAPITAL FORMATION

Finally, we come to the problem of capital formation in the black "nation." In some circles, it is fashionable to argue that "employment" is not important and that "the issue" is capital! No such superficial dichotomy is necessary. It is sufficient to note that (a) most blacks—like most other people—are not going to be holders of capital in any significant sense, but (b) it *is* important to increase the proportion of black capital holders and the proportion of capital they hold as rapidly as possible and to the fullest degree possible. The point simply is that the share of the economy controlled by blacks is so extremely small that, unless measures to alter the position are found, a decisive lagging behind must continue for an indeterminate time.[8]

Capital development is, in any case, a highly competitive enterprise. There are probably three aspects which will have to be overcome. One is the need for an *adequate information base* to identify the kinds of situations into which new people can penetrate because the situations are "soft" and not yet commanded by the international and national giants.[9] (The ability to anticipate computer-related business chances around 1950 would have been pertinent, as would the ability to anticipate the business implications of cable television in the middle 1960's) The second is the need to develop *general managerial competence* to overcome the present characteristics of black business as a peasant or traditional economy. In both these respects, the problem of economic policy links with the problem of educational policy, for the first tactical objective is the rapid improvement of skills which permit one to regard education as a form of capital for penetration of vital sectors of the economy. It is not true that education for the economy fits people merely to be employees. It also fits people for those managerial, professional, and technical roles which lead to the acquisition of equity. It also fits people for penetration into "soft" industries, soft because they are new (as the computer industry was new in the 1950's). Education for the economy also helps to produce an information base from which to identify the business prospects fitting the most serious black needs. This contradicts a traditional criticism of black occupational interests—that too many black people concentrate in education. On the contrary—the increasing importance of higher education in the United States, and the growth of "the learning industry," are jointly creating significant employment pressure—a pressure which will renew itself by the end of the decade. There is, to a constantly increasing degree, a seller's market in this area, an area important because it trains and educates the people who must occupy critical social positions and, therefore, will remain indispensable. Hence, in fact, there is every reason to emphasize the importance of occupations in education, not at the secondary-primary level but at the post-secondary level where the professional is not merely a teacher but a professor of a specific branch of learning which gives him entry into critical social connections in government and industry.

If lack of information is one problem to overcome, and lack of managerial skills a second, the third and undoubtedly most critical is lack of money (or the form of collateral on which money can be guaranteed). This is important because any new enterprise requires money enough for its management to live beyond the start-up period and beyond the period at which all that is earned should be reinvested. Antitrust and tax-reform policies are also appropriate and pertinent to freeing up the competitive situation. But it may be both more important and more feasible to focus upon means of providing the money to be risked. The central mechanism for this purpose undoubtedly must be set up by government action, in the form of some species of Bank for Internal Development, modeled on something like the World Bank complex (see Shonfield, 1962) for international development or the Farm Credit Administration for domestic purposes.

The other major capital-forming procedure calls for deliberate and rational use of government contracting—an historic source of capital formation. This need not be used to build up individually held capital, but lends itself brilliantly to the underutilized device of the cooperative. For instance, the wholesale cooperative organization which serves retailers is well-known but it has not yet been applied widely to the service of the black retailer. To foster such wholesale cooperatives to furnish purchasing, distribution, management and other services might well have the dual result of making the service to black customers more efficient and (thereby) increasing the retailers' earning power). Government contracting permits not only a federal role but also a local-government role in development. Every big-city institution spends money to buy concrete, tar, and steel for roads; food, medicine, equipment, and construction materials for hospitals; and so on. It surely ought to make some difference if an appropriate share of the millions of dollars spent for supplies were routed through merchandisers in the ghetto. It might be entirely reasonable—subject to laws on purchasing—to exercise some discretion as to potential suppliers. Since one box of sugar is about as sweet as another, the purchasing agent might well buy the school sugar through a ghetto cooperative, thus providing that cooperative with an assured income it would not otherwise have. There are still other ramifications. Even though local-government funds are usually on short-term deposit, they are quite useful to banks. Hence, a city treasurer might well evolve relationships under which banks could legitimately consider how to play a useful social role they had not before considered. Nothing would seem *obviously* to prevent a treasurer's persuading the bank that an *aggressive* equal-opportunity policy would enhance the chance of receiving city deposits.

In sum, the political *economics* of the black "nation" calls for a convergent push toward income maintenance, economic growth, antidiscrimination, and capital acquisition.

There is, in addition to education and economic progress, a third area —badly neglected by black strategists—communal order and equal protection under law.

COMMUNAL ORDER AND EQUAL PROTECTION UNDER THE LAW

The third major program element is communal order and equal protection under law. I treat this more extensively here for the reasons that (a) it is basic in social organization, and (b) there is a profound reluctance on the part of black leaders to talk about it. The topic is normally avoided because it involves the issue of crime, an issue more often used by those who would, in any case, be adversaries to black people. Nonetheless, this is one of those issues which cannot realistically be ducked. If black leaders avoid the subject, ordinary black people in the communities do not. Why should they?

Who, after all, bears the brunt but themselves? One definition of a "bad neighborhood"—and one of the commonest which occurs in black people's conversation—is that it is a place where you have a high chance of being harmed! Since neighborhood residence is strongly influenced by income, it is apparent that "bad neighborhoods" *at their worst* are places where poor people prey on other people.[10] (The fact of racial segregation means, of course, that even not-so-poor people are more likely to be crowded into many of the same areas as the very poor,[11] but the very worst areas will be abandoned by nearly all who can pay any sort of higher rent or mortgage installment.)

The consequences are quite practical. Black ladies of middle age, who earn their daily bread as household help in Westchester County or Chicago's North Shore, usually can afford only relatively cheap housing. If one looked at such ladies on any sociologist's SES (socioeconomic status) measure,[12] they would be accounted "lower class." Their rankings would not be much above those of unemployed teenagers, teenagers whom they may well know because they know their mothers, sisters, and cousins. All are in the same social web. These ladies, however, are also the people whom such teenagers are most likely to rob. After all, a boy approaching manhood can rob a middle-aged woman more easily than he can rob a man. Moreover, since there will be a certain amount of personal knowledge—if the robber does not know the robbed personally, he knows someone or can know someone who does—to report the robbery is often an act which the robbed will fear to undertake; the robber or his friends may take later vengeance.

This simple example really makes clear the meaning of "property rights," more often thought of as a "conservative" doctrine for the protection of the rich. Robbery and theft are forms of property transfer, against the will of the property holder and beyond the rules which define "the market." The criminal act of robbing the housemaid is a political act—depriving her of the "property" (the day's pay) which the law declares she is entitled to have—regardless whether the robber has an ideological notion in his head. It is quite the same with the workingman. His weekly pay may be a very modest form of "property," but the law declares that he is entitled to hold onto that, and to release it only for purposes and to persons whom he approves (or for which he has made some commitment, such as paying his rent). If our workingman goes into a tavern and buys a round of drinks, for which he pays a stated price, he has engaged in a market transaction—willing buyer, willing seller. If he gets into a stupor and the bartender cheats him, fraud has occurred. The game has changed still more if, coming from the tavern, the remainder of his money is picked from his pocket without his knowledge. When it is taken by force, or threat of force, we have reached the same situation as that of the house-maid.

Each of the intervening acts, no less than the act of robbery itself, is a form of politics (albeit frequently a politics without ideas).[13] Nor need one choose only the property examples, important as they are. The presumption of a republican regime is that the individual minding his or her own business may go about without let or hindrance. Yet notice the territorial constraints which may actually operate. Imagine a young man, with about twelve years' schooling, married, and steadily employed; imagine also his wife's brother, hardly different from himself except that the brother is not steadily employed, *prefers not to be,* and runs with a danger-ous street-commando group. Indeed, the unemployed brother-in-law claims to play a large role: "I *rule* that neighborhood and nobody messes with my people [family]." If the employed young man lives in that same neighborhood, he may be relieved that no one will molest his wife, because they fear his brother-in-law. But he cannot be very comfortable if she should, say when visiting an old school friend, go into some neigh-borhood where his brother-in-law is unknown. It is, in the latter case, as if she were traveling in a foreign country where the passport might be honored—but again might not be.

I have chosen these examples to suggest the quality of the problem, not to make the case that such situations are universal. It is also true that hundreds of thousands of people live in urban ghettoes, from birth to death, and are never robbed or injured. But a very large proportion of them know some situation where they have actually found scratch marks around their doors, where they have had to frighten off robbers by scream-ing or calling the police, or where they had to hasten a bit on a dark street because they knew they were being followed.[14] This is a problem which deserves, in the interests of the black "nation" to be treated more seri-ously. It cannot be ignored on the supposition that it is an artifact of the hostile white press, although there are papers which exaggerate it all. Nor can it be justified or explained away by the academic romanticism which asserts that, at least in lower-class black areas, people regard dope pushers, pimps, rapists, and holdup men as culture heroes.[15] Those who have been absorbed into such activity, or are about to be so absorbed (as some juveniles), may regard such people as figures for emulation. But common sense defies us to believe that dope pushers and others mentioned are *heroes to their potential and actual victims—who are the people of their apartment buildings, blocks, and neighborhoods.* Nobody likes to be raped, robbed, beaten, threatened, or killed, and nobody hates having dope peddled to his kids so much as a lower-class black parent. The anxiety about crime—notably crime which might involve personal injury—can be found in too many forms to permit the belief that it is accepted, unless "acceptance" be in the manner of medieval people who accepted a plague they did not know how to avoid.

The problem is even more complex when we try to comprehend the social role of street commandoes. Under present circumstances, that role is not easy to comprehend without intensely personal observation. Much of what is said seems very serving the sayer's personal view. According to policemen, these groups are nothing more than hoodlums, miniature versions of Al Capone's gang. That view cannot be *entirely* true. Some activity is distinctly constructive, as in the case of their participation in the "Street Academies" which the National Urban League (with corporate sponsorship) has created to tutor drop-outs, in the hope of returning them to more productive paths. If one listens to some reformers, the street commandoes are at a minimum Robin Hoods, possibly even latter-day emulators of Jesus driving out the money changers. That view cannot be *entirely* true either. Some commando activity is unquestionably shaking down neighborhood merchants and, for that matter, shaking down other young people who are not themselves commandoes. Some activity is neither "elevated" nor "depraved," but the mere "hanging around", much as Irish boys hung around the same neighborhoods forty-odd years ago[16] or as middle-class suburban youngsters "hang around" in their own fashion.

In the present context, we may note at least that some part of the street-commando activity is threatening and is based upon violence.[17] Since there is so great a tendency to suppose that "antisocial" activity is peculiar to black communities,[18] we may note the obvious fact that such threat is by no means limited to black communities but is widely present in white communities. That somebody else has a problem does not relieve you of the necessity to face your own problem, even if the other party is using your problem as an excuse to try to make you feel "inadequate" or "inferior." I have already argued that the weakness of black-community organization, insofar as "youth" institutions were concerned, left a major vacuum for many years which street commandoes filled.

As we know, commando life has taken on an increasingly "political" cast, whether as represented by a group of some ideological pretensions (such as the Panthers) or by the many local groups (such as the Black P. Stone Nation in Chicago). This development was virtually inevitable, once racial political consciousness became really an everyday phenomenon in street discussion. Moreover, there are probably three points of view which have enabled the more politicized commandoes[19] to draw some gingerly, embarrassed, but nonetheless real support. Two of these are represented by white reformers who, in their characteristic manner, seek means to provide from outside the leadership which does not come to their satisfaction from inside. One of these reformer types is the missionary, aware of the stress within poor neighborhoods, convinced of the virtues of "grass roots participation,"[20] and also convinced that—properly guided—street commandoes can be saved from "bad activity" and turned into a constructive force for good (see Fry, 1969). Another type is represented by those reformers who think themselves tough-minded and have taken up a version of Daniel Bell's hypothesis: Illegal commerce has been a major source of capital accumulation for certain major white ethnic communities. Their conception has been that this process would, being repeated, have similar effects on the upward mobility of blacks. I also suspect, but cannot show, that there was also a certain judgment among some black community leaders that the gangs could be used to scare the white leaders of the cities. What this judgment would reflect, assuredly, is the basic political weakness of these leaders themselves. On many critical issues, they could not themselves persuade city leaders, or bargain successfully with them as conventional equals; they could attempt to coerce them by pointing to the threats posed by the gangs. Moreover, one would suppose that the scare tactic sometimes worked. But this is by no means a fully realistic view, and certainly does not take account of the difficult problems of internal order which black communities experience. Commando life encourages young people to think of force as a salve for all their ills, and teaches them that it is legitimate to terrorize and intimidate anyone who even happens to be in their way. We should thus expect them to enjoy the experience of being feared—something which may be part of everyman's fantasy life—and that they would invent moral-sounding reasons to justify enjoyable action.

Several important consequences follow.

The first is that, under present conditions, commandoes' personal needs become mixed in with "revolutionary" rhetoric. But the best guess is that many of the recent attacks on policemen have come as commandoes mentally cast the police in the role of their normal adversaries. This conduct and outlook produce no social policies which might make a major contribution to urban reform. At the minimum, it aggravates police fear and increases police discretion to harass and kill. At a more extreme point, it threatens a politics of terror, energized by the feelings alone, unguided by any rational strategy, and adverse to the best purposes of those who undertake serious and responsible leadership. These situations provide scope for the disturbed, who derive their own therapeutic satisfaction from the act of coercion, and they create pressures such that quite ordinary people (who would never believe themselves able to commit atrocities) become disoriented.

Stressful situations free the madmen to do as they please—if the "reasons" involve "political" or "moral" arguments, one should not take those arguments themselves at face value[21]—and organizational factors often fail to give colleagues the will or capacity to control the madmen. Rules of self-restraint become suspended, in effect, and the situation becomes one of hunter against hunted. The more stressful a situation is, the greater the pressure to apply force as a rational policy measure. But the greater the stress, the less rational will the use of force actually be and the more it will serve the psychic need of individuals.[22] The more decentralized (or merely disorganized) the group which applies force, the less control there will be over pathological excesses.

This absence of control is the real concern raised by the Rackley case. Rackley may well have been a police agent, or he may not; and the charges that the Panther leaders ordered him killed may or may not have had some foundation. But the really convincing point is not what could or could not be presented as legal evidence. The point is that all the participants in the trial—the dead man, the state's witnesses, the accused—had been participants in the organizational life of the Panthers, and had apparently long been regarded as normal people within that environment. Yet in the end, somebody did some rather un-normal things, so that we may conclude either that the organization was insufficiently selective (so that a person disposed to those un-normal things could be regarded as acceptable) or the organization lacked a capacity to maintain effective discipline. Bobby Seale refers to the matter gingerly, as one would expect a prudent man in a clandestine organization to do[23] and during September 1970, Bobby Rush (the public spokesman for the Panthers in Illinois) announced a purge on what seem like similar grounds. Rush reportedly said some of the people being dropped lacked discipline, were dissatisfied with community service work (such as free-breakfast programs), and were too anxious for confrontation with the police.

The purge phenomenon leads to two obvious questions. First: Will the purgees humble themselves and accept discipline for readmission, go outside and fall apart, or go outside and create their own organization for confrontation? The second obvious question is: If uncontrollable pathological excesses are a problem for an organization with at least some overt social purpose—what should we expect of other groups with less clarity about social purpose? In any case, we have no reason to encourage per-

meating the community with people who have adopted doctrines of terror, and who cannot be subjected to any regular control. (See Seale,
1969.)

This problem gains added importance if we suppose that, inevitably,
the tendency to act on coercive presumptions requires demonstrations of
coercive power. In the same manner that politicians choose, when they
can, opponents who look highly vulnerable, one would suppose that the
people most susceptible to ganglike coercion will be those people within
the community who cannot and will not retaliate. Consider, for instance,
the "storefront" church of the sort represented in James Baldwin's *Go Tell
It on the Mountain*. It has recently happened that such churches—deep in
the heart of the South Side—have been invaded on Sunday morning.
Nothing actually happened except that young men of minatory manner
marched through the church, looked at the congregation, and marched
out again—all during the sermon.[24] The people being intimidated are
black church people, for whom the church provides one of their few
outlets for self-expression free of an hostile world. All who wish to participate are welcome, on the sole condition that those who cannot respect the
proceeding stay away. When the rule cannot be enforced—because the
ushers dare not ask people to leave—one has a raw demonstration of
power which will be remembered by those in attendance. In another case,
the events were still more troublesome. A young man—with no visible
record of gang connections—recently discharged from the Marine Corps
was killed at a church by assailants unknown to the church people.

We should expect the problem to be more severe if people within the
community do have real conflicts of political belief or interest. It is quite
easy for the most sincere radicals to say that a black businessman, being
black, is a "worse 'exploiter' " than a white businessman. The argument,
correct in itself, that such small businesses can survive only by extra
charges would simply cut no ice at all. The black contractor, so recently
brought into the building industry, may owe as much to white investors'
fear of roving gangs—a building site is terribly exposed after hours—as
to the persuasiveness of black boycotts or Federal officials. Or, if black
businessmen find new opportunities where white competitors have now
vacated the field, it is easy to imagine the claims that those who made the
new opportunities possible deserve something special. In the end, it would
not be going much further to argue that the entrepreneur ought to pay
a special compensation to "the community." But who decides the amount
and the schedule? Who collects? Who, indeed, except those possessing the
raw power!

There is still a less encouraging prospect. Those who are in the business of crime are always looking for good "fronts." The mood of revolt—and a language of "by any means necessary"—should be expected to be easily assimilated to what is simply crime for profit. Now that revolutionary language and "street language" are so nearly identical, and both sorts of groups recruit from the same personnel pools, we should also expect a good deal of overlap in actual personnel. Moreover, we should expect the police (and other official agents) constantly to confuse the two—accidentally and purposely—thus creating an ecological situation in which they might often have to depend on each other. But "revolution" provides a better front for "crime" than crime provides for revolution.[25] This is the best available explanation for a murder in Boston, where the availability of money—more money than the participants had before seen—in a federally funded manpower-training organization seems to have led to gangland-style slayings among those contending for control. The rhetoric of revolution can lend itself all too easily to extortion.

Nor should we suppose that the commandoes' pragmatism will allow them to remain free from the larger system of "organized" crime. Instead, one should view the major metropolitan underworld as a sort of corporation needing subsidiaries and agents within the ghetto. People do not enter those relationships because they like them, but because they need them. If guns cannot be purchased legally, to take an obvious example, one can only purchase them illegally—which implies a contact with the underworld. Once those contacts are initiated, how are they broken? Or are they broken? This progression at once raises all the problems of clientage, in this "under" world, just as they are also raised in the "upper" world.

The disposition of black leaders to avoid discussing these problems is entirely comprehensible. They set as the first item on their agenda the battle against racism. They know that their white adversaries are forever searching for reasons by which to deny them basic rights, reasons which at the same time can be stated without the language of racism. They know that most policemen appear to believe that blacks are peculiarly disposed to crime (Skolnick, 1966, 80–83) and they are fully aware how much an attack on crime has been adopted in national politics by those who show no interest in equal protection. Within the past several years, the phrase "law and order" has come to be (or be seen as) a code word for police action to "keep the blacks in their place." When they hear Police Commissioner Frank Rizzo (since become mayor of Philadelphia) describe themselves as "animals," or witness the adoption of "crime control" as a major project by national politicians whose interest in racial equality is minimal (as, apparently, Attorney General Mitchell and Vice President Agnew) or negative (as in the case of Senator McClellan), they are properly wary. If in these circumstances the black leaders cannot show that the crime statistics are, in indicating higher crime rate for blacks, *grossly* distorted, then it is frequently better tactics variously to shift the subject entirely to organized crime (a white enterprise), to emphasize the sociological conditions of crime, or to avoid the subject entirely. If blacks are to address their problems seriously, however, they cannot permit themselves to be misled by their adversaries' abuse of an honorable and essential conception.

The moral authority of any political leadership is undermined about as rapidly by the failure, or the incapacity, to face the order problem as by anything. And certainly nothing more undermines the moral authority of *black* leadership than its failure or incapacity in this regard. Not only is it at a discount with white audiences under such circumstances, but it is even more important that black leaders' moral authority is seriously discounted among black audiences for the very same reasons. Nor is the advancing of "sociological" explanations—cast in terms of "poverty" and "deprivation"—wholly convincing. The actual or potential victims of personal crime, black though they be, are very unsympathetic to the hypothesis that "broader social forces" somehow constrained neighborhood aggressors to behave aggressively. Since they come from very similar socioeconomic circumstances, frequently, they cannot see why such explanations apply to other persons, but not to themselves.[26] Instead, they are very likely to regard such explanations as worthless excuses.[27] As Livingstone Wingate said in a 1970 speech,[28] about the mood of Harlem: "Sometimes Harlem frightens me now (a change after many years' familiarity there). When I try to talk to them, my people tell me, 'Whitey! Hell, it ain't Whitey hitting me on the head and taking my pocketbook."

The Rev. Walter Fauntroy, a black political leader in Washington, D.C., spoke of the same reaction. The fear of crime among black Washingtonians was so great, he said, that there seemed little choice except to let the police have wider discretion. Similarly, a black cab driver is not merely a black, but also a *cab driver,* worrying about being robbed or killed. It is understandable that he should sound precisely like a white driver in telling well-dressed passengers, "The trouble in this town is that the police are handcuffed. They ought to let them whip some heads." This is a choice he is willing to take, even though it is childishly simple to show him the basis for Fauntroy's reluctance to agree for more police power: that to the policemen "black" and "criminal" are often synonymous. Black people in this circumstance are fully aware that they are getting anything but equal protection, and this awareness contributes simultaneously to their distrust of other blacks, to their lack of confidence in black leaders, and to their revulsion from due process—which, so far as they are concerned seems merely a defense for successful criminals, black and, even more, white.[29]

The adverse consequences of disorder, within black communities, are so serious that it is short-sighted any longer to evade a serious discussion. No mature politics can possibly avoid more serious attention to the problems of achieving and protecting life, bodily security, property, and physical freedom. No social group can constitute anything worthy of the name "community" unless it makes an effort so to protect its members. Perfect order never exists. But order is approximated to the degree that all these rights are assured in doctrine ("law") and maintained in practice. The failure of *equal protection* thus means that some sorts of people may regularly expect to have less assurance of these rights in practice than some other sorts of people. Both ordinary crime and street commando operations (as normally conducted) impose the severest burdens upon thousands of black urbanites, who are doing their best to make their way in a harsh world. It is working black men and women who find themselves robbed. It is thousands of black school children who find that, in addition to all the other problems of a bad school environment, they are subject to disruptions and privations adverse to sound learning. It is the marginal black businessmen whose commercial success is diminished because neither the official government nor his surrounding community can provide him the minimum level of protection. And it is the internal politics of the black community, quite apart from whatever may happen in the white world, which is threatened by the supersession of rational debate through the imposition of coercion. Consequently, while it is not possible or justifiable to concentrate on this problem alone, the possibilities of serious educational or economic improvement will be diminished by a neglect of the necessity of communal order.[30] Finally, there is one fact of life which goes beyond black politics. As a political reality, the greater the neglect of this issue by black communities and their leaders, the more the general public support of the issue is determined by the propaganda of the police, which is hardly a desirable result.

Finally, this set of issues involves *gross official misbehavior* (police brutality and other), which is a much better known part of the equal protection problem. The indispensability of remedial measures has been clearly delineated in the past several years—particularly since the summer of 1964. is so patent, I do not discuss it further here.[31] Perhaps the one observation merited is that if legalized order does not constitute a viable standard for official behavior, then the many episodes in which policemen have been assaulted without notice acquire a genuine political meaning. They become both a signal of the deteriorated condition of social life, and an incitement to further wildness on the part of police who, themselves, are none too restrained. Clearly, police violation of the law-and-order standard, in its proper sense, only generates a corrosion of the potential community. Everyone has a vested interest in not being killed or seriously wounded by private persons, so everyone has a similar interest in *law*ful official behavior. Yet a goodly share of the black "nation" (perhaps most of it!) cannot feel secure enough to trust the ordinary mechanisms of the law. Black leadership, of whatever persuasion, has been unable to conceive and effectuate appropriate means of defense against what used to be called "police brutality." Such leadership will always be faced with a turbulent and chaotic politics inside the black "nation" so long as most reasonable people cannot be confident that "law and order" does not apply against official misbehavior.

SUMMARY AND CONCLUSION

The central assumption is that the problems of the black "nation" require the same sort of realism that they would require if the "nation" were a separate juridical unit. One aspect of such realism is that blacks and whites have no viable option, whatever might ideally be preferable, except in an integrated polity (a "republic"). The integrated polity does not now exist. Its creation will arise, if it arises, from a process of exchange between black and white amounting to domestic peace *making*. Moreover, our main argument is that this process should be, and can be, substantially consummated during the next five presidential terms (that is, by about 1988), provided that really serious effort is undertaken in the *next five years!* It is analytically sound to argue that the prime role in such peacemaking must be assumed by whites. But it is not sound to argue that blacks have no *autonomous* and *essential* role!

If blacks are to define and fulfill such a role, however, they will have to achieve substantial improvements both in their self-images and in their capacity for collective action. This improvement involves both morale and objective capacity, with a heavy emphasis upon the latter. The idea of a social program is oriented to the problem of enhancing objective capacity. Specifically, the essay sets a five-year horizon for a serious start on three major problems: (1) *improving the education competence of a large number of black students* for performance in *a technological society;* (2) making a critical break in economic issues relative to (a) *income support* for the immobile poor; (b) *breaking the disparity both in unemployment rates and in distribution by occupation* for the working poor and the black bourgeoisie, and (c) initiating a new direction in *capital formation;* and (3) *enhancing the level of communal order and the degree of equality* of treatment before the law. My argument is, moreover, that a serious push on these three elements within the time specified could release new social energies looking toward a reasonable approximation of genuine integration by the time that children born this year are leaving high school.

NOTES

1. For instance, those who lead young people in street commando operations are wrong, but at least have the merit of consistency. Those who stand back, encouraging such activity but themselves shunning its dangers, are hypocritical.

2. See the discussion of defiant heroism and moralism as important themes in black culture, above, Essay I.

3. See, for instance, the discussion of the varieties of *patronage* in *The White Man's Burden,* Essay VI, " 'Sticky' Trade-Offs and Urban Immobilization," relative to party politics.

Perquisites are a highly visible part of the business world, the academic world, and the church. The trade union movement used to protest its disdain for perquisites, on the theory that the union leader ought to live like the rank and file. In reality, the claim that a major union leader lives "simply" is almost equivalent to the old log-cabin motif in presidential politics. Yet few do live so "simply" for long. (Both Walter P. Reuther and James R. Hoffa were often described in these terms, at least to the extent that neither flaunted affluence in his personal visible assets and personal daily life—homes, clothing, or the like.) One very authoritative labor reporter recently noted how unusual Albert Shanker is in receiving a salary about at the same level as a teacher's salary, since most union leaders are *much* better paid. (Raskin, 1967). *Revolutionary* movements frequently have attempted to impose the secular equivalent of poverty vows upon their leaders, but this attitude seems seldom to last more than a few years. There is hardly such a thing as a revolutionary elite in power which does not leave its children with much better opportunities than other children in the same society. Despite contemporary sociologists' interest in "revolution," "social change," and similar categories of events, they seem to have done very little on this subject, For the views of a controversial lay writer on the subject, consult the works of Milovan Djilas.

4. Thus, Kenneth B. Clark has somewhere suggested an improvement in the physical environment and housing stock of the urban ghettoes as a major emphasis. This makes very good sense as a morale venture, but will make still more sense when, it is possible to formulate a housing program which also improves the net capacity for action. I have some hints on this in the ensuing discussion of economics.

5. This is quite different from saying that everyone who alleges discrimination is actually subject to discrimination. It is only honest to remember that blacks also cry wolf and make excuses.

6. A similar conception, applied to higher education for blacks, has been developed in a privately circulated paper, "Education for Black Power."

7. I refer to the three best-known examples of recent times: the bus boycott at Montgomery; the selective-purchasing campaign run some years ago by Leon Sullivan in Philadelphia; and "Operation Breadbasket" run by Jesse Jackson in Chicago.

8. Moreover, capital shortage means increased internal competition (factionalism. (See above, Essay I.

9. For instance, there is a considerable amount of money being made in urban planning and consulting, including planning and consulting on urban social policy. Only in the last few years has the black consulting firm begun to enter this arena, partly because of inattention and partly because of discrimination. See, for instance, Friedman, 1970).

10. I have never seen a study of black people's reasons for moving from one neighborhood to another. But I would expect such a study to find that two reasons were particularly important. (a) People would move in search of a better neighborhood, meaning one where they would be safer on the streets and in their houses. (b) People would move in search of better schools which—often enough—would not mean schools of better academic quality so much as schools free of the disruptive student behavior usually associated with "juvenile delinquency."

11. Harlem is probably a special case here. The density of population in Harlem is so high that one can go *one block* from high-priced apartments occupied by people who are very well off to buildings that are virtually slumlike.

12. SES rankings customarily are composites of schooling, income, and occupation.

13. However, we should never forget how closely revolutionary politics becomes associated with criminal activity, as in the case of those who extort funds or commit robberies to support their political purposes.

14. I am here referring to the cases in which one could be confident that the informant was not hysterical or misinformed.

15. On this point, I have a flat disagreement with my friend and colleague Martin Kilson who, I think, simply misunderstands the command of the pertinent sociological data. (See his 1970 paper.)

16. I refer the reader to depictions in the Studs Lonigan novels of James T. Farrell.

17. The case that the pretensions of violence exceed the practice of violence is made in Miller (1967).

18. There may even be some reason to suppose that the street commando phenomenon—which used to be a lower-class white form—may be creeping into middle- and upper-class white behavior as well. Not only the Weatherman might be interpreted in this way, but so might the rise of group vandalism in middle-class

suburban communities. I have even been told that the problem has been slurred over in the reporting of Chinese-American community life on the West Coast. At least one San Francisco juvenile officer has said that there is an incipient "Red Guard" movement in San Francisco, growing directly out of Chinese street gangs.

19. Some groups have remained what they (or their predecessors) were before, marauders organized for fun and profit.

20. It is not only missionary-reformers, nor even the late Poverty Warriors, who place a high value on grass roots participation. See the same theme in a report published more than twenty years ago under the auspices of the Illinois State Department of Public Welfare, *Bright Shadows in Bronzetown*.

21. The essence of the theory of cognitive dissonance is that any excuse will do to reconcile yourself to what you have done, or what you want to do (Festinger, 1964).

22. Reports of police and National Guard behavior in such diverse situations as Detroit (1967), Newark (1967), Chicago (1968), and Kent State (1970) all tend to strengthen my confidence in this interpretation. Moreover, this is neither a purely contemporary nor purely American phenomenon. I may illustrate what I mean by a case from the Anglo-Irish War in which a British captain killed four people in one evening. Three were journalists—one sympathetic to Sinn Fein, but at the moment trying to organize action against looters—and one was a seventeen-year-old boy returning home from church. Then, having spent the night praying, the captain went on the next morning to kill two others: a city councilman, and a boy whom he shot through the back of the neck, having already made the boy kneel on the pavement for the execution. "The man was unbalanced," says Younger, "but what was unforgivable was that, although the military authorities knew of his crazy crusade, nothing was done to halt it until another officer (with no apparent authority) took matters into his own hands and had him confined" (Younger, 1969, 27).

23. No intelligence organization, for instance, is ever very forthright in commenting on this problem.

24. One case was reported to me by an absolutely unimpeachable eyewitness.

25. Seale (1969, 366–401) for some vague hints which can best be interpreted in light of a broader knowledge of urban crime patterns.

26. This theme is quite common in lower-class black conversation. The idea that people involved in crime want "honest work" but cannot find it is likely to be repudiated—at least when the economy is in reasonably good shape—by other people who have "honest jobs." Much more is involved. For one thing, there certainly is some effect from high levels of unemployment (as among black young adults), even though the effects are not very well defined. At the same time, there are also problems of personality and life style. I thus note the comment of a man of twenty-three (married, but separated from his wife, with two children and jobless): "You are a man with scruples, and I speak to you as a man with no scruples." He made it clear that he was not jobless because he could not find a job. In fact, he had had factory jobs which he quit. "I don't like work. I don't like

anybody bossing me around." At the same time, he emphasized certain limits: "I have too much respect for myself to take a man's money out of his pockets, when he is coming out of a tavern drunk." He was, I am sure calculatedly, imprecise about how he did earn money. He got some from his mother—who had been working at a steady job for more than 20 years—and his estranged wife worked and supported the children.

27. I do not mean to try to develop an explanation of criminal behavior here, although I would maintain my view expressed elsewhere (Holden, 1969) that criminology is fundamentally a subpart of a *political* science. Clearly, the idea that poverty and deprivation themselves are explanations of criminal behavior will not quite hold in view of the fact that some criminal behaviors increase with prosperity. (See Biderman, 1967; Silver, 1967, 2, n. 3.)

28. Wingate is a tough-minded realist, formerly associated in politics with Adam Clayton Powell and former head of the antipoverty program in New York City. He is at this writing Executive Director of the Urban League of New York, and is known in the agency as a man with an intense concern for the immobile poor. These remarks were made at a planning session prior to the 1970 National Urban League Conference.

29. Thus, in the summer of 1970, a group of young blacks (teenagers and young adults) challenged the Nassau County Police, daring them to enter a certain portion of Central Islip, in Long Island. *In this instance, the group was not "Panthers" nor mouthing any revolutionary slogans. Instead, they were attempting self-help because they said the police either were not enforcing the law against narcotics sales or were in collaboration with the narcotics sellers.* See *Newsday* during the last week or ten days of August 1970.

30. There is one school of thought under which it is preferable for black professionals "to remain within their community." Those who move out are subject to severe criticism from this viewpoint. However, one very simple point should be noted. At least as much moving out arises from anxiety about physical safety as from any pursuit of money. Who would, if he could escape, remain if (a) he suspected police inability or disinclination to protect him and (b) suspected that, in addition, people of the surrounding community would decline to support him?

31. But see Essay VII, "A Look at Medusa's Face," in *The White Man's Burden.*

VI

The Next Five Years:
II. Organizational Options

THE "UNITY" PROBLEM AND ORGANIZATIONAL UNDERSTRUCTURE

The customary prescription for increased "power" is "unity." In all the history of black politics no theme is more valued than unity. In reality, one can make too much of the "unity" principle.[1] But, as a practical matter, blacks are not yet at a point where they need to worry about too much unity. The more pertinent point is that if one accepts the prescription, in some broad sense, what is needed is some operational guidance. For it is incontrovertible that "unity" is perennially in the talking stage, and seldom in the action stage. How may it be enhanced? My proposal is very simple. Stop talking about it. Talk normally leads only to recrimination and bitter dispute, with such "unity" as may appear being little more than a superficial accommodation to real or perceived social pressure. Most calls for "unity" are claims that some person or group (within the black community) is a dis-unifer, which is to say that he (or it) is pursuing some logic or need which leads in a direction different from that which the appellant desires.

As a general principle, unity is more easily achieved if parties X, Y, and Z—desiring to work together or perceiving some need to do so—also know that differences among them can be tolerated and will not become the subject of irremediable chasms. This is essential, precisely because much disagreement comes out of real and legitimate difference of need. What is needed is not so much some mystical unity as a common framework for deliberation, clarification, and judgment—even when the end

171

product of these processes may be a rather clear disagreement. This calls for an institutional modification sufficient to implement what has been an off-and-on aspiration in black politics for many years: a modest regularization of the "quasi government" (see above, Essay I) through a common deliberative mechanism.

A MECHANISM FOR COLLECTIVE JUDGMENT

Black leaders at the national level conduct all kinds of exchange and interchange. But this is a highly irregular process, usually limited to a small number of people, often dependent on the vagaries of personalities, and most often called into being by some relatively specific crisis. What would be more useful would be a regular conclave, so structured as to represent the widest possible range of opinions and circumstances—a kind of Afro-American general council. The Leadership Conference on Civil Rights performs some part of this function, but the Leadership Conference has at least two difficulties from the present perspective. Without derogation of its proper functions, one may note that it is an interracial consortium and that it is devoted to lobbying at the federal level. Both those qualities are important, but are not to the point here. The last time the broader approach was tried, the National Negro Congress of the 1930's, it foundered on the rock of Communist penetration and was smashed by the lack of funds and other logistical supports. This experience raises some important technical problems of design (Record, 1951).

One is the simple problem of size. No place in the United States is more accustomed than Black America to the belief that just anybody is entitled to participate in just any discussion. Yet this belief is obviously self-defeating, for it raises representative bodies to such a size that realistic debate is not possible and, even more, to such a size that part-time participants cannot get to know and make their appraisals of each other well. Hence, one would be talking about a deliberative assembly of no more than (say) 150 persons, meeting several times a year in plenary session and (given the nature of work) meeting somewhat more often in committees of smaller size.

The basis of participation is another problem. If one chooses on the basis of organizations, one creates several more problems. Those who wish to enter may, to enhance their influence, create still more organizational claimants to the end that such people would be grossly overrepresented. If organizations are to be represented according to number of members, one has the problem of verifying their claims of size. If one makes financial contributions the basis, one has the problem that a "means test for participation"—the least acceptable form of means test—is imposed. On the other hand, it is probably unrealistic to believe that one can entirely skip over existing organizations.

But this kind of problem in constitutional design has been faced many times before, and is well known to law and political science. It should be possible to design a structure which depends, basically, upon direct election—particularly in these days when there is so much experience with the verification and direction of private elections—and to devise such modifications of the bicameral principle as would take account of the minimum demands of existing formal organization.

Another important problem about which no mistake should be made is the formal authority of such a collective-judgment body. The precise point of the body would be the collective *discussion* of issues and the formulation of collective judgments in a rational way. From that point onward, the influence of such a collective mechanism would have to depend on the reasonableness of the judgments reached and the moral authority which should inhere in the fairness of the procedure. Such a mechanism would also have to be linked to similar vehicles which, in an inchoate sort of way, have begun to emerge in local communities; otherwise the communication back and forth would be severely impeded.

Some such mechanism, however designed, seems the most practical way to remove competition between black leaders from the disorderly practices of recrimination and contradiction to a form which commands moral authority both inside the black "nation" and in the rest of the public audience. This objective does not imply that there could, or should, be some collective determination binding on all black persons, the execution of which would be overseen by some sole leader. Not at all! The recognition of the right of individual action must be complete, without any effort at suppression through group opinion or in any other way.

There is indeed already a leadership process and a leadership structure, generally emergent, generally recognized, generally approved or generally criticized. The point is that this leadership structure and process is undermined by a peculiar process. At any instant, any individual may assert—as he is entitled to do—that the leaders represent no one. In the nature of the case, any such critic always finds dissatisfied souls willing to join him. The latent dissatisfaction is great enough that, on each such occasion, the emergence of the critic almost entirely discredits the predecessor leaders, in the eyes of many people. What is troublesome is that there is no framework of ideas within which legitimacy can be assessed.

SELF-HELP AND THE INTERNAL BUREAUCRACY PROBLEM

If common deliberation is to realize its best potentialities, it will have to be supported by a more refined and sophisticated internal bureaucracy. This support, in turn, will require acceptance, enhancement, and enlargement of the concept of "*self*-help." For many years, this idea—and the very phrase itself—was repellent in black political language. It was used by whites, to suggest that blacks ought to avoid "political" action or pressure upon whites, and that they should concentrate on "improving themselves" instead. "Self-help" in that sense seemed very like a strong nation's advocacy that some weaker nation should engage in unilateral disarmament. Consequently, blacks shied away from the entire concept.[2] But this was an error, for self-help is in no way inconsistent with the ordinary practice or politics or the exercise of citizenship claims. On the contrary, there is nothing more fundamental to ordinary politics than the attempt to aggregate power for the service of one's own interests.[3]

Self-help means, in addition, the utilization of one's own resources, for one's own purposes, without the intervention or association of any external party. Despite the fact that they have been repelled by the ordinary usage, blacks have shared a deep cultural sense of the value of true self-help. This theme has never been revealed fully, given the lack of deep cultural anthropological studies of the black "nation," yet it is very real. Frequently, indeed, the conversational world of black people indicates that black people have practiced more self-help than they themselves realize. I think this is revealed in the discussion one could (in the 1930's, 1940's, and 1950's) hear in almost any barber shop or almost any Baptist church: "We have not done enough for ourselves." In reality, the complex web of fraternal associations, the array of imposing churches paid for by the assessment of rather poor people, and even the proliferation of black colleges would not have been possible except for a serious effort at self-help (Frazier, 1962). The limited ability to support communal institutions fully—a function of limited capital (see above, Essay I)—should not be confused with the absence of hard effort and serious purpose.

The capital resources of the black "nation" are still extremely limited, relative to the demands which might be put upon them for collective purposes. Nonetheless, it is now possible to escape from those forms of grantsmanship which still tend to make some critical activities—and the people who carry on those activities—into *de facto* wards of the foundation system or of those few federal agencies which provide minimal funds.

Absolutely nothing said here implies that blacks should avoid seeking funds from such sources. Quite the contrary. But there is a recognition that many purposes which seem essential, from the interests of the black collectivity, will be regarded as erroneous or explosive from some other perspective. In addition, the self-image of the black "nation" is impaired, not by seeking external support (which is something almost everyone must do),[4] but by the belief (and by practice based upon the belief) that everything important must be financed by an external gift. Moreover, if it is too simple to say that "he who pays the piper calls the tune," it is at least to correct to be aware that the piper who is sent repeatedly to the same payer for his pay will quite probably give some heed to the payer's view about what kind of tune is played. (For this reason one cannot regard *subsidized* "radicals" or "Militants" nearly so seriously as they regard themselves.)

If one accepts this view, the question is how the limited capital resources can be tapped. The first fact of life is that the central source of support must lie in the emergent black middle class engaged in professional and near-professional occupations. How is this class to be approached? Moralistic preachments will not lead people to part with their money in the support of collective ventures, and the difficulties in getting people to part with their money are by no means limited to blacks or even to ethnic groups generally.

The practical problem is finding some private form of assessment which is both reasonably effective and reasonably fair. If assessments are to be effective, they must bear some relationship to reality. One measure of reality, for any geographical area, is the aggregate dollar requirements of all black-supported religious, fraternal, education, and charitable agencies now operating. Computing this will give some indication of the level of support which is actually given. Then one may calculate the required additional support for new activities as a proportion of this base.

The problem then becomes determining what would be a fair level of contributions. Income would be a preferred basis, but most people are not going to reveal their incomes; capital assets might be still more preferred, but the same qualification applies. What basis then? A realistic one would be some obvious consumption indicator, such as the quality of one's dwelling or the value of one's automobile, or both. Either a dwelling or an automobile is visible—indeed, neither can be disguised. The real-estate market and the used-car market permit confident and reasonably accurate appraisal of the expenditure required to maintain dwelling or car. Technical ownership doesn't matter—whether owned or leased, either involves a readily ascertainable amount of expenditure. If there were an agreed institution for making the judgment, it would be possible to arrive at some rough (but fair) estimate of the amounts which different people should pay.

Conceded, many middle-class people do not own or maintain cars, but a large proportion of them do. And nearly all maintain dwellings. Once a fair system of setting the expected contributions of car owners and householders becomes operative, however, it begins to resolve the problem of assessing those who do not own cars or maintain households. If you publish annually a book of contributors, communal solidarity begins to have its effect. Those who are not car owners would be persuaded, if only through invidious comparison, to make contributions approximately equal to those made by people whom they know, and who know them, who are on the car list. This kind of system can be reinforced in other ways; one could be a judicious use of honors for those prepared to meet their collective responsibilities, while the judicious use of silence would bring influence to bear upon the others. If it is objected that such a system is crude, we agree. But the point is that it may provide the initial funds, and that successful operation would indicate the necessity to which other people would then be responsive.

Such a series of local funds, linked to some central fund, obviously would require a carefully developed legal structure and adequate managerial methods. Both would be essential to the confidence of the contributors and to its operation in such a manner that, from year to year, that confidence would rise. But for what purposes would one imagine using this catalytic money? There are essentially three levels of operation, all *badly* needed.

LEVEL I: AN EMERGENCY INFORMATION NETWORK

The first, and absolutely essential, element of self-help is the availability of information on which action may rationally be based. The kind of information which is least available, and most needed, refers to situations of actual and imminent danger. Thus, to take a recent case, on Saturday, October 24, 1970, some newspapers carried a story from Cairo, Illinois, in which blacks were reported to have shot up the local police station. What were the implications for the rest of the black "nation"? What was happening in Cairo? What was its background? Who, if anybody, had shot up the police station? What would be a viable and proper response? There was very little basis for anyone not directly familiar with Cairo to know. Precisely the same situation existed when the Augusta police shot six blacks during a civil disturbance earlier in 1970—apparently all were shot in the back! (*Washington Post*) Then an administrator in one major black organization had to say: "We have a man down there, but as it often happens our field people may get so involved, they forget to call in and give us the details." Yet, from a national perspective, having the details in the national office was the demanding need (even as it is also understandable that the field man should get involved to the depth that cut off communication). The point might be repeated about stories of campus disturbances, Panther raids, and so forth. It is a simple one, however: *There is an urgent and critical need for an emergency information network!*

LEVEL II: MONITORING AND ADMINISTRATION

In addition to the need for clarifying the main options, which would be the function of a "general council," there is need for more intensive monitoring of public operations and for more efficient administration of internal policies. One way to indicate how such a monitoring operation might work is indicated by the problem of police misbehavior. The ways of responding to police misbehavior are various, but one very simple way has been almost *totally* neglected. If a police officer misbehaves, even with the consent of his superiors, he is engaged in an illegal *(ultra vires)* action, which renders him personally subject to civil action at law. If there is anything a large city needs, it is an immediate response to every such case, a response in which the police department is made a defendant and in which, as well, the officer is personally brought into court. If the rate of suits filed were to go up dramatically, then police officers—troubled by the necessity to defend themselves in court—would unquestionably find more reason to be prudent and discreet in adhering to legal standards for maintaining order. This effect would result even if, in the end, the officers often won their suits. For the cost and difficulty of defense against an almost certain suit, not the fact that one may lose, is the powerful deterrent.

There are other immediate problems which require a similar bureaucratic readiness. Many of the important short-term problems which must be met by blacks might be attacked more effectively in rather simple ways. For example, it is clear that much of the open-occupancy legislation is ineffective. Clearly, blacks do not make substantial use of this legislation. (This is not because open occupancy is "irrelevant." People do start to occupy housing when they know that it is available. Rather, that the individual has too many difficulties in exercising his legal right unassisted.) Probably, open-occupancy laws could be made to work by a community reference service which (a) undertook to advise people about the administrative procedures involved, (b) made some strategic choices about what kinds of targets in the real estate industry might be most vulnerable, and (c) undertook a bird-dogging job to make sure that cases did not get lost in the administrative process. This kind of activity calls for a combination of "community organization" skills (in the social work sense) and of public administration skills.

At this level, the problem of communal order becomes relevant in a special way. One of the most important problems in black politics is the development of a politics of prison reform. The prison system, as it exists, contains a disturbing high proportion of black prisoners, whose life in prison is hardly at all related to any chance for their postprison adaptation. Prisons are schools for crime, schools which add to the burdens of the black communities in the large cities by serving that very function. Yet no part of the political system is also more decidedly administrative, and ordinarily closed to public view, than the prison system. In consequence, there is no mechanism which takes account of the prisoners' actual experience and insights, or of their postprison necessities—let alone of the question about what proportion of the prisoners really ought to be prisoners in the first place. One of the functions of a black monitoring operation, therefore, ought to be to make a contribution to communal order (and the broader problem of social peace) by making a persistent inquiry into the conduct of the prison operation and by providing a basis on which black leaders could put forth viable political proposals in this regard.[5]

Black organizational leaders, particularly at the city and neighborhood levels, need opportunities to meet with their counterparts operating in very different situations. Practical discussion of problems and issues, with an adequately prepared background of fact, would do much to break the circle of repetitions that meetings often produce, and this, in turn, would permit people to make their own judgments about appropriate new strategies. An example of need and opportunity is presented in the strengths and weaknesses of the Coleman Report (or the Moynihan Report), which look rather different depending on (a) what kind of activity you are usually engaged in (social work, direct-action civil rights work, or the practice of law), and (b) what kind of community situation you have. The center would function to provide a place to meet and talk about the issues and implication without the heated (and often irrelevant) exchanges which follow debates through the press.

Black organizations faced with specific problems, for example, how to get into the act on planning a Model Cities application, often need consultation services. Consultation is particularly important in the smaller cities, where the ratio of professionals to general population is small and the likelihood of being able to secure accurate and perceptive advice is, consequently, smaller. There are few mechanisms which advise groups on how to design an OEO grant application, or which have been prepared to advise black architects, contractors, and their colleagues of the potentialities implicit in Operation Breakthrough.[6] It is not even possible in most cities to get an impartial analysis of voting behavior without having to ask a white agency or an agency sponsored by a white-based group. Even if one assumes the technical competence, the complete trustworthiness, and the sophisticated insightfulness of the white source, most blacks still feel uncomfortable because they are in a dependent role.

In this economic matter, one possibility in the large cities (500,000 plus) is the creation of economic development organizations which would undertake appraisal and planning functions. For instance, it is apparent that much will depend on the roles assumed by corporate industry. How might industry proceed? Certainly, industry will proceed if it perceives a suitable profit opportunity *and* believes that its investment will be physically safe. (Schuchter, 1968, 319–320). But how should black leaders identify the firms upon which it is proper to make demands? And what demands are reasonable relative to the nature of the firm, its line of business, and the particular characteristics of the black community with which it deals? Handling questions of this order demands a considerable degree of knowledge and close attention to business trends.

Finally, there is clearly a need for continuous training facilities and services. Typically, any national organization is aware of the fact that a replacement of the chairman or president of a local unit with a new man may bring in a whole new group of people who are not yet experienced and skillful at organizational activity. (This is not particularly limited to blacks, by the way.) It would be useful to have a facility capable of designing and executing training courses (somewhat in the manner of industry management seminars)—short courses which would fill people in on the way in which the legislative process usually works, short courses on the strategies of precinct work or the tactics of campaign coordination, or the mechanisms of the municipal bond market.

LEVEL III: AN INSTITUTE OF STRATEGIC ASSESSMENT AND FORECASTING

Popular enthusiasm, moral or physical courage, and tactical shrewdness all are, in some combination, essential to the serious pursuit of power. But they can never be sufficient unto themselves. Modern politics, with these qualities but without the soundest available basis in knowledge, ultimately becomes a study in futility. Much that is pertinent to realistic politics depends upon an understanding of scientific, technological, and social factors which do not carry an obviously racial label,[7] but which will somehow significantly affect the world in which racial politics must be practiced. Consequently, it is urgent to develop some institutional format which brings more penetrating analysis and knowledge into alliance with political purpose. Even if "think-tanks" are in disfavor at the moment with many white intellectuals, black politics urgently requires its own think-tank.[8]

Only by having their own thinktanks does it seem probable that black strategists may, in the short run, escape the trap of which they so often complain: that both "the problem" and "the remedies" are persistently defined from a perspective which is not their own, and which neglects very significant factors. The theme is not new. It has been present in discussions of black politics and social organization at least since the early days of W. E. B. DuBois,[9] through virtually whose entire career it runs (no matter what ideological phase one samples). In the 1920's, it surfaces in Kelly Miller's attempt to create "a Negro Sanhedrin."[10] And it reemerges in the activities of the Howard University social scientists under the leadership of Ralph Bunche (in the 1930's), in the works of Charles S. Johnson, and of course in the entire career of E. Franklin Frazier. But nearly all attempts systematically to employ a broader knowledge have failed.

Often enough, such ideas have been elaborated into proposals such as the "Talented Tenth" doctrine, the conception that black progress would depend on the activity of special, "talented," and educated persons who would "lift up" the rest of the race. In this naive form, the attempt it is obviously self-defeating, for it not only imposes upon a relatively small group an extraordinary burden but simultaneously relieves all others of any obligation *and* insultingly implies that there are no important contributions to be made except by this small elite.

The pressure of urgent necessity has contributed to a doctrine, which most black leaders have accepted in one form or another, that "action" was imperative and "studies" were superfluous of wasteful.[11] One concrete example will show how this view was in error, and even harmful. Until several years after *Baker vs. Carr,* the 1962 case in which the Supreme Court decided to take up the reapportionment issue, black leaders (and audiences) responded favorably to the doctrine of "one-man, one-vote." Yet it was possible, as early as 1962, to discover three things. (a) Although reapportionment was a major problem, imposing limits on urbanites in the South, it was much less an important practical problem in the Midwest. The "underrepresentation" of large Midwestern cities was very small. (b) The demographic trends should have made it perfectly clear that central cities were not going to grow in absolute size, but were going to decline in absolute size. Their color composition might change, but size would go down. Accordingly, it was possible to foresee that the beneficiaries of one-man-one-vote would be suburban constitutencies. (c) In view of the white migration to the suburbs, it should also have been possible to forecast that there would be increasing political conflict between central-city interests and suburban interests.[12] From this tactical perspective, black politicians and black civic leaders ought to have been far more circumspect about the enthusiasm with which they then embraced reapportionment. Fundamental analysis ought to have exposed this view for debate, at the least, much earlier but there was no mechanism for doing so, and it is only in recent years that blacks have come to see it from actual experience.

Even when there has been receptivity to thinktank concepts, the "resource scarcity" problem has been present. The money to sustain such an enterprise has been far too scant[13] and, until recently, the body of blacks with the appropriate range of competences has been too small to constitute a critical mass.[14]

Some of these problems remain. But the situation is much changed. There is some potentiality of internal funding, if appropriate money-raising techniques can be found, and the range of competences (from systems analysis and engineering to law and social science) within the black "nation" is enormously expanded beyond what it used to be. Moreover, there is a widespread and intense desire, among black professionals, to "put our skills at the disposal of the community," but there is not yet a definite and viable model which shows them how to do so.[15] The opportunity now offered, it seems to me, is the supplementation of the deliberative mechanism (proposed above), and of the monitoring operation (also proposed above), with an institute for strategic assessment.

The potential uses of strategic assessment apply to a wide variety of issues and problems. The point of an institute of strategic assessment is to have a mechanism which will identify potential issues well before they become "hot," in order to permit the development of the most useful strategies, and to identify alternative mechanisms for translating general ideas into operational forms.[16] For example, it will be possible to develop better programs for black economic growth if the factual base is sounder. At least the following would be necessary: periodic inventories of consumer expenditure patterns, income patterns, educational and skill patterns, and entrepreneurial behavior patterns within black communities. Some of the information required would have to be secured by special adaptations of survey-research (or market-research) methods, but much of it would be available from existing Census sources. The planning function then would involve recasting this information into forms which would permit the development of year-by-year targets, with recommended means for achieving such targets.

Strategic assessment might also be applied to the important problem—much neglected in all social science—of the *administrability* of legislation. I would speculate that there are certain administrative principles operative which make legislation more or less easy to administer. Assuming that officials have some incentive to act in the first place, the most easily administered legislation meets the following criteria: (1) the beneficiary can be directly identified, (2) the action which he needs to take to secure his benefit is relatively simple, (3) the compliance action by an official is relatively clear (4) the official is relatively immune to sanctions by those who should prefer him not to comply, and (5) those who prefer him not to comply cannot prevent compliance by removing themselves from the process—except at the risk of losing important benefits to themselves (Holden, 1967). These principles would lead one to forecast that legislation of the voting-rights type could be administered relatively easily, whereas legislation proposing school desegregation would be much more difficult. In the latter case, as against the voting rights case, the significant differences are as follows: (1) the action which the black student and/or parent needs to take is not at all simple, (2) it is not clear when administrative officials are trying to comply and when they are "filibustering," (3) the officials are open to sanctions by white students and/or parents who prefer nonchange, and (4) the option of moving out of the school area or district means that a dip in segregation (as in Washington in the first half of the 1950's) is followed by "resegregation."

Perhaps this view is quite in error. But its correctness is not to the point. Rather, what is to the point is the necessity for *some* conception of what the conditions of administrability are, and an appraisal of the various sorts of substantive legislation with respect to those conditions. At a different level, one might desire consideration of the implications of new ways of thinking about policies. If elites are beginning to believe that programing-planning-budget systems are important bases for analyzing policy (Schultze, 1968), what should we expect this approach to do to consideration of racial issues? What effect should it have on the access and influence of black representatives? The same problem would be posed to the emergent idea of "social indicators" (Gross, 1969; Sheldon and Moore, 1968). Again, the same consideration would apply to new substantive ideas (as against the procedural ideas of programing-planning-budgeting or social indicators)? How will the decision-making autonomy of city governments be affected by the emergent national tendency to adopt national policies on land use, air transportation, or power plant siting? How will this tendency affect the power of black constituencies?

Trend analysis might go in still other directions. How should we expect the black communities of the urban North (or the urban South) to be affected by agricultural displacement? By white-collar unionism? By automation? Is it *true*—as many more radical blacks (and some less radical) believe, that the future economy holds no role for black people in large numbers? What *will* the pattern of interaction between black young people and their white counterparts be by the time they reach the stage of being apprentice rulers?

There are still other sorts of important problems. Consider the very serious need for understanding of the implications of *international* changes on the domestic arena. Is it true (as I believe) that international threat increases the likelihood that blacks will be defined as a "dangerous class" against whom special measures will be necessary and appropriate?[17]

Doubtless, someone else might choose different examples. But the examples are less important than the point that there is a serious need for an instrument of strategic assessment, which is what is here proposed. This instrument is conceived as supplementary to the earlier-discussed arrangements for monitoring and administrative activity, and to the urgent need for an emergency information network. All three should be regarded as part of the soundly based internal bureaucracy, requisite under the self-help concept. All three should, at least initially, be financed internally through revenue-establishing procedures (for which some suggestions have been offered) and should be linked to the collective-judgment process for which institutional suggestions (in the form of an Afro-American "general council") have also been made. As I conceive these, they are not claimed to be sufficient measures for all purposes, but they are necessary measures (and for some initial purposes sufficient) to revitalize the *understructure* of black political action. As I conceive that understructure, it would give point and practicality to the attitude of self-confidence which is also essential.

SUMMARY AND CONCLUSION

Serious attention to the real problem of black power, not merely to an emotive rhetoric of black power, surely depends upon a conception of self-help (or self-reliance). This is essential, but needs to be implemented by a regularization of the black "quasi government." Two considerations especially are involved in such regularization.

1. There is some necessity for a minimal level of collective economic

support, sufficient to sustain activity without excessive dependence on external allies. There is a similar necessity for technical support (knowledge) without excessive dependence on external allies.

2. It is essential to have some deliberative process (however formal or informal) for making rational judgments about what black interests require. If this cannot be achieved, then group interests and objectives are presented as merely whatever interests and objectives happen to be advocated in the loudest voice at the moment, and thereby are deprived of the moral authority which is needed to get members of the group actually to perform according to the implications of those interests and objectives. Moreover, "follow-through" is crucial. Interests and objectives, even if agreed, require some kind of administrative process for detailed, persistent, and consistent action. As outlined here, such a process implies an efficient emergency information network, a thoroughgoing procedure for monitoring the administrative process, and an institute for basic strategic assessment.

NOTES

1. There are two reservations about the "unity" principle. The first is that it has to assume that "the other side" is less unified. Thus, if *all* Jews in New York City voted for Jewish candidates (in opposition to non-Jewish candidates) and all non-Jews voted similarly for non-Jewish candidates, then no Jews would ever be elected. (This assumes, for the sake of the argument, that everybody registered, everybody voted, and that the distribution of Jews and non-Jews in the voting age range would be identical.) That is, one could have perfect Jewish unity and a complete Jewish defeat, simply because the city is less than one-third Jewish. If one prefers, one might substitute any other social labels. But "polarization" is complete when both sides are perfectly unified. Thus, in pursuing a unity strategy, one must assume that such a strategy will somehow tend to disunify the opposition. The second reservation concerns practical experience. The "unity" model is too often based on an assumed unity among other groups which does not exist. Even the Jewish community (probably the most unified in ethnic terms) is a cockpit of competition on many matters and the long-standing Jewish unity (merited or not) on the Israel question is beginning to crack.

2. In this respect, "self-help" suffered some reputational burdens (that is, it was made to seem "wrong" and "disagreeable") in the same manner that "economic development" did. But it is clear that black people are now largely over the economic vs. political hangup and recognize the interdependence of the two. In the same manner, there is a difficulty now in accepting the indispensability of "law and order," although one foresees that that difficulty also will pass.

3. From this viewpoint, political lobbying by petroleum producers in defense

of the oil-depletion allowance or by the Catholic Church in behalf of parochial-school aid are among the purest forms of self-help.

4. My guess is that relatively few nation-states in the world raise all their own revenues by their own taxation systems, without depending substantially on foreign loans or grants. However, this is a guess; and I have (in any correspondence with students of international economics and international politics) been unable to find an analysis of the situation.

5. It is an astonishing lapse that, in the summer of 1970, a great political controversy arose over New York City prisons in which none of the black organizations nor any of the black politicians seemed to play any important role. Instead, the point man on this venture was a *suburban Republican* politician. *Since this draft was written, we have had the Attica experience which makes the point even more forcefully!*

6. Breakthrough" is the present HUD effort to develop a mass-production system for housing.

7. An example of pertinent policies with no *obvioulsy* racial label would be airport-planning decisions and their relationships to the local governmental institutions.

8. My comments in this section (and in the preceding section on "monitoring") have been particularly influenced by conversation with James T. Harris, Jr., Benjamin F. Payton, William T. Patrick, Jr., and *particularly* Anna Arnold Hedgeman.

9. In this connection one might invite attention to the social science monographs produced by DuBois at Atlanta University in the early 1900's.

10. Miller, a mathematician, was also dean at Howard University. For a brief note on the "Sanhedrin," see Record (1951, 43).

11. In his *Autobiography,* W. E. B. DuBois is particularly critical of what he deemed the incapacity of his great adversary, Walter White, to appreciate the significance of genuine research. But one might see this opposition in other relationships as well, even now. The role conflict is comprehensible.

12. This argument was, in fact, laid out in a paper based on the Michigan experience (Holden, 1962).

13. In this respect, no major philanthropic foundation—despite much talk about social change—has even now shown little inclination to put its money where its mouth is. On the contrary, the foundation leaders have shown a distinct tendency to prescribe what activity blacks ought to undertake, in return for support, and have tended to make it clear that *their* immediate criteria of "relevance" would not include broad research and assessment.

14. As I have argued before, one reason that legal action has been so much more feasible is that there is (and has long been) something approximating a critical mass of lawyers in the black population.

15. There is, moreover, the practical difficulty that all too many people expect to see immediate payoffs from the use of such skills as they may possess, when fast payoff is simply not to be expected. They may even wish to exercise political leadership through such skills, when that is even less to be expected.

16. The formulation of black issues, in terms such that they become more compelling to the general world of social science, is also very important. Some of the issues and problems which are of practical importance to blacks are also of intellectual importance to social and behavioral scientists. These are often neglected because the intellectual relevance to the main interests of social and behavioral scientists has not been properly identified. *In this regard, the mission would be to inject black-related issues more fully into the major currents of academic analysis, by helping to restate those issues.* One might, for instance, regard the black community as an "underdeveloped economy," with special problems despite the fact that it is not *institutionally or territorially* separated from the larger economy with which it interacts. If this is a reasonable view, then economists might wish to examine the question whether it is feasible to adopt special policy measures to expedite the "growth" of this underdeveloped economy. (What kind of response would one get if people at the Yale Growth Center put their minds to it?)

17. This is an underlying thread in Essay VII of *The White Man's Burden,* "A Look at Medusa's Face." In order to see some of its implications imagine first that there should be a considerable respectability achieved for the view expressed by John Chamberlain that the United States failure to destroy Castro is now being translated into Castroite support for black militants in the United States (See his column as published in *The Chicago Sun-Times,* September 25, 1970.) Then ask what interpretation one might reasonably predict whites would tend to make or accept of two events: one, problems involving black troops in Germany (see *Chicago Sun-Times,* November 3, 1970, 8); another, the establishment of a Panther office in Algeria (see Gramont, 1970).

VII

The Next Five Years:
III. Modifying Political Tactics

THE DETENTE GAMBLE

Everything we say about black politics presupposes a more active role in the public decision-making process. In the immediately preceding essay, we have discussed some organizational options which might make the black "nation" stronger internally. In the same way, we have discussed some elements of a social program which would have the same strengthening effects. The discussion does not imply any wish to encourage some withdrawal strategy. The rest of the world is simply too big and too powerful for blacks to go off in some dream world by themselves.[1] Rather, the point is that both social program and organizational development are meant to enhance capacity for black political competition in a Great World. In order to enhance this capacity, the isolation of the black population must be reduced.

When one thinks of such a problem one is reminded of Bertram Gross's observation that while politics is "the art of the possible," people all to often constrict themselves by narrow perceptions of what *is* possible. Thus, one of the possibilities which is neglected—and to which the most serious attention must be paid—is a detente between the urban Afro-American population and the urban Euro-American ("white ethnic") population.[2] This attention is simply dictated by population structure. *Most of the cities over 500,000 (and even over 250,000) from the Mississippi Valley to New England and north of the Ohio River are composed mostly of Afro-Americans plus several Euro-American nationality-linguistic-cultural communities. By*

187

"Euro-American" I mean, specifically, those people descended from Eastern European, Central European, and Southern European immigrants—most of whom came into the United States after 1880. Other people figure importantly in various aspects of city life (for example, the Anglo-Protestants generally run the big-business sector). But Afro-Americans and Euro-Americans are the people who count when you look at numbers! Moreover, the fact of conflict between them cannot be denied. Its reality can be seen in many industrial plants, in many industrial unions, and in the borderline areas of "changing" neighborhoods.

If you have any two large populations in contest with each other, you don't get a peaceful situation until you somehow get them to extend diplomatic recognition to each other. A fundamental fact of politics is that nobody can really do much that is constructive and intelligent in any of the cities if he has to face the deep-seated and protracted resistance of either of these groupings. In this context, there is a fundamental gamble which blacks have to be ready to make within the immediate future. They have to gamble that they can prepare the ground for a detente, or—as Congressman John Conyers has put it—for "melting hostilities."

This expectation will be inescapable even if many more central cities come to have black majorities and black mayors, black council majorities, and black school boards. It will remain inescapable even as many more Euro-Americans move to suburbs.

Why so?

Because urban politics and social policy is more than city-hall politics. It is also state-house politics. The importance of state-house politics should be easily appreciated by a simple reference to public-assistance benefits. Although the ultimate recipients of public assistance money are not exclusively black, Spanish-speaking, or urban, they are heavily so. The level of their benefit depends on what *state* legislatures and *state* welfare departments do. The same point can be made with respect to urban health policy. The more the Comprehensive Health Planning legislation is implemented, the more urban decisions will be processed through state-level machinery. The same will also be true for policies regarding law enforcement and public order, the development of housing, and the control of education (child and adult, including manpower training). The importance of state-house politics will be acutely increased as the United States moves into some form of revenue sharing between the federal and the state governments.

Certain ineluctable realities have to be faced. One is that "one man, one vote," which many people think of as an urban (central-city) benefit will in the North increasingly be a suburban benefit. It is the power of suburban legislative representatives which will increase the most (and central cities will tend after a while to lose power simply because their total populations will be declining). What does "suburban" mean? It does not mean merely the bedroom communities of top-level Wall Street lawyers. It means preeminently the FHA- and VA-subsidized "tract" suburbs which provide housing for the low income white-collar and blue-collar migrants from the central city. That is to say, *it means the several Euro-American populations!* It means Hempstead and Staten Island as well as Scarsdale. When voting time comes in the legislature, those suburban spokesmen will be either "for" or "against" reasoned and progressive social policies. It would be foolish to increase their chances of being "against" by ignoring the problem here posed. If people interested in forward-moving social policies do not think about this upcoming difference, they will themselves increase the chances for a successful Northern version of the "Southern strategy." Indeed, there is already one wing of the Nixon administration which seems about to adopt this strategy and seems to believe itself on the trail of political paydirt. But I do not think this wing has a monopoly on the digging tools.

Those Euro-American communities are understood to be the central locus of urban resistance racial to readjustment. Yet there is no warrant for saying that they are more hostile toward blacks than is any other community, and there is some evidence that they may be a bit less so. According to recent survey data collected by Louis Harris, and released by the Urban League's Research Department, about "[h]alf of the native whites . . . compared to about two-fifths of the Irish, Italian, and Polish, believe that the push for racial equality has been too fast." (*Urban League News,* 1:2 [November 2, 1970], 8). Thus the idea that Euro-Americans are somehow peculiarly prejudiced, in a way that other whites are not, simply will not bear much thought or examination. The logic is commanding when one notices the racial exclusivism of upper middle-income residential neighborhoods, a fact which is not explained by the absence of potential black purchasers. For there are enough blacks who have had extraordinary difficulty making purchases to dispose of the idea that such exclusivism is a result of money differences. The reason these neighborhoods are instructive is that they are not neighborhoods where one finds many Euro-Americans. The same point could be made about hiring practices in the executive suites.

Indeed, Euro-American hostilities, real as they are, have been exaggerated, have been allowed to develop into a frightening mythology which few people interested in social policy dare challenge. The black man's problem is to master both the critical similarities and the critical differences between his experience and that of the several Euro-American ethnic groups, in order to discover whether an ethnic detente—and "diplomatic recognition"—may be possible. Similarity is frequently denied by black commentators, some of whom perceive (correctly) that comparisons to the Euro-American populations are usually meant to deny the legitimacy of present black claims. Other blacks deny similarity on the independent grounds which lead them to see themselves as unique. It thus behooves black strategists to make every effort to understand the perceptions of "white ethnic" communities and to understand the factual history which is (correctly or incorrectly interpreted) the basis upon which those perceptions rest. History is thus particularly relevant to present political understanding.

The most cursory knowledge of the derogatory view which American literature has taken of the immigrant populations cannot fail to call to mind Ossie Davis's speech, "The English Language Is My Enemy," wherein Davis explicates the synonyms of white and "virtue," black and "evil" in ordinary speech. If one views the Euro-Americans in this light, one concludes that they also, have an experience which leads them to be both "sensitive" and "ethnocentric." Moreover, people tend to speak of the "black poor" as *against* the "white affluent middle class." There is much reality in that categorizing but it is misleading to stop there. The practical mistake, and the analytical mistake, is to ignore the fact that although the Euro-Americans generally are "better off" than "Afro-Americans" they are *not incomparably* better off. Economically and psychologically, they feel profoundly insecure in the contemporary United States. It is reasonable that they should feel so. Not only have their values have been treated with all too little respect—as they might see it—but even their much-vaunted political progress is overrated. Detroit, which will almost certainly have a black mayor soon, has had but three Euro-American mayors in its history (Albert Cobo, Louis Miriani, and now Roman Gribbs); Chicago one (Anton J. Cermak); New York two (LaGuardia and Impelliteri); Boston and Pittsburgh none yet; Philadelphia none until the election of Frank Rizzo in 1971. Cleveland, where all the politicians talk ethnicity a good deal, probably takes the record, with four (Frank J. Lausche, Anthony J. Celebrezze, Ralph S. Locher, and Ralph J. Perk who replaced Carl B. Stokes). The earliest of these (Lausche) came to office in 1941.

One need not argue that the Euro-Americans are "utterly suppressed," nor even take the ridiculous position that they are in no respects better off than blacks. One need only argue that their over-all position is commonly exaggerated in the telling. I am quite sure that something like this also holds in the private sector. If one examined their advance beyond the white-collar jobs into the more central positions of industry, education, foundations, and the professions one probably would find that their progress has been much less rapid than public mythology suggests. I think it also likely that these peoples themselves understand these facts. To say or concede this is not, self-evidently, to adopt the ridiculous position that black movement forward should somehow be sacrificed to Euro-American needs. The point is, instead, that forward-moving social policies will be vastly enhanced when political leadership, *including the leadership of the social-welfare sector,* sets its mind to the creation of a broader urban coalition, encompassing blacks, Spanish-speaking peoples and Orientals where applicable, but also encompassing the great untouched reservoir of Euro-American political energy in the cities. I cannot emphasize too much that if this potential political energy is not recognized and related to forward-moving social policies, it will almost surely be absorbed into retrogressive policies based upon fright.

It is necessary to create linkages between Afro-American communities and Euro-American communities, so that the self perception of each can authentically be communicated to the other. It used to be that the Afro-Euro split was covered over because both groups were linked through (a) trade-union leadership, (b) party-organization leadership in the cities, and (c) liberal Democratic politics at the national level.[3] The trade-union experience probably merits closer study, since the unions had to bridge the gap at the time when management used to exploit it as a means of weakening the unions. To some degree they succeeded.

"Old-fashioned" party leadership is often credited by socioligists and political scientists as playing an integrative role. I disagree. My interpretation is that the dominant party leaders actually played off the subordinate ethnic groups (Afro and Euro) against each other, saying different things in different places, and dispensing just barely enough patronage and symbolic attention to hold both in line. But old-line politics also contributed to the present state of affairs by building up a backlog of resentment and unsatisfied demand on both sides, a backlog which is now rolling down upon them from both sides. "Liberal" Democratic leadership in national politics sought to smother the differences under a joint economic appeal ("grocery-bill liberalism") which pretended that the ethnic considerations simply were unimportant or irrelevant.

At this juncture, the sole institution which shows any sign of recognizing the importance of Euro-American ethnicity is the Roman Catholic Church, even if there may be doubts and debates about the precise departures represented in recent activity of the United States Catholic Conference. The question is: Are there other institutions with credibility and competence appropriate to such a role? Insofar as the answer is "yes," then it should be possible—beginning in a few strategic cities—to carry on quiet private conversations about the ripeness of the time for more direct exchange (perhaps on the model of the Black-Polish Conference in Detroit), and about the appropriate mechanisms for such an exchange. But this approach requires intensely good judgment. Nothing would be worse than to play copycat, repeating in any city a procedure from some other city without careful consideration of the local environment.

Diplomatic recognition is stabilized by joint interest and joint action. In each local area, there will be concrete situations lending themselves to "action" beyond the diplomatic first steps I have mentioned. I cannot speak about those now. But the important problem is also to begin establishing a nucleus of congressmen who perceive the joint prospect in Afro-Euro collaboration. It would be premature to discuss here how precisely to identify the potential members of such a bloc (although that problem can be faced in some other context). Instead, we may note at least two sorts of policy proposals which might contribute to the congealment of such a nucelus even within the next session.

The first is symbolic, but none the less important for all that. This is the Ethnic Heritage Studies Centers bill (introduced by Congressmen Pucinski, Hawkins, Conyers, and others). It was introduced as an amendment to the Elementary and Secondary Education Act. One might have reservations about the specific bill, but the general idea seems useful as an entry point. It proposes that the federal government finance certain teacher-training and curriculum development centers, the purpose of which is to introduce ethnic diversity into the elementary and secondary schools. It is obvious from reading almost any social studies textbook or history textbook that Poles or Italians are as much neglected as blacks, and with similar psychological consequences. The significance of the bill, precisely, is that it marks the first overt recognition that there are joint Afro-Euro concerns which can be facilitated by Afro-Euro congressional action.

The principle can be extended, much more importantly, into economic policy. The administration's "blue-collar" task force has not yet developed specific policy proposals, but merely a kind of "background study." What is *now* important is to develop proposals which would serve the interests of working-class families and individuals of both races. To do this is to widen the base of political support, well beyond the narrow base of *public assistance* policy, and to increase congressmen's incentives. (Congressmen have a natural interest in proposals that have a wide scope. Once these come up, the administration has a much harder time bringing in a less-acceptable proposal, just as it had a harder time with its own voting-rights proposal simply because a different precedent had already been set.)

Finally, "there's different strokes for different folks," a wise comment which points to the specialists who deal with industrial leaders. Large corporations used to play off black workers against Euro-American workers in an open competition. To do this is no longer possible, *without serious industrial loss*. There may be some merit in considering the role of the National Urban League in mobilizing major industrial interest. For if the black vs. white ethnic conflict grows, not only will blacks suffer and white ethnics suffer, but so will the firms themselves. (See, the July 1970 *Fortune* which contains hints of this already.) Consequently, it is very much a part of the interest of the firms to facilitate both internal policies and public policies which are conductive to our purposes as here stated, and social-welfare specialists have some role in helping to make this interest clear.

THE PROBLEMS OF ELECTORAL POLITICS

If favorable governmental decisions are to be achieved, in forms and on a scale suitable to the necessities described in these essays, it will be essential to put electoral politics in its proper perspective. The first step is to cease the plaintive litany "[electoral] politics doesn't work for black people." That view is manifestly wrong, and is not believed by many who state it; otherwise the advocates of this view could logically propose only abstinence from electoral politics. Rather, the basic point is that the trade-off process involved in the exchange of votes for favorable governmental decisions is too slow (and covers too narrow a range) relative to the needs of the occasion. It is not that the process does not work, but it works all too badly.

Moreover, the electoral process is neither sufficient by itself, nor has it any politically sophisticated population ever regarded it as sufficient by itself. The basic rationale for electoral politics, insofar as policy is concerned, is that desirable policies will emerge when there is a clear identity between the interests and values of the elected and of those who elect them.[4] This rationale also requires, of course, that those elected come into command of the appropriate public resources.

In reality, the conditions just described can be met sometimes in local government, but very seldom in metropolitan area or State, not to say national, politics. Thus, the second version of black power is the capacity to use the vote strategically, that is, to shift among alternative candidates and parties. The rationale for this is that the political party[5] will not usually pay much attention to any constituency X if party leaders believe—rightly or wrongly—that all but a trivial proportion of the X vote will go to the other side in any case. The party will try to appeal to X, once it gets the idea that the X vote could be large enough to make some difference and could, practically speaking, be "available." The probability that a party will be responsive to the demands of some constituency is dependent on party leaders' estimates that the constituency under consideration may be available as a potential contribution to the party electorate. The responsiveness of the party will be further dependent on its estimates of the probability that: (a) the constituency—having been gained as a part of the party electorate—may drift toward the opposite party; and, (b) such responsiveness will drive off other actual or potential parts of the party electorate which may be more valuable, or which are already deeply entrenched in the party-as-organization. In practice, the best one can say is that the range of permanent and ineradicable commitments must be kept to a minimum (unless, of course, there is ample evidence that those to whom one has the commitments view them with as much reciprocal attachment).

What has been presented is nothing more than the basic idea of "balance-of-power" politics which is practiced by all sorts of people. Business interests, for example, provide financial support to candidates and parties (by one route or another), but they do not provide such support continuously, if they perceive that such support fails to serve the interests they prefer. In the same way, electorates (as in the case of labor) sometimes define their interests in such a way that party or candidate X can count on support, but only if interest Y is advocated by such party or candidate. This conception of balance-of-power politics has persistently run through the black "nation" for most of the years since the Civil War, but the conception has seldom been made operational and practical. Black Republicans in the North adopted this language in the nineteenth century, but provided no real examples of how to perform. Similarly, W. E. B. DuBois recurrently argued the logic of balance-of-power politics in his swing to the support of Bryan and of Wilson, to the support of LaFollette in 1924, and to his support of Henry Wallace in 1948. But, again, he was able to provide no real guidance on making balance-of-power politics effective. With the black swing to the Democratic party, since the late 1930's (or 1940 at the latest) many publicists have adopted balance-of-power doctrine. But blacks have actually ended by providing support to the Democrats—regardless what the Democrats did or failed to do.

There is a fundamental rule about balance-of-power politics. *Those who would practice such politics must have no permanent and ineradicable commitments, hence no permanent and ineradicable enmities.* (Thus greater flexibility vis-à-vis the "white ethnics" is important.) Such a model, however, is not useful if adopted as an ideological proposition or a secular article of faith. It is purely tactical. Another model which will make more sense in many contexts has the objective of acquiring a strategic position within the organizational decision-making process of the major political parties. Political influence does not require that one be a "majority" in a demographic sense, but only that one discover those points at which one's organizational resources can be concentrated.

Institutionally, how might blacks proceed? There can be no single answer, but only an answer which depends upon the specific features of local situations. The greatest likelihood of influence in state and national politics will, frequently, come through penetration of the regular party mechanisms. The reason is that it is through the party mechanism that one has the greatest chance to do the two consequential things following: (a) establish some definition of one's own interests as part of a broader political ideology, and (b) acquire entry not only to electoral positions (legislative and other), but, *even more important,* develop entry into the "political" aspects of public administration, which is where the center of government in the United States is *and increasingly will be!*

From the point of view of national and state politics, the objective is to achieve a position similar to that which the Irish Democrats achieved between World War I and the Korean Conflict. That is, the objective is to become sufficiently critical a minority that no one could expect the party to perform successfully without the assent of that minority to the party's organizational decisions. The Irish occupied a position within the party which did not satisfy all their interests, but which did provide them with powerful leverage on many important matters. They could enforce some of their interests upon convention decision makers, for instance, and be assured that if convention decision makers reneged after the fact, there would be an inevitable day of reckoning. This experience also has local implications, for a great many congressional districts will be electing (as only a dozen now are) black Congressmen. To control local party machinery is to assure the likelihood of their renomination until they acquire sufficient seniority to become key members of the congressional decision structure (which, thus far, but two members have).

The strategy of seeking to control local party organizations—likely to be more important than the strategy of seeking to control local governments if one must compare the two—probably makes the most sense in Democratic politics, since so many black people are already Democrats and in the practical circumstances of any given election are likely to adhere to their normal party identification. (It would in principle be better if they were more disposed to penetrate the Republican party as well, since this flexibility would increase the Republican incentive to pay attention to their interests and diminish the Democratic incentive to take their continued adherence for granted. However, this maneuver is not quite likely to occur, so long as the Republican party is deemed—and acts as if it were —essentially inhospitable.)[6] The idea of a *national* black party is likely to be unproductive or, at the least, to jeopardize too many relationships which it might be better to cultivate. But third parties can be useful and effective in localized situations and under special conditions.

However, this emphasis on *penetrating* a party, which is not the same as merely *voting for* that party[7] should not constitute a doctrinaire objection to essentially black *third*-party politics. The common belief among social scientists is that the presidential sweepstakes is so important that political participants have to coalesce into *two* opposing sides in order to enhance their chances. There is much to this argument, although it is open to some criticisms.[8] But those who are not themselves directly in the presidential sweepstakes do not have to be bound by this tactical dictum.

Third-party mechanisms will also prove relevant in at least two kinds of situations where blacks cannot expect to dominate the party within it. The reasons may be demographic (as when the blacks are too small a fraction of the whole electorate) or may be institutional (as when the blacks simply face too much opposition from already intrenched partisans. This strategy may prove to be particularly important in some parts of the South (Alabama for instance), if Republican strength stabilizes and the remaining white Democrats prove unable to accept the intraparty consequences of black participation. In that event, a multiparty politics would become a basic bargaining game.

Insofar as the urban North is concerned, the utilization of the minor-party device is potentially important to the extent that it increases black power within the major parties and increases the disposition of black politicians to use for socially relevant purposes such power as they accrue. It is apparent that such black politicians have been and will be, more cautious than their fellow blacks outside the party organization. Indeed, they have, with rare exceptions, stood outside (or even opposed) the black ferment unless it were self-evident that not to join would be suicidal.

Many objectives and strategies of the civil-rights activists have seemed utterly unreal to the major-party black politicians, and they have thus been unresponsive to new claims. Here the ultimate "economics" of politics— the necessity to allocate time, energy, and attention—is crucial. Like other decision makers, they tend to rely on the familar, and lack both inclination and time to search for signs of latent pressure. Even those who have better knowledge, and some degree of shared "feelings" with the activists, are likely to be inhibited by the present realities of party power. As professional politicians, they share the same "practical" and "realistic" judgments to be found among their white colleagues. While idealists may speculate about the power which black politicians will have in 1980, when more cities have black majorities, the realists of the present have to invest much of their time and effort in short-term tactics if they are to be politically alive next year.

This short view is not simply a tendency of black politicians, but an expression of the natural tendency of *partisans to become so absorbed in the logic and rewards of the party-as-organization* that they pull away from the group interests in behalf of which they sometimes have moved into party action in the first place. It is perfectly natural for a *farmer* Republican or a *labor* Democrat, as he becomes more deeply engaged in party management, to become a farmer *Republican* or a labor *Democrat*. In the same way, people who move into party politics out of ethnic considerations also may be moved to emphasize their partisan obligations more openly than their ethnic obligations. Obviously, they will try to avoid a divergence if they can, but it is not always possible to avoid it. Since the party has some immediate capacity for granting or withholding rewards, this tendency will be reinforced, which is precisely what one sees in the party-cum-ethnic politics of Chicago, where the party leaders in the most volatile black wards also closely associate themselves with the interests of the regular organization.

Indeed, parties as they are presently known could not operate, were it not for their ability to absorb and mitigate the demands of the various pressure groups, the elites of which tend to become part of the party's dominant "coalition."[9] However, if a particular pressure group is (as blacks are) in an extremely disadvantageous position, the effect of party absorption of its "representatives" is rather negative. Thus, the group needs some means by which to enhance its claims upon such "representatives." The essentially black local party will sometimes strengthen the black major-party politician's incentives to increase his own pressure upon his white colleagues. He is probably not unwilling to increase such pressure, provided he can get away with it. But if, in fact, he cannot show that there is a demand from his constituency, and cannot protect himself against the retaliation of his white colleagues, then he is more likely to go along with whatever he can tease, bluff, or persuade out of them. The function of blacks in the local party, thus, is partly to increase the black major-party politician's sense of the need to be more aggressive. It is also to give him assurance and protection, by providing his white colleagues with objective evidence that there is some politically realistic demand with which they have to contend. Such white colleagues will perceive that evidence, though reluctantly, if the black minor-party activity actually has disequilibrating effects of the major parties.

The principle can be seen, clearly, in the 1970 gubernatorial election in New York State, leaving aside entirely the senatorial election. Mario Procaccino's defection to Governor Rockefeller and Rockefeller's assiduous cultivation of the Italo-American vote during the campaign will almost surely reinforce the political leverage of the Italo-Americans in Democratic politics over the next several years. The same principle is potentially applicable in other situations, including presidential elections. For instance, the Democrats often win the presidential vote in Illinois by small margins, but the fact that the winner takes all the Electoral College votes makes the Illinois popular vote critical. Consequently, the Democrats would be very much jeopardized if there were a third party in Illinois which threatened to divide the vote so that the Republicans would win. If such a party were to emerge, it would become at once the object of solicitations from the Democrats (fearful of its effect) and of encouragement (probably undercover) from the Republicans (hopeful of its effect). In short, one is concerned with the practicability of nonideological, calculated, spoiling third-party politics of the same type which George C. Wallace adopted. Such a party activity might well be conceived—without valid objection—as essentially "black," at least to the degree that the Liberal party of New York is primarily Jewish and the Conservative party primarily Catholic Irish and Catholic Italian.

This conception of the importance of electoral politics does not at all suppose that the electoral process is sufficient by itself. That supposition is naive in the extreme. Rather, it maintains that the electoral process is important, but that the difficulty which must be overcome is the extreme stickiness of the trade-off process between voting (and party participation) on one hand, and the receipt of favorable governmental decisions on the other. To be *serious* in this conception, then, those who speak of "black power" can really have only one practical meaning. They must mean to focus on the conditions of political success, under conditions where there is strong opposition, some of that opposition coming from people who are more accustomed to winning than to losing. Political success requires some ability (a) to take care of one's own needs without external assistance —although recognizing that this cannot always be done; (b) to confer upon (or withhold) from allies the benefits or incentives which determine their alliance; (c) to impose penalities of some sort (of which physical often are the least pertinent) upon adversaries, but to abate them when that is rational; or, (d) of course, to manipulate both benefits and penalties in such a way as to induce neutrals to move in one's direction.

FROM LOCAL OFFICE TO STATE-FEDERAL POLICY SYSTEMS

As part of a movement beyond collective psychiatry, it is also useful to seek a broader perspective on the limitations as well as the values of *local* office. Except for congressional seats, nearly all the offices for which black competitors have entered have been local, be they county positions, school boards, mayoralties, or whatever. This competition for local office is important. Office is one of the symbols of control. To achieve offices previously reserved for others is to demonstrate one's own political manhood. This effect is equally well understood in places as dissimilar as the city of Cleveland and the small Mississippi town of West Point. Not only is the conquest of local office psychologically valuable,[10] but it may have more practical and wordly values.

First, competition for local office is itself a form of political education, variously for the seekers of office, for those who participate actively in their campaigns, and for those who are the audiences to which an appeal is made. This very process increases the reservoir of persons with political competences formerly less plentiful. Second, the conquest of local office has some definite potentialities for policy influence, particularly in such matters as law enforcement. Southern sheriffs have traditionally been the plantation owners' agents and the allies of white supremacists. The probability that a black sheriff will act as the white plantations owner's agent is less than the probability that a white sheriff will do so. It seems equally valid to believe that where Northern mayors are black the police departments will be constrained to see their roles differently. Similarly, judges in local courts have considerable discretion and in all good conscience may exercise this discretion quite differently, depending on their social values and connections. Hence, awareness of possible social connections and experiences is highly pertinent. One might well imagine that a black judge, known for constitutional strictness, would handle some cases involving "revolutionaries" somewhat differently than would some of his white colleagues. Third, as I have pointed out in Essay V above, there are circumstances under which a perfectly proper and legal use of discretion about local expenditures can be used to facilitate some forms of black economic development. Fourth, when the local offices controlled are at least fairly significant, they provide an incentive for some whites—who would otherwise be at some remove—to seek some rapprochement they would otherwise be less energetic about seeking.

STATE-HOUSE POLITICS AND LOCAL GOVERNMENT

Nonetheless, if we are serious about social change, we must also pay mature attention to the limitations on local government and to the importance of seeking strategic entry into state-federal policy systems. Consider first the state relationship. Assume a medium or large, black-governed city in a midwestern or eastern state.

If there is extreme state-house opposition to city officials' way of doing business, several important possibilities immediately are available. The state legislature can restrict the city's taxing power, make mandatory those expenditures it prefers, impose limitations on personnel management as it sees fit, or even go so far as to reorganize the city government—to the extent of withdrawing powers and vesting them in other bodies which the electorate within the city cannot control. This kind of maneuver has frequently been the occasion for the creation of "special districts" or "special authorities," institutions publicly justified as providing a particular service more "efficiently" or "rationally," but which may also come into being as a way of controlling city policies to which state officials object.

This modern version of "ripper" legislation is a far more serious threat to effective government in the central city than is metropolitan government, which I think blacks reasonably, but unnecessarily, fear.[11] New York's recent experience shows something of how this process may operate, even without racial connotations. Some very important effects on its land use and economic development policies arise, not from any decisions of the city but from the decisions of the Port of New York Authority—an effectively autonomous agency—relative to airport management, to bridge, tunnel, and terminal operations, and to the development of the World Trade Center in Manhattan. Another such decision is the present plan to build a rail link between downtown Manhattan and John F. Kennedy Airport—a link which would serve air passengers, but not necessarily ordinary New Yorkers—in cooperation with the Metropolitan Transportation Authority. Yet in theory the function of the MTA is to plan and operate a "coordinated" transportation system for the New York Metropolitan region, starting with its base in the New York City subway system. MTA, whose chairman (a former political secretary to Governor Rockefeller) is a member of the Port Authority Board, is successor to another "authority" which came into being when the City of New York was seeking state funds in the 1950's. "The Transit Authority was established in 1953 over the objections of the Mayor and other city officials when the Governor and the state legislature insisted that this was a preferable alternative to granting the city new taxing authority to meet the deficits of transit operation" (Sayre and Kaufman, 1960, 323). The background of the Old Transit Authority, of which the MTA is an enlarged version, was that the (predominantly) Republican state government insisted that all costs be met out of earned revenues (which implied a fare raise). The Democratic mayors of New York found it politically more agreeable to maintain a low fare, grant raises to the transit workers—with whose union leadership they were politically allied and which they wished to help defend against intraunion challenges in the late 1940's and early 1950's.[12] They could not do these things without state subsidies, which furnished the leverage permitting the state to insist on moving to the "authority" structure.

New York City has recently seen itself (that is, its incumbent administration) defeated in a fight to prevent the establishment of a somewhat similar organization in the housing field, in the form of the Urban Development Corporation, a state agency whose head is chosen by the governor; and a less autonomous version has been created in a Health and Hospital Authority, demanded by the medical profession to replace the old city departments and to reduce the city government's budgetary control over health and hospital activities. This kind of problem affects not only a politically weak administration such as Lindsay's, but even a politically strong local government such as that of Cook County, Illinois. Within the past year, the usually powerful president of the County Board found himself in a dispute with the professional staff of the County Hospital. Early in the game, he insisted (and accurately) on defining the issue as "who is in control of the hospital?" In the end, he found himself utterly defeated, forced to seek rationalizations to cover his retreat, as the professional staff, in alliance with metropolitan newspapers, the governor, and the governor's party in the legislature won a clear decision that authority would be placed in a special commission favorable to themselves, rather than in the County Board.[13]

Such relationships are developing in many aspects of the city state interaction. They should acutely concern blacks now, lest blacks find themselves inheritors of offices and titles substantially bereft of power. That this power shift could occur seems the more probable simply because it is the suburban areas which will inevitably—by the sheer combination of demographic trends, the constitutional effect of "one man, one vote," and virtually automatic reapportionment—come to dominance. Conflict between central-city and suburban interests will be natural in any case, and some racial problems will exaggerate that conflict. This effect has already been seen in the educational politics of New York State, where it was legislators from the New York City suburban area who pushed antibussing legislation, and might well become an issue in the future politics of public order. I should think that state efforts to assume control over the city police forces would be a relatively early move. It seems very likely that many suburban residents with central-city property interests will want a different enforcement style than will city governments in which black residents have a considerable sway. The fact that these suburban residents will in many cases have still some remaining relatives in the cities will be a factor, as will the fact that many policemen will themselves have become suburban residents, to whom their local legislators would be somewhat responsive.[14]

But the limitations on local power go beyond the state-house relationship. More to the point, still, the kinds of policies which such local governments may adopt are primarily fiscal, rather than economic. The controllers of such local government, be they black or white, would have relatively little capacity to increase economic resources. Without these economic resources, there will be relatively little capacity to improve the material welfare of black populations. Consequently, one caution is that a concern with the acquisition of local and even state office should not be permitted to obscure the ultimate importance of federal politics. There are two overlapping aspects of an attention to federal politics: attention to Congress and attention to administration.

CONGRESSIONAL POLITICS

As important as the presidential quadrennial is, it can never be forgotten that the other side of federal politics is Congress. Accordingly, activity in black politics should be directed not only to the initial election of congressmen but further to the problem of minimizing those effects which would lead to a great deal of turnover in black congressmen. Even if, as is by no means assured, the formal rules of seniority are relaxed, influence in any collective body (Congress among them) is going to be concentrated most among those members who have been there the longest and acquired a certain experience and respect. Therefore, to the extent that black congressmen are sacrificed/replaced, as soon as they falter on some ritual test of "blackness," to that extent will the whole group of black congressmen be relatively inexperienced and ineffectual. Moreover, in particular communities and districts, blacks will have to make—if they are to serve their own interests—far more discriminating judgments about white members of Congress. It is not merely that they will need to be more alert to the deficiencies of congressmen who "sound right" at campaign time, but that they will also have to be alert to the political needs of white congressmen who do have some political incentive to be helpful.

Imagine, for instance, the House Banking and Currency Committee. The committee is pertinent because it handles housing legislation and much banking legislation. Thus, it has influence over two areas which interest blacks: housing policy in the cities and the potentialities of federal support for black economic development. As with most committees, the decisions it reaches are partly influenced by lobbying at some given moment. Some lobbying is pressure, in that it means to induce a congressman to support what he is inclined to oppose. But much lobbying is persuasive, in the sense that it brings to the member's attention considerations of which he is not aware—considerations that he would be disposed to take into account if he knew about them. Thus, in dealing with Banking and Currency, black political strategists would be wiser to determine which members of the committee are—in any event—politically untouchable and to ignore those. The task then is to learn which members of the committee might be committed to housing and development policies preferred by blacks. If that were learned, the pertinent organizations might then do everything possible to inform the black constituents of such members (where relevant), in order to yield political support in the intent to establish future political debts for the member.

As another technique, it would be useful if organizations having need to deal with Congress were to inform themselves more intensively about the nature of the congressmen's constituencies. Congressmen are responsive to other considerations beside constituency demand, but constituency demand is extremely important. If black lobbyists knew, as few do know, which of all the congressional districts have significant black populations, how those populations are organized, what they do for a living, how much schooling they have, what kinds of black splits and agreements exist within those constituents, and so on, it would then be possible to make far more useful judgments about how to exert influence in Washington.[15] Such procedures are not panaceas, but merely some among the many practical methods which can be used in preparing Congressmen to be receptive and in exerting influence at moments of decision.

BUREAUCRATIC-ADMINISTRATIVE POLITICS

The other major aspect of federal level politics is the need for a vast improvement in the practice of administrative politics by blacks. *Adminis-*

tration is so fundamental an element of governance that those who are unsuccessful in penetrating the administrative process are very unlikely to get what they need or want. It is the ultimate "guts" of government.[16] In a "rule" which one derives from the late Paul Appleby: "policy" minus "administration" is nothing: $P - A = 0$. In government, there is a constant necessity to scan the horizon, to collect new information, to put together bits and pieces of knowledge in the planning of policy. Legislation plays some role in this, but the essential role here is—and historically has been—administrative rather than legislative.

In addition, the legislative process almost always leaves ambiguous policy decisions which have to be clarified (resolved, interpreted) by administrators. One reason is that almost any important problem has some ramifications which cannot be spelled out in a statute. The other is that since a legislature represents many diverse elements, the chances of getting legislative agreement are enhanced if the sponsor can find some ground on which some of the diverse elements can agree, even though underneath they may mean rather different things.

Once a statute is adopted, however, implementation requires specific action which is somewhat less ambiguous—although the ambiguity can seldom be removed entirely. Because implementation depends on specific administrative choices, those groups successful in penetrating the administrative process are likely to achieve a good deal of what they want, and those unsuccessful in penetrating the administrative process are likely to achieve relatively little of what they want. This penetration is particularly important in United States politics, where policy changes occur mostly by disjointed incrementalism rather than by large-scale revisions of policy. This incremental process means decision detail by detail and it is in the administrative process that such decisions are likely to be made. If the administrator in charge of policy happens to be incompetent to act within those rules, or simply does not want to act, or is under great pressure not to act, then the policy is likely to be undermined and even completely negated. The old situation remains and the new situation does not come into existence. Hence, he who would have his vital interests protected must intervene in the administrative process. The adroit administrator has considerable ability to manipulate his program in such a way as to serve those constituencies which he perceives as relevant and legitimate, and it is the necessary task for any constituency which would be taken seriously to establish itself in such a position of visibility before the administration. For it is through the day-to-day interventions of administrators that policy outcomes are so shaped that broad mandates are followed, ignored, or wholly controverted. In the emergent Integral State, where *decision making* is increasingly centralized and "public-vs.-private" distinctions decreasingly meaningful, administration is more important than ever.

Federal policy is restricted, much more than the occasion warrants, because the agency staffs are populated by those who have not directly shared any part of the black experience and who usually fail to ask the racially relevant questions. Probably, high-level and middle-level decision makers, as well as those who advise them, suppose themselves to be sufficiently perceptive in these matters. Yet one may be permitted doubts. How else could one explain that three former chairmen of the Council of Economic Advisers and one outside scholar (Nourse, 1953; Heller, 1966; Okun, 1970; Flash, 1966) discuss the Council's work with no special mention of blacks? This might once have been reasonable, but it is questionable now when keeping inflation within "acceptable" limits implies policies adverse to the reduction of ghetto unemployment. It seems rather important to be sure that the CEA considers other options which might serve both the anti-inflation objective and the ghetto-growth objective. For example, it would obviously benefit the ghettoes if the United States might, like the Germans, get close to a zero unemployment rate. But how might this be done within the limits of "acceptable" inflation? Is there anything in economic policy which *might* be done and is not now being done?

The symbol of black exclusion is the White House staff itself. Until the Eisenhower administration, no black executive was on that staff at all. And Mr. Morrow, who came to serve President Eisenhower, had so little influence that he could barely get a secretary. Since then, every administration has had some black staff, but no President has yet permitted black staff to enter his central advisory group.[17] But the pattern is merely symptomatic of the federal bureaucracy to below the bureau chief level.

Black strategists have understood this principle, as they have shown when they have argued for, and criticized the relative absence of, blacks at the "policymaking" levels of the federal administrative establishment. One cannot be naive about these matters. A black man as assistant secretary in, say, the Department of Transportation will hardly do all the things which avant-grade "militants" prefer, nor should he. He is, after all, an officer of the *United States* government and appropriately has to have a broader sense of responsibility. But things are much more likely. The first is that field representatives are much less likely to be cavalier about the relocation problems associated with highways if they must report through such an assistant secretary. The second is that he is more likely, simply as a function of past social experience, to be alert to racial considerations in the policy of his department than will a randomly chosen white alternative appointee. Closely associated with this expectation is that he may have more reason to be alert to the possibilities of implementing what is after all the policy of the government than might be a randomly chosen white.

There is a further, and absolutely critical, element of bureaucratic participation which merits understanding. No executive appointee, no senior bureaucrat, automatically represents the "interest" with which he has, in the past, been most identified merely because of that past identification. The bureaucratic enterprise contains its own incentive which impose directions and constraints upon the functionary. Thus, it is fatuous to expect that a black functionary will automatically "represent black interests" or that, if he attempts to do this he will automatically be effective, without some external relationships. The bureaucracy, like the Congress, depends on constituency relationships. In addition to knowing what the issues and relationships are at a given moment, it is also essential to be able to offer the functionary both criticism and support. Without these, his presence is merely symbolic. With them, his presence is likely to be of value, for he thus becomes a figure of some power in his peer level relationships to others who do not have in mind the same considerations that he does.

The idea of securing a vastly expanded black presence in administration is but one part of the process. The idea is also present in the previous discussion (above, Essay VI) of the need for a more complete monitoring operation. In monitoring, however, there is still a further point. It is necessary to be aware that decision making may be rather centralized, despite the system of federalism; that much that is "relevant" does not have a black label upon it—and that much of what has the black label is likely to be trivial in its potential significance. These two considerations are closely related to each other. It is true that federal officials can seldom make valid and binding decisions on New York in the way that (at least theoretically) British officials can make such decisions without the acquiescence of local officials in Scotland or Yorkshire. But there are some instances where they can. For instance, harmony and disharmony in a community may be profoundly affected by the extent to which television stations are open to both sides or only one side of racial issues. The cases in which this is pertinent have involved no local officials, but rather the judgments of the federal courts as forums of appeal. But apart from these instances, there are still few local policy decisions which do not, at some point, require the engagement of federal decision makers as well. This engagement is closely tied to the federal grant-in-aid system. Most local revenues are already committed to purposes which decision makers do not feel free to repudiate or modify. Consequently, while federal aid is only about one-sixth of all local revenues, it dominates *new* income for *new* purposes. Both the purposes deemed legitimate, and the means of their implementation, are very much influenced by the predilections of national administrative officials. Thus, to be specific, the pressure for "participation by the poor" in the Community Action Programs (OEO) was maintained by a steady stream of administrative directives from the OEO Washington office, directives often in conflict with what would have been the normal predisposition of local officials. Similar administrative inclinations are important to the federal grants for low-income housing and urban renewal, without which virtually no new construction would occur in most cities; for the implementation of federal health policies; for the administration of "law enforcement assistance" grants; and for almost all other major purposes.

Contemporary pressures force still other decisions of great local importance, over which local decision makers have relatively little control and about which black strategists have little reason to think. Consider airport siting and expansion. John F. Kennedy Airport lies along the southeastern edge of Brooklyn, into which black residents will increasingly be moving in the years 1970–1980. But that area will be one of maximum discomfort. It will lie within the heaviest zone of airplane noise. That noise will increase because the Port of New York Authority (the airport organization), the Federal Aviation Agency, and the Civil Aeronautics Board will all tend to support an increase in traffic. All these agencies are *relatively* immune to local electoral politics, have a different constituency in the airlines industry, and operate at a technocratic level invisible to most local citizens or local politicians. The federal role will be enhanced by still other decisions as the country moves to a national land use policy, a national policy on power-plant siting,[18] and implementation of the Environmental Protection Act of 1970.

Since the federal administrative role is so important, conflicting parties in the local areas are seldom willing to consider issues "closed" unless they have pushed them all the way to "Washington," or unless they anticipate that they would lose even on pushing these issues to Washington. In this sense, the whole country is drawn together in a series of vertical "policy governments" linking the specialists in each policy area more closely to each other, regardless of "level of government," than to specialists in other policy areas at the same levels. The net effect is to transform domestic policy into a series of separate games, from which most of which the elected local officials are excluded (or in which they have relatively low leverage) and into which they are constantly attempting—against considerable odds—to get.

Getting in calls for a more sophisticated appreciation of the very process by which ideas float about in the administrative works—before they emerge as policy, but well after the administrators have ceased to be entirely open to all ideas on the subject of policy. This process involves what may be called a kind of "policy analysis core" associated with virtually every aspect of United States government. Ideas float about for a considerable while until a kind of consensus in the technocratic policy-analysis core emerges, and thereafter all ideas which are not reconcilable with the consensus have great difficulty gaining acceptance. The policy-analysis core embodies another element of the Integral State, namely an intensive public-private collaboration in the conception, formulation and implementation of policies.

Moreover, policy analysis is a politics dominated by money plus a technocratic elite, and is largely invisible to most citizens, state politicians, local politicans, and even some substantial fragment of national politicians. Three examples will suffice. One is the idea that the specific way to break down racial barriers outside central cities (and the immediately adjacent decaying suburbs) is to exercise some form of federal preemption of local zoning controls. This rather startling idea has recently floated about among land use planners, land economists, lawyers concerned with the subject, and a few others. Its life history can be traced through a series of government documents which reflect its growing acceptance: the National Commission on Urban Problems (the Douglas Commission), merely said that this idea might be considered; the President's Committee on Urban Housing (the Kaiser Commission) specifically recommended it; and the Department of Housing and Urban Development, in 1970, began to try it out in a rather crude fashion. The idea of comprehensive health planning has floated about in the same way, as the idea of a national air transport policy is now beginning to. The various ideas about the appropriate national role in controlling crime have a similar developmental process.

The pertinent points are twofold. Once ideas have been absorbed into federal policy, they gain influence and prestige by the very fact of that absorption. State and local decision makers, let alone decision makers at the neighborhood ("community") level, find themselves able to maneuver, but mainly within the constraints imposed by such policies and ideas. Yet this process operates in such a way that most participants in the leadership systems of black communities usually do not notice their pertinence until issues have become public in the form of specific proposals. At this point, it is usually very difficult to do more than achieve modest amendments, which are often quite inappropriate to the objectives which blacks would have thought appropriate.

Members of the black middle class fail to play a useful role at this level, when they—out of some assumed sense of guilt—permit themselves to be browbeaten into withdrawal or negativism by the rhetoric of street-level populists, who have neither capacity nor opportunity to enter into the process being described. The problem is to establish a reasonable juncture between the kinds of problems raised by street level populists and the kinds of problems which are dealt with in the policy analysis core. Dichotomous choices are, in fact, merely misleading and not helpful.

If my interpretation of state and federal impacts on urban life is correct, then we need to consider how to penetrate state and federal policy systems. From this point of view, then, there is a clear role not only for a monitoring operation but also for a strategic assessment operation to serve the function of alerting black leadership to broad trends and the policy implications of such trends. Collective action ultimately requires competition in the governmental arena. The view here is that black collective action will be enhanced if the following are possible: (a) an Afro-American and Euro-American detente in the cities; (b) a more sophisticated balance-of-power electoral politics; (c) a clearer understanding of the limits of local office; and (d) a greater emphasis on bureaucratic politics. In the end, however, the effect of any rational strategy in black politics will depend on whites. What is the white capacity for rational adjustment? What would be necessary to turn that capacity into policy? And what policies seem necessary to create a viable politics of social peace?

NOTES

1. On several occasions in these essays, I have noted the importance of the scale of the world and its penetrating effects. One more illustration is the Fiat's total annual sales equal General Motors' annual profits. *New York Times,* Financial Section, February 7, 1971.

2. Ethnic groups are here *defined* as groups whose members are essentially recruited by birth and from which effective social withdrawal is *nearly* impossible. Such groups are "communities," in the sense that their members have a "strong sense of common history, commony destiny, and reciprocal obligation. Ethnic groups tend to encompass more than one social class level—even when outsiders cannot espy any class differentiation. Moreover, both members and outsiders tend to define group characteristics as if those characteristics were genetically transmitted, even though such characteristics may be clearly sociocultural and not genetic. (The case of Ulster Protestants and Ulster Catholics is a superb illustration of treating sociological characteristics as if they were genetically transmitted.)

By this conception, it is superficial and inaccurate to simultaneously define

"Italo-Americans" as ethnics but Anglo-Protestants as nonethnics. Each is as "ethnic" as the other. Moreover, I maintain that there is an implicit snobbery in the ordinary use of the term "ethnic," for it somehow implies that "ethnics" are merely those white people who somehow deviate from the "normal" cultural-political standards of the Anglo-Protestant population. That implicit snobbery has made it possible for social scientists (and others) to suppose that "ethnicity" was essentially abnormal, undesirable, and would in due course "disappear." Such estimates are wrong. Ethnicity is one of the fundamental bases of social organization and social division and is at least as persistent—and often more divisive politically—than social class.

3. Thus, G. Mennen Williams who, as governor of Michigan, commanded *wide and genuine* (as well as genuinely merited) support from black voters, was also a well-known figure at "ethnic" functions and served as head of the "Nationalities Division" of the Democratic National Committee.

4. There is also the function of elections as part of the public personnel system, proving some means of recruiting decision makers, but this is not under consideration here.

5. The situation will be a little different in nonpartisan elections, but the basic pattern probably is similar.

6. *The White Man's Burden,* Essay IV, "The Republicans: Historical Note on the Southern Strategy."

7. Discussed in *The White Man's Burden,* Essay VI, " 'Sticky' Trade-Offs and Urban Immobilization."

8. In all likelihood, the control of state-local election regulations and machinery by the Democratic and Republican parties has probably been much more influential in suppressing third parties than we have acknowledged. Hence, precisely as election administration becomes more honest and routine, and as the requirements for candidacies become less stringent, one might expect third-party efforts to be more frequent and more successful. Moreover, there is no law of nature which requires that ideological cleavage be bipolar instead of multipolar. The current tendency in American politics—an unhealthy tendency, perhaps—for more and more people to define politics according to their "principles" should encourage multiple party efforts, with the result that we may foresee some increased likelihood that more presidential elections will be settled by bargaining in the House of Representatives. (3) To the extent that the president is divested of control over *patronage,* and to the extent that "policy governments" arise in the mammoth federal bureaucracy over which he has less control than is frequently imagined, the incentives to depend on the presidency (and thus the control which this dependence gives a president) also might be expected to diminish.

9. This is developed in greater detail in *The White Man's Burden,* Essay VI.

10. This symbolism was explicitly recognized and discussed by a former SNCC worker who, in the summer of 1970, became a candidate for mayor in West Point. He lost. See the *New York Times,* August 2 and August 4, 1970.

11. There is no way to create a metropolitan government, in the ordinary

sense, without accepting blacks as part of the new electorate for the new unit. If Cleveland, for instance, were merged into a new metropolitan government also including the Cleveland suburbs, the new government would still contain a large black electorate. While such an electorate might have its power diminished, relative to its old-city position, it would still constitute a formidable and (under the circumstances) largely hostile bloc. Intelligent white politicians could hardly desire such a result, although they may blunder into it in one or two metropolitan areas. Once the consequences are clear, however, this strategy will not be widely emulated.

12. See Lincoln (1967) and Sayre and Kaufman (1960). For some additional insights into the wage politics of the New York transit system, see the portrait of Theodore Kheel in *The New Yorker,* August 1, 1970, 36–58.

13. An account of this dispute is being developed in Seth W. Norton, "A Working Note on Hospital Politics," manuscript in preparation as this writing began in 1970.

14. The historical precedents for this kind of move are several. One was the fact that, once the Irish became really important in Boston city politics, the Yankee interest managed to secure legislation putting the force beyond the control of the mayor and under the control of the governor. It so remained for 83 years. See Roger Lane (1967). Victor Jones and Samuel C. Jackson have also pointed out to me that ripper legislation was similarly applied to the police forces of St. Louis and Kansas City.

15. On the whole, this kind of approach to politics has been much neglected except in extreme crisis. For instance, I once spent more than a year trying to persuade members of a black organization's education committee—with which I was associated—that we should simply construct a matrix showing (a) each member of the House Education and Labor Committee, and (b) each member of the organization's education committee who had some personal contact, leverage, or influence with this member. The purpose of such a matrix would have been, at any moment, to permit the organization's leadership to discover what the possible points of initial and personal contact with the relevant congressmen were.

16. This is further examined in a paper in draft: Matthew Holden, Jr., "Administration: The *Central* Political Process," 1970 (available by request).

17. Observe the composition of the Nixon inner circle (*New York Times Magazine,* August 3, 1969, 6–7).

18. The New York city newspapers (July-August 1970) are particularly instructive on this, as regards a Consolidated Edison site in Astoria (Borough of Queens).

Postscript

The preceding essays express some biases which it may be well to set forth in this postscript. The central bias conviction of *black-white interdependency,* concerns politics itself. If politics is a power process, interdependency is its central element. People may be masters and slaves, firm allies, deadly enemies, or bargaining partners. But all of these are interdependencies. All involve the relevant people in a political system. Some of the hardest *political* problems come when, somehow, the very character of the relationships is changing, or even when one of the parties is trying to change those relationships.[1] So it is now with racial politics in the United States.

As a political system, the United States includes the two "sociocultural 'nations' " locked into each other, in a relationship which has historically been "imperial." Imperial, in that the white element has been *dominant* over the black element. The present question is one of encompassing black and white within a *republican* norm—within a political community or a shared moral order understood to be the common enterprise and concern of both its black and its white members. The problem of transforming an internal "empire" into a full-scale republic is that to which, given the bias noted, these essays have been devoted.

Most of the essays were written, off and on, between the summer crises of 1967 and the latter part of 1969, although the basic theme was formulated in 1964 and many editorial or substantive changes were made in 1970 and early 1971. In that interval, we have seen a dramatic rise of

213

public interest in racial issues. We have also seen an apparent decline in such public interest. One reason is that a country never lives its public life on one issue only. Environmental policy, the condition of the economy, the secular desecration which counter-culturists wreak upon older values of patriotism, responsibility, and enterprise, and the gloomy sickness of the Vietnam war all take their toll. Another reason is that people have come to see in racial politics a theatrical bravado—a melodramatic rhetoric, from blacks and from whites, which so far exaggerates reality that it should be treated no more seriously than political realists treat most "campaign oratory." The relative quiescence of 1970, the first apparently quiescent summer in five years, encouuraged this belief. But just as it is foolish for blacks to bluster beyond their capacity, so it is foolish for whites to believe that all that they hear is bluff. The underlying reality is still there, in such observable indicators as rising tensions in military installations and in high schools, or in the evident tendency for black professionals to withdraw from white contact, noisily if they wish to be regarded as "militants" and quietly if they simply think they have no choice. It is also folly to believe that reinforcing governmental coercion will somehow restore a previous quiescence. It might, indeed, do so, but only after a protracted struggle utterly beyond reason.[2]

There is another important bias. It is the belief that *rationality is supremely important to the achievement of desirable political results.* No one could doubt, of course, that politics is a profoundly emotional matter. Politics can become so emotional that conflicting groups may be willing to accept —almost, indeed, to provoke—mutual self-destruction. As hard as it is to find a logic-tight *definition* of rationality, it would be harder still to say that such behavior is rational. Rationality means, at the minimum, some understanding of what wouuld be sensible results (not perfect ones!) and some understanding of the necessary means of action to achieve those results.

Insofar as racial politics is concerned, there has been a near-moratorium on rational consideration. Some of this may be due to the belief that "the worst" is already past. But I think it more likely to come from intellectual and emotional paralysis, a paralysis born of a sense of incapacity to do anything useful and aggravated by preoccupation with other matters. That sense of incapacity arises from three remarkable suppositions, each of which I believe erroneous in important respects.

The first is that the present intense crisis is unique to this time, that "the system" *no longer* "works," with the implication that nothing in American history or social practice provides lessons for good judgment.

The second remarkable supposition is that the problem is somehow *unique to the United States* and related either to some moral flaw in "the

American character" or to the necessities of the private enterprise economy.

The third remarkable supposition is that the problem is peculiarly associated with contact between white peoples and nonwhite peoples. This view is clearly expressed by the emigré South African writer, Ronald Segal, who formulates the problem of racism as a global problem—observing (correctly) that there is no white-ruled state in which nonwhites live under conditions of equality and dignity (Segal, 1967). There is no one of these three statements in which one can fail to find some element of reality. Yet, as indicated, each obscures quite as much as it clarifies.

Consider them in reverse order. Segal's statement is perfectly correct yet so misleading that it provides no insight into useful solutions for our problems. First, the apparent implication of the Segal hypothesis is that states ruled by nonwhites are different from states ruled by whites in their treatment of ethnic minorities, a suggestion which would make it utterly impossible to explain the virulent conflict in countries (Guyana, Nigeria, and others) where none of the combatants are white.

The second implication of the Segal hypothesis is that *white ethnic minorities in white-ruled states* do not encounter problems comparable to those of nonwhite minorities. Again, the case cannot be sustained. If it were correct, we should not observe white-against-white religious communalism in Northern Ireland producing a Protestant quasi militia (the B-Special force) so large that a white-against-black equivalent in the United States would amount to 400,000 organized and armed men beyond the regular public forces.

Even when we deal with *white* racism, the most serious criticism of the Segal hypothesis remains. The hypothesis provides no clues into the development or the sources—and therefore no clues to the possible decline—of white racism. This is a noticeable failure, for one presumes that Segal is not arguing that white racism is biogenetic.

Moreover, nowhere in this world has ethnic diversity been easily reconciled with political order and equality (any more than extreme class disparities have been easily reconciled with political order and equality). These problems are more difficult when they are combined with the criteria of democracy, constitutionalism, and welfare statism. Politics like those of the Soviet Union, which neither pretend to nor desire the terms of democratic constitutionalism, have incorporated the welfare motif (in their own way), but the degree to which they have mastered the multi-ethnic problem is unclear (Armstrong, 1948, 3–49).

The Low Countries have their own persistent problems of ethnicity, despite their small-scale governments, although they also combine democratic constitutionalism and welfarism (Kelly, 1967; Lijphart, 1968; Lorwin, 1966; Schaper, 1960). Even the Scandinavian polities, so often deemed idyllic by United States standards, combining the welfare motif, democratic constitutionalism, and small scale, have recently discovered that ethnicity is not entirely trivial for them. This now becomes a problem in Denmark, it seems, with the importation of Turkish labor; and Danes wake up surprised to find their own version of emergent "racism."

Finally, it is not quite right to think of the United States as a tranquil, consensualized polity in its historical development. There has hardly been a period of more than a quarter century (and never more than fifty years) when the question of the stability of republican government has not been raised. While the Constitution was ratified and operative as of 1789, one could not count the republic even established until the Jefferson takeover of 1801 *demonstrated* that free elections and peaceful change of administrations *actually* were possible. (Moreover, we should not pass without noting that even this change involved an interference with the courts more drastic than anything which the Civil War or the New Deal brought forth, namely the legislation (in the Judiciary Act of 1802) under which sitting judges who had in no way vilated their oaths were displaced from the federal courts. What is even more, this was an act undertaken not by the contemporary "conservatives" but by the contemporary Jeffersonians, in their own political defense!)[3] The Hartford Convention, the Missouri Compromise issues, the South Carolina Nullification controversy, and the struggles after the Kansas-Nebraska Act raised still other questions, questions only answered by the military outcome of the Civil War. It is only since the Civil War that we have had no political insurrections (Rich, 1941). After that, the class war known as the "rise of the labor movement" went on for more than fifty years, with a level of violence which even the 1970's have not touched.

As a matter of intellectual honesty, it behooves us to try to get a better grasp on the issues. To do this is also a major practical necessity. If it all the trouble stems from capitalism, then all solution must depend upon the coming of some alternative economic system. If it all depends upon some global revolt of nonwhites against whites, then the black American population must be regarded as the historical lamb by which the nonwhite hunters of "the Third World" will catch the white tiger. But in that process, both tiger and lamb are destroyed.

Those who hold the three views contained in the remarkable suppositions build a psychological and political trap for themselves and for those who take their advice. No magical transformation of a situation from "bad" to "good" ever occurs all at once. Action has to be taken in pieces.

The practical problem is to choose the right pieces, to multiply their numbers, and to produce them in ever more rapid succession.

Under any of the three interpretations, any pieces of action which *could* be generated must also be defined as "trivial." If this view is correct, and any of the suppositions be adopted, confidence must remain at a low level, the *will* to face down danger must ever erode, and commentators must ever be reduced to woeful lamentation of the dire consequences yet to come. For this reason I avow a bias toward rationality.

Still another bias is a belief that *we need some strategic sense of what is at stake and how people might proceed.* I view the problem as one of *peacemaking* and maintain that the central issue in peacemaking is *reciprocal* deference. "Deference (means) being taken into consideration (in the acts of others and of the self)" (Lasswell and Kaplan, 1963, 55). Success in political reconciliation means the creating of means for the reciprocal sharing of deference and esteem between actual or potential disputants. This is not the same as incorporation of a new population into the older symbol system. It is the devising of new symbol systems common to both populations and which identify the "contributions" of each. I find at least some support for this view in Karl Deutsch's summary of the historical integration of several Euro-Atlantic countries:

It . . . seemed important that each [party] at least sometimes take the initiative in the process [of establishing a peaceful community], or initiate some particular phase or contribution; and that some major symbol or representative of each territory or population should be accorded explicit respect by the others. (Deutsch *et al.*, 1957)

The transformation of American society, from an Anglo-Protestant society to one on which Catholics and Jews (of Continental European background) play a significant role is a demonstration of the possible end product. Cultural pluralism is not some vague state of "good will," nor some appreciation of exotic food and folk dances. It is a recognition of the shift in the structure of society, and in the structure of deference within society.[4]

The requirement for such a shift is posed by the late Adlai Stevenson's observation that the essence of republican government is not command but consent. It is especially the consent of those who at some earlier time constituted the main respectable sources of resistance. Consent of this kind is one of the basic requirements of change in stable societies.[5] By "stable" societies, I mean those where (a) governmental institutions—particularly at the national level—have been operative without interruption for a long time; and (b) wide social agreement has also existed for a long time on whom the social constitution ought to encompass, and how new people should be brought in. Those who argue that power in the hands of the weaker is the most likely means to generate change are correct, but are grossly short-sighted when they stop with this statement. The initiation of "fairly" far-reaching change probably depends upon the obvious beneficiaries of such change,[6] but the confirmation of such change probably depends upon those who are not obvious beneficiaries, or even more upon those who have been disposed to resist.[7] There are only two other options: total victory when those proposing changes can entirely beat the resisters into unconditional surrender, or complete defeat for those proposing changes. The former option obviously does not describe a stable society, but a revolution. If neither option exists, and resisters do not at all yield, the struggle drags on ad infinitum. As illustrations note the following:

1. The position of factory workers, both in the internal government of industry and in the politics and broader social structure of the nation, clearly has changed since 1937. Moreover, it has changed in ways which industrial leaders before the mid-1930's would have often regarded as so "revolutionary" that they *thought* they would never agree to them. But they have agreed to those changes and those changes have become firmly embedded in the operative social constitution.

2. New Deal welfare statism grew out of the politics of the "have-nots," but the welfare state was confirmed only by the acceptance of the Eisenhower Republicans.

3. Government regulation of trade union practices began with the 80th Congress, but government regulation of trade union practices was confirmed by John Kennedy's role in the Landrum-Griffin Act and Robert Kennedy's policies as Attorney General.

4. Federal aid to all schools (including Catholic schools) was initiated by Catholic Democrats in Congress, but federal aid was confirmed by the policies of Lyndon Johnson and the American Jewish Committee's adoption of the child-benefit theory.

All these cases illustrate that people of some party X consider that fighting with party Y would be "bad" for them to do, whatever test of "bad" they should apply. This kind of consent does not mean immediate conversion, but the dissolving of prior certainty into ambivalence. That ambivalence may be grounded in moral preference, economic interest, military necessity, vote calculation or something else; and the new course of action develops as ambivalence is resolved. It does not necessarily follow that ambivalence will be resolved in favor of some accommodative action. People may go to the drastic extreme of trying to destroy the "enemy."[8] People already committed to, and satisfied with, one position *must become ambivalent and then resolve that ambivalence as they acquire a vision of new possibilities.*

The difficult process of joining separate groups places maximum emphasis on the catalytic function of leadership. *Leadership styles and ingenuity must somehow be brought to bear, though within certain limits* ("conditions" or "parameters") *which they can manipulate, but seldom wholly escape.* Broadly, these parameters are of two types. Attitudinal parameters ("values," "belief systems," and the like) are extremely important, and their interposition leads to results which would not be either predictable or rational if attitudes were not taken into account. Structural parameters are those (like "the economy") which tend to determine action even though the action is different from what ought to have been predicted from the actor's beliefs or attitudes.

Parameters cannot ever be safely neglected. Leaders or elites who make these judgments must try to interpret ("sell") them to those followers who could upset the necessary arrangements. But political leaders are not mere prisoners of circumstance, bound to one and only one course of action. When their deals can be achieved, and maintained for some reasonable time, the *de facto* effect is to create a sort of "treaty" arrangement. That is, the deal between the parties requires some presumption of longevity, though not of permanence. At this point, the interests of leaders themselves become terribly important. If the exchanges between the sides result in gains and institutions which the leaders of the sides think valuable, leaders will begin to concentrate on maintaining those gains and institutions. The more they do so, the more they come to have some increased moral appreciation of their counterparts on the other side. One may speak here of elites, with divergent followers of bases of support, having internalized the values of joint action with their counterparts (and having internalized *the values of those counterparts*). Their role in generating and sustaining new visions of "the possible" and "the desirable" is so important that it can comfortably be compared to the role of Machiavelli's prince, engaged in creative intervention in chaotic situations to produce new forms of order. The emergence of the active political community, including the diverse groups, is the end result which sometimes follows.

The most troubling aspect in the Republican crisis in the United States is that there has been at least a temporary (hopefully, not a permanent) cessation of major efforts by political leaders to establish some form of social truce, and to lay the groundwork through which that truce may be developed into a stable social peace. Clearly, my view is that this leadership paralysis must be broken, and the next five years are the critical "turnaround time." It would indeed be appropriate to act so that 1976—the second centennial of the Declaration of Independence—might be celebrated by the birth of a Second Reconstruction, beginning to undo the dammage wrought by the ceremonial killing of the First Reconstruction in 1876. Whether white people have the psychological and cultural capacity to begin so decisive a break with the burden of their history is naturally questionable. But if there were no capacity for adjustment, the United States would already be in far worse condition then it now is. Instead of clear determination, there is a profound ambivalence, ambiguity, and confusion.[9] It is, I argue, yet possible to overcome the ambiguities which white Americans experience on the subject of race, to crystallize the desire for forward movement, and to turn that desire into workable policies. The problem is to find practical options for resolving that ambivalence, ambiguity, and confusion in a direction favorable to Republican government. Practical action seems to me most important, for this purpose, in three major realms: the political economy of racial adjustment; short-term threat reduction, with a particular emphasis on urban arms control and disarmament; and, major institutional modification. Measures of the sort described[10] may be "radical" in their departure from standard suppositions. They may also be "conservative" in the sense that they indicate the realistic prices which it is worthwhile paying to stabilize the United States as a political community.

Neither label is important.

The result is.

NOTES

1. Obviously, we have to recognize that one (or more) parties may wish to change a relationship and may fail in the effort to do so.

2. *The White Man's Burden,* Essay VII, "A Look at Medusa's Face."

3. The Judiciary Act of 1801 created a set of federal judgeships which President Adams filled at the last minute before leaving office. The Judiciary Act of 1802 repealed the Act of 1801 and put these judges out of office, contrary to the life-tenure provisions of the Constitutions, and so amended the Supreme Court's calendar as to make it practically impossible for the issues involved to be brought to litigation. For two accounts of this pair of Acts, see Warren (1923, I, Chapter 4) and Ellis (1971, 33–68).

4. The admission of "labor men" to the Community Chests' boards of directors, in the past thirty years, is a sign that *these formerly excluded are no longer excluded.*

5. The politics of change in stable societies probably deserves at least as much attention as the politics of change or the politics of stabilization in unstable soci-

eties, both of which latter have received considerable attention from students of the Third World nations.

6. I will not try to define "fairly," but I do mean that (a) change which totally revolutionizes the society (as in the Chinese case after 1949) is not here being considered; but that (b) the change which we have in mind must have at least some major structural consequences.

7. The general proposition is based in part upon Coser (1969).

8. It is also possible that the ambivalence will so paralyze them that they can do nothing, which is the extraordinary case of primitive uncertainty. In this case, people neither "know what they want", nor how to "make things turn out right," nor even what "right" is. (Holden, 1965a)

9. This argument is laid out in *The White Man's Burden:* Essay III, "Racial Politics as a Study in Paradox," and Essays VIII and IX on "Public Opinion and Everyday Behavior."

10. Particularly in Essays X–XII of *The White Man's Burden:* "Some Possible Measures toward Social Peace."

References

Ake, Claude. *A Theory of Political Integration.* Homewood: Dorsey Press, 1967.
Armstrong, John A. "The Ethnic Scene in the Soviet Union: The View of the Dictatorship," in Erich Goldhagen, ed., *Ethnic Minorities in the Soviet Union.* New York: Frederick A. Praeger, 1968, 3–49.

Benedict, Ruth. *The Chrysanthemum and the Sword.* Boston: Houghton Mifflin Company, 1946.
Biderman, Albert. "Social Indicators and Goals," in Raymond Bauer, ed., *Social Indicators.* Cambridge: MIT Press, 1967, 111–129
Boulding, Kenneth. *Conflict and Defense.* New York: Harper and Brothers, 1960.
Bracey, John H., Jr., August Meier, and Elliott Rudwick, eds., *Black Nationalism in America.* Indianapolis: Bobbs-Merrill Co., 1970.
Brink, William, and Louis Harris. *Black and White.* New York: Simon and Schuster, 1967.
Brink, William, and Louis Harris. *The Negro Revolution.* New York: Simon and Schuster, 1964.
Burck, Gilbert. "There'll Be Less Leisure than You Think." *Fortune* (March 1970), 82–89 and 162–166.
Bureau of Labor Statistics, United States Department of Labor. *Black Americans: A Chartbook.* Washington: U. S. Government Printing Office, 1971.

Caliver, Ambrose. *Education of Negro Leaders: Influences Affecting Graduate and Professional Studies.* Washington: Federal Security Agency, Bulletin, 1948, No. 3.
Carmichael, Stokely, and Charles V. Hamilton. *Black Power.* New York: Random House, 1967.
Chesnutt, Helen M. *Charles Waddell Chesnutt: Pioneer of the Color Line.* Chapel Hill: University of North Carolina Press, 1953.
Coser, Lewis A. *Political Community and the North Atlantic Area.* Princeton: Princeton University Press, 1957.

Cruse, Harold. *The Crisis of the Negro Intellectual.* New York: Morrow, 1967.

Dancy, John C. *Sand against the Wind.* Detroit: Wayne State University Press, 1966.

Deutsch, Karl W., *et al. Political Community and the North Atlantic Area.* Princeton: Princeton University Press, 1957.

Drake, St. Clair, and Horace R. Cayton. *Black Metropolis,* rev. ed. New York: Harper and Row, 1962.

DuBois, W. E. B. *Autobiography of W. E. B. DuBois.* New York: International Publishers, 1969.

Eldridge, P. J. *The Politics of Foreign Aid in India.* London: Weidenfeld and Nicolson, 1969.

Ellis, William W. *White Ethics and Black Power.* Chicago: Aldine Publishing Company, 1969.

Erikson, Erik H. *Young Man Luther.* New York: W. W. Norton and Company.

Feis, Herbert. *Foreign Aid and Foreign Policy.* New York: Dell Publishing Company, 1964.

Festinger, Leon. *Conflict, Decision, and Dissonance.* Stanford: Stanford University Press, 1964.

Flash, Edward S. *Economic Advice and Presidential Leadership.* New York: Columbia University Press, 1966.

Flax, Michael J. *Blacks and Whites: An Experiment in Racial Indicators.* Washington: The Urban Institute, 1971.

Fleming, Robert W., and Murray Edelman. *The Politics of Wage-Price Decision.* Urbana: University of Illinois Press, 1965.

Fox, Stephen R. *The Guardian of Boston: William Monroe Trotter.* New York: Atheneum Press, 1970.

Frazier, E. Franklin. *Black Bourgeoisie.* New York: Free Press, 1957. New York: Collier Books, 1962.

Frazier, E. Franklin. *The Negro Church.* New York: Schocken Books, 1962.

Friedman, Neil, Agatha White, and Edgar G. Epps. *Attitudes of Southern Black College Students toward Black Consciousness and Integration.* Tuskegee: Division of Behavioral Research, Carver Research Foundation, Tuskegee Institute, January 1970.

Friedman, Saul. "Race Relations Is Their Business." *New York Times Magazine,* October 25, 1970, 44.

Fry, John R. *Fire and Blackstone.* Philadelphia: J. B. Lippincott Company, 1969.

Garfinkel, Herbert. *When Negroes March.* New York: Atheneum Press, 1969.

Garraty, John A. *The Barber and the Historian.* Columbus: Ohio Historical Society, 1966.

Geyl, Pieter. *History of the Low Countries.* New York: Macmillan Company, 1964.

Gramont, Sanche de. "Our Other Man in Algiers." *New York Times Magazine,* November 1, 1970.

Grier, William H., and Price M. Cobbs. *Black Rage.* New York: Basic Books, 1968.

Gross, Bertram M., ed. *Social Intelligence for America's Future.* Boston: Allyn and Bacon, 1969.

Hamilton, Walter Hale. *The Politics of Industry.* New York: Alfred A. Knopf, 1957.

Handler, Joel F., and Ellen Jane Hollingsworth. "How Obnoxious Is the 'Obnoxious Means Test': The Views of AFDC Recipients." Madison: Institute for Research on Poverty, University of Wisconsin, Discussion Paper, January 1969.

Handy, W. C. *Father of the Blues.* London: Sidgwick and Jackson, 1957.

Hannerz, Ulf. *Soulside: Inquiries into Ghetto Culture and Community.* New York: Columbia University Press, 1970.

Heller, Walter. *New Dimensions of Political Economy.* Cambridge: Harvard University Press, 1966.

Holden, Matthew, Jr. "Reapportionment and Legislative Output." Paper presented at the Faculty Seminar, Michigan Center for Education in Politics, December 1962.

Holden, Matthew, Jr. "Committee Politics under Primitive Uncertainty." Midwest Journal of political Science, 9:3 (August 1965), 235–253. (1965a)

Holden, Matthew, Jr. "The Republic in Crisis," in Reza Rezazadeh, ed., *Symposium on Civil Rights.* Platteville: Wisconsin State University—Platteville, 1965. (1965b)

Holden, Matthew, Jr., "Legislation, Power, and Opportunity: The Civil Rights Case." Paper prepared for the United States Conference on Church and Society, Detroit, Michigan, October 22–26, 1967.

Holden, Matthew, Jr. "The Quality of Urban Order," in Schmandt and Bloomberg, 1969.

Holden, Matthew, Jr. *The White Man's Burden.* San Francisco: Chandler Publishing Company, 1972.

Hughes, Langston. *Fight for Freedom: The Story of the NAACP.* New York: Berkley Publishing Corporation, 1962.

Imari, Brother. *War in America.* Detroit: Malcolm X Society, 1968.

Jacob, Philip E., and James V. Toscano, eds. *The Integration of Political Communities.* Philadelphia: J. B. Lippincott Company, 1964.

Jones, A. H. M. *The Herods of Judaea.* Oxford: Clarendon Press, 1967.

Jones, James E. "Equal Employment Objectives of the 1970's." Address to the NAACP Freedom Fund Dinner, Madison, Wisconsin, May 8, 1970.

Kellogg, Charles Flint. *NAACP.* Baltimore: Johns Hopkins Press, 1967.

Kelly, George A. "Biculturalism and Party Systems in Belgium and Canada." *Public Policy,* 26, 316–357. Cambridge: Harvard University Press, 1967.

Kennan, George F. *Democracy and the Student Left.* Boston: Atlantic-Little, Brown, 1968.

Kilson, Martin. "Political Trends in the Black Community in the 1970's." Paper presented at a conference under the auspices of the American Jewish Committee's Conference on Group Life in America, May 22–24, 1970.

King, Martin Luther, Jr. *Stride Toward Freedom.* New York: Ballantine Books, 1958.

Ladd, Everett C., Jr. *Negro Political Leadership in the South.* New York: Atheneum Publishers, 1969.

Lane, Robert E. *Political Ideology.* New York: Free Press, 1962.

Lane, Roger. *Policing the City.* Cambridge: Harvard University Press, 1967.

Lasswell, Harold D. *Power and Personality.* New York: W. W. Norton and Company, 1948.

Lasswell, Harold D., and Abraham Kaplan. *Power and Society.* New Haven: Yale University Press, 1963.

Lerner, Daniel J., ed. *Evidence and Inference.* Glencoe: Free Press, 1958.

Lewis, David. *King: A Critical Biography.* New York: Frederick A. Praeger, 1970.

Liebling, A. J. *The Earl of Louisiana.* New York: Simon and Schuster, 1961. (2nd ed., Baton Rouge: Louisiana State University Press, 1970)

Lijphart, Arend. *The Politics of Accommodation.* Berkeley, University of California Press, 1968.

Lincoln, Albert L. "The New York City Transit Strike: An Explanatory Approach." *Public Policy* 16 (1967), 271–292. Cambridge: Harvard University Press, 1967.

Long, Norton E. *The Polity.* (Charles Press, ed.) Chicago: Rand McNally and Company, 1960.

Lorwin, Val R. "Belgium: Religion, Class, and Language in National Politics," in Robert A. Dahl, ed., *Political Opposition in the Western Democracies.* New Haven: Yale University Press, 1966.

McCain, Rea, *et al. Forty Years in Politics: The Story of Ben Pelham.* Detroit: Wayne State University Press, 1957.

Macaulay, Stewart. *Law and the Balance of Power.* New York: Russell Sage Foundation, 1966.

McKay, Claude. *A Long Way from Home.* New York: Lee Furman, 1937.

Meier, August. *Negro Thought in America.* Ann Arbor: University of Michigan Press, 1966.

Miller, Walter B. "Violent Crimes in City Gangs," in Thomas R. Dye and Brett W. Hawkins, eds., *Politics in the Metropolis.* Columbus: Charles E. Merrill Books, 1967.

Muse, Benjamin. *The American Negro Revolution.* Bloomington: Indiana University Press, 1968.

National Advisory Commission on Civil Disorders. *Report.* New York: Bantam Books, 1968.

Norton, Seth W. "A Working Note on Hospital Politics." Manuscript in preparation, 1970.

Nourse, Edward G. *Economics in the Public Service.* New York: Harcourt Brace Jovanovich, 1953.

Nowlin, William F. *The Negro in American National Politics.* Boston: Stratford Company, 1931.

Okun, Arthur. *The Political Economy of Prosperity.* Washington: Brookings Institution, 1970.

Osofsky, Gilbert. *Harlem: The Making of a Ghetto.* New York: Harper and Row, 1966.

Ovington, Mary White. *The Walls Came Tumbling Down.* New York: Harcourt Brace Jovanovich, 1947.

Paige, Glenn D., "The Rediscovery of Politics," in John D. Montgomery and William J. Siffin, eds., *Approaches to Development.* New York: McGraw-Hill Book Company, 1966.

Palamountain, Joseph. *The Politics of Distribution.* Cambridge: Harvard University Press, 1955.

Parish, John Carl. *George Wallace Jones.* Iowa City: State Historical Society of Iowa, 1912.

Perloff, Harvey S. *The Alliance for Progress.* Baltimore: Johns Hopkins Press, 1969.

Poinsett, Alex. "Dr. Charles G. Hurst—Mastermind of Malcolm X College." *Ebony,* March, 1970, 29–38.

Polsby, Nelson W. "The Institutionalization of the House of Representatives," *American Political Science Review,* 62:1 (March 1968).

Postgate, Raymond. *The Life of George Lansbury.* London: Longmans, Green and Company, 1951.

Raskin, A. H. "He Leads His Teachers up the Down Staircase." *New York Times Magazine,* September 3, 1967, 4–5.

Record, Wilson. *The Negro and the Communist Party.* Chapel Hill: University of North Carolina Press, 1951.

Redding, Saunders. *The Lonesome Road.* Garden City: Doubleday and Company, 1958.

Rich, Bennet M. *The Presidents and Civil Disorders.* Washington: Brookings Institution, 1941.

Rose, Richard E. *Governing without Consensus.* Boston: Beacon Press, 1971.

Rosenau, James N. "Pre-Theories and Theories of Foreign Policy," in R. Barry Farrell, ed., *Approaches to Comparative and International Politics,* 65–71. Evanston: Northwestern University Press, 1966.

Ross, Arthur M., and Herbert Hill, eds. *Employment, Race, and Poverty.* New York: Harcourt Brace Jovanovich, 1967.

Sayre, Wallace S., and Herbert Kaufman. *Governing New York City.* New York: Russell Sage Foundation, 1960.

Schaper, B. W. "Religious Groups and Political Parties in Contemporary Holland," in J. H. Bromley and S. H. Kossman, eds., *Britain and the Netherlands.* London: Chatto and Windus, 1960.

Schmandt, Henry J., and Warner Bloomberg, Jr., eds. *The Quality of Urban Life.* Los Angeles: Sage Publications, 1969.

Schuchter, Arnold. *White Power/Black Freedom.* Boston: Beacon Press, 1968.

Schulze, Charles L. *The Politics and Economics of Public Spending.* Washington: Brookings Institution, 1968.

Seale, Bobby. *Seize the Time.* New York: Random House, 1969.

Segal, Ronald. *The Race War.* Baltimore: Penguin Books, 1967.

Sheldon, Eleanor E., and Wilbert E. Moore, eds. *Indicators of Social Change.* New York: Russell Sage Foundation, 1968.

Shonfield, Andrew. *The Attack on World Poverty.* New York: Vintage Books, 1962.

Silver, Allan. "The Demand for Order in Civil Society," in David J. Bordua, ed., *The Police*. New York: John Wiley and Sons, 1967, 2, n. 3.

Skolnick, Jerome. *Justice without Trial*. New York: John Wiley and Sons, 1966.

Stone, Lawrence. *The Crisis of the Aristocracy*. Oxford: Clarendon Press, 1965.

Strickland, Arvarh E. *History of the Chicago Urban League*. Urbana: University of Illinois Press, 1966.

Thompson, Daniel, *The Negro Leadership Class*. Englewood Cliffs: Prentice-Hall, 1963.

Thompson, Leonard M. *Politics in the Republic of South Africa*. Boston: Little, Brown and Company, 1966.

Torrence, Ridgely. *The Story of John Hope*. New York: Macmillan Company, 1948.

Uya, Okon E. *From Slavery to Public Service, Robert Smalls, 1839–1915*. New York: Oxford University Press, 1970.

White, Walter. *A Man Called White*. New York: Viking Press, 1948.

Wicker, Tom. "Special Introduction" to *Report of the National Advisory Commission on Civil Disorders*. New York: Bantam Books, 1968.

Wilson, James Q. *Negro Politics*. Glencoe: Free Press, 1960.

Wohlstetter, Roberta. *Pearl Harbor: Warning and Decision*. Stanford: Stanford University Press, 1960.

Younger, Carlton. *Ireland's Civil War*. New York: Taplinger Publishing Company, 1969.

Index

229

The White Man's Burden

I

The Crisis of the Republic

THE TWO "NATIONS"

When the Kerner Report held up to public view the specter of "two societies," separate and unequal, some commentators assumed that to be dramatic exaggeration, and most thought it mere forecast. In reality, the Kerner Commission neither exaggerated nor (though it seemed to think contrarily) offered a mere forecast. Instead, it actually described both the past and the present, the sole element of forecast being that there was some danger that this would be intensified in the future. As Disraeli could speak of rich and poor as "two nations" in nineteenth-century England,[1] so it is even more appropriate so to speak of white and black in twentieth-century United States.

The term "nation," when applied to a part of the United States population, is likely to be emotionally disturbing to many, so averse does it seem to textbook notions of "one nation indivisible." But by the term "nation" we need not mean either a separate territory or a separate government. Instead, we mean a sociocultural grouping which constitutes a *moral community,* the persons within which evaluate each other as *legitimate* fellow members whose presence and participation is valuable in itself. The "others" are not merely outsiders, but are sufficiently "alien" that they ought to be outsiders and could not ever properly be considered as potential fellow participants. The development of separate "nationhood" in this sense is the natural consequence of "frontiers," both physical[2] and nonphysical. If "frontiers," physical or otherwise, persist for a long time, the

1

people contained within them will evolve rules for their own association and also rules for interpreting the behavior of the "aliens." In anthropological terms, they will develop some common culture. Since culture is learned and transmitted in cohorts, it also follows that when different cohorts are rigidly separated (as any "average" set of black youngsters and any "average" set of white youngsters are), cultural difference develops and is reinforced over time. *In the black-white case, this was, and is, the natural command of segregation, particularly the forms of segregation so intense that one may call them "unofficial apartheid,"* a form which did not come under really serious challenge until very recent years. (See Essays III and IV, below.)

The frontiers between black and white are not primarily physical, although the existence of black belts in the South and urban residential segregation in the North gives them a physical dimension. But they are just as real, being present in individual behavior and in all kinds of institutions from the corporation to the medical society to the church. The separate development of a black "nation," with some noticeable differences in culture, internal social organization, and quantitative social welfare was simply an inevitable consequence. There is no suggestion that the cultural difference between black and white is absolute. To suppose so would be silly, for cultural difference could not be absolute if two populations must have a good deal of exchange and overlap. Thus, some part of the black population has an *almost* entirely white culture and a good deal of black culture has penetrated into the white system. Nonetheless, the differences are important,[3] as one may observe by comparing black entertainers on television, black clergymen, the styles of "grass-roots" activists, or black political organization against their white counterparts. One must indeed note that the difference between "standard" black and "standard" white is at least as great as the difference between Italo-American and Anglo-Protestant, or that between citizens of Irish and North European descent. (See Levine, 1965; see also James Q. Wilson, 1964.) In the same way, there is a social (institutional) framework which stretches across the entire United States, linking black settlements in places as far apart as Minneapolis and Georgia, Oregon and South Carolina, Kentucky and Massachusetts, even when the local participants in this network do not necessarily have strong links to their local white counterparts. (*The Politics of the Black "Nation,"* Essays I and II.) There is no better vindication of the "two-nations" proposition than the long-term tendency for the material welfare of whites *en bloc* to remain well above the material welfare of blacks *en bloc*. One need not be a statistician to calculate this difference. Anyone who wishes to take the *1970 New York Times Almanac* can carry out the same exercise. For he will find that on all the indicators of things which most people regard as good (income, schooling), blacks get about 50 to 66 percent of their proportionate share. On all the indicators of things which most people regard as bad (unemployment, infant mortality, capital sentences), blacks tend to get at least 50 percent more than their share, if not still more. The employment problem gives us one specific instance. The dreary fact that black unemployment rates run upward from 175 percent of the white rates has been shown so often, and by so many observers,[4] that we need not explore it again here. Unemployment figures (as defined by the Bureau of Labor Statistics) include only *completely jobless persons who say they are actively looking* for work. But "unemployment" figures *do not reveal the full extent of the problem.* They neglect what some scholars call "subemployment." This means "those who say they have *stopped looking in despair,* those who have *poorly paying part-time jobs,* and those able-bodied adults in the ghettoes *who have simply 'dropped out'* " (Altshuler, 1967; emphasis additional). Figures on subemployment are extremely hard to get. But in 1967, the Bureau of Labor Statistics con- ducted an experimental survey in which they tried to get reasonably adequate figures. In the eight cities which they surveyed, the subemploy- ment rates were *three to four-and-one-half times* the official unemployment rates.

There is also a viewpoint from which black population is somewhat comparable to an underdeveloped economy, with too limited supplies of capital. Traditional "Negro business" has been a sort of peasant enter- prise, smaller-than-average in size, necessarily charging higher-than-aver- age prices, and earning smaller-than-average profits. Even the enterprises which within the black community are deemed "big" are actually quite small in the context of the national economy. As of the mid 1960's, in all the United States there were twenty black-owned banks.[5] The average assets of a black-owned bank were about $5.6 (Brimmer, 1966, p. 300). The average United States bank was slightly under five times as big (with assets of $25.8 million). When one takes account of the big banks in the cities, as a part of the total assets of all banks, it turns out that all the black banks held *two-one-hundredths of one percent* of all bank assets. Moreover, this ratio points up the weakness of the black-owned banks, at least in the urban North, in another way. These banks (eight in Northern six cities) (Editors of *Ebony,* 1966 *Negro Handbook,* 218), have to compete for busi- ness in the service areas of some of the biggest banks in the Federal Reserve system—in Chicago, New York, Philadelphia, Los Angeles, Washington, and Kansas City. If one moves over to the insurance industry, which is easily conceded to be the citadel of black capitalism, it appears that the twenty largest black-owned companies, with assets of $811 millions or most of the black-controlled assets in the industry, hold just about *one-fourth of 1 percent* of all assets controlled in the insurance industry of the United States (Brimmer, 1966, 309).

In these economic matters, and in nearly all other quantifiable relationships blacks in any part of the country may be separated from whites in the same part of the country. Richard Scammon, when Director of the Census, had the habit of coloring census tract maps with one color (say, green) to represent areas of high education and income, and another (say, red) to represent areas of high black settlement, and so on. To a visitor one day, so it is reported, he said he had never found a city where the red and green touched (Wattenberg, 1965).

The distinguishability of the two nations is a basic fact of politics. An equally basic fact is their interpenetration, even in the biogenetic sense which purportedly distinguishes a "white" man from a "black" man. It is obvious that a substantial number of "blacks" look "white" (and most have some non-African ancestry), while a substantial number of "whites" could easily be taken for "black" in any part of the city where "whites" do not normally appear, and no one knows how to calculate the substantial number of people with "black" genetic ancestry who have long since "passed" into being "white." But the interpenetration is far more extensive in politics, in the economy, and particularly in the military.[6]

Interpenetration poses the political problem particularly if one observes the elemental facts of demography. The demographic pattern must be clearly understood, for almost every expressed political strategy assumes some particular population pattern. For instance, the original school integration strategy assumed the pattern of legal segregation and assumed a demographic pattern in the South where white and black students, though occupying homes near each other, were quite artificially separated for purposes of school administration. In contrast, it was only after the fact that people began to appreciate the genuine significance of racially segregated neighborhoods in the urban North, where the tradition of the "neighborhood" school had more impact. We must once more regain a sense of the importance of demography, for the black "nation"—taken as a whole—links the Southern bands and the islands and islets of the urban North into a *social* system. Whatever is put forth as strategy or policy affects the social system across the whole country, and similarly affects the white social system across the whole country. In the former Confederacy, there are wide bands of black and white spread adjacent to each other. In the Mississippi case, for instance, there are regions (notably the Delta) in which for miles on end whole counties have black quantitative majorities, with scatterings and islets of white residents. There are other regions (such as the hill counties of northeast Mississippi) in which the white-to-black ratios are reversed, and blacks are few or nonexistent. There are still other counties, in large number, where very sizeable black minorities (25 to 40 percent or 45 percent) coexist with white neighbors. The rest of the country is rather different in the sense that it has its most highly concentrated black islands in the large cities, surrounded by white urban and rural populations, as in the case of Detroit relative to the rest of Michigan or of Chicago (about a third black) to the rest of Illinois. Outside these large cities, there are smaller but still sizeable black islands in the smaller cities, but their ecological relationship to whites is similar to that of blacks in the larger cities. There is a quantitatively insignificant proportion of the black population which, whatever its social connections to the rest of black United States, is physically scattered in almost imperceptible ways. Such is the case for blacks in the Upper Midwest or the Great Plains, once one gets outside the cities of Milwaukee or Minneapolis-St. Paul or Omaha or Des Moines. The demographic pattern is not likely to change very much, except that the urban islands will grow somewhat larger and the black proportions in the *rural* South may grow somewhat smaller. There is no likelihood that either white or black will make any voluntary decision to change the space it occupies, except that individuals may decide to move from one place within the United States to some other place within the United States, decisions which will be affected (under ordinary circumstances) mainly by changes in the economy. There is no likelihood that any number of persons, large enough to make a difference, will voluntarily cease to occupy some physical space *in North America*. This is the fundamental political fact, for it necessarily forces people to adjust somehow or other to people unlike themselves with whom they cannot escape contact, direct or indirect.[7] Dissimilar peoples who cannot escape each other's presence must adapt either by mutual adjustment (which may include ignoring each other) or by some order of dominance (the effort to establish which may result in the fight to the death). To put it another way, the question of black-white relations is a question of the political necessities imposed by demographic (and other) facts. How many two conflicting "nations" relate to each other in a defined physical space called "North America"?

The problem is accentuated by scale. If, by some miracle, blacks were physically removed into a separate nation-*state,* the new unit would have a population twice the size of Algeria or Ceylon, the Netherlands or Tanzania, and four times the size of Ulster and the Irish Republic combined. It would exceed that of Argentina or Yugoslavia, Burma or East

Germany, Canada, or North Vietnam by anything from 20 to 40 percent. These imaginings point up factors whose size and complexity make more difficult the problem of intelligent action, a problem which will be sufficiently difficult in any event merely because of the burden of hatred and conflict which is the offspring of racial history in the United States.

THE SOCIAL CONSTITUTION AND RACISM

If people would overcome the fact of two "nations," with the attendant political strains, they would also be obliged to deal with the *operative social constitution* (or, as synonym, the *aggregate* rules-of-the-game)[8] expressed in the body of common beliefs, practices, and operational commitments by which the society runs.[9] It is through the social constitution that people allocate physical security, material welfare, and symbolic deference, which themselves may be thought the goods over which political strife occurs (Lasswell and Kaplan, 1963). It is by thinking about the social constitution that people may come to terms with the idea of the United States as a "racist system." This idea proves remarkably troublesome in conversation or serious analysis. Part of the reason is that the term has moral tones of deprecation and suggests something wrong with the white man as an individual. But that connotation is largely beside the point. The concept of a racist system no more asserts that every white man is a racist than the concept of capitalism asserts that every man is a capitalist. It would perhaps be clearer and less threatening if we spoke of "racial hierarchy," for the point is to note a certain systemic fact: that there are interlocking and self-sustaining social patterns which have the persistent effect of depressing a particular racial population.[10]

Racism is the social principle which sets race as the first test of "merit" under the social constitution, or sustains racial hierarchy. It specifies that in any relationship, the man of one race is always and inevitably to have the advantage and the man of some other race to suffer the disadvantage. We can properly describe a system as racist if the social constitution provides for race as a basis for purposeful discrimination, if persons are treated unevenly when "normal" criteria would lead us to predict even treatment. We are thus considering the chances that—regardless of the social identity "race"—people will have equal or unequal likelihoods of achieving some respectable level of material wealth (income or other), physical security, and social respect and deference. It is thus fair to describe the United States as racist because—as we know—the probability[11] that any given black person will receive more undesirable results and fewer desirable results is higher than that any similarly circumstanced white person will receive such results in the same combination. Consider, thus, the specific rules-of-the-game which define the social constitution in the United States. To be a citizen of the United States (or even an *apparently* law-abiding human being with money) is minimum qualification for admission to the "membership" circumstance of occupying a house in some community X. There are, of course, manifold and complex limitations on white persons' occupancy of houses, for not every community is fully open to everyone who can pay the money price (Norman C. Thomas, 1966). But it is beyond question that any black occupant A is considerably more likely to encounter various screening mechanisms than his white counterpart B who might compete for the same property. That is to say, one man (black) is deemed a more questionable potential member of the community than some similar man (white). Similar probabilities can be cited for every other contact. It was only after several days that commentators, sharing the nationwide anxiety after the Kent State episode, *discovered* the fact of a similar episode at South Carolina State College the year before. That is, the substantive output of physical safety is believed to be available to white persons at a considerably higher probability than to their black counterparts. By this line of reasoning, we might also add a similar judgment about the reception of *undesirable* results. The chances are that any given black person will often receive more undesirable results than white persons who would, if he were white or they black, be expected to receive the said undesirable results. In other words, racism in this institutional sense (racial hierarchy) can—at least conceptually—be distinguished from attitudes. But it seldom can be distinguished so neatly, and two attitudes should at least be mentioned. The first is racial prejudice or the contemptuous assertion of "natural" ("biologically inherited") superiority with or without its reflection in the policies and operations of institutions. This is the racism of the popular culture. The second is the *"quasi racism" of cultural ethnocentrism.* This second tendency is reflected in the judgment that there is nothing inherently inferior about the genetic structure of the subordinate people, that if they had had the same cultural experiences as other people, they would be equal in fact, but that in fact they have obviously not had that experience, and could not be expected to develop it instantaneously.

In fact, cultural ethnocentrism, racial prejudice, and "objective" necessities have tended to reinforce each other, although they are sometimes separable. To agree on this is not to deny, of course, that there have always been contrary pressures and explicit advocacy for ameliorating the conditions of black people. Some years ago, those whom I call meliorists—

generally now called "liberals"—took the matter as a kind of missionary problem in which virtue could be indicated by the good works of helping the less fortunate.[12] More recently, meliorism has been taken as a kind of welfare matter to be handled by clergymen, social workers, women, and professors. But the fact of racial hierarchy (or "institutional racism") has almost always been taken for granted by most realistic people.

This taking for granted meant that, in the perception of most white people, the only people to whom a change in the pattern of racial hierarchy could be urgently desirable were the blacks. The change did not, in the *practical* sense, "mean" anything to most whites, except insofar as their consciences were troubled by the disparity between what they could see everyday and the beliefs which they professed about how United States society ought to work. There was no conception that the society would, in a realistic and practical sense, be "worse off" if some significant change in racial hierarchy did not occur. Moreover, it is still true that many white people see no social advantage in a change, and still think of any modification as some version of home mission work or social welfare. But the everyday realities ought to make it clear that racial strife does bring into question the essentials of the political order.

There has never been a time when any significant and identifiable part of the black population cheerfully accepted its fate. The undercurrent of resistance has always been present. But this spirit of resistance, more accentuated of late, has become ever clearer. Even in the early 1960's it was possible to see it in civil rights litigation (Holden, 1963, 777), which now is mistakenly interpreted as "tame." Clearly, the insurrectionary spirit has grown and taken other forms, now saturating the very simplest every day experiences. Consider:

On September 8, 1969, the *Pittsburgh Press* carried a UPI squid from Hightstown, New Jersey, that "(a) curfew was imposed on this small community yesterday following a brawl between about 100 white and Negro youths on Main Street."

On November 22, the *Milwaukee Journal* carried a front-page, five-column photograph of five white officers grabbing a black young man, as a number of other officers and white youngsters watched and participated in the melee. The focus was a high school which had been under heavy turmoil four days running, since "four black girls refused a police order to go to their classes or leave school."

In March of 1970, Madison, Wisconsin—a city with a very small black population (less than 3 percent), hardly any ghetto, and dominated by the State Capitol and the University—found it necessary to close temporarily one of its high schools, after some sort of encounter between militantly black students and militantly white students whom the principal described as "Nazis." This much appeared on the front page of the local papers, but what did not appear was the report that the police had set up barricades near another high school, at least six miles away on the west side of town. Their report, which fortunately proved to be wrong, was that "the east-side kids were out to get the west-side kids."

Fights between ebullient high school kids are nothing new, and one would not ordinarily take such incidents as signs of a large political danger. But there can be hardly any reader who has not observed high school disputes of the Madison-Hightstown variety, or who has not seen authentic[13] reports of this sort. It is precisely because of such a tendency[14] in race relations that people do now properly worry. The matter obviously neither begins nor ends with high schools. Two indicators relating to the military are so striking that they make the point more sharply than any other data of which we can think. First, in American society, the presumption of "civilian control over the military" also involves the idea that civilian politics are to be free of overt or covert military intervention. The idea has never been fully honored in practice, but it is now being denied in a noticeably troublesome way: systematic military spying upon peaceful black groups, *demonstrably committed to legal means of action alone,* on the rationale that such spying is required to plan for military action in possible situations of tumult. Second, the presumption of any armed establishment is that its members are subject to discipline (and accept discipline). Practically speaking, this means that they are largely immune, so long as on active service, to the demands which might come from their other identities in civilian life. If, as has occurred, strains from the civilian realm do penetrate the military so that this presumption can no longer be accepted as an article of faith, we may reasonably conclude that a systemic crisis exists, that race now presents, as a problem to be solved, the achievement and maintenance of a viable social peace within domestic society. But this demands a certain clarity about what we mean when we consider social peace.

SOCIAL PEACE AND REPUBLICANISM

Social peace does presuppose, as its minimum condition, the reduction and ultimate elimination of any significant degree of private political force in society. The reason that private force has to be excluded from society is that its use involves a natural tendency to expand in irrational and irreversible ways, a natural erosion of any system properly described as "law." For force is always *implicit* when hostile parties address each other in a language of menace, and it is only in unusual circumstances that such parties can successfully bluff without having to go beyond the language to the fact of actual use.[15] Yet each party in a conflict will assume that the *other* parties will yield to the language (or the fact) of menace in ways fully satisfactory to itself, regardless how unsatisfactory those ways may be to those other parties. The language of menace may achieve victories. It is just as likely (if not more so) that coercive politics will become irrational, leading into "the dynamics of mutual "alarm" (Schelling, 1966, Chapter 6), with consequences which none of the parties actually desire.

To concede this condition is not at all to suppose that social life can transcend the fact of power. But it is to suppose that social life becomes nearly unbearable if people cannot surmount *pure* power politics in which there are no constraints at all. If a polity, in which there are divergent elements, is a *pure* power system, we may more reasonably call it an "empire"[16] and if it is a stable "empire," it has the stability of the quiescent order which depends on simple technical superiority by one side over another. This is not the sort of problem to which, until very recently, people in the United States have given much thought. Part of the reason, I suppose, is that they have tended to forget the element of violence in their own national history (Graham and Gurr, 1969), not to mention the fundamental importance of violence in politics around the world. Even those who think themselves tough-minded realists stick mainly to the idea of politics as bargaining and log rolling (Banfield, 1955; Buchanan and Tullock, 1962; Riker, 1962). They have accustomed themselves to the idea that politics actually will be limited, nondisruptive, and easily responsive to important issues. When they talk about "coercion" they usually have in mind fairly limited forms of coercion from which the victims eventually recover.[17] The more agreeable version, as official morality describes it, is that political fights take place under rules of "reason," that arguments will be "sound," that no one reputable will reject sound arguments without offering sound counter arguments, and that there will be some logical connections between arguments and decision. It is exactly as these optimistic assumptions are disappointed that one might expect a ritualistic reaction (and ritualistically reactionary politics) just as one might expect children to fly into rage when they happy dreams are not satisfied.[18] In short, Americans have neglected the lesson of *Federalist* #10, that social peace is always in danger, and thus have failed recently to think about its requirements.

It should be clear that social peace is not to be confused with the sort of quiescent order existent between Montague and Capulet—formal obedience to the law against feuding so long as the magistrate's men are present and violent confrontation as soon as they are gone. Nor is it to be confused—as those who have made the honorable idea of law and order into a phrase of party warfare have done—with a prison-farm society, in which one part of the population is held down by the omnipresent guns of the other. Peace exists when violent means are avoided not simply because the other side might turn out to be bigger and tougher but rather because participants *"feel" uncomfortable* about employing them, would rather not employ them, and believe that *losses suffered for the failure to employ violent means will not be irreparable.* This peace presupposes then, from the viewpoint of the several parties involved, a political system that is not only a power system in which dominance can be enforced, but one that incorporates a shared moral order (political community) in which there is wide agreement on the essential rules-of-the-game which define "the presence of justice." The creation of a political *community* (which is the end state of "integration") is precisely equivalent to the creation of peaceful handling of conflicts of interest, beliefs, and values.[19]

The achievement of peace within societies is not a new problem but a very old one, the difficulties of which can be read in political records as various as the Bible, the oral histories of African politics, or the statecraft books of Asian philosophers. No one has discovered how to "solve" it, but there are insights into how it may be "handled" with reasonable effectiveness. Most commentators formulate the problem as one in "democratic" politics. However, the term "democratic" is by now somewhat debased, through our loss of memory about what political problems the mechanisms of democratic politics have been most often intended to alleviate. The historical problem of democracy was to get "minorities" (aristocratic, plutocratic, or other) off the backs of "majorities" and, collaterally, to establish the idea (and sometimes the practice) of "majority control" over those who held the signs of office. Our current usage of "democracy" emphasizes too much the question of who shall *rule* over whom else in the polity. It specifies (or tends to specify) the right of the majority, and to the extent that critics believe the United States polity falls short of being "democratic" it is on this account.

As a practical matter, counting heads is a feasible method of legitimating a governing group, particularly when the option is to override the sustained preferences and clear interests of the majority if one is going to decide on some other basis. But any society in a real world (not some imagined Utopia) will be composed of various majorities and minorities —be they political parties, social classes, regions, religious communities, ideological groupings, or whatever. *However, majority rule does not by itself do anything to resolve the critical problem of avoiding internal war and of achieving social peace.* The central insight is that those who are "on top" at any moment must be willing not to grind the losers into the dust, and those who are losers must be willing to be losers for the time being. It cannot be denied that stability requires, to a certain degree, the exclusion of the losers. If it were otherwise, the winners would find their "victory" utterly meaningless. It would be as if the Labor Party won in 1945, but proceeded to institute all the Churchillian domestic policies and refused to institute nationalization or socialized medicine. Or, it would be as if black men won control of city governments in the urban North and proceeded to do everything which their white opponents had been doing, and refused to do anything which their supporters had expected or desired.

But there are limits. The losers are not to be excluded from the benefits of the society and its law, but only temporarily from a certain access to office and only temporarily from a certain influence on policy. Those excluded must understand that their miminum interests will be respected. Otherwise, each change of officials would lead to a complete change of policies, the consequences of which no society could tolerate. *But much more important, those excluded must understand that sooner or later they themselves will become the government or some important part of the government.* These limits are most viable when the polity exists not merely as an institutional framework within which people are bound willy nilly, but when it exists as a *shared moral order* (Long, 1960). This does not mean some ideal state free of conflict.[20] Conflict is real, is vociferous, and may become divisive.

The stresses now experienced make it more appropriate to emphasize racial politics in the United States as a problem of "republican" government. In the modern world, the idea of republican government subsumes three important features: (1) that government is "democratic," or in some sense responsive to majority rule; (2) that government is "constitutional" or in some sense subject to regularized restraints on the exercise of power (Friedrich, 1950), even when that power is sanctioned by majority opinion (Gans, 1969), and (3) that government has the obligation to maintain a state which looks to the "welfare" of all its citizens. Such a regime depends upon one important consideration which is often left unstated: that citizens have *common* rights, *common* opportunities for participation and self-fulfillment, a *common* sense of membership, *and perceive a common responsibility for rational adaptations in the interest of the future well being of the political system.*

These common qualities do not mean the absence of real enmity between contending groups. Their presence does mean that contenders, though hostile, are extremely unlikely to carry their enmity to its utmost extreme, to the point where it threatens to break up the whole system. As a very simple example, Democratic and Republican presidential contenders have often been genuinely antagonistic to each other, and their supporters have often believed that the other side took unfair advantage. But they have usually been prepared to stop short of any physical contention for control of the Executive Branch. If they believed all those things they say about each other (they sometimes do and sometimes do not) to the extent of being prepared to act on them there would be a threat of interparty civil violence after each election. Instead, such violence has seldom developed in national politics, and but little more frequently in state politics.[21] This restraint might be contrasted to conditions in the large number of nation-states in which the losers of the election are quite ready to redress ballot-box defeat by physical means if they can get away with it. In industrial relations, management and workers have more often been ready to define "the public interest" as equivalent to their separate interests, and thus to go on the physical means if other means did not work. But this pattern—though not eradicated—has certainly been diminished since 1937, even though each still seeks clear advantage over the other.

The achievement of a firmly republican system is, as James Madison knew very well,[22] highly problematical. And the one aspect of United States politics in which it has unquestionably never been achieved is in the white-black relationship. White citizens have, on the whole, not been prepared to regard blacks as *fellow*-citizens. Instead, the standard relationship, now under enormous pressure for modification, is *"imperial."* That is, the two nations are joined in the same *power* system, with the prestige, protections, and perquisites of that system being unevenly distributed. It can persistently and accurately be predicted that the balance of advantage will go to persons of one identity and of disadvantage to the other. Moreover, it can be argued effectively that the maintenance of the "imperial" relation is not exclusively accidental, but contains significant elements of calculated purpose. Since so much attention is given to material considerations (and they are important), it is perhaps well to emphasize that some of the more pervasive and troubling inequalities relate to the politics of insult and respect. The matter is illustrated by a vignette from *Time* magazine (in the summer of 1970), regarding school integration in the South. The first act of the new (white) principal, when a black school was desegregated in Louisiana, was to paint over the murals of Booker T. Washington and George Washington Carver. This psychological version of Dred Scott clearly asserted that black people had no symbols which whites in that Louisiana town felt obliged to respect. The intent was patent and is the sort of thing which also explains the anger which black students, in recently desegragated Southern schools, have shown at the playing of "Dixie."

In discussing political life, there is a certain tendency to ignore one very simple fact. People tend recurrently to construct rank orders of esteem and contempt, and those who find themselves low in those rank orders are likely to be far more incensed by that fact than by any sheer material privation. Who, indeed, wants to be "treated like dirt"? In this sense, it is easy to see that one of the critical demarcations between the white "nation" and the black is that the former, as the dominant party, imposes a persistent order of disesteem upon the latter. Everywhere the supposition has been that the perceived demands of blacks could be met only if they did not put "too much" strain on the system—did not, that is, alienate more than a small proportion of the white participants. In contrast, the supposition has also been that the perceived demands of whites would more likely have to be met, even if they alienated a substantial proportion of blacks in the system. As black pressure has risen of recent years, the resulting race schism now constitutes a much more serious crisis in the unfinished republic of the United States. Self-evidently the republican principle is threatened whenever the polity contains conflicting elements which define each other as *the enemy to whom no quarter can be given*. Precisely because there is some tendency to define "white" and "black" as mutually exclusive enemies, I have found it more fruitful to formulate these thoughts on race schism as problems in republican politics.[23] The strategic question is whether a *large-scale* government, on republican principles, can also cope with the question of "integration." This is not so much the question of *integrating the black man into white society,* as dealing with the residues of white supremacy over a black internal "colony" and *discovering what* (if any) *conditions will transform the "two nations" so as to create a common political order* consistent with the requirements of republicanism.

Both theoretically and practically, this formulation raises important questions about the mutual adjustment capacity of whites and blacks under the present circumstances. The element of mutuality should be emphasized, for there is a tendency to speak as if the outcomes hinged on the unilateral action of one party or the other. But in no two-party relationship is it likely that one and only one party can determine outcomes. And it is certainly not the case now that blacks are so utterly helpless in all respects that no action, except white action is pertinent. (See *The Politics of the Black "Nation,"* Essays IV-VII.) At the same time, mutuality does not mean that each party is "equally" required to adjust in some quantitative sense. If a satisfactory joint outcome is to be achieved, the party having the greater range of relevant resources will have to make the greater effort. If the limits of white adjustment capacity have already been reached, then three main options seem likely. (1) It would be possible that semianomic disorder, violence-as-protest, and recurrent political rioting would become standard, normal, "institutionalized."[24] (2) There would also be the possibility of internal war, as black-white commonalities should be further and futher eroded. (3) There would, finally, be the attempt to forestall either of the first two possibilities by the development of a systematic method of public (and public-private) coercion calculated to cow the black population into utter submission. Each of these alternatives would, from the viewpoint adopted here, be grossly unsatisfactory. Each would inevitably precipitate a state based upon sheer main force. Mississippi before the civil rights movement, with the refinements of computerization, would thus constitute the model for the whole country.

One element which permits us to appraise white capacity is an understanding of the fluid word "racism," some manifestations of which I consider in the following essay and some limitations upon which I again consider in Essays VIII and IX.

NOTES

1. Harold Laski points out that this rigid division persisted until well after the middle of the century. The "British people," Laski notes, meant—in usual political language—the aristocracy, the middle classes, and some part of "the respectable poor," but excluded the vast number often referred to as "the mob." See his *Reflections on the British Constitution* (1951).

2. On this, my thinking has been greatly influenced by the work of the Dutch historian Peter Geyl. See his *History of the Low Countries* (1956), 15-16 and *passim*.

3. So far, I have been referring to the political factors leading *to* a separate black culture. My main concern in later essays is to consider the political consequences *of* black cultural differences. See particularly Holden, *The Politics of the Black "Nation,"* published simultaneously with this present volume. Occasions for referring to *Politics of the Black "Nation"* will be numerous and the form for reference will hereafter be simply the title.

4. For a useful introduction to the economic position of blacks, see Ross and Hill (1967).

5. This number will now be out-of-date with the creation of some new banks in the big Northern cities in the past few years, but the picture does not change significantly and will not until the new banks are firmly established. The number also excludes whatever banks are secretly controlled by blacks, but I have known of only one.

6. As I note later on, the participation of blacks in the United States military

establishment has been far more than an "interesting story." It has been a vital part of the black experience and vital to United States military success in the sense that no war since the Mexican War (including the Civil War) could have been fought without black troops.

7. That is, the ghetto black youngster may see white people in the flesh only in very small numbers (although description of this isolation can easily be exaggerated), but he cannot be unaware of their presence in his environment, and so somehow adjusts his action to their presence.

8. The concept of the *rules-of-the-game* is important in politics (and political science), but seldom made explicit. One useful way to make this a little more explicit is it say that the social constitution is a set of five interlocking sets of understood rules. *Membership rules* prescribe which sorts of persons will be full members entitled to all prerogatives in the polity, what sorts entitled to limited prerogatives, and what sorts entitled to no prerogatives, but dependent solely on the grace of those who are members. *Substantive-output* rules specify what policies shall be regarded as mandatory, permissible, or proscribed and forbidden. *Recruitment rules* define the reservoir from which officeholders shall be drawn and the recruitment processes (lottery, examination, election, or other) which shall be necessary to choose amongst those who are eligible. *Decision-process rules* indicate the way in which decision-making officials shall deal with their superiors, their equals, their subordinates and various classes of outside parties. These rules answer the questions about who shall act contemptuously, mutually respectfully, deferentially, obsequiously, and so on with respect to whom. *Amendment rules* specify how the "constitution" is to be altered and under what circumstances.

9. When ordinary people think of the term "constitution," they usually mean some formal enactment in words, which purports to lay down "basic" rules for the operation of a government, a union, or some other defined human association. But the term may be used more broadly. Anthropologists' field reports from Africa, historians' accounts of the Venetian Republic, or our common knowledge of life in the military barracks, the corporation, the union hall, or the college campus all converge on at least one major point. Every known human association is bound up in some body of common belief, practice, and operational commitment which is well understood to those who are members of the association. Everybody who "knows the score" is able pretty well to predict what action will be accepted by whom, and what will not. Sometimes this body of common belief, practice, and operational commitment—this aggregate rules-of-the-game—will be reflected in the positive law. Often it will be supplementary to the positive law, and on many occasions it will directly contravene the positive law but be effective nonetheless.

10. In the United States, the version which is most prominent is black-white. But there have been few, if any diversified societies in which race (or some other ethnic identity with similar social meanings) constituted no basis for distinguishing between "inside" people and "outside" people. The Roman Republic and Empire, recent China, Ulster, India, and contemporary Africa are all cases in point.

11. If the statistician conceives that something is *certain* to occur, he says that "the probability of such an occurrence is 1." If something is certain not to occur, the probability of such an occurrence is 0. If the chances that the event will occur and the chances that it will not occur are judged equally likely, he says that "the probability is .5." (This is exactly the same as the common term "fifty-fifty chance.") Every possible occurrence may be placed somewhere on the continuum from 0 (no chance at all) to 1 (certainty). Naturally, use of this measure assumes that the person making the judgment has sufficient knowledge of the situation to calculate probabilities.

12. See particularly the discussion of conservative meliorists in Essay III below: "Racial Politics as a Study in Paradox."

13. The *spurious* reports are legion!

14. We should emphasize that the word is *tendency*. Clearly it is by no means *yet* true that all social relationships are structured by race and nothing else. If that were so, then all books on the subject would be superfluous, except as exercises in self-satisfaction for the authors.

15. The phrase "language of menace" is borrowed from Joseph Hamburger (1963), describing the tactics of the Reform leadership just before the act of 1832 in Great Britain. On the same point, see Critchley (1970).

16. On the conceptions here utilized, see Holden (1971).

17. Note that people fired from their jobs, and publicly calumniated, may often outlive their pursuers and return to places of prestige and reward. The cases of Otto Otepka, John Paton Davies, and Adam Clayton Powell are illustrative.

18. In contrast, one might argue that the reason British politics has been able to surmount several major situations of internal menace (such as the crisis just before 1832 and the General Strike of 1926) is that the assumptions of British society were less *ephemerally* optimistic. The optimism, instead, was the confident expectation of a ruling elite that it itself would have to be responsible for the overall outcome and that it itself would have to choose rational strategies to merit its self-confidence. There is, at the moment, no comparably self-confident (as against self-delusive) element of leadership and influence in United States society.

19. I have, in this respect, been particularly influenced by the studies of political "integration" generated by Karl W. Deutsch. See, particularly, Deutsch *et al.* (1957), notably 30-38.

20. The effort to get rid of all conflict is dangerously Utopian, leading not to social peace but to thought control and mass graves. The only way to get rid of all conflict is to control the minds of some people and to kill off those whose minds are resistant to control.

21. Republicans in 1960 seemed very much inclined to believe that President Kennedy's narrow electoral margin was achieved only by unfair practices in Illinois, but they were able to "live with" this loss—not going even so far as to raise any possible court challenges, let alone any other. Physical competition for control of governmental machinery appears to have increased in United States politics as

one descended from national to state to local politics. But no very precise measure of such physical competition has yet been developed. I plan to enlarge on this matter in "Aspects of Force in American Politics" (draft manuscript in preparation).

22. *Federalist,* #10. Perhaps the Madisonian insight really is that a republic can never be quite finished. For if "faction" is a function of difference, economic, technological and other changes will recurrently produce new differences which are so important that they generate new forms of faction. Thus, there are now at least six other elements which merit attention but which cannot be treated here. These are (a) the profound alienation of United States intellectuals from the national society—a process which has been going on since the time of Henry Adams at least; (b) the "youth rebellion" and the erosion of the idea that any sort of authority is valid; (c) the development of an apparently semiautonomous military institution with a different view of social necessity and extremely great significance for the allocation of economic resorces; (d) the persistent rigidities in the distribution of wealth, so that at least a sixth of the nation is genuinely poor by United States standards—and more than half of the poor being white; (e) the much neglected problem of white ethnic groups in large cities; and (f) the empathy gap between the more educated people (who become the upper-middle and upper classes) and the less educated (for which the term "hard hat" is but a shorthand stereotype) upon whom the more educated act through major public and private institutions. Some, though not all, of these elements are treated in Theodore J. Lowi, *The End of Liberalism* (1969).

23. As I have worked on the matter, it has also become apparent that some parts of the problem are—rather surprisingly—closely connected with the capacity for governance which lies (or does not lie) in the Republican party. There are two reasons for this concern with the Republican party.

First, my assessment is that the most important time for forward movement is in the next five years. See, below, Essays X-XII on social peace; also, *The Politics of the Black "Nation."* In the most important part of that time, the Executive Branch will be controlled by the Republican party which, this far, has shown a rather restricted insight into these matters of race.

In addition, however, the Republican party is *inherently* important to the adjustment process because (a) the most important adjustments will depend on the relatively more conservative elements of the United States polity, and (b) it is likely that only Republican political leadership can provide the interpretive role to capture the attention of those more conservative elements.

My concern with the Republican party is, however, inadequately reflected here (chiefly in Essay IV, "Historical Note on the Southern Strategy," and in the final Essay XII on social peace). This volume was simply too far along when I began to come to some perception of the special relevance of the Republican *party.* (As with most social scientists, I suppose, my own biases have entered unconsciously to preclude my appreciation of this aspect.)

24. This pattern is known in some Third World countries (and there is a good deal of it in India and Japan), but it has not been recently found in the industrial nations (except possibly Japan). For an historical examination, see the discussion of England down to the end of the eighteenth century in George Rude, *The Crowd in History* (1964).

Racism in the United States Polity

INSTITUTIONAL RACISM

Within the past five years, the phrase "institutional racism" has come into fairly wide use. How, exactly, may we use it to convey a fairly precise meaning? To speak of "institutional racism" is to say that a given institutional pattern systematically and regularly discriminates in favor of one set of claimants (in the United States case, white people) and against another set of claimants (in the United States case, various nonwhite peoples, notably blacks). No one has ever tried, so far as I know, to measure institutional racism, and it is possible that such a task would be too complicated to be worthwhile. But the meaning of institutional racism might be clearer if we were to proceed as if we could develop a measure. Imagine, now, that chattel slavery based upon race were still fact of law and life in the United States. If that were so, the slave would have literally no chance to equal a white man in any measure, and the free (legally nonslave) black man could live only in such a precarious circumstance that his chances to equal a white man would be very small. Hence, we could intelligently say that the society scored 0 on the integration measure and 100 on the institutional racism measure. In between, one might score the society somewhat as shown in the scale on page 21.

It is not necessary to attach too much importance to such a scale to see the main point. "Institutional racism" is *what we would measure* if such a scale (or a better version) existed, by observing the extent to which the wide variety of *social roles* ("voter," "priest," "husband," "TV repair-

20

A Scale of Institutional Racism and Integration

Imagined Institutional Racism Score	Condition Described	Imagined Integration Score
90	Legal freedom, combined with actual peonage as the normal condition of the subordinate population.	10
80	Official regulations requiring extensive separateness in most aspects of life (official apartheid).	20
70	"Unofficial apartheid:" meaning legal equality but actual persistence of segregation and of widespread unofficial measures (to which official measures would most often be supportive) for enforcing the dominance of the superordinate group.	30
60	Some measure of freedom greater than implied by unofficial apartheid, but nonetheless such widespread inequalities that the chances for any subordinate individual would be rather limited, even if he acted efficiently on the Avis principle of trying harder.	40
50	Very great inequality, but some few perceptible breaches.	50
40	Some lessened inequality, but with some increased likelihood that acting on the Avis principle of trying harder would have some effect.	60
30	Substantial economic opportunity (somewhat achievable on the Avis principle), and great political and social limitations.	70
20	Substantial political opportunity (on the Avis principle) and economic equality, with noticeable and injurious but not unbearable political limitations and social limitations.	80
10	Economic-political equality, with minor social irritations; for example, the exclusion of rich Catholics or rich Jews from social clubs can be regarded as a minor social irritation. It is insulting to them, but it does not stop them from living effective lives within American society.	90

man," "policeman," "lodge brother," "customer," "luncheon companion," "ditch digger," "trade unionist," and the likes) should regularly be predictable on the basis of race. If one trusted the scale at all, in the actual conditions of this year 1971 in the United States, one probably would have to conclude that the country scores about 60 or thereabouts on the institutional racism scale (at most, about 40 on the integration scale).

This point is cleverly put by James E. Jones, a law professor at the University of Wisconsin, in a discussion of Daniel Patrick Moynihan's (possibly) misinterpreted case that blacks had made such "remarkable progress" in recent years that the racial issue could now profitably suffer from "benign neglect." Citing Andrew Brimmer, Jones says:

[Brimmer] notes that median family income, for example, for 1959 showed nonwhite families earnings [sic] 54% of that of whites. In 1968, the ratio was 63%. [Jones then notes that the figures may not be wholly informative since black families tend to be larger than white families, with the result that the per head income—the actual money available to be spent on the needs of each family member—is still lower compared to white per head income.[1]] But take the figures at face value. Is an increase from 54% to 63% in ten years progress? In 1787, in Article I of the Constitution, we started out as three-fifths (60%) of a white man for purposes of apportionment of Representatives and taxes. Now, black families, without regard to size, have a median income of 63% that of whites. (Jones, 1970)

In a certain sense, Jones's argument really is that blacks are sufficiently excluded from those social roles which produce income that , at best, they average out having something like 60 percent the chance of whites to earn reasonable incomes in this economy. Or, in our terms, they are—at best — 60 percent integrated into the economy.

There are other data, in common experience, which also point to persistent institutionalized barriers. Perhaps this is best demonstrated by looking at those institutions which have an explicit doctrine of facilitating integration.Such a trade union as the United Auto Workers is pertinent for our purposes. The UAW has had large black membership since the days when the industry was unionized; the national leadership of the National Association for the Advancement of Colored People was instrumental in helping to persuade the black leadership of Detroit that the blacks ought to join the union (White, 1948, 213-217); and the UAW frequently verbalizes its commitment to policies of integration. In that light, it should be noted that it took more than fifteen years' political pressure before the union could find a device by which to introduce a black member into its International Executive Board (Stieber, 1962, 41-45 and 83-88).

The major philanthropic foundations show evidence of the same problem, noticeable in their case *because* several of these foundations have, for a long time, sponsored work calculated to reduce the inequalities between black and white. In determining what is important, foundation executives have particularly wide latitude. Yet is seems seldom to have been possible for any major foundation to create racial diversity in its top-level executive staffs. And when particular projects are delegated to other agencies, the same pattern tends to hold. Example: for many years foundation officials (and federal officials concerned with education) have expressed concern about the quality of the black colleges and universities. But the striking fact is that they have persistently defined the issues in the cultural terms already most familiar to the "Establishment." This includes defining the relevant persons in terms already familiar to the "Establishment." Thus, the Ford Foundation's recent expressions of interest in this subject have been channeled through such agencies as the American Association of University Professors and the American Academy of Arts and Sciences. Similarly, the recent Carnegie Commission at first in no way dealt explicitly with the special problems of the black institution; neither did it even have a black member. These channels are legitimate, useful and relevant —but the use of these channels alone amounts to a continued skewing of the issues, since they are not the normal channels in which the largest likelihood of eliciting the responsible interest of serious black scholars and administrators would be found.

Precisely the same point is made easily in the public sector. Consider the cruciality of the racial variable as a determination of eligibility for the presidency. Any black politician is considerably less likely to receive the Democratic or the Republican presidential nomination, between now and 1976, than is any a reasonably comparable white politician. For example, we may say that (assuming no change in his present *personal* reputation), Senator Edmund Muskie's chances of being a Democratic nominee (in 1972) are "reasonably good." (We could not say that his chances are .4 or that they are .5 or that they are .9, because that involves too fine a calculation for any knowledge we have.) On the other hand, we would almost certainly say that, whatever Muskie's chances are, Senator Edward Brooke's chances on the Republican side (or the chances of a Democratic Brooke, if one existed) would be lower than Muskie's chances. The *legal* constitution merely limits the presidency to native-born citizens over 35. But the *social* constitution limits the presidency to native-born, white (male?) (Gentile), citizens over 35. By now, nearly every reader will have become impatient with this example, regarding it as tedious—everybody knows, the reader will say, that a black man cannot be president! Exactly.

But consider, for instance, those appointments which are open to presidential discretion. It is hardly credible that only one black man in United States history was suitable for the Cabinet (Robert C. Weaver in the Kennedy-Johnson years). Yet only one black man entered the Cabinet. It is even less credible that until the Eisenhower administration there was but one black man able to meet the normal political criteria (other than race) for sub-Cabinet appointments. Yet it is the case that, except for one

Assistant Attorney General (William H. Lewis) in the Taft administration, no black man reached the sub-Cabinet until the appointment of J. Ernest Wilkins as Assistant Secretary of Labor in 1953. It is also fact that no black man went onto the White House executive staff until 1955. For the sake of a baseline, let us merely note that 1969-1970 college freshmen would then have been three to five years old! Each president since Eisenhower has made some similar appointment—yet the old pattern holds. For no knowledgeable observer, of whom I am aware, claims that these black appointees have at any point been part of the White House inner circle. Perhaps the most striking indicator is a very small thing. E. Frederic Morrow, the black man on the Eisenhower executive staff, found it difficult to get what every senior executive must take for granted: a *secretary.* Mr. Morrow reports that he finally got a competent secretary when one *volunteered* to work for him, out of a sense of religious obligation (Morrow, 1963, 11-12).

I have not actually studied the pattern of gubernatorial and mayoral appointments across the country. But common sense impressions are that the pattern has not been noticeable different, even in such a place as New York.[2] Nor do state legislatures (where key positions are mainly at the command of colleagues and under little influence from the larger public audience) seem much different. In no Northern state has a black man reached the speakership, and but two (so far as I can tell) reached a floor leader's position (the Democratic [majority] leader in Pennsylvania and the Democratic [minority] leader in Iowa, 1969).

In each of these illustrations—union, foundations, government—we are talking about evidences that admission to a given social role is restricted on racial criteria. As far as the private sector goes, we could illustrate the visible uneven admission of blacks—as compared to whites —in almost any part of that sector. The union example and the foundation example are not chosen because the union and the foundations are more restrictive than most institutions. They are pertinent, exactly because they are less restrictive! One would find a distinctly narrower range of options if one were to examine the executive staffs of large corporations, the directorates of medical societies and bar associations, and the leadership structures of other institutions in which the constituency is less attuned to "social change." In virtually all these, the regular exclusion of blacks from certain roles is as clear as if these instituions really were as "private" as one's home, from which any stranger may properly be excluded. In the private sector, however, there is often a special problem of interpretation. It will often be argued that the disparities are a result of history, since it is the result of history that too few blacks are qualified for the private-sector roles which are open. This argument is not entirely fallacious—assuming the going definitions of "qualified"—although the claim is often fraudulent. But the particular kind of public sector roles I have been discussing override that problem entirely. It is unquestionable that the present situation affords a plentiful supply of black political functionaries, comparable to those whites who are in the fact elevated to the pertinent roles. Thus, the problem of racism is more sharply defined, not only because the supply situation is not a barrier, but also because the *formal* theory[3] of representative government in the United States overtly denies the pertinence of racial criteria.

Thus far, we have been suggesting that—at best—the United States social system, taken as a whole, would score out at about 60 percent on an institutional racism scale (if one really existed). But since we still live with the heavy hand of history, it should be emphasized that it was until *very recently*—and in some places and respects still is—the case that "unofficial apartheid," implying a higher institutional racism score, was the dominant rule. This dominance could be suggested if we looked not at the actual recruitment of decision makers, for instance, but at the decision-process rules which decision makers are expected to follow. Once the recruitment rules have been modified, so that a formerly closed social role is deemed open, it is important to ask if the criteria for role performance differ from one sort of person to another. To the extent that blacks are under constraints which whites in the same roles would not be under, the phenomenon of institutional racism may be said to be present. The extreme case was the Southern black policeman, authorized to arrest only black persons.

The net effect is a sort of unofficial apartheid. Unofficial apartheid may be illustrated in quite different ways, one of the more interesting of which is the economy. That is to say, one suspects a careful study of the years between 1900 and 1950 would show that black men were simply defined as nonexistent for many aspects of the economy. Through the private restrictive convenant as a central technique, the pattern of urban residential segregation was developed and maintained. The substantive output guaranteed was a residential area confined to persons of one race only, regardless what decisions consumers might have themselves made with their money had they had free choice. It created a market restricted to white purchasers and renters, and a mixed or marginal market in which both might operate—with the mixed market inevitably tending to become black (or, in rare cases, white). One may call this condition apartheid for it amounts to saying to consumers: here is a defined piece of land which, given your race, is the only one you may occupy, and here are other pieces of land which you will, under no circumstances, occupy. The enforcement mechanism, in the end, has been the display of coercive private violence.

To call this "unofficial apartheid" should not lead us, however, to miss the role of the federal government itself. The Federal Housing Administration played a key role in encouraging the real estate industry's doctrine that it was desirable policy to maintain homogeneous residential areas, on the ground that these enhanced property values (Abrams, 1955, 158-164 and Chapter XVII). Considering the leverage which is exerted through the insuring functions of FHA, one probably will never be able to measure how much FHA did contribute to the new reinforcement. Still another constraint on consumership was a restriction on the right to buy whatever educational services one's means would afford. Until the very late 1940's, Northern private universities kept black registration to a minimum, either by not admitting blacks at all (as in the case of Princeton) or by the maintenance of small quotas.

Another aspect of apartheid is the explicit reservation of particular occupational categories for particular ethnic groups, above and beyond any limitation which the blind operations of the market would itself produce. If this was not required by public law, it was nonetheless the predominant practice of management and of the trade unions. It is reasonably well known, for instance, that between 1890 and 1920, black men were substantially displaced from a number of occupations in which they had traditionally been employed. They were replaced by the continental European immigrants who were just coming into the cities in large numbers. The replacement, however, was not merely a market phenomenon, but the result of specific desisions by managers with the intent to replace black with white (Bloch, 1969).

In the public sector, one can find other illustrations. In such a city as Pittsburgh, the public school system did not hire black teachers at all until near the end of World War II. (The option offered black parents was black teachers and segregated schools or continuation of mixed schools with white teachers.) Other cities, such as Chicago and Detroit, hired black teachers, but regularly assigned them to black schools exclusively. The teachers who were first able to expect a reasonably high chance of being assigned to nonblack schools are in the generation that was graduated from college about the time of the Korean conflict. The restrictions are still more apparent when one considers administrative personnel in urban public school systems. Chicago appointed its first black high school principal in the early 1940's, New York City appointed its first black senior-high school principal in 1968(!), and no big city system has yet appointed a black superintendent.[4] If one examines the trade union side one sees a similar pattern. There were a few occupations, such as longshoreman, in which blacks had long constituted an important part of the labor force. In some of these trades, black admission to the unions was widely practiced. But apart from these trades, the policy of the unions was generally to exclude black members—a policy which did not change substantially until mass unionization under the CIO during the 1930's (Spero and Harris, 1968; Cayton and Mitchell, 1939; Wesley, 1927).

Still other constraints in the economy could be found, some in seemingly small events. Witness the problem of Robert S. Abbott, the founder of the *Defender* newspaper chain. Like many another self-made man, once Mr. Abbott was rich, he wished to indulge himself in the visible signs of richness, one of which was a Rolls Royce. To his chagrin, he found that he could not buy a Rolls Royce in Chicago, because the Chicago agency would not sell to a black man (Ottley, 1955). Abbott solved his personal problem by getting a white man to buy the automobile and transfer title, but the incident was an earnest of more important things. One would hazard that one of the impediments to black entrepreneurship has been not only the weak credit position and the absence of managerial skills, but beyond these the simple refusal of financial institutions to regard black men as part of their normal market.

Institutional racism is, in part, a function of historical accident. If two racial groups, living in the same polity, occupy uneven positions, then it is predictable that—regardless of policymakers' or citizens' attitudes—the superordinate-subordinate relation will be maintained by the ordinary necessitites of governing. This experience is clear enough in the present national concern with macroeconomic policy. If the control of inflation be taken as the supreme domestic objective, and if deflationary measures produce unemployment, then it is predictable that those who are at the bottom on the economic scale will be hit first. Since blacks in cities are the people who fit the category "bottom of the economic scale," it follows that black unemployment will rise rapidly, just as if policymakers had specifically meant blacks to carry the burden of the whole economy's adjustment.

But, obviously, institutional racism is not merely a function of historical accident. It is also a function of social doctrines about the relationships which one racial group ought to have to another. In this sense, we are also talking about racial attitudes as an underlying support for an institutional pattern. What we ordinarily mean when we speak of white racism, then, is a doctrine of white supremacy or white predominance.

It is possible that John Morley (the British historian-politician as authentic spokesmen of upper bourgeois rationalist liberalism) and Senator James K. Vardaman (Democrat, Mississippi, as apostle of poor-white populism) never heard of each other. But each offered a clear statement of political racism in the rule that there were some situations in which men could become entirely unacceptable role holders by sheer fact of race or color. Austen Chamberlain recites a dinner conversation (in 1907) about India saying:

> . . . I said I was dead against [admitting an Indian to the highest government circle] . . . because [inter alia] our whole position in India rested on the admission that we were different from and in a different position from the natives. We could not and ought not to submit to coloured rule, etc., etc. . . . Morley said he pretty much agreed with my conclusions, though not with all my reasons. He knew he would not submit to be governed by a man of colour. (Chamberlain, 1937, 59-60)

About the same time Vardaman offered an identical view, as he spoke on the black man's right to vote. "I am," said Vardaman, "as opposed to Booker T. Washington with all his Anglo-Saxon refinements and accoutrements voting, as I am to . . . the little kinky-headed coon, who shines my shoes every morning." Either statement adequately expressses that *white* racism which has been so notable a feature of European culture, "from the Atlantic to the Urals," for much of the last four hundred years.

What is the explanation for white racism? One explanation is that white racism is based upon a narrow and nasty, but distinctly rational, calculation of advantage. It is the rational dimensions of racism to which scholars most often turn for explanation. Moreover, there is some justification for their doing so. But racism may also be pathological.

RACISM AS PATHOLOGICAL DOCTRINE: THE BASES OF CONTEMPT AND FEAR

The first element of pathological racism is a white sense of contempt for nonwhite peoples, resulting from a long-term convergence of religion, science, and power. There is (and long has been) a body of racist religious doctrine the Protestant version of which is the equation of black people with the descendants of Ham. Catholic doctrine is more complex, and a little less favorable to the ultimate denial of *human* qualities although it is patently not averse to the development of systems of ethnic stratification. Active, assertive Biblical racism may well have been associated with the fact that the most important part of large-scale European contact with nonwhite peoples came in the times of the Protestant Reformation, when a self-conscious attention to the Scriptures was acutely in vogue. Religious dogmatism probably contributed to Europeans' experiencing in Africa what is now called "culture shock" (which is one sure source of ethnocentrism), particularly after the mid-eighteenth century. It is most reasonable to believe that the culture shock was due as well to differences in technology, to the disparities between African technology after the mid-eighteenth century and the technology that Europeans then knew.

A second element in the basis of pathological racism is science. The science that the common man believes in any generation is the science of a previous generation. In the eighteenth century, educated men assumed some natural and hereditary mental difference between whites and blacks. But the tone of the eighteenth century is different from the later tone. Whereas eighteenth-century whites could send a black man (John Chavis) to Princeton as an "experiment" to see if Princetonian learning would "take" on a black, it is almost inconceivable to imagine such an "experiment" being proposed in the nineteenth century. Nineteenth-century evolutionism provided an intellectually respectable basis for slavery which had not been present in the world of the Enlightenment.

Slavery was a means of getting extremely cheap labor and in that sense was rational from the perspective of the slaveholder. The plantation owners' tyranny had some of the same elements before mechanization hit the Deep South. And racism was a rational managerial tool in the pre-Union days, for it created one more source of friction and thus increased management control over the labor force. From the same perspective, the late V. O. Key tried to show, candidates appealing to "white supremacy" fared best in the "black belts" of the South, where presumably black voting would have most threatened white control. From the same perspective, the rational fear of economic competition is advanced to explain white resistance to black entry into the building trades of the urban North. It is even possible to argue that racism stands as a barrier to the lower-class solidarity which, otherwise, would increase the chances of a redistributive economic politics in the United States. In the United States today, more than half the poor people—defined in "War on Poverty" terms—are white, not black. Politically, there could be no losses to either whites or blacks were they to cooperate in joint ventures to increase the level of public subsidy for poor people, yet the fact is that cooperation between the white poor and black poor is one of the less likely prospects in the politics of this country.

If racism were purely rational, why should white working-class people be so reluctant to cooperate with black working-class people in their common interest? If racism is purely rational, why are the evidences of prejudice so perceptible among upper-middle and upper-class industrial managers, even where there is no opportunity for using the racial cleavage to control the workers? Our view, instead, is that—apart from rational dimensions white racism has a pathological quality which is a function of history and culture, a quality which explains the importance of racism as a social doctrine. By the last of the nineteenth century, it was broadly agreed—in the most influential intellectual circles, no less than among public men—that there was a racial hierarchy, of which blacks were the absolute mudsill.[5]

Religious dogma and scientific doctrine provided the intellectual and perception basis for whites' belief in their own natural superiority. But we must also take note of power. People do not so easily manifest contempt for those who have retaliatory capacity. The earliest venturers to the African coast were not some agents of predominant power, but rather concessionaires operating much at the tolerance of local rulers. The very language of contemporary traders and explorers' journals is indicative. When European power on the coast was weak, these sources spoke of the African polities as "kingdoms" ruled by "kings." Only in the mid and late nineteenth century, with white dominance, did African polities become "tribes" ruled by "chiefs" (Anderson *et al.*, 1967, 29). And with this, the "white man's 'burden'" became an important theme. As the power balance shifted, so that white men were dominant in virtually every part of the earth, there must have been a devaluation of nonwhites, consistent with religious and scientific belief, in the same manner that there has been a partial upward revaluation of the Japanese since 1905 and of the Chinese since 1949. The devaluation process amounted to a full institutionalization of the idea that to be other than white was to be less than fully human, to be legitimately an object of contempt. This sense of contempt has pervaded the white American's conduct of his private relations to a degree which shocks those few whites who have been able literally to put themselves in black men's shoes (Griffin, 1962), and it has similarly pervaded the policies of public and private institutions to a degree incompatible with any rational policy.

The other element which has even more limiting effects is that of white fear. "The Negro needs the white man," Martin Luther King said, "to free him from his fear. The white man needs the Negro, to free him from his guilt." Whatever one might have said of this view, an element of white racism is white fear. A participant in a Detroit archdiocesan seminar told Professor Alvin Rose, "Can't you understand? We don't run from dislike. We are literally frightened to death of you!" (Citron, 1961, 13). This person was speaking a more profound truth than it is ordinarily convenient for either blacks or whites to recognize. Only nameless, unreasoning fear

—to borrow Franklin Roosevelt's phrase—of the same quality as fear of "the Oriental hordes," "the yellow peril," or "the savage, heathen redskins" could explain the persistent and virulent racism which leads to so much irrational white behavior.

The evidences of fear, historical and contemporaneous, are at least as widespread as are those of contempt. During the American Revolution whites had been appalled by Lord Dunmore's offer of freedom to those blacks who should support the Crown. During the Haitian Revolution a few years later they were appalled and frightened. Their successors were even more frightened by the episodes of the 1820's and 1830's, even by the mildest discussion of gradual emancipation, projected through such conservative bodies as the American Colonization Society. Yet for the most part, the colonizationists had in mind an African destination (and Liberia is one result), though it was occasionally proposed to settle blacks in some reserved portion of the public domain. One New York congressman who urged inquiry into such a projuct apparently felt obliged to assure his colleagues that he did not contemplate eventual statehood or congressional representation. He was merely looking for a place to put the blacks. Even this was profoundly disturbing. The lesson is contained in Frederic Bancroft's study of the colonization movement. In 1828, says Bancroft:

William Harper, recently United States senator and soon to be chancellor of South Carolina, insisted that the publications of the American Colonization Society, with all their mildness, were dangerous because they spoke of emancipation as desirable; and he pictured the mental condition of many when he wrote: "It is with no pleasant feelings that we see members of our families turn pale at observing a pamphlet of the American Colonization Society on our tables." (Cooke, 1957, 177)

Harper's critique brings to mind another side of the situation: the slave revolts. Whatever one may say of Styron's *Confessions of Nat Turner,* we may believe he captures appropriately the degree to which the Turner uprising (and most other slave revolts) created consternation among whites. Marion deBunsen Kilson reports the white response.

A slave revolt resulted in a three-step syndrome; an initial period of panic in which vengeance was wrought not only upon known insurgents, but often upon innocent Negroes. During this period of mob panic and activity, aggression might also be vented upon white moderates within the area and upon outsiders who were disliked but not directly involved with the revolt. (Kilson, 1969)

Flurries of mob panic were followed by more systematic "armed oppression to enforce the threatened slave system," and capped off by new legislative measures to strengthen the public authority (Kilson, 1969).

The hypothesis of fear would seem to explain better, than any alternative, still another feature, namely the first responses to Reconstruction. "Military government," says Dunning, "was declared to be preferable to [N]egro domination: better the tyranny of the intelligent one than that of the ignorant many" (Dunning, 1965, 187). Whites began to participate in the civilian politics of Reconstruction only when it became clear that a civilian politics would proceed, regardless whether the whites abstained or not. But the rationale of "the ignorant many" cannot explain the white response (despite white acceptance of doctrines of natural inferiority), in light of the well-known intellectual level of the white South. It was not so much "ignorant" politics that was frightening as "black 'domination.' " The image of "black domination," which so long itself dominated historical accounts, cannot be sustained. But a truly fearful people would quickly seize such an idea, on very limited evidence, and hardly yield it.

Fear would also explain the unwritten "law" of twentieth-century Southern rural politics, challenged on a large scale only in our own lifetimes. David Cohn and Richard Wright—two emigré Mississippians— would have agreed on little, but Wright would surely have agreed that Cohn was accurate in stating the basic Delta proposition "that a Negro must not raise his hand to a white man" (Cohn, 1967). To live in the Delta as a white man was to live surrounded by those whom one trod upon, and if one lived in a culture of vengeance, one would expect to prevent one's own destruction only by the insistent pressure of draconian arbirariness.

The fear hypothesis, one may believe, is appropriate even to ordinary experience in the metropolitan culture. In almost any black neighborhood there are a few white residents, usually very elderly people and often living alone, who are remarkable exceptions to almost any rule one may lay down. Frequently, their children and grandchildren will long since have moved twenty miles to some all-white suburb, where they live in exasperation that Mamma or Papa will not come along. Sometimes these whites will be abused by young toughs in the neighborhood, but more likely they will be left to their own devices or even given such protection and aid as their neighbors themselves can muster. But the usual pattern, to which they are precisely exceptions, is the well-known "flight." With some judicious assistance from realty dealers, a neighborhood can be turned over from white to black in a couple of years; left to nature, it will take five or six or seven or even ten years. Blacks most often attribute the turnover to simple prejudice (and economists to fear of economic loss). Neither factor is irrelevant, but we suggest that simple physical fear would be a far more potent explanation.

Again, only such fear could account for the characteristic white over-reaction to whatever modes of black resistance occur. Thus, in the early 1960's, when both the practice and the overt doctrine of nonviolent direct action (moral opposition) was dominant, most white respondents said that this was illegitimate.[6] In the same way, many whites now react *as if* guerrilla warfare had already been carried into their living rooms, even though much of what they react to is but black rhetoric about "violence" and even though actual "violence" is no more violent than parallel actions by whites in recent times. The ghetto rebellions of 1964-1968 were *almost* entirely assaults upon property, although it certainly would have been possible for blacks to invade white neighborhoods, as white rioters used to invade black neighborhoods, had the participants so desired.

White student radicalism may be aimed at an utter demolition of the social structure of the United States. But black activism on campus, though disturbing and in some contexts not acceptable, has been much more conventionally American. Black student "takeovers" of university build-ings have, in fact, usually been a pressure device comparable to trade unionists' sit-down strikes in the auto industry in 1937 (Bernstein, 1960). Welfare clients, led by the Reverend James Groppi, created a furor when they took over the Wisconsin State Assembly chamber in the fall of 1969; but that action could reasonably compare to a farmer group's similar taking over of the same chamber in the early 1930's. The Black Panthers' defiant harassment of judges—in contrast to an escaping prisoner's *appar-ent* actual killing of a judge[7]—could compare to similar action by a farmer group opposing mortgage foreclosures in Depression-time Iowa (Shover, 1965). The number of deliberate political killings of whites, by blacks, since 1960 cannot match—for instance—the number of deliberate politi-cal killings of blacks, by whites, since the same year. This statement would hold even if we counted every recent ghetto murder of a policeman—which may be unwarranted despite the rhetoric of some *soi-disant* "revolu-tionaries" who proclaim every such death as a "political" execution.[8] There are indeed several small groups which openly advocate a politics of "armed rebellion." There are more people who use a language which *suggests* that they believe in "armed rebellion," though their language is actually not clear. The evidence is that they are nonpracticing believers who will never practice unless driven to the last extremity. Otherwise, the casualty rate would already—and *long* ago—have been far higher. Those groups which do advocate "armed rebellion" openly are themselves *very small* (no more than a few hundred people) and no suggestion or evidence of still more secret groups, to be taken seriously, has yet arisen to view. Finally, those groups which do advocate "armed rebellion," such as the Panthers, show at least some judgment in recognizing at least some of their present incapacity to act on their arguments. In brief, despite the rhetoric, virtually all black activists, however "militant," actually conduct their politics within the conventional formats of lobbying, litigation, party competition, and propaganda.

If racism in the George Wallace sense were dominant, the failure to understand black politics would make sense. But, as we shall show, racism in that sense is not dominant. Hence, the only coherent explanation we can find is that whites tend so quickly to be *fearful* of nonwhites that imagination and perception atrophy. This is the essence of political pathology. To say that the fear is pathological does not mean that it is beyond explanation, but only that it immobilizes its white victims' capacity for reasonable judgment and imagination. *But why such fear?*

In part, white fear of nonwhites is a function of historical experience, experience from which certain cultural doctrines have been learned and relearned over many generations of Western history. One fundamental element has been an accommodation to the problems which white world imperialism posed *for white people*, particularly from the eighteenth century onward. White imperialism was based on a slender use of numbers and a temporary (historically "accidental") superiority of technology and economics. It is inconceivable, for instance, that an English army armed in the manner of Henry V's troops at Agincourt should ever have survived in Africa. But it was perfectly conceivable that, armed in nineteenth-century style, they should overcome resistant Africans. European imperialists were dealing with people whose natural resources (numbers, and skill in the use of weapons derived from the local physical environment) were far superior. Hence, the Europeans could never afford to relax, and always were forced to fear the possible uprising. It is perfectly natural to be fearful of people whose natural resources are greater than one's own.

This kind of experience, repeated around the world, inculcated a deep fear of the latent possibilities of the "savage races," at the same time that technical and economic superiority provided a basis for contempt. This much is ecological in origin: a simple adjustment to the facts of potential danger, and the development of a cultural image out of that adjustment.

A second very important element in white fears derives from the culture of white people themselves, a culture in which the prediction is that a man who has been offended will seek to redress the offense by taking vengeance. American folklore celebrates this belief in stories of poor whites who burn the barns of their more prosperous neighbors, of gunfights at the O.K. Corral, of the underworld's code of "honor." We do not have to believe that people act this way often—although the crime statistics are too poor to allow us to conclude that they do not—but merely to recognize a kind of social mythology which emphasizes the possibility that they will act this way. Moreover, we have to note that—whatever may be preached on Sunday morning—the popular culture does not in fact esteem "turning the other cheek."

If white fear of nonwhites was already endemic to the broad culture of the West, a function of historic experience, it was reinforced in the American case by the Southernization of the literate American's interpretation of race. We can hardly overestimate the extent to which, as Southern-oriented historians dominated academic historiography until nearly World War II, so writers of Southern culture dominated the book-club output. David Cohn, whom we have just quoted, is perhaps one of the clearest examples. To read Cohn's books is occasionally to get a glimpse of white gentility fighting the "rednecks," and in the spirit of *noblesse oblige* protecting (and when necessary, gently correcting) the dangerous child, the black man. The significance of Cohn "[*Atlantic* Editor Edward Weeks' cabinet member for the South] is not simply in himself, though that may have been substantial."[9] It was in his role (along with Faulkner and many others) in teaching the nation-at-large what it was ready enough to learn in any case, that the black man was inherently dangerous and had always to be controlled.

If white men's fear of retribution, their own cultural interpretation of the likely consequence of an historical experience they had actually lived, is one important element, it is at least subject to some rational comprehension. Of no less importance, in all likelihood, is a deeply ingrained psychosexual pathology. Beyond all else, psychosexual motives have proved more compelling justifications for racist actions than almost any others we can imagine. In the history of black lynchings, for instance, it seemed mandatory to defend the act by proclaiming the sacrosanctity of white womanhood—even in the preponderance of lynching cases where there was no hint of sexual affront by the person killed. The same obscure relationship is reflected in an account of a recent mob scene in the South. The federal agent who reported the case[10] thought the fascinating fact was that in the large crowd outside a building, it was the white women who kept screaming that the blacks inside should be emasculated. One need only recall the reports of young white girls being raped in Chinese laundries (Miller, 1969), the mid-nineteenth century avidity for "scandals" of the Maria Monk variety, or the Hollywood movies in which frontierswomen embattled are soberly told to save the last bullet for themselves. How this is all to be explained, we cannot say, although there is a broader experience which suggests some connection between proscribed groups and sexual fantasy. "Would you want your daughter to marry one?" may be an absurd question when the overt issues concern voting, but it is usually there on whatever issues of policy are most overtly concerned with race. Walter Kaufman, a sociologist, first raised this speculation in discussing the politics of resistance to public assistance, a speculation more recently raised in Gilbert Steiner's comment that public assistance involves "problems of race, of sex, of religion, and of family relationships . . . four areas most American politicians would rather avoid" (Steiner, 1966). It also permeated school politics, as a recent (North Carolina) effort to meet the integration problem by separating on sexual lines—a point anticipated by Walter Lippmann a long time ago—would suggest, and as is equally suggested by the fact that the whites readiest to flee central-city residence (at great economic cost to themselves) are those who have school-age children.

The psychosexual question serves to alarm those who (consciously, though perhaps silently—or unconsciously) are somehow concerned with maintaining the boundaries which will make outcasts of anyone marrying beyond the boundary of "one's own kind." To raise the issue is to mobilize the formidable bias which is not only associated with the idea that "the others" are biogenetically inferior, but the even more formidable bias associated with the subject of sex. Some writers of psychoanalytic bent treat this as fear made stronger by the thought of succumbing to suppressed attraction. The great fear is that the racial boundary of sex and/or marriage will be crossed, by whites themselves who are simultaneously frightened and thrilled by the idea of the crossing. If this ambivalent fear were not present, it would not be possible to make money selling so many bad historical novels (as nearly every drugstore now does) about white slave mistresses and their seraglios of black men. The explicit white preoccupation with sex and marriage becomes one powerful support for racism —immune to rational discourse—because it focuses all the hostilities, antagonisms, attractions, and fears into a determination to remain dominant where contact is essential, and to remain utterly separate where contact can be avoided. This becomes, above all, "the poor man's racism," the racism of the popular culture.

"QUASIRACISM": CULTURAL ETHNOCENTRISM

Institutional racism is a set of practices which, once having been initiated, may continue for a long time even though few—if any—of the people participating in them may operate with racist assumptions or purposes as ordinarily understood. Racism as a social doctrine, in the ordinary sense, is the set of values and beliefs which have to be held by *persons* and which broadly assume the biogenetic inferiority of one set of human beings and the superiority of another. There is a third dimension which may, in practice, be akin both to racism-as-doctrine and to institutional racism although it may be most often manifest in people who think of themselves as unprejudiced, and who may indeed think of "prejudice" as intellectually shallow and morally vulgar. But there is often a certain shallowness in the failure to recognize that those who repudiate doctrines of biogenetic inferiority may nevertheless hold to a cultural ethnocentrism which sustain white over black in both policies and institutions. People who reject biogenetic interpretations may, intellectually and psychologically, accept the black person as a worthy person to the degree that he approximates values and behaviors peculiarly associated with a Euro-American tradition.

This is clearer whenever policies are discussed on the supposition that race is not "really" the issue but a spurious cover for other issues. Daniel P. Moynihan did not *show how and why* having different family patterns within a multiethnic industrial society would produce the results he described. Nor did he show that the black family pattern he described[11] was the significant barrier to black progress. But virtually all comment (that of *The New York Times* editorial board for example) seemed to suppose that he had said so, and to suppose that he was correct. In the same way, it is often argued that the "real" problem is the Vietnam war, welfare reform, or something else which more easily fits the world view of the educated, book-reading, upward-mobile person whom Eric Goldman (1969) calls "the Metroamerican," the man oriented toward a metropolitan (even cosmopolitan) world.

The root problem is this educated man's persistent Eurocentric definition of "culture" whereby, for example, a longshoreman who knew all of Mark Twain or European classical music, but nothing else, would be thought more "cultivated" than a longshoreman who knew all of Paul Laurence Dunbar or West African music (but nothing else).

Let us make this point in the context of the social world of social science. Cultural ethnocentrism in social science causes the practitioner of the science to miss E. Franklin Frazier's point—far more important than his readily accepted caricature of the black bourgeoisie[12]—that the study of race in the United States is central to the theoretical concern of social science. As a general rule, appreciation by social scientists' of the racial crisis, *and its implications for their work,* is limited not because they are malevolent but because they are insufficiently perceptive. Being insufficiently perceptive, *they have failed to do their homework on the cultural anthropology of United States society!*

Consider political science on the subject of race. If political science had been really perceptive, it would more clearly have perceived the state of mind in the black "nation," and the emergent tendency toward black political withdrawal. In order to have done this, two things would have been necessary: (a) more serious treatment of black politics as a problem in political science, not as mere exotica for curious whites[13] or a subject with which to get rid of black Ph.D. candidates; and (b) serious consideration—though not automatic rejection of—the correctness of many political scientists' implicit proposition that the American polity does work well, though perhaps slowly, to "solve" all really major problems. The political-science example should not mislead us, however, into supposing that the difficulties are the difficulties of that discipline. Sociology purports to pay more attention to social class and stratification than any other social science, yet the attention to black class and stratification is virtually a repetitious series of slogans. Economics is even worse, for there is virtually no consideration of so simple a matter as whether "black capitalism" makes any sense, or makes excellent sense, in the context of economic theory.

The cultural ethnocentrism which underlies this scholarly neglect affects not only the content of social science but its social structure as well. Moreover, as social scientists generally concede, the underlying cultural suppositions of the social scientist have something to do with what he writes and teaches. People can recognize this, and simultaneously deny that the experience (which is the forming pool of "culture") of being *black* is pertinent to the assessment of data and the translation of the same into formal scholarship. It might be hard to develop a Middle Eastern Center which actually included Jews and Arabs, because of the predictable social strains. But, in principle, a Middle Eastern Center staffed only by competent Israeli scholars would be rather astigmatic, as would such a center staffed only by competent Arabs. The parallel need not be labored.

There is a second effect in the social structure of social science. Most social scientists accept the proposition that a colleague (white) ought to work on whatever problems interest him, whether the subject matter is race or not. But until the irruption of the black-studies mood, the common presumption was that a black social scientist ought not to articulate a racial component in his work, lest he "damage his career" by being thought "unprofessional." Since the development of the black-studies mood, and all the intrauniversity stress associated with it, a different fashion has emerged. The rule of thumb often appears to be that it is inappropriate (or improbable?) for a black man to participate in the common enterprise except *as* a black man, it suggests that *as economist* he will not (or should not) really have anything to say about the theory of value, but that he is competent to explain "ghetto economic development." The reason that cultural ethnocentrism is important is that it frequently constitutes a barrier to realistic exchange between blacks and whites, even when the white parties recognize the significance of institutional racism and are personally as free of psychological racism as it is reasonable to imagine that a human being would be.[14]

NOTES

1. For a further critique of median income as a useful conception around which to compare blacks and whites, if one has equalitarian objectives, see Robert S. Browne, "Barriers to Black Participation in the American Economy" (paper presented at the National Urban League Conference, New York, July 1970).

2. New York is noteworthy because its black community conceives of itself as the most aggressive and sophisticated in the country, and because the Lindsay administration has a reputation for energetic attention to racial issues. Nonetheless, there is little evidence that either the mayor's personal staff or his Cabinet or the leadership of the civil service is much more penetrated by blacks than is the case in (say) Chicago or Detroit.

3. I emphasize *formal* because no informed observer can seriously maintain that, in practice, racial criteria are ignored.

4. Since this essay was drafted, Hugh J. Scott has become superintendent in Washington, D.C.

5. The intellectual acceptance of a thoroughgoing ethnic hierarchy is nicely discussed in Solomon (1965).

6. On the implications of this white view, as seen at that time, see Holden (1965 b).

7. We have learned, however, to be very careful in making judgment about what did happen in these complex events when we have nothing on which to go except newspaper reports.

8. Apart from the fact that political murders themselves are not to be countenanced, we cannot believe every *sub rosa* group which claims "credit" for every such death. It is just as reasonable to believe that some such deaths grow out of the policeman's relationship to the underworld. For the underworld has every

reason to want its role obscured from the public, while "revolutionaries" have, as they mistakenly see it, reason to *want* "credit."

9. The quotation is from the introduction by James W. Silver to Cohn (1967, viii). Silver says that Cohn functioned as speech writer for J. W. Fulbright, Averell Harriman, Estes Kefauver, Sam Rayburn, Adlai Stevenson, and Stuart Symington —which suggests a man of at least modest political influence.

10. In a social encounter some time after the event.

11. I pass over the substantive question: whether Moynihan even described the black family pattern correctly.

12. It is curious that S. N. Eisenstadt, much of whose work has been on the tiny society of Israel, should have had considerable intellectual impact, while Franklin Frazier should have had almost no intellectual impact except to generate a caricature of "the black bourgeoisie."

13. For all my disagreements with its thrust, I have to say that *Negro Politics* (James Q. Wilson, 1959) is one of the few books which attempts to meet a proper standard on this subject.

14. See the comments on the philanthropic foundations on pp. 22–23 of this essay.

III

Racial Politics as a Study in Paradox

THE DRAKE PROBLEM

St. Clair Drake, a black American of West Indian background, belongs to the "age-grade" (to borrow a term) which knew at first hand the Depression, the Mississippi and the Chicago about which Richard Wright's novels speak, and the college life of *The Invisible Man,* and which was the cohort of the penniless African exiles who became the ruling "independence generation" from Ghana to Kenya to Zambia. He is also a social anthropologist who has studied aspects of race in the United States and in England and aspects of urbanization and social organization in Africa. It is natural that such a man should have a perspective deeper and wider than his academic colleagues whose intellectual scope is not matched by the full experience, than his practical contemporaries whose action experience is not matched by the intellectual scope, and surely wider and deeper than the perspective of his juniors.

From Drake's perspective comes a question critical to a proper interpretation of the republican crisis and its potentialities: *Why is not the United States more like South Africa?* As of World I, he suggests, the racial patterns of the two countries were remarkably similar, but their broad tendency since then has been divergent.[1] This is a surprising observation to those of us with a more parochially American experience, but there is much to be said for the supposition of similarity. In the North of the World War I period, the black man (like his counterpart in the former Cape Colony) possessed and used the right of franchise. From it, he got some minimal political favors (which were important, considering how little he had), but his rights as citizen were remarkably limited. In daily life, he encountered a persistent pattern of discrimination far more pervasive than that which now exists, and in moments of crisis he could count on legal protection for his right to exist far less than he is now able to do. In the South of that period he lived (as did his counterparts in Transvaal, Orange Free State, and Natal) under a systematic public-private regime of coercion such that "baas" and "boss" were virtually indistinguishable.

If we may infer from the historical record, we must believe that a Louis Harris study of racial attitudes, conducted fifty or sixty years ago,[2] would have shown white supremacy to be a dominant public norm. The proper answer to the Drake Problem is not clear. But the fact of *any* change points to some paradoxes in United States social history. If some earlier Harris had been operating, his survey would have discovered several such paradoxes. Among whites, there has always been some residue, though quite tiny, of opposition to the very idea of white supremacy as a basis for social organization (Cable, 1888). Yet those who did not accept the doctrines tended to accept the fact, even when they sought meliorist policies within the framework (Bailey, 1968). The survey would also have revealed an acceptance of white supremacy, an opposition to change, but no particular supposition that any action to maintain white supremacy was necessary. Finally, the survey certainly would have revealed a vast body of active prejudice, of the sort associated with the politics of the Ku Klux Klan and the most vociferous spokesmen of the Southern Democrats.

If there had been a simple, homogeneous, uniform white conception of the black man and his place, there would have been no room for the changes which we can all too well document. We have to believe of people fifty or sixty years ago what we know about them now: that their attitudes and opinions are complex, so that what they will do under changing circumstances is by no means easy to anticipate, particularly since the combinations of circumstances are themselves so difficult to anticipate. The facts of history and the logic of survey research agree[3] and lead us to an "obvious" but important point. White supremacy is (like "national security," "black power," "changing national priorities," "democracy," "free enterprise," "states' rights," "constitutional government," and others) an ambiguous symbol. It means different things to different people. It is not difficult to see this ambiguity in white supremacy even in television's old movies. About 1970, there was a rerun of *The Sun Shines Through,* based on the Judge Priest stories of Irvin S. Cobb. The judge, leader of the Confederate war veterans' post, was patently as much dedicated to white supremacy as anyone and a contemporary viewer might well be sickened by the groveling posture in which the script writers cast black actors. But in another sense, the judge as hero stood for "law," providing an opportunity for a black defendant to be saved from a lynch mob until the real rapist (a white man) should be caught. The spirit of *The Sun Shines Through* is somehow different from the spirit of *The Birth of a Nation*.[4]

The politics of the South has persistently been faced with exactly this question: Does white supremacy mean rampant lawlessness? (The advocates of law and order have not always had the best of it in answering this question.) The Carswell case similarly brings the matter of ambiguity to the surface. Judge G. Harrold Carswell did not cut a very distinguished figure in his presentation of himself. But anyone who understands Georgia politics of the Eugene Talmadge era will know what he was *trying* to claim in 1969, when he said that his 1948 speech pledging undying fealty to white supremacy was the "liberal" position. In context, he apparently meant to claim that he too favored a guaranteed position of preference for whites, but that he favored less *aggressively* hostile postures toward blacks. Whether Carswell's description of his own history is factually accurate is something we cannot tell. But it is similar to the statement that Huey Long did not exploit the race issue. What people mean by this is not that Huey Long supported black advancement but rather that he was willing to countenance some benefits for blacks along with some greater benefits for whites.

Not only is white supremacy an ambiguous symbol in the sense that it means different things to different people; it is also a symbol to which the same people respond ambivalently. If white supremacy has some clear meaning, shall the individual accept that meaning and accept the action which its acceptance entails or shall the individual reject that meaning and action? Shall a Judge Priest, knowing that lynching is wrong and lawless, himself abstain but permit the mob to take a prisoner (and salve his own conscience by saying they would have killed him anyway had he resisted)? Ambivalence in the individual is brilliantly demonstrated in the actual behavior of Thomas Jefferson. As a single human being, Jefferson advocated manumission, kept title to his own slaves until death, offered the slave trade as an inequity justifying revolution against George III, maintained seriously that blacks were intellectually inferior, carried on a learned correspondence with Benjamin Banneker, and apparently agreed to the action of his Postmaster General, who helped draft legislation forbidding the use of black mail carriers.

AMBIGUITY AND AMBIVALENCE IN POLICY: HISTORICAL PERSPECTIVE

Ambiguity and ambivalence are something more than the problems of discrete individuals. When there are substantial blocs of opinion or interest in disagreement about some matter, it is also possible to perceive collective ambivalence, and to perceive ambiguity in the statement of policy. This is an obvious fact of United States politics—what people usually mean by "compromise politics." What is not so clearly understood is the significance of pragmatic and moral ambivalence in racial policy in the United States.

Such ambivalence has served to inhibit pursuing any policy to its full implications. The policy of white supremacy, in the period from the Constitutional Convention to the Civil War, is inescapably obvious. But the hidden counterpoint is nicely illustrated in the opinions of the Attorney General in the James Monroe administration, an officer who could hardly have *considered* denying white supremacy. Congress had long before prohibited black militia, and administrative rules prohibited black service in the standing forces. But in the War of 1812, Captain Perry's crews could not be filled without arming blacks. "Veterans" of the war were entitled (apparently by Congressional act) to land bounties on the public domain. The question for the Attorney General was whether this promise extended to blacks. Since the Attorney General found that Congress had no more intended black men in the standing forces than in the militia—which latter was explicitly proscribed—it would have been consistent to deny their claims. In fact, however, he took note of the fact that the men had been in the service, and he ruled that they were legally entitled to the land bounties.[5] Virginia adopted legislation requiring that free black seamen, coming into port from other jurisdictions, should be jailed until their ships were ready to depart. The Attorney General ruled this an unconstitutional act in violation of the federal government's plenary rights under the treaty power. The seaman's ruling is understandable since many of the merchant seamen were British subjects on British vessels, at a time when a contrary ruling might have produced diplomatic problems. But why should an Attorney General—in the last administration of the Virginia dynasty—have been so scrupulous about a land promise made nine or ten years before?

Antislavery politics raises equally complex issues. Very few people were ready for aggressive action to eliminate Southern slavery. Moreover, it is evident that the black man was not a welcome member of Northern society in the slavery years. But it is also clear that there was much practical resistance to enforcing the Fugitive Slave Act of 1850. There was then no Department of Justice, nor any other very extensive federal law-enforcement mechanism. Hence the Fugitive Slave Act could not be effectively enforced without the cooperation of the states. Some states, however, adopted "personal-liberty laws," which forbade judges and sheriffs to assist slave catchers, granted black fugitives the right to trial by jury, and sometimes required prosecutors to stand as counsel for such fugitives.

Presumably, such legislation would not have been likely without fairly wide public support. Moreover, such support probably was more than symbolic. This would seem the natural implication of cases such as the "Oberlin-Wellington Rescue," an episode in which students of Oberlin College in an early display of direct action forcibly interfered with the slave catchers who had arrested certain persons for return to the South in 1859. The resultant trial, in Cleveland, produced an outpouring of public support for the rescuers, with the leading members of the town's bar acting as their counsel.

The ambivalence hypothesis gains credibility if we notice that the people of the same states (Ohio for one) were divided about the Civil War, gave some support to Copperheads during the War, refused to approve the Fifteenth Amendment, and (as late as 1912) rejected a proposal to delete the word "white" from the state constitutional prescription of those entitled to vote. Just as ambivalence obstructed the full fruition of white supremacy when that was public policy, so it obstructed the fruition of equality when that became public policy. This ambivalence is quite acute in the Reconstruction experiences.

Reconstruction was really a low-grade undeclared civil war following the official Civil War. It did not take place in either a social or a technological vacuum. The parties to that war were the majority of the white Southerners against the freed blacks and some indeterminate proportion of white Southern allies. *But the decisive variable had to be sustained intervention from the North,* made operational through the federal role. As William A. Dunning wrote:

The maintenance of order was but a negative function . . . ; [the] positive and most characteristic duty was that of creating in each state . . . a political people. Having given to such a people a definite existence, [military government] was furthermore to communicate to it the initial impulse toward the organization of a government for itself, and then to retire into the background, maintaining an attitude of benevolent support until Congress should decree that the new structure could stand alone. (1965, 176)

Moreover, Reconstruction was meant to be (and required for its fulfill-ment) what we would now call "planned economic and social develop-ment." An administrative agency, known as the Freedmen's Bureau, was supposed to facilitate the development of schools, necessary to provide a quick rise in literacy. It was also supposed to resettle the freed population, aid them in securing land which they might develop as independent farmers—which would have called for breaking up plantations—and also in securing seed, tools, and animals to do the farm work.

From the point of view of black officeholding, Reconstruction had some effect. This can be shown in the only easily available data (see Table III-1), dealing with electoral participation and officeholding in the constitutional conventions held in 1868, the congressional delegations elected in 1870, and the state Houses of Representatives for 1870–1871.

Table III-1, Black Membership in Constitutional Conventions, Congressional Delegations, and State Houses of Representatives

Percent of Members Black	Number of States			
	Constitutional Conventions, 1868	Congressional Delegations		State Houses of Representatives 1870–1871
		1868	1870	
50% or more	1		1	1
25 to 44%	2	1	1	2
11 to 24%	5	1	2	3
1 to 10%	2			2
Less than 1%		9	7	
Not shown in source	1			3

In the eleven Confederate states, there were three conventions in which the black delegates were 25 percent or more of the total convention delegates and one in which the 1868 congressional delegation was 25 percent black or more. In another five, the black convention delegates were from 11 to 24 percent of the total, and one more in which the congressional delegation between 11 and 24 percent black. In the remain-ing three states, the convention participation was 10 percent or less, or not known. In all the remaining states (nine), blacks were not yet elected to Congress in 1868. For 1870, one congressional delegation had a black majority, one had more than a quarter but less than half, two had less than a quarter but more than 10 percent, and the remaining seven had none.

For the state House of Representatives (1870–1871), one had a black majority, two more than quarter but less than a majority, three more than 10 percent but less than a quarter, two 10 percent or fewer, but three are not known.

This is a substantial rise, considering that Appomattox occurred not more than five years before, even if it is not the picture of black domination painted by so many writers. If this participation were to be made stable, however, it would inevitably have required a more intensive and more extensive support than it got. Intervention in civil wars can be effective only if the intervenor is prepared to pay a high cost and to remain a long time. But the Northern intervention was never really adequate, even in technical or military terms. Throughout this whole region, with a white population of 5,000,000, the army could deploy no more than 20,000 troops *at any time,* and these troops operated under technological circumstances far more constraining than we now experience: no hard roads; no telephone; no radio; miles of mud between railroad lines.

The South—after an initial period of sullenness—turned an increasingly diplomatic face to the North. Distinguished and prominent figures, some with political antecedents from before the War, returned to politics speaking the language of "peace" and "conciliation," others to business speaking the language of "prosperity" and "common interest." What blacks saw, quite realistically, was the white mask of the KKK—and informed Northerners can hardly have failed to know it. The internal politics of the South was profoundly violent, a calculated and pervasive terror meant to convince blacks that the existence of formal citizenship rights was not a guarantee that those rights could be exercised. White supremacy itself need not have been a main goal for Northerners, but they were ambivalent about how far they should (or could) challenge it, just as whites (North and South) have been ambivalent about how far white supremacy should be pressed or what forms it should take.

There were those who wanted to continue that social reconstruction. But there were others. Some merely wanted to re-establish their prewar Southern contacts, economic and otherwise. Some wanted to establish a new political arrangement based upon the emergent industrial economy. Some wanted to continue Reconstruction, but also wanted to reunify the country politically, which meant including the whites. Those who preferred to bring blacks within the polity were thus faced with an ineluctable fact: the process cost more than they could persuade any significant body of Northerners to assume. Only a vastly larger army would have worked unless—as white people were not ready to accept—the United States government was simply to arm the whole black population. The latter measure would have elicited great political resistance even in the North, and the former (larger army) would have been unacceptable on various grounds: people did not want to serve during the War, and *certainly* not in "peacetime"; the budgetary costs would have been far too great; and (with industrial strife rising in the North) it is doubtful that public opinion would have tolerated a large standing army. Then, unlike now, the Republican party had strength to conserve among the working classes as well as among others. Deep engagement in Reconstruction over a long time had other risks, as people probably saw it then. One aspect was the battle of the civil service reform politicians against the more conventional users of patronage. (Not only were the politicians most interested in the South deeply embedded in the patronage system of the North, but they were also using the South itself as one of the largest patronage engines the country had then seen.) Withdrawal from Reconstruction was, perhaps above all, the response to industrialism as the emergent corporation made its way through the economy.

The decision was to cut the losses and get out. Once the decision to withdraw was made, it became necessary to accept a Southernization of Northern opinion, precisely because there was always an undercurrent of Northern politics calling for re-intervention in the politics of the South. After all, black participation did not stop with 1877 and the Hayes-Tilden settlement, but continued into the twentieth century. But that participation was increasingly being narrowed by the coercive pressure of white antagonists in the South. It is reasonable to believe that black Republicans in the South would have tried to activate their Northern colleagues (white and black) to provide support. If the situation were to be stabilized, from a Southern perspective, it was essential to make the point that "the black man is not fit for politics." In the North, this argument was credible for some because in the North itself white racism was a powerful factor (Fishel, 1969). It would win the credence of others because they could reinterpret it to mean "the black man is not yet fit for politics," and so persuade themselves that when he should become fit, he would be accepted.[6] The upshot of this was the argument expressed in academic historiography and popular fiction, that Reconstruction was a "mistake," and its reinforcement by the invocation that "Lincoln would not have done it, but the Radicals miscarried the nation."

But the Southernization of Northern opinion had other elements. In its simplest form, it invoked the claim of "unreasonable prejudice" against the South, as if Northern criticism were simply founded in ignorance, and ultimately became a threat—"if you want cooperation, be quiet." To make this Southernization really viable required both exclusion of any definition of the black man as essentially human and reinforcement of definitions of the black man as essentially subhuman. The great maneuver for this purpose was the lending of national legitimacy to lynching. In the late nineteenth and early twentieth centuries, six or seven blacks were being lynched every month somewhere in the South. But antilynching propaganda was distinctly unwelcome. Floyd Crawford, an historian, notes the bitter response to Ida B. Wells's antilynching tour in England (1894):

[*The New York Times*] observing editorially the fact that, immediately following the day of Miss Wells' return to the United States, a Negro man assaulted a white woman in New York City "for purposes of lust and plunder," sarcastically commented on the crusader's [travelling about] the British Isles to set forth the brutality of white men and the unchastity and untruthfulness of white women. "The circumstances of [this] fiendish crime," [the *Times*] concluded, "may serve to convince the mulatress missionary that the promulgation in New York just now of her theory of Negro outrages is to say the least, inopportune." Commenting finally on her responsibility for organizing the Anti-Lynching Committee, the *New York Times* stated that her purpose "plausibly" might have been considered one of income rather than outcome. (Crawford, 1968, 16)

There is little to indicate that the *Times*—then essentially a Southern newspaper in a Northern city (Talese, 1966, 80–92)—was very different from other papers, or that most people disagreed. The asserted justification of "protection of white womanhood" was persuasive although the evidence was that most lynchings had nothing to do with sex at all. Lynching meant much more than a mere extralegal hanging, based upon "community opinion"; it very often meant castration, mutilation, immolation, sheer bestiality. Apart from its elements of white sexual pathology, lynching was *functionally* a vital element of the terror required to maintain an inert and submissive population. Through the intentional cumulative intensification of this terror the white South managed so firmly to consolidate its hold that, in the last decade of the nineteenth century, it could actually begin the process of joining legal restriction to extralegal force to create a new regime.

THE THRUST TOWARD APARTHEID

The distinguished historian Rayford Logan has described the period after 1877 as the "nadir"—the low point—in the black man's experience after the Civil War. The nadir can be located even more precisely. It is not simply "after 1877" but *after 1900 and before the 1920's.* In these years, it would have been reasonable for any intelligent observer to believe that virtually all white resistance to white supremany was gone, that ambivalence was completely resolved to the disadvantage of the black man. Another of the paradoxes of American racial history is, in other words, that the United States came then closer to apartheid than it had come at any time since the Civil War and that (the Drake Problem) it somehow veered away thereafter.

The best test is in very simple things. If there is anything central to the "civil religion" of American society it is that the law-abiding man who bothers nobody is to be left alone, and that the law-abiding man who tends to his own business and acquires property is to be respected. A series of vignettes will show how absolutely this proper behavior failed to bring to individual human beings the expected rewards of simple toleration and simple respect.

Some time around 1900, a preacher living near the town of Liberty, Mississippi (anomalous name!), was a bit more than ordinarily prosperous. He pastored four churches (one for every Sunday of the month), was active in the affairs of his church association, served as trustee of a little Baptist college, and ran (with a very large family) a farm of some five hundred acres or so (which he owned). What catalyzed the enmity of his "White Cap" neighbors is not clear, but he found himself subjected to mysterious threats such as miniature coffins atop his gatepost early in the morning with warnings to "be gone by sundown." Two men living in Mound Bayou, Mississippi (a black town in the Delta) had similar experiences about the same time. One recounted that he had owned a farm of some hundred acres in Coahoma County, Mississippi.[7] Living there, he had been under the necessity to carry a gun and a pair of shears in his car each time he went from home and returned—the gun for fighting and the shears for cutting barbed wire strung across his road in the dark of night. Another had been driven from his 160 acres in Hinds County (near Jackson) about 1910, after he had committed the offense of buying a new car before any of his white neighbors. Of the same motif is Walter White's account of the mob approaching his father's home in the 1906 Atlanta riot shouting, "That's where that nigger mail carrier lives! Let's burn it down! It's too nice for a nigger to live in!" (White, 1948, 11).

If the simple problem of being threatened in, or driven from, legally acquired and legally held property is one test, there are others with which scholars are more comfortable.[8] Public legislation is a more common test. The elements of apartheid existed in a degree which, from the perspective of 1970, seems a little startling. The version coming closest to apartheid, as we know that term now, was specifically meant to restrict the physical presence of black persons in places where white persons might also congregate. There is, logically and behaviorally, very little difference between this practice and admitting white and black to the same shops, with white always having first claim on the clerk's time. Public accommodations are one sort of example. Except for a brief period, when the Civil Rights Act of 1873 was still in force, the pressure was toward deciding that a black man might not buy a meal, or a railroad seat, or have access to a theater if whites were also to be present. *Plessy v. Ferguson* (163 U.S. 537; 1896) could be interpreted as a statement of the right of the seller to choose his customers. But it is more convincing to regard it as a judgment that the public authority could be used to require segregation—even if the seller were willing to operate otherwise. The process was exacerbated after 1900. The process which Woodward calls "the strange career of Jim Crow"—beginning in the nineteenth century—was the assertion of Southern state authority in the direction of apartheid. The Berea College case is a clear demonstration of this. Berea, a small but distinguished school, has long been oriented to the service of poor students, black and white. The Kentucky legislature in 1904 forbade Berea to admit black students, as was then its practice. The Supreme Court (211 U.S. 45; 1908) thus permitted Kentucky to impose a degree of segregation which South Africa's universities were not required to adopt until after the Nationalist victory of 1948. Kentucky presents us with still another version. In 1914, Louisville adopted an ordinance forbidding persons of one race to acquire residential property in areas where the majority of residents was of the other race. In consequence of a law suit, the Supreme Court ruled the ordinance unconstitutional (*Buchanan v. Warley* 245 U.S. 60; 1917). The ordinance had already been adopted in similar form by other cities (Baltimore, Richmond, and St. Louis, and several small towns). Had the Supreme Court reached a contrary decision, it is quite possible that many more cities would have adopted such an ordinance, and that legal apartheid might have arrived in the United States well before it eventuated in South Africa.

There is another parallel which is as close to being fundamental as anything can be: the franchise. Until the Act of Union (1911), the present four provinces in South Africa were separate colonies with separate franchise systems. In three (Orange Free State, Natal, and Transvaal), there was no such thing as a black franchise. The Cape operated, on the other hand, with a property qualification, which has been misunderstood since few blacks could meet the property test. The point is that those blacks who did meet the test were a significant proportion of the whole electorate in their respective constituencies. In those constituencies, they determined the fates of candidates and significantly affected the balance of power in the Cape Parliament.

One of the most widely shared points of agreement in the Union Convention was the elimination of the Cape franchise. As a means of getting past the British Parliament (which had to ratify the constitution), the Union Convention substituted a special category of representatives to be elected by blacks but from white candidates only. The United States case was more complex, taking place at the state level in the South. Under the Reconstruction Amendments, it was not possible to outlaw black voting per se, but the clear and explicit purpose was accomplished by the design of educational, poll tax, and other restrictions which had to be interpreted at the discretion of registration officials. The net effect was similar: to reduce black participation to a nullity.[9]

White resistance to this disfranchisement seems to have been about as effective in the one case as in the other. Histories of the Republic of South Africa recount the opposition of one former Cape Prime Minister (W. P. Schreiner), who carried his forlorn fight all the way to the Parliament in London, as if Schreiner were utterly quixotic. One finds a similar expression about one of the last holdouts in the Republican party. When "the South, with Populism safely dead, was making bold finally to nullify the Fourteenth Amendment and formally disfranchise the Negro," says W. J. Cash, "Henry Cabot Lodge would shrill practically alone on the floor of the Senate regarding the pressing need to send down bayonets upon the land again—and to galleries that only grinned" (Cash, 1941, 203).

At that point, the Republican party made a decision from which it has yet to recover, a decision to accept the thrust toward apartheid. Perhaps most people assumed that, as President Taft later told a group of black students, "Your race is destined to be a race of farmers," with the implication that their future lay in the South. If people so assumed, then disfranchisement in the South would free the Republican party of the onus of being a black party in the South and would thereby permit its lily white faction to compete effectively with Democrats. Certainly, the Republican leadership began to pull back. President Theodore Roosevelt had begun a departure from past practice of appointing black federal officials in the South, using the now well-known argument of Northern hypocrisy which has been revived recently. He did not see, said he, why black officials should be appointed in the South but never in the North. If the implication was that black officials would be widely appointed in the North, it proved misleading, for there were very few.

The more appropriate implication, to judge from the Roosevelt practice, was that blacks ought to be less deeply engaged in politics. The test here is that the Progressive Convention of 1912 (a fully Roosevelt convention!) simply refused to admit black delegates at all. Taft continued the Republican pullback, initiating the beginnings of segregation in federal departments and insisting that he would not make appointments in local communities offensive to those communities. Since "local communities" meant white people, Taft was in effect announcing that he would appoint no blacks if whites objected. Since they could be expected to object under most circumstances, Taft's decision was itself a decision to reduce black appointments still more. In disillusionment, some fragments of black leadership began to search for a viable connection to the Democrats.

. . . [T]he president of the Washington NAACP branch, J. Milton Waldron, who was also leader of a Negro Democratic club, obtained an interview with Wilson. Waldron's memorandum on the interview stated that Wilson desired the support of Negroes. There was nothing to fear from a Democratic Congress, he assured Waldron, because he as President would veto hostile legislation, administer the laws impartially, and would not exclude Negroes from office on the basis of color. (Kellogg, 1967, 157)

Despite Wilson's repudiation of this memorandum, some people (including DuBois, who had also backed Bryan in 1908) convinced themselves that Wilson was a superior choice to the Republicans, and to Theodore Roosevelt's Progressives who had refused to admit black delegates to their 1912 convention (Kellogg, 1967, 156).

Those who persuaded themselves so were soon disappointed. The President was not a "hater" of the Vardaman type, but if he was a gentleman he was both a *Southern* gentleman and the leader of a Southern-based party. The early signs were sufficiently adverse that even Booker T. Washington's persistent optimism seemed to flag: "I have never seen the colored people so discouraged and bitter as they are the present time." Charles Anderson, a New York Republican (see Osofsky, 1966, 161–168), spoke a language very like that being used today to describe the Nixon administration. The most serious thing about the Wilson administration was:

" . . . the reflex influence of the Administration's attitude toward us." This Anderson considered to be more hurtful than all of the removals, demotions, and segregation put together, because it inspired enemies of the Negro all over the country to run amuck at any time without fear of punishment and notified the oppressor that oppression was safe and protected by the highest authorities in the land. (Kellogg, 1967, 166)

Other events seemed to confirm the Anderson diagnosis. Southern congressmen were presenting bills to require segregation in several areas of national life, absenting themselves from hearings if NAACP spokesmen came, and with the NAACP itself regarding it as a blessing merely that Congress should have failed to adopt this new legislation (Kellogg, 1967). The nation was racked by riots in the cities. The Justice Department began to survey black newspapers for signs of seditious agitation. At the end of World War I, a gubernatorial candidate in Massachusetts found it possible to denounce "the Afro-American Party, whose hyphenated activity has attempted to stir up troubles among Negroes upon false claims that it can bring social equality" (Litt, 1965, 31). ("Social equality" in those days meant interracial marriages.)

All told, the years between McKinley's second election and that of Warren G. Harding probably were the worst of any twenty-year period since the Civil War. Yet in all this there is a double paradox. For the first time since blacks were admitted to the franchise, their more adventurous spokesmen were looking for a political connection, but neither party wanted the black vote. That vote held no interest for the Democrats, who were still a Southern party; and it was losing its appeal for the Republicans, who developed the essentials of the "Southern strategy" from which they have yet to escape.

Just at this point, we see still another of the paradoxes. Precisely when apartheid approached its apogee, white people began to lose their confidence that white supremacy was unquestionably right and inevitable. Congressional ritual provides a major key. Most new bills are rituals of activity, meant to impress someone, be it the "folks back home" or some other audience. They are not considered seriously, nor are they meant to be. But the values celebrated in the ritual are instructive. Between 1903 and 1947, the ritual was seen in 129 bills explicitly relevant to race; 20 were antidiscrimination bills of one sort or another and 22 were segregationist bills of one sort or another.[10] The bills supporting segregation were almost all introduced in the years between 1903 and 1923, while bills professing to attack discrimination were almost all introduced between the early 1930's and 1947. By 1947 not even one segregationist bill was being introduced. The inference we draw is that, almost unnoticed, public approval of the rituals of segregation had begun to taper off in the 1920's. Unconsciously, without so intending, whites had begun a glacial retreat from apartheid.

THE UNCONSCIOUS RETREAT FROM APARTHEID—A NEW
AMBIVALENCE

In each decade since World War I, black pressure against white dominance has been stronger than in the decade before. (See *The Politics of the
Black "Nation."*) The retreat from apartheid might possibly be explained
as a response to such pressure. Such an explanation is pertinent; but it is
not complete. *The whole point in the Drake Problem is that North American
whites, like South African whites, might have adopted progressively harsher programs of coercion, but did not.* This does not mean that racial equality was
now taken seriously and intently by a great many people, nor (for the most
part) that there was much calling into question of the position of whites.
But there was a new approach appropriately described as meliorism: simply making things somewhat better. From segregation as public doctrine,
through meliorism, the path eventually leads to the liberal rituals of antidiscrimination.

Although "liberalism" and "civil rights" are now closely associated—
and both likely to be joined to Democratic politics—they were not always
so. Until the New Deal years, "practical" liberalism was largely disjoined
from black advancement. (See below, Essay V, "The Democrats. . . .") The
most notable advocates and practitioners of meliorism were conservatives
and (usually) Republicans. Though they were, on the racial question,
deviant conservatives (and *deviant* Republicans), *they were noteworthy precisely because they were not then matched by liberals of similar stature.*[11]

Conservative meliorism did not start generally with an advocacy of
equality (surely not of "integration" in any current sense, decidedly not
of "black self-determination"), but with an advocacy of relaxing what
seemed unnecessary or inappropriate constraints. Meliorism could be sentimental, as in the case of Bernard Baruch's memory of his mother's
admonition to "do something" to help the pathetic blacks. But the most
important conservative strand had less to do with pity *or* rights than with
efficient management, or what would now be called "welfare colonialism."

Conservative meliorism operated in the South, from the late 1890's.
This is one source of the revived tradition of the Southern Moderate (and
the Southern Moderate's Northern ally), the white man prepared to argue
that the black man "deserved better" (if only as "Christian decency"), that
he *might* yet actually be irredeemably inferior and that, in any case, black
improvement would be good for the white man. This tradition centered
upon a network of whites who accepted—pragmatically or morally—the
fact of white supremacy and chose to put different policy preferences

within that framework. The general doctrine was that if the black man were "properly" educated, whites would permit him to assume a somewhat different status—and that this would be good for the South. Who were the advocates of this view? For the most part, they were members of a kind of "education Establishment": white state-university presidents (including David F. Houston of Texas, later Wilson's Secretary of Agriculture), officials of the United States Bureau of Education, Northern businessmen (including such men as Robert C. Ogden of Philadelphia, for many years President of Hampton's trustees, and William H. Baldwin, Jr., a railroad executive),[12] and precursors of the contemporary foundationeers (such as Edgar Gardner Murphy, executive secretary of the Southern Education Board). The Washington group had close relations with the conservative meliorists. The meliorists were likely to prefer the Booker T. Washington types and to be rather impatient with the more militant and demonstrative blacks, regarding such activities as NAACP as "silly." Naturally, more militant blacks reciprocally had no use for them. Indeed, from the point of view of some other blacks, the meliorists were both a powerful and an unacceptably paternalistic group. Relative to blacks, they *were* powerful. There was then no such thing as any consequential federal aid to education. The distribution of the *extremely* limited state funds was in any case discriminatory. Blacks simply could not support the educational institutions they needed, out of their own resources, despite great concern and strenuous efforts (Bond, 1966, 145–146; Frazier, 1962). Consequently white sponsors with private money, or with access to private money, were overwhelmingly important. Moreover, such sponsors were clear in their own minds about how they ought to proceed. The character of many black institutions is still powerfully influenced by the fact that such white sponsors then made their own decision that "industrial (vocational) education" as advocated by Booker T. Washington was what ought to be encouraged, and that "professional" or "classical" education ought to be discouraged.

Powerful as these men looked to blacks, they themselves felt constantly exposed and under the necessity to defend themselves from more hostile whites. Moderates of this sort depended to a large extent on Northern philanthropy, and even more on some minimal toleration from influential Southern whites whose audience they sought. The moderates persistently deemed it futile to attack segregation, and often found it prudent to abstain from overt politics. As Hugh Bailey describes the businessman Robert Ogden, President of the Southern Education Board:

Although not personally prejudiced . . . he completely accepted the philosophy that the Southern Negro must wait for advancement until the Southern white had been enlightened. . . . He did not foresee that education would simply provide more sophisticated rationale for segregation. "We cannot meet the views of our colored friends and must be content to be greatly misunderstood for the sake of the greater usefulness. . . ." However, he was distressed by what he felt he must do. For fear of offending the white South, he consistently refused to invite Negroes to the annual conferences, and of this he wrote, "I am greatly ashamed, but, nevertheless, it is worse than useless, at present, to quarrel with conditions we must accept because we cannot control." (Bailey, 1968, 150)

To advocate "giving the black man a 'better' chance" was about as far as any white meliorist seriously *expecting to influence other white people* would go.[13] If they had a relatively limited effect on policies, they meant to have (and probably had) at least some effect in mildly shifting the structure of public opinion. Within the limits of segregationist reality, they provided one form of attack on white supremacy—a criticism by indirection, relying upon "facts" and "persuasions," oriented to the "modernization" of the South.

In the North, conservative meliorism was related to a pragmatic and managerial response to the fact of black urbanization. We do not understand this process very well, nor will we until there is a more serious examination of the role of the big businessmen of the early 1920's. Such businessmen were seldom (if ever) advocates of racial equality in any sense. But they were also not mere Babbitts or Dreiserian Titans, utterly unaware that the migration had important implications for themselves. Most businessmen were perfectly well aware that black laborers were now an important part of their industrial establishments. Some had the distinct intent to use black labor as counter pressure upon white immigrant labor.[14] And some few (*very* few) entered the picture for other reasons. Victor Lawson, the publisher of a major Chicago paper *(The Daily News)* was one such, to whom the matter was a sort of home mission work. (Lawson was so rigorously Presbyterian that he refused to publish a Sunday edition of his own paper.) In a remarkable anticipation of the Urban Coalition reasoning, Lawson had his own energy renewed by the riots of 1919, on the postmortem commission for which he served. The role of the businessmen had to be even more important then than it is now, because so much of what is now in the public domain then rested under private charity for which they paid.

The businessmen defined the black situation (with help from social workers) as primarily a "welfare" issue, but needed interpreters to keep them abreast of the details. Two organizational results were attendant. One was to generate the creation of a new black leadership structure, based upon social work and financed by industry, in the identity of the Urban League (Strickland, 1966). The other effect was to create a small corps of white men, Northern and Southern, who in later years would come to be called "race-relations professionals." The function of the race-relations professionals was to mediate the side effects of the cityward black migration, to maintain contact between blacks and the businessmen.

The race-relations professionals had a dual problem. On one hand, they had to maintain their own credibility and monopoly as the expert advisers to the businessmen and the foundations. On the other hand, they had to maintain some rapport with their black counterparts and points of contact. Out of this dual need there developed the small corps of such advisers as entrepreneurs of social reform, defining the situation of blacks, defining for blacks what avenues would be most useful in approaching white private leaders,[15] and defining for white leaders what sorts of activities in black communities would be most productive. The essence of what has come since to be called "welfare colonialism" rests in this relationship, but in context this relationship was also part of the process of raising a certain white awareness from simple assurance about white supremacy to a level of some ambiguity and ambivalence.

Still another strand of meliorism runs to the churches, particularly to the Protestant denominations. In the North, the Protestant denominations —through the Federal Council of Churches of Christ[16]—became a vehicle for what was actually often thought of as equivalent to "home-mission" work. Most people—properly—would think it absurd to place much emphasis on "Race Relations Sunday" once a year. But in the 1920's, it was rather important that George Edmund Haynes should have managed to create this device under the auspices of the Federal Council, because it was the one sure way in which ordinary, respectable white people would be brought to hear some reasoned discussion of racial problems.[17]

Perhaps the factor which most catalyzed new opinion was a growing revulsion against lynching. The problem was to establish a public conception of lynching as a repugnant act. Lynching was the gross offense, beyond others, to which expositors of all persuasions directed attention— Washington no less than his radical critics. The first vocal expression came from radical white journalists and social workers—moved by the 1908 Riots in the symbolic "home of Abraham Lincoln," Springfield, Illinois— and led to a linkage with the black Niagara Movement to produce the NAACP. But it was the South in which lynching was standard, and against which propaganda could be directed. Some part of the change came through radicals' capitalization upon the basic idea of "decency," which did not call for equality at all, but simply meant no excessive abuse of the weaker. The most important symbol evoking the idea of decency probably was lynching. In this context, we probably have to assign much weight to the role of so distinguished a lawyer as Moorfield Storey. Storey made himself the center of respectable opposition, induced so solid a figure as William Howard Taft to join in the public propaganda, and gave credibility to the idea that Congress had power to punish lynchers. The left wing was relatively unimportant for most symbolic purposes. What was more important was the activation of conservative meliorism, with its emphasis upon law, fair trial, and due process.

This convergence of a grass roots notion of decency, of a conservative emphasis on law and orderly process, of a radical bias toward what would now be called "human rights," and of some notion of "modernizing" the South all became part of the broad thrust against lynching, an important crack in the older conceptions of unlimited white supremacy. But it had somehow to be transformed into a set of ideas perceptible to those people who do not bother much to think about social structure and social organization. Hence, one may suggest, the critical role was that of the press. A good part of the more adventurous, and sometimes more prestigious, *reporting* press (but not necessarily the *commenting* press, such as Alsop or Evans-Novak) has since the 1920's generally been sympathetic to the more advanced part of whatever was deemed a movement for black improvement. The working reporters, who had actual experience of covering the lynching situation, tended to develop a problack bias in much the same way that the reporters who regularly cover contemporary ghetto politics tend to develop such a bias. Lynching provided the reporters, as rioting later provides their successors, with an occasion both to achieve the drama which is their professional lifeblood and an opportunity to play the role of cynical but aspiring moral censor which is so much a part of their professional culture. The idea that lynching "protected white womanhood" probably was once believed by most people who heard it. But detailed publicity made clear to people who had never thought about it before that lynchings had nothing to do with sex. In its natural pursuit of drama, the press brought the elite perceptions and themes into a common pool of public ideas. In turn, the role of the press was to convey to the nation-at-large, even to those components themselves committed to white supremacy, the image that the South was wantonly and needlessly doing the black man a great wrong.

Still another element entered: The Ku Klux Klan of the 1920's simultaneously became the symbol of lynching and made itself the antagonist of certain sorts of Southern conservatives (such as Oscar Underwood, whose opposition to the Klan apparently diminished his chances for getting the 1924 presidential nomination), urban Catholics (who were a critical part of the Democratic party in the North), and urban Jews (who were some substantial part of the intellectual leadership of American liberalism). To give publicity to lynching, and to the Klan, was to create a new perception among the antagonists chosen by the Klan: those who lie about us probably are lying about everyone else as well.

Two other elements deserve notice. One was the discovery of Harlem (and the little Harlems elsewhere) by the avant-garde world of art. The "Harlem Renaissance" was not a political movement, but its effects were political. It generated new states of mind among the younger people to whom the artistic *demi-monde* had appeal, a process of intellectual and sensory contact across racial lines never before experienced, and left complex residues in the attitudes of the people so engaged. It was a part of the process by which the black artist and musician began to break somewhat out of the world of unofficial apartheid, and which would lead them in the next decade straight into radical politics—which in turn would make some concern with blackness a part of one's credentials as a genuine white radical.

The other current was the shift in the direction of serious scholarship. Franz Boas's anthropology led, through his intellectual descendant Melville Herskovits, to "cultural relativism." In true positivist spirit, he insisted that there was no *scientific* basis on which to regard one "culture" as higher than another. Left at this, cultural relativism leaves open the road for the most arbitrary "I like what I like" judgments, but it certainly did undermine the rationale for discrimination. Herskovits did not particularly mean to draft a political program, but the political effects of relativism are beginning to come to the fore, most particularly in giving scientific credentials to the notion of Africa as a legitimate place with legitimate cultures, and this notion is undermining the imputations of "Negro inferiority."

More directly, psychologists began to search for ways to deny the inferiority which World War I testing had led many to attribute to blacks. By 1940, historical revisionism was able to make some (though minor) impact on Reconstruction studies—something black historians had tried vainly to do—and the general thrust of social scientists (if not other scholars) and some leading journalists was toward "improvement." And sociologists were immersed, particularly at the time of the

New Deal, in studies of the actual conditions of Southern servitude.

The sum of all this was to begin to make respectable a sort of discussion which, as late as the Wilson years, had been regarded as utterly radical and unacceptable. By the middle of the 1920's, the opinion-making part of the country had begun to have a different appreciation of the racial problem, an appreciation which would not have generated any urgent action but would have created and sustained ambivalence.

The broad pattern of American society has been an increasing ambivalence in social decisions about race, somehow related to changes in both the practical circumstances of life and in the body of ideas deemed respectable. One may, of course, reject the ambiguity-ambivalence hypothesis, but it is difficult to do so and still explain not only the visible constraints on blacks but also the modification of those constraints. Only on the ambiguity-ambivalence hypothesis does it seem possible to explain behaviors which can be seen any day of any week, without simply falling into endless conundrums.

The process by which the new ambivalence came was very complex. Part of it stemmed from radical politics. But much more stemmed from the invocation of conservative values and the activation of very simple common sense notions of decent behavior, sufficient to undermine the old idea that white supremacy was *the* valid public philosophy. The first consequent was mere meliorism. It has long since become apparent that mere meliorism is not adequate to the requirements of the United States polity. The atmosphere which encouraged meliorism developed into a new form of ambivalence which made it possible for government to consider some positive action, the end of which chain was the idea of "civil rights" as championed by black moderates and Trumanite liberals. Even the question whether "civil rights" as redefined by the Trumanite liberals is sufficient seems to have been answered in the negative. From the time of the 1947 *Report* of the President's Committee on Civil Rights until now, the question has been increasingly sharpened until it hardly can be mistaken: can a contemporary republic stand, containing within itself a second "nation" virtually as if that second "nation" were an unassimilable body of aliens? It is about this particular question that white ambivalence presently focuses.

The theoretical (and the policy) question now is whether we should foresee a slowing down or a reversal of the increase in ambiguity which has been characteristic so that—after all—the United States may experience something like the South African pattern. This discussion we save for later essays.[18]

NOTES

1. Whether Drake has ever written about this is not clear, but he certainly made such observations orally when teaching at Roosevelt University in the 1950's.

2. An imaginary precursor of Brink and Harris (1967).

3. Fenton (1960) is a good layman's introduction to survey analysis. For a more sophisticated exposition, see Mendelsohn and Crespi (1970).

4. A social scientist interested in changing American values might profitably study the black-white relationships depicted in movies since World War I as one very good indicator.

5. See Leon Litwack (1961, 32). Litwack does not discuss whether these men actually got the land bounties, a question which would perhaps naturally occur to students of administration.

6. Bailey (1968) discusses this conception as entertained by Northern businessmen who supported education in the South.

7. Clarksdale, the birthplace of the writer Lerone Bennett, and the residence of Dr. Aaron Henry, now Democratic National Committeeman, is the county seat of Coahoma County. The anecdotes are childhood stories. The preacher was the author's grandfather and the two men neighbors.

8. In these days when Afro-American studies have become fashionable, one wonders if any scholar has put his mind to the problem of quantitative analysis of this element of history.

9. It would be useful, in keeping with our discussion of ambiguity and ambivalence to ask why federal legislation or constitutional amendment for this purpose was not adopted. What was the political barrier preventing its adoption, at a time when the Democrats did not desire the black vote, the Republicans were losing interest, and the black vote by itself was not yet *self-evidently* too big to prohibit such a practical possibility?

10. The remainder were bills calling for various kinds of study commissions, which (since they implied a need for change) might be associated with the intent of the antidiscrimination bills, or bills dealing with ceremonials, pensions for individuals, and so forth. In the discussion of these matters, I rely on some memoranda prepared for me by a former research assistant at Wayne State University, Mrs. Asha Borgaonkar Vattikutti. The memoranda, so long as they last, are available in mimeographed form to interested colleagues.

11. The roll call includes Henry Cabot Lodge, virtually the last senatorial advocate of black enfranchisement by federal coercion; Moorfield Storey, self-conscious heir of the Charles Sumner tradition, advocate of the NAACP, but also Boston railroad lawyer, sometime President of the American Bar Association, nemesis of Louis Brandeis (on Storey's role in the fight against Brandeis's court appointment, see Alpheus T. Mason, 1946); Senator Joseph B. Foraker (R., Ohio), senatorial advocate of the Rockefeller oil interests, and bitter critic of President Theodore Roosevelt's handling of the "Brownsville riot" case (see Foraker, 1916); and, indeed, the Rockefellers themselves.

12. Among the many underdeveloped subjects in black-white history is a study of the philanthropists who were interested in problems of the black South. It would be useful to start with a biographical and sociometric analysis of the supporters and managers of the various educational foundations reported in Horace Mann Bond (1966), 130–150. Baldwin is one such whose name crops up in many connections and whose widow was one of the original sponsors of the Urban League (see Strickland, 1966). The Rockefeller interest is another. John D. Rockefeller, Jr., reportedly became interested in the Southern Education Board (which put most of its effort into white education) when convinced that white education was a necessary precondition for black education in the South (see Bailey, 1968). From the biographical sociometry or "prosopography" as historians apparently say (see Stone, 1971, 46–79), one might usefully proceed to a study of the policies and outputs of these foundations.

13. However, they should be distinguished from others, such as the Alabama editor John Temple Graves, the Mississippi Senator LeRoy Percy, or the writer David Cohn (above, Essay II), who are also called moderate by Northern observers. These latter really differed from the Vardaman lynch-mob segregationists only *on questions of manners,* yet it was the good-mannered segregationists to whom the Northern popular and elite audiences were often more responsive.

14. On the importance of white immigrant labor, see Leiserson (1924). On the specific in black labor as counterpoise, see Abell (1924).

15. In the South, and in national politics, the race-relations professionals also had a certain monopoly of access to public leaders. In Northern *local* politics, they did not have it; the avenue was directly through the professional politicians, black and white.

16. Predecessor to the National Council of Churches.

17. I would comment, in passing, that there is no comparable forum for raising today's *comparably* "far out" racial issues.

18. Notably, Essays VI-IX.

The Republicans:
Historical Note on the Southern Strategy

The crisis of republican institutions is intimately associated with some problems within the Republican party as an organization. Black people frequently argue that "we have been excluded deliberately," and often they are correct—though like most complainants they may exaggerate the process while whites, like most defendants, may minimize it. But if there is any perceptible place of exclusion from genuine public politics, apart from the ballot box in the South, it is in the Republican party since about 1900. That history accentuates our understanding of the problems which the Republican party must now solve *if* it is to have a desirable effect on the quality of republican institutions in this generation.

BLACK REPUBLICANS BEFORE 1890

The first major proposition is that black Republicans in the South, but not the North,[1] *before 1890 had a position within the party about as favorable as that of black Democrats in the North between 1960 and 1969.* The seven black Congressmen (Republicans) elected in 1872 and again in 1874 were a larger number than the national capital would again see until after the election of 1968. The comparison is still valid *after* the apogee of Reconstruction. In four of the five Congresses starting with 1880, blacks were yet able to send to Washington one congressman from each of two states, in addition to the single senator from Mississippi elected in 1874. This was very ordinary politics, hardly enough to shake the world, but it was more

64

than blacks again were able to accomplish until the past decade. Moreover, if—*ceteris paribus*—the single actor in a small group carries more weight than a single actor in a large group, we might possibly attribute slightly more importance to these congressmen than might otherwise be thought. They were members of small or medium-sized state delegations in contrast to the larger delegations of which black congressmen presently are members. (The largest state delegation having a black member was the 10-man Virginia delegation, which included John M. Langston—elected 1888—in contrast to the somewhat larger delegations of Illinois, New York, and Michigan down to 1958.) The likelihood is that these black members played a more than trivial role[2] in a House two-thirds the size of the present House, with a more fluid power system in which both committee and seniority counted for less than they do now (Polsby, 1968, 144-168). Even more to the point is the black politician's role in internal party decision making. Some historians note, for instance, the election of Congressman John R. Lynch (Mississippi) as temporary chairman of the Republican National Convention of 1884. What is important about this is that Lynch was elected as the first test of strength between the James G. Blaine forces and the anti-Blaine forces (of which the most important element was the Chester A. Arthur group). Lynch was by no means an agreed candidate. The Blaine group, controlling the Republican National Committee, recommended another candidate; Lynch, placed in nomination by Henry Cabot Lodge for the Arthur people, was elected with 424 votes, a 40-vote margin or by 52.4 percent of the recorded vote. One may suppose that the Lynch candidacy reflected several normal elements of convention politics. One would have been the desire to get whatever advantage might accrue from having the chair in friendly and competent hands during the fluid organizing stages. Lynch, a former speaker of the Mississippi House and former Mississippi State Chairman, was admitted by all observers to be competent[3] and, on this occasion, he certainly was aligned with the Arthur group.

But another aspect of the candidacy would have to do with the normal requirements of bloc politics. One student of the Democratic party describes the candidacy (quoting *Harper's Magazine*) as intended to "conciliate the [N]egro vote" (H. C. Thomas, 1919, 159). This seems a very reasonable interpretation in light of two facts. One is Lodge's own nominating speech, in which he referred to support for Lynch as support for those Republicans who were steadfastly supporting the party in their home states, even when doing so produced the risk of great physical danger to themselves. The other is the size of the black delegation in the convention. The precise number of black delegates in 1884 is unknown, but it probably cannot have been less than 10 percent, if we note that as much as eight years later (when black participation was beginning to decline), there were 120 black delegates in a convention total of 905 persons.[4] If we recall that the black delegates at that time had a great incentive to hold on to their places, and if we consider what would now be the implication in a national convention of a "black caucus" of 13 percent (the 1892 share), we may reasonably guess that the name of the game was "get the black delegates on our side." There was not just partisan hyperbole, but much realism in Frederick Douglass's claim that "the Republican party is the ship; all else is the sea."

THE BLACK FRANCHISE AND WHITE SOUTHERN SUPPORT

The second major proposition is that the black Republicans of the South began to lose when their interests could no longer be effectively merged with the political interests of a significant element of Northern Republican conservatives. Such a comment requires us to reexamine the supposition, which many analysts read backward from now into the past, that racial adjustment was then a political property of the "liberal" or "progressive" forces. "Conservatism" was no more of one piece than the "liberalism" of the New Deal period, when some liberals had racial adjustment high on the agenda and others were liberals on "everything but the race question." Some saw the continuation of the black franchise as essential to the fortunes of the party.

The assignment of the 19 Southern electoral votes to Hayes was crucial in 1876. But from 1880 onward, the Republican vote within each state was insufficient to deliver the electoral vote for the Republican candidate in any Southern state. Cleveland's 1884 victory was accounted for, in the *post hoc* opinion of one Republican commentator, by the fact that the Republicans lost the South. Had the black vote been maintained, so this commentator thought, the Republicans would have won, even without some important Northern states such as New York (Foraker, 1916, II). It is also possible that maintenance of Republican strength in the South would have made some difference to the party's position in Congress. For instance, the 43rd Congress (elected 1872) had a Republican edge of 43 seats, 41 of which were accounted for by Southern members, most of whom were white but a good share of whom must have depended on black votes. In only two of the next ten Congresses were there Republican majorities and these two paper-thin: a majority of one in the 47th Congress (elected 1880), with six Southern Republicans, and a majority of three in the 51st Congress (elected 1888), with nine Southern members.

The underlying politics of the state legislatures had somewhat similar effects on Southern senatorial representation.

There were, of course, many other factors beside race and Southern representation, including Republican vicissitudes in the rest of the country. But the exclusion of blacks by force and fraud was an important consideration, which Republican national politicians sometimes acknowledged. President Benjamin Harrison, in one message to Congress, referred vaguely to the need for protection against ballot abuses, which people seem to have taken as a reference to attacks on the Southern black (hence, *Republican*) franchise. Politicians seem, at that time, to have considered two possible responses. One was, under the second clause of the 14th Amendment, to reduce the Congressional representation of the South so that only that population entitled effectively to vote would be counted in the apportionment of seats. This might have been thought a form of pressure on the South to save its overall allocation of seats by leaving the black franchise alone. But such a strategy seemed unproductive, particularly from the viewpoint of black politicians. Their fear was that this would merely encourage the South to settle for a smaller number of guaranteed white seats.

The main alternative, which Southerners called a "force bill," was to provide for federal administrative supervision of Southern elections. The Federal Elections Bill of 1890, the principal drafter of which was the then Congressman Henry Cabot Lodge, broadly anticipated the Voting Rights Act of 1965. It would have put Federal officials on election boards, in any part of the country, upon petition of 500 voters in any given district. Such boards would have been authorized to inspect and verify returns, to pass upon the qualifications of voters, and to receive ballots refused by local officials. After narrow passage through the House (where the Republicans had a three-vote edge) the bill was entangled in a 33-day filibuster on the Senate side, and was finally defeated in some complicated politics involving both silver legislation and a tariff bill sponsored by then Congressman William McKinley. " 'The bargain [to kill it] was carried out,' Lodge wrote sadly in his Journal. 'It was sold & sold for dishonest money. A bare and miserable business' " (quoted in Garraty, 1953, 120). The diary note can be reconciled with the rest of what we know only on the assumption that some part of the nineteenth-century conservatives had a doctrinal commitment to their conception of "the Constitution" and of "the Abolitionist tradition."

The Lodge bill of 1890 also makes it clear that the late-nineteenth-century conservatives had no doctrinal attachment to state's rights. Nothing could be more centralizationist than a measure to permit a federal takeover of local election machinery anywhere in the country. This fact is the more obvious when one of its principal sponsors specifically says that the key provisions have been copied from election legislation in the United Kingdom,[5] where the very idea of anything like state's rights is absurd!

Defeat of the Lodge bill should probably be accounted one of the major events of the decade. For had it been adopted and implemented, the process of legalized disfranchisement initiated by the Mississippi Constitution *of the same year* could not have been carried to fruition.[6] But, by January 1891,

. . . the Force Bill was completely dead and the whole question of Federal supervision of elections was assigned to the limbo of discarded issues. By 1892 even Lodge had given up hope of reviving it, telling a constituent that he had decided not to offer a bill on the subject, since it would have no chance of getting out of committee. (Garraty, 1953)

Thus, the greatest significance of the Lodge bill's defeat was that the politically active conservatives thereafter abandoned racial adjustment as something they had the political power to affect. *They were defeated by their copartisans who were attached to other traditions and interests.* As a matter of high politics, the Republican party never again made a major stand on a question of reducing the social constraints upon blacks.[7] How is this to be explained? We suggest two considerations. In the first place, Republican conservatives had two cross-pressuring interests. They had, as some saw it, an interest in the Southern franchise, but that put them at odds with the Southern Democrats. At the same time, they had an interest in industrial protectionism, for which some measure of Southern collaboration (or, at least, nonobstruction) was essential. Thus, in the franchise case—as in the earlier Hayes-Tilden dispute—the Republican party settled for industrial benefits which were open to interpretation as contrary to the electoral interests of the party.

In the second place the Republican party was not really a solid national party. It had won in five or six[8] of the eight presidential elections from 1868 through 1900. But the underlying stability of the Republican majority can all too easily be mistaken if we depend on the presidential accounting alone. Congressional politics provides a quite different point of view. Sixteen Congresses were elected in this same period, in five of which (1868, 1870, 1872 and 1898 and 1900) Republicans were elected to majorities in both houses. In five others (those elected in 1874, 1884, 1888, 1890, and 1894) the Republicans and Democrats split control of the two houses. In the remaining, the Democrats controlled both houses. Hence, the Democrats actually controlled more Congresses than did the Republicans in the years from the presidency of Grant through that of William McKinley.[9] In all likelihood, an analysis of local and state elections would show an even greater reserve of Democratic strength. There were then Republicans, as there are now Republicans, convinced that an appeal to a white electorate—without the onus of being a "black Republican" party—was a more prudent way to diminish the Democratic reserve.

The confluence of protectionist politics and Republican lily white ambitions probably accounts for the defeat of those interested in the black franchise. With the clear indication that those with the strongest personal and political incentives to support black suffrage would no longer be able to interfere, Southern politicians were freed to move rapidly ahead with exclusion of blacks throughout the region. In the next fifteen to twenty years, the discussion went into other veins, mainly the reduction of representation under the 14th Amendment.[10] The reduction of representation never reached the same degree of seriousness as had Lodge's 1890 bill and, in any event, was more controversial among advocates of black suffrage, white and black.

THE DOWNGRADING OF BLACK REPUBLICANS

The third major proposition, thus, is that the conditions for an explicit Southern strategy existed as soon as Northern conservatives ceased to discuss how to make black suffrage effective and instead considered whether it should be defended at all.

Disfranchisement in the Southern states did not eliminate the black Republicans, but it decisively weakened their position within the party over a series of years. The consequence of attempting to reduce their influence was to be expected. The principle can be stated simply. If national party leaders find that one local or regional constituency is no longer available to them, they will tend to listen more to the claims of others who seem to be effective substitutes. If a collective decision-making body contains members with different sorts of resources, those who most provide the resources for supporting the organization will also want the organization to be most attuned to their constituency interests. They will consequently resist the influence of those who participate in the collective decision but who lack the capacity to help implement the collective decisions or who have incentives not to help implement those decisions.[11] If the basis for participation is some presumption of electoral representation, then those who lack an electoral base which their colleagues can treat seriously will be stigmatized as "rotten-borough" representatives. Efforts will be made to get rid of the real or alleged "rotten-borough" effect and to replace it with some more "useful" set of contributions.

Under this logic, it would be expected that—once the prospect of serious black enfranchisement had receded—the Republican party would pay less attention to its "black-and-tan" ("integrated") factions and more attention to its "lily white" ("segregated") factions. Because the black Republicans were obliged to work in a situation where they were more and more threatened with violence, and after 1890 more and more disfranchised by apparently legal means, they could not offer protection to their members. Thus, they could maintain only the shells of their former organizations. Their organizations became, instead, rather small clubs and cliques of associates. Those few who remained active were the same people who recurrently represented their state and local organizations in the national conclaves, and their position in those conclaves was rather similar to the position of legislators from extremely safe districts. Because they still had convention votes—and some symbolic importance for black audiences on a national scale—they could still be influential at key moments. But their latitude extended mainly to the ability to bargain for themselves. As participants in the national scene, they could do whatever they liked because they were so extremely safe back home.[12] They were in fact, no longer representatives but rather "owners" of the local organizations.

The attack on the black Republicans then took the form of widespread allegations of "corruption." It is by no means impossible that many such allegations were correct. For one thing, such allegations would reflect not merely the political behavior of blacks in the 1890's and early 1900's, but an important element in the style of all politics in the United States. Moreover, it should be predicted that members of collective bodies who do not have constituencies to which they must answer will do one of three things (or possibly all three in combination). They may behave in a very "statesmanlike" way, taking the "broad" view of what is "right" because such activity costs them nothing. They may also behave as doctrinaire advocates of very special points of view, points of view which their colleagues in competitive situations cannot afford. Or, finally, they may use their trading ability to secure individual perquisites for themselves.

If their colleagues need their support, however, the likelihood of an emphasis on the individual perquisites will increase, since these are the only form of persuasion their colleagues will usually be able to afford. However, since the competitive colleagues will feel themselves "put upon" by having to achieve the support of those who cannot help to implement the decisions, such colleagues will seek ways at the earliest possible moment to exclude the "safe" members if they can. This is what happened in the Republican party, and would have happened to some degree—assuming a declining black vote—even without any attribution of "racism." As early as 1884, there had been pressure to cut down the Southern (hence, black) representation in the convention by making it contingent on support at the general elections.

Naturally, the black delegates resisted such a move, the more so because their colleagues—acting through Congress and the presidency—would not help them maintain the conditions required for a high Republican vote, namely enforcement of the black franchise. In due course, the party began to cut down on Southern representation, with very clear effects on the black delegates. As of 1892, the Southern delegations constituted 24.7 percent of the names listed in the official proceedings (244/905), of which about half (120) were black. Twenty years later, these delegations constituted a little more than 16 percent (252/1550) of the total convention, of which a fourth (65) were black. Under the amended rules in 1916, the Southern delegations constituted about 18 percent (174/987), of which a fifth (35) were black. By 1924, the Southern delegations were still about 16 percent (183/1109), of which now about a sixth (32) were black. In short, the party's decisions about how it would structure itself somewhat reduced Southern representation and decidedly reduced black representation in the years we have been considering. John Lynch, still living and active in 1924, might well have pointed out to his younger successors how sharp had been the decline since his own high point in 1884.

THE DYNAMIC OF THE SOUTHERN PARTY STRATEGY

The fourth major proposition is that a Southern strategy has been pursued vigorously, and with sharp national attention, only at the behest of Republican presidents or presidential advisers, not at the behest of Republican congressmen, even when those congressmen have been in alliance with antiblack Southern Democrats. The reason is that congressmen, whatever their policy preferences, have no need to think of national majorities, while presidents do, and Republican presidents have needed (or thought they needed) to think of consolidating national majorities including the dominant proportion of the white South. This outlook was early also reflected in the Republican presidents' handling of patronage questions. Although winning elections cannot be regarded as the prime objective of party leaders, the objective to which they will always defer anything else, it is certainly an important secondary purpose. If party leaders cannot win a sufficient number of elections, or otherwise sustain their organizations on local resources, then their organizations will die off unless external resources are made available. In the years we have been considering, patronage was still the prime external resource, and for the black Republicans of the South this meant federal patronage. Straight through the 1880's and 1890's, Republican presidents had kept alive at least skeletal organizations by appointing blacks to federal positions in the South. Both Southern Democrats and lily white Republicans objected, the former because they objected to black officeholding at all, and the latter both for that reason and for the more important reason that they wanted the patronage in order to build up their own organizations.

Acceptance of lily whiteism as a policy became apparent with Theodore Roosevelt, whose "problack" reputation has been dramatized repeatedly, on the basis of some rather special episodes. One was the public denunciation which he received across the South for his famous breakfast with Booker T. Washington, but another was his closing of a Mississippi post-office when local whites objected to the appointment of a black lady as postmistress.[13] Too much attention to these episodes put the matter out of focus. Only a superficial search for heroes and villains could obscure the fact that Theodore Roosevelt was equally vigorous in defending himself under attack from any quarter, and that even less egocentric presidents than TR are quick to defend the "prerogatives of the office." If we really leaned on the episodes, we should equally have to say that Roosevelt was antiblack for having discharged three companies of black infantry without honor, under circumstances where all the available evidence was on their side.[14] One historian, working from Roosevelt's papers and correspondence, offers a very simple explanation. TR simply did not quite appreciate how vigorously the Southern critics would react (much as Robert Kennedy misunderstood Ross Barnett) until after the fact, and—though holding on tenaciously in specific cases where he was attacked—quickly modified his policy to diminish Southern criticism. He paid less and less attention to those advisers who recommended "black-and-tan" alliances, and more and more adopted the lily whites wherever that maneuver seemed profitable. Above all, the key feature was his fear of losing the presidential nomination in 1904:

Roosevelt was faced with the detrimental political consequences of a policy that too many people condemned. . . . The Negro question was a problem that could determine the vote of Southern Republican delegations. [Mark] Hanna controlled both 'lily white' and mixed delegations; therefore, Roosevelt concluded that he must follow a similar policy. If an anti-Negro policy could secure the vote of a delegation, he would use it; and on the opposite side, if a pro-Negro program meant the control of a delegation, this was the policy to follow. (Scheiner, 1962, 180)

The explanation which Scheiner offers makes sense for the second administration as well as the first. Roosevelt was no longer trying to get himself renominated, but he was interested in dictating his successor (as he eventually succeeded in doing). As a matter of politics he could hardly expect to have much hope in the South for his Secretary of War if he did not prove to white Southerners that the Army might give black men guns, but not for use against whites. Once in office, however, the Taft administration also adopted a Southern theme. Extending the Roosevelt policy, Taft not only made fewer appointments in the South, but announced that he would not make appointments unless they were acceptable to the people (the *white* people) of the local communities in which appointees would have to work. What was happening was that the Republican party, having been unable or unwilling to pay the price for enforcing black suffrage, now proceeded to destroy the remaining basis for black participation in the politics of the South.

Even at this point, however, the Taft people left themselves sufficient leverage that they could secure the "black-and-tan" delegations in the 1912 Convention, for the Roosevelt forces by that time had adopted the lily whites almost everywhere (Nowlin, 1931, 56; Walton, 1969, 51).[15] In a series of credentials fights, the Taft managers recurrently seated the "black-and-tans," but the basis for essentially autonomous black participation in the Republican party had been eroded. Black Republicans in the North would try to counteract this erosion by claiming that the black electorate constituted a "balance-of-power" vote in key states, but they had been making this claim at least since 1880 without having been able to verify it in practical politics (Fishel, 1969, 64).[16] They were, in fact, isolated from influence in national politics.

There were some brief signs of a potential departure in the Harding administration. The most publicized of the recent Harding biographies also lays great emphasis on the President's October 1921 speech in Birmingham, interpreting this as a call for a new policy (Russell, 1968, 470–473). We cannot, the President said, "go on, as we have gone on for more than half a century, with one great section of our population, numbering as many people as the entire population of some significant countries of Europe, set off from real contribution to solving national issues, because of a division on race lines."

A single speech is never conclusive evidence of a presidential policy, and in fact black Republicans interpreted this one as a continuation of the TR-Taft position, in its acceptance of segregation and social barriers. Moreover, Gosnell claims that Harding's "official actions showed that he agreed with the Taft policy of insisting that Negroes appointed to federal positions in the South (be) acceptable to white communities (Gosnell, 1967 ed., 29). On the other hand, the Southern senatorial reaction was stronger than one might expect in response to a genuinely segregationist position. And there is still another fragment. Speeches apart, Harding became the first president to endorse federal antilynching legislation. It would be inappropriate, without careful inquiry, to attribute the House passage of the first such measure to the President's role, but the coincidences at least suggest some connection, the more so because it was less than a decade since the very idea of such legislation was "radical" and since no other president until Harry Truman would take the political risks of endorsing it.

But Harding was, in any event, not one of the presidents who would leave the mark he desired on policy, and the Coolidge-Hoover positions substantially reestablished the Southern strategy as a central feature of their politics. The notable feature is that the Republicans were unable to get beyond a Southern strategy when, because the controverted issues concerned little more than basic political participation or basic legal rights, their lattitude was greatest. Presidents even proclaimed themselves unable to act against lynching, and lawyers seemed to have forgotten the Civil Rights Act of 1866. Particularly after 1900, the problem of blacks already active in politics was to maintain a defensive fight against their further exclusion from Republican politics. *If we recall that much of this fight was going on during the heyday (1895–1915) of Booker T. Washington, we may also understand more clearly how those blacks actively involved in politics frequently resented his strategy of overt nonparticipation (The Politics of the Black "Nation,"* Essay II). What is apparent is that they thoroughly and decisively lost that fight.

Beyond that fight, the practical problem was to resist the trend toward apartheid, which accounts for the terrible importance of the franchise question (on which the blacks were making little progress), and the equally pressing problem of segregation. For, within and without the federal government, the problem of segregation was gaining in importance, not diminishing. On this matter, the Taft administration was curiously mixed and began to permit the official segregation of government installations in Washington, thus setting the precedent which would be widely extended by the Wilson administration. The submerged theme in the Taft administration was curiously contrary to lily whiteism. For Taft also appointed the first black sub-Cabinet member (an Assistant Attorney General), who was the only such sub-Cabinet member until the Eisenhower administration (1953). Similarly, Taft's Attorney General (George Wickersham)[17] apparently had the political freedom to lead a fight against segregationist policies within the American Bar Association. Nonetheless, the Taft administration's main policy direction was unmistakably lily white. Of the ensuing Republican administrations little is to be said, for little happened that was different. (Hoover, curiously enough, could separate his lily white conception of Republican politics from his administration of the Department of Commerce, and at first earned considerable approval from blacks because he reportedly abolished segregation within the Department.) The labor and black contingents had not been allied before, union policy requiring racial exclusiveness and black leadership responding in opposition to unionism. But some groups (notably the Urban League) were already trying to get the American Federation of Labor to modify its exclusionist policies. No one broke through this until President Hoover's nomination of John J. Parker gave blacks and unionists a common political issue. Parker had acquired an antiunion reputation, which made him a target for the AFL. At the same time, his history as a lily white Republican candidate for governor (North Carolina, 1920) made him a target for the NAACP. Parker's rejection, and the subsequent defeat of some pro-Parker Northern senators, mark the operative beginning of the reputation of the "alliance" between black and organized-labor interests.

THE CRISIS OF THE PARTY

The fifth major proposition is that the Southern strategy in Republican presidential politics has been obscured by two important facts. One is that the only Republican president between Hoover and Nixon seemed at once *sui generis* for his personal attractiveness and above the ordinary techniques of political manipulation. When Dwight Eisenhower declined to support integration as a broad principle, it could be said that as a career soldier, he simply did not understand the needs of a changing civilian society. When he refused to endorse *Brown v. Board of Education* (347 U.S. 483; 1954), arguing that the President should not judge the Supreme Court, it could be argued that he simply did not understand the presidential role. The other important fact was that the Congressional version of the Southern strategy was less visceral, less calculated to stir up the public at large, than the presidential version. If Republican congressmen, happily collaborating with their Southern colleagues in the "conservative coalition," contributed nothing to the solution of national problems, they contributed less to their exacerbation. At least, they had no need to dramatize racial prejudice, which is quite different from the needs of the presidential version.

The final proposition is that the matter now becomes particularly acute because the incentives of presidential competition are just as strong while the issues are vastly more complex. The Republican party proved to have too little capacity to deal with relatively simple and individualistic citizenship issues, which in no way threatened the basic interests of the party's social infrastructure. The broader issues of social policy—of attempting to use a political position in order to generate new policies—would naturally impose more constraints on them. But these issues simply did not yet exist on the public agenda. Neither the conception of positive governmental action to secure racial equality (equal employment opportunity statutes, open-occupancy statutes, or the like) nor the broad range of relevant social welfare or economic policies were then contemplated as governmental functions.[18] Once these issues, with all their implications for class politics and the politics of redistribution, should begin to arise, the Republican party would naturally have greater difficulty coping with them.

The fact that of the Southern strategy has been inherent in Republican presidential politics, not merely the creation of Mr. Kevin Phillips or Attorney General John Mitchell, dramatizes the sense in which the republican crisis is also acutely a Republican crisis. This is all the more true now that the issues of racial politics go beyond simple citizenship and involve extremely complex problems of social esteem and, in a real sense, some form of redistributive politics. Whether the Republican party, which as the "conservative" party has an indispensable function, has or can acquire the relevant capacity is the question. It is a question of the party's ability not merely to pursue politics but to conduct government, if we understand government to mean the rational and responsible ordering of society. Or, perhaps, it is a matter of knowing that the Republican party fully possesses the capacity for "smart" politics, but wondering if it has the capacity for "wise" politics.

NOTES

1. The black position in the local parties of the North was extremely weak. See Fishel (1969, 56–75).

2. The sole study of the subject, which we find superficial and lacking in an understanding of the legislative process, is Samuel D. Smith's (1940).

3. For a sketch of the Lynch career, see Gosnell (1967 ed.), 23–35. In retirement, Lynch put some of his effort into historical writing. See, for instance, his *Some Historical Efforts of James Ford Rhodes* (Boston: The Cornhill Publishing Co., 1922).

4. The total number is taken from the official proceedings of that year's convention. The count of black delegates is taken from Nowlin (1931).

5. The bill's Senate sponsor (George F. Hoar, Massachusetts) is so cited in Schriftgiesser (1944), 106, n. 1.

6. The bill suggests the utility of a study of communication and alliance patterns of the sort now common to students of decision-making behavior. For instance, while the bill was being considered, how much were congressmen aware of the details and implication of Mississippi's constitution-making adventure? How much would Lodge have been aware that John R. Lynch (whom he had nominated for Temporary Chairman of the Republican National Convention in 1884, only six years prior) was one of those to be driven from Mississippi politics by the new constitution? How much difference would any of this have made or did any of this make?

7. Thereafter, conservatives interested in racial meliorism were, as compared to their normal *political* associates, somewhat deviant and obliged to act outside the framework of "practical politics." See the preceding essay.

8. The count is five if we exclude the Hayes-Tilden election of 1876.

9. This paragraph is based upon a table showing (a) votes needed to organize each house, (b) Republican votes, and (c) Southern Republican votes for the sessions 1867 through 1901. This table (available by private request to the author) was prepared by Miss Alberta Sbragia, a Project Assistant in the Department of Political Science, University of Wisconsin.

10. A Library of Congress bibliography on the suffrage question, published in 1906, mentions neither Lodge nor the question of administrative supervision.

11. In Congressional politics, for instance, this is the basis of conflict between members who accrete seniority and power because they have safe seats and members who operate from highly competitive constituencies where they are in perpetual danger. The process can also be seen in the public accounts of United Mine Workers politics. Convention delegates representing locals whose members actually work in the mines were apparently more likely to support the candidacy of Joseph Yablonski, in opposition to those representing locals of pensioned miners who were more responsive to the appeals of W. A. (Tony) Boyle.

12. In this respect, they were like a recent Massachusetts Republican congressman who neither campaigned for reelection nor even maintained an office in his district!

13. The postoffice was in Indianola, the county seat of Sunflower County (from which comes Senator James O. Eastland).

14. This was the Brownsville affray of 1906. Three infantry companies were

moved into a military post near Brownsville, Texas, over considerable local objection. In due course there was a shooting episode in which one white man was killed. No evidence was ever developed by the Inspector General to connect any man of the post with the shooting, but the IG concluded that they had all been in a conspiracy of silence to cover it up, and so recommended discharge without honor for all 270 men. This led to a bitter two-year public political fight, including a face-to-face debate at the Gridiron Club between the President and Senator Joseph B. Foraker of Ohio. See Foraker (1916).

15. When the Roosevelt people bolted to the Bull Moose convention, they seated the black delegates from the North (who were not objectionable to their local communities), but "the credential [sic] committee offered a resolution which was adopted by the convention stating that every Negro delegate from the lower south be excluded from the meeting."

16. My only guess is that they *could not* have sustained this claim in any except the most extraordinary circumstances unless the two-party vote split were otherwise extremely close. The reason is that, before World War I, the black population was actually so small in nearly all the Northern cities except New York and Philadelphia that it could not have had much effect on the elections. But careful analysis may lead to rejection of this hypothesis.

17. As a further instructive sidelight in how the same social issues persist over time, the Wickersham Commission (National Commission on Law Observance and Enforcement) appointed by President Hoover covered much of the same terrain as the later National Crime Commission and some of the Eisenhower Commission terrain. One of the Wickersham Commission's task-force reports on the policy, entitled *Lawlessness in Law Enforcement,* covers some of the same terrain as the Walker Report to the Eisenhower Commission.

18. Federal aid to education once had a different status, being specifically conceived as a Reconstruction measure. Like the later Lodge bill on the franchise, it was far more centralizationist than anything since conceived, for it merely proposed that wherever a State did not provide an adequate common school system the federal government should do so. By the twentieth century, this was out of phase with the Republican conception of governing, and so represents another element of the Republican party's failure to come to terms with the requirements of a republican regime.

V

The Democrats:
Racism, Black Votes, and White Liberals

BEFORE THE NEW DEAL

If the Republican adoption of a "Southern strategy" is one sort of paradox, so the near-equation of "civil rights" with Democratic politics is another. For the Democratic party, for most of its history, has patently contained the Southern strategy in a clearer fashion than the Republican. Not only has this been true because of the party's dependence on the white South until fairly recently, but also because the Northern Democrats have frequently been rooted in constituencies (like Mr. Dooley's Irish) decidedly averse to blacks. There were, of course, the exceptions which make this generalization a little suspect, as any generalization must at times be. It is ironic, for example, that the Massachusetts Democrats should have nominated one of the first two blacks known to have been elected to an American legislature (1866) (Moon, 1948, 88–89). Some local Democratic politicians, notably in Chicago and New York, had begun to stretch out for black votes late in the nineteenth century, but the Democratic party did not make a serious effort to reach such votes until well after the black shift toward the Democrats was already under way.

The potentialities of a black Democracy had existed for some considerable while before Franklin D. Roosevelt became President. W. E. B. DuBois was a little unusual, both as a personality and as a black radical, but he and a few others of his circle had endorsed Bryan in 1908 and Wilson in 1912. Moreover, some more hard-headed types had gotten into Democratic ward politics for the "fishes-and-loaves" incentives (Moon,

79

1948; Osofsky, 1966). But it took more than twenty years before the party could treat the black prospect seriously. There was apparently some interest as of 1912. At any rate, this is the implication of Moon's comment that Wilson's campaign managers had received reports that from 20 percent to 40 percent of the Northern black vote had gone to Democratic congressional candidates in 1910. Thus, says Moon, in 1912

. . . the Democratic party was definitely out for the Negro vote in the three-way fight of that year. Hoping to capitalize upon the Negro's resentment against the Republican party and against Taft and Roosevelt, the Democrats sponsored the organization of the National Colored Democratic League and other political outfits among Negro voters in the North. . . . They sent speakers to address Negro groups and advertised in the Negro press. . . . It was, however, an uneasy and restrained association, almost clandestine. (1948, 94)

By 1928, the Democrats (or at least Alfred E. Smith) seem to have reduced their Southern anxieties somewhat; Walter White reports an approach from Smith, suggesting that he himself come in to help direct the campaign in an open quest for black votes. But, White also reports, Smith later withdrew this agreement on the purported advice of Southern Democratic senators, one of whom was his running mate (White, 1948, 99–101). Nor was Franklin Delano Roosevelt more adventurous, either before or after his entry into the White House. The correspondence of Louis Howe, his personal manager, is full of skittish warnings about how to handle what Howe called "the colored brethren" (Rollins, 1962). One could not imagine Roosevelt brooding, like Henry L. Stimson, over "the original crime of slavery," nor worrying too much about the question of legal rights like Moorfield Storey, nor even recalling like Bernard Baruch his mother's admonition to do "something" to "help." He was mainly alert to his interpretation of the political necessities. When Walter White sought his support for antilynching legislation in 1935, Roosevelt was quite explicit in his refusal. He told White that the Southerners controlled all the key committees and would retaliate by bottling up his economic program. Roosevelt seems to have had ideas of decency just as conventional as his ideas of black and white. As a decent man he could try, by personal conversation, to get the Governor of Alabama to intervene in the Scottsboro case. But deliberate policy, no. The political incentives were against it, and there were no apparent political incentives in favor of it. As is fairly common in party politics, the Democrats did not see the black potentiality until *after* blacks had already begun to shift toward the Democratic party. There was no image of an available and useful black vote. Instead, there was virtually no appreciation that blacks were not sentimentally Republican, but responsive to the fact that at each stage in the twentieth century efforts to go aboard the Democratic ship had been repelled by those already aboard. Rather, the image of an available vote developed during the first term, and it seems that Roosevelt himself was interested only after he saw that possibility. Harold Ickes notes and gleefully reports how Roosevelt agreed to more black public housing after having seen his picture in every window of a black Indianapolis neighborhood.

It was, however, necessary that the President's attention should be called to the policies which might encourage this political development. (Some policies would, of course, be self-activating. Any noticeable spillover at all from its economic programs could not but have an attractive effect upon the black population.) The operative mechanism for calling the President's attention to racial matters was, in very large part, the group whom we have since come to call "white liberals."

"WHITE LIBERALS" AND "RACIAL ADVISERS"

It is particularly important to understand the role, for the "white liberal" has been one of the transformers, one of the entrepreneurs of social reform, in the area of race relations. The insistent pressure toward black self-assertion, which makes that role now less viable, should be understood in context of what that role is. The white liberal is necessarily ambiguous and ambivalent. He has not seen his role as that of educating the mass white public. Nor has he seen his role as that of an independent power wielder, capable of operating against other power wielders. Instead, he has seen himself as an "external" leader of black people and spokesman for their needs. His political role thus has depended on his monopolizing something other people might value, namely knowledge about black people (which white power wielders would not have) and knowledge about the inner details of high politics (which black people would not have.)

This role has required the white liberal to practice what C. P. Snow calls "court politics," dissimulation and intrigue to catch the favorable attention of the ruler (also see Reedy, 1970). In other words, white liberals could not operate except on the readiness of major political decision makers to believe that there was a substantial black problem requiring attention, somebody who knew what attention it required, and a substantial political incentive to give it favorable attention. The white liberal has thus had to maintain a certain monopoly of access to the most important decision makers because his value to those decision makers would be reduced if blacks had equal access and equal credibility. He is, to blacks, the man who "knows where it's at" (to use a new phrase) both as to the social condition and as to workings of power. At the same time, he is unreliable, for he cannot afford to press his white superior too hard, lest he lose credibility for realism. The role is, like many marginal roles, lacking in great nobility. At the same time, the role has been critical in establishing a more direct connection between issues of race and decisions in public policy. The white role could not be operative, in the form it has taken, until several social conditions could exist supporting a *critical mass* of "white liberals."

There was a distinct shift in the attitude of the interpreters of social events (the opinion-making community) toward problems of race. Until the academic community and the journalistic community (from which the individual functionaries in the white liberal role so often come) began to repudiate the Southernized opinions which so long reigned, there simply could not be very many people to play the role. Moreover, the existence of the "white liberal" in critical mass depends on the existence of some white group the interests of which require it to support policies which, frequently but not always, could be served by legislative, administrative, and judicial decisions sufficient also to cover some of the interests of blacks. "Liberalism" in this sense has been most pertinent when it could simultaneously cover the problem of "antidiscrimination" ("human rights") and the problem of economic policy. Historically, the former thrust has found its roots mainly in the necessities of the Jewish community, while the latter has found its roots in the emergence of the "industrial" (as against "craft") labor union movement.[1]

These conditions were, of course, developments of the years after World War I. Before then, the elements of "progress" which might have been latent in Democratic administrations could not be fulfilled. One might have supposed, for instance, such elements to be present during the Cleveland administration. For ironically, Cleveland—the first Democrat since the Civil War to occupy the White House—followed policies at least as open as those of his Republican contemporaries in the years just before the Republicans settled on the Southern strategy. He continued Frederick Douglass as Marshal of the District of Columbia, argued that the black voters should split between Democrats and Republicans, and issued appointments to other black men (including the interesting innovation of sending a black man to a white embassy, instead of to Haiti as was usual). In a world where political symbolism was acutely important, Cleveland even invited Frederick Douglass (with Caucasian wife) to White House social functions nearly twenty years before the Booker T. Washington breakfast which earned Theodore Roosevelt bitter criticism in the South. None of this behavior suggests any excessive commitment to the more rigid demands of the South. But Cleveland lacked the supportive and prodding influence of an entourage which would push his administration toward a more open policy and help to formulate that more open policy in workable terms. The first hints of the "white liberal" role are to be seen in the Wilson administration, but the potentiality was minuscule and of little effect. The principal "white liberal" was not a member of the Wilson administration but was a strong supporter: Oswald Garrison Villard, who was at the same time editor of a New York newspaper and a major figure in the internal politics of the NAACP.

It was Villard (even more than the black Democrats) with whom Wilson discussed his racial posture in 1912 and in the first two or three years after inauguration. Recognizing that the President was not going to take any more positive action, Villard tried to get him to appoint a "National Race Commission" which would really have been a kind of combined Myrdal study and Kerner Commission. Its purpose was

to engage in "a nonpartisan, scientific study of the status of the Negro in the life of the nation, with particular reference to his economic situation." Areas proposed for study were physical health and efficiency, homes and property, work and wages, education, religious and moral influences, citizenship, legal status, and participation in government. (Kellogg, 1967, 161)

The correspondence went back and forth, and Villard was in and out of the White House consulting Tumulty on the project, advising on means to evade Congressional resistance, and at one time thought he had a commitment that the action would be taken. (He also counted on the assistance of the "inside" white liberal, Walter Hines Page; but whatever influence Page might have had was lost when he was removed from the scene by being appointed ambassador to London.) In the end, nothing came of the project, for Villard's energies were diverted into the more urgent project of opposing the administration policy on segregation— necessary activity if he was to maintain his NAACP role, but utterly adverse to maintaining much further influence with the President.

As is well known, the Wilson administration went in the other direction. With the President's subsequent (if not advance) approval, black participation in the Civil Service was cut to an absolute minimum. The federal buildings were themselves resegregated, and the resegregation—which would last more than forty years—returned to the city as a whole. As far as the available studies show, only two more favorable results came forth. As a response to the great Northward migration—from which the present black communities derive—the Labor Department created a Division of Negro Economics, apparently a sort of study section. Even this measure, which we would now regard as trivial, must have been thought of some importance, considering that the politically influential South was doing its best to stem and reverse the migration. The other direction in administration policy was responsive to the military-manpower situation. Over the objections of Southern whites (always apprehensive about blacks with guns), blacks were enrolled in the United States Army and, following what was then a "radical" demand (for which DuBois was a major spokesman) segregated camps were set up to train black army officers.

If the "white liberal" role was to be played, there would have to be a fair number of such persons, in different public and private institutional settings. They would have to have some capacity for mutual support and there would have to be a sufficient number that if any one became expendable,[2] the role could be filled by someone else. Only after the transformation of the 1920's was this even possible, as a matter of the sheer "political economy of personnel." Until the 1920's, the atmosphere had not permitted enough such persons to survive. By the time of the first Franklin Roosevelt administration, there were enough such that they entered the government in many roles, including the critical category of "advisers on Negro (or racial) affairs." The clearest example was Will W. Alexander, a one-time Methodist clergyman who became the majordomo of the Rosenwald system (Dykeman and Stokely, 1965). Alexander had been a key figure in the Commission on Inter-racial Cooperation (later the Southern Regional Council), the first executive officer of Dillard University, and virtually "Mr. Race Relations" in the foundations-university-government system between the 1920's and World War II. How his connection to Franklin D. Roosevelt was established is not clear, but he served as an official in the Resettlement Administration and performed other chores for the President. Although he does not seem to have been asked to work for Roosevelt as race relations man, it was quite natural that he should carry with him into government his conception of a meaningful approach on that subject. The conception was essentially to emphasize the need for overall Southern economic development (a point of view to which Roosevelt was responsive) and, within that, to emphasize a subtle mix of "diplomacy" and "research" in order to emphasize the utility of "inter-racial cooperation." In providing the President with ideas about Southern poverty and Southern tenancy, it was inevitable that Alexander should also provide ideas about racial policy. Stanley High, a White House administrative assistant, picked up this note for a time, and was the 1936 link to the black community. David Niles, with strong connections in the Jewish community, also sometimes functioned as a race specialist, perhaps more so in the Truman administration. All these were white "friends of the Negro."

The prime function of these "racial advisers" was to provide a channel for black complaints and, generally, to facilitate the delivery of services to blacks as well as to whites. Previously, black people had no administrative entree worth mentioning, and no means of securing the services that other people secured. As the New Deal programs began to move, it could not be taken for granted that blacks would be covered under these programs at all. It could not be assumed, for instance, that the public-housing authorities being created in local areas would build housing projects in black areas, and it could easily be assumed that blacks would not be admitted to projects being built elsewhere. This was precisely the problem in the Chicago case, and was repeated in Detroit and probably other cities. Nor could it be assumed that black farmers would be advised of, and admitted to, their rights under agricultural subsidy programs or permitted to purchase farms under the Resettlement Administration, or that blacks would be admitted to commodity-distribution programs. The racial advisers' *modus operandi* has never yet been studied in a major work, but it seems to have developed almost by accident, out of the concerns of various individuals who had direct access to the President.

Idiosyncratically, the "white liberals" were also helped by the fact that foremost among themselves was Eleanor Roosevelt, whose role as reforming politician probably deserves new consideration. The idea that Mrs. Roosevelt was merely a naive do-gooder seems very dubious. She had been directly engaged in practical politics since 1922. She had demonstrated interest in her husband's *political* career. And she is not recorded as having done anything which she thought harmful to his interests, or which he really wanted her to avoid. Moreover, Mrs. Roosevelt's political role probably increased—with Louis Howe's—precisely because there were so few others left in the Presidential circle who knew him well. She appears to have played a liaison role between the White House and the National Committee in 1936, making detailed inquiries on a wide range of matters including the black vote.[3]

On public policy, the President could ignore anything she did or said which turned out badly by treating it as a personal opinion to which she had a personal right. But for this reason, she was a useful weather vane.

The President's wife became the prime symbol of racial change, a role which she dramatized by public castigations of segregation, by sitting in the aisle between white and black sections of a meeting in Birmingham, rather than sit on the white side, and by renouncing membership in the Daughters of the American Revolution after the DAR refused to let Miss Anderson into Constitution Hall. It is almost as if a President's wife were joining open-occupancy committees in Arlington or subscribing funds to an Angela Davis defense committee.

Probably, the most important line administrator to take an interest in racial issues was Harold Ickes, the Secretary of the Interior. Ickes's interest was mainly personal, not departmental. Interior's main job concerned public lands, grazing rights, fisheries, petroleum, and other natural resource questions. (He also had independent and personal duties as head of the public works program.) His only official connection to ethnic issues was through the Bureau of Indian Affairs and Howard University. But Ickes—who had long before been president of the Chicago NAACP—went well beyond the minima required by the politics of the Department. When the public housing program was going into effect (1936-1939), Ickes was the conduit by which the fight of some Chicago blacks to get a project located in the South Side ghetto was placed before the President. When the DAR barred Marian Anderson from Constitution Hall, it was Ickes's Interior Department which granted permission for a concert before the Lincoln Memorial, in circumstances calculated to produce the maximum publicity. No other Cabinet officer had this measure of interest, and indeed, most Cabinet recollections from the Roosevelt years barely mention the race problem, even when it is critical to the particular department.

BLACKS IN THE FEDERAL BUREAUCRACY

But there was one other innovation which merits attention, and which is directly related to the "white liberal" role. It was the introduction of blacks to the federal bureaucracy. At the agency level, a number of black people were appointed, usually to staff rather than line positions. Interior first broke with the general pattern of excluding blacks from positions having to do with policy. William Hastie,[4] who came into the Interior Department as Assistant Solicitor, and was later appointed United States District Judge in the Virgin Islands at Ickes's recommendation, although the influential Senator Pat Harrison (Mississippi) was backing a different (and white) candidate. Robert C. Weaver[5] is probably the best-known alumnus of the agency group, although it was the training school for a number of other people who have played important roles in the black community since then. The sole black staff with any apparent *White House* entree was Dr. Mary McLeod Bethune, the Negro Adviser in the National Youth Administration. The press gave this group the sobriquet "the Black Cabinet." It seems that they were almost always staff personnel, never possessing line authority. (That pattern, incidentally, remains. Since Eisenhower, there have been black senior staff in the White House itself, but the central role in racial issues is filled by a white member of the staff.) They had to work with whatever backing they could get from top-level administrators known as "liberals" (like Ickes) or from persons with White House influence (notably Mrs. Roosevelt), and whatever influence they could develop by overt and covert collaboration with the black press and such organizations such as the NAACP. Even more than the "white liberals," they were obliged to rely almost exclusively on "court politics."

In the Chicago housing case, for instance, the relevant man went back and forth negotiating with the local authorities, checking to see what had been done, advising the agency administrator what might be done next. Nonetheless, the real significance of the Black Cabinet should not be underestimated. It was a positive gain that black men should be employed in large numbers on WPA crews, that they might get any sort of subsidy payments under federal agriculture programs, that they might at all buy farms under the Resettlement Administration,[6] and that sizeable numbers of black young people should be admitted to the Civilian Conservation Corps (CCC), or the National Youth Administration (NYA) programs.[7]

That the Black Cabinet could have some effect on details, but not on major policy, was consistent with the Roosevelt style and the strategic context. The ambiguous position of the Black Cabinet expressed the ambivalent attitude of the administration. But even then, the Roosevelt administration's policy position remained rather ambiguous; it was in favor of good things, but doubtful about the price to be paid. The effective function of the Black Cabinet, and even more that of their "white liberal" sponsors, was constantly to emphasize the options which the administration might pursue on racial issues. The more successful they were, the more they contributed to black interest in Democratic politics, and the more they did so, the more they generated new pressures for some form of adaptation. But, by 1940 at any rate, the general idea of meliorist policies was fairly well established. Yet the administration had not yet made a commitment to active policies of "civil rights," as such. This lag is illustrated in the War Department's resistance to nondiscriminator per-

sonnel policies in World War II, a resistance strong enough that William
H. Hastie, the racial adviser (with the title of Civilian Aide to the Secretary of War) resigned in public protest. The Hastie resignation was nearly
unprecedented, both because it made an issue explicit and because Hastie
gave up a job paying $8,400 a year, in 1943 a nearly astronomical salary
for a black man (and substantial for any bureaucrat).[8] By this gesture,
Hastie made himself a hero in the black political circles, though one may
guess that Hastie's style did not make a favorable impact on Secretary
Stimson. Hastie is not mentioned by name in the pages of the book dealing
with racial discrimination in the Army (Stimson and Bundy, 1947,
454–461). But the Secretary was reported to have had a very high opinion
of his replacement, who operated in a very different manner. By implication, this suggests that the Secretary was less sympathetic to the Hastie
role.

FAIR EMPLOYMENT PRACTICES

The problem of job discrimination was the issue on which blacks were
able, somewhat successfully, to go beyond court politics. On June 25,
1941 the President issued Executive Order 8802:

I do hereby reaffirm the policy of the United States that there shall be no
discrimination in the employment of workers in defense industries of
government because of race, creed, color, or national origin, and I do
hereby declare that it is the duty of employers and of labor organizations
in furtherance of said policy and of this order, to provide for the full and
equitable participation of all workers in defense industries, without discrimination because of race, creed, color, or national origin. . . .

Congress had, in 1933, written a formal policy of nondiscrimination on
Federal personnel into the Unemployment Relief Act. In 1940, the nondiscrimination proviso was extended to the civil service generally, by an
amendment to the Federal Classification Act. Nonethless, this legislation
applied only to federal government employment, and, in any event had
been only indifferently administered, which is to say that the built-in
patterns of active discrimination in the civil service continued. Executive
Order 8802 dealt more broadly, however, with the principle of nondiscrimination private employment, so far as such employment was in de-
fense-contract industries.

It is not possible to say how far the black majority for Roosevelt in 1940 —not 1936—and the conception of that vote as "the balance of power" in industrial states affected the White House decision to issue the Order. But it does seem, from the record, that the decision was much influenced by a projected "March on Washington" to protest discrimination in the burgeoning defense-production industries. The planners (chiefly A. Philip Randolph and Walter White) seem to have been surprised at the *promises* of support which came unsolicited from black communities across the United States. In the end, they raised their crowd prediction from 10,000 to 100,000—although they themselves never knew whether they could actually achieve that result. This enterprise represents the first genuine case of black influence, if not power. The President was already politically entangled with the black population, and had to recognize the possible payoffs from that population. Moreover, at least some of his liberal advisers probably were sympathetic. But the more important fact is that, for the first time in United States history, a president responded primarily to pressure emanating from the black community itself, organized by the established black leadership.

In this respect, Executive Order 8802 represents something new in United States politics, something new in specifically assuming a governmental obligation to foster equality of treatment in the private sector, as in the public sector. For that idea had gone into disfavor before 1870. The fact that the Order was limited to government and defense-production industries probably was not so important. During World War II, almost everything of importance in the United States could reasonably have been classified that way. It was more important that the Order existed under the President's temporary wartime emergency powers, for its effect would expire when those powers should expire. The important problem lay in administrative politics. To administer the Order, President Roosevelt created a Fair Employment Practices Committee. But as is common with new agencies taking on unpopular tasks, the Fair Employment Practices Committee began with a very small staff (too small for its job) and very limited budget. Moreover, its location in the chain of command made it subject to powerful administrators (like James F. Byrnes and Paul V. McNutt) who were either indifferent or hostile. The Committee lived a tumultuous life and, before it was five years old, was killed by Congressional withholding of appropriations. But the issue never died. On the contrary, "FEP" legislation became one of the central items on the black legislative agenda, until its incorporation in Title V of the Civil Rights Act of 1964.

"CIVIL RIGHTS" AND A SHIFT TOWARD A NEW POLITICAL PROGRAM

By the end of World War II, the very limited notions of meliorist policy which existed in the beginning of the New Deal were transformed into a new political program. The Democratic party was deep in a bitter fight over "civil rights"—an agenda then limited mainly to anti-lynching, anti-poll tax, and "FEP" proposals. Truman's political brain trust (self-appointed), consisting of Oscar Chapman (one of the old Ickes crowd, later himself Secretary of the Interior), Clark Clifford, Benjamin V. Cohen, and others, began to see "civil rights" as one of the necessary components in a 1948 campaign. How far this entered into the appointment of the President's Committee on Civil Rights is not clear. But the Committee report (*To Secure These Rights,* issued 1947) had some of the effects which Villard had sought in the proposed National Race Commission thirty years before. It provided public credence for civil rights as a major public issue, and provided the specific objectives on which liberals—who now claimed a virtual mortgage on civil rights issues—would fight for the next seventeen years, beginning with the Democratic platform fight of 1948 in which a group led by Hubert Humphrey forced through a platform originally rejected by President Truman, but on which he ran successfully. We suspect, but cannot prove, that the President was actually not too dissatisfied with the result. As a border-state man—with Southern connections—the President may well have understood the gravity of racial conflict more than FDR or most other Northern Democrats. If so, he might also have better understood the need for *serious* measures, once he decided some measures might be appropriate. But on this supposition, he could only reduce the costs of being a "traitor" to old allies if civil rights were forced "down his throat." And his ability to accept political force feeding would have been enhanced by the fact that the more rigid Southerners broke away to run a ticket headed by Strom Thurmond. In any event, President Truman's narrow victory depended on the major industrial states that year. This dependence, like President Kennedy's similar dependence on those states in 1960, once more refurbished the image of the black vote as a balance-of-power factor, capable of determining the fortunes of the Democratic party.

Naturally, no Democratic nominee or president has had a political incentive to be single-minded on the subject. Indeed, there has been considerable variety in the behavior of the five nominees (including two presidents) since Franklin D. Roosevelt's death. Adlai Stevenson was the most ambivalent, even uncomprehending, a civilized gentleman averse to a politics of prejudice, but also a doctrinal and temperamental conservative more attuned to the feelings of the South. Stevenson never understood, apparently, the fact that the Southerners whom he most respected —for instances, his speechwriter David Cohn and Senator J. William Fulbright—represented only the elegant face of what was, in fact, a racial tyranny. Kennedy was verbally facile, condemnatory of Eisenhower's inertia, ostentatiously parading his appreciation of "qualified Negroes," promising even to outlaw discrimination in housing by "the stroke of a pen." But Kennedy showed no real understanding of how important the issues were, either to blacks *or* to Southern whites. Only with the demonstration of 1963—and the white reaction—did the Kennedy administration realize that civil rights involved a social earthquake not to be stilled by graceful rhetoric. Hubert Humphrey might be regarded as personally much more serious, having shown an interest in the subject from his days as mayor of Minneapolis. In the end, he came to appreciate the compromises required for his Southern colleagues in the Senate, but it is doubtful if Humphrey ever appreciated the gut Southern reaction. The two presidents most serious on civil rights were Harry Truman and Lyndon Johnson. It makes sense that they should have been so. For, if they understood the tactical reasons for emphasizing civil rights, Truman and Johnson were themselves "Southern" enough to know that the issue could not be treated casually or merely as a political debating item. The Democratic party could be safe only if, instead of treating civil rights as a permanent issue, it looked toward the relatively early resolution of the issue.

With all the variety, however, presidential campaign politics have been based on the supposition that capturing the electoral vote in the urban-industrial states was essential. Since these states have large black populations, the vote of which is deemed "pivotal," it has been understandable that presidential campaign planners should seek to hold that vote to the party, and thus seek to emphasize civil rights as an issue. The tendency would be further reinforced by the continued penetration of Democratic party organizations, and thus of Democratic national conventions, by those unions (Auto Workers, Steel Workers, Packinghouse Workers, and others) whose leadership had—because of black constituencies—to offer at least symbolic (if not always real) interest in "civil rights." This reinforcement, in turn, would interlock with the penetration of Democratic politics by black politicians coming up through state and local organizations, who, though lacking a capacity to ensure actual performance, could constantly press the party toward declarations of faith on the subject.

Moreover, Democratic presidents have continued to talk a civil-rights language, whatever their actual practice. Some have been led—partly by their own electoral calculations and partly by the liberal mystique of White

House advisers—to lay some emphasis on new actions which would demonstrate their *bona fides.* For all these reasons, a simple Southern strategy was not any longer feasible in Democratic presidential politics and "civil rights" loomed larger.

This is not to deny the very important countercurrents associated with *Congressional* Democratic politics. The Congressional Democrats could be divided into four groups. The first were the civil rights doctrinaires, the perennial presenters of civil rights bills, cloture petitions, and proposals to evade the House Rules Committee. This relatively small body of members sat for constituencies in which blacks, Jews, or others with a vested interest in civil rights were sufficiently large that the members had no choice. These were the members ready to support the "Powell Amendments" of the 1950's—antidiscrimination riders which Adam Clayton Powell, anticipating Title VI of the 1964 Civil Rights Act, used to attach to nearly every kind of federal legislation. In view of the Southern bloc's power, such riders spelled death to a bill, and thus were repugnant to the economic (and other) measures dear to the second group: the pragmatic "grocery bill" liberals[9] on the public record, the Northern "grocery bill" liberals—who had their bases either in the urban party "machines" or in the trade unions—were ready to defend civil rights proposals. But they seldom, if ever, were prepared to take a position so far out that their pragmatic concerns would be jeopardized. On the public record, the Southern "grocery bill" liberals—who were *against* civil rights—were generally reluctant to use the language of white supremacy,[10] but nonetheless consistently defended policies which sustained white supremacy.

The third group were the Democratic "moderates," a category of men with no close commitment to Roosevelt's New Deal or to Truman's Fair Deal. Evans and Novak (1966, 39) have revived an old nineteenth-century term to describe these Northern (and more often Western) members who, on racial question, shared Southern principles. They call them "doughfaces." Some shared Southern principles simply because they agreed with them on race itself. Others agreed with the Southern idea of action, or rather *in*action, called for in Congress, because they had similar conceptions of how Congress ought to operate (no antifilibuster rule), or because race meant nothing in their constituencies, or simply because the Southerners were good allies and bad enemies. Finally and fourth, there were the cohesively hostile Southerners. The centers of Congressional power were approached in the order mentioned, so that Congressional Democrats who *might* have been interested were immobilized by the need to pay more attention to the requirements of "getting along" in Washington. In consequence, the "programs" and "platforms" recommended were frequently evaded or negated when Democrats were actually elected to office.

In the absence of very strong external pressure, Congressional Democrats treated race at best as a ritual issue—until 1957, the year of the first Civil Rights Act. But the pattern clearly had changed from Wilson's years to Roosevelt's, from Roosevelt's to Kennedy's, and has changed even more since. *Some* notion of racial equality has become part of party symbolism, and its upholders diffused through the party power structure. The question of their realism, and present capacity to act, is another matter.

NOTES

1. See the discussion of NAACP politics in *The Politics of the Black "Nation,"* Essay II.

2. The expendability of the "white liberal" or anyone else playing the court politics game is illustrated by the sacrifice of Adam Yarmolinsky in the initial days of the antipoverty program. See Sundquist (1968, 149).

3. Gosnell (1952, 155) refers to a memorandum from Mrs. Roosevelt to James A. Farley, saying that this memorandum required *twenty pages* to answer!

4. Hastie retired in 1970 from the United States Court of Appeals, Second Circuit (Philadelphia).

5. Weaver apparently worked for Clark Foreman, a white Georgian whom Will Alexander brought from the Commission on Inter-Racial Cooperation into the Government.

6. The black farmer in the Deep South who might, under Resettlement programs, possess his own 40-acre farm, complete with newly built, *painted* house, and electric lights was a distinctly fortunate figure.

7. In these days when Job Corps experience is before us, we may imagine how extremely difficult it would have been had young black people been wholly excluded from the Civilian Conservation Corps—which was the Jobs Corps model —or the National Youth Administration.

8. When E. Frederick Morrow went to work in the Eisenhower administration, thirteen years later, he was thought to be putting a high value on his services when he insisted on $10,000 a year in salary. See Morrow (1963), 8–9.

9. There were, of course, those remarkable combinations of populism and racism who were never reluctant to speak the language of white supremacy. The archetype in recent times, probably, was the late Senator Theodore G. Bilbo of Mississippi.

10. See, for instance, Munger and Fenno (1962), 14 and 150–152.

VI

"Sticky" Trade-Offs and Urban Immobilization: The Tension between Party and Ethnicity

In the first two years of the Johnson administration, people actively concerned with race relations and urban affairs were beginning to find a certain attractiveness in the idea that the management of programs for social change and for racial-conflict resolution ought to be devolved more and more upon urban local governments. The idea of "decentralizing" decision from federal to urban government has several roots. The one I examine here was that made so influential by Robert K. Merton and recently restated by Robert A. Dahl—the view that urban party politics had been a significant (if not the prime) vehicle for the social integration of conflicting ethnic groups. The present essay was intended to show why the analysis seemed to be inconsistent with the organizational requirements of political parties, or ethnic groups, and defied the observable experience in city politics.[1] Except for stylistic changes, the essay remains as originally written, with two or three footnote comments on points which have or have not developed as then expected.

TRADE-OFFS AND SOCIAL INTEGRATION

Sooner or later, the idea of "resolving" social conflict requires us to consider the process by which the resources of the conflicting parties might be made available to (traded-off against) each other, to produce joint satisfaction. Trade-off processes might be sticky or fluid. If A takes some action to B's advantage, and B reciprocates quickly, we call that a fluid trade-off. I hypothesize that social peace is a function of fluid trade-offs, and social conflict one of sticky trade-offs. If either side perceives the situation as so sticky that it has to *compel* delivery, then the chances of social peace go down accordingly.

For a long time, some very distinguished social scientists—Henry Jones Ford (1914, 306-307), Robert K. Merton (1957, 71-82), and Robert Dahl (1962, 34), among others (McKitrick, 1957, 502-514; Pomper, 1966, 79-97)—have believed that the trade-off process between urban parties and urban ethnic groups has been a significant vehicle, if not the prime vehicle, for social integration. Like many other writers on politics, they assume that party politicians want, above all else, to win office, that to win office they have to build up a large enough bloc of votes, and that to hold those votes they have to dispense rewards to the voting-bloc members. Since even the most deprived of groups has "the marketable commodity of the vote" (Lane, 1959, Chapter 17), it follows that favorable decisions will be traded-off for the delivery of said votes. But these favorable decisions (patronage and the like) are social resources which provide ethnic groups with instruments for upward social mobility thus diminishing ethnic consciousness and ethnic conflict. *Simply: the desire to maximize votes leads to fluid trade-offs, which lead to social integration.*

I believe this view, though plausible, is mistaken. It underestimates the stickiness which arises from the organizational problems of parties and the organizational problems of ethnic groups. This underestimation of stickiness has also led to a mistaken view of the *degree* of previous ethnic integration. This, in turn, leads to an excessive optimism about the degree of *further* integration to be anticipated from the normal workings of urban party politics.

ORGANIZATIONAL PRESSURES TOWARD STICKINESS

The first proposition I offer is that *the vote-maximization assumption seriously violates observed experience.* There are almost no large cities in which the minority party maintains an effective organization, carries out sustained efforts to develop the support by which the ruling party might be brought down, or constitutes an effective source of opposition. At some times, John Doe, as party chairman, may be observed to adopt vigorous "win" strategies. At other times, he will be observed in active collusion with Richard Roe, his formal opponent in the other party, for the defeat of his own candidate. At still other times, he will be observed in tacit collusion, by behaving lazily or by fighting with his intraparty antagonists so hard that he has no resources left to fight the opposition (Sayre and Kaufman, 1965, 170–180; Shames, 1958, 109–114 *et passim*). If we assume that vote maximizing, aimed at electoral victory, is the dominant rule, then such behavior is simply crazy. But we do not believe that, on the whole, party managers are crazy. Hence, we choose the assumption that existing party leaders are themselves the prime beneficiaries of party decisions[2] and that they act first on the *Rule of Closure:* "Hold what you've got!" What they have and seek to hold is control over the existing party organization. They seek to hold control in order to allocate *to themselves* whatever goods (prestige, ideological satisfaction, or material returns [patronage])[3] the party can command. The control sometimes comes through *electoral* victory, but sometimes comes through biparty deals and in other ways.

If John Doe, party chairman, goes all out to recruit those who are presently not his voters, he risks the disaffection of some who already are his voters. Moreover, he is not dealing with "just voters." His party elite is not simply that shown on the official table of organization, but a coalition of elites from what political scientists *normally* regard as party neutral pressure groups. They are not party neutral. The medical society leaders are somewhat more Republican than Democratic. The "moderate" civil rights leaders are somewhat more Democratic than Republican. The big business leaders are somewhat more Republican than Democratic. And so on. While these pressure group leaders have nonparty interests, their prior histories tie them more strongly into one party organizational system than another. They play an actual role in party "internal" decisions.[4] The price they pay for such internal influence is to "moderate" their constituencies' demands, to adjust their constituencies' claims toward the party center of gravity. Their several constituencies may often put pressure upon the leaders to be "completely independent." But this is more than the leaders can do. Instead, what they are usually able to exact, as their price from party leaders, is some minimum attention to their own and their constituencies' needs. If they are put into a position where John Doe's decisions —as chairman—undermine them "too seriously" with their own groups, then the structure is shaken and John Doe himself, as one of the prime beneficiaries, is jeopardized. Hence, the Rule of Closure.

This setup leads to sticky trade-off situations, as far as the newest groups are concerned, because all the old-time participants have vested rights to be considered first. The setup has a direct limitation with respect to party-ethnic trade-offs. At any moment, some members of the coalition of elites will be there because they are regarded as leaders of the ethnic groups with which they are associated or identified. Other activists, desiring to enter the coalition of elites on a similar basis, will tend to find their way impeded by an ethnic order of precedence which asserts that these newer claimants are not important enough to be represented (Gottfried, 1962). Such an order of precedence would be even more rigid by reason of the fact that existing groups, let alone new ones, would already tend to demand more in total than coalition managers have at their disposal. In order to protect themselves and keep down dissension, the coalition managers have to have some rules of allocation. The operative rule of allocation— or *Rule of Dividends*—is expressed in the maxim "Take care of your own!" The distribution of rewards is guided by a norm that the obligation of leadership is to regard claimants according to their just deserts, the primary test of which is the past performance of the claimants (Costikyan, 1966, 252–268; Moynihan and Wilson, 1964). Since there is a strong tendency toward moralistic judgments about who "deserves" what within party, the Rule of Dividends has much the same effect as the private economic allocation expressed in the maxim "last hired, first fired." It is exactly the newcomers who are most sharply restricted by the Rule of Dividends.

Actions based upon the Rule of Closure and the Rule of Dividends tend eventually to become pathological, because they repel new votes so far as to jeopardize what the party already controls. When expansion of the party vote is necessary to maintain the goods to be distributed, then the *Rule of Expansion* ("Get more benefits") becomes applicable. If it were feasible, party decision makers would simply expand benefits without the hazards of competition. But since this expansion tends to require electoral victory in order to secure resources controlled by somebody else, party leaders have to seek new votes. Expansion of the existing force of workers is a normal prerequisite to expansion of the vote. The Rule of Expansion has provided the historical basis for most entries of new ethnic groups into the party mechanism. But admitting such groups into the party has little or nothing to do with admitting them to any share of political power. It is, rather, similar to one writer's conception of the Disraelian Tory approach to the British working class. "For most [Tories]," says Paul Smith, "the essential problem was not how to take the newly enfranchised working men into partnership, but how best to reconcile the acknowledgement of their novel political influence with the maintenance of their economic and social subordination" (Paul Smith, 1967, 320).

The basis for opening up at all is simple. When the acquisition of more benefits becomes contingent on electoral victory, there is a need for additional workers as well (a requirement which television will surely alter). But taking in workers raises the basic managerial problem of security. As do competing firms and opposing armies, parties seek to infiltrate and conduct espionage in each other's organizations, with the result that the maintenance of internal security becomes urgent. Familial cooptation[5] is particularly useful since it facilitates gradual screening to determine reliability and reinforce loyalty; a man brought into the party organization by his cousin who is already active is automatically enmeshed in a web of associations which help to keep him under observation. But the critical importance of familial-and-ethnic cooptation is that this is the procedure out of which groups of ethnically related partisans come into being and form subparty caucuses. The trade-offs which occur then focus on these subparty ethnic caucuses as nexuses between the party as an organizational system and the ethnic group as an organizational system. Out of familial cooptation the networks of ethnic subparty groups are formed and, once formed, are threatened by the appearance of new groups even if the "party" (defined in some organic sense) has considerable "need" (by some objective criterion) for such new groups. Hence there must always be a substantial lag between the search for new workers and new votes and the willingness to permit ethnic newcomers to share in critical decisions and critical rewards.

The relative slowness with which the lags are taken up is a function of the interaction between party organizational requirements and ethnic leadership requirements. This becomes clear if we note that ethnic politics is simply that form of politics in which the actors calculate their strategies upon the basis of estimated gains and losses with respect to communities of birth and descent. Within the party, this strategy means multiethnic politics, but such multiethnic politics also entails the requirement for a political leadership within each group. Except in rare instances, ethnic groups do not constitute formal organizations—although there are many formal organizations whose members come from specific ethnic groups. Whole groups may, however, be regarded as proto-organizations with hierarchies (how else could one refer to "Slovenian leadership" except that some Slovenes can give direction to others?), reward and penalty systems (why else should any black worry about being called an "Uncle Tom"?), and some sense of common interest (how else could one speak of something as being "good for the Jews"?).

The central organizational feature of the ethnic group is that *it depends less than most organizations upon individual decision to participate,*[6] but it is based upon pre-existing marriage rules which inevitably fix membership on the basis of descent (Plotnicov, 1962; Shibutani and Kwan, 1965). It may be perfectly true that social behaviors have no genetic basis, but there are behavioral tendencies associated with particular groups and these behavioral tendencies are mythologically identified (both in the minds of members and nonmembers) with traits of descent.[7]

It is sometimes suggested that ethnic politics is largely devoid of policy interest, but reflects some mysterious "fellow feeling." This approach, which then makes ethnic politics "irrational," is by no means essential nor even apparently correct. If we adopt the Lasswellian scheme of political values, we find that policies distribute physical protection, income, skill, and enlightenment discriminately. So much for the "welfare" values. It is even clearer that the "deference" values—power, respect, rectitude, and affection—are discriminately distributed. If such values are unevenly distributed among ethnic groups, then it is entirely rational for the less favored to act *as groups* to modify the distribution, and it is equally rational for the more favored to act *as groups* to maintain the distribution. The absence of policy interests is, accordingly, more apparent than real. However, collective action to serve those interests has been obstructed by three factors. (1) Until quite recently, the internal cultural imperialism which asserted that the United States was, and of right ought to be, English-speaking and Protestant coercively repressed the expression of collective interests by groups other than Anglo-Protestant.[8] (2) As an organizational factor, most such groups have been such small fragments of the population that their specialized policy interests provided no realistic basis for working coalitions. (3) As an even more critical factor, collective ethnic action does not follow automatically from the existence of a collective ethnic interest, any more than any other form of collective action follows automatically from any other kind of collective interest (Olson, 1965). Before collective action can take place, there must be a perception that collective ends could be served, a disposition to act in their service, and a capability for action. Such a result presupposes an interaction between ethnic leaders and ethnic followers such that collective ends may be redefined in operational strategies, sanctions may be imposed upon those deviant members who undermine the strategies, and rewards may be conferred upon those who aid the strategies. Members of subordinate groups constantly make efforts to escape the "boundaries" set for them, so as to escape the penalties associated with those boundaries. One of these penalties is to have one's options set by another who claims to be one's ethnic leader, but whom one does not accept as such. It is an offense to have some X assert "I am your leader" by his own notion and with full knowledge that he is more likely to profit from such an assertion than any other member of the group. Those members who seek to escape must often regard any particular person's claims to leadership as mere supererogation. This renders the group organizationally weak because leadership is rendered less capable of enforcing upon individuals *decisions to produce* (that is, to meet the requirements associated with membership) (March and Simon, 1968).

Within ethnic groups, as any other types of groups, disagreements about proper operational strategies are natural. The authority and power of leaders is essential to the practical settlement of such disagreements. With rare exceptions, there is no mechanism for authoritative designation of leaders. Ethnic leaders are, then, likely to be self-appointed leaders, without authority or power, confirmed only by subsequent "success." Now one of the practical sources of "success" for any kind of group leader is access to governmental decision makers. Much politics within pressure groups is a fight over which leadership claimants are going to deal with government. The bargaining election and NLRB certification, the industry committee in the regulatory process, the farmer committee system and the producer referenda in agriculture, all are authenticating mechanisms in such fights. But in United States politics, ethnic groups lack the constitutional legitimacy which permits their direct participation in government matters of group concern and, therefore, also lack the authenticating mechanisms.

Deprived of such authenticating mechanisms, ethnic leadership is circumscribed in its ability to stabilize its control over its own followers. Those who would become ethnic leaders are often able, however, to establish effective control over the group by using support from the leadership of some more powerful group. Decision makers outside the group are able, in short, to intervene in the internal politics of the subordinate group to choose group leaders who become the outsider's clients.

It also follows that the ethnic group is often incapable of offering rewards which make it possible for members of the subordinate group to resist the coercive pressures from the dominant which tend to proscribe discussion of issues which might be raised by the subordinate. One factor determining capability to resist counter pressure is the prior existence of voluntary organizational structures (financial institutions, welfare systems, educational systems, and the like) which increase or decrease the group's necessity to depend on public government. There is considerable variation from group to group on this score and one might hypothesize that the tendency to seek governmental action in favor of group objectives is mainly residual, inversely related to the complexity and strength of the voluntary organizational structure which the group is able to support at the time that its sense of "need" is greatest. In any event, so long as weaker groups remain weaker, the party organization will have an "imperial" character. Decision makers from ethnic groups, oriented to their "own," will deal with all the others as "colonial" appendages. These latter will be able to change their position only by struggle, which implies ethnic mobilization.

URBAN RETROSPECT

Whether our view comes closer to the facts of the case, or whether the transitional hypothesis seems better, cannot really be determined conclusively. But the historical experience will provide some guidance. If the fluidity hypothesis is sounder, then the historical data should show that new ethnic groups appearing in the community have gained fairly quick access to party influence and to the major public nominations and benefits open to party influentials. This is not so. The trade-offs for the prior ethnic groups have been rather sticky on the whole. Even the opportunity to acquire any sort of visible office, let alone substantial and prominent power, has been fairly limited.

The historical experience upon which we rely is divisible, for each group, into three main phases of ethnic development and mobilization. (This is represented in Table VI–1.) In the first phase, when the subordinate ethnic group is inexperienced or seriously deficient in organizational skills, the initiation of trade-offs rests mainly with dominant politicians. They can decide what they want from new groups and choose those trade-offs which have the most favorable cost-benefit ratios for themselves. The trade-offs which they choose have become well known. The need for deference is met largely by genuflection to group heroes, group values, or group achievements. The Cabrini Hospitals, Pulaski Drives, and George Washington Carver High Schools are offered as signs that the emergent Italian, Polish, or black populations have the "good will" of dominant leaders. In the same general phase one finds highly divisible welfare allocations (such as aid in a fund drive for the parochial school) or the well-known standby jobs on the public payroll. Welfare allocations are intended not *only* to indicate a sense of "good will" but also to establish a sense of obligation on the part of the particular recipient to lend his support to the benefactor at the right time. Trade-offs of this sort simply could not have any substantial effect toward increasing the recipients' autonomy over major welfare values or major deference values, or any significant influence on the particular ethnic group's collective standing in the party. Since organizational limitations of the ethnic group are so acute, it follows naturally that the dominant groups are usually able to retain control over the weaker at a price which they themselves can set.

Table VI-1. Phases of Party-Ethnic Trade-Offs

Phase	Welfare	Deference	Initiative Taken by
		Type of Political Good Allocated	
I	Highly divisible; to particular persons; establishes obligation to patron	Patronly "recognition" of heros, values, achievements	Dominant leaders within party
II	Marginal ticket-balancing; middle-management returns (policy returns mainly at judgment of dispenser)	Ritual identification with values and interests	Both party leaders and ethnic leaders; party leaders dominant, able largely to resort to forestalling tactics; ethnic leaders using doubtful bluffs, being unable to *enforce* claims
III	Access to major offices; opportunity to control other people's benefits; access to preferment; some realistic policy satisfactions	Critical values and interests become actual public policy; some serious enforcement	Initiation from within party, but by *ethnic* partisans; great responsiveness of decisionmakers who are not themselves members of the strong ethnic groups

It is inevitable that the products of these trade-offs initiated by the dominant will fall short of the preferences held by the subordinate. It is equally inevitable that this disparity will evoke the restiveness which makes later ethnic mobilization possible.

Ethnic mobilization begins after there is a sufficient change in the occupational structure of the subordinate group that there are some individuals who are more-or-less independent of the dominant group. (There is a "critical mass" problem here, for not all individuals who are more or less independent will have leadership skill, nor will all who have skills wish to exercise them.) Some of these more or less independent individuals may go farther and try to set themselves up as independent (nonclient) ethnic leaders. They may begin to make demands on the dominant groups' leaders, claiming the support of their own followers as the sanction to justify or enforce these demands. Ordinarily, such initiatives taken from within the ethnic groups themselves are backed up by threats of retribution at the polls. Most such initiatives are bluffs, but there is sometimes enough reality in them to make some of the dominant politicians uncertain.

Although the actual possibility that ethnic leaders can enforce their demands will usually be dubious, dominant party leaders may respond in two major ways. On the symbolic side, they may try more clearly to identify with group goals in some more important sense than the trivial expressions of "good will" found in the first phase. Cultural pluralism begins to take life with the implications that, if the specific values of the group are not represented in public action and policy, in any event public action and policy should not be offensive to the values of the group in question.

Even so, the new efforts to identify are likely to be ritualistic. They tend to refer to things which the subordinate group finds important but about which the dominant politician making an appeal is realistically able to do little or nothing. The big-city mayors who, during the New Deal years, urged antilynching legislation were talking about something important to blacks, but these mayors had little influence over such legislation. They avoided, on the other hand, local housing and zoning policies, over which they had some realistic influence. There was something of the same ritual when, a few years ago, one might find a candidate for the State Senate earnestly reminding a Polish community that he favored Cardinal Wyczynski in preference to Mr. Gomulka.

The indicator of ethnic emergence to which most commentators have pointed, however, is the balanced ticket. Undoubtedly, the balanced ticket has been used by politicians as a device for managing ethnic problems. But when tickets are balanced, it is the existing leadership which does the balancing. This existing leadership is most unlikely to offer to the new ethnic participant *opportunities commensurate with the importance of his group in the voting constituency of the party.* Consequently, the balanced ticket cannot have had much to do with making the trade-off process more fluid when it came to deal with the occupational income capital structure of the group, nor when it comes to giving the group a more favorable place in the prestigearchy.

In the first place, the balancing process has customarily taken place much too slowly. In the nineteenth century it apparently took the Boston Irish (Blodgett, 1966), the New York Irish and Germans (Ernst, 1949, 162–163, 165–167, 169–170), the New York Jews (Rischin, 1964, Chapter 11), and the various nationalities in New Haven[9] *at least* one full generation to make their first entries into such local offices as state legislatures and city councils. Yet, we presume, no one is about to argue that the mere election of councilmen and legislators is an indicator that any group has actually achieved a critical position.

In the second place, the extreme slowness of this process is not accidental, but reflects the time it takes for new claimants to fight it out with older groups who are trying to bar the way. If, for the individual ethnic politician, the new step increases his personal rewards, for the group its importance is the precedent which it establishes. Groups make strenuous efforts to establish the idea that once "they" have received any place, they should have first mortgage on that place in future, *with the implication that other groups are estopped.*[10] Much of the time is consumed in the processes which develop and test the organizational strength of the particular ethnic groups involved. In the early aspects of ticket balancing, the subordinate ethnic groups are peculiarly susceptible to clientage. Here we return to the "critical mass" problem previously mentioned. The extent to which the outside group can intervene depends on two considerations: (a) whether any particular ethnic leader has so few options that he can be fairly easily "bought" by the dominants, and (b) whether the ethnic community is capable of replacing him if he is bought. The general tendency has been that those ethnic leaders who initiated new claims, and thus inconvenienced the dominant leadership, were themselves quite unlikely to profit. The more common pattern has been that if leader A actually broke the pattern by making a new claim, a fight would ensue before the claim would be honored. In the eventual process of compromising the fight, the results would show up in the political promotion of leader B, more disposed to accept client status with respect to powerful external patrons (Dahl, 1962, 110–111; Seltzer, 1956; James Q. Wilson, 1960, 52 and 78–82).

Another feature of this process needs to be made explicit. When party leaders have deemed it necessary to admit newcomers to new political roles, they have sought to open up only those roles which would cause little or no disturbance in the whole organizational system. To appoint a newcomer as assistant prosecutor is profitable to the individual, but only honorifically useful to the group. To agree that the next nominee for a legislative seat will be of group X, when the constituency is already X but the sitting member is Y, is the same kind of gesture. One of the possible indicators—although we are less sure about this—is that ethnic newcomers to elective office may be admitted into legislative bodies, even though their entry into executive positions would be resisted. The reason is not merely that there are more legislative posts, and accordingly more possibilities of sharing, but that the legislative influence on party resources is secondary while executive influence is direct and immediate. This is true not only for "major" offices such as big-city mayoralities, but also for "minor" offices such as court clerkships or auditing departments. These are the positions which permit their holders to acquire bargaining parity, rather than clientship, because these holders are able to exert some control over the claims which other people would wish to make. All have the key feature that the occupant has some considerable likelihood of independent action with respect to the control of personnel and public funds and, accordingly, some prospect of independent power.

Against this background, we find that the urban Democratic organizations have been particularly resistant to the upward movement of those New Men produced by the post-1880 migration. The Irish leaders have attempted to prevent other ethnic New Men from rising above client status, even when this kind of attempt jeopardized the possibilities for immediate electoral victory. This stickiness has been particularly noticeable in the urban Democratic parties, despite the Democrats' *patently greater reliance on a multiethnic voting constituency.* The political scientist Elmer Cornwell has shown this in a study of Providence, Rhode Island (Cornwell, 1960). Specifically, Cornwell shows that in 1900 the Irish faction commanded just about three-quarters (73 percent) of the Democratic ward-committee positions in the city. At the same time, the Yankees commanded about 94 percent of the Republican ward-committee posts. In 1957, when the replacements in both parties were primarily Italian, the Irish still held 50 percent of the Democratic committee posts, or about two-thirds what they held in 1900. By contrast, the Yankees held 29 percent of the Republican positions in 1957, or a bit less than one-third their 1900 share. In other words, the Providence Italo-Americans, the largest "new" group in that city after the Irish, had much greater difficulty penetrating the Democratic party, which the Irish controlled, than they had in penetrating the Republican party, which the Yankees had controlled.

Rather similar interpretation seems merited by the political career of Fiorello LaGuardia even if it is true (which is not clear) that LaGuardia was not chosen by his party leaders (Republican) as representative of the New York Italo-American (Glazer and Moynihan, 1963, 210). LaGuardia survived until his hour of glory in the Republican party, not the Democratic party, although his entire Congressional and mayoral career showed the most remarkable *policy* differences with those who constituted the Republican center of gravity. He (like other Italo-Americans at the same time) had extremely limited career options in a party where the Irish spoke of themselves as "natural rulers." He surely exploited the ethnic appeal to his fellow Italo-Americans before he became mayor (Mann, 1965) and it is reasonable to suppose that his Democratic antagonists evaluated him as "Italian." It makes sense, in this light, that he should have been an active Republican for most of his premayoral career.

The point comes through again in the last sixty years of Cleveland political history. As early as 1910, the successor to Mark Hanna as Republican leader in Cleveland came out of the Jewish community and this man retained his leadership for about a quarter-century. Of more recent years, the most successful Jewish politicians have been Republican "New Dealers"—despite the fact that Ohio Republicans were not warm to their "moderate" wing and despite the Democratic proclivities of the Jewish electorate. Even by the 1960's, no Jewish Democrat was able to exercise an independent leadership role in his party. There is a similar experience for the Italians. By the late 1950's, Italian Democrats had come to hold a number of key offices (including the mayoralty of Cleveland), but their control over party machinery was much more doubtful. By contrast, the Republican chairman in this period was an Italian businessman-politician whose political career went back to city council in the 1920's and later service as city-council president, long before any of his Democratic compatriots were able to attain comparable places.

Democratic politics in Cleveland is almost the textbook example of Closure. The period between 1931 and 1941 was one of sharp intraparty struggles between Cosmopolitan[11] New Men trying to escape clientage and the Irish elite seeking to maintain their existing overlordship. In five consecutive elections the Irish group gave approval to one of its own members, evoking such sour responses as a Polish-language editorialist's observation that "for the Irish the politicians always have plums, and for the Poles, promises, for which we fall." The rigid application of Closure cost the Democrats four of these elections in a row and threatened to erode the very base on which the Democratic leadership rested. Then, a temporary rapprochement occurred, signalized by the nomination of Frank J. Lausche in 1941. Even then the Irish group (which still controlled the official machinery, the county offices, and the federal patronage) soon found it preferable to try to eliminate both Lausche and his most important Cosmopolitan successor, Anthony J. Celebrezze. As late as 1958, the Irish caucus successfully sponsored a change in nomination rules, only to find that even under the new rules it had no viable candidate. At this point, it grudgingly endorsed Celebrezze. The final sign of its defeat was its inability to control the federal patronage under the Kennedy Administration—as it had under the Roosevelt and Truman Administrations—so that Celebrezze was first appointed to the Secretaryship of Health, Education and Welfare and then to the United States Court of Appeals.

The pattern seems relatively clear. The interval from the time that most ethnic groups have become quantitatively significant, as a proportion of the local population, until they are able to acquire the entry-level political offices (state legislatures, city councils, and the like) appears to be about a quarter-century or a little more. But, as was noted, no one argues that merely electing a few councilmen or legislators confers major power over party machinery, let alone over public policy. If we treat the mayoralty in a large city as a significant office, it appears that about fifty years from the zero point has been required for such groups to begin capturing such offices. Thus, the vaunted Irish began to acquire this modest measure of ceremonial recognition and power in the mayoral "firsts" of Cleveland, Boston, and New York during the 1880's. The various groups of continental European descent began to be numerically significant in the population about this time, and began to get into the entry-level political roles about the time of World War I. Their mayoral "firsts" began with La-Guardia (1933), Lausche of Cleveland (1941), Celentano of New Haven (1945), and continue on to such figures as Addonizio of Newark in the 1960's. The elections of Carl B. Stokes in Cleveland (1967) and Richard Hatcher in Gary (1967) seem to conform to the same broad pattern: something around fifty years after the blacks first became a significant proportion of the urban Northern population. In each case, the lags did not just happen. They reflected fights between groups which had already come into some fair measure of influence and were trying to consolidate the rewards thereof, and other groups trying to make that entry.

Why Democratic politics has been stickier than Republican politics probably has to do with the availability of alternatives. The recognition of preferment makes it convenient here to note that the opportunity structure of the whole polity is probably the critical determinant of how much conflict there is as one ethnic group comes in on the heels of another. The existence of ethnic networks among decision makers, decision makers' sensitivity to the prizes of influence, and the ramifications of some of the more consequential prizes (such as preferment for economic enterprises in the ethnic community) all contribute to the maintenance of ethnicity as a politically relevant criterion. The attack by one ethnic group on the political position of another is, like the black attack on discrimination in crafts unions, partly an attack on an existing system of "property rights" which are ethnically defined.

The narrower the surrounding opportunities, the more important preferment becomes. The more important preferment is, the stickier the adjustment process. These facts probably explain why the Republicans have had fewer ethnic disputes in the urban setting than have the Democrats. Since the Anglo-Protestants, the dominant ethnic group in the Republican electorate, have also been the main beneficiaries of industrialization and openings in industrial management, many of them have secured many more benefits from the executive life than the political life. Moreover, the executive life has been continually increasing its demands on the time and energy of its participants. Consequently, Anglo-Protestants have had many fewer incentives to compete for those opportunities that are specially dependent on overt politics. This interpretation by no means says that they gave up influence, but does say that they cut down overt and continuously visible participation; they proceeded to exercise influence through the checkbook (Holden, 1966a; Cornwell, 1960; Peel, 1935). The Irish Catholics, on the other hand, have actually needed the influence which political engagement gave them if they were to acquire money and prestige at a rate any faster than the snail's well-known speed. Hence, the greater Democratic inhospitality to the entry of new groups which might disturb the structure of control.

As ethnic groups have risen, however, they have been less than content to stop short with merely economic gains. The hard tests come with the attempts to secure favorable public policies and, particularly, to incorporate the prime values of the group into the policies of the whole community. Success is not success for the group until the group can reasonably often count on public vindication of its symbols and public embodiment of policies which it desires. The greater the pressure along these lines, and the wider the implications of ethnic change, the greater the likelihood of counter pressure by other ethnic groups. Previously dominant groups which, in the face of sheer necessity, may yield the paraphernalia of office still possess numerous means to resist shifts in actual policy.

Resistance by dominant groups merely sets the scene for further conflict as subordinate groups try to break that resistance. It sets the stage for what we may call politics as collective psychiatry. Even if the rewards being contested are purely material, the resistance of dominant groups evokes from newcomers the sense that they are being held back by prejudicial conspiracy and repression. This result is particularly the case when such newcomers are able to see that, by the apparent criteria for "service," their claims ought to be received well. Offense to the collective self-esteem of the newcomers then evokes the effort to acquire power as a weapon. The purpose of pursuing power as a weapon is to achieve victories which will make the presumptively subordinate groups "feel better" because it will have forced the opponents to "show respect."[12] This provides a basis on which the ethnic New Man may organize to develop autonomous power. But the process is slow. Client-politicians become major participants only by watchful waiting, testing the lines of resistance through minor conflicts, achieving minor gains, withdrawing in defeat, consolidating in victory until they are ready to try the next stage.

Such situations develop slowly because the ethnic New Man, as client-politician, owes debts upon the repayment of which his former patrons will insist. The form of payment upon which the patrons are most insistent is that he do his all to defend them, when they are under attack by other members of his "own" group. To violate this obligation is to invite grim retribution. The obvious difficulty is that the client-politician makes himself a target of hostility within his group and provides opportunity for other leadership claimants within the group to organize against him, using such terms as "flunkey," "sell-out," and "stooge" as their points of reference. Moreover, client-politicians may eventually come to be dissatisfied merely with the ability to dominate their own groups, while themselves being dominated by external patrons. What they will then seek is to make themselves equals so that they may enter into bargaining relationships with the leaders of other critical groups. To achieve this position the client-politicians have to demonstrate to the outside world that they already have power. To show that they already have power is to show that their "followers" will do whatever they request and for this must exploit or even create a sense of "peoplehood" within the groups from which they come. Only when the client-politician can actually plot and enforce a collective strategy upon "his" group will erstwhile patrons swallow their anger at his "ingratitude" and accept his independence as ineluctable reality.

The ethnic New Man's success in this sense may be taken to mark the entry of his group into the third phase. But ultimate success is not easy, because the questions which ultimately make a difference in the urban arena have to be resolved in national politics. National politics, however, is much more difficult. The few groups which have had considerable success in capturing local offices have had a very hard time developing the coalitions necessary for national success.

Again consider the experience of the Irish. Despite the rapid acquisition of local offices in the 1880's, the Irish were still stuck in the second phase down to the 1920's. The Smith nomination of 1928 is, in fact, the demonstration of the power of the urban Irish to force the party to accept what the rest of the Democrats did not want but could no longer avoid. This was the clear measure of the urban Irish entry into the third phase, when their autonomy was explicitly recognized by other contestants. Few Anglo-Protestants, even if disposed to bargain with the Irish-dominated urban organizations, were prepared to accept the consequences of cultural pluralism in major public policies. Yet it is not truly until the Kennedy nomination that the results of this process are consolidated beyond question. And we forget, at the peril of complete confusion, that the process begins all over in the cities with the challenges of the various Cosmopolitan groups to the urban Irish. Moreover, we have to note that the use of ethnic politics as a species of collective psychiatry is by no means always successful.[13] Rather, departure from the interests of the ethnic groups may be productive for the individual politician, once he has used the group as an initial source of political strength, if he can find other groups willing to accept him on nonethnic terms (which really means if he is willing to accept the terms of other ethnic groups). Unless the group itself has made substantial progress, however, this shift may often stigmatize him as a "traitor" to "his own" group,[14] reinforcing the sense of collective grievance, and igniting new chain reactions or ethnic political conflict.

PARTY, RACE, AND URBAN PATHOLOGY

This view suggests that party must introduce further pathological dimensions into the presentation controversies of race. Those controversies activate the interests of too many other sectors of the urban polity. Far from being irrelevant, party is highly relevant to the determination of urban policy outcomes. Party decision makers do tend to share judgment about policy values (Flinn and Wirt, 1966), and seek to influence public policy (Bowman and Boynton, 1966), not so much through broad and systematic formulations as by intervention on details. An aggregation of successful interventions may significantly divert decisional outcomes from the directions which "broad" policy decisions may have seemed to imply.[15] Party decision makers have some leverage, notably through control of the machinery of nomination and election, which can be used to impose penalties upon public decision makers who refuse to deal with party decision makers when that refusal goes beyond what the party decision makers believe to be tolerable limits.[16] On this basis, our further knowledge that ethnic communities do expect their political representatives to function as ambassadors to the outside world (Gans, 1962) leads to the conclusion that the more salient the ethnic issues become, the greater the likelihood that party interests will require interventions which may freeze the racial status quo in the urban North.

If one were to consider the stress between urban black communities and police departments, one would immediately recognize that the characteristic method of party intervention would be to seek alleviation of particular penalties and grievances without touching the fundamental structure of police organizations. This method makes sense. In the first place, urban police departments are not simply public organs, but organs which well serve urban party leaders as tools to expedite the flow of funds to party, as sources of patronage, and as instruments of political espionage.[17] Second, since urban police departments are disproportionately composed of particular ethnic groups, and presumably regarded somewhat as ethnic preserves (Moynihan and Wilson, 1964, 297), it may reasonably be supposed that policy changes initiated by other ethnic groups would elicit ethnically oriented responses from policemen and their compatriots in the pertinent ethnic organizational systems. On both counts, it is prudent for urban decision makers to move with extreme caution in making basic changes. Yet it is also clear that the relationship of the police to blacks is at such an order of crisis that characteristic incrementalism cannot produce a new relationship which is stable and mutually agreeable.

School politics may be even more instructive since it is often believed that this realm is independent of party politics. Experience in Chicago strongly suggests the contrary, where the Mayor (who is also the Democratic leader)[18] appoints the Board of Education. An initial boycott (1964) resulted in the absence of about 240,000 students, mostly black, and caused great embarrassment to the Board of Education and indirectly to the Mayor. When a second boycott was projected, the Mayor maintained official disengagement. Through party channels, however, precinct captains were moved through the main black wards in an effort to head off another embarrassment.

That second boycott was less effective than the first, drawing off about 175,000 students (Blackwood, 1965), or about 29 percent fewer than the first. But the defeat for the party was far more severe. This organization, which ordinarily could dictate most major results in the South Side community (James Q. Wilson, 1960), had, by its own movement into the issue, demonstrated for all but the most naive that its power was seriously curtailed. Such self-injuring action arose from the combined necessity of party leaders to forestall action which might force the Board into policies adverse to white communities' interests[19] and, equally, from a simple failure of its intelligence system. It did not know what it was fighting.

But this is an increasingly common pattern in the urban North: intelligence failures and the emergence of claims which are mutually exclusive. This pattern precludes attention to the kinds of problems we have been citing, and raises to focus the pathology which we perceive: the strategies consistent with the mandates of the larger system and the strategies meant to change those mandates may be equally self-defeating in the end.

As numberless commentators have said, American politics depends on coalitions in which the price of success is the ability to serve others as well as oneself. The strategy seems improbable in the present context because it cannot be imposed by external leadership but must be developed from within the ethnic community. The sense of grievance which gives vitality to ethnic politics cannot be reduced except by real environmental changes and it is those which internal leadership is presently incapable of providing. The relevant resources do not exist within the ethnic community alone. When the issues are diffuse and pervasive so the politics takes its increasingly psychiatric form, then leadership which seeks to follow the coalition-service strategy runs the risk of self-destruction. That strategy works only if the ethnic group is already sufficiently powerful that others see it as dangerous to violate its vital interests *and* if the ethnic group possesses a sufficient capability for collective action outside of politics that the burdens on the governmental channels are sharply contained. There is, is this respect, a certain realism in the confused rhetoric of "black power." The element of realism is basic politics: power is the necessary price for effectiveness. The strategy implied by the exponents of "black power" is dictated by the historical experience of powerlessness, by the extraordinary internal fragility of the black organizational system, and by the rigidities of the larger urban system. The effort is to rely exclusively upon the ethnic group and thus to achieve a measure of power which can be directed against points of resistance. It is to seek means to put on a convincing show of force. In its simplest sense, the strategy calls for the most vigorous use of those issues and appeals which will elicit the most intense response from black constituencies.

But this appeal precludes any strategic choice of allies, because no allies can be assured that their vital interests will be deemed consistent with the vital interests of the black claimants. For example, if the strategy were to focus on official representation in public bodies *on racial grounds,* it is probable that urban Jewish leadership would find it objectionable. But it is also possible that Jewish leadership would accede to such a strategy. One purpose would be to support the *end* of rectifying historic black under representation. But another purpose would be to maintain a working alliance with black groups—an alliance which, in any event, Jewish leadership feels is threatened by real or putative black anti-Semitism. On the other hand, it would be entirely unlikely that urban Slavic communities which believe, quite correctly, that they are also underrepresented could accede at all to such claims. They would, rather, perceive such claims as likely to preempt places which their interests would better require them to occupy.

If, on the other hand, the strategy called for eliciting black community support by dramatizing commonsense economic grievances (food prices, credit terms, or rent levels), then one would rather expect it to be ignored by urban Slavic communities. Such a strategy would almost certainly cause great discomfort in urban Jewish communities because a significant proportion of the small entrepreneurs with whom the black lower class deals are, among other things, Jewish. It is entirely likely that in the heat of a propaganda campaign the generalized hostilities would be focused on "the Jews."

The possible combinations of issues and targets are virtually infinite, but it is essential to note that any combination is likely to involve some specific groups. (To the extent that it involves simply "whites" as targets, the problem of polarization develops the more rapidly.) Affected white claimants are, to a considerable degree, likely to perceive that their own needs are being neglected in order to serve the black interests. Their predictable resistance does not arise solely because there are material conflicts in interest, but also because of the psychic impact, on the urban white groups, of the perception that blacks are getting special attentions which, in earlier stages of the history and even now, the whites did not get or are not getting (Coles, 1966; Lamson, 1966). (Blacks and whites are, of course, merely seeing different dimensions of the same action. For blacks it is a proper emphasis in policy which reflects previous exclusion and neglect. For the pertinent white claimants it is a radical shift from the existing baseline.) To the extent that racial politics became more explicit, there would be a tendency to magnify this perception and to turn it into a large-scale political grievance.

The problem of escalation in racial politics is basically comparable to the problem of escalation in international politics. If we assume that neither side is or will be disposed to retrench, then the longer prospect is polarization or immobilization. Let us then indicate, even at the risk of being foolhardy about prognostication, what might seem most likely to ensue, taking as our warrant the view that the harshest of all analytical tests is the problem of indicating direction, if not degree.

1. *The initial result* would be to discredit black leadership claimants who possess skills in the normalities of American politics. Out of this collapse several results are conceivable. The most likely is the further fragmentation of the urban black organizational system, so that leadership becomes genuinely "elemental." The initiatives would be exercised, from the black side, in the ultimate forms of psychiatric politics: uncontrollable action, bereft of strategy, by those emotionally prepared now to express their psychic state through the simplest forms of direct action—highly symbolized defiance of the public order. It would be unreasonably, however, to expect that those within that community who seek action within normal politics would entirely vacate the field. Nor would it be reasonable to expect that those knowledgeable about the normal ways of politics (but also prepared to resort to more elemental methods) would not use violence within the group as well. To put it bluntly, black internal politics might well become saturated with assassination, much as did Irish politics fifty years ago.[20]

2. *The incidence of violence,* whether in the forms of disorganized riots, incipient rebellion, or merely the politics of assassination, would constitute a threat to the public order which no government could be expected to ignore. Thus, one might well see a new era in which the specialists in race relations would be found not among social workers, planners, and administrative generalists, but among the city and state police, the federal investigative agencies, and the National Guard.

3. *The expectation of future violence* would spur the development of private organizations of violence. The nuclei of such organizations appear already to exist in (a) the various paramilitary organizations associated with what some observers call "the radical right," (b) the "scores of neighborhood, block and building protective organizations . . . *particularly in fringe areas where white and Negro neighborhoods meet"* which reportedly exist in New York (*New York Times,* January 14, 1964; emphasis added), and (c) such an organization as the Deacons for Defense and Justice[21]— which set up at least one Northern unit (in Chicago), allegedly on the invitation of a fraternal order in 1966.[22]

All these organizations indicate a phenomenon which is the very essence of faction in the Madisonian sense: a level of distrust about the probability of being left alone by others and a sense of uneasiness about the effectiveness of the machinery of public order which provide people with the incentive to create their own private mechanisms of force "just in case." If we keep in mind the problem of escalation, what we have to consider is what would happen to such ordinary people in the event of more pervasive troubles.

4. If our view of the stresses on party, and the reactions of party, is at all sound, then we may expect *a sharpening of the central-city-suburban cleavage* within the political parties of the metropolitan areas. Since central cities are presumably going to increase their black concentrations and suburban areas their white concentrations, the parties must take note. What happens would be expected to have important implications for legislative politics.

Suppose, for example, that the black political influence in the central city were likely to make significant impacts on police administration. What shall one expect from those suburban residents concerned for their physical safety lest disorder from the city spill over—and from some of those people who are concerned for their investments in the properties of the city? Together they may reassert Dillon's Rule—the legal doctrine of plenary state power over cities—and place the police administration under state direction. Such a procedure need not (and probably would not) be justified overtly on racial grounds so much as on the ground that the metropolitan area provides a more appropriate framework for law enforcement—a ground which an intellectual atmosphere where systems analysis flourishes would support. As the history of Boston, Detroit, and New York itself will indicate, this would not be the first time that those groups most influential in the legislatures "took over" the urban police when they were anxious about the consequences of letting those groups appearing to become dominant in local politics obtain that control.

Public education raises a similar kind of problem. If racial diversity seems a desirable criterion for educational policy, then it would be reasonable to expect efforts to apply that criterion by mixing white suburban pupils with central-city black pupils whenever so doing should be feasible. If resistance to racial diversity is so strong that suburban legislators sponsor legislation to limit state administrators' authority to require diversification, then one would expect even greater resistance when measures for diversification also involve the troublesome political problems of school consolidation.

Such issues must present extremely urgent considerations for both political parties, which then would tend to force both parties to opt for the "white" side of the issues and against the "black" side of these issues. The Democratic party, apart from its historic problems of Closure, must increasingly invest effort at building suburban strength unless it wishes to forgo both legislative and gubernatorial control in future. This imperative is the practical consequence of "one man, one vote." The Republican party must compete on the same ground (a) because more of its vote is to be found in suburban areas, and (b) because *the Republican suburbs* would not face race as a salient problem for themselves, thus relieving the party of pressure to compete for the central-city black vote.[23]

5. Finally, *federal strategy would have to be distinctly altered.* Particularly since the beginning of the Kennedy administration, and even somewhat before that, federal civil rights strategy presumed that even if white Northerners found certain aspects distasteful, they would, on balance, feel sufficiently few disadvantages that their political support would not be withdrawn from the administration on racial grounds.

If the federal administration were to perceive a shift in support, that perception would ultimately be reflected in efforts to compensate by modifications in policy. Two main lines would seem to be likely in such a compensatory modification:

(a) Reliance on administrative devolution in the historic pattern of federal domestic programs, and emphasis on the need for local action for ultimate solutions, would relieve much of the pressure on the Federal Government. This shift means a natural increase in the discretion of the local decision makers who have, in the past, either shown a profound lack of perception about the thrust of the issues or have shown a particular need to be responsive to political claims other than those which the civil-rights issues have articulated.

(b) It would be essential for the political reputation of any administration, whatever its ultimate objectives, to take the position that internal disorder cannot be tolerated. Insofar as the administration followed the preferences of the most recent years, this emphasis would be coupled with efforts at ameliorative policies, but the emphasis on order would increase as disorder increased. From the judicious mix of Office of Economic Opportunity grants and National Guard detachments, the natural escalation seems to be OEO grants and United States marshals, after which the next level is OEO grants and United States Army detachments—until the end result becomes the substitution of the military planner entirely for the social planner.[24]

NOTES

1. An abbreviated version of this paper was published as, "Party Politics and Ethnic Politics," in Wingfield (1967), 117–131. The publisher's permission to use that earlier paper in this volume is gratefully acknowledged.

2. For a different thesis, see Schlesinger (1965), 765–768.

3. There is a tendency, among current students of party, to de-emphasize patronage. We believe this is misleading. It probably is not patronage *qua* patronage which had declined, so much as one trivial form, namely petty payroll appointments. *Preferment* opportunities, that is, opportunities to increase net worth, which also require some form of sponsorship, remain critical. These special opportunities, based on one's political sponsorship—to secure referee appointments, insurance contracts, public funds for deposit in one's bank, urban-renewal land made cheap by eminent domain and the federal write-down, or bulk sales of one's product to a public agency—are particularly valued and may be much more alive matters in the "regulatory state." These opportunities are peculiarly the province of decision makers and those associated with them, precisely because of the skills and sophistication which their pursuit requires. On the general nature of incentives for party action, see the views of a scholar and of a practitioner, respectively, in Sorauf (1964) and Costikyan (1966), 296–307. For more specific discussion of some cases the following are pertinent: Meyerson and Banfield (1955), 19; and Francis Tannian, a recent study of a major political district in Washington, D.C. (unpublished; University of Delaware).

4. The point is obvious once stated, but *it is not obvious in the literature on parties.* It was most forcibly suggested to us by remarks of Mrs. Mary Barnes during a seminar (for foreign visitors) on the dynamics of the American political system, Office of Cultural and Educational Exchange, University of Pittsburgh, August 1964. On other aspects we have had the benefit of Robert Agranoff's intensive knowledge of the differential alignments between major farm-organization leadership and national party leadership. Calkins (1952) is also relevant.

5. See Salisbury (1965–1966), particularly at 561–562. Salisbury's information shows that 18 percent of the people in his survey cited family influence as responsible for their specific organizational membership. Forty percent (40 percent) cited family influence as being responsible for their general interest in politics. A "high proportion" who did not specifically *mention* family had politically active parents. This is the more persuasive because Salisbury is more conservative on the issue than we are.

6. On individual decisions to participate in formal organizations, see March and Simon (1968), Chapter 4.

7. See Gordon (1964). For more limited definitions consult Dahl (1962), Wolfinger (1965), and Grace M. Anderson (1966).

8. See the discussion of "Anglo-conformity" in Gordon (1964).

9. Dahl (1962, 36) presents a table showing stages of ethnic development.

10. Maiale (1950) and *New York Times,* March 21, 1966, on a debate between New York Mayor John V. Lindsay and certain Puerto Rican spokesmen over

positions which had been held by Puerto Ricans during the preceding Wagner administration.

11. "Cosmopolitan" is a term Clevelanders apply to persons (other than Jews) descending from the post-1880 migration. This collective noun initially indicated a purely artificial category, but the conflict processes have tended to turn it into a term referring to an actual social system. See Holden (1961).

12. See Mann (1965, 192–193) on "the politics of resentment," and Lubell (1956b) on "the politics of revenge."

13. Pomper (1966) refers to a case of failure in Newark. Hapgood (1960) is a narrative of success.

14. This is a second point on which Glazer and Moynihan (1963) seem to accept a less than adequate interpretation. At p. 213, they point out that when "LaGuardia defeated O'Dwyer in 1941, he did worse in the Italian districts than in the city as a whole." Yet it is quite reasonable to argue that since LaGuardia as mayor refused to play the ethnic game with the Italo-American community, the 1941 election could easily be interpreted as their revenge at having been disappointed.

15. On the significance of "small decision" see the discussion of "anti-suboptimization" in Holden, (1966); and, from an analysis of the market process, Kahn (1966).

16. The displacement of former Mayor Martin H. Kennelly by Richard J. Daley in the 1955 Democratic primary in Chicago presents such a case.

17. Considerable evidence that this is sometimes done at the state level was adduced in a legislative investigation of the Pennsylvania State Police in 1966. See the Pittsburgh, Harrisburg, and Philadelphia newspapers during the period January-May 1966.

18. The two positions automatically go together by local custom, and highly dysfunctional consequences ensue when they do not. See Meyerson and Banfield (1955).

19. The *party* leaders' need to contain the pressures emergent from black communities was again demonstrated in a contest for school board president in 1970. The board was deadlocked for several weeks between a black candidate (not a part of the mayor's group) and a white candidate (closely associated with the mayor's group). Only when the mayor filled a vacancy on the board did the new appointee become the swing vote, obviating the choice of a black school board president in Chicago.

20. I may be mistaken in this estimate. At least, the politics of assassination has not unfolded as rapidly or intensively as I thought it would, although the Panther-US relationship persuades me that the basic analysis probably was right as written four years ago. Still the best historical situation for understanding this, I believe, is the Irish experience in the World War I era. Younger (1969) appeared too late for me to make use of its remarkable depth, but it seems to me a book which is greatly worth pondering.

21. The Deacons, a kind of functional analogue to the Irish Volunteers or the

Haganah, first came to national attention in 1965, from their home base in Louisiana (*New York Times,* February 21, 1965).

22. *New York Times,* April 16, 1966. The reader should know that, in my opinion, the *direction* of this comment was correct as written originally, but the *identification* was wrong. What I find compatible with the analysis, *but did not anticipate, was the form of action now represented by the Panthers.*

23. This is the clear implication of Rogin (1965–1966).

24. I have not seen reason to change this paragraph from the way it was written more than four years ago. But the public evidence—*The New York Times, The Washington Monthly,* several trials in the federal courts, and Congressional hearings—seems substantial and complex. Were I now beginning to write on this point, a much more sophisticated analysis would be both possible and mandatory.

VII

A Look at Medusa's Face:
On the Possibilities of Internal War

WHAT SHOULD WE EXPECT?

Some matters were better not discussed, except that failure to consider them would not reduce their likelihood. It would be intellectually and morally irresponsible even to discuss racial war without such a caution. After all, such a war's result would not be like losing the World Series (or even a prolonged strike). It would be the death of thousands of human beings and the abortion of the nearest approach to a *large-scale* multiethnic republic yet seen on earth. We are reasonably clear that a racial war would not command much support from blacks, except in direst extremity. Nothing would be less desired by most black people, even if (as is not always the case) they contain within themselves—or give voice to—powerful hostility toward whites. Some blacks oppose aggressive violence on the prudential grounds that it will backfire. Others oppose violence on the ground of very moral principle. But most of all, they respond to the fact of their own increasing engagement in the social and economic life of the country.

That engagement is by no means without its pains. Yet, pains or not, the persons so engaged have ever more reason to prefer the engagement with the pains than to prefer disengagement without the pains. If, as we believe, there is now some critical mass of blacks so engaged—some number sufficient that these persons themselves constitute not mere "exceptions" but a strategic element in the black population itself—then we have a clue to their importance. These participants are among the most vigorous advocates of doctrines of "black self-determination," yet it is not really physical separation or armed rebellion they are talking about, but "caucus separatism."[1] If in one sense caucus separatism is politically trivial, there is another in which it is politically important. It expresses the upward-mobility strategy of a sector of the black population which, whatever its rhetoric, has no intention of withdrawing from the political economy of the United States. It is thus absurd to believe that any significant number of these participants take doctrines of "armed rebellion" seriously enough to be ready to lend support to them. All the revolutionary rhetoric (and even the recent series of bombings) cannot obscure that any group having any large body of *active* black followers operates within the understood rules of lobbying, litigating, and propagandizing. Even those who talk of "armed rebellion" have thus far done more talking than anything else. The Black Panthers, despite their emotional similarity to the Irgun or the Irish Republican Army, have not in any sense approximated those groups in action. And while many other people express some sympathy with the doctrines of violence, there is so little evidence that they have considered even the technical side—let alone the political or moral issues—that we feel compelled to treat most of such talk as fantasy or deception. Black politics may be rhetorically violent, but it is still predominantly a legal politics-without-guns. In the same way, it is clear that most white people contemplate racial war with no enthusiasm.

No one should treat internal war as a foregone conclusion. On the other hand, the possibility is serious enough that it should not be utterly disregarded. Prediction as to how likely it is (or when it might be expected) is another matter. Though economists have some theory which helps to "anticipate" depressions, other social scientists have no theory which helps to anticipate social disintegration very well. Social science, under the impact of left wing thought, used to attempt to explain revolution and other forms of social strife as a function of some groups being *deprived* in some absolute sense, for example, declining in absolute well-being. However, it can be observed that much disruptive behavior has come, not when people were particularly badly off, but when they were in *some* process of measurable improvement. The concept of *relative* deprivation[2] merely states that groups become rebellious when they see a big block between what they think they are entitled to and what they are likely to get. Relative deprivation is also interpreted *mainly as a problem of material goods*. But the significant point is that it also has to do with individuals' perceptions of themselves as members of collectivities which are subject to deprivations of esteem. As Ross Stagner says, from a background in industrial psychology,

It has become clear that money is not the answer to all problems of discontent and rebellion by industrial workers; that questions of ego status, power, and security often dominate and push economic issues aside. It is only sensible for us to keep this thought in mind as we approach the social problems of urban discontent and disturbance. (Stagner, 1969, 14)

Relative deprivation really means *a sense of grievance* (not mere disappointment), a sense of *being "put upon,"* of *being abused and insulted by the world.*

If people perceive themselves as deprived—through somebody else's real or putative malevolence—and if they believe change practicable, then they are likely to embark upon a politics of *"collective psychiatry,"* the main thrust of which is to make the claimants feel better about themselves by forcing others to show deference and respect. Politics as collective psychiatry comes from the sense of being put upon. It leads directly to limitations on the abilities of leaders to interact. It can hamper leaders in groups A, B, C, and so onward not only from extending to each other overt professions of legitimacy, but even from cooperating *de facto*[3] with each other. Such hampering destroys intergroup "bridging," a leadership function which is as important as the simple advocacy of the group position *completely, only, and without limitation.*

DEGENERATIVE INCREMENTALISM

If the sense of being put upon were to produce internal war in the United States, this development probably would not come through the deliberate intention of any significant leadership element, or through the desire of any significant number of people. It would more likely come through some domestic analog of the *Guns of August,* some dynamics of mutual alarm, some *degenerative* incrementalism with whites taking actions which would frighten blacks into taking actions, which would frighten whites into taking more drastic actions, which would frighten blacks into taking still more drastic action, until by the escalatory spiral a point of no return should have been passed. To understand this potentiality, we must reemphasize the difference between hope and sheer Micawberish optimism. One should not discount the possibility merely in the optimistic belief that if people are unwilling to meet the *extreme* costs, they will take none of the precipitating actions which an impartial observer could predict would bring down those costs. In the language of the Old Testament, "where there is no vision, the people perish"; and we are precisely talking about a situation which beclouds and destroys vision. In the formal language of social science, we are talking about *attitude salience,* about the prospect that people, when the chips are down, will accept what they now sincerely reject.

The possibility of degenerative incrementalism is most often brought into discussion via some effort to deal with the problems of Afro-Americans or others believed to be "the worst off" in United States society. Social scientists and journalists, sympathetic to their conception of what "the disadvantaged" need, have done a great deal to foster this idea. The perceptions of "the disadvantaged" are a vital part of the matter, but they are not the only part of the matter nor the part which, alone, could give us understanding. The same psychic problems are experienced by other groups, and it is the interaction between groups which is pertinent. Upper-middle-class university students in this country, having nothing in their historical experience to feel deprived about, nonethelesss have shown a certain tendency to develop an ideology of deprivation virtually immune to evidence. Other groups, having previously held a favored position, may see themselves as losing that position and so develop images of being unfairly abused by the world; thus we may explain the behavior of white Southerners faced with the consequences of the civil rights movement. Still other groups have had a historical sense of their own deprivation, but also have had some experience in rising above the deprived position. If these groups see still others entering the same social arenas, in ways which seem to forestall their own fulfillment, they too experience "relative deprivation"; thus we may interpret the behavior of certain white ethnic groups (such as the Polish-Americans or the Italo-Americans) in response to the black upsurge which they interpret as "the Negroes getting everything." Degenerative incrementalism is more likely if there are several such populations which simultaneously have images of themselves as being unfairly deprived, and which perceive the need for taking decisive action to arrest, forestall, or reverse that process.

The legitimate basis for worry is that these simultaneous and mutually exclusive senses of insult and being "put upon" would join with the natural human tendency to let wish and fear take precedence over thought and judgment (Holden, 1968; also Holden, 1965a). This is no trivial matter. In any extreme situation, each side is likely to believe that it desires "peace" but that the others are "aggressive," that its motives are "good" but that the others are "evil." This impasse is the more likely if side A has taken what it believes to be measures which the other side B ought to recognize as valid concessions. Side A will tend to believe that side B knows such "concessions" have been made, but that side B is being perversely stubborn in refusing to reciprocate.[4] Hence, the response we should predict is action to make it "too expensive" for the other side to persist in its perversity and stubbornness: *escalation,* the ultimate expression of which is *brinksmanship.*

Escalation may sometimes work, but it may also lead to consequences which those initiating it neither desired nor thought likely, and which the initiators themselves, in advance, would not have wished to see followed through to their logical extremity. The precise fallacy in escalation theory is its presumption of a complete rationality which would make clear to all parties concerned just who stood to gain and who stood to lose under a given set of circumstances. Escalation makes sense on the presumption that the opponent is rational and will lose his nerve before you lose yours. If the opponent's nerve breaks first *and he is very rational,* then the strategy is very good. If the opponent's nerve does *not* break first or if he is really mad, then the results can be very bad indeed!

High social costs, like extreme physical pain, are more bearable when people have the opportunity to build up to those costs slowly. Escalation as a social policy tends to be defended on the basis that one more turn of the screw will break the will of the enemy and bring him to the bargaining table. It will be argued that each such action will lead to some early "turning of the corner" toward a more satisfactory future. But each side adjusts to the penalties and pains which the other imposes, without at all reducing its own disposition to fight.

These are the potentialities of degenerative incrementalism, the sense of being put upon, a politics of collective psychiatry, and the naturally imperfect rationality of decision making. Degenerative incrementalism would tend to turn the people (black and white) interested in social peace toward ambivalence; those already ambivalent mentally toward polarization; the mentally polarized toward readiness for physical fights; and those ready for physical fights toward active combat. If, as we believe, not many people would willingly contemplate such a result, what are the behavioral indicators (the "signs" to be read)[5] which should give us specific concern?

SHORT-RUN PROSPECTS OF DEGENERATIVE INCREMENTALISM

We have no real basis to be sure about our time horizon. But we should *guess* that the short run might mean something like the next two to four years. In this period, the two main dangers are (1) a disruptive process evoking wide white mob violence, or (2) escalation of the feud between the police and young black rejectionists.

One possible focus would come from the general atmosphere of black-white fear, in an unstructured situation where no one who is white can convincingly promise blacks safety, and where no one who is black can convincingly promise whites safety. Everybody "knows" what he means by "black" and "white," yet there is no way for Mr. Everyman to define the boundaries around black and white (for the purposes of deciding what he ought to do in a conflict situation), nor is there any stabilized relationship between "black" and "white" leaders. How, except when dealing with public officials, is the ordinary black man to know who "represents" whites? Are most blacks best represented by the man who will go out of his way to show that he hates white men or by the man who will go out of his way to show that he does not hate anyone? Are most whites best represented by men who show nothing about their feelings (but who, by that action, may tend to "vote with the stronger")?

The *individual* man has no obvious basis on which to decide the question, and should be expected to seek safety by choosing the most pessimistic assumptions. Each member of a group must decide for himself how to interpret the behaviors of members of the other group. Thus, the most reasonably basis for action is to interpret the most "hostile" sound as the voice of the most "representative" persons. This is the way to minimize the risk of those very severe losses from which recovery might not be possible.

If this were so, then the individual would have little security against unprovoked violence. The black man reading gas meters in a suburb of whites might all too easily find himself the target of anger which he did nothing to create; this is what happened to a couple of people in Cleveland during the June 1968 crisis. The white fireman, normally performing what everybody would usually admit is a service, might find himself shot at with greater and greater frequency during his runs through black neighborhoods. In short, the juvenile defense of turf (Suttles, 1968; Yablonsky, 1966) might be carried to the adult level, and thus transform social relations entirely from the present ones whereunder daylight passage—at any rate—through strange areas is mutually acceptable. Persons of either identity might more and more find themselves under the necessity to be fearful of persons of the other.

How might such a process by catalyzed? We should think that one way would be an expansion to a higher level of the pattern of bombings experienced in New York in March 1970. Imagine, for instance, that someone were to bomb a school and kill a number of children—black and white. If white parents thought the bombing source black, one might be quite sure that they would view any black at random with more suspicion, demanding that he prove himself to be among the harmless. And the more irrational types would merely be out for revenge on the collectivity, so that personal guilt would not matter. Similarly, one would expect people to *try* (however futilely) to protect their homes or their employments, as well as their physical safety.

This possibility indicates, incidentally, the peculiar vulnerability of blacks in one respect. Since the normal supposition is that they are more dangerous than other people, any dangerous action is more likely to be attributed to them. Hence they become natural patsies for the fringe types, both Right and Left, who think it desirable to bring things to a head.

Under circumstances of this sort, the greatest likelihood of white mob violence—which would naturally elicit defense measures by some blacks—would come from action attributed to blacks, *whether validly so or not.* For one thing, we should predict more overt activity by the several private organizations (such as the Minute Men) who since World War II have been stockpiling weapons to resist what they foresee as "Communist invasion." But more ordinary people would be drawn into the process. If, for instance, a specific building or area were "known" to be "headquarters" for the bombers, one could almost certainly forecast some group's getting together to "go in there and clean it out." Other moves would be made. Most cities have some sort of "police reserve" which does not normally do much. But we can easily imagine some high school principal or some postman activating his commission in the police reserve and taking it upon himself to decide which crowds of black youngsters on some downtown street should be arrested.

The other serious short-run threat is that the police and young black males (for example the Panthers) will so far escalate their private feud[6] that all conciliatory influences become immobilized. These two elements are remarkably similar. Each possesses and uses guns, the one illegally and the other under color of the law. Each appeals to broad values, which many other people share: "black liberation" and "enforcing the law." Each tends to act upon an implicit theory of coercive brinksmanship. And each tends to think of itself as the proper and exclusive interpreter of the values it ought to serve.

That the police prefer "tough" policies is evident. Such policies are frequently defended on the ground that, though unpleasant, they are necessary to control crime and social disorder. We may make more sense of what happens if we believe that much police behavior relates to the psychic needs of policemen on the job, that it frequently conflicts with the technical requirements of achieving physical order, and that it almost never contributes to social peace.

On the whole, the working policemen are recruited from the world of the white working class, where problems of status, the fear of contempt and disesteem, and the resentment at being held in contempt and disesteem are extremely powerful. As policemen, they experience daily peril (and a sense of peril) as "society's" agents, for the control of whatever elements are defined as "disorderly" and "threatening." What they now experience is that those middle-class and upper-class elements who define the social "good," in whose interests they work, are repudiating the latitude formerly allowed to the police. Instead, at the same time, these beneficiaries of police operations appear often to side with "the disorderly," obstructing what policemen themselves deem "good police work." At the same time, the same beneficiaries continue to demand—and other people increasingly demand—that "order" be maintained. As the policemen also experience an increasing sense of disesteem, problematic situations are likely to make them literally *enraged* and, thus, to make them not *reasonable* in action.

The problem for the policemen is especially troublesome since he is inevitably experiencing an actual and realistic sense of threat, greater than he has before experienced. This sense of threat is, for instance, reflected in the widespread reports of "sniper fire" in the urban rebellions, although very little evidence of sniper activity ever has been placed on the public record. Though police work always involved perils, it is a new experience for policemen to face the prospect that they may be fired upon at just any time, by just any unidentified person, simply because they are policemen. The sense of being literally imperiled cannot but be enhanced.

If policemen and firemen come to experience more unprovoked attacks in black areas than they experience elsewhere, then it is reasonable to predict that they will see all blacks in those areas as potential terrorists. Even if (which would normally be contrary to fact) they were without racial prejudice, they would have no realistic option. After all, they would have no way to identify beforehand which black man might be a terrorist and which might be an undercover policeman. The more the sense of threat or peril increases, the less reasonable one should predict police action would become. At some point, one should expect the same process reported from studies of battlefield stress: that discipline will collapse entirely and the use of violence become a psychiatric problem for the user (soldier or policeman). The present police tendency is to think of the city as battlefield, with blacks, particularly such groups as Panthers, as "the enemy."

The more the strain is increased, the greater the likelihood that policemen and firemen would respond with a great deal of unprovoked brutality and violence of their own. Under these circumstances, commanding officers would tend to condone or overlook such behavior, or to lose influence over their men.

But this examination calls forth a situation in which the Panthers and similar groups are in a state of mind remarkably similar to that described by a now-recusant Zionist who joined Irgun Zvai Leumi in the late 1930's:

Arab terrorism was raging in the country . . . Jews were being ambushed and killed every few days. The British seemed incapable of putting a stop to these acts, and the Jews, even suspicious of British perfidy, believed that the British were secretly supporting the Arabs . . . [I]t looked to me as if our established leaders, preaching havlaga or self-restraint, were acting like cowards. . . . There was only one way a boy could respond to the situation. We had to kill Arabs in return, kick out the British, and our own official leaders, the people of the Jewish Agency, out of office. . . . The place of every self-respecting, upright young Hebrew was in the Irgun. (Avnery, 1968)

Something very like this spirit is what the young black people of the Panthers represent, not without historical and current justification. Yet it is clear that to the extent that they act on this spirit, they generate new waves of hostility and lawlessness in the official users of force, and these in turn reinforce rejectionism, in a circular process.

A closely related aspect of degenerative incrementalism is the corruption of the court system and the loss of judicial legitimacy. Somewhere about 1962, when the King protest movement was nearing its crest, President Kennedy urged that "[these issues] be taken out of the streets and into the courts."

Such a statement was good politics for a President who needed to show sympathy for blacks without being coercive toward whites. Yet, taken at face value, it illustrates one of the most serious deficiencies of liberal politics since the Supreme Court switched to the New Deal: a tendency to overload the courts with issues requiring a subtler but more far-reaching type of decision making. There is no *automatic* magic about judicial decision making. The key, questions, even if frequently masked, which first must be understood are: (1) What does the litigation mean, psychologically, to the litigants?; and (2) How much side taking does the judge do, and how frequently is he on the same side?

The problem becomes most troublesome when litigation has a "constitutional" function, not in the sense of interpreting the formal Constitution of the United States—though this may be part of it—but in the sense of defining men's actual status under the "social constitution."[7] Constitutional litigation in this sense is similar to insurrection. It amounts to a contention between the established order and those challenging the presumptions of that order, with the allegiance of some third party as the stake or prize.[8] This likeness is quite applicable to civil suits in which, under "ordinary" circumstances, only the overt parties would be much interested, and to criminal trials. Civil rights litigation was mostly a series of civil suits, technically directed to the rights of particular individuals. But it was actually a kind of insurrection without arms—a signal of increased racial tensions sufficient to break through the bonds of Southern apartheid under which all signs of tension had before been suppressed. This much was perceptible quite some time ago. (Holden, 1963, 777–778). *The sociopsychological function* of these law suits was to express the latent black spirit of defiance, to challenge the old order of white supremacy and bring it down. Although this challenge and defiance was conducted with the fullest display of good manners and not a whisper of violence, the real purpose was fully understood by Southern whites.

The reason for the "Impeach Earl Warren" signs, displayed by Southern whites and their Northern sympathizers, was that the federal courts became more and more an instrumentality by which a once-suppressed group (black) could effectively fight its suppressors (white). The fact that this struggle was political, in the most agonistic sense, was reflected in the Southern resort to litigation as a filibuster device, the endless generation of new technical issues (some patently inconsistent with what the courts were holding, and in that sense not serious) as a means of delaying compliance as nearly forever as possible. The litigation filibuster did not end, but it appeared to subside only when the tactics of black people—and the policies of the federal government—moved the racial issues into the Congressional and administrative arenas.

If we wish to know how much cleavage is occurring between whites and blacks, we should watch this indicator among others: How much should we suppose that disputes requiring civil adjudication are governed by the racial identities of the parties in question? If the Nation of Islam, for instance, brought suit in the trial courts of St. Clair County (Alabama) to protect its contested property rights in some piece of farm land (*New York Times,* November 23, 1969; also February and March, 1970), how much confidence would we have in their getting a "fair shake" before the local judge? A single case, or a few cases, in which litigants do not get a "fair shake" may be regarded as deviations from the norms of the law, but a pattern of such deviations tells us something about the atmosphere of the polity in which the litigation takes place.

The criminal law process offers the same sort of clues, but in a more intensive form since the criminal law is inherently the regularization of force-and-intimidation in the interests of those who are already on top.[9] In the criminal process, the "state" becomes an active litigant (in behalf of the social values embodied in "law"). It is the "law" that *regularizes and limits* force-and-intimidation by applying strict rules of "evidence" to sustain "fairness" and "due process." The theory of the criminal law is that the State-as-litigant agrees to these limitations and the business of the trial judge is to assure that the limitations are at least approximately observed.

We can see this process in decay (though not necessarily irreversible decay) whenever the criminal law takes on a *preventive* function against unpopular group actions which are not themselves directly on trial, and not necessarily themselves in technical violation of the law. When it takes on such a role the court itself becomes the antagonist of the defense, serving a *witchcraft* function, carrying out a "ritual" to avoid "dangers" which "society" imagines (and which may or may not have some basis in reality).

When this occurs, the charge and specific evidence against the individual defendant will predict less about the conduct and outcome of the trial than will the identity of the individual. If a society were *completely* polarized, even the most trivial offenses would bring very severe sentences to those with the "wrong" social identity. There is a little evidence which suggests that matters had not gone to this extent, at least by 1966 in so tense a city as Detroit.[10] There is, however, good evidence in the contrary direction, the most highly publicized piece of which comes from the trial of LeRoi Jones. As one event growing out of the July (1967) experience in Newark, Jones was brought to trial in November (1967) and sentenced in January (1968), the charge having been illegal possession of guns. According to an analysis by two responsible scholars (Dolbeare and Grossman, 1969), the trial and sentencing were distinctly more affected by Jones's ideas (he is and long has been, a professed black "nationalist") and personality (he is apparently a dramatic and tempestuous man) (Dolbeare and Grossman, 1969, 7–10) than by the formal charge and evidence. Jones and Jones's attorney both comported themselves in a manner which would have reduced such chances for acquittal as did exist. But the main point here is that "both the judge and the prosecutor . . . [acted with] what seemed a single-minded dedication to the conviction and severe punishment of LeRoi Jones, and . . . this dedication could not be explained [by] . . . the nature of the offense charged in open court but . . . only [by] . . . the defendant's role as a severe critic of white society" (Dolbeare and Grossman, 1969, 21). According to this account, the trial judge went out of his way to retain control over the case when it was removed to another county (even though substitution of another judge would have been conventional and preferred procedure). He took an unusually active role in questioning witnesses, in such a way as to accentuate testimony adverse to Jones. And he made it clear that some of Jones's poetry—published after the trial but before sentencing[11]—constituted part of his grounds for the sentence. Perhaps the Jones trial was unusual in its starkness. But there are other experiences of the same general sort, either in the actual conduct of trials or in the preliminary decisions of prosecutors or grand juries.[12]

The tendency to use the criminal law machinery severely against blacks is but one dimension. What is equally suggestive is the frequency with which public authorities (notably policemen) alleged to have acted beyond their proper authority either are not charged, or are released without penalty when they have been charged. It would be unrealistic to believe that *every* time a black person accuses a police officer of improper practices the accusation is accurate. That is not the issue. Rather, the issue is that it is even less realistic to believe—in the fact of all other evidence —that there are *no* occasions when major charges are well founded. (Thus, the death of Fred Hampton was declared by a coroner's jury to have been a proper exercise of police power, despite awkward evidentiary questions. In the same manner, the three men finally charged as a result of the Algiers Motel incident (Hersey, 1968) were also acquitted after trial.) What one may more properly believe is that images of "black criminality" in general (or "black militancy," which is something else again) serve as a basis on which administrative hearing officers, judges, and juries assume that the action of the police officer was right and proper.[13] This pattern thus describes the use of the judicial process as a political weapon in the coarsest sense, and leads on to the other side of the problem: black rejection of the legitimacy of the judicial process as constituted.

If courts (or quasi-judicial tribunals) act in this way often, or are believed so to act, it is to be expected that any victimized class of potential defendents will regard the court as a mere instrument of arbitrary and illegitimate power. This proposition erodes any basis for defendants' adherence to the obverse of "fairness" and "due process," namely the "decorum" which permits the court to proceed. The social danger signal is thus manifest in other situations: the complicated case of a young black lawyer in Detroit who emerged from the courtroom calling the judge "a racist honky dog"; the confrontation between Judge Murtaugh and Panther defendants in New York (*Newsweek,* February 23, 1970); the anxieties that people had about the trial of Bobby Seale in New Haven (*New York Times,* March 22, 1970); threats made by young blacks that other blacks who continued to function as judges in the normal court system will be deemed "Toms" and "traitors," and be "dealt with"; the probable increase in difficulty of getting black jurors. The more such situations occur, the more we may say that levels of social tension (of dispute between groups) are rising to immobilize the legal process and turn it into sheer tests of power, whether one is dealing with Virginia in 1774 (Eckenrode, 1916, Chapter 4), with the Congo in 1959 (Legum, 1961), or with the cities of the United States today.

SOME LONG-RUN PROSPECTS OF DEGENERATIVE INCREMENTALISM

The erosion, corrosion, and corruption of the legal process is one of the warning signals. But there are others to which people are inattentive until situations become quite delicate. One is the political significance of what we normally regard as "good manners." Richard M. Nixon's visit to an NAACP National Convention, late in the 1950's, offers an example of an event with far more political meaning than most commentators then recognized. The convention—composed of respectably middle-class delegates—was very rude to the then Vice President, not on his own account so much as because its members resented the "go slow" posture of Eisenhower's administration. The delegates hissed and booed the Vice President so badly that he could not speak until Roy Wilkins arose, rebuked them for rudeness to "an invited guest," and enabled the proceedings to go on. As of the last 1950's, this was simply an astonishing departure from the norm, for the country had not become accustomed to high-level personages being quite unable to make themselves heard unless their messages agreed with the predilection of the audience.

When people begin to behave in ways they themselves would normally regard as improper—and when they do so in some systematic way (as *whites* behaving insultingly to *blacks* but not to other whites and conversely)—we may regard this as a straw in the wind. What it signifies is their rejection, rightly or wrongly, of those private authority symbols and social rituals which maintain social structure and which are normally not challenged. Some of these "inappropriate" behaviors are not at all illegal, while others are "technical" violations which seem to have no more immediate consequences than a traffic violation. It is not illegal to boo a speaker, but some people will find it offensive, saying that one should either listen or leave. It is not clearly illegal for a civilian to keep his hat on when the flag passes, but to do so in the presence of a middle-aged Legionnaire is to invite anger. It probably is "technically" illegal to sit in a courtroom with one's hat on (at least if the judge says to remove it), but it surely does not obstruct the presentation of evidence or the deliberation of the jury and might thus be ignored. Yet one may suspect that a group of Panthers who did this would evoke nearly as much anger as a Jehovah's Witness child refusing to salute the flag, or a seventeenth-century Quaker insisting on remaining covered in the presence of the sovereign.

If such activities are writ large, rather than merely occurring as individual deviations from a norm, then it is possible to regard them as a form of *secular desecration*. The significance of secular desecration is that it *anticipates* a more extreme challenge, namely a direct challenge not only to those symbols which are not protected by force of arms but also to those which are. Not "everyone" begins to behave differently; some people do not change, and are grossly disturbed or upset by what seems to them "inappropriate" behavior in public places. What we then have to anticipate is that those adhering to the old values will respond to secular desecration by taking action which they formerly would have thought inappropriate. Some such actions may be possible without direct confrontation. It is possible to have not only an antiwar demonstration but also a prowar demonstration. The problem begins to arise when the psychological states and the physical distribution of the competing parties do not permit them to remain disengaged.

The problem thus arises, for instance, when a high school (as one did in Madison, Wisconsin) finds itself with an activist black element which refuses to accept most of the normal high school modalities and, at the same time, finds itself with a "Nazi" element which also refuses to accept those modalities. In the long run, it is precisely this sort of relationship with which people in the United States have to deal. We may reasonably suppose that a number of black children are now growing up "Black Panther in mind," as we may also suppose that a number of white children are growing up with more active—not latent—racial prejudices than was the case just before the middle 1950's. But both the blacks and the whites are growing up in an era where the notion of social self-restraint is less accepted, and the notion of coercing other people into one's own values is more accepted. If we project this situation ahead, say about ten years, then—in the absence of countervailing forces—we should expect to have a college-age population no less active than the present one, but far more openly divided. We should also expect, by the active pressure of contemporary communications, to have this activity and division more deeply inserted into the high school population. If that is so, then we should have to expect the Harvard-Berkeley-Wisconsin pattern greatly enlarged, and therefore much more dangerous to social order. (Imagine, in the same vein, the effects on politics in the early 1980's of the present course of the Nixon administration. Whereas white young people in the South in the 1960's had begun to reach near-adulthood with the idea that integration was "inevitable," and "perhaps right," one would predict that the recent turnaround would bring forth a new cohort convinced—as post-Reconstruction whites were convinced—that the blacks had temporarily gotten out of hand and had to be put back in their places.)

If we follow this scenario to its natural conclusion, there is still another feature which may be pertinent. An increase in physical conflict would, for physical and psychological reasons, tend to run counter to the recent tendency to absorb blacks into the broader range of economic and occupational structures. If, for instance, the Army becomes more and more an instrument for controlling blacks inside the United States, one would have to predict at some point the emergence of an American reverse version of the "Curragh mutiny" in which British officers threatened to resign their commissions rather than fight against Ulstermen. The American version would be that black officers and noncoms would be under ever greater pressure—both within themselves, from their civilian contacts, and from their military ties—to get out rather than accept their duties. The harbinger of this *potentiality* is to be found in the police world, where, in more than one city, black policemen have found it obligatory to form ties with each other, not only for departmental reasons but also as a measure of protection for blacks in the hands of the police. If the situation became more intense over the next several years, this process would be reflected in a number of civilian occupations as well: the exit of black professors from "white" universities; the disinclination of black potential bureaucrats to accept government appointments; the reduction of the usefulness of blacks in corporate life; and so on.

But what offers the most serious long-run problem is the present tendency toward a collapse of public leadership. The process of decay can be arrested only by an exercise of the public leadership function which discovers and articulates possible forms of action sufficient to enlist the wills and energies of large numbers of people who would normally be on both sides of the chasm. It is the function of public leadership to generate new symbols and policies sufficient to attract the attention and enthusiasm of potentially dissentient elements, to devise measures which will enhance confidence in the potentialities of intelligent choice. Polarization may be reflected in a disappearance of leadership suggestions for handling social issues or by the disappearance of all suggestions which are not strictly keyed to one side or the other. Practically speaking, the public record itself becomes a source of information on polarization (although an inadequate record), for it is there that one can measure the presence or absence of leadership suggestions with some appeal to more than one faction. What the public record contains—in the last five years—is a set of suggestions which would appear, on careful examination, to be self-defeating for the purposes in the name of which they were advanced.

The influential and responsible conservatives (examples being Stewart Alsop or Walter Lippmann)[14] do offer ideas, but these have clearly counterproductive implications. Lippman's case is particularly noteworthy because it is the most respectable statement: that blacks must be made to learn that forcibly disruptive behavior, outside the law, will not produce desirable outcomes, but that legal approaches will produce desirable outcomes. Under the Lippmann doctrine, once order is restored, progress can begin anew.

In the policy-making community, it is possible to interpret the course of the Nixon administration as an operational version of the Lippmann doctrine. Attorney General Mitchell's advocacy of preventive detention is expressly directed to "criminal" behavior in the conventional sense. But we should reasonably expect that were preventive detention expanded, it would surely be applied to the more obstreperous forms of black political activism. Similarly, the Attorney General's advocacy of wiretapping could be interpreted as a more coercive approach to domestic politics—the more so because even the November (1969) Mobilization against the Vietnam war is, from his point of view, "violent" activity. But the most convincing evidence of a federal turn toward coercive restraint is that even those black groups known to have a full and verified history of peaceful, legally correct, politics have been subject to military surveillance.[15]

Even if such surveillance is rather crude, possibly initiated by military authorities who somehow have been given no guidelines as to how far they should go, the prospect could easily be regarded as sinister. For such a surveillance operation also implies that judgments about who is "dangerous" and who is not so will be made. And one distrusts those judgments, particularly when the makers are likely to be allied with the needs of a Justice Department capable of cooperating in the detention of almost 900 Mississippi black students and their transportation to Parchman (*Madison Capital-Times*, March 26, 1970, 44), one of the nation's most notorious prisons. We suspect, though we cannot prove, that most conservative whites would approve (or at least not object to) this action because they think racial change has gone "too far," "too quickly," or "too far and too quickly." But the Lippmann doctrine (and even more its practical application by the Nixon administration) has one practical difficulty: from the point of view of social peace as a policy objective, it is inherently unproductive. The error is one which Lippmann (above almost all intelligent critics) would instantly spot if the subject were international politics rather than domestic racial politics, and it is the same error committed by black advocates of "armed rebellion." The doctrine neglects to ask: How will those against whom action is directed interpret the action? Nothing would —or should be expected to—alarm blacks more than these activities unless the administration should overtly endorse the detention program called for by the House Internal Security Committee (formerly House Un-American Activities Committee).[16] Our prediction is that those against whom the action is directed in this case (blacks) could only be expected to become more averse to the legal order rather than less so.

As far as our knowledge goes, Alexander Gerschenkron, the student of Russian economic history, has never addressed himself to domestic racial politics. But Gerschenkron offers an interpretation which seems enlightening in this context. *Revolutions have emerged,* he argues, when economic *well being had been increasing and then began to decline* (Gerschenkron, 1964, 204). Logically, this is a refinement of the relative-deprivation hypothesis offered by sociologists and psychologists. If, according to our own refinement of the relative-deprivation hypothesis, the issues are more than material, then Gerschenkron's argument becomes instructive. The revival of coercive policies should be expected to be interpreted as an explicit sign of racial prejudice and the expression of a determination to avoid what is "obviously right." This interpretation may be factually correct. But it does not have to be factually correct, since the trend of policy will go in the same direction as if it were. The cause lies in the political necessities of developing an approach to policy, and to the instructional necessities and ambitions of those who actually have to administer the policy.

If a government identifies group A as troublesome, it must develop a psychological-political climate in which it will have wide discretion to penalize those identified as A. It cannot simultaneously develop a climate in which a friendly posture toward A is taken. Only a relatively small portion of the constituency from which support must come will be ready to tolerate the "wishy washy" program which seeks to combine both "toughness" and "reconciliation." Policies have to be administered by some particular agency or complex of agencies, and each agency tends to acquire a vested interest in any policy area where it acts. Each interprets the policy issues in terms of its going ideology and to generate constituencies favorable to its techniques of decision. As social work agencies almost never argue for coercion, police agencies almost never argue for conciliation. Under ordinary circumstances, police doctrine has been that disorder

—from individual "drunk-and-disorderly" conduct to large social disturbance—is best handled by coercion anyway, and that the best man to
administer the coercion is the police officer himself, unrestrained by legal
"niceties." Police doctrine—not written in manuals, but revealed both in
street conduct and in conversation—also has been and is that blacks are
particularly troublesome people, to whom tough measures are properly
applicable. The more the police agencies are loosed to act upon this
doctrine—reinforced by a vast public propaganda—the more one expects
them to *become* what black activist rhetoric has always called them: quasi-
military armies of ghetto occupation. If this were accepted as command
doctrine, then the consistency of such doctrine with the felt necessities of
the working policeman (described above), would tend to generate greater
and greater pressure for coercion. Policy would tend steadily to diverge
away from the conciliation alternative, the more so because going back to
the conciliation side would reduce the importance of the police organization and upgrade the importance of other kinds of organizations.

It is less clear what the military doctrine would be. On the one hand,
we have the testimony of S. L. A. Marshall that the dominant doctrine of
the United States Army has been to remain clear of domestic disputes
(interview with Matthew Holden, Jr., and David H. Blake, August 1969).
But there is a contrary historical thrust. The top-level military commanders' view of such groups as Coxey's Army and the Bonus Army seems to
have been that these were subversive conspiracies, without moral justification, and to be dispelled by force as rapidly as possible. We do not know
if this was generally accepted doctrine for the whole period between the
1890's and the 1930's, but we may suspect that it was; and we may further
suspect that it was usually of no *practical* significance because the working-
class population was large enough that politicians could not long afford a
simple policy of coercion. The problem of the blacks as a potential "permanent minority," in a political sense, might offer us reason to believe that
the abstinent role in labor history would not be followed under present
circumstances. The fact that the military would come, under circumstances
where most whites were grossly disturbed, to be regarded as protectors
against the "black hordes" would be an asset in appropriations politics; the
spillover of domestic racial disputes into the internal discipline of the
services would provide a reinforcing incentive; and the tendency of certain black radicals to adopt Third World revolutionaries as their symbolic
heroes would be conclusive.

Consequently, one should best predict an increasing order of coercion
and a decreasing order of conciliation. Police and military would each feel
free and compelled to behave more roughly with suspected persons, to

define their criteria of suspicion more and more on sheer skin color, and to assert their discretion (on the basis of "emergency" conceptions) to inspect, penetrate, or supervise black populations more and more crudely. But the more they should do this, the more would they generate sympathy for suspected terrorists, even among people who might actually be opposed to terrorism. What would occur would be an uneasy collaboration between the "respectable" (and "responsible") members of black communities and those more closely associated with clandestine organizations.[17] But this process is circular: the only conceivable police response to that pattern is still freer and freer searches (as in the house-to-house search for guns in Newark, 1967), more and more casual detention, less and less circumspect means of interrogation, the taking of hostages unofficially and the actual movement (under some circumstances) into policies of preventive detention. Out of this process could come an expansion of urban guerrilla warfare as terrorist groups seek to protect themselves, a tendency toward more overt racial clashes, ending in forms of more or less open confrontation in many centers simultaneously. That such a process would also be madness *is* our present contention, but the contention also is that such a process would tend to emerge if other factors did not intervene.

In this context, the coercion-plus-conciliation approach could hardly be more viable than it was in the Anglo-Irish struggles of 1880–1922, or in the British-Arab-Jewish politics under the Palestine Mandate, or in the British-Kikuyu interaction at the time of the Mau Mau emergency.

THE COSTS OF INTERNAL WAR

So far as we know, the growing sense of alarm has not led anyone to write seriously about the potential costs of internal war. Neither the advocates of severe official repression, nor the advocates of "armed struggle," seem ready to ask: What, *exactly,* would happen to whom? What would this process mean to the American social system? It is not possible, with my present information and skills, to estimate these costs in quantitative terms. But it is possible to indicate the kinds of losses which are reasonably imaginable, and even in qualitative terms these are far beyond anything which should be regarded as "supportable."

The costs for blacks, were this process to continue, would be self-evidently bad. But what should also be understood is the error of the implicit assumption that the white population would come out of this essentially "all right." *Nothing seems less likely* and this is inherent in the mixed physical distribution of whites and blacks throughout the economy and across space. Blacks and whites are tied to each other. The political system is in part a function of their historical relationship. The fact that they speak the same English language (even with subtle differences) and must use the same radio-television-newspaper-book-magazine industry means that it is not possible to communicate ideas to one without the potentiality of awareness by the other. The physical interspersal of whites and blacks in the same land area, an interspersal which could not be changed except by one of the largest population exchanges in history, points to another tie. And it is patent that they are tied in as components of the same economy. *The costs which black Americans would suffer cannot be disentangled from those which white Americans would suffer.*

The first sorts of costs are merely the most obvious: *economic costs.* If one reads the papers carefully, one will usually find that after a major civil disturbance, certain costs have to be counted. The insurance industry needs to count up the damages it must reimburse and compute how its subsequent premium schedules will be affected. Precisely how the insurance industry calculates such costs, or how expensive they have been until now, is not clear, but they must sometimes have been substantial. Public officials have been faced with a different sort of economic cost, such as overtime pay for policemen and firemen, or claims (sometimes denied by courts) by individuals that city governments did not give adequate protection to their property. Economists and businessmen may try to calculate the costs to "the community" or "society as a whole."

In all these costs, it is possible to get some dramatic claims. For instance, the manager of the Detroit Board of Commerce (chamber of commerce) claimed that the 1967 crisis cost Detroit a billion dollars! He was trying to calculate all the economic losses from having all banks, major factories, major stores, and other places of commerce or employment closed for three days, plus a measure of assumed deterrent to future growth. His retrospective estimate was many times that of any other Detroit source and —in light of chamber of commerce analytical methods—probably should be regarded as exaggerated. We lack the analytical technique or the conceptual frame to establish quantitative forecast estimates, but some basic appraisals can be made by indicating the order of the problems. For example, the distribution system depends on transportation by rail and by major highway. In most major American centers, these lines pass directly through the ghettoes. It is not feasible to build or man a wall along every mile of freeway and railroad. It follows, therefore, that under conditions of internal war, goods could be transmitted only under heavy armed guard. Imagine, then, that some group declared a ghetto off-limits to whites, tried seriously to enforce their declaration, and had even a modest capacity to do so. Such an industry as steel would suffer little more than inconvenience. Those dealing in products directly consumed or used by individuals would be highly vulnerable. Nothing is more vulnerable, for instance, than a shipment of new cars or of gasoline.

The vulnerability of downtown is another element in potential economic costs. Despite the long-term *economic* trend toward metropolitan decentralization, downtown is still the critical center. To immobilize downtown is to immobilize the economy. What would happen to the newspaper industry if printing plants (all in the central city) were no longer secure,[18] or if loads of newsprint could not come in? How would business be conducted without banks, clearinghouses, stock exchanges, and communication services domiciled in downtown? Under the conditions imagined, it would be essential for the downtown areas—which contain the post offices—utterly to be sealed off if the mail delivery system on which a complex, literate society depends would continue operating.[19]

The second sort of costs refers to changes in ordinary everyday social relations and in political behavior. Very mundane examples will make their nature clearer. One is control over people's physical movements. It is, and will remain, impossible to impose severe controls over blacks without imposing similar controls over whites. The simple fact is that twentieth-century urban Americans have already given up much of one of the simplest and most elemental rights ordinarily taken for granted. *It is no longer possible for a law-abiding man not obviously misbehaving to be reasonably sure that he may go wherever he likes in the country, at any hour of day or night.* This is what an institutionalized curfew system establishes. Imagine, then, the growth of police doctrine that any young (say under 30) white male in a black area after dark is "suspect" as a member of some revolutionary cadre. What out-of-town reporter then could do a "depth" study of "urban conditions"?

Surveillance would be the area of another change. Imagine such a city as Detroit—renowned for its luxuriant variety of "nationalist" groups. The city produces, via Wayne State University, young blacks who become junior executives at the auto companies and the public utilities. In turn, it would be predictable—indeed, strange were it not predictable!—that some of their childhood friends and classmates will have become active in various groups as restrained as the NAACP or as radical as the Republic of New Africa. Police practice being what it is, certain consequences seem probable. If policemen think it appropriate to watch *obviously* clandestine groups, they will probably also wish to watch people who have *any* associations or ties to people in clandestine groups. Moreover, it would not be usual for policemen to exclude the prospect that people would be using their jobs as "covers" for their illicit activities. If this possibility were pursued, we should also expect surveillance over any organization in which there were common black-white participation (such as the head-quarters of a company with black executives). From this it would also follow that whites associated with blacks in any very intensive roles (say as office colleagues) would also have to maintain very severe social distance *(far more than is now customary)* if they would escape all suspicion. How this development would affect, say, a personnel man trying to learn more about what companies call "the hard core" is not hard to imagine. Consider, similarly, the practical problems of running a trade union. How could one ever hold an executive board meeting at night and how could one be sure the meeting was not bugged? But if union meetings were bugged, how could unionists be sure their secrets were not being peddled to management?

Finally, this surveillance and control would entirely disrupt virtually all the usual forms of thought about political strategies, which assume the viability of electoral competition. Politics in the North would be more like politics in the South after Populism. Successful or rational white politicians would have to accept an implicit deal—a modification of the social constitution, as it were—such that the black man be considered not part of the legitimate electorate. The change would so contract the Democratic constituency that one of two results would be foreseeable: a nearly permanent Republican majority or Democratic-Republican competition for a white electorate. Either result would reduce liberal politics, as recently known, to nothingness, except as liberal politics should be redefined as *white* "bread-and-butter" populism.

The third sort of costs refers to foreign policy. In essence, the United States would lose its capacity to be effective, and would be driven to sit simply as an armed and hostile menace to most of the world. One might expect the Soviet government to try to keep out of domestic racial matters. The Soviets might have as little desire to see a real upheaval in the United States as the government in Washington might have to see a real upheaval in the Ukraine. (This assumes the Soviet Government to be motivated more by pragmatic interests, including a perceived need to act, explicitly or covertly with the United States for the limitation of international disorder.) It would be folly to suppose that the non-European governments would have similar interests. It is also not difficult to imagine the interlocking chains which might be possible.

Jews who worry about black anti-Semitism may or may not have their facts straight. (No really reliable analysis of the amount or strength of this phenomenon has ever been made, so far as we know. Those who find that black anti-Semitism is weak usually seem to have some vested interest in friendly associations with the Jewish community, which perhaps beclouds their judgment. Those who allege that it is strong have no data at all, and also have axes to grind.) But imagine that black university students continued to learn to think of Israel as a part of a "white imperialist" camp, with the Arab states in the role of the fraternal black victim. Surely, Arab governments—with access to oil money—would have every incentive to seek means whereby the New York Jewish population could be politically immobilized.

The growth of a "Third World" conception—which allies blacks with Spanish-speaking peoples, American Indians, and Orientals—has other implications. If Afro-Americans indentify with Africa, would we expect a more restive young population in the Chinatowns not to identify with China? But if blacks regard Chinese as their allies within a domestic "Third World" grouping, must they not also regard China more favorably than the United States? On the other side of the equation, if Mexican-Americans overlap (in their ordinary social and informational systems) with Mexican nationals, what happens if political turbulence inside Mexico grows? Or what happens if nationalist or revolutionary sentiment grows in Puerto Rico and the Caribbean, feeding into the Puerto Rican and West Indian populations of New York City? Pierre-Elliott Trudeau anticipated this possibility better than anyone. He was, he said, less concerned for Canada's role in NATO than with the potentiality that internal strife in the United States might spill over the borders, linking itself to linguistic and class revolutions in Canada and Mexico.

To what has been suggested we need add only certain other ingredients. Historically, black people have been able to use moments of national crisis to lessen their own burdens, partly because their leadership has been able to show the contrast of patriotic services to the reality of discrmination. Such a trade-off would be less and less possible. If the black manpower pool were already defined as less reliable—for resisting domestic antiblack assignments—and the United States were now obliged to assist South Africa or to fight some "Third World" insurrection, what should we expect? Public opinion would, perhaps by deliberate manipulation, be made more inflamed and hostile. There would, under those circumstances, be almost no legal or political defense if a president chose to interpret severe repression as a military necessity and acquiescence by whites as a patriotic duty.

Would it really be possible to resist legally or politically if another president chose to invoke the precedent of Lincoln in the suspension of the *habeas corpus?* Would there really be a basis to resist if some latter-day Henry Stimson were to say that detention was "personal injustice" to some "loyal citizens," but nonetheless a military necessity? (See Stimson and Bundy, 1947, 406.)

The ultimate cost would be the destruction of the United States, not in a physical sense but in a political sense: the destruction of even the present imperfect approximation of a republican government and the emergence in its place of a sort of concentration-camp society, with the police and the military at its core but supported by a thoroughly paranoiac and frightened white population. *We do not mean to argue that anybody intends this result.* The point is that the lesson of the Japanese internment is *not* fully learned, because no society ever fully learns that lesson. Americans are impressed with the restraint and civility of British governmental methods, yet they seem not to notice either the brutalities of the Anglo-Irish war (or "collective punishment" in Malaya, Palestine, and Kenya), nor do they notice that the British anticipated the Germans by nearly forty years in the creation of concentration camps (Hancock, 1961, 13n1). These camps were not created, moreover, by white racists for the detention of blacks but by British commanders for the detention of Boer women and children.

It should be emphasized that we do not predict such an end result *will* come, but rather point out that it *could,* if the whole chain of events to which we refer were in fact to eventuate.

CONCLUSION

In ancient lore, to look upon Medusa's face was to be turned to stone. But that was the thought of an essentially pessimistic people ("count no man happy until he is dead"). To look upon Medusa's face now is salutary, if the *will* to overcome adversity be energized by the knowledge that inertia—the paralysis of will if not actually being turned to stone—itself is the invitation to social decay.

We have accentuated the negative because there is too great a tendency for ordinary people—notably the middle-of-the-roaders and the intelligent conservatives—genuinely to believe that everything *must and will* work out right. We think that belief is wrong. The history of the world is the story of people doing what they would never have imagined. Rationally, therefore, the question is: How might the country be put on a different path of development? Carmichael and Hamilton (1967) may properly have defined the racial problem in the United States as one of "political modernization." The problem is that of creating a "social system that can constantly innovate without falling apart" (Apter, 1965, 67).

The degenerative tendencies are apparent, and the country has gone some uncomfortable distance on the wrong road. *But there is, we believe, considerable turnaround room, much of which is not being utilized.* There is room in which to initiate a process of modernization, in which to create a politics of social peace.

NOTES

1. For more on this topic, see *Politics of the Black "Nation,"* Essay II, "Clientage, Opposition, and Withdrawal."

2. Ted R. Gurr is the political scientist who has used this idea most systematically. See Gurr (1968).

3. Political analysts are fully attuned to the necessity for group leaders to look after the welfare of their own constituencies first and foremost. But they are not always so sensitive to what this necessity means in practice. If groups are *ecologically* interdependent, so that to some degree the well being of the one depends on the well being of the other, then a certain amount of *de facto* cooperation is essential. Else, the relationship is one in which both (or all) parties lose more than any one of them gains. This can easily be demonstrated in industrial relations. It will often occur that union leaders, knowing how much the company can really afford, must restrain their own followers' pay demands—lest the company be put at some disadvantage relative to its competitors, and in the end deprive union members of jobs or future pay increases. Similarly, company negotiators must sometimes refrain from trying to drive the union to the wall, because dealing with a structured group, by giving more stability to labor relations, may be better than dealing with a mass of disorganized employees. The same may be true in international relations. The classical balance-of-power conception precisely was that no potentially opposing state should be permitted to get too strong; hence, no third state—potentially a limit on the opposing state—should be utterly destroyed, even if it were hostile to the first state. Similarly, a national decision maker may act in a way he believes helpful to a *particular* decision maker in a hostile foreign government, if he believes that the alternatives within that hostile state would be worse for himself.

4. It seems likely that this is a better explanation than any alternative now available of the manner in which the United States became engaged in the large-scale Vietnam war.

5. This part of the present essay has been adapted from Holden (1969a).

6. "Police and the Panthers," *The Black Politician*, 1:3 (January, 1970); *Newsweek*, February 23, 1970, 26–30.

7. See above, Essay I.

8. On the nature of insurrection, see Huntington (1962), 19–22.

9. This is further discussed in Holden (1969b).

10. See Jaros and Mendelsohn (1967). There are two caveats about the Jaros-Mendelsohn article. (a) They deal with the lowest level and most routine offense —traffic violations. But if their data had shown racial discrimination in these offenses, it would have been taken as evidence of polarization. *Ergo,* their contrary showing is also fair evidence of absence of polarization. (b) More important, however, is that their data came from a period (1966) antedating the sharp discussions following the 1967 crisis summer. A study of something as simple as traffic violations would be indicative, we suspect, if one took violators during the week when the city was under curfew.

11. The trial was in November and the sentencing the following January. The poem was published in *Evergreen Review* in December (Dolbeare and Grossman, 1969, 8–9).

12. See, for instance, the NAACP's house organ *The Crisis* (November 1969, p. 370) for a story on an indictment growing out of student disturbances at San Fernando Valley State College in 1968. Whatever the campus situation may have been, it seems a little odd that if "some 300 students, many of them white members of Students for a Democratic Society, were involved in (a) three-hour demonstration, only 26 Negro students and two others (one Mexican-American and one Asian) were indicted on the serious charge of conspiracy to violate state laws."

13. Commissioner Patrick V. Murphy (New York) got into political difficulty in Washington (where he was Director of Public Safety) because, among other things, he adopted a different policy. Murphy's policy was that an officer who shot someone was placed on administrative leave until the facts of the case had been resolved. This is not only sensible policy, but—we maintain—ought to become part of a general strategy of reducing social fears and tensions.

14. Alsop's main contribution is the argument that school segregation should be accepted so that the country can get on with "education," utterly neglecting both the problem of what "education" is about and the *political* problem of what accepting segregated education means for the operational effectiveness of the republic.

15. Since this draft was written a good deal of information has been made public which makes the pattern seem even more extensive than was before suspected. I have not, however, tried to assimilate that more recent information into the present discussion since it seems to change nothing in the major argument here.

16. *Guerrilla Warfare Advocates in the United States,* Committee on Un-American Activities, House Report 1351, 90th Congress (Washington: United States Government Printing Office, 1968).

17. As a harbinger of the kind of process one could imagine, note the declaration of a "black curtain" (or unofficial curfew) against the entry of whites into the black community after 6 P.M., following the death of Fred Hampton. This particular curfew was not enforced, but any sane man would have to be disturbed at the implications of such an event. In the absence of some greater display of political intelligence by public leadership, in the broadest sense, someone in some city will,

on some occasion, be obliged to take some such action and try to enforce it. But can anyone imagine that a city government could afford to accept it? But can anyone imagine the consequences of such a direct confrontation between the public authorities and newly constituted private authorities?

18. In 1968 *The Detroit News* remodeled its headquarters plant, giving it a fortresslike appearance. *News* management reported that it had not done so *because of* the 1967 rebellion, but had been going to do so anyway. In any event, the same kind of judgment about vulnerability is implicit.

19. The 1970 mail strike—which occurred after this passage was drafted—dramatizes the point.

VIII

Public Opinion and Everyday Behavior: I. Notes on Confusion and Ambivalence

SOCIAL PEACEMAKING: THE WHITE MAN'S BURDEN

When white people were still extending dominion over nonwhites, the term "white man's burden" came forth. The burden, so it was argued, upon the white man was that of "civilizing" the nonwhites through the imposition of a new order of power upon them. This rationalization of white rule has long since been abandoned. But in a more profound sense there is now a genuine white man's burden. In United States domestic politics,[1] the white man's burden is to achieve what has never before existed: a level of political rationality which will permit black and white peacefully to inhabit a common republic. This achievement implies an active process of social peace*making,* a set of deliberate efforts to slow, halt, and reverse racial faction; to achieve a reciprocal renunciation of force between black and white in domestic controversy; and ultimately to achieve a shared moral order encompassing both peoples.[2] This conception assumes that the achievement of social peace is something more than an "organic growth," and that—within some limits—deliberate acts of *human will* make a difference about how things will go (Long, 1963, 1–6). Obviously, there is an essential black contribution in such a process.[3] But the outcome will depend mainly upon cultural and psychological capacity of whites. No level of rational politics in the black world can, given the disparities of black-white power, compensate for irrational politics in the white world. The central question about the beginnings of peacemaking is what capacity whites have to initiate, or to accept, measures which will break the back of *institutionalized* racism, will break those institutional patterns which have the ineluctable effect of maintaining whites *en bloc* in a favored position relative to blacks *en bloc*.

In part, this capacity (or incapacity) is contingent on "structural" factors such as the short-run or middle-run conditions of the economy. If political-economic imperatives make inflation control more important to the government than anything else, then black progress will be retarded. The reason is that even white "full employment" (4 percent unemployed for the country as a whole) usually equals a black-ghetto recession; and a white recession is a black-ghetto depression. Or, consider the common assertion that automation creates more jobs than it eliminates, and consequently that technological unemployment is an overrated problem. Perhaps so, but if the new jobs require skill which the displaced people do not have, then blacks really are not better off (assuming many of those displaced people to be black). These are merely illustrations of "structural" factors which I mention here merely to keep the ensuing discussion of *cultural and psychological dispositions* in perspective. People often do what they swore beforehand they would never do—in consequence of structural constraints and opportunities. But human choice is not governed solely by the "structure" of a situation. It is also governed by the ability of men to discover alternatives within their "structures," by the values men bring to the handling of their problems, and by their ways of adapting, retaining, maintaining, transforming, or rejecting those values as they work on those problems.[4]

For these reasons the values implied by the word "racism" are important, as contrasted to the structural patterns involved in "institutional racism." The question, therefore, at this point in the discussion is whether whites are inseparably wed either (1) to *cultural ethnocentrism* under which blacks are defined as "worthy" only to the degree that they approximate norms and behaviors drawn from a European-North American cultural stream; or (2) to a *pathological prejudice* which defines blacks as inherently unworthy or threatening. (See above, Essay II, "Racism in the United States Polity.")

Public officials, newspapermen, and social scientists now rely, in trying to answer such questions, rather heavily upon "public opinion polls" or "survey data." Interviewers go about asking people questions about what they know, believe, or think. If the sample (the people actually interviewed) is well chosen, it is possible to take a small number of answers and learn a great deal about what large masses of people will do: vote for or against Republican candidates, go on relief or seek new jobs if they lose their old ones, buy new houses or old ones, and so forth.[5] There have been a great many surveys recently on the subject of racial policies and racial attitudes. If one believes the more common interpretations of these surveys, the white capacity for adjusting to the black upsurge is extremely low. If about one-third of white adults believe that Martin Luther King, Jr. brought his assassination on himself; that equal opportunity employment laws, open-occupancy, interracial dating and marriage, and school desegregation are bad; or believe that the black minority is itself most to blame for the plight of blacks in the United States (Rokeach, 1970, 36–37), then a certain ground for pessimism exists. Such attitudes, if indicative of what people will support and oppose, point to a major obstacle against public action favorable to social peace. Such attitudes bespeak a preference not even for the present, but for the *status quo ante* 1954. Other public opinion polls suggest similar estimates of that part of the white population which can be called "racist" with little or no qualification. Five years ago, 28 percent of the white respondents in a Harris survey said that blacks were *not* discriminated against (Brink and Harris, 1967, 125). It would be utterly unreal to suppose that these respondents could be *cognitively unaware* of limitations to which blacks were exposed, from which they themselves were protected. It probably really means that the respondents thought blacks were not being deprived of *anything to which they were entitled,* in other words that whites thought it *proper* that these limitations were imposed.[6] Other polls show an even stronger racist residue. In a 1968 Columbia Broadcasting System poll, one question was whether it would not be better if all blacks left the United States and went somewhere else. To this, 38 percent of white respondents answered "yes." But the figures offered do not provide a clear basis for knowing what capacity American whites have for a more rational approach to racial politics.

If one were disposed to be optimistic, one might point out that the racist proportion, estimated at something between a quarter and a third of whites now, has declined significantly since it was apparently about two-thirds of whites thirty years ago (Sheatsley, 1966, 222). Moreover, the decline seems to continue. Despite all that is said about "backlash," the aura of polarization in the last few years does not seem to have revived the basic core of prejudice so widespread as of World War II. National poll data seem to show a slight increase in the total number of whites who, as of 1969, regarded the status of blacks as unfair, despite all the anxieties about urban tumult (Scammon and Wattenberg, 1970). Those data seem consistent with white public opinion during the 1968 campaign, which was surely the point at which polarization ought most to have been revealed in new forms if it existed in new forms. As of 1968, the University of Michigan Survey Research Center (SRC) asked people whether they thought most of their neighbors were more hostile to blacks than they used to be and whether they themselves felt more hostile. People said their neighbors were more hostile, but they themselves were not. Could they have been lying, hiding their own feelings under statements about their neighbors? Of course they could. But were they? I should think not. Indeed, if the neighbors were more hostile, people should themselves have felt more secure in expressing hostility also. Hence, we reason they were telling the truth. They were *not* more hostile. But since most people gave this answer it follows logically that hostility really had not increased. Instead, they were attributing to their neighbors what they heard was happening "everywhere."

Moreover, it is not true that the responses given by the most hostile people *obviously* mean that they have some determined purpose to roll back the calendar of social change. It is not at all clear what they mean. For instance, what did those people mean who thought it would be better if all blacks left the United States and went somewhere else?[7] A man might believe that and ardently desire it to come about, but he might also accept it in resignation, frustration and despair. No one can tell what was on the minds of the CBS respondents. But one can be sure that few people were expressing any serious interest in the idea, for there is virtually no reflection of such interest in national politics. Did people mean that they would support this alternative if it ever became an important policy question? Such uncertainties could well mean that we are all overreacting, and that the presumptions of intense polarization and probable conflict are taken much too seriously. That argument, in turn, is also open to challenge. It could well be said that the slow decline of racist attitudes over the past thirty years is too slow for practical usefulness, since the adjustments required call for more rapid and urgent action than the rate of attitude change will allow. The fact that we can go back and forth, without a conclusive answer, probably indicates serious weakness in our own analytical capacities. We do not know how to discern the right answers from the available data. One might say that survey data represent the current *social weather* (today's temperature or, at best, tomorrow's temperature), but we need a more profound understanding of the *social climate* (the *general dispositions* of people which give point and meaning to the specific opinions they express). To gain this understanding requires that we use public opinion survey data, but that we also go beyond those data to various indicators from everyday behavior.

The need to go beyond survey data is demonstrated by the ordinary answer to the question "Who's a racist?" Virtually every poll reports that white people expressing support for "integration" are likely to be upper-middle-income, college-educated, professional people. Those expressing opposition to "integration" are disproportionately among the white poor or the white working class. From this kind of report, it is all too easy to leap to the conclusion that racism is essentially a working-class (blue-collar) posture, but that it has little significance among the well-to-do.

Alas! Racial prejudice is demonstrable in middle-class and upper-class life, and does have significance.

One might start with the doctrine that white people are biogenetically superior to those who are not white. This doctrine is seldom expressed openly. The well-to-do people have great respect for higher education, above all "scientific" education. Either they come from families in which, for at least a couple of generations, higher education has been taken for granted ("traditional"), or they have become well-to-do partly because of being educated themselves, or (if not so highly schooled) they may find in their everyday work a great need for the expertise which it confers. This orientation to education inhibits their open expression of doctrines of racial superiority and inferiority, for those doctrines have been vigorously attacked in the last generation's higher learning, and denied respectability even as hypotheses, by memories of the Nazi barbarities. Nonetheless, biogenetic hypotheses are often latent in the well-to-do culture, providing an ever-recurrent potential audience for such writers as A. R. Jensen, William Shockley, and Carleton Putnam. These hypotheses are more often revealed obliquely. In Madison, Wisconsin (a city with a tiny black population and little residential segregation), the revelations come in little ways, such as a kindergarten teacher's repeatedly asking the two black children to perform for the others. With an almost unbelievable naiveté, she explained to the angered mother of one that she did so because "black people have so much rhythm." More astonishingly, she explained to the same mother that she had first learned this information from her husband —also a school teacher—who told her that blacks were good at music and athletics, but not good at mathematics or science. Precisely the same bias was noted by a university mathematician who had given a group of natural scientists and engineers some papers written by a research-minded black physician. The mathematician said: "It was important (in reshaping their attitudes) that they should see those papers; they were impressed, because they just didn't believe a black man could do work like that."

Biogenetic determinism may not be expressed often on the record, and people may even refuse to accept its propositions privately. But it is much easier to hold on to a well-to-do version of cultural ethnocentrism. The crude version is expressed by a high school music teacher, now on a Middle Western university extension faculty. This musician recently undertook a study of "youth music" (rock), in the course of which he encountered a large number of black combos. Describing the Spartan regime which the teacher (a talented, but untutored garage mechanic) had set for one combo, he said: "These blacks *will* take discipline!" His tone said clearly: "I had never seen black ghetto youngsters before, except on the television news, and I did not believe that they could take the constraints I normally expect of other youngsters who want to be musicians." This was perhaps one of the more naive cases, but it cannot be so far from the statistical norm as to be bizarre.

Attitudes of the sort just described are influential long before people have to make any personal decisions about the relationships they themselves will enter. But signs of racial prejudice in the middle and upper classes are the clearest when decisions are raised about the institutions which people define as "private." "Private" does not really mean "free from the presence of other people," for only one's home is private in that sense. "Private" applies to any set of roles in the "nongovernmental" sector where one does not normally expect to encounter "strangers." Experience with the housing market is noteworthy. It is less "intangible" than the questions we have just been discussing, and involves the claim that one is entitled to choose not merely one's house, but the occupants of other houses in the same territory. Housing experience shows that a black family moving into a white lower-class neighborhood is more likely to face direct physical harassment than a similar family moving into a middle-class or upper-class neighborhood; the same is true of a black child in a working-class school. It is quite true that white lower-class people are more likely to give open expression to the simplest forms of prejudice, not only in words but in personal and direct action. But none of this proves the point, nor even lends credibility to the absurd argument that the real core of racism is the blue-collar man.

Grosse Pointe (Michigan) demonstrates that if lower-class people are those more likely to take some direct physical action against black neighbors, middle-class and upper-class people have their own methods. Perhaps the vignette which makes the case as powerfully as any was the experience of Joseph L. Hudson.[8] After the Detroit civil crisis of 1967, Mr. Hudson became chairman of the New Detroit Committee—an organization which served more or less as a prototype for the local Urban Coalitions. Among other things, he went about making open-occupancy speeches. This activity involved no "outside agitators"—the charge frequently laid against open-occupancy advocates[9]—but a man of substance, who lived in the immediate area and was on intimate terms with the other men of substance in the area. For his effort, Hudson found himself being thoroughly booed in this upper-middle-class, upper-income community. (The booing, I am informed, was led by the wife of the millionaire owner of a food products chain.)

Had Grosse Pointe been a working-class neighborhood, one might possibly give credence to the fear that property values would decline. But such a fear in an area where houses cost over $30,000 is an absurdity. It might also have been possible, of course, to have interpreted Grosse Pointe's hostility as a fear-ridden reaction, bred of the panic which followed the 1967 crisis, except that Grosse Pointe had seven years before (when urban disturbances were unheard of) been the focus of a complex legal action when the Michigan state government tried an action against restrictive housing practices (Norman C. Thomas, 1966).

Grosse Pointe could much better be explained as a place in which a distaste for black associations was profoundly developed among a very large number of its white residents. When Martin Luther King, Jr. went to speak there he did find a receptive clique, for the area is home to a good many of Detroit's "limousine liberals."[10] But he also found a middle group troubled by his presence, and a right wing clique openly hostile. Whitney Young journeyed to the same suburb and opened the speech in his puckish manner, saying that he was glad to have the chance to appear in a stronghold of the country's most segregated organization apart from the Ku Klux Klan—"the Junior League."

If racism were not itself a powerful element in industrial executive suites—participation in which is one measure of upper social class—then it would not be the case in 1970 that less than one one-thousandth of the directors (and senior officers) of large industrial corporations should be black. But that is the case (Egerton, 1970)[11] and—despite recent shifts in hiring policy—is the inevitable consequence of many years' practice of unofficial apartheid in industry. Similarly, if the usual statement of the inverse relationship between racism and social class were correct, then the country club set would not be nearly so "uptight" at the appearance of the first black guest, let alone the first black member. Yet this "uptightness" does exist. In the same way, the *private* world of most directors of the Urban Coalition includes the dozens of clubs where business may be transacted, but where even a black guest would be unwelcome. Millionaires' luncheon clubs are not so tightly closed for "rational" reasons. It is most unlikely that the 89,865 nonblack millionaires are going to be inundated by the 135 black millionaires! Reluctance to accept change in the present black-white pattern, and even vigorous hostility toward blacks, is—I have been suggesting—not limited to any social class. Instead it is significant in all social classes, although the reluctant or hostile factions of each class may differ.

The fact that one can discover significant signs of prejudice in those parts of the population which report "integrationist" opinions sharpens our sense of how difficult the peacemaking problem is. But it is even more complex (and thus more difficult) than that discovery suggests. Some important elements of conservatism on racial policies arise not only from specific attitudes about blacks, but also from more general assumptions which people take for granted; assumptions which people find it hard to modify, even if they are not prejudiced against blacks per se. [12] The fact that people can hold attitudes about blacks which one could call "racist" only by a travesty of meaning and still adopt specific actions adverse to racial reconciliation is clearly shown in the following statement about a group of Los Angeles people, more than half of whom were Yorty voters in the Yorty-Bradley election.

They do not believe in racial differences in intelligence, and there is virtually no support for segregated schools, segregated public accommodations, or job discrimination. Moreover, most of this group recognizes the reality problems that blacks face in contemporary United States society. They perceive blacks as being at a disadvantage in requesting services from government, in trying to get jobs, and in general in getting what they deserve. And they feel that integration can work: they feel the races can live comfortably together (Sears and Kinder, 1970, 16; emphasis as in the original text.) If such people can vote for a Mayor Yorty in large numbers, then something more than "racism" in the simpler sense of prejudice (or even cultural ethnocentrism) must be operative. Moreover, one might think that there is something more complex at work in even larger bodies of the population who show a conservatism (understood as resistance to change) on racial policy. In the next section, I wish to discuss two such population elements which are particularly important to racial politics in the urban North. Both are "conservative" in the sense of resisting the racial changes most under discussion these days, although it does not follow that they are necessarily conservative on the broad complex of civil liberties, racial, foreign policy, educational, and economic issues which are so often lumped together. [13] I call them (even oversimplifying a bit here) "Euro-American[14] conservatives" and "managerial conservatives."

EURO-AMERICAN CONSERVATISM

It is particularly believed, by many observers, that Euro-American prejudice against blacks is so much more intense than that of other whites that it is qualitatively different. Whether this qualitative difference really exists is not so clear. Andrew Greeley and Joe Spaeth, two men associated with the National Opinion Research Center, have offered some evidence that this belief is true, at least as far as Poles are concerned (Greeley and Spaeth, pp. 12–14). But the available survey evidence is that if Poles appear to be more hostile to blacks than do Irishmen and Italians, they are less hostile than are "native" whites. That question is too hard to resolve now. There is a more important point. If Euro-Americans are simply as hostile as the average white, that fact is crucial. The reason is that the racial struggle is urban and metropolitan, and since Euro-Americans constitute the main share of the metropolitan white population, and are immediately adjacent to blacks both on the social scale and (often) in physical space, no program of social peacemaking seems likely to work if it ignores them. Consequently, any serious interest in peacemaking demands the same kind of empathy for Euro-Americans as must be extended to blacks, and by blacks to others, before the process ultimately reaches fruition.

My hypothesis is that Euro-American reaction to blacks is a partly psychiatric response to adaptation problems which Euro-Americans faced in the past. Some of their resistance is based upon the supposition that the path they now believe they followed is the one blacks now should be expected to follow. Some deny that the Euro-American experience is in any way similar enough to black experience to merit consideration. Others seem to maintain that the two are so alike in essentials that the former constitutes a model for the latter. Neither choice seems quite right, for both similarities and dissimilarities are pertinent. When blacks say that nothing else is as important as the fact that the Euro-Americans are "white," they are entirely correct. Being white meant that they never experienced the sustained and all-encompassing oppression which has formed the black "nation" in the United States. The Euro-Americans escaped the particular experience of chattel slavery and the web of private force. And, while their first generation in the United States was extremely deprived, the worst of their North American life lasted but about thirty or forty years. Out of that, they have come—not without government assistance—to an economic and educational level which is roughly close to the national norm and far above that of blacks.

But the similarities are also important, and provide some clue about the Euro-American situation relative to contemporary politics. The Draft Riots of 1863, for instance, are much better understood if we keep in mind the recent bitter strife of hawk and dove, the shrill cries of "Hell, no! we won't go!" and the pervasive doubts that any government in Saigon could be worth American lives, above all black lives. To the Irish rioters, the case must have been rather similar. To be drafted and sent South was an inconvenience at best. At worst, it was danger and death. The Irishmen had no contention with Southerners. Nor had they any interest in the freedom of blacks. Emancipation meant something to the dignity and well being of blacks, to the politics of the Union leadership, and to the ideology of Abolition. But it meant little more to the transplanted Irish peasants in New York than a Kurdish revolt means on the South Side of Chicago. As far as the urban Irish were concerned, it was an extreme and unreasonable privation in the interest of altogether alien or hostile elements, and government action to suppress them could have been little more acceptable than the draft now is to young black nationalists.

Euro-Americans were similar to the later blacks in another respect. There was a great deal of violent action associated with them, unsanctioned by law or in defiance of law, both for social ends and for narrow personal ends.[15] Predictably, public opinion and public officials outside those communities stigmatized whole communities with complicity in such violence. In all, there was some perception in the rest of the populace—perhaps widespread—that these communities somehow bred people who constituted a threat to the public regime, and were culturally incompatible with its stability. Each set of violent actions, whether coming from or merely attributed to the immigrant populations, produced a distinct enhancement of the capacity of the governmental forces to suppress what might come next: a recurrent use of federal troops, not to mention the development of the state police, the mobilization of the National Guard, and the assimilation of the courts to the side of employers; a plethora of new laws against the underworld—although, if we believe the Justice Department, they cannot have been enforced[16]; and even a certain amount of private force and intimidation.[17] If current language about "cultural 'genocide' " might be too strong to apply, retrospectively, it is at least proper to speak of Anglo-Protestant "cultural 'imperialism'." Wilson and Theodore Roosevelt, the two twentieth-century presidents who counted themselves highbrows (before John F. Kennedy laid such claims) are the best examples. Roosevelt's stern hostility to "hyphenated" Americans who would not completely adopt the Anglo-Protestant style is well known, but it is surely matched by Woodrow Wilson's assertion ". . . Any man who carries a hyphen about with him [represents himself as Irish-American, German-American, or the like] carries a dagger which he is ready to plunge into the vitals of this Republic" (1919). It was quite legitimate to advocate aid to "our English cousins" in their efforts to repel attacks from "the Huns," but it would have been absurd to speak of "our Russian" or "our Italian" cousins, and treasonable to have defended "our German cousins."

Anglo-Protestant cultural imperialism was also inherent, and unapologetically expressed, in the legal system. Civil courts imposed a new family order at variance with bewildered immigrant fathers finding that "the law" interfered with their traditional ideas about how children should be trained,[18] and the joint effect of law, education, and management policy was to erect a triumphant policy of English monolingualism. The fact that we now speak of "cultural pluralism" is not a testament to the early purpose, but to the commanding fact that even the severest Anglo pressure could not quite produce the submergence of other ethnic cultures. When linguistic communities move *en masse,* it is not "natural" for them to lose their original language quickly. Instead, they will retain and use the original language if there is any latitude at all. Language habits are extremely hard to change by deliberate policy, whether the policy intent is to suppress a language or to revive one.[19]

Against this persistence of the various European cultures, the relationship to blacks must be considered.

1. *Cultural Identity.* The problem of maintaining cultural identity is mixed with a certain natural competition for physical space. Even now, with the vast processes of metropolitanization at work, much of the "ethnic neighborhood" remains. It remains not only in the "old neighborhood" in the central city (Binzen, 1970), but it reemerges in suburbia, even if no particular ethnic group is so tightly clustered in suburbia as its predecessors were in the central city.[20]

The pressure which blacks experience to find new housing space drives them inevitably toward the Euro-American neighborhoods. If it is true, however, that these various groups prefer to be free from strangers of any sort (Gans, 1962), then it is to be expected that the entry of blacks will activate rather sharp antagonisms. It would do so even without prejudice, simply because blacks *are* the newest strangers. These antagonisms would be most sharply focused in the lower-class and working-class neighborhoods, not because these people are more "prejudiced," but because they have less escape room. If the neighborhood bar is frequented by Italian regulars, the new black man in the neighborhood will be a threat to the equilibrium of the existing group, but it is hardly reasonable to expect that he will not seek the use of the bar. The same problems of mutual accommodation will arise in the use of the local boys' clubs (or the boys' informally staked-out turf), of the ladies' access to the church clubs or the gossip system of the local beauty parlor. The relationships would be much the same if white strangers came into such a black area. But, as it happens, the demographic-economic history of the cities means that the newer migrants normally are black. When these migratory processes occur, the most common result is physical resistance followed by either some delicate set of "tacit bargains" about who will go where,[21] or the eventual withdrawal of one group to another area in which it feels more satisfied.

2. *Organizational Conservation.* The contact pattern is also associated with all sorts of complicated organizational defense problems. If the Catholic Church were seen in this light (Wakin and Scheuer, 1966, particularly at 27–28 and 105–106; Glazer and Moynihan, 1963, 203–204), we would have a deeper insight into the roles of bishops, clergy, and laity in the urban racial scheme. Twenty years ago, it is informally reported, a delegation visited Samuel Cardinal Stritch, asking his support for integrating public housing facilities (which would naturally have a large black residency) into white neighborhoods—an issue then current before the city government.[22] The Cardinal allegedly declined to intervene on the argument that the nationality parish was the foundation of the Church in Chicago, and he would not risk the disruptions which would occur in the parishes if large numbers of blacks were suddenly introduced.[23]

In the late 1960's, when the atmosphere on race relations was somewhat different, this issue came to the fore in Detroit in a different way. John Cardinal Dearden was seeking to abandon the nationality parish format and convert to a straight system of territorial parishes. But many of his Polish priests, through the medium of a "Priests' Conference on Polish Affairs," were actively trying to persuade the Cardinal to change his mind. Thus, it would be possible to interpret the Detroit priests' dissent as "racism" just as it would be easy to interpret Cardinal Stritch's response as racist. And such an interpretation might be correct. But it would not be self-evidently correct.

An even simpler problem of organizational defense arises in electoral politics. The fact that ethnic alignments are related to central-city community structure and voting behavior has been demonstrated more times than one need cite. But this relationship is specifically relevant to suburban politics as well. It has been shown in at least some cases that when one white ethnic group becomes numerically dominant over another, there is also a change in the ethnic character of suburban office holders (Walter and Wirt, 1966). If this change happens in suburbia, where some evidence suggests that class outranks ethnicity (Gans, 1967), then *a fortiori* it might be true elsewhere. Since we believe that politicians will normally be more disposed to hold what they have than to expand their horizons,[24] we must also believe that the first reactions of local politicians—of any group—will be to safeguard the territorial integrity of their units, if they can.

3. *Ethnicity and Status.* The most important of all contemporary facts refers to the status and conditions of the various Euro-American groups, most acutely those whose parents or grandparents came into the United States after 1880 or 1890. Euro-Americans are clearly not subject to the gross penalties of black men. Nonetheless, as far as evidence exists, there is a real sense in which very many members of the Euro-American groups have not "made it." Two statements probably would be correct. (1) Euro-Americans are likely to be overrepresented, statistically, in one set of influentials (unionists) and in a number of blue-collar and middle-class occupations (for instance, salesman). This must mean that, compared to blacks, they lead "comfortable" lives. (2) But it must also mean that—as we guessed—to speak of their having "made it" in a more fundamental sense is simply wrong. We should be reinforced in the belief that the European-descended groups constitute exactly that part of the working class and urban "middle class" upon whom black pressures impinge the most heavily.

We may start with a simple observation about those public issues which concern "neighborhoods" in the most local sense. In some cases, such as the area of Philadelphia about which Binzen writes, the level of community action is remarkably like that which was widespread in black communities a decade ago, and which is quite widespread even now. People show a notable incapacity to try to do anything about the mundane social services which are so often under discussion (Binzen, 1970). Or, if they try, they find themselves frustrated by precisely the same problems of complex government which have been so well advertised in black communities in recent years.[25]

It is particularly notable that the two most visible of Euro-American groups (Italians and Poles) are not actually markedly well off in the most significant and reputable parts of the power systems of United States politics and United States business. Their problem of overcoming barriers to public esteem has been particularly acute and so remains. Ask the following question: *What kind of personal deviation from the social "average" will make a candidate more attractive and what will make him less so?* The answer is definite. It is much better to be an upper-class—which is almost tantamount to saying also "Anglo-Protestant"—figure. Thus, Franklin D. Roosevelt, John F. Kennedy (far more openly "Harvard" than "Irish"), Adlai Stevenson, Joseph S. Clark, or (nowadays) John V. Lindsay. It is not nearly so good to be Al Smith, Michael Musmanno, Mario Procaccino.

In local politics, the probability that the civic notables, who hand out political "Good Housekeeping seals of approval," will rate a Euro-American candidate "highly qualified" is simply smaller than the comparable chance for an Anglo-Protestant candidate. Moreover, in the case of the Euro-American, his chances of general acceptability seem closely related to the extent of his demonstrated adoption of the Anglo-Protestant language and cultural style. Even then, such a man—as, for instance, Mayor Joseph Alioto (San Francisco)—is almost by virtue of his surname an open target for character assassination.

National politics similarly provides indicators. In the present years, Spiro Agnew and Edmund S. Muskie exemplify the proposition that a Euro-American's chances are increased exactly as he stops being such. For Agnew is no more a "typical" Greek-American politician, and Muskie is no more a "typical" Polish-American politician, than Edward W. Brooke is a "typical" black American politician.[26] It is quite realistic to say that the political culture of the United States is just beginning to change in response to Euro-American demands, desires, necessities, perceptions, and ambitions.

The ethnic factor also plays at least a moderately important role in other social institutions. This factor is less noticed in literature on the corporate world. But the incidence of Polish-name or Italian-name executives in the *Fortune* "500" companies—a significant test of the status of a group— seems to be virtually nil, although the data are uncertain. (Jewish exclusion is better advertised, probably because the Jewish defense agencies are more vigilant.) The executive suites are mainly Anglo-Protestant, in stark contrast to the assembly lines. It could be argued, of course, that the life-styles and cultural values of Euro-Americans lead them into other worlds than politics or commerce. If this is so, we should find other prestigious or profitable institutions where Euro-American overrepresentation compensates for underrepresentation in politics or commerce. But where should we look, except the trade unions—the one sector in which the compensation probably is manifest? Surely not in universities.[27] And we suspect that careful study of medical socieites, symphony guilds, and other private institutions would reveal an even greater shortfall in these other sectors.

This line of reasoning leads to the belief that Euro-Americans, emotionally insecure, realistically perceive themselves as struggling still against their predecessors and now against their challengers. When such people say that blacks are moving too fast, some part of the judgment may be attributed to racism. There are ordinary people who say, in effect, "I do not believe that blacks are as good as I am, and I do not believe that they should be equal." But there are others who say (with or without judgments about whether blacks are as "good as they are") that "they should have an equal chance, but they should not have special opportunities and, above all, they should not have even an equal chance if that means practical limits on my chances." This translates into the objection to "Negroes getting everything," which means an objection to seeing rapid improvement for blacks while they themselves (not markedly better off as they see it) are not improving in position (or even, as they see it, are worsening in position). For such a man, appreciation of blacks as humans is represented by the emergence of a lowbrow TV comic strip caricature of integrationism, instanced by the emergence of double-edged jokes about open-occupancy on "the Mothers-in-Law," the sugar sweetness of "Julia," or a painful effort by the "Bonanza" script writers to cope with the ambiguous position of the black man in the Old West. This is the man who has just reached the point at which he is confused about believing in natural biological inequality, uncertain when his remaining belief in biological inequality justifies discriminatory behavior, uncertain about the fashionableness (or legitimacy) of resorting to his traditional use of mob violence and overt prejudice, willing to use the phrases about "equality of opportunity," and confronted with mighty coercive forms of black politics which he does not in any sense "understand." I frankly concede that much of this is speculative, and that really good evidence is hard to find. But my interpretation is that, in the metropolitan areas, this is substantially the population described by Brink and Harris. By "the end of 1966" they say, "alienation was far greater among low-income whites than comparable, low-income Negroes." This conclusion is based upon the answers given to a series of statements which the Harris interviewers read to the people they interviewed (see Table VIII-1) (Brink and Harris, 1967, 135). It would be reasonable to predict that such a population,

Table VIII–1

	Total Public, %	Blacks, %	Low-Income Whites, %
Sometimes feel that:			
Rich get richer, poor get poorer	48	49	68
What you think doesn't count much	39	40	60
People in power don't care about us	28	32	50
Other people get lucky breaks	19	35	37
Important events in the world don't affect me	18	12	26
Few understand how I live	18	32	36
Nobody understands problem I have	17	30	40

conceiving itself to have lived within "the rules," would be disturbed to see a competitor population "rewarded" for "breaking" those rules.

MANAGERIAL CONSERVATISM

On the whole, the Euro-Americans are the less well educated and less prosperous part of the urban white population, although there are some exceptions to this statement. But there is another important sector whom one may call "the natural Republicans," ranging from the very rich and top-level leaders of commerce, industry, and the cognate professions through the middle-management people (plant managers, personnel managers, and such) and their noncorporate equivalents (federal field officials,[28] insurance brokers, lawyers, and their peers) down to the very small business man. On the whole, they have little sustained personal experience with racial problems, except insofar as these arise in the management of personnel under their supervision. In the latter case, they seem to depend very much on conventional stereotypes, at least if one may infer from one field study by a Michigan-based team. In New York, this team found that to a black interviewer, executives said the lack of black advancement in the industry resulted from:

. . . discrimination and barriers to advancement . . . resulted from race; to [the black interviewer's] white colleague, they reiterated all the negative stereotypes about the [blacks'] lack of ambition, poor work habits, and even the pathology of their family structure. (Cousens, 1969, 32)

The more prosperous and better educated part of Middle America encounters some adjustment problems which are contingent on the dominance of a "conservative" business culture and on the standards of judgment inherent in what one may call *the managerial ethos.* The problems exist not because the business culture is "inherently conservative" in the sense of resisting "change" in general; on the contrary, there is a sense in which no part of United States society is more radical. In dealing with the rest of the world, the corporate institution and its personnel argue with fervent emotion the notion of "progress," defined as an economic-technocratic imperative to which all else must give way. The impact on other institutions can be at least as pervasive as any form of explicit "political radicalism" yet imagined (Hamilton, 1957). Moreover, there is no other institution in the country which keeps itself in such a feverish state of reorganization, or which dispenses with prior personnel and practices so ruthlessly as does the corporation. (Compared to the corporation, the university—purportedly a center of social radicalism—is a study in the most extraordinary organizational conservatism.)

At the same time, the radicalism of the corporate institution—and those who absorb its values—is constricted. What is really dominant is a managerial ethos—a radicalism dedicated to the search for the "best" answer within very narrow parameters. If society could be organized on the model of the Weberian bureaucracy, modified by the conference technique, the managers would be content. "Politics" is not welcomed as an ordinary part of the common life—a necessity for the social organism —but practiced "realistically" as a means of defense against the ills which the adversary will inflict upon you, if you also do not practice politics.[29]

The values of the well-to-do—well reflected in publications of which *Fortune* constitutes the "left" wing—are profoundly committed to the idea of "profit" as the central test of rationality; to property and the sanctity of property as something to be achieved and safeguarded[30]; and to the transcendent importance of competent and prudent management. "Good management" is a religious test. The Elect who succeed have little sympathy for management sinners who fail, be they private or public.[31] And those who fail expect and greatly fear execution for their sins. As one corporation president—whose firm was able to pay him $75,000 a year plus perquisites ten years ago, which meant that it was a substantial, though not a "big" firm—said: "You can't imagine the pressure of having to show a profit from month to month, from year to year."

Those whose normal working life is dominated by such criteria should be expected to value privatism. The Salina (Kansas) High School reunionist who told his classmates of his last ten years by saying "I have raised a family and enjoyed life" is prototypical. This is the lesson of a man who has learned to adhere to the rules of "minding your own business" and "keeping out of trouble." Middle Americans learn and relearn it through virtually their entire career histories. The consequences for attention to civic issues, except when a consensus has already been developed on those issues, is reflected in the Salina tenth-year reunion. When one alumnus "took the speaker's stand with an urgent yet soft-spoken speech about pollution, ecology, cities, racism, and the war," 17.9 percent of his fellow reunionists (35/195) endorsed his views by a letter to President Nixon; 7.7 percent signed a counter petition. It is impressive that *twice as many* (and a little more) *came out for what would now be regarded as the "change-oriented" side.* But it is more important that *all those who took some stand were outnumbered almost 3:1 by those who did not* (Time, July 13, 1970, 14).

It is natural that people who have to be responsible for something very specific, and who expect to pay high penalties for failure, will place great weight on expertise, on authority (knowing their own need for authority in doing their own jobs), and on breaking large problems down into small and manageable bits. But "challenge" in the most general sense is not welcome or comfortable, and this marks a difference between Metroamerican and Middle American responses to racial issues.[32] While Metroamericans may talk about "broad restructuring of institutions," Middle Americans assume the system to be "fundamentally good and sound." From this latter viewpoint, racial issues may be treated as if they were similar to United Fund drives or traffic safety campaigns.

Such conservatism means that those who share it are usually not very adaptive. If a man is a personnel officer in a firm where black girls have never been in a secretarial pool, he does not know if the *particular* girl standing before his desk will "fit," or if he dare take the risk. Nor does he know if it is "worth it" to break the normal routine of recruiting secretaries by word of mouth—through the present secretaries—and so cooperates with the standing pattern. If a black family shows up on his block, again he does not know what he should do about their disliked presence (although he might well know what to try in order to forestall the appearance of a family if he "heard" that one "might" appear).

Part of the inhibition arises not only from personal beliefs about race, but also from beliefs and judgments about other relationships. One of these is the importance of "getting along," "being practical," "fitting in," and generally being "nice," or "polite" to those with whom one normally deals. The actress Marcia Rodd captures a part of it, I think, in describing her home town and childhood.

If there was one thing that did throw me, it was that Midwest, middle-class standard of behavior. The *polite* image: be nice to people, be pleasant, don't ever show an anybody what's inside you. *(New York Times,* March 14, 1971, Theater Section, 1)

Whether this is particularly Midwestern one may doubt, but there does seem to be something acute about this view of middle-class life.[33] Such a life style prevents one's going off the deep end. It means, for instance, that to become a member of an open-occupancy committee is going much too far for the ordinary man, even if he himself genuinely has no "personal" objections to nonwhite neighbors. But the same style of life means that, provided some buffer space for the protection of his own privacy is guaranteed, he can also adapt reasonably well in the face of a *fait accompli.* (It is easier if the *fait accompli* comes by "proper authority," that is, if the boss assigns a black man to his work section and makes it clear that the man is to stay there, and if the measures necessary for evasion are inherently irritating to himself.) He may refuse to adapt if beyond the attention or control of "higher authority." Thus, real estate brokers may say they accept virtually all the rules of thumb being suggested, and yet persistently evade open-occupancy statutes, mainly because evasion is easy.[34] One sort of *fait accompli* is the presence of the black family, which presence itself might not have been desired. Once such a family is present, most people will simply "leave them alone" for a time until they gradually work out an "ecological" adjustment at the superficial level of neighborliness. (On the other hand, the middle-class rules of politeness may be activated in the other direction. Thus, it will frequently happen that the one man on the block who insists on making his disdain for the black family *evident* will often enough find that his normal friends and neighbors will, though maintaining their own relations with him, not support him in that effort.)[35] That is, once he begins to make his feeling obvious, as if he were the local representative of George Wallace, then he begins to violate the politeness norm more than most of his neighbors are willing to follow.[36]

This sort of "conservative" social behavior is affected by something more than politeness, and the old-fashioned word "conscience" (if not leaned on too heavily) is perhaps a good label. For some years, one of the major sources of white civil rights interest was found within the churches. Most laymen, of course, were not much interested, and many were even uncomfortable that their clergy should be so active. But most were not utterly unmoved. As one black woman said, "When nothing else works, I can always throw Jesus on them." "Conscience" provides a gound for what is a sort of home mission approach, bringing Mississippi children to Wisconsin families for the summer, or raising money to aid a Sunflower County co-op. That activity is a far cry from the active interest desired by blacks, and frequently sniffs of what they mean by "paternalism." But it is one root of the concept of "decency" and "fairness" which transforms "conservative" behavior into "moderate" behavior.

The "moderate-conservative" notion of decency and fairness is quite distinct from "liberal" or "radical" postures of zealous reform. One finds it not only in race relations proper, but in social policy and in questions of law and privacy under the present information revolution. People may criticize welfare "free-loaders" and "immoral mothers," or may even have broader ideological criticisms of the "welfare state." However, when pushed to the ultimate conclusion, they are much more likely to reverse course and argue that there has to be some public support for poor people, because "you can't let people *starve* in this country." This moderate-conservative feeling can be tapped in discussions among state legislators or county board members almost anywhere in the urban or semiurban parts of the country.[37]

Such ideas of fairness and decency do not, in the minds of those who hold them, require energetic campaigns in behalf of black-white equalization, and may be grossly offended even by the integrationist advocacy which characterizes such a group as the NAACP. Such ideas do not preclude the private practice of discrimination,[38] more often than not assume a great deal of cultural ethnocentrism, and frequently contain more than a tinge of belief in the biogenetic superiority of white people. But moderate-conservative "fairness and decency" is different from the most intense racism because it does assume that there is something "wrong" with the status of blacks, and that *part* of the responsibility lies with whites. It is this approach which is so often described as "hypocritical," for "pointing fingers" at someone else (say the South) when the home situation is "really just as bad." At the same time, it also assumes that "most people" really could "improve themselves mainly by their own efforts." Therefore, if you ask people who see the world that way who is most to blame for the black situation, blacks or whites, they will answer "blacks are most to blame." Comprehensibly, the more specific and immediately relevant to themselves racial situations become, the more moderate-conservatives hold on to to their ideas of fairness and decency, but deny (or at least doubt) that those ideas require them to do anything specific that blacks want them to do.

Thus, managerial conservatives are pulled in at least two directions: recognition that a different racial pattern might be desirable to some degree (or merely necessary) opposes irresistible pressure toward defining one's own job as if racial patterns did not have something to do with them. Merely to illustrate. Within the past two years I gained a modest familiarity with airport-planning policy. The airport planners whom I met defined their task in a strictly "technocratic" sense. This technocratic definition of mission excluded serious attention to the fact that an airport-expansion program could have the most serious impact upon housing supply, community facilities, and crime in an adjacent urban area of 1,000,000 people—and would probably acerbate racial conflict. In short, the airport planners' acceptance of a managerial ethos made it impossible to learn much from the recent experience of the urban highway planners.

Most Middle American activity on racial policy is, therefore, still quite mundane. Again to illustrate. The American Bar Association created, sometime in the last two years, a committee to develop a new statement on "the role of the police in a democratic society." Astonishingly enough, it apparently did not occur to the ABA leadership that such a committee simply ought to have a black lawyer among its members, until during one of the early sessions the issue was raised by one white member, a judge with a long history and great sophistication in these matters. At the outside, some fragment of corporate leadership (and the commercial communications enterprises) has adopted the role of trying to obscure the intensity of racial conflict and (at the same time) to exploit that conflict in order to justify certain "technocratic" changes in the ordinary pattern of racial contact. As examples of the latter, we may observe the propagandistic role which such institutions as the Advertising Council has adopted, the role of the National Alliance of Businessmen in popularizing the idea of hiring the "hard-core unemployed," or the idea now being popularized that the application of business expertise will "solve urban problems." But, we repeat, the matter is not seen as so urgent that most responsible people keep it on their minds and seek viable responses.

CONVERGENCE OF THE TWO SORTS OF "CONSERVATISM"

The two sorts of "conservatism" have rather different experiences underlying them, but they converge to produce the single most important factor about Middle America: its commitment to the normative rule that "it's all right to press your case, but by all means do so within the rules." Such a rule means that its advocates believe the system is "fundamentally sound and good."

Even if Euro-Americans concede that blacks have been under an unfair disadvantage, and that rectification is desirable, they are likely to insist that it should take place within "the rules." The Euro-American self-image— we suspect—is that of tough people who overcame great odds by their own unaided efforts.[39] Accordingly, it makes sense to them when they argue that any rectification should take place the same way they imagine that it took place for themselves in the past. In other words, no group should get anything "special." The rule is that rectification should take place in the "normal" way, without causing undue disturbance to those who have already acquired vested rights. There is a cognate tendency to react at first—whatever subsequent thought may produce—on an almost unspoken conception that the "most" rights "naturally" belong to those who are "there" (in whatever favored position) first.[40] Finally, it will be believed that no group should even *make claims* in any way which does not already fit the common idea of "proper" means of action.

The upholders of the managerial ethos are usually unable to understand —without a very painful learning process—the political implications of cultural ethnocentrism. Nor do they exhibit, or have, a ready basis for comprehending a legitimate challenge to systemic features which maintain large racial disparities over long times. "Racism," in short, means very little to them, unless it refers to specific, overt, and unjustified manifestations of prejudice by individual persons. Since they have these outlooks, they also have little basis for comprehending why any established social or organizational priorities should be altered. In the practical terms, this limitation means that people are expected to observe carefully the niceties of social behavior, to maintain proper behavior in public places so as to cause others as little mental or physical discomfort as possible (James Q. Wilson, 1969), that there is nothing *sufficiently* wrong to warrant disruptive, nonlegal, or even grossly unusual behavior.

The net effect is that the tendency to avoid conflict is enhanced. The feeling that issues should be settled on neutral ground, which Robert Lane tapped in interviews with white workingmen, is equally potent for this group.

There are several routes to the 'neutral ground' they seek. One is to *deny that there are real differences* of interest among men, and this often follows from their position on the reality of a true public interest. Another is to stress the reconciliation of apparent differences by *bringing the conflicting partisans together.* (Lane, 1962)

This is the bias of "practical" people, committed to the defense of their own interests, anxious to be "fair," and holding a vision of themselves and the world which they believe to be decent and rational.

Such an approach structures the perception of racial issues—even without racism—in ways which make Middle Americans rather unreceptive to black politics. As Lane said in the same book:

One discloses this penchant in his belief that the "race problem" might be solved by bringing the parties together. Discrimination in certain areas is "not the American way of doing it," he says, and in a pleading and rather desperate tone, he adds, "But I should think there should be some way of bringing it out between them." It is his vain hope that the Negroes could be persuaded to accept a segregated arrangement, and thus relieve him of what is really a rather bad conscience. (Lane, 1962)

The more highly schooled Middle Americans have shared this hope. Now when they are unable to avoid racial conflict, these "practical" people are afflicted with a terrible—indeed, terrifying!—uncertainty and very little understanding. They are uncertain as to "what the blacks *really* want," as to what measures are "fair" by some general standard and effective in the particular case, as to what values and interests of their own really are so essential that no compromise is possible.

It is erroneous to expect Middle America to be actively "committed" —almost in a religious sense—to some grander ideas of justice. Decisive action as that phrase would normally be used, is not to be expected from Middle Americans, unless their own sense of interest is *immediately* touched. Their "commitment" *is* to mind their own business, and their emotional attachment is to a "decent" and "orderly" world. But it seems wrong to think of them as advocates of a new police state or even a sheetless version of the Ku Klux Klan. The truth is that they themselves do not know how to answer the question of what is essential, what is nonessential; what is permissible, what is not permissible.

NOTES

1. I would note, though I do not here try to analyze, the sense in which there is also a global version of the new white man's burden.

2. I would note that the idea of *reciprocal* renunciation of force is the decisive idea. It is all too easy to suppose that one means merely the exclusion of force from the black political armory. But the far more important idea is that, contrary to their normal expectation in American society, blacks should be able *realistically* to believe that their engagement in political controversy will not activate official or *unofficial* white force against themselves.

3. The black contribution is the focus of discussion in *The Politics of the Black "Nation."*

4. It is perhaps natural that this problem should have been examined somewhat more fully by students of foreign policy than by most other specialists. After all, it is particularly important for them to understand what "public opinion 'demands' or 'permits' " in the conduct of foreign affairs. See Bobrow (1969) and Caspary (1970).

5. Mendelsohn and Crespi (1970), Chapter 1 and 2, will be instructive on how survey organizations operate.

6. Of Southern white respondents, 47 percent denied that blacks were discriminated against, which so obviously denies their daily experience that we can only interpret it to mean that they limited the term "discriminate" to mean unfair limitations as they themselves interpreted "fair" (Brink and Harris, 1967).

7. The problem of interpretation is still more complicated because black nationalists could believe the same thing, yet they obviously are not antiblack.

8. Mr. Hudson, now vice-chairman of the Dayton-Hudson Corporation, was then president of the J. L. Hudson Company, one of the nation's great department stores. He lived in the area and was, at the time, president of the board of trustees

of the Grosse Pointe University School, hardly a position for the "outside agitator."

9. On a complex case in a Chicago suburb (Deerfield) beginning in 1959, see Rosen and Rosen (1962).

10. Grosse Pointe, though always Republican, also always returns about one-third its vote for the Democratic candidate.

11. In *Race Relations Reporter*, a newsletter issued by the Race Relations Information Center, Nashville, Tennessee.

12. For useful comments on this matter, see Hadden (1970).

13. I am disturbed by the tendency of social scientists to oversimplify on these matters, as if the people disposed to accept change on racial issues are, and of necessity must be, theological liberals (if not agnostics), social democrats (if not disguised socialists), against the Vietnam war (if not pacifist), and the like. This is one of the difficulties in the analysis by Rokeach (1970).

14. By "Euro-Americans" I mean those people whose ancestors moved into the United States between 1880 and the cutoff under the Immigration Act of 1924 (although for these purposes I also include the Irish, whose high tide was earlier).

15. The best published data on this are contained in Graham and Gurr (1969a).

16. Otherwise, we should not have heard Attorneys General Kennedy, Clark, and Mitchell on the seriousness of organized crime.

17. New Orleans, for example, is famous as the site of a mass lynching of Italians, but it is doubtful that this was the only place where the regular processes of the law were suspended for the "foreigner" who "got out of line."

18. On this sort of relationship, see Thomas and Znaniecki (1920).

19. Revival is apparently nearly impossible, even if the language to be revived is associated with ideological symbols which people presumably value and if the government in question provides special incentives for revival. The hard test here is the virtual failure of De Valera's policy of re-Gaelicization. See Heslinga (1962).

20. So far as we know, this idea was first expressed by Lubell (1956a). It seems natural that Lubell should make this discovery since he was himself out interviewing people at their homes, and would accordingly pick up social cues. We have discovered this ourselves in an analysis of Cleveland area suburbs, using 1960 Census data. We find distinct clusterings of Slavic populations in one set of suburbs, Germans and Irish in others, Jews in others, and Italians in still others.

21. "Tacit" bargains are the sorts of accommodations which A and B make to live without fighting each other, but which they do not negotiate formally. See Schelling (1960). For a recent case study of an Italo-Chicano-Black area on the Near West Side of Chicago, see Suttles (1969).

22. The broader controversy is that reported in Meyerson and Banfield (1955).

23. This information was provided some time ago in private discussion with St. Clair Drake, then in the Sociology Department of Roosevelt University. It was

never verified in the strict sense, and thus is only indicative. But it seems realistic, since we know on independent authority that some Roman Catholic parish priests in the late 1940's and early 1950's were active leaders in formulating community resistance to the entry of blacks. It would have been strange if the Cardinal, as administrator, had felt no concern for maintaining some rapport with the greater proportion of his constituency.

24. Above, Essay VI, " 'Sticky' Trade-Offs and Urban Immobilization."

25. On this, I rely on descriptions offered by Mrs. Patricia Cooper (of the Pennsport Civic Association in Philadelphia) and by Miss Barbara Mikulski (of the Southeast Community Association in Baltimore). Both made presentations on this topic at the National Consultation on Neighborhood Government, Institute of Human Relations, American Jewish Committee, New York (March 1, 1971).

26. It is also interesting that *all three*—Agnew, Muskie, and Brooke—developed outside the usual framework of ethnic politics.

27. For instance, the number of reported political scientists with identifiable Polish surnames is even smaller than the number of identifiable black political scientists. See Wandycz (1969). Is this so for other disciplines?

28. If one attends gatherings of middle-level civil servants, their similarity to gatherings of businessmen is remarkable. Although Leiper Freeman does not discuss this point explicitly, I think it is supported by his study of field officials in the South. See Freeman (1962).

29. The company-sponsored literature on "practical politics" courses for executives is most illustrative here.

30. As a resident of a city afflicted with much student disturbance (Madison, Wisconsin), I have the impression that many nonuniversity citizens are even more profoundly disturbed by property damage (which does not touch them) than by physical danger to persons (which does not touch them). At least, I have *felt* that antistudent comment, based on "damage to property" was *volunteered* more often than antistudent comment based on danger to persons.

31. *Signature,* the house organ of the Diners' Club, has recently been publishing articles which might be called "very light social comment." One article on urban problems, by Mayor Lindsay, drew forth two letters. One said: Why should New York be the responsibility of the state or the federal government? The other asserted that the article was image-building for Lindsay's presidential campaign, and that the shortage of funds in New York City was due to the "extravagance" of the Lindsay regime. Such an article, said the writer, had no place in *Signature.*

32. The term "Middle American" might seem to be self defining, but editors ask for a definition. In my discussion I have in mind the rather standard lower middle-class (blue collar) and standard bourgeoisie (Chamber of Commerce types), in contrast to the people Eric Goldman has called Metroamericans.

33. I do not think it is exclusively middle-class either. What we are *told* of upper-class life (which social scientists normally do not have the opportunity to observe) and what we know of "working-class respectables" is rather similar to this.

34. Open-occupancy statutes do not *have* to be easy to evade, but usually are so because of the design of the specific statutes in force and the control systems which operate within the real estate industry. Evasion is common in personnel management if a new—black—person is hired, but hostile supervisors or coworkers know that (because of the boss's inattention or collusion) it is permissible to harass the said employee.

35. In the specific case of the neighborhood, the matter would merit the attention of a good anthropologist. Frequently, it appears, the social distance is bridged first by the *children*—not because, sentimentalists to the contrary, children are racially unaware or unprejudiced. It is rather that "play" takes so important a role in child life that new play opportunities are likely to be welcomed, and parents are marginally drawn into the play relationships. To show how complicated these matters can be, however, I would cite the case in which the first contact occurred at the level of the *women.* Mrs. A (whose husband was the neighborhood bigot) and Mrs. B (generally an Agnew sort of conservative) were close friends (and their husbands were friendly). The neighborhood custom was to hold a "coffee" for any new woman. Mrs. B did so for Mrs. C (the black newcomer) *immediately and with apparent full knowledge* of Mr. A's disposition invited Mrs. A., who could not or did not refuse. Thereafter, the C's were regular invitees to all the neighborhood houses (except the A house) and invitations were reciprocated and accepted. Moreover, Mrs. A and Mrs. C worked out their own *modus vivendi* (morning visits, sugar borrowing, and the like). The A's never invited the C's for "social" occasions, nor obviously did the C's invite the A's. The A's reached the point at which they invited the C's to "political" fund-raising cocktail parties (which the C's never accepted). Distance remained greatest between the *men*. Once Mr. A reached the point at which he made chit-chat about the hot weather or the grass, Mr. C. acknowledged such chit-chat if it were rude for him to pretend not to hear, but refused to have anything to do with Mr. A if it were possible to do so.

36. This apparently holds on some occasions even when there are no blacks directly present to observe. The following illustration will make the point. A few years ago, an attorney for one of the large steel firms was particularly vociferous at a cocktail party. The wife of another attorney for the same firm finally interrupted him, saying, "if those are your feelings, why don't you just keep them to yourself?" The incident was reported without verification. If it occurred, it is instructive, because there was nothing "reformist," "crusading," or "liberal" about the overt behavior of the woman on the occasions when it was possible to observe her directly. She was merely a polite, well-bred member of the Episcopal parish, married to a professional man with a good income and a good future.

37. One also finds it in the editorial approval which a conservative Republican paper gives to Secretary Richardson's suggestion that "some" safeguards should be established over federal data collection and use (*Wisconsin State Journal,* March 17, 1971).

38. Pages 41–62 of this book.

39. The claim to having overcome by self-reliant activity is somewhat romanticized. Those who are better off are so because of gross changes in economy and society, and even of governmental help, more than is usually known.

40. This conception of some *droit de premier occupant* is not merely an American value, but is virtually universal. The illustrations are legion. The internal politics of the Congo, at independence, were much affected, for instance, by an assertion of BaKongo leaders that their people had *droit de premier occupant* against other Congolese peoples. In South Africa, it has taken the historical form of competition between Afrikaners and blacks over their nearly simultaneous entry into what was largely unoccupied land. In Malaysia, it has taken the form of a Malay opposition to the Chinese preponderance in the economy.

IX

*Public Opinion and Everyday
Behavior: II. Is There Latitude
for Peacemaking?*

EVERYDAY BEHAVIOR AND HOPEFUL SIGNS

Everyday behavior provides, the preceding essay might suggest, a good deal of evidence which supports the grimmer interpretations of public opinion data. Some of that behavior is quite clearly associated with pathological prejudice. Some, however, is not associated with racial values, so much as with a deeper social conservatism which makes racial adjustment more difficult. At the same time, it is simply not realistic to pretend that all the signs in the United States are adverse.

As a first step, we need some sort of baseline. One way to set a baseline is to imagine or to recall the world that existed when black young people now emerging from high school or college were born. One full generation ago, any black man rationally expected to encounter an uncountable number of social limitations due primarily (if not solely) to his racial identity. These limitations were present in every aspect of social life and reinforced each other. For that reason, I have earlier described the social regime as one of "unofficial apartheid." An ordinary member of the 1970 high-school graduating class might have been born in 1953, the year that the Supreme Court ruled that a long-thought-to-be-dead statute prohibiting segregation in downtown Washington restaurants was still effective (the Thompson Restaurant Case). Before then, a black could not count on a meal or a hotel room unless he chose his places carefully. A young person graduating from college in 1970 might well have been born in 1948. In this case, he would have been born the year the Supreme Court first decided (in *Shelley v. Kraemer,* 3344 U.S. 1) that public courts could not be used to enforce private restrictive covenants against blacks. A 1970 college graduate might go to law school in the fall. If he were 21, he would be of the generation born when the bar association (which he may enter upon passing the bar examinations) probably *first* began to admit black lawyers to membership at all. One might make exactly the same statement if he were a medical student, with a modification to read "medical society" instead of "bar association." He would, if he went to a business school instead, be of the first generation to be reasonably sure that he would not be rejected if he sought an executive trainee position in one of the *Fortune* "500" chosen randomly.

In other words, it is only within the past generation that there has been any serious challenge to unofficial apartheid. That is the baseline. Against this baseline, we also lack systematic indicators (Gross and Springer, 1969) of how much cracking has taken place in unofficial apartheid, whether and how soon we should expect unofficial apartheid virtually to crumble, just as we also lack systematic indicators of the extent to which new elements of apartheid have entered or might enter. My hypothesis, however, is that there are at least three sorts of common sense indicators which suggest a greater potentiality for the collapse of unofficial apartheid than might ordinarily be supposed.

"THE FIRSTS" AS CRUDE SOCIAL INDICATORS

The public press pays a certain amount of attention, these days, to the phenomenon of the "first" black to enter one or another social role. The roles may be grandly visible to the whole world (the first Nobel Prize winner or the first member of the Supreme Court) or they may be rather more mundane (the first officer of a union local, the first man on a local police force, the first family in a particular part of town, or even the first member of the Rotary Club). Without a social accounting method, one cannot know what the pattern of "firsts" actually is in the present decade. However, it seems reasonable to believe that a careful accounting would in fact show an increasingly rapid occurrence of firsts, in wider and wider areas of social life, with more and more presumption that such firsts do constitute precedents available to other people. A decidedly unsystematic listing[1] of some such events shows such diverse items as the following:

October 31, 1961: The appointment of two black policemen in Biloxi, Mississippi, who, according to their mayor, "would patrol Negro districts" (*Detroit News,* UPI, 10a).

November 7, 1962: The election of a black man as state treasurer in Connecticut (*Detroit News*, 6b).

March 27, 1963: Selection of two black naval officers—one of whom was also the first to graduate from a midshipman's school (1944) and the first to command a United States warship (1962)—for the Naval War College (*Detroit Free Press*, 2b).

April 26, 1963: Appointment of a cabinet officer in the city government of Cleveland (*Detroit Free Press*, UPI, 1).

July 1963: Choice by the Norfolk school board of a local black attorney to fill a vacancy (*New York Times*, August 1, 1963, 17).

July 1963: Federal court order admitting a black girl to the University of South Carolina; and a separate order by the same judge that state parks be desegregated (*New York Times*, July 11, 1963).

July 1963: Entry of black students into the medical schools at Duke, Emory, and Johns Hopkins (*New York Times*, July 13, 1963).

The "firsts" wave tended to come more rapidly in recent years. Within one recent year, we note the following:

May 22, 1969: The addition of two black members to the board of the United States Olympic Committee (*New York Times*, 63).

July 1969: The inauguration of Mayor Charles Evers in Fayette, Mississippi.

August 17, 1969: The acceptance of a black osteopath as an "interim member" of the Detroit Yacht Club (*Washington Post*, C13).

September 19, 1969: The appointment of a black policeman in Madison, Wisconsin (*Wisconsin State Journal*, Section 2).

October 7, 1969: The election of a black vice-mayor in Atlanta (*World Almanac*, 1970, 928).

October 17, 1969: The designation of a black president at Michigan State University (*New York Times Almanac*, 1970, 28).

November 1969: The election of a black physician as president of the American Public Health Association.

January 18, 1970: The installation of a black Episcopal bishop in Massachusetts (*Wisconsin State Journal*, UPI, 4).

January 1970: The awarding of the first black-held franchise for a MacDonald's hamburger stand, after a somewhat difficult controversy extending from several months before.

January 18, 1970: The appointment of a back retiring lieutenant general of the United States Air Force as Director of Public Safety in the City of Cleveland (*Milwaukee Journal*, Part 6).

February 1970: The victory of "loyalist" Alabama Democrats over Wallace Democrats in providing blacks access to the party's state executive committee.

Blacks used to take a certain pride in acquiring those "first" roles themselves, or in sharing those roles vicariously. The pace of the revolution in black self-images has so far accelerated that blacks themselves no longer pay the "firsts" much attention, or may even deprecate them as "tokenism" or as "irrelevant to the larger problems of the black masses." Both these skeptical, even cynical, reservations have merit.

Nonetheless, life is lived in details, and "firsts" are details which provide a significant measuring rod. One reason they have some sociological importance is that they indicate the degree to which unofficial apartheid existed in the past, and the degree to which its residues are alive in the present. The very fact that something is a noteworthy "first" usually means that the event would have passed notice, except for the fact that the persons involved were black.

Except for unofficial apartheid, which dictates that a black person is ineligible for that which comes to a similarly circumstanced white, the fact of blackness would have little relevance. A "first" would not merit attention. This is apparent in a newspaper story that "Frank Robinson became the first black to manage in the major leagues today, leading an all-star team against the Yankees in an exhibition game" (*New York Times,* March 14, 1971, Section 5, 1). In that story, Robinson was quoted thus:

I don't think any place is barred to a black manager. I think this is the same situation as when the first player broke into the majors. I think they are trying to find the right person and the right situation.

I think the climate keeps changing. Each year they get a little closer to it, and the chances of it happening get better. I forsee it happening in the next few years.

Robinson's comment made explicit the presumption that "firsts" will not become permanent "onlies," but will constitute precedents so that those roles will not thereafter automatically be closed to other blacks, but will be open with more or less ease. *They begin to take on major sociological importance, when, within a given time, they occur in an increasingly wide selection of institutional settings and social roles and occur at an increasingly rapid rate.* If "firsts" do not constitute precedents, do not occur in increasingly wide institutional settings, and do not occur at an increasingly rapid rate, then it is realistic to emphasize their "token" quality. *If they do constitute prece-*

dents, do occur in increasingly wide institutional settings, and do occur at increasingly rapid rates, then they become real indicators of change in social structure.

INDICATORS OF WHITE IMAGES OF "SELF," "OTHER," AND "APPROPRIATE" BEHAVIOR

Amid all the strong evidences of racial conservatism there are also interesting clues to changes in white people's images of themselves, of others (blacks, in the instant case), and of the behavior which is appropriate in the relationship between themselves and the others. This is best seen in those instances where blacks have not been sufficiently numerous to constitute a "threat" in any realistic sense, but have nonetheless occupied a distinctly subordinate position.[2] Thus, the behavior of public officials in circumstances where the black electorate could almost never carry an election, or cause anyone to lose an election, is instructive. If a county has a very small proportion of blacks (less than 3 percent), there is little reason to expect its elected officials to be responsive to black *political* pressure, for no pressure exerted by so small a group could make much electoral difference. When such a county board spends long hours debating a resolution denying "county privileges, such as dance hall permits . . . to clubs that practice 'invidious discrimination,' " it seems reasonable to believe that the motivation comes from some sources such as I indicate. The view is reinforced if the resolution purports to forbid county officers to belong to such clubs and for that very reason is openly criticized by a powerful bloc leader in the board, who angrily tells his colleagues "nobody is going to tell Ed Hickman what do do." If one had time and opportunity to analyze the editorials of moderately conservative papers in the Middle West, one would—I hazard—find this kind of theme repeated, as one would also in the suburban papers of the great metropolitan areas (Long Island for one).

Both the Haynsworth and Carswell nominations to the Supreme Court also bring to the surface a similar kind of disposition. As much as anything, both judges lost because judicial white supremacism has lost respectability at least as much as because of the "conflict of interest" or the "mediocrity" issues. Such cross currents are also suggested by mid-1970 polls on people's ratings of Presidential performance. On the issue of "law and order" President Nixon got a 37 percent favorable rating and a 56 percent unfavorable rating (*Wisconsin State Journal,* December 29, 1969, Section 2, 1; same, December 21, 1969, 1; *Madison Capital-Times,* December 31, 1969, 2). On handling race problems, he got 35 percent favorable and 58 percent unfavorable (Harris poll, *Washington Post,* June 8, 1970, A2). It is to be presumed that some of the negatives were from people who wanted him to be even "tougher" on black rebellion. Yet it is not to be presumed that these were all. It is also reasonable to believe that some people were negative for the contrary reasons, which suggests no decided consensus in either direction.

There are also evidences of deeper changes in the self-images of parts of the white population, changes sufficient to drive those parts to actions more encompassing than those of a moderate-conservative disposition would themselves entertain. At the time of the Poor People's March, the Johnson administration appeared to have "backed off" on civil rights and racial equality. But acceptance of the idea of racial equality, and of positive action toward equalization, had by that time become fairly common doctrine among members of the bureaucratic elites living in the Washington area. Some of its members were ready and willing to risk the antagonism of their neighbors by carrying open-occupancy petitions around the neighborhoods. Others were ready and willing to create still more delicate situations by making an issue over discrimination in the tennis clubs which they attend. Still others were willing to "help," as they saw it, by making financial contributions to the March or by opening their homes to the Marchers.

There are more elements, important though nearly intangible, associated with white self-images and with white other-images (in this instance, images of blacks). The best single test of self-imagery is the rapid reception of the concept of a "racist" society. The Kerner Report doctrine came into vogue quickly, rather like the ready acceptance of Freudian psychoanalysis: a means of reveling in some kind of cultural "sin," a means of expressing the moralistic self-deprecation which runs deep in American culture, but also a means of absolving oneself from responsibility for action. That such a report should have come forth under the aegis of the "United States Government" merely lends to its authority as a new gospel in the current political religion. Others reject it utterly as if to deny the perfectly human tendency to the uncomfortable with strangers.

The parallel question is what "other-images," in contrast to "self-images," one is prepared to respect. At still another level, we have hardly begun to understand the impact of cultural relativism at work, but its signs are present in the Black Academy of Arts and Letters. The existence of such an academy is a sign of a barely emergent white recognition of a new dimension in the literary world. It has the same implications of general interest as recent debates over "black theater." The people interested in "art" or "theater" a decade ago could hardly have cared less, and what we now perceive is their painful approach to black people as producers of "other-images" capable of being valued. Other indicators may be seen in the readiness with which university faculties adopted "black studies" once that issue was raised.

Another important clue to the remaking of images is the crystallization of attitudes expressed in the "student 'rebellion'." However much sentimental nonsense is talked on this subject, particularly by people carrying adult responsibilities who seem to wish to pass off the responsibility for social change onto young people whose judgment is still uninformed and whose power is almost exclusively the power to create disruptions. It would be all too easy (particularly in light of the events of 1968–1970) to overestimate the beneficial social effects, or even the intelligence, of student upheaval. In the first place, much of the student response to racism is grossly superficial, for the college generation may often remind one of missionaries looking for primitives to practice upon. Indeed, their fascination with certain marginal aspects of black life may properly be compared to their predecessors' discovery of Harlem in the 1920's—a temporary escape from their own world and their own lives. Moreover, no matter how much destructive impact they may have upon current policies and current rulers, the reality is that the students themselves will not come to the rulership of key United States institutions (nor participate much in the rulership of any except the universities) soon. It is difficult to explain the fascination which Malcolm X and Eldridge Cleaver hold for students, unless one can suppose that racism really is less persuasive to them than it has been even for their parents. Nor, in view of the national revulsion brought on by the 1969 television showing of black Cornell students emerging from an occupied building carrying guns, can one neglect a very important fact: When the Cornell faculty finally yielded (April 24) to the demands of the black students, there was a reported "roar of approval" from 7,000 students conducting a sit-in at the Cornell gymnasium (New York Times, April 25, 1969). Obviously, these 7,000 Cornell students might have been wrong (or right), but they could not all have been black. In other words, the black rebellion and the naive idea of black revolution have become a part of the symbols of good to much of the upper-middle class population which the youth rebellion represents. (The lower-middle and lower-class youth are another matter.) Consequently, we should forecast that—unless the student population continues on its present emotional binge, and thus commits suicide as a potential elite by infuriating the entire nation—we should expect a still more responsive opinion-making community in the next decade than in the last decade.

Perhaps the most important change is the respectabilization of black-white marriage, something never on anybody's formal political agenda.

The image of "self" as good and of "other" as repellent is most sharply defined by the marriage rules. There is a modern version of what was called in Roman law *conubium,* the doctrine which defined within what group party A was marriageable and beyond what boundaries marriage was utterly to be rejected. Those who, by virtue of their birth, are automatically defined as beyond the conubium are, by that very fact, defined as less than fully human. There was, indeed, philosophical insight in Hannah Arendt's argument, some years past, that the civil rights movement should have focused its main attack on marriage laws rather than on school laws (Arendt, 1959). It did not, as everyone knows, but there are evidences that cultural and psychological dispositions are beginning to move toward the same result which Arendt might have preferred. What people will tolerate in the fantasy world of the theater, even when they have no intent of practicing it themselves, is one clue to the changes which the culture is undergoing. It is for this reason that James Earl Jones's rise to stardom *(The Great White Hope)* is important. For Jack Johnson, the real-life model of the hero in that play, was roundly deprecated by his contempories (Lucas, 1970) to a greater degree than Muhammad Ali in the present generation. Johnson was a virtual "black beast" in white men's eyes, not because he was so formidable a boxer, but because he flaunted his addiction to white wives almost as if he anticipated and wished to verify *Soul on Ice.* To imagine the successful production of *The Great White Hope* even so late as the time of *Strange Fruit* (1944) is a virtual impossibility.

Beyond fantasy, there is everyday reality. One aspect of everyday reality is the dating pattern, a public display of intimacy which implies that the partners wish that they might enter a permanent relationship. Such displays can be risked in circumstances now where they would have been quickly suppressed a short time ago. When one sees a white woman with a black escort at night in an Atlanta bar, and the next day sees a black girl (complete with Afro hairstyle) casually sauntering across a Georgia college campus hand-in-hand with a white in full daylight, one perceives that something is changing in Georgia.

The Metroamerican world is now capable of absorbing mixed couples with no visible difficulty. University communities which used to find black students unwelcome, and never entertained the idea of black professors at all, now find the mixed couple hardly worth comment. Nor does the change stop there. The well-publicized series of recent marriages, involving partners prominent in themselves or because of their families, indicates that the white partner no longer suffers a perception of lost caste. This is not to argue that the powerful weapons of prejudice no longer have any effect, and surely not to argue that the number of such relationships is large; prejudice is important, and the number is small. But the phenomenon is important because its public tolerability, at minimum, indicates a weakening of the caste-like boundaries between white and black. No one set out to produce this result. Indeed, had anyone acted on Arendt's advice, as an organizational policy, he would have been guilty of an utmost tactical folly. But the fact, the shift itself, is a shift in one set of attitudes which stood as parameters of black-white politics. It is one more illustration of the profound black-white ambivalence and ambiguity discussed in these essays.

INDICATORS FROM CHOICES MADE UNDER HARD CIRCUMSTANCES

Finally, the best short-term common sense indicators are those revealed when people have to make choices in particular and dramatic action situations. One such situation is an election. What do people do when race is clearly a major element of electoral choice? The evidence will not support the proposition that the country is becoming more and more polarized with no countervailing effects. Observe, for instance, the small city of Chapel Hill, North Carolina (14,000), very much dominated by the faculty of a large and important university. Like much of the rest of the country, Chapel Hill participated in a ritual of respect for the late Martin Luther King, Jr., but its ritual of respect was to adopt an open-occupancy ordinance by public referendum. One need not examine the practicality of open occupancy—either in general or in Chapel Hill—as a substantive policy contribution; one need only regard this action as a form of indication that the people of the community wanted somehow to address the problem. One may, moreover, treat their ritual of respect seriously if one notes that the same city voted for the black candidate for governor in an election shortly thereafter, and that the city elected a black mayor in the next years.

Electoral politics elsewhere provides still other pragmatic indicators. In the urban North, about 15 to 25 percent of the white electorate has shown themselves prepared to vote for black candidates in preference to a white candidate in a series of elections where the racial line was tightly drawn. One out of every six white men has accepted such a man (though one's overall estimate of the future would depend on whether one imagined this vote ratio to be a floor or a ceiling). In the *Washington Post* (August 20, 1969, page 1), there is a simple box showing the Democratic primary results for attorney general of Virginia. The important fact about this is that the losing candidate had tried hard to make "law and order" his principal theme in the campaign, but was still defeated two to one by a candidate explicitly identified as "liberal" (in a "nonliberal" state) who had rejected the law-and-order theme. If white supremacy were the dominant theme on electors' minds, however, such a result would have been inexplicable. In Virginia the same year, a Republican governor—Mr. Nixon's state campaign manager in 1968—was elected. Linwood Holton defeated the candidate of the Virginia Democratic establishment—whose speeches, though moderately phrased, carried Mr. Agnew's themes, "if you've seen one slum, you've seen them all" and "people make slums." The pertinent fact is that, once in office, the new governor did not seek to "out-backlash" the backlashers, but instead made himself the first governor in the state's history to set racial equality as an important part of his administration's official program.[3] This departure from the "Southern strategy," we must emphasize, occurred in the home of "massive resistance"—at the same time that the national administration, domiciled but a bit more than one hundred miles away, was accentuating the "Southern strategy" as its way to make the Republican party into a national majority. The same paradox is presented by Republican senators from states which do not support doctrinaire liberals (such as Ohio and Illinois), who differ with the administration's interpretation of the 1968 election as a call for retreat from domestic reform. If such Republicans do not necessarily interpret the political necessities as blacks themselves would interpret them, neither do they interpret them as calls for a new apartheid. The inference may properly be that, as on other occasions, there are contrary themes and currents in American politics. The inference is even more sharply defined in crisis situations which threaten *immediate violent confrontation.*

In view of the panic which follows each dramatic instance of black violence, it is noticeable that the wave of white counter violence has been far less extensive than either American history or the widely reported metropolitan arms races[4] might have led us to expect. The open-occupancy legislation of 1968 was not the only possible response to the uprisings which followed the murder of Martin Luther King, Jr. A possible alternative would have been to apply ever greater coercive force against blacks than actually was applied under those circumstances. In the actuality, the main political response was dominated by the Congressional liberals, who somehow were able to persuade their colleagues that this was the time to pass the open-occupancy legislation, although it would be surprising if some congressmen did not advocate full use of the Army or even agitation of white mobs as a counter force.[5]

The Cornell 1969 experience probably had an incalculable effect upon white televiewers, for this was not an anomic riot but instead a calculated move in which young black people, with arms, occupied a university building. It would not have been surprising, on ordinary logic, if the event had fueled anxieties to the point that white-black fights might have taken place elsewhere, all across the country.

The relative quiescence of working-class whites, who have historically been the most active source of violence against blacks, at least as far as the early winter of 1971, is also instructive. This group has not yet been activated to adopt large-scale violence against blacks, *under circumstances where its emotional attachment to white supremacy might have led one to expect that it would.* Considering the social history of the South, one would not be surprised if white truck drivers, subjected to physical attacks in circumstances which they as individuals had done nothing to produce, should have replied with force, or if their sympathizers in the community had attempted to impose retribution. Hence, it requires notice when such truck drivers (or their sympathizers) did not do so. The case being cited did occur in 1968 in Greensboro, North Carolina, where discontent in a black high school spilled over into a local black college, and where the young people then went into an adjacent main street, stopping trucks, pulling drivers out of cabs, and actually beating some of the drivers.

A Detroit episode in the spring of 1969, less than two years after the big crisis of summer 1967, is instructive in the same way. At a Republic of New Africa (RNA) meeting there was an exchange of shots between the police and some other persons. One policeman was severely wounded and another killed, and more than a hundred arrests were made. The night judge[6] appeared in the police station, held hearings expeditiously, and released a small number of persons whom the police and prosecutor wanted to detain. The initial press reporting said that the judge had released a very large number of persons, and implied that the judge had acted in complete and obvious defiance of proper legal standards. Legislators prepared to launch an investigation; demands that the judge's conduct be investigated by the Judicial Tenure Commission were put forth; and— with the patrolmen's association in the lead (the sergeants and lieutenants' associations were more circumspect)—proposals for impeachment were vigorously urged.

The city appeared to be divided on racial lines more seriously than it ever had been. The critical role—which no one else could have played— was that of New Detroit, Inc., the local version of the Urban Coalition. The president of New Detroit—a black lawyer—publicly praised the judge as "an authentic hero of these trying times." Within a very brief period, the chairman (the actual top man) of New Detroit—a rich Republican businessman whose "closeness" to President Nixon is much advertised in Detroit—also issued a declaration supporting the judge.[7] He understood, he said, that the judge was a fine lawyer who knew the law in these matters, and he thought the judge had just exercised "good common sense." As part of the ritual process by which the racial cleavage was blurred, *the judge got the benefit of an ambiguous statement supporting his right to make a decision* (but not necessarily the substance of his decision) *from the President of the American Bar Association* (a prominent Detroit lawyer associated with Ford), *the presidents of the Detroit and State bars, and of the black bar association.* The ambiguity of the statement was that it said the judge's action raised grave "legal and constitutional questions," but that it clearly affirmed his right to decide. To say that it raised questions (and what decision in a local court would not?) was self-evident to lawyers, but it permitted the judge's critics to say that they were right. At the same time, to say that the judge had the right to decide got rid of the public clamor that the judge had simply and clearly behaved beyond the bounds of propriety. What editorialist could make that claim any longer in the wake of a statement from four bar-association presidents? Thus, though both white critics and black supporters could get something out of the report, the main beneficiary was the black side, which had the label of legitimacy pasted upon the action of the judge.

PROBLEMS OF WHITE LEADERSHIP

The main question in this essay has been whether the white capacity for political rationality is favorable or unfavorable to carrying the burden of social peacemaking. No fully satisfactory answer seems possible. There is sufficient confusion and ambivalence that neither a capacity for rational politics nor an incapacity for rational politics is self-evident. If we leave aside entirely "the liberals" (whom I have not yet discussed anyway), it is still possible to discern contrary currents in the flow of white public opinion. There is an uncomfortably numerous category of whites whom it would be proper to call "racist" in the most restricted sense. It is not justifiable to suppose that any more than a trivial proportion of the racists would follow up their unpleasant words by other behavior. After all, the lesson of unionization is that even very prejudiced whites can learn to adopt another style, when there is some sufficiently rational compulsion or influence. Moreover, it must be that many people who are really antagonistic toward blacks are somehow uncertain whether they can justify that antagonism or how they ought to express it. Otherwise, it would not have been necessary for Wallace's supporters in 1968 to find such code words as "law and order." They might have done what people like them have done in other circumstances: come right out and say "we don't like the blacks" and "we do want white supremacy."

In addition to the racist core—disguised or undisguised, granite-hard or shrinkable—there is the powerful body of conservatism. The argument in the preceding section has been that conservatism is only partly based upon explicit racial values. Much of that conservatism is also based upon the conception that "America is a *good* society, that anybody who challenges that idea in any extent is malevolent, and in any event, nobody has a good enough complaint to warrant acting outside the rules." On the other hand, there is also a body of opinion—frequently the same people as those properly called "conservative"—which is moved by rather conventional ideas of decency and fairness. This attitude does not make them into radical reformers, nor prevent their acting conservatively on many occasions. But it is a part of the broad pattern of internal contradictions, confusions, and ambivalence that one can discover among white Americans. Because people are confused and uncertain, one cannot take good results for granted, but neither can one take for granted their impossibility.

Ambivalence, confusion, and uncertainty are hard for human beings to tolerate. They create too much stress and strain. But, in highly factional situations, they also provide opportunity for change. Whether change that is desirable can be brought to fruition depends on many things. One of the things which is pertinent is the identification of who is ambivalent and who sure, and what he is ambivalent or sure about. Only out of this knowledge is it possible to create new alternatives capable of unifying people whose tendencies are otherwise toward division.

THE FAILURES OF THE LIBERALS

The formulation of initiatives which might contribute to social peace does lie with the white people most willing to consider change in the racial structure of United States society. It is not necessary to play the fashionable game of "whip the liberals," the main white leadership center on racial issues, to note that they have always been a weak leadership center and are in disarray. This disarray is most noticeable in the *opinion-making community,* as contrasted to the actual policymaking community.

Why the disarray exists requires a prior discussion of "who are the liberals?" What does the term mean? The term "liberal" is in reality a little misleading. In the first place, when used in conjunction with racial issues, it implies a greater consistency between racial policy preferences and actions and other policy preferences and actions than may exist. In the second place, it implies a bit more doctrinal consistency than may exist. Eric Goldman's term "Metroamerican" may be more in point. The prototypical Metroamerican was (and is):

. . . youthful, educated, affluent, more likely to have some minority blood in his veins [when compared to the rest of the country]. *His mind had been shaped by an environment which had been good to him.* (Emphasis added.) It was no less formed by an American scene of aggravating big organizations, brassy media and grinding social dislocations, and by a world situation of wars and threats of still worse wars. *His thinking and his attitudes were a tangle of ambivalence.* (Emphasis added.) The Metroamerican was avidly on the make, economically and socially, but he shied away from the appearance of sheer moneymaking or sheer caste and preferred the manner of public-spiritedness and cultivation. He had ideals but was skeptical of other people's—and even a bit, of his own. He was liberal but without ideology; tolerant but intolerant of do-goodism; flexible, pragmatic and a devotee of the ironic edge. (Goldman, 1969, 16)

The clearest view of the liberals (Metroamerican breed) comes in national affairs. They are the people who specialize in producing ideas for the political storage bank, ideas from which policymakers (notably, but not exclusively, Democrats) will later draw. Sometimes, if the right sort of president is in office or if they know the right congressmen, idea producers will also be commissioned to help turn their own (and other people's) ideas into the program. Outside the gilded circle of the national idea producers, the liberals are the idea repeaters, the people who help to give "forward-looking" propositions circulation as these become less and less wild ideas and more and more domesticated for serious public debate. In a sense this description fits the readership of the most prestigious papers—*New York Times, Washington Post, St. Louis Post-Dispatch, Louisville Courier-Journal,* and so on. It takes in the people who combine the reading of weekly magazines (*New Republic, Newsweek,* and others), the reading of monthlies and quarterlies more or less explicitly addressed to college graduates (*Harper's, Atlantic,* and the *Public Interest*), book-club subscriptions, at least modest contribution to "good causes," and possibly even some active political work. It embraces the people who, in the 1960's, were for "urban renewal" and against "Negro removal," but who refused to believe—when warned in the 1950's—that *the one would mean the other.*

It also implies activity, organizational activity: in Americans for Democratic Action or the American Civil Liberties Union, in "reform" Democratic clubs, in local human-relations committees, regional-planning commissions, and the whole paraphernalia of institutions vaguely associated with "rationality," "progress," and "social justice." In the end, it comprises Kennedy Democrats and Lindsay Republicans. In the 1960's and the 1970's, this group became heir to the "white liberal" tradition of the 1930's, except that the new liberals existed in the thousands (where the old "white liberals" existed in the dozens).

The collapse of the liberals, perhaps only temporary, can be seen most clearly in two respects. The first is that they have so far lost confidence in themselves that they are almost embarrassed to be called "liberals," unless they call themselves so belligerently as if daring anyone to smirk. The second is that—quite without the possibly misunderstood advice of Mr. Moynihan—they manage benignly to neglect serious thought on racial issues, even though their national exponents show no lack of energy on matters as diverse as ABM, the Sakharov Memorandum, interest rates vs. tax rates as inflation-control devices, the desirability or undesirability of revenue-sharing and federal financing of welfare costs, or the propriety of Senate intervention in the conduct of the Defense Department.

The collapse of idea production is the most obvious part of the situation, for liberal senators can yet muster skill and votes to drive through open-occupancy statutes and to block the confirmation of Judges Haynsworth and Carswell in succession. In the stress of the last few years, the liberals have lost a clear vision of the problems at stake. In fact, they have gone three ways. Some have reacted strongly to "violence" and "black racism," and—as in the case of the Californians—gone the Yorty route without ever losing faith in the desirability of "integration." Many others have gone the route of "radicalization" which, in the application to black politics, means a disdain for all blacks who do not make them feel uncomfortable or threatened and an infatuation with those blacks who speak of "picking up the gun." The center remains the center, doubtful about whether "integration" will really do any good for the blacks who need it most and prone to commit themselves to everything from manpower programs to family planning to "community control."

All this variety reflects both intellectual and political difficulties which Metroamericans have not learned yet to solve. The first and basic intellectual difficulty was that *Metroamericans never understood the black situation,* as I also maintain that they never understood the Euro-Americans.[8] This vagueness was partly associated with a rather *sentimental* left wing politics (not a *doctrinal* left wing politics) in which good people had to be on the side of the downtrodden. Blacks were to be sympathized with, and aided, not only because it was "good politics,"[9] but because they were the *downtrodden.* The image of sweet, well-behaved little girls being abused by howling mobs in Birmingham, Little Rock, and New Orleans were quite factual, and the image of Martin Luther King's well-disciplined moral protest movements was also quite factual. But this sweetness, morality, discipline, and courage were nearly all that the liberals could permit themselves to see. They could not permit themselves to see in advance the turbulence of the past five years. Once it happened, they not only found themselves less able to argue convincingly to white audiences; they also found themselves bitterly impugned by black audiences.

Second, the liberals have largely ignored a lesson from one major liberal figure, Reinhold Niebuhr. They have largely maintained a faith in the "goodness" of humanity and have built upon this an optimistic expectation of "progress." Thus they obscured from themselves their own ambiguity, and have made it hard to remember that the forms of social conflict are not simply between the good and the bad, with the good winning, but are often *genuinely nasty and bitter to the extent that the main problem is simply finding a viable basis for reconciliation.* It was easy to make this mistake in the wake of the New Deal. For the New Deal confirmed, in the liberal mythology the older "Jacksonian" and populist mythology, that there is nothing to politics except the conflict between the "interests" and the "people" needing to be treated decently as to money, and encouraged the hope that the exercise of power by the "people" will compel "the interests" to do precisely that. To deny money conflict or/and class conflict in politics would be superficial,[10] but the liberals had gone so far in the other direction that they could not comprehend a politics of esteem. That is, they thought that any problem could be "solved" if adequate material resources were available. Furthermore, even in economic terms, they were short-sighted. They could conceive no policies except those which might be carried out consistently with the developed pattern of the New Deal and post-New Deal welfare state. This means that they championed modifications in such things as the welfare system, but took for granted the broad complex of economic measures (both in the manipulation of fiscal policy and in the specific regulatory policies which associate industry and government). To put it another way, they not only maintained that black economic progress was contingent on increasing white economic progress (which is probably true), but also maintained that the normal conceptions of economic policy must govern that process. These are intellectual problems. Political difficulties follow from them.

The first political difficulty arises from the very necessities of this liberal category of people. To be "on the make" required them to find roles from which they could exercise influence, but since they had neither capital nor large popular followings, they could not maintain those roles once national political sponsorship failed to provide "cover" for their activities. So long as White House politics covered an energetic push on civil rights, the liberals were safe. But they were terribly exposed once that cover was withdrawn. So long as the national situation were more favorable than not, blacks' problems provided some potential roles of influence for liberals because their own careers could be enhanced as providers of expertise to presidents (directly or through intermediaries) and as providers of advice to blacks on how to approach centers of power. Moreover, once the black movement began to jettison "white leadership of black people," their credibility was terribly damaged.

The second difficulty arises from the fact that the liberals do not seriously know the country as a whole, but are prone to take those interpretations which are provided through the highly literate (and essentially Boston-Washington-New York) circles which find their way into the papers and journals they read, into the foundations, and into the university world. The consequent trouble with liberal leadership was not that its specific programs were wrong in themselves, but that the liberals' basic interpretation of the racial cleavage was wrong. Liberal power has depended on the liberals' peculiar role as linkers between several competing groups, notably Euro-Americans and blacks in the urban North. The liberals acted as brokers in a coalition where these groups provided the muscle but liberals the policy ideas. In their emphasis of grocery bag issues, liberals acted within the understood and conventional calculus of American politics: political incentives are "rational" in the end only if they can be turned into dollars-and-cents bargaining.[11]

Liberals could reconcile their ideas to black politics on the theme that "more"—more cash, more shoes, more jobs, more houses—is itself the end in view. This theme is fundamentally wrong. If material considerations were dominant, certain other relationships should have been found. (1) There should have been substantial evidence of poor-black plus poor-white alliance in these disorders, but to mention this very possibility reminds us how ludicrous it is—in light of ordinary social history and social experience. (2) There should have been a simple inverse correlation between income level and black participation in rebellious disorders; but the relationship is not as simple as that. Neither of these possibilities has been found in fact. We suggest, instead, that looting and similar behaviors are not integral parts of any disposition toward rebellion, but are mere epiphenomena which develop once a violent or volatile disorder has occurred.[12] If material privation were the principal clue, then it would be impossible to explain why the black middle class and the black gentry are *and have always been* critically important to black protest against white dominance.[13] It would be impossible to explain why the present black middle class is emotionally prepared to sympathize with even the most avant-garde militants, no matter how much they themselves may hold back from the same activity. It would be impossible to explain why the black students in Ivy League universities who are most prepared to adopt revolutionary language and cultural nationalism and least interested in the adaptive learning of a technocratic society, are not the newcomers from the poorest ghetto, but third-generation students.[14]

The misfortune of the liberals, in the past few years, has been to see that their verities did not work. Neither improved welfare programs, nor public housing, nor greater material well being proved sufficient to obviate racial conflict. Thus, it is said, the possibility that blacks are better off compared to themselves than they were before matters less than the fact that they are still about as badly off (possibly just as badly off) as they ever were, when compared to white counterparts. The liberal interpreters have lost authority, not so much because racism has increased as because they cannot show other audiences why, amid this greater prosperity and security, black rebellion grows apace. In the effort to reestablish a rational focus, consistent with their own political ideas and authority, the liberals have adopted the relative-deprivation hypothesis. The relative-deprivation explanation makes sense in one respect. If what is at stake is not absolute well being, but the sense of one's own well being compared to others' well being, then the material of strife does become more clearly understood. But the point is still blurred so long as the materialistic bias ignores deference itself.

The paradoxes disappear if we assume that black politics is basically a politics of deference seeking, responsive to the stigmata of contempt, disesteem, and doubt about the capacities of blacks so visible in the culture. Obviously, I do not limit this emphasis on deference to blacks. Nothing is clearer than that foreign-policy disputes become harder to handle, as soon as "national *interest*" issues become entangled with "national *pride* and loss of face." Similarly, a labor negotiation may be stalemated utterly if one side challenges the legitimacy of the other,[15] and departmental life in a university may be made unbearable by "personal" considerations. The problem now demands a political appreciation of the case for cultural relativism long ago made by Melville Herskovits. There was, he said in true positivist spirit, no *scientific* basis on which to regard one "culture" as higher than another. The problem of applying this proposition in politics is particularly difficult. Cultural values—in contrast to technological aspects of culture—are among the least manipulable aspects of human life.[16]

As I have said, this failure of the liberal initiatives is not subject for gleeful finger pointing. The substitutes presently offered for faulty policies are not very illuminating. On one hand, there is the new populism which urges that "when (the) people give any clear indication that they are ready to move (away) from materialism and apathy and complacency and the vulgar know-nothingism that so often passes for common sense along Main Street—leaders will be there to lead."[17] Even worse are the grim repetitions of the words "backlash," "repression," and "impending doom," all without benefit of the slightest hint of who might do what to produce a more desirable condition.

THE DEMANDS ON THE PARTIES

Far more important than the failure of the liberals is the failure of the party elites, for party elites have more to do than anyone else with the conjunction of public opinion, the actual organization of power, and the policymaking process. Party provides a mechanism by which diverse interest-group leaders are brought together—sometimes in concord and sometimes in conflict. Party is still the most important agent in the recruitment of public policymakers, and provides some leverage over the decisions which they actually make. The party platform—often denounced for its irrelevance—provides the one forum (perhaps even more than Congress) in which the concerns of the nation are symbolically expressed in verbal format. Above all, party provides the symbolism to which most people— not themselves politically active—are responsive, except when particular issues or items touch their feelings or pocketbooks in some special and different way. Accordingly, the party mobilizes the individual's bias, when he has no reason to take a counter view, so that he is more likely to be responsive to whatever is represented as the party view. Hence, party leadership on issues—though not consistent or stable (as it purportedly is in some countries)—is of great importance. But parties may fail to provide the requisite leadership in two main ways: by a failure of nerve and confidence or, despite nerve and confidence, by a failure of insight and foresight. In the present racial crisis, the former is rather more the Democratic problem, the latter more the Republican. Thus, there is *at least a temporary* failure of confidence in "practical" Democratic national leadership. From the Civil War to the New Deal, the Democratic party rather consistently occupied white supremacist ground, but in the New Deal paradoxically started an abandonment which gathered force after World

War II until the Democrats acquired a near monopoly of "civil rights."[18]

Moreover, the concern with racial equality has penetrated that party's life so far that it regularly concerns some major Congressional figures in a way not imaginable twenty years ago. One reason is that the penetration of blacks into the party structure is so much deeper. Another is that purity on these questions has so much more intense attraction for some part of the white constituency—just as it repels others. Still another reason probably is that Congressional Democrats have some pride in a structure of policy they helped to create, pride of authorship quite apart from beliefs and doctrines. At the same time, the strains created by the rising crescendo of black political demands, the backlash problem, the Republican invasion of blue-collar territory, and the Agnew strictures against "radical-liberals" all threaten to make the Democratic party a minority party. The normal expectation: defensive retrenchment, *particularly* when it can be disguised. Democratic policymakers have little further confidence that they know how to deal with racial tension, or that measures they propose would be acceptable to any *significant* white audience *they can reach.* An effective Democratic party role will depend on two things.[19] One is a rediscovery by Democratic policymakers of the practical terms in which the racial issues may be addressed. There are both attitudinal and structural signs that this rediscovery is possible, although no major Democratic politician has yet articulated the elements of a relevant program. The second need is a new maturity among the Democratic idea producers which takes simultaneous cognizance of the welfare and the esteem problems of the black population and of the Euro-American population with which it must come to terms. There is possibly a third—and even more significant consideration: the emergence of mechanisms within which the community leadership of blacks and the community leadership of Euro-Americans in the cities can create an ethnic detente, as the first step toward depolarization and eventual construction of a common political community.

It is particularly troublesome in Democratic politics that the elites have shown little recognition of or interest in the fact that on many measures of political "alienation" (such as statements like "nobody [important] cares about people like me"), lower-middle-and lower-class whites often show stronger signs of alienation than do blacks. This tendency is rather dangerous, for the working-class white population (or the black population, for that matter!) accords automatic deference to no one. In consequence of the elites' indifference, the white lower-middle and lower-class role in putting forth policies, receiving deference, and influencing critical decision makers in the modern bureaucratic state is also very limited. Between the rank and file and the educated elites of the nation (the "establishment," the "technostructure," or whatever) is *an enormous empathy gap!* (Holden, 1971) This empathy gap tends to reinforce overt indicators of racist feelings and the disposition toward racist policies.

This same kind of failure in Democratic politics is represented in the white reformers' preoccupation with the internal politics of the black "nation"—which is but an effort to provide "leadership" from without, on the supposition that only a change in the activity of *black* people will make a significant difference. It is the obverse of the same liberal-moderate reformers' failure to understand the problems of the white blue-collar lower- and middle-lower class, the so-called silent majority, and to examine the problem how that part of the population can—without self-sacrifice —be brought to understand the need for black liberation and for black-white reconciliation. When the need for activity in the Euro-American population *has* been recognized, the task has been left to one (or more) of three institutions: the trade unions, the political party local organizations, or the Catholic Church. The first, in the days of "grocery bill liberalism" dealt with the blacks and Euro-Americans as two irreconcilable parties linked by the Democratic politico. Neither ever knew what the mediator told the other. He balanced them off by keeping them apart and —incidentally in the process—by maintaining his own leadership over both. At least for now, "grocery bill liberalism" is not adequate for either black or Euro-American. But neither party (nor any union) has discovered a new *modus operandi* and only the third Euro-American institution—the Catholic Church—has shown the comprehension of the reconciliation problem, and that rather recently.[20]

In the short run—say, the next five years—the Republican role and the Republican problem may be even more important than the Democratic role and the Democratic problem. The liberal failure is less important than the conservative failure for two reasons. The first is that, unless the country becomes Mississippianized, the liberals will inevitably be penetrated by the value shift which can be perceived in the present conflict of generations. But that will take a longer time, and my focus in this essay is on those things which need urgent initiative within the next five years. At least until 1973, the Executive Branch will be in "conservative" hands, since Republicans will be in control there. That fact is crucial, since the presidency of the United States is a kind of secular priesthood-kingship, *from which the nation as a whole and not merely the current government officials tends to take its cues.* It is possible for a president to fritter away his capacity for leadership by misunderstanding the situation of the nation or his own situation. When that occurs, nothing very constructive happens until the president regains his own confidence and the nation's confidence, or until he is in time replaced with a president more suited to the demands of the occasion. But if a president has the capacity to elicit trust in himself, the prime national issues become those in which he is concerned, and his interpretation of those issues tends to take precedence over other interpretations. In this role, President Kennedy contributed much to the civil rights movement (1962–1963) by helping to redefine civil rights as a "moral issue." He so focused interest that many private parties, including those not notably sympathetic to blacks (such as presidents of the American Bar Association), were far more responsive to the moral appeals enunciated by the active civil rights leadership of the time. The urban rebellions since 1964, the natural emergence of the "backlash," and the national preoccupation with the Vietnam war, have blurred—if not destroyed—that focus.

Under the specific circumstances of the moment, the dictates of middle-of-the-road politics impose a special historical responsibility upon the Nixon administration. Precisely because that administration represents those most resistant to social change, it is the option of that administration to formulate a new framework in terms which may elicit the enthusiasm of blacks and the assent of whites. This option also focuses the sense in which specific facts of current politics make the republican crisis into a Republican crisis. The Republican crisis arises out of an incapacity to play a resolute role in pursuing social peace while the Republican party attempts to pick up the Southern and urban white ethnic remainders of the Democratic electorate by appealing to the older sentiments of racial separatism. This duality inhibits the adoption of a critically important presidential role which might make a useful contribution.

The social structure of the Republican party contains two elements which, rationally, have an extraordinarily high interest in the achievement of social peace, not in mere quiescence. One is major industrial leadership, which would be utterly foolish if it did not begin to comprehend the realistic costs of social disorder.[21] The other is the urban Euro-American population, which is itself just beginning to break through the historic layers of Anglo-Protestant dominance to find its own role in the redefinition of American society. Nothing has been more important to the liberation of Euro-Americans than the black upsurge, which has made attention to ethnicity a viable and respectable theme in social, intellectual, and political life. Precisely because that population is urban, it stands in need of a detente and ultimate settlement with the black population, much as the black population stands in similar need vis-a-vis the Euro-Americans. From that perspective, one may argue that Mr. Agnew, as the symbolic spokesman of the administration and the Republican party, is *misleading his natural constituents.*

Why should this misdirection have occurred? The answer is a simple phrase: "practical politics." It is unimportant whether the Republican leadership has a *calculated* "Southern strategy," although most of the evidence contradicts official denials that it has such a strategy. The political judgment seems to have been twofold. (1) In any event, one might imagine White House strategists arguing, the blacks (and others most interested in racial resolution) are not going to vote for the Republican party, so that any action which might suit their desires would be a wasted political investment. (2) On the other hand, there are sufficient whites, North and South, alarmed, anxious, disturbed, that catering to those will provide a firm national majority for many years to come. If that judgment was in fact made, then certain other implications follow. The first is that the United States is ready for celebration of the 200th anniversary of the Declaration of Independence, and the 100th anniversary of the Hayes-Tilden settlement, with a new retrenchment. It would mean a readiness to abandon the prospect of a Second Reconstruction, even if the price were that a tenth of the country should be driven willy nilly to blind and self-destructive armed revolt. That readiness could only be justified on still another set of presumptions: (a) that the adoption of a more coercive posture by the government would induce a new and indefinite era of black quiescence, or (b) that even without quiescence the costs of coercion would be high for blacks, but low for all others. Such reasoning might, at first glance, seem practical. Yet its practicality is extremely dubious, particularly when deference considerations play so important a role, for it has been effectively argued that such a strategy produces bad results even when mainly material considerations are at stake (Gerschenkron, 1964).

It is not necessary to suppose that such calculations were reasoned to their very end. Indeed, reasoning about them to their very end makes them utterly bizarre, so that only madmen could easily adopt them. What is more likely is that the first step was taken, in a simple calculation of "practical politics," without stopping to inquire whether the politics being adopted were, in fact, so practical. Politics is, indeed, the art of the possible, but the possible is not intelligently to be equated with the "clever," the "smart," or the "cheap." Thus, what has been lacking—and what makes the republican crisis a Republican crisis—is a deeper sense of history and social change. To assume away the black vote is "natural," but who could have (in 1928) foreseen the day when the black vote would be securely committed to Democrats? Surely, as we have noted above, the Democrats did not. Only after they had begun to adopt policies which made a black vote switch plausible to black voters did the switch take place. In this very simple way, the Republican strategists have failed to see the implication of 1956 (when a drift toward the Republicans began), much as the Democrats failed to see the implication of the drift in their direction which took place on more than one occasion before 1936, but was reversed by Democratic politics itself.

What is even more important, it can be argued with some conviction that present Republican strategy misunderstands the white portion of the electorate, no less than the black. The essential argument of this essay is that the white portion of the population is *not* agreed on the dominant drift of the administration in office. Rather, it is profoundly troubled and confused. In that trouble and confusion, many kinds of contradictory behavior are to be seen, and could be seen even before the 1970 election. The little signs were apparent when Charles Goodell began his remarkable transformation—a transformation which is partially explained by a reading of the New York electorate.[22] It could similarly be seen in the presence from Pennsylvania (a truly right wing state when Mr. Nixon began his political career) of two senators (Scott and Schweiker) far more alert to domestic reform than the administration. It could be seen similarly in the disposition of Ohio Senator Saxbe to argue that he did not agree with the administration that the 1968 election meant a domestic demand for retrenchment rather than reform. It could even be seen in the vacillation of the unfortunate Senator Ralph T. Smith on his first big test when he got to Washington: the Haynsworth nomination, and the even greater deviation of his Illinois colleague Percy. Nor was there anything about the 1970 election which made the administration's interpretation of the national trend seem more persuasive. The fundamental point is that "modern Republicanism" probably has more adherents in the electorate than it had when the phrase was coined in the Eisenhower days. This discussion is not to argue that there is a powerful national *demand* in the direction contrary to the Administration's preferences, but that there is a web of ambiguity and ambivalence, which it is the function of political leadership to resolve, and that the tendency to resolve it against "change" in general is far less "practical" than Nixon administration strategists have supposed.

If there is any reasonable interpretation of the recent experience, it is *not* that there is a national demand for the Mississippianization of the United States. Rather, it is that a vast and confused white population desires a "decent" resolution which will, at the same time, be not too inconvenient for itself. It will, if events seem to dictate so, accept an ultimate movement in the reverse direction, not because it desires so, but because it will—in that event—come to see such a result as "inevitable," "unavoidable," and "practically necessary."

It is in precisely such confused situations that political leadership is the most important, the most decisive, and when perceptive the most constructive. Whether one maintains that the Nixon administration is calculatedly antiblack (as does Bishop Stephen Spottswood), or that it merely has no policy (as does James Farmer), is not necessary here to resolve. Nor is it necessary to evaluate Attorney General John Mitchell's claim that criticism is either insincere or ill-informed.

The main point is that—whether by lack of energy, latitude, or insight —the tendency of the Nixon administration in its first two years has obstructed rather than facilitated the search for social peace. (It may even be that a Democratic administration would have found itself in the same position.) It is perfectly reasonable, by ordinary political logic, for an administration to praise itself by comparing itself to prior administrations. Such was the response (through Mr. Leonard Garment's office) to the Spottswood criticism: We, said Mr. Garment, have appointed more blacks to high positions than any prior administration. But a careful study of the actual list of appointees suggests at least two considerations: (a) the number is nonetheless minuscule, though larger than before, and (b) the appointments were, even more than before, to roles which can only by the most extraordinary stretch of the imagination be called "policymaking." The search for "Southern" judges has meant a search for judges thought likely to adopt the narrowest possible interpretation of civil rights obligations. The initial effort to extend the Voting Rights Act into the North is of the same unhelpful quality. In principle, it is sound to argue that literacy restrictions are not more defensible North than South. But the practical fact is that it is in the South, and only there, that literacy restrictions have been systematically exploited to reduce the black franchise. To propose diffusion of administrative attention to the whole country, at a time when the black franchise is now beginning to be consolidated in the South, is too clever by half! The same argument can be made about the obfuscation of residential desegregation questions in the urban North, and even about a "revenue-sharing" proposal which could not but reinforce the political power over the central cities of state governments notably averse to new departures in urban policy. It is too much, perhaps, to belabor Mr. Moynihan's colorful rhetoric, yet the predominant tone of the Nixon administration's "liberals" is that some rather ordinary things will, if left alone, produce highly beneficent results. No one need, thus, attack the merits of early childhood programs (of the sort which Mr. Moynihan finds attractive) or of family assistance programs to note the obvious fact that they do not address the central issues of racial strife. Similarly, one cannot necessarily fault the party or administration for the woeful failure of black capitalism.[23] But one needs to note that an extraordinary verbal emphasis was placed on "black capitalism" *as a substitute* for other measures, while the administration has been unable or unready to make the major investments which "black capitalism" would require. Similarly, one may observe the level of party and administration attention by noting that there is even less attention than in prior administrations to the questions of the racial impacts of macroeconomic policy.

The minimum conclusion which the pattern can justify is that a low evaluation of the racial battle exists. The Nixon administration shows every evidence of regarding racial issues as trivial. In part, it has simply tended to choose its domestic reform proposals from among those least susceptible to criticism (although the family assistance plan is contrary evidence). More to the point, it has seemed, it either stirred up those forms of resistance to reform which would utterly negate new action on the racial dimension, or else encouraged those specific forms of black action which it itself could use to frighten a white audience into voting for it. Thus, there would be no partisan attack but mere recitation of fact to use in 1970 or 1971 the language which a black Republican used of Woodrow Wilson: that its "reflex influence" served to notify all who were hostile that the government stood on their side (Charles Anderson, quoted in Kellogg, 1966, I, 1). By this test, the Republican party in power has tended to resolve ambivalence, not in the direction of social peace, but in the direction of catalyzing further white resistance and undermining further black confidence in the regime.

Both Democratic and Republican party elites now act in a way which gives point to an answer which black separatists have been fond of offering in the past several years. When "black power" came to be a persuasive phrase, white liberals frequently asked: "But what role does that leave for me?" Usually, the black separatist answer was, "You will have to figure that out" or else "Go and work in your own community." Apart from rude gamesmanship, the answers do contain a germ of realism. The starkest leadership need is not among blacks, great as it is there (see *The Politics of the Black "Nation"*), but among whites. The task of party leaders is to bring to fruition the potentialities which are inherent in the hopeful aspects of everyday behavior, and to abort those which are inherent in the unpleasant aspects. The most delicate feature of the present time is not racial faction itself, but the present incapacity of national political elites— notably in party leadership. The Democratic case amounts to a palsied nerve and the Republican to an utterly misdirected judgment. Yet it may be here that one major point of departure is the task of political elites to give direction to events in moments of great social uncertainty.

This is the business of *political* elites, that is to say, of clusters of people who make it their business to generate ideas for the public agenda, to carry on debate about those ideas, to resolve the debated ideas in the formulation of new policies (or the reaffirmation of old ones), and to see to the implementation of policies once they have been formulated. It is understandable but regrettable that political leadership should have shirked so hard a problem. Both liberal and conservative elements of leadership in United States politics have failed to reintroduce elements of political rationality. The former have seen their bread-and-butter verities turn to nothing and have witnessed the decline of their capacity to lead the traditional Democratic coalition. Conservatives, in the broadest sense, have had a clearer appreciation that racial reconciliation depends on reciprocal deference. This is the best meaning of the Eisenhower-Goldwater-Buckley position that racial reconciliation depends on changes "in the hearts of men." But the conservatives have actually been as much incapacitated as have the liberals, through their disposition to treat "government" as some alien presence which should be kept out of the affairs of "society."

Thus, while conservatives have uttered words more indicative of an understanding of the problem of deference and esteem, they have taken action quite as heedless as that of the liberals—the more so as they have tried merely to capture dissident elements of the old Democratic coalition into a new Republican coalition. But what is required is a rediscovery of politics in a sense more fundamental than the traditional politics made possible (Paige, 1966).

This rediscovery is not easy in a culture with an antipolitical bias which, in many respects, is becoming an anti*elite* bias as well. Why political elites excite such antagonism is unclear, but it does seem that they do. Such elites are frequently under criticism not only by the man in the street but also by members of other elites (businessmen, soldiers, scholars, artists) who think that the "rational" way is to "get on with" their proper business without "political interference" or "self-serving wrangling." Such criticism is acute when life seems so stable that "politics" is pointless or when it is so turbulent that "politics" seems dangerous. This antipolitical bias is not only Utopian, but also unites people of the most dissimilar persuasions. Many big businessmen would probably be astonished to discover their emotional kinship to the Marxist-Leninists desiring to replace the "government of men" with "the administration of things."

Yet from time to time events emphasize that the human problem is the government of men. The present situation might remind one of Joseph Charles's interpretation of the period from 1787 to 1800:

We hear much of eighteenth-century optimism, and the achievements of this generation would have warranted it, but we are studying a period when thoughtful men were frequently subject to despair; apprehension and despair . . . . These men had no narrow conception of their differences; they thought in terms of 'fixing the national character' and of choosing the path the new nation should follow. (Charles, 1969, 6)

APPENDIX—ON PEACEMAKING

The late E. Franklin Frazier once argued:

If . . . studies [of the black situations were] undertaken in a fundamental manner, they would enlist the interest of the most competent scholars and the results of these studies would have a scientific validity and significance far beyond the [black situation itself]. (Quoted in Caliver, 1948, 41n2)

I agree, and for that reason have throughout the preceding essays, from time to time, digressed to comment on some broader issue, an understanding of which seems pertinent to the specific problems of race in politics and society. For the same reason, it seems useful to set down some very preliminary notes (motivated by the problems discussed above) on the requirements of *peacemaking* as a generalized human process.[24] Unfortunately, both the experienced decision maker's common sense and the scholars' more abstract models are still so limited[25] that one is driven to be somewhat speculative.

The point of departure is that theories of political change which depend exclusively on coercive power, which suggest that politics is *nothing but pure power or a capacity for blackmail,*[26] are distinctly misleading. They obscure the *obvious* fact that a challenging group—whether a foreign nation or an internal faction—usually has the power to express its own discomfort or ambitions by creating a sense of disturbance among its adversaries. This is almost always a prior condition to achieving a new situation which it can find satisfying. But it is not the same thing as having the power to create that new situation. The new satisfying situation does not automatically or inevitably follow from the fact of disturbance, nor even from specific actions in technical compliance. If it did, party X (the defender) would merely adjust to the wishes of party Y (the challenger) and that would be that. Under that theory, Mississippi would have been a tranquil biracial polity before 1900, the Kohler strike would not have occurred, and peace would now reign in Vietnam and the Middle East. Such theories not only ignore the residue of hatred which another party builds up if you compel him to eat dirt. They also ignore the high risk, in any current situation, of mutual alarm, madness, and a politics of self-defeat.[27] *If some very bad situation exists between parties X and Y, peace seems achievable only on a kind of "social installment plan."* It is sometimes possible that the only route to a healthy accommodation is through the agonistic struggle which results in stalemate.[28] Sometimes people learn that they have to coexist only after they have tried unsuccessfully to beat each other into the ground, and learn to live peaceably only after they have faced the fact of coexistence, even if this bargaining is purely amoral. But to place bets on this possibility or process is extremely risky.

Suppose some party X is "sure" that he is doing what his interests and beliefs require, and that anything else would make him worse off than he could "tolerate." The best prediction is that he may respond coercively to any proposal for change, and almost surely will respond so to somebody else's coercion. From which, the agonistic struggle. The end result would be some fight between the two, leading to a stalemate or to some victory by one over the other. The first problem in installments, thus, is to terminate actual battle where it exists, or to prevent its eruption where it threatens.

Battle (or the immediate threat of battle) provides its own stress, which exaggerates the chances of a politics of self-defeat! Men often lose sight of what their real objectives are, *or decide that they have "no choice"* but to act in ways which defeat the objectives they have in mind, even though they usually *will* not understand this fact until after the event. Studies of international politics are highly suggestive here. Only in this way is it possible to understand World War I, for it can hardly be supposed that the Russian, Austro-Hungarian, and German elites meant to set in motion a process which would destroy themselves. Yet they did so, moving blindly into a corner from which they had no escape, all the while interpreting themselves as friendlier to the enemy than the enemy was to themselves. Masao Maruyama, a Japanese political scientist, reports a similar process of ill-informed and self-defeating decisions by the leaders of the Japanese government before World War II (Maruyama, 1963), while —if Robert F. Kennedy is to be credited—the Cuban missile crisis was a scene where the President sought to avoid putting Khrushchev into a corner, a course which he could adopt only by ignoring some of the most considered judgments of his advisers (Kennedy, 1969, 73, 76, 124–128). The point is also well known in industrial relations, where the union leader's demonstration of his power often requires the calling of a strike. But, in union folklore, "anybody can *call* a strike; but not anybody can settle a strike."

Only if parties avoid mutual alarm, and begin to move toward some form of truce, does the first installment occur. Truce is the suspension of arms, whether general (all armed clash ceasing) or limited (some forms continuing). Truce, whether born of the parties' mutual exhaustion (or of some more constructive intent), permits some measure of bargaining. Armistice is an extension of truce, with the expectation that the suspension might last for a considerably longer time. The question which next occurs is how stable the armistice itself could be. When conflicting parties hate, despise, and distrust each other, almost the only basis for stabilizing an armistice is the sense of practicality. Parties may recognize (or believe) that the costs of continuing active conflict are greater than the gains to be achieved thereby. However, stability is more likely if the parties have simply worn each other down to the nub, for it is here that men may become realistic about mutual loss possibilities, sufficiently to seek to put their relationships on a new and less dangerous footing. Doing this requires making choices about which men have discretion, and thus seems to emphasize bargaining. Bargaining itself is truly important, but genuine peacemaking—in contrast to the negotiation of treaties (Nicolson, 1965) or union contracts (Douglas, 1962)—is far more complex.[29] Bargainers do have to negotiate deals, but the deals require more than short-term implementation. The nature and scope of a shared moral order—wherein conflicting parties *reciprocally* renounce coercive force against each other —is indicated by the operative social constitution ("rules of the game"), not merely by the legal constitution let alone the contractual language on a particular deal. Questions and disputes are widespread about all the rules of the game: those defining membership in the polity and exclusion from the same, which members are eligible for recruitment to which posts, how those who hold responsible positions are expected to treat other people, what specific social outputs (universal education, private property, and the like) are regarded as necessary or not, and above all what rules shall govern the changing of any other rules.

It is evident that most of what I have said on these points is highly speculative, justified only because reasoned speculation is—though inferior to precise scientific analysis—superior to standing mute on questions too important to be neglected.

For scholars, there are at least two major implications. One is that the "fields" of political science and political sociology as presently constituted offer all too little guidance to the important problems. The problem of overcoming Madisonian faction is not merely a United States problem of race, but one that can be found repeatedly in the confrontations of French-speaking and English-speaking Canadians; or of Serbs, Croatians, Macedonains and others in Yugoslavia; or of Hindus and blacks in Guyana; or of Walloons and Flemings in Belgium; or of Melanesians and Indians in Fiji; or of Indians and whites in the countries of Latin America.

The other implication is that the study of "conflict resolution" (or of peacemaking as I have here chosen to say) needs to be treated far more intently. For all the importance of precision and methodological refinement, that is not the first order of business, since the minute studies of bargaining situations and situations of escalation provide no organizing focus for a proper analytical theory. Yet what people need—much as they need bread—is a serious understanding of the central processes involving the de-escalation of serious conflicts and the rearrangment of hostile relations into more peaceful relations as here defined. At this point, we are thus back to the previous comments on the limitations of "field" thinking: peace*making* is not a problem which can easily be defined by "level of government" or by the formal characteristics of the units interacting. It is a problem such that the conceptual boundaries of "international" politics, "comparative" politics, and "American" politics almost entirely disappear.

NOTES

1. These are merely items which I chanced to cull. A systematic search—though very tedious—would probably produce material for a profound social history of the decade. Dates from newspaper sources are those of publication; other newspapers of the same or nearly the same dates also carried much of the same information.

2. I refer to this sort of case because it is useful to get away from the grosser notion that blacks are "accepted" when they are "few" in relation to the number of whites. While there are some circumstances which lend support to this proposition, the fact that blacks are distinctly unwelcome in the poor-white hill country of the South (where they are very few in numbers) and in much of the rural Midwest runs counter to the "threat" hypothesis.

3. Professor William P. Robinson of Virginia State College first called my attention to the Holton phenomenon. Since this draft was written, state elections have brought to office Governors Dale Bumpers (Arkansas), Jimmy Carter (Georgia), Rubin Askew (Florida), and John C. West (South Carolina), all of whom explicitly reject the older posture of discrimination in state government. What eventual outcomes may result one need not predict; here the point is that all these governors adopt a posture consistent with the pattern to which I am referring.

4. Thus far, there is not a good public analysis of the metropolitan arms races, although some fragmentary work apparently was done for the Eisenhower Com-

mission on Violence by the Stanford Research Institute. However, a doctoral dissertation on metropolitan arms races is apparently in preparation now by Mr. David Seitz in the Political Science Department at Yale University.

5. I find it surprising that none of the Washington correspondents, and none of the political scientists studying the legislative process, has yet produced an analysis of the discussions among Southern senators at this time. *That would have been most informative.*

6. The criminal court in Detroit (Recorder's Court) has one judge assigned to night duty for matters which cannot wait until the normal court hours. By sheer chance, the judge on night duty in April was black.

7. Since New Detroit was making a serious effort to remain noncontroversial, without being ineffectual, it is unclear whether the president acted solely on his own or with prior consultation. But it seemed clear that the president's position would have been tenuous had he not been supported by others.

8. Indeed, it could be argued that they never tried understanding the former until about five years ago, and have only now begun to try to understand the latter.

9. Hubert Humphrey—whom many liberals, with gratitude sharper than a serpent's tooth—repudiated and deprecated some time after 1965, is in fact the archetypal liberal.

10. Here they were somewhat led astray by John F. Kennedy. For if Kennedy taught them anything, it was that "class" conflict could not be a viable basis for contemporary politics. The validity of the Kennedy lesson is by now not so clear.

11. The intellectual history of political liberalism is beyond my present scope of capacity, but it merits attention by someone. It seems to have at least three elements: Marxism (or pseudo-Marxism), social democratic ideology of the British Labour model, and American populism.

12. Moreover, if people wanted goods, they could better get goods by organizing themselves as criminal gangs.

13. See *The Politics of the Black "Nation,"* Essays I and II dealing with the internal politics of the black "nation" and with clientage, opposition, and withdrawal. Also see Drake (1969).

14. For this judgment, which is consistent with whatever else I know, I am indebted to Charles J. Hamilton, Jr.

15. Thus, one commentator claims that Theodore Kheel's particular success as a mediator depends upon his recognition of the personal needs of the negotiators, in contrast to the more "neutral" reliance upon the "merits" of the disputes (*New Yorker*, August 1, 1970, 36–58).

16. Observe the persistence of Confederate symbolism in the South, although Union symbolism in the North now has less effect. So strong a hold does that symbolism retain in the South that the custodians of respected tradition in Maryland have maintained a Confederate Room in the State Capitol, even though Maryland remained in the Union during the War. On the other hand, it was not until 1968 that the keepers of the faith opened a Union Room as well.

17. Tom Wicker, column, *Wisconsin State Journal,* December 30, 1969, Section 1, 8.

18. For historical background, see Essay V above.

19. It is possible that the Democratic malaise will be overcome by the explosive emergence of new situations, and some decisive new political genius as Roosevelt in 1932. But this is inherently unpredictable.

20. The activities of the United States Catholic Conference are pertinent here. See, among other things, "The Work of Depolarization" (editorial), *Commonweal,* October 2, 1970.

21. See above, Essay VII.

22. Even now, we should not be confused by the Goodell defeat. Senator Buckley is a *senator,* but he is a "minority" senator (40 percent of the vote), and the likelihood is that he will be far less "conservative" in performance than the election campaign indicated.

23. This is not the same thing as saying that all specific "black capitalism" *projects* have failed, for that is untrue.

24. This question is not much discussed even in the literature on "conflict resolution." For two useful contributions, exceptional in this regard, see Levi (1960) and Levi (1964).

25. Compare the discursiveness of the essay on peacemaking in Hancock (1961) with the clarity and elegance of the discussion of war in the same volume.

26. For the satisfaction of black cultural nationalists, one might substitute "whitemail."

27. Of course, a politics of self-defeat may arise under less stressful conditions as well; see Holden (1968).

28. Peaceful social change cannot mean, unfortunately, a complete absence of violence since society itself cannot exist with a complete absence of violence. But the idea is, generally, that violence *should* be contained so far as possible and its residue washed away as soon as possible. We merely declare this proposition here, without advancing a full normative argument. In the context of racial policies, however, we are quite clear that violent politics can only be destructive of the republican principle in general and of the conditions for a desirable life for blacks specifically, and can have no beneficent effects for any significant number of people in United States society in this generation.

29. This is most clearly shown in international politics, where one encounters the seldom-solved problem of creating more or less permanent peace between two (or more) nation-states. One of the rare cases is the establishment of peace between Norway and Sweden. See Lindgren (1959). In today's world, the problem is also faced acutely in the effort to reconcile warring (or potentially warring) populations within states hitherto presumed to be political communities (examples are in Canada and the United States) or to create viable states out of populations where that presumption of community had before not been entertained. See Ake (1967), Deutsch and Foltz (1963), Jacob and Toscano (1964), and Zolberg (1966).

X

Some Possible Measures toward Social Peace: I. The Political Economy of Racial Adjustment

Black and white may realistically be regarded as two "nations" in a sociocultural sense. But their fate is inevitably common. Therefore, each has a rational self-interest in the achievement of social peace, for which a political community (or a "republic" to use the old-fashioned word I have chosen to use) is the securest defense. If white leadership accepted this view, what sorts of policies might the leaders fruitfully consider. I suggest three: (a) a political economy of racial adjustment; (b) short-term threat reduction; and (c) major institutional modifications.

By the term "political economy" I mean what Robert C. Wood claims is "the dictionary definition of the phrase—'the art of managing the resources of a people and a government'."[1] I choose this emphasis in order to say that *merely* improving somewhat the economic conditions of blacks in the United States cannot be the appropriate objective. *The objective is to make economic decisions which will be calculated to have the political effect of improving the likelihood of social peace.*[2]

This objective means that public decisions will have to focus upon the connection between national economic policy and the options which present themselves to people operating within "the ghetto economy," and upon the strategic direction and measures which would seem appropriate. My contribution is necessarily somewhat amateurish, but that cannot be helped. For there is still very little analysis of the black ghetto considered as an "economy,"[3] and even less of the national policy relationship.[4] Consequently, I am not able to tell, from economists' writing, when they would regard my view as nonsense, *nor—more important—what policy options they would offer.*

THE REPARATIONS CONCEPT

The political economy of racial adjustment can, in my view, legitimately rest upon a pragmatic reparations policy. The rational form and procedure of such a policy cannot lie in permitting some black man to designate himself as the agent of "all black people," and thus to make whatever he believes a valid claim upon whatever white person or institution he should choose.[5] Nor can the rational basis of such a policy lie upon the supposition that living white people are somehow *personally* "guilty" for whatever may have happened in the historical past. That is an absurdity which does not contribute to clear thought. It leads to the confusion reflected in John Marchi's[6] argument that he had no responsibility to deal with the inherited disadvantages of blacks, because during the time of slavery his ancestors were still eating spaghetti in Italy. The issue is not a personal guilt issue, although it could theoretically be closer to a property dispute (in the sense that were my great-grandfather's property stolen—under the law as it existed in 1890—I might now issue an action against somebody for some form of recovery). But even the legal analogy would be strained and unworkable.

Reparations must be conceived within a contemporary structure of public law and policy as a means of coping with the consequences of history, without attributing present moral responsibility to anybody for whatever somebody's past action may have been. It is certainly reasonable to maintain that most whites in the present economy—even those whose ancestors were somewhere else before—are now real beneficiaries of the historical practices of discrimination. Most blacks lag behind them, not only for personal reasons, but because of the structure of inequality which grows out of that same set of historical practices. To say the one thing is to say the other. The present disparities did not "just happen." Generation-by-generation, blacks were systematically held back, not by the mysteries of "the market" but by deliberate policy; not by the inevitable logic of "capitalism" but by a violation of the principles of capitalism. Considering land, labor, and capital as the three basic "factors of production," the exploitive utilization of uncompensated (slave) labor can be ranked with the exploitation of vast quantities of available natural resources. Nor did this stop with the end of legal slavery. Instead, it continued with the peonage-plantation system of the South since 1865, which New Deal policy seldom challenged and sometimes abetted, and the formidable wall of economic discrimination in the North which increased the opportunities available to the white lower class (including the European immigrants of the late 1890's and early 1900's)(see Essay II, above). This provides ample justification for a pragmatic reparational approach. It is eminently reasonable to modify economic and social relationships, growing out of the historical development of the economy, much as we are now entering into a modification (rectification, reparation) of the *environmental* damage which was inherent in the historical growth of the economy. It is eminently sensible to repair, so far as possible, the cumulative economic damage, simply as a practical matter but without reference to any secular versions of original sin.

WHITE LEADERSHIP AND THE REPARATIONS RATIONALE

In an earlier essay, I have argued that the discovery of means toward social peace is preeminently a problem of white leadership. White leadership would make a strong contribution to social peace if it might face the reparations problem directly. But it cannot do so without a careful interpretation for the benefit of white audiences which would naturally tend otherwise to reject the idea. (Brink and Harris, 1967; Sears and Kinder, 1970, Table 5).

The white objection which may be treated most seriously arises out of simple and honest self-interest. No one wants to be put at some positive disadvantage in order to aid someone else, even if the other party has a valid claim. However, few people propose anything which would displace or limit white economic options. Political leadership may reasonably take the position, moreover, that special policies need not be "discriminatory" against whites in the sense of imposing special burdens upon whites, any more than a special regional program (such as TVA or Appalachia) imposes special burdens upon the rest of the nation. Instead, the principle is one aiding national objectives by filling in weak spots in the national economy.

The rationale for such a policy is threefold.

1. *Precedent.* Action to provide "special" favors for a group is both reasonable, if the criterion is not arbitrary, and fully consistent with the tradition of public policy in the United States. On a large scale, a good part of the movement of migrants to the United States in the nineteenth century was systematically organized and financed by the governments of the states. State governments put "emigration commissioners" into the

field in the same way that they now put industrial teams out to secure new plant investment. And the federal government sponsored a job-referral system with the purpose of decreasing congestion and unemployment in the Eastern immigrant centers, and of forwarding the movement of labor to regions where labor was in short supply, out of which the present employment security system developed (see Rourke, 1957).

Nor is this practice simply something from the dead past. Government programs and agencies are pervaded by decisions meant either to correct misallocations of resources or to redistribute income, and these programs and agencies are specifically directed toward identifiable parts of the population. Some of these programs and agencies are specifically calculated to overcome difficulties which are essentially the same as those of blacks, when blacks are considered in the aggregate: monopolistic impediments restricting the flow of funds to particular sector or area: the fact that people operating in a particular sector or area may have too limited present knowledge of the available investment opportunities; or the fact that they may encounter excessive operating costs, because of monopolistic competition in financial markets.[7] Such activities by the government are manifest in many fields: in the plethora of housing programs (from those specifically aimed at veterans to the more general programs administered by the Department of Housing and Urban Development); in the development of the Export-Import Bank as a means of encouraging the export businesses; in the existence of the Small Business Administration; in the oil-import-quota system meant to protect the financial interests of domestic firms (see United States Senate, . . . , 1969); in the recent debates over how much and what form of protection the aviation industry ought to receive; and in the manipulation of tariff regulations. All such programs make it amply clear, as does the very content of the executive budget (see Special Analyses, . . . , 1970), that the idea of "special" benefits for "special" parts of the population is neither novel nor generally regarded as illegitimate.

2. *Political Benefit.* Such action is politically desirable to overcome *national loss which comes with having a permanently depressed sector within the population.* There are two subreasons. The first is that wide economic disparities are a problem in deference for blacks and a consequent source of political volatility. The second reason is that an increase in economic autonomy is essential to the independent self-help capacity of blacks, which is in turn essential to their mastery of the afflictions of white contempt and their capacity to extend genuine deference to valid white symbols.

3. *Economic Benefit.* Such action is also economically desirable, in view

of the *economic costs* which discrimination imposes on the country as a whole. Carolyn Shaw Bell discusses this as a problem of the *loss of production* due to unemployment, and "undereducation" (Bell, 1970, 238–239). Only crude estimates of the economic losses are possible. As far as unemployment effects are concerned, Bell says that if "unemployment among blacks were reduced to the rate prevailing among whites in 1969, some $5 billion annually would have been added to output." Moreover, if Bell is right, there would be substantial gains to the economy were blacks as well off as whites. If they were so, about $16.5 billion would be added to total national income. To the "consumer goods industries—for firms that make clothing, food, furniture, appliances—it would be the equivalent of adding several small states, or one the size of Florida or Massachusetts, to their markets." Bell argues, I should think reasonably, that the losses from underemployment and undereducation (bad education or no education) must also be substantial, though it is not possible now to quantify them. But those direct costs which can be measured amount to "a loss of production which exceeds that during the Great Depression and both World Wars, and a loss which continues each day" (Bell, 1970). The problem, therefore, is to focus upon special policies for the purpose of achieving the closer integration of black and white within the national economy. And the idea of a special governmental role is fully consistent with past policy, political necessity, and economic desirability.

ELEMENTS OF A PROGRAM: THE EXCLUSION OF UNREAL
ALTERNATIVES

What, then, might be the elements of a program? It is particularly important to avoid debating unreal alternatives. By unreal alternatives I do not mean these which seem politically impossible in 1971. For while some constraints must be accepted as given, an important part of political leadership is to widen the existing set of constraints. *By unreal alternatives, I mean alternatives which could not produce a desirable effect, even if the alternatives could be adopted, or alternatives which obscure rather than clarify the problem and the course of action.*

Three such unreal alternatives should be noted.

1. *Escape and Autarchy.* Many people who recognize that there is an extra dimension of unemployment, underemployment (which I shortly redefine as *bad employment*), and poverty in the black population often fall into a debate whether black economic problems should be solved by encouraging people to move out of "the ghetto economy," or by develop-

ing the "ghetto economy." In part, one's answer depends upon the extent to which one means the word "ghetto" to refer to the *territorial* ghetto or to the social system composed of black people. But in either event, no one could imagine realistic conditions under which all blacks (or even half of the black people) would actually move out of "the ghetto." Therefore, it makes sense to search for policy measures which would have their effect within "the ghetto." On the other hand, the idea that developing the ghetto could be a sole economic policy is unworkable. Neither the dynamics of the modern economy, nor the constitutional requirements to the American polity, would permit autarchy.

2. *Pumping the General Economy.* Some people argue that black economic welfare depends solely upon the state of the larger economy. Thus, they say, momentary and fiscal policies which keep the whole economy hot will serve black economic needs, and policies which fail to do that will impede black economic needs. Others maintain that special policies are required, an argument often based upon comparison between the "ghetto economy" and the developing nations of the world. Every laid-off plant worker, who must decide whether it is worth his while to go jobseeking again, understands the first argument. Such a worker knows that blacks have much better chances when the economy as a whole is growing, and that their chances are constricted terribly when it is not. But the choice between the former and the latter arguments is still unreal. The same plant worker knows that there is a residual body of black unemployment, underemployment, and poverty—even during good times—and that this residual body is greater than it would be if blacks were evenly distributed throughout the whole economy (Wolf and McEnally, 1970).

3. *Pumping the "Ghetto Economy."* Finally, some largely unreal alternatives in the ideological and rhetorical styles of the Democrats and the Republicans. The former emphasize the norm of governmental action in the public interest and the latter prefer to speak of letting voluntary decision-making proceed with little hindrance. In keeping with these stylistic differences, it was possible for highly placed Democrats (such as Hubert Humphrey) to adopt Whitney Young's language and speak of a "domestic Marshall Plan for the cities." In contrast, Republicans have talked more of "black capitalism" (rechristened "minority enterprise") and of getting people off welfare rolls and onto employment rolls. Each set of styles provides the party with a language to speak to its main constituencies, but neither has provided a genuine clue to what those parties would do once in office. I am, in reality, strongly favorable to the "Marshall Plan" conception, but I argue that it has no close relationship to the favored symbols of either party. Operationally, it can be made

compatible with the requirements of either party and still have some practical significance.

ELEMENTS OF A PROGRAM: ECONOMIC INTEGRATION

The real objective is a set of policy measures of large scale, calculated to achieve economic integration and to make some major initial step toward that purpose by 1976.[8] These measures can be examined under two heads: income parity and capital development.

INCOME PARITY

We are obliged to accept, as a point of departure, a policy of seeking a *major start toward income parity between blacks and whites within that time.* By "income parity" I mean that similarly circumstanced blacks and whites would be coming closer to achieving similar (closely comparable) incomes.[9] Income parity will not be achieved within five years, but the policy problem is to make a start on those measures which will move in that direction. A politics of income parity would require national attention to two major problems: employment parity and job discrimination.

Employment parity is a condition for income parity. Hence the first measures would entail a departure from a posture which permits the United States to define as "full employment" an unemployment rate of 4 percent. This rate, which is well above that of either Britain or West Germany, *prohibits* a serious attack on black unemployment and, indeed, requires that black unemployment be left permanently at a level nearly as high as the "permanent" unemployment which contributed so much to British political volatility during the 1920's.[10] Under our present national policy, white "full employment" means a black recession, and a white recession means a black depression. In a recent *Social Science Quarterly* article, Harold A. Wolf and Richard W. McEnally report that, in the twenty-year period 1948-1968, white unemployment ran at an annual average of 4.5 percent while black unemployment ran at an average of 8.5 percent (Wolf and McEnally, 1970).

Black unemployment still runs at about that level, at minimum, and is far worse in many cities. Moreover, the economic problem is worsened by the fact that much of black *employment* is what economists call "subemployment" (or about what they call "underemployment"). In plain English, one may call it *bad employment*—jobs far too cheap to produce a fit income by any reasonable test. The "bad employment" rates are hard to measure, but the best available information is that you can figure it out by multiplying the unemployment rate anywhere from 3.5 to 5 times. In other words, if we take 8 percent as about the average black unemployment rate around election time in 1970, we could estimate that bad employment would have been anywhere from 28 to 40 percent in the same communities. In addition, unemployment/employment is all tangled up with anti-inflation policies. But the language in which anti-inflation policies are described disguises some simple realities. The idea of "cooling off" the economy means, in practical terms, that somebody is going to have to suffer; that suffering is not equally distributed among all people in the economy. Inflation-control policies, under present interpretations, require that somebody who has a job must lose it, and that somebody who wants one must go unemployed even longer.

Obviously, when people must lose jobs, those most recently hired are the most likely to be dropped.[11] To the degree that black workers were those most recently hired, they are also those who must first pay the price of reducing inflation. And they will also be unemployed the longest, either because their lack of seniority will put them toward the back of the line when workers are recalled or because they will be among those last hired on the new cycle when investors regain confidence that an expansion is taking place and new workers are needed.

But we should note that it is not simply a matter of inflation (and high employment) favoring blacks, relatively speaking, or of disinflation (and lower employment) impeding blacks. It is that within present suppositions about policy, blacks get cut *in either case*.

If, for the economy as a whole, greater weight is given to price stability, the consequence in the form of unemployment is concentrated in the nonwhite sector. If higher employment levels are chosen, the costs must be paid by those groups which cannot adjust to inflation—possibly including the nonwhite sector of the labor force. (Wolf and McEnally, 1970)

Although Wolf and McEnally nowhere use the *phrase* "institutional racism," they have here provided a clear *description* of the phenomenon. They show that the usual economic policy choices assume—explicitly or implicitly—that it is less undesirable for blacks to carry the severest burdens than for anyone else. As national policy, this choice is unintelligent because it violates the essentials of peacemaking. It demonstrates to blacks that, no matter what words policymakers use, blacks are "worth less," not only in the estimates of private decision makers but in the calculations of major public decision makers as well. So long as the black population was politically inert, it was not pragmatically necessary to consider the implications of such a policy. But if, as I have argued above, black politics is now a highly energized and volatile process, the policy is no longer supportable.

Moreover, one would argue, the policies most often advocated—as a partial response to that new energy and volatility—are (though useful in themselves) secondary to the main purpose. I refer particularly to welfare (public assistance) programs (and in a lesser degree to manpower training programs). Welfare (public assistance) reform is much more fashionable, whether in the formats proposed by the Nixon administration, the Congressional Democrats, or the Welfare Rights Organization. In addition to welfare reform, manpower training has its day. It is not necessary here to praise or to condemn any of these approaches. All may have their merits. But the central point is that none of them can serve the decisive role needed in setting income parity objectives, without an attack on the unemployment problem.

As important as manpower training programs may be, they can neither provide the sufficiency of jobs nor be operative quickly enough to make the required impact. As important as welfare (public assistance) reform may be, it cannot do the main task either, for there are too many black poor people, the cost therefore too high to make a policy of income parity through such subsidy measures acceptable to a sufficient number of whites (or black employed, for that matter). In this political context, the political necessity demands a major effort to dry up the reservoir composed of those who are forced by the normal circumstances of the economy to become more or less casual laborers. What is required from government and economic analysts is a precise conception how this might be done—presumably not excluding the favored conceptions of public spending, human capital development, and increasing the rate of private expansion.

Job discrimination demands correction if income parity is an objective. Ending it calls for a new effort (past efforts having never been so seriously pursued as they might have been) to carry the doctrine of equal employment opportunity to the extent of permitting the Peter Principle to apply to blacks as well as to whites.

Obviously, discrimination is less intense than it used to be. But it remains pervasive; no sophisticated analysis is necessary to show its pervasiveness. The "eyeball-inspection" method will show that black persons should have infinitely greater access than they do have to the same occupational lines and pay levels that are open, with little question, to whites of comparable skill. I may illustrate the problem by a simple sort of example: the diverse jobs to be found in airline terminals. On one recent trip, I went from Detroit to Louisville to Nashville. Each of these cities has a large black population. But among them the visible presence of black insurance agents, travel agents, lunch-counter personnel, baggage personnel, or airplane maintenance personnel was quite different. Black people in these various jobs were most visible in Detroit, but it is hardly to be believed that this difference means black Detroiters have fewer superior job options than their counterparts in Louisville and Nashville. The likelihood is greater that the personnel managers in Louisville and Nashville have yet to learn to treat "equal employment opportunity" even as seriously as personnel managers do in Detroit.

The eyeball-inspection method need not involve comparing cities. On a similar visit to Atlanta (in June of 1969), I walked down a line of airline ticket agents and counted thirty-six persons, including two or three who appeared to have managerial responsibility and one wearing a porter's cap. Only the man in the porter's cap was black, but it is doubtful that a random selection of Atlantans in the twenty-to-thirty-year age bracket would have produced the same result. Neither is it to be believed that, in a major midwestern university in a city with more than 600,000 blacks, one would randomly fill a typing pool with fifty or sixty girls—and hardly a black young lady in sight.

What is the problem? Is it that to hire blacks one would "relax standards"? Possibly. But the more likely point is that relatively few employment institutions—public or private—actually make a serious effort to hire the available blacks who meet whatever the existing standard is. Instead, what exists (in all the rhetoric about "qualified Negroes") is a search for blacks of competence superior to that of their white counterparts, and when such blacks are not available, the employer then hires the white person who is mediocre in preference to the black who meets the standard.

Neither a policy of drying up the casual laborer reservoir, nor a policy of equal employment opportunity, is *by itself* adequate. But taken together and pushed with a major effort, they might logically go far toward achieving the objective of income parity.

CAPITAL DEVELOPMENT

Economic integration also calls for another major policy effort to achieve a quantum change in the character of black entrepreneurship. Black *participation in the capital structure of the nation* must be enhanced, if the objective of equal participation is to be taken at all seriously. Accordingly, it is insufficient to propose merely that business should become interested in applying its techniques to solving social problems, and at a profit to itself. Obviously, it is intelligent and proper for business to seek a profit, profit being largely what business is about. However, it would be entirely possible for business to provide desired services without making any noticeable contribution to the capital wealth of the urban black community itself. The housing case is an easy demonstration. The stock of housing obviously needs improving. If "Operation Breakthrough"—HUD's effort to encourage use of present technology for mass-produced housing—had proved successful, it would then have been possible to replenish the urban ghetto housing stock much more rapidly. Yet cheap and easy housing, yielding a profit to the housing manufacturer, would not have inherently improved the capital situation of the people who lived in the houses, any more than cheap cars improve the capital situation of the people who ride in the cars.

Indeed, it would be quite possible to develop a set of private interests adverse to the growth of the stock of capital in the ghettoes. Accordingly, it follows that one important measure—not the less important for having been advocated without much success over seventy years—is a massive change in the scale and character of black entrepreneurship.[12] The reason this measure appears natural is simply that insofar as there are economic activities to be conducted in the ghettoes, the black entrepreneurs already are there. Their major difficulty is that their business is really close to a form of peasant proprietorship: short of capital, destined to charge prices too high if they are merely to survive, lacking informational resources about the larger economy. Moreover, so long as the black businessman is destined to operate exclusively (or almost exclusively) in the segregated market, his own options must be so limited that they handicap him. Consequently, it is particularly important that he should be able to break out of the ghetto and operate in the larger economy. In fact, this process has already begun, as is evidenced by the enterprises of Leon Sullivan in defense contracting and by the emergence of new management consultants whose entree to industry is their expertise in race relations.[13]

However, the process will inevitably be slow unless major business institutions and governmental institutions adopt a calculated policy of expediting large-scale expansion. Present policies hamper it. As one illustration of the difficulty, a man with government experience got a small contract ($190,000) to evaluate certain manpower training programs, but had so much difficulty getting a bank loan to cover his startup costs that he did the job on a shoestring. The would-be borrower attributed his difficulty to two factors: that he had a "software" contract and that he was black. Another such man had similar difficulty, even to the extent of having a banker call the government agency to see if he had stolen the contract (Friedman, 1970, 52). It would be possible, if one put oneself in the bankers' shoes, to imagine nonracist explanations. If banks are doubtful about financing software contractors—and the article indicates that much larger white firms also have some difficulty—much of the decision would be nonracial. Moreover, if the loan seeker happened to deal with a security-conscious loan officer (as might well be in these days of large-scale stock and paper thefts), the call to the government agency might have been explained otherwise. But it is just as plausible to argue that racism was operative.[14]

Whichever explanation one prefers, the banks with which these men dealt had assuredly not learned to deal with novel situations involving potential black business borrowers. The first point, then, is that if corporate enterprise takes the racial situation seriously, it does have to cultivate a capacity for dealing with novelty which is not part of its ordinary experience.[15] More fundamental, however, is the need for a policy which encourages relationships between existing business institutions and emergent black entrepreneurs. For much that is needed will be possible only if external alliances can be developed. And there are numerous sorts of possible relationships with black economic planning organizations of the sort proposed in Essay X.

However, the most important changes in the entrepreneurial pattern will not come without a very active governmental role. One possible role is governmental encouragement of corporate activity. This has many versions, one of the more prominent of which is the tax-credit idea proposed by some members of Congress, and by the the Kerner Commission (on the recommendation of its Private Enterprise Task Force).[16] The basic idea is that the principle of the 7 percent tax credit for new plant (adopted by the Kennedy administration) should be increased and substantially extended to investments in real property and plant in poor areas and that provision should be made for rapid amortization down to as little as five years. Whether the tax-credit approach is sound has been open to challenge, but there is a basic point to be made on the assumption that it is sound. Any such public policy decision should be geared to requirements for local participation. If, for example, the federal government is going to encourage large-scale corporations to set up subsidiaries in territorial ghettoes, it might also require provision for accrual of equity rights to investors living within such ghettoes, possibly even for such holders of equity to come to majority control of the subsidiary corporations.

A more direct approach, however, would be through the creation of a Bank for Urban Development. The Farm Credit System might provide a crude model, appropriately adapted to present conditions.[17] The Farm Credit System consists of thirty-seven (37) farmer-owned banks and 1,100 farmer-owned local associations.[18] At the apex stands the Farm Credit Administration, an independent agency within the executive branch.[19] This system encompasses real estate loans on farms through the federal land banks, agricultural loans and discount facilities for the production-credit associations, and credit for farmer cooperatives. During the fiscal year 1969, farmers and farmer cooperatives borrowed more than $10.7 billion from the Farm Credit System. Not only does this System provide more than 20 percent of all credit used by farmers and farmer cooperatives, but the system exerts a wider influence because other lenders tend to adjust their terms to those used by the System. The System is now farmer-owned, but it was developed through government investment and only as of 1969 was that investment fully retired by farmer payments. In other words, from 1916 until 1969, the United States Government itself built up this System—which farmers now more or less control[20]—by putting in the essential risk capital and by providing many of the equally essential management skills.[21]

The central thread, in any case, is not the particular device mentioned, but the urgent need for action calculated to start a new process between now and 1976. Since economic relationships provide ample warrant for treating seriously the "two-nations" formulation, it is reasonable to adopt serious measures for economic improvement, to make sure that those measures are perceived by the putative beneficiaries as so intended, and to make sure that they are sustained until some form of takeoff occurs. The argument merely is, therefore, that rapid economic adjustments depend on the application of historic governmental practice to the special economic circumstances of the black "nation." The desired results will obviously not be accomplished all at once. Nothing important is. But there is a critical turnaround time, a period both of risk and of opportunity, which lies within the next five years.[22]

NOTES

1. Wood (1961), 2. I do not know what dictionary Wood was using, but the one at my desk while this sentence is being typed defines "political economy" as "economics." However, I find Wood's usage much more compatible with my purpose.

2. It may seem strange to move into this from a discussion of deference and esteem, but the point is fundamental. Money is important, not merely for what it will buy at the store, but because the amount of money available to X is likely to be interpreted by X (and Y and Z too) as a partial indicator of the social esteem and deference which he receives or does not receive.

3. Four useful, though dissimilar, contributions which have come to hand since this draft was initially written may be worth the readers's attention: Bell (1970), Downs (1970), Levitan *et al.* (1970), and Tabb (1970).

4. Of the books cited in the preceding footnote, I find Bell the most helpful on the broader problems as well. For a more explicit treatment of the broader problems, also see Wolf and McEnally (1970).

5. Thus, I disagree with the "reparations" idea as put forth by James Forman and others in 1969. The Black Manifesto issued at that time led to a demand that certain private institutions (church groups with large endowments were the main target) should pay compensation of $500,000,000 to provide the basis for autonomous black economic development. The Manifesto language implied that individual persons ought to accept its recommendations or demands, as an admission of personal guilt. While it was fair—if ironic—that such a demand should be focused upon institutions which professed other worldly values (for example the Episcopal Church) but which subsisted off portfolios of stock in quite this-worldly institutions (Chase Manhattan, General Motors, as examples), it did not in fact provide a reasonable basis for action. Two main criticisms might be offered. (a) The first is that the black role in the development of the United States has been too critical to be marked "paid for" with a specific settlement *less than one year's welfare budget in the state of New York!* (b) The second is that, while it is quite reasonable for any white institution to provide money to any black institution it wants to, that transaction could only be a transfer between private parties. *There is no rational or authoritative basis on which such private transfers could constitute a valid and legitimate social settlement.*

6. Senator Marchi, a New York State senator from Staten Island, was the Conservative party candidate in the New York mayoralty election of 1969.

7. In this section, I have relied a good deal on Polakoff (1969), Chapter 11. For a general introduction to the government role in the economy, see James E. Anderson (1966).

8. This should be read, as should the ensuing pages, in light of the earlier discussion. Also see the three concluding essays in *The Politics of the Black "Nation."*

9. This is one point at which analysis must compromise with a certain sort of political reality. The well being of the United States would be served if we could achieve a substantial political program for income *redistribution,* between the very rich and the people at or beneath the median United States income. This would call for a major modification of taxation policy and probably of antitrust policy, which is simply not in the cards at all. Anything more than a modest redistribution is a political pipedream, beyond virtually all other pipedreams in United States society. *Not even "the poor" will support this!* The experience since the adoption of the federal income tax in 1913 should be conclusive on that point. And if the New Deal, which had a much bigger coalition of the poor behind it than any administration is now likely to have, did not tackle the redistribution problem in the way desired by Michael Harrington, Herbert Gans, and others, the likelihood that anyone else will do so is much smaller.

10. A. C. Pigou, author if the influential book, *The Economics of Welfare,* has been quoted as giving the label " 'the intractable million' [to] the hard core of 10 percent of the working population which remained out of work during the inter-war years." (Blake, 1970, 219).

11. The problems of the professionals in the 1970 recession is a special case.

12. See the discussion of Booker T. Washington in Essay II of *The Politics of the Black "Nation":* "Clientage, Opposition, and Withdrawal."

13. In the normal course of events, it is to be predicted, these management-consultant firms will expand to other aspects of the consulting business and will spin off people who go directly into general management. On the race relations consultants, see Friedman (1970). On the expansion of *black enterprises* in the general economy, also see the new publication, *Black Enterprise.*

14. Since both banks were in Washington, D.C., it is not absurd to attribute racism, for it is reasonable to guess that bank loan officers are probably good representatives of the Washington metropolitan area middle class which—when not in the government—has little obvious inclination to adopt new styles in race relations.

15. It is not to be expected that this will be easy. Here one should take account of the rather limited world view of the managerial types.

16. The task force chairman was Charles B. Thornton (Litton Industries) and the other members were executives of North American Rockwell, General Mills, the Bank of America, and the National Industrial Conference Board, along with a tax-law professor from the University of California.

17. For a general introduction, see Cochrane (1966) and Talbot and Hadwiger (1968).

18. In this section, I have been greatly assisted by Mr. Nicholas J. Peroff.

19. Twelve federal land banks (and the related federal land bank associations which number about 650); thirteen banks for cooperatives; twelve federal inter-mediate credit banks; and 450 production credit associations which are financed through the intermediate credit banks and the banks for cooperatives.

20. The Farm Credit Board, which is the policymaking agency in the Farm Credit System, consists of thirteen members appointed by the president, subject to senatorial confirmation. The governor of the Farm Credit Administration is also a presidential appointee, subject to senatorial confirmation.

21. Even now, the Farm Credit Administration provides for the member banks and associations such facilities and services as credit analysis, development of land appraisal standards and policies, preparation and distribution of information on farm credit, preparation of budgets and reports, assistance in financing and invest-ments, and custody of collateral for bonds and debentures.

22. My argument for this particular time horizon is offered in *The Politics of the Black "Nation,"* Essay IV, "Toward a Black Regrouping."

XI

Some Possible Measures
toward Social Peace:
II. Short-Term Threat Reduction

DEFERENCE, THREAT, AND THE NEED FOR AN ARMS-FREE SOCIETY

Economic measures are important to social peace. For men are obviously likely to be in conflict if over prolonged time they see themselves persistently poorer than other men—without what they believe "rational" justification. They fight not only from hunger but from the sense of disesteem which being paid less than other people get imposes. Material and psychic privations are not the only elements. Another important element is fear and insecurity. The deference problem is thus intimately connected with physical threat. For when a man reasonably believes that he comes low on the public scale of deference he must realistically doubt that the public authorities will extend as much effort to protect him as they will extend to protect other people. This sense of threat is also a critical part of the republican crisis.

It is possible for the United States to experience many forms of social disruption and yet survive with its basic political system intact. But the chances for that survival are greatly reduced by any continued movement of an already incipient pattern: blacks and whites threatening each other with force. To permit the escalation of that incipient pattern is to court the travail of internal war. When parties have so high a level of mutual distrust, it is of very little immediate use advising them to change their fundamental and long-term attitudes. There are too many *complicated* aspects having to do with the reducing of the actual conflicts of interest and perception from which highly factional disputes emerge. The short-run necessity is to reduce the sense of threat which people convey to each other. The purpose of threat reduction is to create an environment in which conflicting parties may have the option to adjust to new states of fact which, in turn, may modify attitudes.

Therefore, a first-step truce would be a reinterpretation of the present national passion for "law and order." The intermediate objective should be to show every realistic sign that the public policy is to afford physical security to all persons—*specifically, clearly, and crucially black persons no less than white persons.* This point is so simple that it might be regarded as trite. Yet it is so obviously at variance with public policy as administered that it could hardly be more important. The white fears of black violence are so well advertised that it is hardly necessary to say more—despite the fact that remarkably little black violence has been visited upon white persons. But what is seldom understood, particularly by whites most committed to the maintenance of the regime, is the realistic basis for comparable black fears—black fears of white violence.

The minimum requirement of a "truce" is that each side must be able realistically to perceive that a knockout blow—a first strike—by the other is improbable, not because the other may not desire it, but because the other has not the capability to achieve it. Each side must be able *to feel safe,* despite its distrust of the other side's motives. *That feeling must be realistic!* Hence, the purpose of policy—in the current realities of politics in the United States—is to provide both black and white with reciprocal clarity that neither would have the capacity to assault the other en masse.

This policy implies a program of domestic arms control and disarmament, looking toward the policy objective of an arms-free society.

Domestic disarmament will not work unless people have confidence that they will not suffer by cooperating. In this process a clear and visible fairness in the application of the arms-control and disarmament process is essential if people are to have confidence in it. Since it is evident, from demonstrable experience, that law-enforcement systems offer better protection to whites than to blacks, a significant amount of white disarmament prior to black disarmament would be essential from the black point of view and not irrational from the white point of view. The reason is that blacks would be in no position to move upon whites (a) because the police and other enforcement agencies would in any event prevent their doing so, and (b) because public opinion would be particularly hostile if blacks were to move on whites while an arms-control mechanism was being put into effect. If blacks should see a visible measure of white disarmament and arms control, then black participation would be both desirable and relatively easy to achieve, which in turn would enhance white confidence, thus enhancing black confidence further. If this confidence could be achieved, then any future racial disorders could be subject to more flexible controls, the provocations of meaningless slaughter could be reduced, and those prepared to use the policy threat as an occasion for provocation could be deprived of credibility with their audiences. Thus, a first consideration should be given to controls over the use of present arms.

CONTROLLING THE USE OF PRESENT ARMS

Some people are very emotional about their right to keep guns. Moreover, the fact is that some actually need guns, at least if one accepts hunting or the protection of one's store (say) as legitimate activities. But most of the people who own the 25 million handguns or the 65 million long guns do not, in fact, need such weapons. Rather, they keep them out of fear (and sometimes do themselves more harm than they do to anyone else with these weapons which they are incompetent to handle)[1] and they probably would be happier if they could be reasonably assured that they would not suffer without them.

However, to think practically about these matters requires a focus on those small, but important, groups which are convinced that they do need weapons. Two of these groups, police officers and street commandoes, tend to interact with each other, creating an atmosphere of hostility which then absorbs the attention and energy of many other people. The measures required to offer an assurance to these two sets are also measures which ought to have a much wider beneficent effect (Lough, 1969). The basic requirement is to make it extremely painful and expensive for any private person to shoot (or shoot at) any other person—whether the other person should be in a private or an official capacity—for any reason. Just as the law distinguishes between killing which is premeditated and killing which is spontaneous, just as the law distinguishes between assault with one's fists and assault with a deadly weapon, so it ought also to distinguish between categories of weapons. Unless we are prepared to say altogether that penalties have *no effect,* we ought instead impose the severest possible penalties upon private persons at any time inflicting death or injury on other persons with any firearm or other projectile instrument.[2]

The formulation of legal penalties in these terms would obviously benefit private parties, if such penalties could be made operative in a practical sense.[3] The concept here is meant to benefit a specific and well-defined group: the police. The reason is that the police are the one social group who have some legitimate claim to be armed and who are exposed to danger. But, as I shall shortly note, reduction of their armament is also essential. However, it is neither reasonable nor practical to expect much success in this area, unless as a matter of social policy we impose severe sanctions upon those who visit physical harm upon policemen, so long as policemen are doing their duty in conformity with the requirements of legality and ordinary tests of decency. If social policy does define the physical person of the police officer as beyond violation, and does implement the sanctions appropriate to such violation, then it is possible to deal with the next key problem: reestablishment (or establishment for the first time!) of conditions under which people will have a reasonable degree of confidence in the policeman's own adherence to legality and ordinary tests of decency.

Establishing these conditions requires modernization of police ideology, police organizational practice, and police relationships to political authorities. The imposition of new restrictions upon private use of arms must also be calibrated to new restrictions on the use of official firearms by the police. The reason is that restriction on private use is not going to be credible unless those people can be reassured who, with no criminal intent, nonetheless fear police. Such new policies governing the use of firearms are essential in an era when unwise exercise of police discretion in the use of firearms may have domestic consequences that are catastrophic. The new policies are needed not because policemen are malevolent "pigs" but because the policeman—as a human being—will suffer the stresses and tensions of other people. The consequence is that he should be protected from, and relieved of, those as much as possible.

POLICE PRACTICES IN THE USE OF FIREARMS

There will, of course, be many situations where firearms must be used. Those situations call for a new approach to police training and police competence. In training, the present "shoot-to-kill" ideology must be replaced with a "life-saving-and-damage-reducing" ideology. Even in criminal matters the fleeing suspect is likely to be another human and citizen—not "the enemy." Yet the police officer is asked to carry the burden of deciding whether to kill the suspect or not (and the burden of deciding how to use weapons under tense crowd situations).

A life-saving and damage-reducing policy would imply, however, that policemen should be aiming their fire at extremities rather than at the center of the body. This would mean, particularly, at the legs. Such a policy may well require a vast improvement in technical competence with arms. In a sense, the modern policemen must become a good enough marksman that he may shoot swiftly and accurately at very small and mobile targets. If it should be technologically feasible, the police might be equipped with some sort of tranquilizer projectile for dangerous or deranged persons, and police thus armed given further instructions to withdraw and call for a special tactical squad armed with lethal weapons if such a person were himself or herself armed.

ADMINISTRATIVE CONTROLS ON THE USE OF FIREARMS

Basic modifications in administrative control are also pertinent. For example, the acknowledged strain on the individual officer might be reduced by vacating the characteristic policy of permitting or requiring off-duty officers to carry weapons. Instead, off-duty officers should be obliged to check their weapons into an armory room (as is done in the Army) when going off-duty. It is no longer necessary or profitable to operate on the supposition that the officer might have to use his weapon, even when off duty, so frequently as to require the off-duty possession of a weapon. Decisions about police use of firearms should be advanced to the highest administrative level possible, at least to the senior officer on the scene. In "ordinary" cases, firearms should be used only for the *emergency defense* of the officer. It is grossly unfair to policemen, so many of whom are very *young* men, to ask them to decide alone who should be killed and who should not. Above all, "riot" situations should—in the manner of presidential control in the military—be under the direct control of the civilian political authorities, and not delegated to lower levels. It seems appropriate to assert, for the first time in urban history, the principle of civil political control over domestic coercion, much as we have also asserted the principle of civil political control over military action.

India, a very diverse and large country—with more than twice our population and with many riots—has a procedure which might well be adopted and extended in our practice. When weapons are used, the Indians sometimes follow up with a special inquiry into the circumstances (Khera, 1964, 132). This special inquiry is apparently not mandatory in India, but under the circumstances of the United States, it probably should be mandatory. The purpose of such an inquiry would include fixing blame (and praise!), but it should not be so limited as that. Its purpose really should be to raise to clear public view—and to the view of administrators and legislators—factors and processes which work against the public peace. Moreover, the presumption of stigma upon the particular officer might be removed if the inquiry were automatic, much as inquiry is automatic following an air crash—a search for explanations.

Such an inquiry could well be created whenever any person (or persons) should be killed by the police, die in police custody, or die within some specifiable time (say, a week) after having been in an encounter with the police. But such an inquiry should also be alert to the special problems of police work, and should be convoked on any occasion when a policeman might be killed. In order to facilitate serious examination of the issues —rather than to permit the development of routinized whitewash investigations—the dead person and/or his (her) heirs should be represented by a member of the Bar on automatic assignment. If the idea of automatic assignment is to be taken seriously, the Bar itself will have to be associated in such a way that counsel in these cases should be drawn from the most prestigious, experienced, and competent personnel available.

Since there is already a visible interest in the "ombudsman" function in the United States, it might be associated with this form of inquiry in order to bring the ombudsman function into the most serious public problems, rather than having it develop as a means of dealing with mere minor social hangnails. But there are other possibilities. The automatic inquiry might be associated with the United States Civil Rights Commission, with the Community Relations Service, or with comparable state-local bodies, or with a corps of special examiners comparable to those which already operate in the various federal regulation agencies. Or it might even be possible to use judges on special assignment for the conduct of such inquiries if such judges and the public would distinguish the *inquiry* from a *trial*.

Another administrative arrangement might be a system of citizen-observers, particularly *but not exclusively* from the black communities who might be stationed in departments, much as students on fellowships might be, with freedom to move around, to talk to people, to learn by observation how decisions are made. Undoubtedly this plan would present certain administrative problems, but such problems should not be insoluble. It might even make sense, if one wants to enhance communication, to go to some length to open such citizen observership to active persons whose normal disposition would be to distrust official authority. Just as it takes the conservative to authenticate change, so it takes the more radical to authenticate authority. This approach would be particularly relevant if one could develop panels of such persons who might, for limited periods, have the legal right to walk into any police precinct, at any hour of the day or night, and ask to be shown any part of the operation whatsoever.[4] This specific proposal has at least two advantages. (1) It would provide a high degree of uncertainty, on the part of officers disinclined to act circumspectly, because they could never tell when they might be observed by someone having access to authentic information and having a capacity to issue a report. In this respect the proposal is an improvement over the review board concept. (2) Because the proposal involves frequent turnover of citizen-observers, it would have the effect of limiting the extent to which any particular outside observers would be psychologically co-opted by the police system.

The control of official use of firearms also lends itself to other administrative decisions, one of which is the allocation of personnel in such a way that they have an incentive toward self-restraint. Thus, it is essential to increase the proportion of black patrolmen, so that it matches the proportion of blacks in the city, *but not for use in black areas.* On the contrary! As far as possible, black patrolmen should be assigned to predominantly white areas, and white patrolmen to predominantly black areas.

The theory of deterrence may, thus, reasonably be applied to the policeman's control of his own behavior, in the expectation that some other policeman will similarly adapt. If this process worked at all well, policemen would learn a considerable restraint in the use of their weapons, and it would soon become apparent to most policemen that in the ordinary course of work they would have no *need* (other than psychological) for their weapons.

PUBLIC RESPONSIBILITY FOR POLICE FIREARMS POLICIES

In addition, it would make sense to seek an increase in public responsibility for firearms policies. Such policies presently are based upon little more than intuition, with little consideration of the ends to be achieved or of operational necessities. By operational necessities, I mean the degree of threat which policemen do experience. Little actual consideration is given to this. There is no doubt that policemen consider their work very dangerous, and there is no doubt that it is dangerous. But it is not established that the degree of danger demands the degree of discretion in the use of firearms upon which police doctrine presently insists. How can this adjustment be improved? Partly by a kind of technical-cum-political review of what actual practices are, and what social objectives those practices are meant to achieve.

For example, police department might well emulate *other governmental agencies* in coopting the private citizens' advisory committee or task force, the purpose of which is to review a policy and to consider the technical means of serving the policy ends (Boyer, 1964, 31–35). This method is extremely common in such matters as municipal tax policies and health policies, and might well be adapted to law enforcement. For instance, it would be most useful to have such an advisory committee review the extent to which (a) policemen are actually threatened in the performance of duty—for it is doubtful if most such threats presently are reported, (b) policemen actually are obliged as they see it to draw their weapons, (c) policemen actually fire their weapons, and (d) policemen actually injure or kill other people in the line of duty. Such knowledge would establish a much better basis for consensus about policy, and might more adequately form the basis for legislative action.

Since policemen are very sensitive about their "status," "respect," and "professional" perquisites, it is too much to expect that they will welcome such innovation. Policemen are likely to resent the demand that they show their *bona fides*. This is a very human resentment. After all, no occupational group easily accepts the idea of external regulation or inquiry—as the public experience with lawyers, physicians or—surely!—university professors must indicates. Moreover, one might hope that, in due course, the police would themselves come to see how such an institutionalized procedure would actually work to their advantage. Yet they must acquire the maturity to know that being like Caesar's wife *is* a necessary condition of public life.

CONTROLLING THE AVAILABILITY OF ARMS

As is well known, the problem of gun control involves some very complex constitutional issues. But, in the context developed, the matter deserves much closer attention. It simply cannot be maintained, as a matter of common sense, that "the right to keep and bear arms" should be subject to no limitation. That right, presumably, is no more valid than the crucial right to private property, yet there is no general agreement that the right to private property means that one is entitled to hold that property in the form of gold. On the contrary, the right to hold private supplies of gold has long since been reduced (except in certain marginal cases—jewelry and the like) in the interest of national economic policy. Similarly, the right to free speech clearly does not mean the right of a ham radio operator to use the airways without limitation, but rather that he may use the airways under certain well-defined conditions.

Even more important than the strictly constitutional questions are the political questions. As the constitutional complexity is widely advertised, so the potency of the highly organized gun lobbies is well advertised. As far as I know, the extent to which these lobbies have real support in the wider population is uncertain. But one study, by a young political scientist at Pittsburgh, Michael Margolis, is at least suggestive. Margolis compared gun owners, people who lived in gun-owning households but who were not themselves gun owners, and people who lived in nongun households and were not gun owners. As might have been predicted, gun owners were less favorable to various controls than were nonowners.

Considering the furor made by antigun control organizations whenever new regulations are proposed , the level of support for specific new gun control regulations *among gun owners* is surprisingly high. Nearly two-thirds of the gun owners favor testing hunters before issuing licenses, 56 percent favor a 48-hour "cooling off" period between purchase and delivery of a rifle or shotgun, and 50 percent favor registration of handguns. A majority of both groups of nonowners favor each of these proposed regulations. (Margolis, n.d., 13)

If Margolis's Pittsburgh survey is at all representative, then, we can be sure that there is at least no passionate attachment to unfettered gun freedom. What is more to the point is that most people simply do not have an intense interest in the matter, even if they themselves have guns. Margolis buttresses this by analysis which indicates that at the minimum, Senator Joseph S. Clark's strong gun-control position—for which he was vigorously attacked by sportsman's groups—probably lost him no votes in Pittsburgh. (His opponent was thought to be against gun control.)

To begin with, only 35 percent of the voters claimed to know either candidate's position. Of these fewer than half attributed "a great deal" or "some" influence to these positions in making their voting choice. Those attributing such influence split two to one favoring Clark's position over [his opponent's]. The data imply, therefore, that if anything, Clark's position on gun control helped rather than hindered him in Pittsburgh. (Margolis, n.d.)

A lone survey from a lone city is obviously not conclusive, and many questions are unanswered even within the limits of Margolis's analysis. Nonetheless, the implication might well be that achieving gun control is not impossible, and that the reason the gun lobbies have been so successful thus far is that no one else has perceived opportunity and incentive to create a viable counter lobby.

If one is to consider limitations on the holding of private weapons, it is also essential to consider the administrative practicality of various limitations. On the face of it, one might argue that no gun legislation now could be effective because it requires widespread compliance, and so many people already possess private weapons that no restriction could be made very workable. Milton Eisenhower's estimate that there are about 90 million private weapons in the United States points up the problem. This suggests that just about every other person owns some form of firearm. However, the implication that popular support for keeping private firearms is so widespread in the population may be much less valid than we have believed in the light of such figures and the vigor of the gun lobby. The private keepers of firearms can be divided into two main categories: those who have arms for *legitimate* purposes and those who have them for *strongly doubtful or clearly illegitimate purposes.*

I have seen no studies of what gun holders *do* with their weapons, but the guess on which I would bet is that a substantial number of the weapons are held by private persons who do not use them or carry them, except on very rare occasions. A personal illustration may make the point. Until I was 13, my parents farmed in the South and my father owned a shotgun which I can remember his firing once: to kill a hawk threatening the chickens. My grandfather also owned a shotgun, which I can remember having seen fired once: to kill a snake. After the family moved North, neither my father nor my grandfather ever owned a weapon at all, and the only uncle whom I can remember with a weapon owned a .38, which he used to fire into the air on New Year's Eve. In my guess, I am speculating that a very large number of individuals are similar. They have weapons to which they have no great attachment, and would not be particularly disturbed if those weapons were surrendered. They keep weapons, do not carry them, and, frequently enough, could not find them on the spur of the moment were a robber coming through the window. They are not antigun; they just are not much interested.

A second category of legitimate weapon holders are those people who do have reason to keep weapons immediately available, or even to carry them: merchants, rent collectors, sometimes even politicians.[5] A third category are people whose weapons are immediately available, though they do not commonly carry them, and are brought out for frequent or regular use. Hunters probably account for more of this category than any other. It is very likely that some people in the second category and most people in the third would have very strong attachments to their weapons.

The weapons held by legitimate owners are important for administrative reasons. There is no way to impose a control on the whole weapon-supply system unless one can be sure that weapons will not move out of one set of hands into less legitimate sets of hands. Moreover, insofar as racial disturbance is concerned, some part of the problem is to keep very ordinary people—who would usually be very law abiding—from digging out their dusty weapons and using them in highly tense situations. Consequently, the practical problem is twofold: (a) to create a climate of opinion in which most of the legitimate gun holders would understand why their holding weapons works against public order; and (b) to create sufficient assurances and incentives that they will not mind ceasing to hold such weapons. There are several possibilities which merit considerations.

There would be merit to a sustained program of voluntary and symbolic agitation against the private possession of guns. Imagine the public-relations effect if every member of Congress, the big city councils, or the state legislatures who holds a private pistol were—on an announced day—to surrender that weapon to the authorities in full view of television! The reasonableness of such a gesture would be clearer if people understood how much accidental harm is caused by people like themselves, with no malice intended, and communicating that fact is one important problem. Another important problem is the improvement of the technical quality of law enforcement. Those people who do not use their weapons, and might even have to hunt around the house for them, may have some residual image of the gun as a protection piece, "just in case." The "just in case" will almost certainly refer to some unusual criminal threat, and the problem of law enforcement is to do its job well enough that people can perceive that public action as more effective than self-help. It would even be reasonable to consider monetary incentives, such as a massive public purchase program, to persuade people who haven't touched the weapon in years to give it up altogether.

From such a combination of symbolic and pragmatic measures, public policy might also move to a program of storing the sorts of weapons for which people have a legitimate use other than self-protection, such as hunting rifles. As a simple measure, the federal building (or local post office) in each city might be designated as a storage area for private weapons, in which individuals might deposit their weapons (as they deposit papers in bank storage vault or as soldiers keep their assigned weapons in arms rooms except when on duty). Hunters might withdraw these weapons if they wished to go hunting. This should be no more unworkable than the Friday afternoon trip to the bank for weekend travel cash. In tense situations, the fact that everyone wanted to go hunting would provide signals for law enforcement officers and appropriate controls could rapidly be imposed or forces mobilized.

State and local governments have a very important role, insofar as privately held weapons are subject to licensing. If a license is a privilege, rather than an absolute right, then all licenses might be revoked and criteria for new licenses made clearer and more precise. This seems reasonable, for if one does not have an absolute right to drive a car or to operate a food-dispensing service as a means of earning a living, then one surely cannot have an absolute right to the gun license. Obviously, the nonlegitimate gun holders will, if sufficiently motivated, find means to evade the licensing requirement. But that is precisely the point. Public policy might be made much more stringent about the treatment of unlicensed gun holders or gun users on each occasion when such a discovery is made. Just as it would make sense to impose sharper penalties for gun killing (contrasted to similar killing without guns), so it would make sense to impose sharper penalties for mere possession of unlicensed weapons.

It makes some sense to try to estimate who the nonlegitimate gun holders and gun users will be. In all likelihood, they will be of two sorts. First, there are those engaged in ordinary crime (robbery, extortion, and the like), for whom the gun is a rational instrument. These will include both the individualistic criminal entrepreneur—the robber who as "the small businessman of crime" holds up stores—and organized criminal enterprises which are supported by a systematic kind of private military force. Second, there are those who expect to practice, or do practice, some form of gun politics in the overt public sense.[6] Under present circumstances, most people will immediately think of the Black Panther party or some of the white New Left groups. There will be a certain relevance there, but the public record indicates that the armory of the Panthers (at any rate) is trivial, compared to the armory of certain private white groups (the so-called Radical Right). To judge from press reports as late as three or four years ago, these groups collected not mere rifles and shotguns (the heaviest weapons reported from any of the many raids policemen have made upon Panther offices) but machine guns, bazookas, grenades, and other surplus Army equipment.

The natural consequence is that federal gun-control legislation ought to be directed, with great precision, against possession of such military weapons. Hunting is a legitimate enough activity, and it is to be expected that practical problems will arise when people with nonlegitimate purposes hold rifles, claiming that they only mean to hunt with them. But there is no justification for a civilian holding grenades or machine guns, and the same principle which justifies antibombing legislation also justifies a serious administrative effort to detect and disarm such groups and to shut off the flow of weapons to them. Doing this ought not to be be too difficult, if police organizations are in fact skillful, for the potential sources of supply —though numerous—can be identified with reasonable ease by those who specialize in the study of this matter (which is what police presumably do).

Therefore, the broad pattern of federal legislation would call for some combination of the following elements: (a) a complete registration of all weapons, in order to separate legitimate from nonlegitimate holders; (b) severe penalties for nonregistration; (c) use of the registration in the manner of the gambling stamp law, whenever a private weapon should be discovered in an illicit use, in order to identify the holder more precisely; and (d) the imposition of really severe taxation upon new gun purchases to discourage casual acquisition.[7]

Obviously, if those people who choose voluntarily to yield up weapons, or who have weapons only for legitimate use under controlled situations, see that the pattern of law is not being enforced, their own discomfort will rise and the whole process become less workable. The natural consequence of this, therefore, is that both the design of legislation and the practice of administration must be directed toward efficient discovery of violations and severe sanctions against them. Some process of the sort outlined here would make an important contribution toward the creation of an essentially arms-free society, which is its purpose.

CAVEAT

We should merely restate that this proposal is raised in the context of the racial disputation. Internal arms control and disarmament is, for this purpose, of the greatest importance. But its requirements must be understood clearly. It will not contribute to the process of conflict resolution unless it is conducted in a way which realistically assures black men that they will not stand in greater peril under arms control and disarmament then they would stand without it. Domestic arms control and disarmament is only one necessary phase in establishing a social truce and turning that truce into an armistice so that political conflict may remain within nonlethal channels. *It is not by itself to be confused with actual achievement of social peace, but only to be seen as a down payment through the assurance of physical safety.* In time, one could use this process to create a dynamics of mutual relaxation in contrast to a dynamics of mutual alarm.

NOTES

1. It would be useful, for instance, to have a study of the accidental deaths in consequence of people having bought weapons, after the metropolitan arms races began in 1967 and thereafter killed people whom they had no intention of killing.

2. There is a practical problem here because people can substitute one sort of weapon for another.

3. Lasswell and Arens (1961) make the thoroughly valid point that at present the penalty clauses in legislation are "tacked on" with little thought as to their actual effectiveness.

4. For another version of this idea, see the "thirteenth juror" idea in Raab (1967, 251–255).

5. Two or three years ago, the Detroit newspapers ran a list of politicians who had licensed pistols, and one Congressman said "yes," that on his making the rounds he sometimes had to go into some pretty rough places, where one never knew what would happen.

6. I refer here to the use of guns as a means of competing in the ordinary political arena, by those who cannot win under (or will not accept) the ordinary political rules. This distinction is important because, as I have pointed out in *The Politics of the Black "Nation,"* even ordinary robbery is a political act in its effects.

7. The less casual the acquisition, the greater the presumption of some threat in the acquisition.

XII

Some Possible Measures
toward Social Peace:
III. Institutional Modification

PRIVATE PARTIES AND INSTITUTIONS

Both economic adjustments and short-term threat reduction depend, to a very considerable extent, on the actions of official decision makers. However, important contributions are not limited only to "important" people who get their names in the papers. Many activities involving less prominent individuals can be pursued to good effect, when their general result is to enhance blacks' and whites' realistic perception of the complexities of each others' lives. Realistic perception is very important because it often is rational for hostile people, unperceiving, to assume "the worst" rather than "the best" about real or putative adversaries.[1] Moreover, frightened and tense people tend to believe "the worst," even though it may be demonstrably false, particularly if they lack the information or the contacts to assure themselves realistically that it is false. The problem is illustrated by the spasm of fear which a young Catholic seminarian generated in an eastern suburb of Detroit after the 1967 crisis. The seminarian's intention was to show his suburban coreligionists that they had better do "the right thing," and quickly. For, he pointed out, the 1967 crisis had cost lives and damage mostly in black areas, but there were groups of blacks talking about going to the suburbs *next* time, to make sure that some white people also were hurt. (Apparently he even reported that there were people ready to select white children in order to make sure that the white injury would be most painfully felt!) In reality, there were very few blacks saying any such thing, and no evidence that any such language

236

was to be treated as more than empty (though vile) threats, asserted in a vaccuum, by people who had no inclination to take the risks involved.

But the suburban audience had no reality criteria. And the seminarian was an "authority" not merely as a potential priest but as a man who had been "to the ghetto," much as an earlier missionary might have been "to China." Consequently, the audience took him at face value and became very much alarmed and frightened. But they did not become either more responsive or sympathetic. Instead, they began to talk more of arming themselves for self-protection, and now could feel morally justified in being antiblack. They had been threatened by nameless, faceless people with an unjustifiable penalty for a social condition they had not created. It is not at all necessary to misunderstand the reality of conflict of interest, nor to pretend that all difficulties are a function of "misunderstanding." Nor is it necessary to believe that increased clarity about one's adversary will always lead to improved relations. But it is reasonable to believe that social peace will be impeded if most blacks and most whites see each other only through the highly selective processes of gossip, rumor, and the two-minute shot on the six o'clock news.

Consequently, reciprocal contact mechanisms at all levels of society are important in order to give blacks and whites fuller reality criteria by which to appraise each other. The voluntaristic tradition of United States society permits and encourages a wide variety of reciprocal contact mechanisms, and the need now is for adapting those mechanisms so that whites may educate themselves about blacks and blacks about whites to a far more sophisticated extent than they now are. Such important reciprocal contact mechanisms can be developed as an extension and fulfillment of a tradition which itself has come to be held in some disdain—the "Brotherhood Week" tradition—and with good reason. "Brotherhood Week" was usually conceived as a once-a-year affair, calculated to smother rather than to explore differences,[2] and was never designed to resolve the contradiction between "high-toned" rhetoric and the ordinary behavior of the participants. Good reciprocal contacts are most important between the black and white lower-middle-class and middle-class parts of urban society, where such mechanisms have seldom been initiated. It is not nearly so important that whites should "do something for the ghetto." What whites *do* need is a systematic program of intensified contact with black men more or less like themselves in occupation and tastes, even though it is almost certain that the initial meetings will turn out to be "confrontations."

For example, some of the trade unions associated with the Alliance for Labor Action have invested their funds (and some of their staff work) in such projects as unionization of housing authority tenants, sponsoring ghetto-based credit unions, and assisting the development of ghetto medical centers (*Wall Street Journal,* November 17, 1970, 10). These are important contributions. But they will never be the most important contributions to social peace until the unions (a) attack the problem of racism within union politics, and (b) begin to create reciprocal contact mechanisms which facilitate black-white contact in broader community affairs. The formation of black caucuses in the unions somewhat helps to bring the intraunion racial issues to the surface. But those issues need to be formulated in such a way as to elicit both white consideration of what they are about, and black consideration of the white responses. It would, moreover, be helpful if the various union educational programs could be managed in such a way as to direct attention to racial issues which go beyond union politics. Just as the union tries to mobilize its members for electoral politics,[3] so the union might well create settings in which its *black members and its white members begin to face openly the fact that it is they themselves whose gun purchases constitute "the metropolitan arms races."*

The large-scale corporation is also important in this process. The importance of the corporation is directly related to the managerial ethos[4] and the fact that corporate leadership sets many styles of behavior which are adopted (or, at least, considered seriously) by subordinate personnel, even when *these styles* are not company policy. Something as simple as personal dress is indicative. Any visit to a corporate headquarters will show that the deep pink shirts (for example) will be much less obvious among the middle and junior staff than will white shirts, if only because there is an unspoken dress code. Within the past two or three years *The Wall Street Journal* reported on a survey of personnel officers' inclination to view an applicant favorably or unfavorably because of his hair style. Long hair was emphatically disapproved and about a quarter of the personnel officers were wary of mustaches! Corporate attitudes on overt political activity are at the other end of a scale from dress codes, being much more formally expressed. Note thus that 553 large firms (53 percent of those covered in a National Industrial Conference Board study a few years ago) had some kind of political-education program. Just about half of these (278) had actual in-plant courses while the other half (275) relied upon printed material, once-in-a-while oral presentations, and once-in-a-while films (Epstein, 1969, 55). If this activity is legitimate, and corporations maintain increasingly that it is (Epstein, 1969), then it is also legitimate for firms to extend this kind of educational program to cover such policy matters as race relations. Moreover, it is also legitimate for firms to reconsider the impacts of their spoken and unspoken racial codes. How might this be approached without unnecessary and inappropriate incursion into employees' private lives? The first step, surely, is that corporate leaders should so behave visibly that their employees understand that no sanctions (no imputations of being "unsound") arise when they themselves show an interest in racial issues. Thus, when a corporation discourages a black employee from fighting his own open-occupancy case, it clearly also signals to white employees that they should not associate themselves with open occupancy issues. Or, when a corporation's real estate department happily cooperates with segregationist policies in suburban development, it similarly puts out signals to the watchful.

These matters are also pertinent to much smaller institutions operating in a much more limited scope. "Service" clubs (Kiwanis, Rotary, Lions, and their ilk) abound in every city. What they *do not need* is some "charity" project to do something "for" the "poor ghetto kids" at Thanksgiving or Christmas time. Whether such clubs recruit one or two black members, as some have begun to do, is of some importance. What they *do need* is a deliberate effort to meet on common ground with their black counterparts in large numbers, regardless of their membership structures.

The approach suggested here has implications for other sorts of private institutions as well. Thus, many university "urban extension" departments have underatken "do-good" projects "in the ghetto." These are, perhaps, not to be condemned. But the sorts of projects undertaken (legal aid, consumer education, and similar helps) could be more useful if they were designed not "to help the ghetto residents" but instead to create frameworks within which comparable blacks and whites might meet for mutual and common education and action. "Comparable blacks and whites" might be PTA presidents in blue-collar neighborhoods; "mutual education" might be discussion of racial problems; "mutual action" could focus on problems of dealing with an unresponsive school administration.

One of the *most* critical ventures is the achievement of a detente between the urban Euro-American populations and the urban Afro-American populations. The relationship between the two has been usually uncomfortable, frequently suspicious, and sometimes overtly hostile. But the relationship is uncertain rather than clearly and irrevocably hostile. The elements of reciprocal adjustment must be cultivated, simply because social peace in the nation depends upon peace in the cities, and the possibility of peace in the cities does not exist, except as these two populations are reconcilable. I have argued elsewhere that the effort to create a detente, as a prelude to a soundly based social peace, is one of the problems which black political strategists must face,[5] however unwelcome it may be under their normal assumptions. Within the framework of the present essay, the other side of the coin is equally indispensable. *Detente must also be a major concern of those who assert various types of leadership within the several Euro-American communities.* This calculated search for the grounds of detente may depend upon several kinds of leadership, but it probably can be carried on most effectively by the leadership of the trade-union movement and the leadership of the Roman Catholic Church.

It is too much to ask the Church bluntly to repudiate the outlooks of its Euro-American constituency. No institution is likely to do that, and it would be unwise in any event. It would merely leave that large body of the urban population also feeling alienated and neglected. The more sensible function for the Church is to facilitate the meeting (and even confrontation!) of whites and blacks in the interest of reciprocal clarity and, in the end, of reciprocal deference.

I have emphasized these sorts of contacts because one social need is to multiply transracial contacts manifold and in short order. The emphasis on reciprocal deference must be maintained and sustained. Obviously, other approaches are possible, including adaptations by institutional leaders which do not reach deeply into the bodies politic of the various institutions. But, in the end, little is to be expected of superficial policy adjustments by white institutional leaders if their followers regard blacks as "niggers," who must be accepted on the job but for whom a basic disrespect remains untouched and with whom all nonutilitarian contact is to be avoided. Nor are adjustments likely to be fruitful if, whatever policy changes occur, blacks increasingly learn to think of ordinary whites as "honkies," properly subject to overt or covert hostility.

The problem of reciprocal deference can be approached on still other levels. There are private institutions which may affect the structure of deference by very simple decisions. Observe something as simple as haircuts. From the point of view of reciprocal deference, there would be much to be said for a symbol's being posted in every barber window on the same day, the symbol indicating that all legitimate customers were welcome. Or consider real estate. There simply is no longer an economically rational basis for the resistance of real estate boards to the unification of the real estate market, nor is there any logic to a racial test (explicit or implicit) for membership. A basic decision by these agencies to adopt a forward new policy, drawing a curtain over the past, would be particularly important, regardless of the volume of black purchases which thereafter might ensue. In fact, the volume would be rather limited, but what would be altered is the calculated social insult involved in being evaded and shunted —now contrary to law, but still practiced—when one chooses to look at a house or an apartment in an unusual (that is, a nonblack) location.

GOVERNMENTAL INSTITUTIONS AND THEIR ADAPTATIONS

CHANGES WHICH CAN BE MADE WITHOUT NEW LAWS

Governmental institutions are subject to two kinds of adaptations. Some adaptations are open to immediate action, without requiring many (if any) changes in existing law and in full compliance with existing policy norms.

Enhancing Communications. In state and municipal governments, it would be desirable to fulfill an early thrust in the specialized agencies dealing with race relations: the tradition of mediation and conciliation which originally entered into the design of the various "human rights commissions." In the 1940's, when these agencies began to emerge in most cities, the emphasis on mediation and conciliation was deprecated because there was no enforcement machinery which operated at all. Without enforcement machinery, and without a strong sense of public necessity, mediation and conciliation were trivial. Consequently, the human rights commissions—virtually the only agencies then concerned with race in an overt way—sought various enforcement powers.

Retrospectively, it is not necessary to judge whether the strategy was then wise. More to the point, it is now particularly important for someone to adopt this role, for there is now no one whose task it is to bring together the various sorts of black and white counterpart groups (or conflicting parties!) mentioned in the preceding section. From this point of view, the principle of the United States Community Relations Service, as a conciliation service, is sound. Not that antidiscrimination *enforcement* mechanisms are unnecessary. On the contrary! But in race relations as in other matters, a simultaneous presentation of conciliation measures and enforcement measures produces better results in most cases than a simple reliance on either. Thus, the city and state "human relations commissions," which have so long futilely sought to function as enforcement agents alone, might adopt an energetic policy of pushing conciliation ventures. It would make sense, for example, if a city human relations commission set out calculatedly to enhance a wide variety and large number of across-the-lines contacts among local neighborhood leaders, such as block club presidents from one end of town and their counterparts from the other end of town.

Enforcing the Laws. At the same time, the variety of agencies which are officially entitled to adopt enforcement policies is actually extremely wide. The political reality has been that, in the same manner that the federal agencies have long neglected their environmental enforcement powers,[6] so local and state agencies have neglected such powers in the race relations arena. Consider only the following examples:

In virtually every state, the district attorney is an officer with extraordinary powers to initiate investigation of *any* behavior which may be in violation of the law, yet it is seldom that a district attorney has chosen to initiate investigations of discriminatory behavior which is already outlawed under one or another statute of his state.

In many states, the elected county auditor has the legal right and duty to determine whether each payment of money by the county conforms with the law. It would be entirely reasonable for an auditor to determine that the payment of money to a contractor who discriminates in employment violates the statute forbidding racial discrimination in the letting and the execution of public contracts.

County and state treasurers have no authority to determine how much the taxes will be or for what purposes public revenues will be expended. But they do have the right and duty to decide which private banks will receive short-term funds on deposit. It would generally be legal and reasonable for a treasurer to determine that those competitive banks which had employment and lending policies most nearly consistent with public policies of equality would be the most suitable candidates for the receipt of such funds.[7]

There are other agencies in which more aggressive enforcement might well be in order. Thus, instead of evading the responsibility to police antiblack real estate practices, the state licensing agencies might adopt the counter posture and insist that the retention of a license to sell would require fair service to any customer.

The governmental modifications thus far discussed may take place at the state and local levels with little more (and it is a very important "little"!) than a political decision.

Effecting New Social Policies. There are similar options, requiring little or no change in the present statutes, which might be taken up by federal decision makers. In this context, the presidential role is critical, and one major aspect of that role is reconstruction of the federal bureaucracy itself. Federal domestic policy now is limited by the overwhelming dominance of people who have directly shared no part of the black experience and who *usually* neglect to ask the following key questions:

How far, and in what respects, will any proposed decision increase or decrease racial faction?

How far would any proposed decision increase or decrease the chances of racial reconciliation?

What practical option would be better, from the point of view of the chances of racial reconciliation?

This is demonstrated by our discussion of economic policymaking.

Edwin G. Nourse (1953), Walter Heller (1966), and Arthur Okun (1970) have all written accounts of their service in the President's Council of Economic Advisors. But none of them so much as mentions that the peculiar status of blacks was ever a factor in high-level policy discussion.[8] It would be hard to believe that the Bureau of the Budget or the Treasury Department would ever have been more forward looking. *Policymakers have—by accident or design—at no time considered it worthwhile to pursue a policy of "full employment" (even at the 4 percent rate) for blacks.* How should one justify so extreme a statement? Simply by noting the finding of Wolf and McEnally that, in order for orthodox monetary and fiscal measures to get black unemployment down to the approximately 4.5 percent average rate for the total labor force it would have been necessary to reduce unemployment in the white sector to about 2.5 percent (Wolf and McEnally, 1970). I would add, though Wolf and McEnally do not say so, that a rate of 2.5 percent for the white sector was never given serious policy consideration —although even that exceeds the British and German rates! This must also mean that policymakers either (a) never considered bringing the black rate as low as 4.5 percent, or (b) considered this, but decided it was not worth what it would cost the overall economy. In translation: the politics of normal economic policy must rest on the policy—explicit or implicit— that blacks will have to be disproportionately numerous among those carrying the burdens under any circumstances. It is precisely for the purpose of changing such unexamined policy assumptions that cultural pluralism needs to be introduced into the federal bureaucracy.

To make a start would require nothing more than a determination to use the executive patronage. Presidential appointments clearly are made —and are understood legitimately to be made—to provide all kinds of "representation." As patronage decisions give "representation" to different farm constituencies in the Department of Agriculture, to different union constituencies in the Department of Labor, to both "industrial" and "conservationist" constituencies in the Department of the Interior, and so on, so such patronage decisions might also give representation to the peculiar needs of the black population. It would also be possible to go beyond an *ad hoc* decision about patronage management to provide for a thorough executive reorganization. To do this is also simple because reorganization is mainly a presidential prerogative, subject to some congressional and interest group constraints. The principle to be invoked would be that established during the Cold War, when containment of the Soviet Union was defined as the prime national objective. Every agency of consequence had, as natural and proper administrative adjustment, a senior officer assigned to responsibility for the international aspects and implications of that agency's work.

On this principle, every department should be restructured to contain an "Undersecretary for Afro-American Development" and to have a functional equivalent of such an undersecretary.[9] The business of such an undersecretary (or other top-level adminstrator) would be to assure that each major policy decision within the agency should be considered in light of the need to facilitate a realistic integration (as we have defined that term) of black and white. This is a minimal step, not to relieve other departmental officials of the responsibility for looking to racial implications, but to provide an official with power to assure that other departmental officials would not avoid looking at racial implications.

Such arrangements should extend throughout the Executive Office agencies, and it would be appropriate to supplement them by having a progress report on Afro-American development built into each State-of-the-Union message and a program for further development included in each budget message. Finally, it would be possible and important to seek out constitutionally valid mechanisms for consultation of black interest groups in the same manner that the farmer-committee system under the Department of Agriculture, the collective bargaining elections and labor representation under the Department of Labor, and the various industry advisory groups provide for the group participation in the ordinary and continuous govermental decision process.

No single innovation to permit the pressure for black liberation to flow realistically into the power system of American life, rather than to "confront" that system by force of arms, is more important than this kind of opening of the federal bureaucracy to black access. The beauty of it is that it requires little or no new legislation! Not only would this form of "down payment" influence the content and realism of federal policies, but *it would also provide moral and political leverage to influence the elites who compose those private institutions which count for so much—the major foundations, the university system, and the Fortune 500.*

CHANGES REQUIRING NEW LAWS

Changes requiring new legislation are almost innumerable. But we might begin with two very conventional proposals. One is the idea that there should be a Joint Congressional Committee on Social Peace, an idea originally proposed more than twenty years ago by President Harry Truman in his advocacy of a Joint Congressional Committee on Civil Rights. Another is a refinement of the ideas, recently advanced, for a Council of Social Advisers and a Social Report of the President.[10] This would require much improvement, for the prototype social report advanced in 1969 is rather weak and shallow on the subject of race and social mobility. Legislation should be elaborated to provide that the prime task of this Council would be to consider problems of achieving and maintaining racial peace, to design indicators of conflict and accommodation, and to propose legislation which would be directed to such problems. Both of these proposals have as much to do with "administration" as with increasing the scope for Congressional attention to racial issues.

Beyond such proposals, however, one may come to certain ideas based upon the need for a new "political agreement," a new *legal* Constitution, which would reflect movement toward a new "social constitution."[11] The essential element of a new political agreement is to provide means by which the upsurge in black electoral politics may produce both a significant increase in political representation at the highest levels and a significant opportunity for emergent black elected officials to perform their administrative and policy functions well. The expression of electoral politics is, at this point, most dramatic in the persons of the new mayors in such cities as Cleveland, Gary, and Newark (not to mention many smaller cities). However, important as black-controlled city governments may be, they cannot fail to prove disappointing if the prime load of social development must rest upon them. The reason is simply that "local government" —black-controlled, white-controlled, or mixed—is an inherently weak enterprise.

URBAN STATEHOOD

A new political agreement (constitution) is so important that people who are serious about politics might wish Mr. Norman Mailer had stuck to writing novels, for his mayoral campaign took the need to find a new constitutional status for large cities and turned that need into something which people might treat as a joke or a fiction. In fact, there is serious reason to provide, by constitutional amendment, statehood for the cities over 500,000 in population. The population cut-off is necessarily subject to judgment, and different judgments might be offered about the precise level which should be considered. However, the cities so identified are actually very complex social entities—larger in human population than about half the independent states in the world.[12] Moreover, one may choose the population criterion of 500,000 since it is in the cities of that size that the political problems most concerning us exist. These very same cities not only exceed in population the state with the smallest present population (Alaska, with 300,382) but they also exceed Vermont (444,-330), Wyoming (332,416), and Nevada (488,738). If these have a rational basis for statehood, with the concomitant of senatorial representation, these the largest cities of the United States have an even greater basis for statehood.

Under recent conditions, we have tended to assume that the number and size of the states was fixed, and, *unwarrantably,* that there was no reason to reconsider the arrangements. But most existing states are now territorial units for which there is no particular social justification. However, many of the states historically began as communities with social meaning—not only in the seventeenth-century settlement of such places as the Maryland colony open to Catholic toleration, or the Pennsylvania settlement open to Quakers, or Rhode Island open to other dissenters, but also the nineteenth-century example of Utah and the Mormons. There is now the most profound social justification for considering new approaches to statehood, adequate to black self-expression and development within the framework of United States constitutionalism, without serious dislocation in the *whole social structure* of the nation.

If urban statehood were developed on the basis suggested, the new array of states would be 69, rather than the present 50, ordered as shown in Table XII-1.

It should be emphasized that this proposal is in no sense magical. Unquestionably, there will be some situations in which the same political forces internal to the cities would be dominant in the city-states. Thus, the black population of Chicago would still have to discover means to overcome its complex problems vis-à-vis the Daley organization, just as it now does. The same point would hold for Philadelphia, Los Angeles, Houston, or any other city which under this proposal would acquire state rank. The point is, however, that under present circumstances, once blacks have managed to overcome their internal adversaries, they come into office in governmental units which have too little power and status for the requisite purposes. This is the situation the proposal is meant to overcome.

Moreover, it would be fatuous not to recognize that there are critical political and technical problems standing athwart the achievement of the proposal. But it is not useful here to digress into those problems of execution, even though they are extremely important![13] These problems exist *in the projection;* they are both technical and political; and they present both magnitude and complexity. But the proposal is intended to deal with

Table XII–1, Rank Order of State Populations, before and after Admission
of Proposed New City-States

	Population, 1970 Census	Rank in 1970	Adjusted Population,* 1970 Census	Rank after New Admissions
California	19,953,134	1	15,724,630	1
New York	18,190,740	2	10,322,980	2
Ohio	10,652,017	6	9,448,590	3
Pennsylvania	11,793,909	3	9,325,183	4
Texas	11,196,730	4	8,465,374	5
NEW YORK CITY			7,867,760	6
Illinois	11,113,976	5	7,747,019	7
Michigan	8,875,083	7	7,363,601	8
New Jersey	7,168,164	8	7,168,164	9
Florida	6,789,443	9	6,789,443	10
Indiana	5,193,669	11	5,193,669	11
North Carolina	5,082,059	12	5,082,059	12
Massachusetts	5,689,170	10	5,689,170	13
Missouri	4,676,501	13	4,677,399	14
Virginia	4,648,494	14	4,648,494	15
Georgia	4,589,575	15	4,589,575	16
Tennessee	3,923,561	17	3,924,164	17
Minnesota	3,804,971	19	3,805,069	18
Wisconsin	4,417,731	16	3,700,834	19
Alabama	3,444,165	21	3,444,165	20
CHICAGO			3,366,957	21
Kentucky	3,218,706	23	3,219,311	22
Louisiana	3,641,306	20	3,049,709	23
Connecticut	3,031,709	24	3,032,217	24
Maryland	3,922,399	18	3,016,643	25
Washington	3,409,169	22	2,878,338	26
Iowa	2,824,376	25	2,825,041	27
LOS ANGELES			2,816,061	28
South Carolina	2,590,516	26	2,590,516	29
Oklahoma	2,559,229	27	2,559,253	30
Kansas	2,246,578	28	2,249,071	31
Mississippi	2,216,912	29	2,216,912	32
Colorado	2,207,259	30	2,207,259	33
Oregon	2,091,385	31	2,091,385	34
PHILADELPHIA			1,948,609	35
Arkansas	1,923,295	32	1,923,295	36
Arizona	1,770,900	33	1,770,900	37
West Virginia	1,744,237	34	1,744,237	38
DETROIT			1,511,482	39
Nebraska	1,483,493	35	1,483,791	40
HOUSTON			1,232,802	41
Utah	1,059,273	36	1,059,273	42
New Mexico	1,016,000	37	1,016,000	43
Maine	992,048	38	992,048	44
Rhode Island	946,725	39	949,723	45
BALTIMORE			905,756	46
				(continued)

*Populations of existing states minus populations of new city-states.

Table XII-1, Rank Order of State Populations, before and after Admission
of Proposed New City-States *(Continued)*

	Population 1970 Census	Rank in 1970	Adjusted Population* 1970 Census	Rank after New Admissions
DALLAS			844,401	47
Hawaii	768,561	40	768,561	48
WASHINGTON, D.C.			756,510	49
CLEVELAND			750,903	50
New Hampshire	737,681	41	737,681	51
MILWAUKEE			717,099	52
SAN FRANCISCO			715,674	53
Idaho	712,567	42	712,567	54
SAN DIEGO			696,769	55
Montana	694,409	43	694,409	56
South Dakota	665,507	44	665,507	57
SAN ANTONIO			654,153	58
BOSTON			641,071	59
ST. LOUIS			622,236	60
North Dakota	617,761	45	617,761	61
NEW ORLEANS			593,471	62
Delaware	548,104	46	548,104	63
SEATTLE			530,831	64
PITTSBURGH			520,117	65
Nevada	488,738	47	488,738	66
CINCINNATI			452,534	67
Vermont	444,330	48	444,330	68
Wyoming	332,416	49	332,416	69
Alaska	300,382	50	300,382	70

*Populations of existing states minus populations of new city-states.

problems that exist *now,* that are not merely projected; they too are political and technical; they too are great in magnitude and complexity; and above all *they must be dealt with.*[14]

This approach would provide a contribution to the handling of three major problems: (a) improving the black-white relation, (b) remedying the neglect of urban interests by the present state governments, and (c) stimulating more serious federal interest in urban development.

1. *Black State Governments.* The proposal would provide, and would be meant to provide, a certain number of black-governed states without the absurdities of "separatism," although probably about half those new states would have white majorities and white or mixed governments. Under the proposal, all persons in the United States would maintain their existing residence (and rights as citizens) if they desired to do so, but those who wanted to move to other residences could do so on private initiative. This black self-determination is particularly important in the Northern cities because of (a) the large number of white persons who are voluntarily

moving to suburbia anyway, and (b) the large number of black persons who are voluntarily moving into the central cities anyway. In contrast to separatist proposals, it would let population transfers take place "naturally," without any enforcement or administrative intervention whatsoever. Government would retain all its normal rights and responsibilities to enforce the federal civil rights laws and policies fairly, and (b) the Senatorial Congressional bloc from the city-states would be able to provide political assurance (the best kind!) that this enforcement would be done. At the same time, the rulers of the new city-states would have every incentive to enforce their own laws fairly, with respect to their white constituents, since it would be political folly to anger the rest of the country by abusing those residents.

Symbolically, such an approach would be useful because it would make a new cluster of important black politicians visible to the country as a whole, and particularly make their visibility known to their own constituencies. The new cultural dimensions of black politics would doubtless be influenced by the emergence of a series of "relevant" city-state universities oriented mainly toward a black population. But the real gain would lie in opening the more important vehicles of political influence. Observe that each city-state would have a governor, one congressman at minimum, and two senators. Although each city-state would continue to have a significant white population, a sufficient measure of skill and wisdom would virtually assure at least one black senator from each of the city-states with more than about 30 percent black population (Chicago, Detroit, New Orleans, and Philadelphia) and would probably assure two in the case of Washington, D.C.[15] Some such result would be likely, though not so assured, in the cases where the black population is large enough to be politically consequential but less than about 30 percent Moreover, one might normally expect even white representatives from such areas to be alert to the necessities of their black constituencies.

2. *Urban Influence in National Politics.* The statehood concept would obviously modify the black position in national politics, for it would provide the nucleus of a senatorial bloc with a major interest in federal urban expenditures, much as Arizona senators have a natural interest in federal water investments or Washington senators a constituent-based interest in defense contracts. The usual log-rolling process would operate. Simply by virtue of the facts of Congressional life, the city-state delegations would have every incentive to go through the usual routines of building up their own power. The same would be true for the governors of the states. The joint roles of such governors and such members of Congress would, further, create a far more responsive and imaginative

attention to racial and urban issues than one now sees from any federal department or regulatory agency.

The fact that the city-states would, to some degree, be dependent on federal channels for certain revenues, would provide a legitimate framework for Congressman Henry Reuss's proposal to tie in the Heller plan to state modernization programs.[16] The tie-in would have the salutary effect of forcing black politicians not merely to articulate the feelings and grievances of their constituencies, but even to carry out responsible governmental programs to serve those constituencies.

3. *Urban Influence on Economic and Fiscal Programs.* Urban statehood would provide an *institutional framework for domestic Marshall Plans,* since we have a long historical tradition of federal grants-in-aid to states. It would cut channels controlled by black men through which such aid could flow—and no other channel presently exists for this purpose, nor can any other be effectively created at present.

Unlike the same territories now organized as cities, *the city-state governments would have the capacity to make economic policy decisions, instead of mere fiscal decisions.*[17] Therefore, these governments could pursue their interest in making decisions to reverse the tendency for industries to move away from the urban locations. In the light of the industries' interest in social peace, one might expect corporations to cooperate, except when clear economic or technological reasons forbade. (In brief, if Chrysler once manufactured automobiles in the city of Detroit, there is no reason why it should in future not invest in new plants in the state of Detroit.)

4. *Urban Autonomy.* Not only would urban statehood provide a new framework for the black-white relation, but it would also make a useful contribution to the general problem of city-state relations. We may note this point by saying that the late Senator Dirksen—much criticized by urbanites because of his attack upon "one man, one vote"—actually pointed up the essential issue. The prime beneficiaries of "one man, one vote" in state legislative politics are not the residents and officials of the large central cities, be those cities predominantly white or predominantly black. The prime beneficiaries are, instead, the suburban rings around the central cities.

As the suburban legislative blocs increase in power under present conditions, one may expect them to exert their influence along lines incompatible with central-city needs in public order, school finance, public assistance, transportation planning—indeed, along nearly the whole range of public policies. This influence will be particularly exaggerated if some form of "general revenue sharing" (block grants) from the federal government provides a broad grant linked to some "function" (such as education or health or law enforcement), letting the states decide exactly how they will spend money within the specially supported function. Whatever the states are, state legislatures will have to make decisions about *how to distribute* funds within the states, and the balance of power under present conditions will most often work to the benefit of suburban constituencies and against the central cities.[18] Urban statehood would here provide an important corrective, for it would mean that the central cities (reconstituted as states) would themselves be the direct recipients of federal grant support, leaving the states of which they were formerly part to make their own decisions relative to their shares of federal support.

It is apparent that realization of this proposal in practice is highly speculative. Apart from technical difficulties and emotional reactions that "it just can't be done," existing state governments would provide major sources of resistance. The resistance would be based primarily on their view of the central city properties and productive facilities as major sources of revenue, a claim that states assert even while they are arguing that the state governments are incapable of making adequate provision for program needs in the central cities. A second source of resistance would, in all likelihood, be those major economic interests which are comfortable with the regulatory structures that have been built into state government over the years. Since many of those interests are domociled in the central cities, though anxious to detach themselves from the problems associated with the needs of central city residents, they might be expected to prefer the *status quo*. A third source of resistance might be Democratic liberals who themselves reside beyond the central cities, who seek statewide office, and for whom the central-city electorate is an indispensable base of voting support.

Consequently, no one could possibly deny that the political odds, under ordinary circumstances, are against the basic idea of urban statehood. On the other hand, at least four factors might well work in its favor. The first is that state decision makers may well find that their processes will not sustain the political and fiscal burdens of constant fights between the central cities and the suburbs. In this event, some will find the costs of reorganization less burdensome than the costs of paralysis in state decision making. The second factor is that, in reality, major economic interests have a great deal to gain from projected city-states if such interests can detach themselves from social fictions. The reason simply is that the central cities need to arrest economic decline, and are therefore likely to favor probusiness policies whenever there is any realistic hope that such policies will attract or sustain investment within those cities. In this regard, central-city decision makers are moved quite differently from present state decision makers, who have only to concern themselves with investment in the state, and who often prefer that it should be elsewhere than in the central cities. The third factor is that *if* central-city Democratic liberals develop the mythology that their statewide aspirations depend on retaining the central cities within present state boundaries, out-of-city conservatives can correspondingly discern that their advantage would be served by urban statehood. The conservatives probably could not hope to win the city-states themselves, but by excising such territories from the existing states they could go far to guarantee themselves nearly permanent tenure. The fourth factor is that, once the now-emerging black local officials discover how little real power lies in control of any conventional city government within present states, they will—given the extraordinary social demands of their constituents—have to seek means to increase their own power. Then two possibilities unfold: (a) Their white colleagues within the Democratic party will have to yield to them far more than any present sign indicates they will; or (b) the emergent black politicians will have to gravitate toward the urban statehood concept as their best available alternative. It will, of course, lie within the capacity of the Democratic liberals to resist either. But it will not be within their capacity to resist both and at the same time function as an effective political party. For resistance to both will produce the sort of paralysis seen sixty years ago in the delicate balance between Britain's Liberals and the parliamentary Irish Nationalists. Black politicians will not be free to act less vigorously than did Irish politicians, for underneath themselves there is, and will remain, the potentiality their own Sinn Fein—a potentiality only to be dismissed as far as there is some reasonable sign of the kind of social improvement best described as a remarking of the social constitution.

ENLARGING THE PRESIDENCY

A major option, requiring new law and also making profound good sense, is a reconstitution of the presidency of the United States. So long as the top level of the United States government is a center of *white* power (with both disposition and capacity to decide how much or how little of black interest will even be heard), the potentiality for social division remains. But it is not difficult to think of a useful alternative. One might advocate another constitutional amendment to create a plural executive, to recreate the presidency by adding some number of vice presidents (the number being chosen to constitute an odd-numbered presidential executive). With appropriate draftsmanship, such an amendment could guarantee that at least one of these would be a black man. The normal political logic would inevitably thereafter result in at least one black vice president. In the natural course of politics, he would come to have a strategic role in domestic programing, and his realistic function would be to assure that black interests were regularly raised at the highest levels—a function which would be performed inevitably by virtue of the emergence of "black caucuses" in the political parties from which he would be unable to keep free. This conception indicates the point which is essential to the whole idea in this volume—that the problem of remaking the social constitution to cope with racial dispute is also a problem of dealing with other needs in the republic.

In this matter, as in others, the basic lesson comes home once more. The measures which are appropriate to overcome racial faction have potential benefits far beyond the black population itself. For it is by now clear that the position argued so long by maverick political scientists—such as Herman Finer and Rexford Tugwell[19]—is sound. The presidency of the United States concentrates responsibilities on one human being to a degree which is, given the scale of contemporary decision, beyond the psychological, intellectual, and physical capacities of a single man. In that light, the case for moving to a plural executive is very compelling. A plural executive is not merely a means of introducing cultural pluralism at the highest level of government. It is also a means of overcoming the monarchic mystique described by George Reedy,[20] and of enhancing the flows of information and debate necessary to a higher level of rational judgment in politics.

NOTES

1. Above, "A Look at Medusa's Face," Essay VII.

2. For some other models of ways to explore differences, see Burton (1969), and Doob (1970).

3. I am not unaware of the fact that union influence on members' electoral decisions is limited, but it is clearly not ineffectual.

4. Above, Essay VIII, "Public Opinion and Everyday Behavior—I. Notes on Confusion and Ambivalence."

5. See *The Politics of the Black "Nation,"* Essay VII, "The Next Five Years—III: Modifying Political Tactics."

6. The criticism which the House Subcommittee on Natural Resources (under the chairmanship of Congressman Henry A. Reuss) has directed against the Corps of Engineers for neglecting certain of its powers under legislation which dates from as long ago as 1899 is in point here.

7. It is reported, though I have not yet verified, that Senator Adlai E. Stevenson (when State Treasurer in Illinois) adopted exactly such a policy.

8. Nor is the racial disparity mentioned in two outside analyses: Flash (1963) and Pierce (1971).

9. There are other kinds of administrative reform which may be pertinent, such as decentralization in some cases and dual control (appointment of coequal black and white administrators) in others. I would view the decentralization of federal activities with some reserve, however, for its most likely effect is to enhance the political leverage of state governments in which black political influence is going to be least in the near future.

10. United States Department of Health, Education, and Welfare, *Toward a Social Report* (Report of the Panel on Social Indicators) (Washington: Government Printing Office, 1969), especially Chapter II.

11. Above, Essay I, "The Crisis of the Republic."

12. If one put New York City in its proper category among nation-states (between 5 and 10 millions), it would compare with such countries as Belgium or Cuba, Sweden or Uganda. Chicago, Los Angeles, Detroit, Houston, and Philadelphia (in the group between 1 and 5 millions) would compare with such countries as Costa Rica, Israel, Ivory Coast, or Norway. Baltimore, Dallas, Washington, and others in the group less than 1 million would compare with such countries as Cyprus and exceed noticeably such countries as Barbados.

13. Obviously, the critical problem is the political problem of securing assent from those who presently dominate decisions in the states whose boundaries would have to be rearranged.

14. One could devise other technical formulae than that which I have offered. For instance, on the 500,000-plus criterion, one might conceive of making New York City into more than one city-state.

15. A large minority, with sophisticated leadership, could almost certainly assure itself one Senate seat, but it would have to do this on the basis of a certain amount of coalition politics with some elements of the white population. If it sought to take both seats, it would find its resources for political combat overcommitted, and probably would lose both.

16. The idea of a systematic sharing of federal revenues with the state governments has been widely propagandized by some economists, notably Walter Heller. The Heller plan, put forth during the preceding Democratic administration, was put forth in modified form by President Nixon in 1970–1971.

17. On the need for urban economic policy decisions, not merily fiscal management decisions, see Long (1972).

18. The threat of "ripper" legislation is another potential area of conflict.

19. See Finer (1960). The idea of a plural Executive is also offered in Tugwell's hypothetical new constitution. In neither case need one commit oneself to the precise details (nor even the precise details in the present argument!). But the essential point needs attention.

20. George Reedy, *Twilight of the Presidency,*

Postscript

The preceding essays express some biases which it may be well to set forth in this postscript. The central bias, conviction of *black-white inter-dependency,* concerns politics itself. If politics is a power process, inter-dependency is its central element. People may be masters and slaves, firm allies, deadly enemies, or bargaining partners. But all of these are interde-pendencies. All involve the relevant people in a political system. Some of the hardest *political* problems come when, somehow, the very character of the relationships is changing, or even when one of the parties is trying to change those relationships.[1] So it is now with racial politics in the United States.

As a political system, the United States includes the two "sociocultural 'nations' " locked into each other, in a relationship which has historically been "imperial." Imperial, in that the white element has been *dominant* over the black element. The present question is one of encompassing black and white within a *republican* norm—within a political community or a shared moral order understood to be the common enterprise and concern of both its black and its white members. The problem of transforming an internal "empire" into a full-scale republic is that to which, given the bias noted, these essays have been devoted.

Most of the essays were written, off and on, between the summer crises of 1967 and the latter part of 1969, although the basic theme was formu-lated in 1964 and many editorial or substantive changes were made in 1970 and early 1971. In that interval, we have seen a dramatic rise of public interest in racial issues. We have also seen an apparent decline in such public interest. One reason is that a country never lives its public life on one issue only. Environmental policy, the condition of the economy, the secular desecration which counter-culturists wreak upon older values of patriotism, responsibility, and enterprise, and the gloomy sickness of the Vietnam war all take their toll. Another reason is that people have come to see in racial politics a theatrical bravado—a melodramatic rhetoric, from blacks and from whites, which so far exaggerates reality that it should be treated no more seriously than political realists treat most "campaign oratory." The relative quiescence of 1970, the first apparently quiescent summer in five years, encouraged this belief. But just as it is foolish for blacks to bluster beyond their capacity, so it is foolish for whites to believe that all that they hear is bluff. The underlying reality is still there, in such observable indicators as rising tensions in military installations and in high schools, or in the evident tendency for black professionals to withdraw from white contact, noisily if they wish to be regarded as "militants" and quietly if they simply think they have no choice. It is also folly to believe that reinforcing governmental coercion will somehow restore a previous quiescence. It might, indeed, do so, but only after a protracted struggle utterly beyond reason.[2]

There is another important bias. It is the belief that *rationality is supremely important to the achievement of desirable political results.* No one could doubt, of course, that politics is a profoundly emotional matter. Politics can become so emotional that conflicting groups may be willing to accept —almost, indeed, to provoke—mutual self-destruction. As hard as it is to find a logic-tight *definition* of rationality, it would be harder still to say that such behavior is rational. Rationality means, at the minimum, some understanding of what would be sensible results (not perfect ones!) and some understanding of the necessary means of action to achieve those results.

Insofar as racial politics is concerned, there has been a near-moratorium on rational consideration. Some of this may be due to the belief that "the worst" is already past. But I think it more likely to come from intellectual and emotional paralysis, a paralysis born—of a sense of incapacity to do anything useful and aggravated by preoccupation with other matters. That sense of incapacity arises from three remarkable suppositions, each of which I believe erroneous in important respects.

The first is that the present intense crisis is unique to this time, that "the system" *no longer* "works," with the implication that nothing in American history or social practice provides lessons for good judgment.

The second remarkable supposition is that the problem is somehow *unique to the United States* and related either to some moral flaw in "the typical American character" or to the necessities of the private enterprise economy.

The third remarkable supposition is that the problem is peculiarly associated with contact between white peoples and nonwhite peoples. This view is clearly expressed by the emigré South African writer, Ronald Segal, who formulates the problem of racism as a global problem—observing (correctly) that there is no white-ruled state in which nonwhites live under conditions of equality and dignity (Segal, 1967).

There is no one of these three statements in which one can fail to find some element of reality. Yet, as indicated, each obscures quite as much as it clarifies.

Consider them in reverse order. Segal's statement is perfectly correct, yet so misleading that it provides no insight into useful solutions for our problems. First, the apparent implication of the Segal hypothesis is that states ruled by nonwhites are different from states ruled by whites in their treatment of ethnic minorities, a suggestion which would make it utterly impossible to explain the virulent conflict in countries (Guyana, Nigeria, and others) where none of the combatants are white.

The second implication of the Segal hypothesis is that *white ethnic minorities in white-ruled states* do not encounter problems comparable to those of nonwhite minorities. Again, the case cannot be sustained. If it were correct, we should not observe white-against-white religious communalism in Northern Ireland producing a Protestant quasi militia (the B-Special force) so large that a white-against-black equivalent in the United States would amount to 400,000 organized and armed men beyond the regular public forces.

Even when we deal with *white* racism, the most serious criticism of the Segal hypothesis remains. The hypothesis provides no clues into the development or the sources—and therefore no clues to the possible decline—of white racism. This is a noticeable failure, for one presumes that Segal is not arguing that white racism is biogenetic.

Moreover, nowhere in this world has ethnic diversity been easily reconciled with political order and equality (any more than extreme class disparities have been easily reconciled with political order and equality). These problems are more difficult when they are combined with the critieria of democracy, constitutionalism, and welfare statism. Polities like those of the Soviet Union, which neither pretend to nor desire the terms of democratic constitutionalism, have incorporated the welfare motif (in their own way), but the degree to which they have mastered the multiethnic problem is unclear (Armstrong, 1948, 3–49).

The Low Countries have their own persistent problems of ethnicity, despite their small-scale governments, although they also combine democratic constitutionalism and welfarism. (Kelly, 1967; Lijphart, 1968; Lorwin, 1966; Schaper, 1960). Even the Scandinavian polities, so often deemed idyllic by United States standards, combining the welfare motif, democratic constitutionalism, and small scale, have recently discovered that ethnicity is not entirely trivial for them. This now becomes a problem in Denmark, it seems, with the importation of Turkish labor; and Danes wake up surprised to find their own version of emergent "racism."

Finally, it is not quite right to think of the United States as a tranquil, consensualized polity in its historical development. There has hardly been a period of more than a quarter century (and never more than fifty years) when the question of the stability of republican government has not been raised. While the Constitution was ratified and operative as of 1789, one could not count the republic even established until the Jefferson takeover of 1801 *demonstrated* that free elections and peaceful change of administrations *actually* were possible. (Moreover, we should not pass without noting that even this change involved an interference with the courts more drastic than anything which the Civil War or the New Deal brought forth, namely the legislation (in the Judiciary Act of 1802) under which sitting judges who had in no way violated their oaths were displaced from the federal courts. What is even more, this was an act undertaken not by the contemporary "conservatives" but by the contemporary Jeffersonians, in their own political defense!)[3] The Hartford Convention, the Missouri Compromise issues, the South Carolina Nullification controversy, and the struggles after the Kansas-Nebraska Act raised still other questions, questions only answered by the military outcome of the Civil War. It is only since the Civil War that we have had no political insurrections (Rich, 1941). After that, the class war known as the "rise of the labor movement" went on far more than fifty years, with a level of violence which even the 1970's have not touched.

As a matter of intellectual honesty, it behooves us to try to get a better grasp on the issues. To do this is also a major practical necessity. If all the trouble stems from capitalism, then all solution must depend upon the coming of some alterative economic system. If it all depends upon some global revolt of nonwhites against whites, then the black American population must be regarded as historical lamb by which the nonwhite hunters of "the Third World" will catch the white tiger. But in that process, both tiger and lamb are destroyed.

Those who hold the three views contained in the remarkable suppositions build a psychological and political trap for themselves and for those who take their advice. No magical transformation of a situation from "bad" to "good" ever occurs all at once. Action has to be taken in pieces. The practical problem is to choose the right pieces, to multiply their numbers, and to produce them in ever more rapid succession.

Under any of the three interpretations, any pieces of action which *could* be generated must also be defined as "trivial." If this view is correct, and any of the suppositions be adopted, confidence must remain at a low level, the *will* to face down danger must ever erode, and commentators must ever be reduced to woeful lamentation of the dire consequences yet to come.

Still another bias is a belief that *we need some strategic sense of what is at stake and how people might proceed.* I view the problem as one of *peacemaking* and maintain that the central issue in peacemaking is *reciprocal* deference. "Deference (means) being taken into consideration (in the acts of others and of the self)" (Lasswell and Kaplan, 1963, 55). Success in political reconciliation means the creating of means for the reciprocal sharing of deference and esteem between actual or potential disputants. This is not the same as incorporation of new populations into the symbol system of the other. It is the devising of new symbol systems common to both populations and which identify the "contributions" of each. I find at least some support for this view in Karl Deutsch's summary of the historical integration of several Euro-Atlantic countries

It . . . seemed important that each [party] at least sometimes take the initiative in the process [of establishing a peaceful community], or initiate some particular phase or contribution; and that some major symbol or representative of each territory or population should be accorded explicit respect by the others. (Deutsch *et al.,* 1957)

The transformation of American society, from an Anglo-Protestant society to one in which Catholics and Jews (of Continental European background) play a significant role is a demonstration of the possible end product. Cultural pluralism is not some vague state of "good will," nor some appreciation of exotic food and folk dances. It is a recognition of the shift in the structure of society, and in the structure of deference within society.[4]

The requirement for such a shift is posed by the late Adlai Stevenson's observation that the essence of republican government is not command but consent. It is especially the consent of those who at some earlier time constituted respectable sources of resistance. Consent of this kind is one of the basic requirements of change in stable societies.[5] By "stable" societies, I mean those where (a) governmental institutions—particularly at the national level—have been operative without interrruption for a long time; and (b) wide social agreement has also existed for a long time on whom the social constitution ought to encompass, and how new people should be brought in. Those who argue that power in the hands of the weaker is the most likely means to generate change are correct, but are grossly short-sighted when they stop with this statement. The initiation of "fairly" far-reaching change probably depends upon the obvious beneficiaries of such change,[6] but the confirmation of such change probably depends upon those who are not obvious beneficiaries, or even more upon those who have been disposed to resist.[7] There are only two other options: total victory when those proposing changes can entirely beat the resisters into unconditional surrender, or complete defeat for those proposing changes. The former option obviously does not describe a stable society, but a revolution. If neither option exists, and resisters do not at all yield, the struggle drags on ad infinitum. As illustrations note the following:

1. The position of factory workers, both in the internal government of industry and in the politics and broader social structure of the nation, clearly has changed since 1937. Moreover, it has changed in ways which industrial leaders before the mid-1930's often regarded as so "revolutionary" that they *thought* they would never agree to them. But they have agreed to those changes and those changes have become firmly embedded in the operative social constitution.

2. New Deal welfare statism grew out of the politics of the "have-nots," but the welfare state was confirmed only by the acceptance of the Eisenhower Republicans.

3. Government regulation of trade union practices began with the 80th Congress, but government regulation of trade union practices was confirmed by John Kennedy's role in the Landrum-Griffin Act and Robert Kennedy's policies as Attorney General.

4. Federal aid to all schools (including Catholic schools) was initiated by Catholic Democrats in Congress, but federal aid was confirmed by the policies of Lyndon Johnson and the American Jewish committee's adoption of the child-benefit theory.

All these cases illustrate that people of some party X consider that fighting with party Y would be "bad" for them to do, whatever test of "bad" they should apply. This kind of consent does not mean immediate conversion, but the dissolving of prior certainty into ambivalence. That ambivalence may be grounded in moral preference, economic interest, military necessity, vote calculation, or something else; and the new course of action develops as ambivalence is resolved. It does not necessarily follow that ambivalence will be resolved in favor of some accommodative action. People may go to the drastic extreme of trying to destroy the "enemy."[8] People already committed to, and satisfied with, one position *must become ambivalent and then resolve that ambivalence as they acquire a vision of new possibilities.*

The difficult process of joining separate groups places maximum emphasis on the catalytic function of leadership. *Leadership styles and ingenuity must somehow be brought to bear, though within certain limits* ("conditions" or "parameters") *which they can manipulate, but seldom wholly escape.* Broadly, these parameters are of two types. Attitudinal parameters ("values," "belief systems," and the like) are extremely important, and their interposition leads to results which would not be either predictable or rational if attitudes were not taken into account. Structural parameters are those (like "the economy") which tend to determine action even though the action is different from what ought to have been predicted from the actor's beliefs or attitudes.

Parameters cannot ever be safely neglected. Leaders or elites who make these judgments must try to interpret ("sell") them to those followers who could upset the necessary arrangements.

But political leaders are not mere prisoners of circumstance, bound to one and only one course of action. When their deals can be achieved, and maintained for some reasonable time, the *de facto* effect is to create a sort of "treaty" arrangement. That is, the deal between the parties requires some presumption of longevity, though not of permanence. At this point, the interests of leaders themselves become terribly important. If the exchanges between the sides result in gains and institutions which the leaders of the sides think valuable, leaders will begin to concentrate on maintaining those gains and institutions. The more they do so, the more they come to have some increased moral appreciation of their counterparts on the other side. One may speak here of elites, with divergent followers of bases of support, having internalized the values of joint action with their counterparts (and having internalized *the values of those counterparts*). Their role in generating and sustaining new visions of "the possible" and "the desirable" is so important that it can comfortably be compared to the role of Machiavelli's prince, engaged in creative intervention in chaotic situations to produce new forms of order. The emergence of the active political community, including the diverse groups, is the end result which sometimes follows.

The most troubling aspect in the republican crisis in the United States is that there has been at least a temporary (hopefully, not a permanent) cessation of major efforts by political leaders to establish some form of social truce, and to lay the groundwork through which that truce may be developed into a stable social peace. Clearly, my view is that this leadership paralysis must be broken, and the next five years are the critical "turnaround time." It would indeed be appropriate to act so that 1976—the second centennial of the Declaration of Independence—might be celebrated by the birth of a Second Reconstruction, beginning to undo the damage wrought by the ceremonial killing of the First Reconstruction in 1876. Whether white people have the psychological and cultural capacity to begin so decisive a break with the burden of their history is naturally questionable. But if there were no capacity for adjustment, the United States would already be in far worse condition than it now is. Instead of clear determination, there is a profound ambivalence, ambiguity, and confusion.[9] It is, I argue, yet possible to overcome the ambiguities which white Americans experience on the subject of race, to crystallize the desire for forward movement, and to turn that desire into workable policies. The problem is to find practical options for resolving that ambivalence, ambiguity, and confusion in a direction favorable to republican government. Practical action seems to me most important, for this purpose, in three major realms: the political economy of racial adjustment; short-term threat reduction, with a particular emphasis on urban arms control and disarmament; and major institutional modification. Measures of the sort described[10] may be "radical" in their departure from standard suppositions. They may also be "conservative" in the sense that they indicate the realistic prices which it is worthwhile paying to stabilize the United States as a political community.

Neither label is important. The result is.

NOTES

1. Obviously, we have to recognize that one (or more) parties may wish to change a relationship and may fail in the effort to do so.

2. Above, Essay VII, "A Look at Medusa's Face."

3. The Judiciary Act of 1801 created a set of federal judgeships which President Adams filled at the last minute before leaving office. The Judiciary Act of 1802 repealed the Act of 1801 and put these judges out of office, contrary to the life-tenure provisions of the Constitution, and so amended the Supreme Court's calendar as to make it practically impossible for the issues involved to be brought to litigation. For two accounts of this pair of Acts, see Warren (1923, I, Chapter 4) and Ellis (1971, 33-68).

4. The admission of "labor men" to the Community Chests' boards of directors, in the past thirty years, is a sign that *these formerly excluded are no longer excluded.*

5. The politics of change in stable societies probably deserves at least as much

attention as the politics of change or the politics of stabilization in unstable societies, both of which latter have received considerable attention from students of the Third World nations.

6. I will not try to define "fairly," but I do mean that (a) change which totally revolutionizes the society (as in the Chinese case after 1949) is not here being considered; but that (b) the change which we have in mind must have at least some major structural consequences.

7. The general proposition is based in part upon Coser (1969).

8. It is also possible that the ambivalence will so paralyze them that they can do nothing, which is the extraordinary case of primitive uncertainty. In this case, people neither "know what they want," nor how to "make things turn out right," nor even what "right" is (Holden, 1965a).

9. This argument is laid out above in Essay III on "Racial Politics as a Study in Paradox" and in Essays VIII and IX on "Public Opinion and Everyday Behavior."

10. Particularly in the three essays immediately preceding.

References

Abell, John B. "The Negro in Industry." *Trade Winds* (Cleveland: Union Trust Company), March 1924, 17–20.

Abrams, Charles. *Forbidden Neighbors*. New York: Harper and Brothers, 1955.

Ake, Claude. *A Theory of Political Integration*. Homewood: Dorsey Press, 1967.

Altshuler, Alan. "The Politics of Managing a Full-Employment Economy." N.p.: American Political Science Association, 1967.

Anderson, Charles W., Fred R. von der Mehden, and Crawford Young. *Issues of Political Development*. Englewood Cliffs: Prentice-Hall, 1967.

Anderson, Grace M. "Voting Behavior and the Ethnic-Religious Variable." *Canadian Journal of Economics and Political Science*, 32:1 (February 1966), 27–37.

Anderson, James E. *Politics and the Economy*. Boston: Little, Brown and Company, 1966.

Apter, David E. *The Politics of Modernization*. Chicago: University of Chicago Press, 1965.

Arendt, Hannah. "Reflections on Little Rock." *Dissent* (Winter 1959), 45–56.

Armstrong, John A. "The Ethnic Scene in the Soviet Union: The View of the Dictatorship," in Erich Goldhagen, ed., *Ethnic Minorities in the Soviet Union*. New York: Federick A. Praeger, 1968.

Avnery, Uri. *Israel without Zionists*. New York: Macmillan Company, 1968.

Bailey, Hugh C. *Edgar Gardner Murphy*. Coral Gables: University of Miami Press, 1968.

Banfield, Edward C. "Notes for a Conceptual Scheme," in Meyerson and Banfield, 1955.

Bell, Carolyn Shaw. *The Economics of the Ghetto*. New York: Pegasus, 1970.

Benedict, Ruth. *The Chrysanthemum and the Sword*. Boston: Houghton Mifflin Company, 1946.

Bernstein, Irving. *The Lean Years*. Boston: Houghton Mifflin Company, 1960.

Binzen, Peter. *Whitetown USA*. New York: Random House, 1970.

265

Blackwood, George D. "Civil Rights and Direct Action in the Urban North." *Public Policy* (1965), 292–320. Cambridge: Graduate School of Public Administration, Harvard University, 1965.

Blake, Robert. *The Conservative Party from Peel to Churchill.* London: Eyre and Spottiswoode, 1970.

Bloch, Herman D. *The Circle of Discrimination.* New York: New York University Press, 1969.

Blodgett, Geoffrey. *The Gentle Reformers.* Cambridge: Harvard University Press, 1966.

Bobrow, Davis B. "The Organization of American National Security Opinions." *Public Opinion Quarterly,* 28:2 (Summer 1969), 223–229.

Bond, Horace Mann. *Education of the Negro in the American Social Order.* New York: Octagon Books, 1966.

Bowman, Lewis R., and G. R. Boynton. "Grass Roots Party Officials." *Journal of Politics,* 28:1 (February 1966), 140–141. (Tables 9 and 10)

Boyer, William W. *Bureaucracy on Trial.* Indianapolis: Bobbs-Merrill Company, 1964.

Brimmer, Andrew F. "The Negro in the National Economy," in John P. Davis, ed., *American Negro Reference Book.* Englewood Cliffs; Prentice-Hall, 1966.

Brink, William, and Louis Harris. *Black and White.* New York: Simon and Schuster, 1967.

Browne, Robert S. "Barriers to Black Participation in the American Economy." Paper presented at the National Urban League Conference. New York, July 1970.

Buchanan, James, and Gordon Tullock. *Calculus of Consent.* Ann Arbor: University of Michigan Press, 1962.

Burton, John W. *Controlled Communication.* New York: Free Press, 1969.

Cable, George Washington. *The Negro Question.* Garden City: Doubleday and Company, 1958. (First published 1888.)

Caliver, Ambrose. *Education of Negro Leaders: Influences Affecting Graduate and Professional Studies.* Washington: Federal Security Agency, Bulletin, 1948, No. 3.

Calkins, Fay. *The CIO and the Democratic Party.* Chicago: University of Chicago Press, 1952.

Carmichael, Stokely, and Charles V. Hamilton. *Black Power.* New York: Random House, 1967.

Cash, W. J. *The Mind of the South.* Garden City: Doubleday Anchor Books, 1954. (First Published 1941.)

Caspary, William R. "The 'Mood Theory': A Study of Public Opinion and Foreign Policy." *American Political Science Review,* 64:2 (June 1970), 536–547.

Cayton, Horace R., and George Mitchell. *Black Workers and the New Unions.* Chapel Hill: University of North Carolina Press, 1939.

Chamberlain, Austen. *Politics from Inside.* New Haven: Yale University Press, 1937.

Charles, Joseph. *The Origins of the American Party System.* New York: Harper Torchbooks, 1969.

Citron, Abraham F. *The "Rightness of Whiteness": The World of the White Child in a Segregated Society.* Detroit: Michigan-Ohio Regional Educational Laboratory, February, 1971.

Cleaver, Eldridge. *Soul on Ice.* New York: McGraw-Hill Book Company, 1968.

Cochrane, Willard W. *The City Man's Guide to the Farm Problem.* New York: McGraw-Hill Book Company, 1966.

Cohn, David L. *Where I was Born and Raised.* Notre Dame: University of Notre Dame Press, 1967.

Coles, Robert. "The White Northerner: Pride and Prejudice." *Atlantic Monthly* (June 1966), 53–57.

Cooke, Jacob E. *Frederick Bancroft, Historian.* Norman: University of Oklahoma Press, 1957.

Cornwell, Elmer E. "Party Absorption of Ethnic Groups." *Social Forces,* 38:3 (March, 1960), 205–210.

Coser, Lewis A. "The Termination of Conflict." *Journal of Conflict Resolution,* 5:4 (December 1959), 347–353.

Costikyan, Edward N. *Behind Closed Doors.* New York: Harcourt Brace Jovanovich, 1966.

Cousens, Francis E. *Public Civil Rights Agencies and Fair Employment.* New York: Federick A. Praeger, 1969.

Crawford, Floyd W. "Ida B. Wells: Her Anti-Lynching Crusades in Britain and Repercussions from Them in the United States." Unpublished typescript, October 22, 1958.

Critchley, T. A. *The Conquest of Violence.* London: Constable, 1970.

Dahl, Robert A. *Who Governs?* New Haven: Yale University Press, 1962.

Deutsch, Karl W., and William J. Foltz, eds. *Nation-Building.* New York: Atherton Press, 1963.

Deutsch, Karl W., *et al. Political Community and the North Atlantic Area.* Princeton: Princeton University Press, 1957.

Dolbeare, Kenneth M., and Joel V. Grossman. *LeRoi Jones in Newark: A Political Trial?* Madison: University of Wisconsin, Center for Law and Behavioral Science, Working Paper No. 5, October, 1969.

Doob, Leonard W., ed. *Resolving Conflict in Africa.* New Haven: Yale University Press, 1970.

Douglas, Anne. *Industrial Peacemaking.* New York: Columbia University Press, 1962.

Downs, Anthony. *Urban Problems and Prospects.* Chicago: Markham Publishing Company, 1970.

Drake, St. Clair. "The Black Middle Class, 1948–1968." Paper for symposium on *The Black Man in America.* Wayne State University, 1969.

Dunning, William O. *Essays on the Civil War and Reconstruction.* New York: Harper and Row, 1965.

Dykeman, Wilma, and James Stokely. *Seeds of Southern Change.* Chicago: University of Chicago Press, 1965.

Ebony, Editors of. *Negro Handbook.* Chicago: Johnson Publishing Company, 1966.

Eckenrode, H. J. *The Revolution in Virginia.* Boston: Houghton Mifflin Company, 1916.

Egerton, John. "Black Executives in Big Business." *Race Relations Reporter,* 17 (October, 1970).

Ellis, Richard. *The Jeffersonian Crisis: Courts and Politics in the Young Republic.* New York: Oxford University Press, 1971.

Ellison, Ralph. *The Invisible Man.* New York: Random House, 1952.

Epstein, Edwin M. *The Corporation in American Politics.* Englewood Cliffs: Prentice-Hall, 1969.

Ernst, Robert. *Immigrant Life in New York City.* New York: King's Crown Press, 1949.

Evans, Rowland, and Robert Novak. *Lyndon B. Johnson: The Exercise of Power.* New York: New American Library, 1966.

Fenton, John M. *In Your Opinion.* Boston: Little, Brown and Company, 1960.

Finer, Herman. *The Presidency: Crisis and Regeneration.* Chicago: University of Chicago Press, 1960.

Fishel, Leslie H., Jr. "The Negro in Northern Politics," in Meier and Rudwick, 1969.

Flash, Edward S. *Economic Advice and Presidential Leadership.* New York: Columbia University Press, 1963.

Flinn, Thomas A., and Frederick M. Wirt. "Local Party Leaders: Groups of Like Minded Men." *Midwest Journal of Political Science,* 9:1 (February, 1966), 77–98.

Foraker, Joseph B. *Notes of a Busy Life.* Cincinnati: Stewart and Kidd Company, 1916.

Ford, Henry Jones. *The Rise and Growth of American Politics.* New York: Macmillan Company, 1914.

Frazier, E. Franklin. *The Negro Church.* New York: Schocken Books, 1962.

Freeman, J. Leiper. "Socio-Economic Characteristics of Field Officials in the Federal Civil Service," in Lynton K. Caldwell, ed., *Politics and Public Affairs.* Bloomington: Indiana University, Department of Government, Institute for Training for Public Service, 1962.

Friedman, Saul. "Race Relations Is Their Business." *New York Times Magazine,* November 8, 1970, 44–69.

Friedrich, Carl J. *Constitutional Government and Politics,* rev. ed. Boston: Ginn and Company, 1950.

Gans, Herbert. *The Urban Villagers.* New York: Free Press, 1962.

Gans, Herbert. *The Levittowners.* New York: Pantheon Books, 1967.

Gans, Herbert. "We Won't End the Urban Crisis until We End 'Majority Rule.' " *New York Times Magazine,* August 3, 1969.

Garraty, John A. *Henry Cabot Lodge.* New York: Alfred A. Knopf, 1953.

Gerschenkron, Alexander. "Reflections on Economic Aspects of the Revolution," in Harry Eckstein, ed., *Internal War.* New York: Free Press, 1964.

Geyl, Pieter. *History of the Low Countries.* New York: Macmillan Company, 1964.

Glazer, Nathan, and Daniel P. Moynihan. *Beyond the Melting Pot.* Cambridge: MIT Press and Harvard University Press, 1963.

Goldman, Eric F. *The Tragedy of Lyndon Johnson.* New York: Alfred A. Knopf, 1969.

Gordon, Milton M. *Assimilation in America.* New York: Oxford University Press, 1964.

Gosnell, Harold F. *Champion Campaigner.* New York: Macmillan Company, 1952.

Gosnell, Harold F. *Negro Politics.* Chicago: University of Chicago Press, 1967 ed.

Gottfried, Alex. *Boss Cermak of Chicago.* Seattle: University of Washington Press, 1962.

Graham, Hugh Davis, and Ted Robert Gurr, eds. *The History of Violence in America.* New York: Frederick A. Praeger, 1969.

Graham, Hugh Davis, and Ted Robert Gurr. *Violence in America: Historical and Comparative Perspectives.* Washington: United States Government Printing Office, 1969.

Greeley, Andrew M., and Joe Spaeth. "Stratification and Social Conflict in American White Ethnic Groups," 12–14. Paper prepared for publication by *Daedalus* and made available by courtesy of Fr. Greeley.

Greer, Scott A., *et al.*, eds. *The New Urbanization.* New York: St. Martin's Press, 1968.

Griffin, John Howard. *Black Like Me.* New York: Signet Books, 1962.

Gross, Bertram, and Michael Springer. "Developing Social Intelligence," in Gross, ed., *Social Intelligence for America's Future.* Boston: Allyn and Bacon, 1969.

Gurr, Ted Robert. "Urban Disorder: Perspectives from the Comparative Study of Civil Strife," in Louis E. Masotti and Don R. Bowen, eds., *Riots and Rebellion: Civil Violence in the Urban Community.* Los Angeles: Sage Publications, 1968, 51–67.

Hadden, Jeffrey K. "Reflections on the Social Scientists' Role in Studying Civil Violence." *Social Science Quarterly,* 51:2 (September 1970), 335.

Hamburger, Joseph. *James Mill and the Art of Revolution.* New Haven: Yale University Press, 1963.

Hamilton, Walton E. *The Politics of Industry.* New York: Alfred A. Knopf, 1957.

Hancock, Keith. *Four Studies in War and Peace.* New York: Cambridge University Press, 1961.

Hapgood, David. *The Purge that Failed: Tammany v. Powell.* New York: Holt, Rinehart and Winston, 1960.

Heller, Walter. *New Dimensions of Political Economy.* Cambridge: Harvard University Press, 1966.

Hersey, John. *The Algiers Motel Incident.* New York: Alfred A. Knopf, 1968.

Heslinga, M. W. *The Irish Border as a Cultural Divide.* Assen, Netherlands: Van Gorcom, 1962.

Hedgeman, Anna Arnold. *The Trumpet Sounds: A Memoir of Negro Leaderhip.* New York: Holt, Rinehart and Winston, 1964.

Holdon, Matthew, Jr. *Decision-Making on a Metropolitan Government Proposition.* Unpublished Ph.D. dissertation, Political Science, Northwestern University, 1961.

Holden, Matthew, Jr. "Litigation and the Political Order." *Western Political Quarterly,* 16:4 (December 1963), 777–778.

Holden, Matthew, Jr. "Committee Politics under Primitve Uncertainty." *Midwest Journal of Political Science,* 9:3 (August 1965), 235–253. (1965a)

Holden, Matthew, Jr. "The Republic in Crisis," in Reza Rezazadeh, ed., *Symposium on Civil Rights.* Platteville: Wisconsin State University—Platteville, 1965. (1965b)

Holden, Matthew, Jr. "Ethnic Accommodation in a Historical Case." *Comparative Studies in Society and History,* 8:2 (January 1966), 175–176. (1966a)

Holden, Matthew, Jr. *Pollution Control as a Bargaining Process.* Ithaca: Cornell University Water Resources Center, 1966. (1966b)

Holden, Matthew, Jr. "Decision-Making on a Metropolitan Government Proposition," in Greer *et al.*, 1968.

Holden, Matthew, Jr. "Internal War and Social Peace: Some Questions for Indicatorists." Paper read at American Political Science Association, 1969. (1969a)

Holden, Matthew, Jr. "The Quality of Urban Order," in Schmandt and Bloomberg, 1969. (1969b)

Holden, Matthew, Jr. "Problems of Achieving Order and Stability," in Harvey J. Perloff, ed., *Toward the Year 2000: The Future of U.S. Government.* New York: George Braziller, 1971.

Holden, Matthew, Jr. *The Politics of the Black "Nation."* New York and London: Intext Educational Publishers, 1972.

Huntington, Samuel P. "Patterns of Violence in World Politics," in Huntington, ed., *Changing Patterns of Military Politics.* New York: Free Press, 1962.

Jacob, Philip E., and James V. Toscano, eds. *The Integration of Political Communities.* Philadelphia: J. B. Lippincott Company, 1964.

Jaros, Dean, and Robert I. Mendelsohn. "The Judicial Role and Sentencing Behavior." *Midwest Journal of Political Science,* 11:4 (November 1967), 471–488.

Jones, James E. "To Secure These Results: Equal Employment Goals for the 1970's." Madison, Wisconsin: Address to the NAACP Freedom Fund Dinner, May 8, 1970.

Kahn, Alfred E. "The Tyranny of Small Decisions." *Kyklos,* 19 (1966), 23–47.

Kellogg, Charles Flint. *NAACP.* Baltimore: Johns Hopkins Press, 1967.

Kelly, George A. "Biculturalism and Party Systems in Belgium and Canada." *Public Policy,* 26, 316–357. Cambridge: Harvard University Press, 1967.

Kennedy, Robert F. *Thirteen Days.* New York: W. W. Norton and Company, 1969.

Kerner Report. *See* National Advisory Commission on Civil Disorders.

Khera, S. S. *District Administration in India.* New York: Asia Publishing House, 1964.

Kilson, Marion deB. "Towards Freedom: An Analysis of Slave Revolts in the United States," in Meier and Rudwick, 1969.

Lamson, Peggy. "The White Northerner's Choice: Mrs. Hicks of Boston." *Atlantic Monthly* (June 1966), 58–62.

Lane, Robert E. *Political Life.* Glencoe: Free Press, 1959.

Lane, Robert E. *Political Ideology.* New York: Free Press, 1962.

Laski, Harold. *Reflections on the British Constitution.* New York: Viking Press, 1951.

Lasswell, Harold D., and Richard Arens. *In Defense of Public Order.* New York: Columbia University Press, 1961.

Lasswell, Harold D., and Abraham Kaplan. *Power and Society.* New Haven: Yale University Press, 1963.

Legum, Colin. *Congo Disaster.* Baltimore: Penguin Books, 1961.

Leiserson, William. *Adjusting Industry and the Immigrant.* New York: Harper and Brothers, 1924.

Levine, Edward M. *The Irish and Irish Politicians.* Notre Dame: University of Notre Dame Press, 1965.

Levi, Werner. "On the Causes of War and the Conditions of Peace." *Journal of Conflict Resolution,* 4:4 (December 1960), 411–420.

Levi, Werner. "On the Causes of Peace." *Journal of Conflict Resolution,* 8:4 (March 1964), 23–35.

Levitan, Sar A., et al. *Economic Opportunity in the Ghetto: The Partnership of Government and Business.* Baltimore: Johns Hopkins Press, 1970.

Lijphart, Arend. *The Politics of Accommodation.* Berkeley: University of California Press, 1968.

Lindgren, Raymond E. *Norway-Sweden: Union, Disunion, and Scandinavian Integration.* Princeton: Princeton University Press, 1959.

Litt, Edgar. *The Political Cultures of Massachusetts.* Cambridge: MIT Press, 1965.

Litwack, Leon. *North of Slavery.* Chicago: University of Chicago Press, 1961.

Long, Norton E. *The Polity.* Chicago: Rand McNally and Company, 1960.

Long, Norton E. "The Political Act as an Act of Will." *American Journal of Sociology,* 69:1 (July 1963), 1–6.

Lorwin, Val R. "Belgium: Religion, Class, and Language in National Politics," in Robert A. Dahl, ed., *Political Opposition in the Western Democracies.* New Haven: Yale University Press, 1966.

Lough, Thomas S. *Urban Disarmament: Summary and Notes of an Exploratory Conference.* Kent, Ohio: Center for Urban Regionalism, Kent State University, November, 1969.

Lowi, Theodore J. *The End of Liberalism.* New York: W. W. Norton and Company, 1969.

Lubell, Samuel. *The Future of American Politics.* Garden City: Doubleday and Company, 1956. (1956a)

Lubell, Samuel. *The Revolt of the Moderates.* New York: Harper and Row, 1956. (1956b)

Lucas, Bob. *Black Gladiator.* New York: Dell Publishing Company, 1970.

Lynch, John R., *Some Historical Efforts of James Ford Rhodes.* Boston: Cornhill Publishing Company, 1922.

McKitrick, Eric L. "The Study of Corruption." *Political Science Quarterly,* 72 (December 1957), 502–514.

Maiale, Hugo V. *The Italian Vote in Philadelphia from 1928 to 1946.* Unpublished Ph.D. dissertation, Political Science, University of Pennsylvania, 1950.

Mann, Arthur. *LaGuardia Comes to Power.* Philadelphia: J. B. Lippincott Company, 1965.

March, James C., and Herbert A. Simon. *Orgainzations.* New York: John Wiley and Sons, 1968.

Margolis, Michael. "Gun Control: A Little Dab Won't Do You." Unpublished draft made available by author.

Marshall, S. L. A. Interview with Matthew Holden, Jr., and David H. Blake, August, 1969.

Maruyama, Masao. *Thought and Behavior in Modern Japanese Politics.* New York: Oxford University Press, 1963.

Mason, Alpheus T. *Brandeis.* New York: Viking Press, 1946.

Meier, August, and Elliott Rudwick, eds. *The Making of Black America.* New York: Atheneum Publishers, 1969.

Mendelsohn, Harold, and Irving Crespi. *Polls, Television, and the New Politics.* San Francisco: Chandler Publishing Company, 1970.

Merton, Robert K. *Social Theory and Social Structure,* rev. ed. Glencoe: Free Press, 1957.

Meyerson, Martin, and Edward C. Banfield, *Politics, Planning, and the Public Interest.* Glencoe: Free Press, 1955.

Miller, S. C. *The Unwelcome Immigrant.* Berkeley: University of California Press, 1969.

Moon, Henry Lee. *Balance of Power.* Garden City: Doubleday and Company, 1948.

Morrow, E. Frederick. *Black Man in the White House.* New York: Macfadden Books, 1963.

Moynihan, Daniel P., and James Q. Wilson. "Patronage in New York State." *American Political Science Review,* 58:2 (June 1964), 286–300.

Munger, Frank J., and Richard J. Fenno, Jr. *National Politics and Federal Aid to Education.* Syracuse: Syracuse University Press, 1962.

National Advisory Commission on Civil Disorders. *Report.* New York: E. P. Dutton and Company, Bantam Books, New York Times Company, 1968.

Nicolson, Harold. *Peacemaking.* New York: Grosset and Dunlap, 1925.

Nourse, Edwin G. *Economics in the Public Service.* New York: Harcourt Brace Jovanovich, 1953.

Nowlin, William F. *The Negro in American Politics.* Boston: Stratford Company, 1931.

Okun, Arthur M. *The Political Economy of Prosperity.* Washington: Brookings Institution, 1970.

Olson, Mancur, Jr. *The Logic of Collective Action.* Cambridge: Harvard University Press, 1965.

Osofsky, Gilbert. *Harlem: The Making of a Ghetto.* New York: Harper Torchbooks, 1966.

Ottley, Roi. *The Lonely Warrior.* Chicago: Henry Regnery Company, 1955.

Paige, Glenn D. "The Rediscovery of Politics," in John D. Montgomery and William J. Siffin, eds., *Approaches to Development.* New York: McGraw-Hill Book Company, 1966.

Peel, Roy V. *The Political Clubs of New York City.* New York: G. P. Putnam's Sons, 1935.

Pierce, Lawrence. *The Politics of Fiscal Policy Formation.* Pacific Palisades, California: Goodyear Publishing Company, 1971.

Plotnicov, Leonard. "Fixed Membership Groups." *American Anthropologist,* 64:1 part 1 (February 1962), 97–103.

Polakoff, Murray E., *et al. Financial Institutions and Markets.* Boston: Houghton Mifflin Company, 1969.

"Police and the Panthers." *The Black Politician,* 1:3 (January 1970), 17–19.

Polsby, Nelson W. "The Institutionalization of the U.S. House of Representatives." *American Political Science Review,* 62:1 (March 1968), 144–168.

Pomper, Gerald M. "Ethnic and Group Voting in Nonpartisan Municipal Elections." *Public Opinion Quarterly,* 30:1 (Spring 1966), 79–97.

President's Committee on Civil Rights. *Report.* Washington: United States Government Printing Office, 1947.

Raab, Selwyn. *Justice in the Back Room.* Cleveland: World Publishing Company, 1967.

Reedy, George. *The Twilight of the Presidency.* New York: World Publishing Company, 1970.

Rich, Bennet M. *The Presidents and Civil Disorders.* Washington: Brookings Institution, 1941.

Riker, William H. *The Theory of Political Coalitions.* New Haven: Yale University Press, 1962.

Rischin, Moses. *The Promised City.* New York: Corinth Books, 1964.

Rogin, Michael. "Wallace and the Middle Class: the White Backlash in Wisconsin." *Public Opinion Quarterly,* 30:1 (Winter 1965–1966), 98–108.

Rokeach, Milton. "Faith, Hope, and Bigotry." *Psychology Today* 3:11 (April 1970), 36–37.

Rollins, Alfred B., Jr. *Roosevelt and Howe.* New York: Alfred A. Knopf, 1962.

Rosen, Harry, and David Rosen. *But Not Next Door.* New York, Avon Books, 1962.

Ross, Arthur M., and Herbert Hill, eds. *Employment, Race, and Poverty.* New York: Harcourt Brace Jovanovich, 1967.

Rourke, Francis E. "The Politics of Administrative Organizations; A Case History." *Journal of Politics,* 19:3 (August 1957), 461–478.

Rude, George. *The Crowd in History.* New York: John Wiley and Sons, 1964.

Russell, Francis. *The Shadow of Blooming Grove.* New York: McGraw-Hill Company, 1968.

Salisbury, Robert H. "The Urban Party Organization Members." *Public Opinion Quarterly,* 29:4 (Winter 1965–1966).

Sayre, Wallace W., and Herbert Kaufman. *Governing New York City.* New York: W. W. Norton and Company, 1965.

Scammon, Richard, and Ben J. Wattenberg. *The Real Majority.* New York: Coward-MacCann, 1970.

Schaper, B. W. "Religious Groups and Political Parties in Contemporary Holland," in J. H. Bromley and S. H. Kossman, eds., *Britain and the Netherlands.* London: Chatto and Windus, 1960.

Scheiner, Seith M. "President Theodore Roosevelt and the Negro." *Journal of Negro History,* 47:3 (July 1962), 180.

Schelling, Thomas C. *Arms and Influence.* New Haven: Yale University Press, 1966.

Schlesinger, Joseph A. "Political Party Organization," in James G. March, ed., *Handbook of Organizations.* Chicago: Rand McNally and Company, 1965.

Schmandt, Henry J., and Warner Bloomberg, Jr., eds., *The Quality of Urban Life.* Los Angeles: Sage Publications, 1969.

Schriftgiesser, Karl. *The Gentleman from Massachusetts.* Boston: Little, Brown and Company, 1944.

Schuchter, Arnold. *White Power / Black Freedom.* Boston: Beacon Press, 1968.

Sears, David O., and Donald R. Kinder. "The Good Life, 'White Racism,' and the Los Angeles Voter." Paper, Western Psychological Association, April 15, 1970.

Segal, Ronald *The Race War.* Baltimore: Penguin Books, 1967.

Seltzer, Louis B. *The Years Were Good.* Cleveland: World Publishing Company, 1956.

Shames, Sally Olson. *David L. Lawrence, Mayor of Pittsburgh: Development of a Political Leader.* Unpublished Ph.D. dissertation, Political Science, University of Pittsburgh, 1958.

✓ Sheatsley, Paul B. "White Attitudes toward the Negro." *Daedalus* (Winter 1966), 222.

Shibutani, Tamotsu, and Kian M. Kwan. *Ethnic Stratification.* New York: Macmillan Company, 1965.

Shover, John L. *Cornbelt Rebellion.* Urbana: University of Illinois Press, 1965.

Smith, Lillian. *Strange Fruit.* New York: Harcourt Brace Jovanovich, 1944.

Smith Paul. *Disraelian Conservatism and Social Reform.* Toronto: University of Toronto Press, 1967.

Smith, Samuel D. *The Negro in Congress.* Chapel Hill: University of North Carolina Press, 1940.

Solomon, Barbara Miller. *Ancestors and Immigrants.* New York: John Wiley and Sons, 1965.

Sorauf, Frank J. *Political Parties in the American System.* Boston: Little, Brown and Company, 1964.

Special Analyses, Budget of the United States, Fiscal Year 1971. Washington, United States Government Printing Office, 1970, 65–80.

Spero, Sterling D., and Abram L. Harris. *The Black Worker.* New York: Atheneum Publishers, 1968.

Stagner, Ross. "Frustration, Aspirations, and Satisfactions." Paper, American Political Science Association, September 1969 (mimeographed).

Steiner, Gilbert Y. *Social Insecurity.* Chicago: Rand McNally and Company, 1966.

Stieber, Jack. *Governing the UAW.* New York: John Wiley and Sons, 1962.

Stimson, Henry L., and McGeorge Bundy. *On Active Service.* New York: Harper and Brothers, 1947.

Stone, Lawrence. "Prosopography." *Daedalus* (Winter 1971), 46–79.

Strickland, Arvarh L., Jr. *History of the Chicago Urban League.* Urbana: University of Illinois Press, 1966.

Sundquist, James L. *Politics and Policy.* Washington: Brookings Institution, 1968.

Suttles, Gerald D. *The Social Order of the Slum.* Chicago: University of Chicago Press, 1968.

Tabb, William K. *The Political Economy of the Black Ghetto.* New York: W. W. Norton and Company, 1970.

Talbot, Ross B., and Don F. Hadwiger. *The Policy Process in American Agriculture.* San Francisco: Chandler Publishing Company, 1968.

Talese, Gay. *The Kingdom and the Power.* New York: World Publishing Company, 1966.

Tannian, Francis. Unpublished study of a major special district in Washington, D.C.

Thomas, Harrison Cook. *The Return of the Democratic Party to Power in 1884.* New York: Columbia University Press, 1919.

✓ Thomas, Norman C. *Rule 9: Politics, Administration, Civil Rights.* New York: Random House, 1966.

Thomas, W. I., and Florian Znaniecki. *The Polish Peasant in Europe and America.* Chicago: University of Chicago Press, 1920.

United States Department of Health, Education, and Welfare. *Toward a Social Report* (Report of the Panel on Social Indicators). Washington, United States Government Printing Office, 1969.

United States House of Representatives, Commiteee on Un-American Activities. *Guerrilla Warfare Advocates in the United States,* House Report 1351, 90th Congress. Washington, United States Government Printing Office, 1968.

United States Senate, Subcommittee on Antitrust and Monopoly. *Hearings on Government Intervention in the Market Mechanism, Part 1: The Petroleum Industry.* Washington: United States Government Printing Office, 1969.

Wakin, Edward, and Joseph F. Scheuer. *The De-Romanization of the American Catholic Church.* New York: Macmillan Company, 1966.

Walter, Benjamin V., and Frederick M. Wirt. "Political Competition in the American Suburbs." Paper, American Political Science Association, September, 1966 (mimeographed).

Walton, Hanes, Jr. *The Negro in Third Party Politics.* Philadelphia: Dorrance and Company, 1961.

Wandycz, Damian S. *Register of Polish-American Scholars, Scientists, Writers and Artists.* New York: Polish Institute of Arts and Sciences in America, 1969.

Warren, Charles. *The Supreme Court in United States History.* Boston: Little, Brown and Company, 1923.

Wattenberg, Ben, in collaboration with Richard Scammon. *This U.S.A.* Garden City: Doubleday and Company, 1965.

Wesley, Charles H. *Negro Labor.* New York: Vanguard Press, 1927.

White, Walter F. *A Man Called White.* New York: Viking Press, 1948.

Wicker, Tom. Column, *Wisconsin State Journal,* sec. 1, p. 8; December 30, 1969.

Wilson, James Q. "Generational and Ethnic Differences among Career Police Officers." *American Journal of Sociology,* 69:5 (March 1964). 522–528.

Wilson, James Q. *Negro Politics: The Search for Leadership.* Glencoe: Free Press, 1960.

Wilson, James Q. "The Urban Unease: Community vs. City," in Schmandt and Bloomberg, eds., 1969.

Wilson, Woodrow. Speech at Pueblo, Colorado, September 25, 1919; reprinted in *The Congressional Record,* October 6, 1919, 6424.

Wingfield, Clyde J., ed. *Political Science—Some Perspectives.* El Paso: University of Texas at El Paso-Texas Western Press, 1967.

Wolf, Harold A., and Richard W. McEnally. "The Unemployment-Inflation Trade-Off, 1948–1968: A Multiple Phillips Curve Analysis." *Social Science Quarterly,* 51:2 (September 1970), 274–284.

Wolfinger, Raymond E. "Development and Persistence of Ethnic Voting." *American Political Science Review,* 59:4 (December 1965), 896.

Wood, Robert C. *1400 Governments.* Cambridge: Harvard University Press, 1961.

Yablonsky, Lewis. *The Violent Gang.* Baltimore: Penguin Books, 1966.

Younger, Calton. *Ireland's Civil War.* New York: Taplinger Publishing Company, 1969.

Zolberg, Aristide. *Creating Political Order.* Chicago: Rand McNally and Company, 1966.

Index

277